The Art of the Italian

RENAISSANCE

The Art of the Italian

RENAISSANCE

Architecture Sculpture Painting Drawing

edited by Rolf Toman

h.f.ullmann

FRONT COVER:
Michelangelo Buonarroti:
The Prophet Isiah, c. 1509
Fresco, 365 x 380 cm
Rome, Sistine Chapel
Photo: akg-images / Erich Lessing

BACK COVER:
Bernardo Rossellino (1409-64):
Tomb of Leonardo Bruni (1369-1444)
c. 1448-50 (marble)
Italy, Florence, Santa Croce
Photo: The Bridgeman Art Library

© 2005/2007 Tandem Verlag GmbH
h.f.ullmann is an imprint of Tandem Verlag GmbH
Original title: Die Kunst der italienischen Renaissance
ISBN 978-3-8331-1040-5

Editing and production: Rolf Toman, Espéraza, Birgit Beyer, Cologne
English translation: Deborah Ffoulkes, Fiona Hulse, Michael Hulse, Michael Scuffil
and Karen Williams
Cover Design: Werkstatt München

© 2007 for this edition: Tandem Verlag GmbH
h.f.ullmann is an imprint of Tandem Verlag GmbH
Special edition
ISBN 978-3-8331-4674-9

Printed in China

10 9 8 7 6 5 4 3 2 1
X IX VIII VII VI V IV III II I

Contents

Rolf Toman

Introduction

Anyone who approaches the Italian Renaissance for the first time, wishing to find out why it is considered so great an era in world art, will usually have some ideas on the matter already. The word "Renaissance" is normally translated as "rebirth"; and this is associated with the idea of an ill-defined yet radiant new beginning, the opposite of the (equally ill-defined) notion of the Dark Ages. This polarity is germane to the points of contrast which define the concept of the Renaissance, a concept generally perceived as altogether positive. "The Renaissance marks the rise of the individual, the awakening of a desire for beauty, a triumphal procession of joyful life, the intellectual conquest of physical realities, a renewal of the pagan pursuit of happiness, a dawning of consciousness of the relationship of the individual to the natural world around him." Such is the enthusiastic explanation that the Dutch art historian Johan Huizinga puts into the mouth of a fictitious Renaissance enthusiast in his essay 'The problem of the Renaissance'. If one adds to this the fact that most people imagine the Renaissance to refer back to the spirit of antiquity, and that it for the first time uses a sense of perspective to add depth in paintings, that probably sums up the most important elements that go to make up our picture of the Renaissance.

As the editor of this volume on the art of the Italian Renaissance, I have proceeded on the assumption that my readership will have just such an idea about the Renaissance and will be acquainted with a few Renaissance artists. Beyond this, I also envisaged a work that could serve the many students of art history as an access point to this complex subject. This served as a guide to the authors in terms of the presentation and difficulty of their texts. It also applies to this introduction, meaning that the above outline of the Renaissance, which poses some problems, is in need of further amplification.

The contrast between the Middle Ages and the Renaissance is normally over-emphasized. It might nevertheless be considered necessary to explain why a volume about the art of the Italian Renaissance, which is normally dated as starting around 1420, should devote so much space to the late Middle Ages. One response might be that of Alick McLean, the author of the first two chapters on architecture: in order to characterize what Italian architecture of the eleventh to sixteenth centuries had in common, he suggests a broadening of the concept of the Renaissance so that it can be understood as an ideological tool of papal power (including propagandist architecture) during this time, as a deliberate restoration of classical antiquity within Christian parameters. This view of the Renaissance both breaks the traditional boundaries of these ages and ignores the usual architectural stylistic classifications of this time. It is used only by McLean in this book, and does not apply where the other genres, such as sculpture and painting, are dealt with.

The traditional strict division placed by art history at around 1420 is questioned from other directions, however. Giorgio Vasari (1511–1574), the famous sixteenth-century author of the *Lives of the Artists*, dated the great renewal in Italian art from the end of the thirteenth century; he associated it with the Florentine artists Cimabue (c. 1240/45–after 1302) and Giotto (1267–1337). Giotto, wrote Vasari, had opened the portals of Truth for all those who had since brought art to the state of completeness and greatness it had attained in his own century; in saying this he was asserting the existence of a continuity in the development of art from Giotto to Michelangelo, the contemporary genius whom Vasari used to measure all other artists by. Vasari used the term *rinascità*, rebirth, to cover Giotto's own lifetime; he saw the great renewal in art as being the imitation of Nature, which for him was practically the same thing as a return to the antique. Vasari was not the first to emphasize Giotto's outstanding part in this: Boccaccio (1313–1375) and Lorenzo Ghiberti (1378–1458) shared his opinion. Both praised Giotto's fidelity to Nature and, in doing so, highlighted a formal characteristic of art in the late Duecento (thirteenth century) and early Trecento (fourteenth century) that was to be a prominent feature of fifteenth-century Renaissance art. The point is that one should talk of a *series* of renaissances rather than of *the* Renaissance.

It is fascinating that even more modern suggestions for defining the epochs of Italian art, ones that take into account the fruits of research into social and economic conditions, never question Giotto's dominant role; in his essay 'Defining the Periods in Italian Art', Giovanni Previtali states, "One cannot actually talk about Italian art as such until Giotto and other artists of his generation appear with their solutions – just as one does not talk of Italian literature until the appearance of Dante and his contemporaries..." He sees a flowering of art in central Italy, and above all in Florence, between 1290 and 1320, which anticipates many of the features that reappeared and came to fruition in the Florentine Early Renaissance of the Quattrocento. This repetition in the Florentine Renaissance was therefore, to a large extent, a reflection of the city's own great epoch of the early Trecento, the age of Giotto. This, then, is the reason why so much space is devoted to the late Middle Ages here.

Alexander Perrig, writing in this volume on the development of painting and sculpture in the thirteenth and fourteenth centuries, talks of this flowering of the late Duecento and early Trecento in terms of the birth and development of a new natural style. Admittedly, he draws quite different conclusions concerning the causes of this flowering and its success. He does not subscribe to the

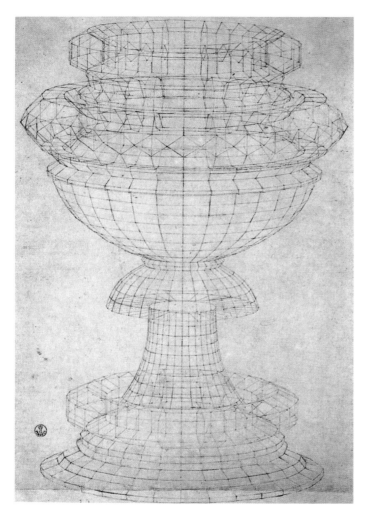

general adulation of Giotto: "The innovative energies that revolutionized painting in central Italy between 1280 and 1345, and placed a region which previously had been an extra into the centre-stage limelight, derived neither from a chance accumulation of regional talent nor from the miraculous powers of one great genius." I will not anticipate what Perrig considers to be the driving force behind the rapid development of Italian art at this time; suffice to say that any questions posed by the above will be answered in due course.

What, though, is the justification for talking of the Renaissance, to begin with of the Florentine Early Renaissance of the Quattrocento, as something new? Which criteria apply and account for this traditional break? What about the much-cited secularity of the Renaissance? There can hardly be any question of such a thing if we refer to the themes of Quattrocento paintings, as Peter Burke reminds us with the statistics in *The Italian Renaissance*. These statistics are based on 2033 Italian paintings from between 1420 and 1539, each one dated and classified according to its subject matter; Burke interprets this material as follows: "Since so much has been written about secular values in Renaissance Italy, the fact that the overwhelming majority of dated paintings are religious deserves emphasis."

In her essay on painting of the Early Renaissance in Florence, Barbara Deimling, at the end of her discussion of Masaccio's paintings, all of which have a religious theme, arrives at a conclusion that reads like a gloss on what Burke has written, but in greater detail – and this without reference to his sources. She concludes that "the world view of the Renaissance was not really shaped by a secularisation of the world and art – people during the Renaissance were just as concerned about the salvation of their souls in the life to come as people during the Middle Ages – though there was an endeavour to illustrate God's order by those means that were available so as to make it an even more intense experience for the faithful."

Deimling uses the expression "those means that were available" to refer both to the naturalism of Masaccio's figure and landscape paintings and to the illusion of depth produced by the central perspective of his paintings. She is also referring to the particular features that lead people to date the beginning of Renaissance painting to Masaccio (1401–1428). Filippo Brunelleschi (1377–1446), Ghiberti, and Donatello (1386–1466) are given equally prominent places as Florentine innovators, the former in the field of architecture, the latter two in sculpture. To go back to the original attempts, during Giotto's time, to find a solution to the problem of how to show depth in paintings, these artists made every effort to define spatial values more precisely and to rid themselves of their earlier compositional faults. It was Brunelleschi who discovered a scientific rather than empirical solution to this problem by identifying the mathematical rules governing perspective. The following generation of Florentine

Classical sculptures and torsos in the inner courtyard
of the Conservators' Palace
Rome, Capitol Hill

Leonardo da Vinci
Canon of human proportions based on Vitruvius
Ink drawing, 34.4 x 24.5 cm
Venice, Accademia

artists busily applied these. It was not until the middle of the fifteenth century that this interest in spatial values spread outside Tuscany, but this broadening of interest in an idea no longer new seems to have led to a loss of excitement about it. In the Cinquecento (sixteenth century), other problems, such as portraying motion (Leonardo and Michelangelo) and the dissolving of drawn contours by the use of colour (Titian and other Venetians), pushed perspective into the background.

Let us consider another characteristic of the Renaissance, the emergence of the individual. This touches on one of Jakob Burkhardt's basic ideas, which he develops in all its nuances in his masterpiece *The Civilization of the Renaissance in Italy*: "*Objective* views and treatments of the state and all the various things of this world made their first appearance in Italy; parallel to this, however, is the powerful rise of the *subjective*, man becoming a spiritual individual and recognising himself as such." In order to avoid getting involved in old debates about Renaissance Man, I will limit the cultural perspective to art history.

The revival of portrait painting around the middle of the fifteenth century can be taken as an indication of the growing self-awareness of people in that century; this was a genre of painting that had almost completely disappeared from the scene since the late classical period. Apart from princes, noblemen and high-ranking clerics, it was mainly commoners such as merchants, bankers, craftsmen, humanist scholars and artists who had their portraits painted. These last had only enjoyed privileges and social respect for a few decades, and it was not easy for sons from good families to manage to achieve their desire to be a painter or sculptor against their fathers' wishes. The good reputation of the family might be at risk.

The path that an artist had to take was laid out right into the fifteenth and sixteenth centuries along the same lines as in the Middle

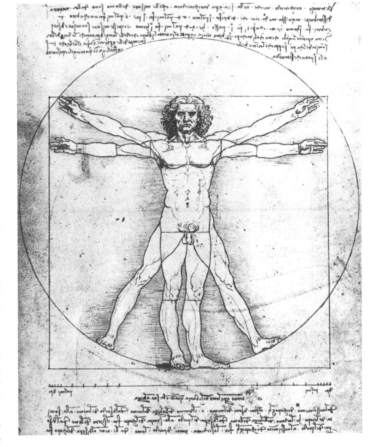

Ages: he had to be apprenticed to a master, just like an ordinary craftsman, and work for him for many years. The Tuscan painter Cennino Cennini, who was born in 1370, writes about this laborious training of the artist/craftsman in his treatise on painting, the *Libro dell'arte* (The Book of Art): "First of all, it will take at least a year for you to learn how to draw on small panels; then you will join the master in his workshop until you have learnt all the branches of our art. Then you will start to learn how to prepare paints, to cook lime, to paint on plaster, to apply plaster, to emboss it, scrape, gild and roughcast it; this will take six years. Then practical attempts at painting, practising fresco painting – another six years." This was certainly not the royal road to the universal man, the ideal artist versed in many disciplines. In reality few lived up to this ideal, though there were noticeably more such artists in the fifteenth and sixteenth centuries than in the fourteenth. They include Brunelleschi, Ghiberti, Leon Battista Alberti, Francesco di Giorgio, Donato

Bramante, Leonardo and Michelangelo. They were exceptional even amongst the creative elite of their age. It is worth noting that most of them were also architects, which says something for the social status of that profession.

Architecture was not considered a separate craft and did not have its own system of training. Any architect would normally have received his formal education in a different area, would have proved his worth in that area and would then have moved on to greater things, which required a knowledge of arithmetic, geometry and the theory of proportions in classical architecture. The task of designing, and the training needed to be able to do so – i.e. the reliance of architecture on the "liberal" arts – ennobled the architect. Painters and sculptors were also able to gain respect – to the extent that people realized that they were not ordinary craftsmen. According to the classification of the Middle Ages, painting and sculpture were not "liberal" but "mechanical" arts. The *artes liberales* were taught at universities; they included the basic subjects of grammar, logic and rhetoric (the "trivium") and the higher subjects of arithmetic, geometry, music and astronomy (the "quadrivium"). Ghiberti was one of the first to realise how important a higher education was for the liberation of the artist. His view was that painters and sculptors should study grammar, geometry, arithmetic, astronomy, philosophy, history, medicine, anatomy, perspective and "theoretical design". Ghiberti himself was one of the first artists to demand a high level of authority in the design of his own works, and even to secure such rights contractually. Uwe Geese demonstrates this using the example of Ghiberti's Gates of Paradise, the east door of the Baptistery in Florence, which in many ways mark a turning point in art history.

Right into the fifteenth century, the term *artista* meant a student of the *artes liberales*, not a painter or sculptor. It was artists such as Ghiberti who were to free themselves progressively during the course of the fifteenth and sixteenth centuries from the theological agenda and requirements of their clients, and finally to create the term "artist" as we understand it today. It can be safely asserted – though it should not be exaggerated – that a rise in social status went hand in hand with this.

The change from mediaeval stonemason to architect, and from viewing sculptors and painters as craftsmen to seeing them as artists, corresponds to changes on the part of the clients, and both in their turn are connected to a change in the function of art. From the fourth to the seventeenth centuries, the Church was *the* patron of European art. But in Renaissance Italy most of the paintings were already being commissioned by the laity. A clear differentiation and diversification of the type of clients can be seen taking place there during the course of the fifteenth and sixteenth centuries. The laymen or clergymen acted either as private clients or as representatives of various corporations. One group of corporate clients were the guilds, such as the Arte della Lana or the Calimala in Florence, who were responsible for the cathedral and the

Baptistery respectively and commissioned many larger works, mainly sculptures. Other corporate clients included confraternities that were dedicated to religious or charitable tasks, and which involved themselves in political and cultural matters. The Venetian name for such groups of citizens was *scuole*, and there were many of these, mainly small, though there were also (around 1500) six highly respected ones, the *scuole grandi*. And finally, another important client was the state or government itself.

It makes little sense to draw a distinction between public and private clients when dealing with regent princes. They tended not to distinguish between their public and private roles and, being used to ordering and commanding, were frequently rather impatient clients. Nonetheless, some artists were given regular commissions by them, and even occasionally a permanent position. Mantegna was the court painter in Mantua, Leonardo in Milan, and these are just two of the better-known examples. From the artists' point of view, there were usually two sides to such a position: on the one hand, there was greater economic security and a rise in prestige; on the other, there were certain duties of attendance and greater dependence in the work itself.

Where the clients themselves are concerned, three main motives can be identified that prompted them to order pictures and sculptures: piety, prestige and pleasure. The last motive is the most interesting, to the extent that it was the newest, and was to gain in importance during the course of the fifteenth and sixteenth centuries. "This desire to acquire works of art for their own sake is found above all in individuals who have something else in common: a humanist education." Peter Burke's remark suggests that an educated understanding of paintings heightened the enjoyment to be derived from them. Humanist teachers found some of their most receptive students amid the ranks of princes and members of important families, and these in turn were key patrons of art. Probably even the artists themselves, however, occasionally had to consult humanists when it was a matter of paintings that overtaxed their own knowledge of classical mythology and ancient history. It is debatable whether they were pursuing a personal educational interest or were simply receiving instructions that related to their commissions.

Finally, where the relationship of the Renaissance to the classical age is concerned, humanist lovers of literature were the originators of this appropriation of classical tradition. Here, too, the essential impetus dates back to the Trecento, when an enormous revival of the classical age took place, together with a renewed familiarity with its literary heritage. Petrarch (1304–1374) was the most influential advocate of this "new learning"; he communicated his enthusiasm for the classical age to many disciples, amongst them Coluccio Salutati. The latter was summoned to Florence in 1375 as Chancellor, where he developed into the leading champion of classical philology. His students were amongst the most important

Giacomo Barozzi, called Il Vignola
Fountain with river gods, and view of the garden façade of the Palazzina Farnese,
begun c. 1560
Caprarola

humanist scholars of the following generation: Leonardo Bruni, Pietro Paolo Vergerio, and Poggio Bracciolino, to name but a few. "The Chancellor was the link between the world of learning and education and the world of trade and politics." The essays in this book show how the humanist reception of the classical age blossomed in the Renaissance, how it was systematized – in terms of theory – in the fifteenth and sixteenth centuries, put on a scientific basis and – in practical terms – made ideologically usable. The relation of the Renaissance to the classical era is indeed the recurring preoccupation of all the essays. However, the importance of this should not cause us to ignore the Middle Ages.

These essays will also deal with such matters as the dividing line between the Early and High Renaissance, and the Renaissance and Mannerism. The editor and the various authors agreed that, in giving such prominence to the Middle Ages, the volume should not neglect Mannerism, which, as the terminal phase of the Renaissance, is often equated with the Late Renaissance by art historians. Advisedly, too sharp a division has been avoided here too. The reader will find precise definitions in the glossary.

Alick McLean

Italian Architecture
of the Late Middle Ages

"Painting contains a divine force which not only makes absent men present, as friendship is said to do, but moreover makes the dead almost seem alive… Some think that painting shaped the gods who were adored by the nations. It certainly was their greatest gift to mortals, for painting is most useful to that piety which joins us to the gods and keeps our souls full of religion."
– Alberti, *De Pictura*, preface to Book II

"…when the belief of the vulgar is founded on the arguments of learned men and then corroborated and confirmed day after day by great edifices that stand as perpetual monuments and testimonies seemingly eternal, as if fashioned by God, then the belief of those, both living and to come, that behold these miraculous constructions will be continually promoted. In this way belief is conserved and augmented, and with belief conserved and augmented, a devotion, based on wonder, will be established and secured."
– *Nicholas V, according to Manetti, in The Life of Nicholas V (Muratori, RIS III.2, (Bologna, 1977-), col. 949–50)*

Towards a definition of Renaissance

The first quotation is by arguably the first Renaissance man, Alberti, who combined the qualities of a brilliant humanist, art and architectural theorist, and architect. The next is by the third Pope to hold office since the return of the papacy to Rome, after a 100-year absence in Avignon: Nicholas V, who was also one of the great builder-Popes of the Renaissance. The Pope's application of Alberti's ideas on painting, as a tool of piety, to architecture should not be surprising. Alberti was employed in the papal Curia while Nicholas V bore the tiara, and may have served as advisor to the pope's own scheme for rebuilding the Vatican. However, the Pope imagined architecture to manifest its divine force differently from painting. Architecture could not make the dead alive, the absent present, or imaginary gods real as painting could, simply by depicting them as breathing, tangible men and women. It could, however, achieve the same ends by representing the places where the distant, past or divine resided or reside. Architecture could also go one step further in its magic – by appearing itself eternal, it could make the persons and institutions it represented appear to exist not only in the present, but also perpetually.

These peculiar attributes of architecture made it, and not painting, the subject of Nicholas V's speech, and the focus of his artistic policy as one of the 15th century's great patrons. With buildings he could bring back to life an empire long dead, and then go on to inhabit it, not with ancient pagan worthies and potentates or their images, but with the Christians of his own day, and, at their head, the new *pontifex maximus,* the Pope himself. By rebuilding the original St. Peter's as an even more "admirable" and antique edifice, Nicholas V and later Popes could make it appear as a "perpetual monument" made by God Himself, as an "eternal testimony" supporting the Popes' claims not only to the ancient seat of earthly power in Rome, but also to the keys to heaven and earth, handed from Christ to the first Pope and foundation of the Church, St. Peter (p. 13).

It is this notion, of a wilful recreation of the antique as an eternal Christian empire, which will serve as the definition for Renaissance architecture in these pages. Renaissance is not a style, but a persuasive tool, developed during and inextricably linked to a specific period in Italian history, when it was used to legitimize simultaneously temporal and spiritual authority. Other Renaissance architectural surveys have not, however, been incorrect to focus on style. Emulated, imitated and even stolen architectural elements from the antique were the means for making the monumental buildings of late mediaeval Italy look as if they had existed and would continue to exist forever. However, the so-called "errors" that occurred in the process of recreating antiquity should rather be explained by the presence of another exigency, namely, that the new antique had to be a Christian one. This second requirement led the architects and patrons of late mediaeval Italy to mix Early Christian

The Dome of St. Peter's, 1546–64
Rome

The Atrium of Old St. Peter's, begun c. 319–22
Drawing by G. A. Dosio

and early mediaeval sources with classical ones, and thereby consciously to create a style that was not a reiteration but a transformation of the past.

The above definition of Renaissance architecture as a persuasive tool based on a hybrid building style requires us to reexamine its time-frame. Hybrid classical architectural forms had in fact been used in religious and secular building since the time of Constantine (bottom right and p. 20). At any intervening date between then and today, a hybrid classicism could be seen as a means for legitimizing institutions by linking them to classical and Early Christian antiquity. There are good grounds, however, for limiting the Renaissance of papal architecture to the 11th to 16th centuries. This was the era of the papacy's greatest power, framed by movements of religious reform. The reform of the 11th century was directed by the Church and helped to extend its spiritual power, and to establish, for the first time seriously, its claim to temporal dominion. The Reformation of the 16th century, catalyzed by Martin Luther, was led by forces peripheral to Rome, was ignored by the Church, and thereby led to the undoing of the Roman papacy's already tendentious claim to universal spiritual and temporal authority.

The consistent element throughout this period was the Church's efforts to cultivate the faith of a rapidly growing constituency – Nicholas V's "vulgar," cognate with the Italian *volgare* – the non-noble laity. Before the 11th century these vulgar had been mostly scattered in feudal enclaves or small towns in Italy, tied to the fields or to the secondary agricultural economy for their sustenance. With the reopening of the Tyrrhenian Sea and the entire Mediterranean for Italian commerce by such ports as Pisa, Genoa and Amalfi at the beginning of the 11th century, the wealth from long-distance trade allowed these and other large cities literally to be born again: they developed commercial and industrial economies, and, in turn, nurtured ever larger populations up to the 14th century. The *volgare* were therefore becoming more wealthy, more numerous, and more concentrated in cities. And they were also becoming more worthy of the attention of the Church, and more accessible to what was, apparently, one of the most effective means of papal propaganda, architecture, which was itself becoming more affordable.

A definition of Renaissance going back as far as the 11th century has the advantage of stressing the continuity not only of papal patronage, but also of architectural iconography, style and building practices. Changes did occur, but less in the classical and Early Christian content of architectural imagery than in the stylistic elaboration of this imagery and in the building types to which classical and Early Christian forms were applied. The new styles and building types that appeared are generally attributable to the diverse institutions investing in architecture. These included not only the papacy, but also institutions created by the same vulgar that were the subjects of papal architectural propaganda. The architectural

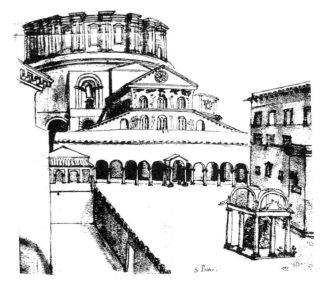

self-construction of these institutions was part of a gradual process of the decentralization of the image of imperial authority. Between the 11th and mid-13th centuries, the citizens of growing centres such as Pisa began to use sacred architecture and planning to represent their cities simultaneously as new Romes and new Jerusalems, independent of papal Rome. Between the 13th and late 14th centuries, the leaders of other commercial towns began to use a mixture of sacred and secular architecture and planning to sanctify and institutionalize their authority over internal and neighbouring antagonists. In the 15th century, private individuals and families increasingly applied classicizing architectural forms to their urban and suburban residences, constructing new centres for urban political and courtly life. In the mid-15th and 16th centuries these same individuals and families began to build villa and garden complexes outside the city limits, which became new centres for the growing court culture. Each of these stages persisted after the arrival of the next, though each new scale of building and patronage tended to be the locus for the greatest changes and innovations. The exception was in papal architecture itself, whether at Rome or at the monasteries, cities, and courts allied with the papacy. Popes showed themselves to be extremely responsive to the innovations of both their architectural supporters and antagonists, and continued to refine their own means for expressing universal, imperial Christian rule in religious architecture, thereby maintaining their buildings as the gold standard in the booming economy of architectural representation.

The continued role of the papacy may have prevented the bankrupting of the imagery of its universal power despite its reproduction by so many cities, institutions and individuals. Nicholas V's "miraculous" architecture sustained its sacred potency up to the final century of this survey, when the wave of northern religious reform began to breach the Alps. It took Luther's 95 theses on the portal of Wittenberg, and the subsequent radical iconoclasm of the Anabaptists and Calvinists, to attack directly the magical properties attributed to holy objects, images and buildings, and thereby to precipitate a sustained abandonment, for the first time in Western Christendom, of the image of universal theocratic authority, and to splinter the Church as an institution.

The "Protorenaissance" and the Construction of a Papal Roman Empire

The first major building campaigns in Italy to be engaged in by the papacy and allied bishops since the Carolingian period began in the 11th century. There was an unusual concentration of these projects in Florence, at the Baptistery, San Miniato al Monte, Santa Reparata, the Archivescovado, and the Badia di Fiesole. These structures are distinct from contemporary Romanesque structures elsewhere in Italy or the North. They are characterized by a remarkable delicacy and refinement of classicizing elements, set into polychromatic compositions, usually of dark green Monteferrato stone and white marble. The degree of sophistication in the use of classical orders and elements, and their similarity to structures designed in Florence in the early 15th century, have led most art historians to name this period the "Protorenaissance." This term implies a break in Florentine building culture between the time of these buildings and their "Renaissance" imitators. Such a disjunction is indeed suggested in chroniclers as early as Villani, who, in the early 14th century, speaks of the Baptistery as an antique Temple of Mars, rebuilt by Charlemagne. However, attempts to fix dates on the two most important of these structures, the Baptistery and San Miniato, have revealed that they were probably in a state of continuous evolution, from the time of the latter's reconstruction, in 1018, and the former's consecration, in 1059, up to well into the 15th century. The case of the Baptistery is particularly revealing. Its polychrome cladding and double-dome structure had been begun at the latest by the time of the entombment of Bishop Ranierius in the church, in 1113. The lantern capped the dome in 1150. The square apse was completed by 1202. The vaulting must have been completed around the same time, certainly by the beginning of work on the Byzantine-style mosaics, in 1225. In 1293 the banded exterior corner pilasters framing each of the remaining 7 elevations were added. The first bronze doors were made in 1330–36 by Andrea Pisano, with the second and third sets completed by Ghiberti in 1403–24 and 1425–52 respectively. Similar sympathetic additions to San Miniato are documented, the

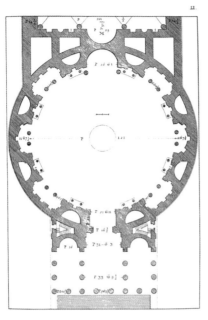

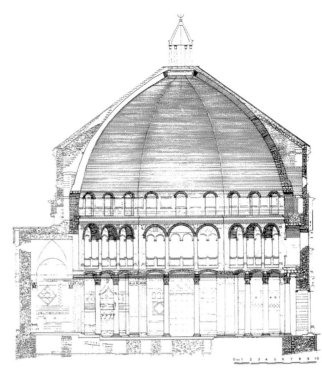

last and perhaps most remarkable being the 1448 tabernacle by Michelozzo, utterly consistent with the refined classical ornament of the 11th- to 14th-century façade and interior walls, to the point of convincing the viewer that it and the entire church were composed and completed at one and the same time.

The major monuments of late mediaeval, or rather, Renaissance Florence were therefore not the products of single instants of inspiration by individual geniuses. These buildings indeed challenge such a notion, suggesting that their greatness was achieved by a continuous building tradition, which itself defies the sequence of periods by which Florentine architecture has generally been divided, the Protorenaissance, Gothic, and Renaissance. Rather, with these structures Florentine church builders of the first five centuries of our millennium were displaying their unbroken affinity for a sophisticated, polychrome classicism. Architects and masons established the principles of this style quite early, in the 11th century, and continued to refine and apply them through the time of Brunelleschi, Michelozzo and Alberti.

A closer view of San Miniato (p. 17) with the Baptistery (p. 16) helps to establish just what these principles were. The entire composition of San Miniato al Monte is regulated by classical architectural iconography and by geometry. The architectural iconography consists of two superimposed classical types. The first is the imperial palace façade, established at the five arched bays and three portal openings of the ground-level portico. The second is the temple front, poised above this palace façade base.

These architectural iconographies fit into a rigorous overall geometric order, with the entire elevation inscribed by a square, as is the upper-storey temple front. This geometry is overlaid by the tripartite rhythm first expressed at the three portals, an ordering scheme which recurs at all levels of structural and ornamental articulation of the façade, down to the three inscribed vertical rectangles beneath each of the portico arches. It also appears at the triple-bay divisions of the nave interior, and even at the articulation of the contemporary Baptistery elevations.

As abstract as such an ordering scheme must seem, it is consistent with the typical imperial-palace scheme of three doors set into a horizontal portico beneath a window or gallery opening, as well as with the generally square geometric frame of the classical temple front. The one seemingly inconsistent element in this bichrome, classicizing façade, the gold and polychrome mosaic at the centre of the temple front, provides a clue to the figurative significance of this triple-in-square geometry. The mosaic depicts three figures: Christ, flanked by the Madonna and Saint Minias, the saint to whom the church is dedicated. The three arches in the pediment frieze above correspond precisely to each figure, and the intarsia star above Christ even reinforces his greater status, something echoed by the cross and eagle above, as well as by the window beneath him and the more elaborate intarsia within the central arch of the portico below. The architectural geometry is consistent with the origins of the imperial palace façade, in the Republican theatre *scaena*: it serves to frame dramatic characters. As the geometry is amplified to

15

The security provided by the Canossa allowed Gebhard an unusual freedom to express the aspirations of the reform movement and papacy in architecture. The support that began with the Canossa continued with the consular government established in the following century, with the Guelph league, with major guilds and banking families in the 14th century, and up through the Medici as both papal bankers and de facto rulers of Florence. In this context the development of the temple front and palace façade images at San Miniato takes on specific meaning. The former is the divine, as a temple, placed above the latter, the secular imperial residence. The consistent square geometry and triple rhythm then interlace these two images, establishing Christ as an emperor inhabiting both the literal attic temple and its larger-scale reiterations at the ground level and at the entire façade. The harmonic compositional order created by the scaled repetition of the square and triplet rhythm, when combined with the delicate treatment of the classical orders and the balanced use of bichromy, reinforce the image of divine and imperial order embedded in the architectural iconography.

The peculiar articulation of the window beneath Christ introduces a tension into this order. It appears to be an open portal more than a window, but is nonetheless inaccessible due to its height and the powerful presence of Christ above it, as if guarding over passage through it. The simultaneous offer and restriction of entry reinforces the power of Christ and of his papal surrogates on earth. It imputes to the latter a weapon more threatening than any fortress or army – the ability to deny the access of adversaries to the gates of heaven. The façade's architectural framework and iconography help to broadcast this alternating image of salvation and damnation not only to the city of Florence below, but also down along the Arno valley that San Miniato faces, towards territories potentially hostile to the Pope.

The Pisan Renaissance

One potentially antagonistic city downstream from the glowering façade of Florence's San Miniato was Pisa. During the 11th to 13th centuries Pisans were also engaged in substantial construction projects. The resulting buildings – Pisa's Cathedral, Baptistery, Campanile and Campo Santo – were radically different in style and sensibility from Florence's Baptistery and San Miniato. Pisan structures were sculptural in their overall form and unrestrained in their infinite decorative encrustations, where Florence's were planar and proportionally restrained. The cathedral architects, Buschetus, Rainaldus and Guiglielmus, achieved complex, rippling patterns of light and dark on their elevations with arrays of deeply-carved blind arcades, detached dwarf galleries, and elaborate relief carving that, though accentuated by intarsia, were never dominated by it. This was in contrast to Florentine architects, who used relief minimally, less for readings of depth than to complement the role of bichrome intarsia in outlining the buildings' harmonic geometries and

the scale of the entire façade, so is the sacred presence of these figures.

The manipulation of these two particular classical types and their geometries as a means for framing the three divine figures animating the church and its façade was probably not accidental. San Miniato and the Baptistery were built at a critical moment not only in the history of Florence but also in the history of the papacy, and they express in stone the revolutionary changes occurring at this time between the papacy and the Holy Roman Empire. Since the mid-11th century the papacy had begun to assert its independence from the Emperor on three levels: the shifting of the election of Popes from the Emperor to the college of cardinals; the assertion of the Pope's right to appoint bishops, which precipitated what has become known as the investiture conflict of the late eleventh century; and the assertion of the right of the papacy to crown the Emperor himself, with the attendant claim that the Pope alone had full sovereignty over both spiritual and temporal power on earth.

The role of Florence in this confrontation began quite early, with the ascent to power of the anti-imperial Canossa in Tuscany and Emilia Romagna, and their establishment of a seat in Florence. The Canossa provided just the political and military backing the papacy needed to pursue its reform mission, which the Canossa fully supported. As a result, Florence became a haven for papal reformers, including the very bishop of Florence, Gebhard of Burgundy, who dedicated the Baptistery in 1059. This same year Gebhard was appointed as Pope Nicholas II (1059–61) in the newly established practice of non-imperial election.

San Miniato al Monte, begun c. 1090
Florence

contained rhythmic sequences. Most noticeably, Pisa's buildings were on a far grander scale than those of Florence, and the perception of that scale was amplified by their elaborate ornament and remarkably open setting, in the Campo dei Miracoli.

The scale, sculptural sensibility and profuse galleries of Pisa's Cathedral and Baptistery linked the church to the Romanesque buildings of Northern Italy and beyond the Alps, such as at Parma and Speyer, or along the pilgrimage route through France and Spain to Santiago de Compostela. The decorative elaboration was closest to that of Spanish and Sicilian Romanesque and to their sources in Islamic architecture. Indeed, there is evidence that Pisan architects were directly influenced by Islamic architecture, whether in Sicily or elsewhere in the Mediterranean. Two inscriptions on the cathedral façade itself indicate just how this connection was established. The first recounts a series of four naval victories over the Saracens at Sicily and Sardegna, between 1005 and 1034. The second tells of how the booty from yet another victory, in 1064, was used, "By

which spoils it was established that these walls be erected" (*Quo pretio muros constat hos esse levatos*). Pisa Cathedral was built from Saracen plunder, and the unending field of Islamicizing decoration embedded in its elevations the image of the vanquished.

While these inscriptions reveal the Pisans' debt, literally, to Islam, they also indicate a more profound debt, to antique Roman culture, that brought the Pisans to use the same classical architectural iconographies that the Florentines did, but for quite different policy ends. The letters of the inscription are carved in classical Latin, in a style imitating classical epigraphy, and in the three-portal setting established by Rome's conquering generals and emperors, the triumphal arch. As at San Miniato, these portals are framed in the horizontal arcade of the imperial-palace façade type, though at Pisa the militaristic inscriptions emphasize more the triumphant element in this hybrid typology. The contemporary chronicles of Maragone indeed indicate that the Pisans were not only vaunting their antique Roman heritage at this time, as the great port city of *Pisae*, but were constructing themselves as a new Rome, as triumphant as antique Romans in their conquests of the Saracens. Such an interpretation is reinforced by another form of *spolium* embedded in the church elevations. Blocks of marble with inscriptions from ancient Roman monuments were built into the walls, with the words apparently intentionally positioned either sideways or upside down. The Pisans were at once appropriating Rome and proclaiming the triumph of their own empire, built with the ruins of the ancient one.

The particular use of antique architecture at the Pisa cathedral appears therefore to have been intended more to construct the identity of the Pisans as conquerors and empire builders in their own right, and not, like the Florentines, as the faithful vassals of a temporally ambitious papacy. The treatment of another familiar antique architectural iconography at the Pisa cathedral further suggests that the Pisans saw themselves as Christian empire builders. The temple front appears here as well, similarly poised above the palace façade portico and triumphal arch portals as at San Miniato. In place of the triple rhythm of the San Miniato temple front, the Pisans used a continuous, unbroken sequence of freestanding arches. The only indication of hierarchy given these arches is to be found with those within the pediment, where they are forced by its geometry to get larger as they approach the apex. At the centre of the pediment are two arches, divided by the tallest column, above which is perched the Pisan answer to the Florentine Christ at the temple front of San Miniato: the Madonna, also with Christ, but with the latter now as the Christ child, cradled in the arms of the larger-scale Virgin.

The statue of the Virgin at the apex of the cathedral temple front is consistent with the religious identity of the church and the entire city. The church was dedicated to the Virgin, to whom the Pisans offered the sanctuary in return for her protecting their naval and maritime fleets in battle and in commerce. The triumphs of the

Pisans over the heathens, while certainly in collaboration with the Pope, as the leader of the crusades and head of the Christian Church, was nonetheless done primarily for the Virgin, and therefore for the Pisans themselves. By transforming their booty into a temple in the Madonna's name, the Pisans sanctified their imperial ambitions, in a similar way that the Venetians robbed the remains of St. Mark from Byzantium, and used his relics to found a church that was to be the new centre of their civic identity, as, interestingly enough, a new Byzantium.

There may be one other way, besides its fusion of Islamic, classical and Marian imagery, by which the Pisans were constructing themselves as a holy imperial city. While still at work on the façade of the cathedral, in 1153, the Pisans hired the architect Diotisalvi for another building project, the Baptistery. It replaced an older one that had been beside the cathedral, and is now dead centre with the axis of the nave. The Cathedral and Baptistery were designed to complement one another, and certain specifics of the latter suggest why.

The Pisan Baptistery differs from most centrally planned baptisteries or churches of the time in that it is a circular plan, rather than a polygonal one. This necessitated more sophisticated masonry and vaulting techniques than churches built of flat wall planes. The Baptistery also differed from its counterparts in the scale of its two-storey gallery, and was almost unique in the height of its cone-shaped roof, which, in its original form as well as its current one, was clearly expressed on the outside of the church, and far more visible from near or far as an architectural attribute. Indeed, each of these distinguishing features of Pisa's Baptistery set it off from all but one building, which was the prototype for many of the centrally planned structures of Christendom, the Anastasis of the Holy Sepulchre in Jerusalem (p. 20, top). Numerous art historians have observed that the Pisa Baptistery was in fact a copy of the Holy Sepulchre, adding that any differences between it and the original are attributable to the difference between the mediaeval idea of a "copy" versus the modern idea: mediaeval copies needed only to resemble in the abstract. It would therefore be arguable that all centrally planned structures, including the octagonal Baptistery of Florence, were "copies" of the Holy Sepulchre. However, it may be that the Pisa Baptistery constituted the first break in the sequence of abstracted copies of the Holy Sepulchre in the unprecedented literalness of its resemblance in section. Its failure to be a perfect replica may be due to the fact that it was simultaneously copying two Jerusalem structures, not only the Holy Sepulchre, but also the other great centrally planned building of the Holy City, the Dome of the Rock, known to the Pisans and their contemporaries as the Temple of the Lord. The latter had an even more overtly expressed dome than the Holy Sepulchre, and one that was furthermore visible from great distances, as it stood almost isolated within the walled precinct of the Temple Mount, towering above the entire city, with only one other major building beside it.

Section of the Church of the Holy Sepulchre and the Anastasis, begun c. 335
Jerusalem

Baptistery, 1153–1256
Pisa

The adjoining monument that shared the Temple Mount precinct with the Dome of the Rock was the Mosque of Al-Aqsa, known to the Pisans and their contemporaries alternatively as the Temple of Herod or the Temple of Solomon. It was a multi-aisled structure, located on an axis with the Dome of the Rock, establishing the same relation between a linear and centralized structure isolated on a sacred plane as Pisa's Cathedral and Baptistery. As if to confirm this interpretation, the Pisans constructed in the next century a long, wall-like structure as a backdrop to this point-and-line composition, the Campo Santo. They then filled the burial grounds within this "holy field" with dirt that they had dug from Mount Golgotha in Jerusalem. With the replication of the Temple Mount at Pisa's Campo dei Miracoli, the Pisans provided themselves with a burial place in a transplanted Jerusalem, constructed first with copies of Jerusalem's architecture, and completed with the actual earth of the Holy City.

The particular ways in which the Pisans took over architectural images from Islam and Rome, dedicated them to the Virgin, and then placed them in a "Field of Miracles" embodying the places of Christ's *pathos* and burial, can all be seen as means of establishing a unique, sacred identity for the city. By constructing such an image of their city, the Pisans furnished themselves with an independent path to God, through the divine intercession of the Virgin, and through locating their own Jerusalem not only in their city, but at the site of their baptisms, masses, triumphs, and, equally important, burials. Indeed, the replica and actual earth of Jerusalem may have been conceived to provide the Pisans with direct passage to that other, Heavenly, Jerusalem, namely eternal salvation.

The reason behind the Pisans' extensive efforts to establish an independent path to salvation may have been to insulate them from conflicts with the Papacy, and therefore from resulting threats of excommunication and damnation. By the time they started work on the Baptistery, the Pisans were at odds with the papacy over their failure to participate in the second Crusade, and subsequently over Pisa's continued metropolitan status – and therefore its right to maintain colonies in Corsica and Sardegna. There was no ideological rift between the Pisans and the Popes, such as existed between the latter and the Emperors, even though the Pisans often sided with the Empire. Rather, the Pisans simply had a different agenda than supporting unconditionally the temporal power of the papacy and the reconquest of the Holy Land. They had their own empire to build, one based on both naval and economic power. The Pisans nonetheless adopted imperial images that were being deployed by the reform and crusading papacy, but to serve their own imperial leader, the Madonna, and to make their own city both a new Rome and a new Jerusalem.

Campo dei Miracoli, 1063–1350
Ground plan of the entire complex (bottom left)
Section of the Cathedral (bottom right)
Pisa

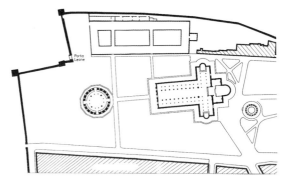

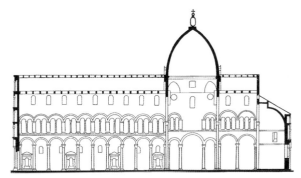

The Impact of the Mendicant Orders on the Merchant Communes

The 11th- and 12th-century architecture of Florence and Pisa established new paradigms for sacred architecture throughout Tuscany. By the 13th century, as religious reform and the wealth of long-distance trade filtered across the region, cities such as Lucca, Pistoia, Prato, Arezzo, and many others to the north and south of the Apennines and Arno valley were beginning to construct their own religious identities with urban design and architecture. This first generation of projects was followed by a phase of experimentation, encouraged by another period of religious revival. Though short-lived – indeed, less than eighty years in most cases – this phase left a permanent mark on how communes sited their monumental structures in piazzas and distributed religious complexes throughout their cities.

The religious revival of the 13th century began with the foundation of pious institutions that catered specifically to the emerging urban classes. Two new religious orders were approved by the visionary Innocent III and Honorius III, the Franciscans in 1210 and the Dominicans in 1216. These orders, together with the Augustinians, Servites, Carmelites, and others that were modelled after them, were largely made up of middle-class artisans, traders and financiers. Though they dressed like monks in simple brown, white or black habits bound by rope belts and were even more rigorous than their cloistered counterparts in their vows of poverty, friars embraced the physical world and the mores of the city. They wrote sensuous, lyrical hymns to the Madonna, and even to the sun and moon; they preached in the vernacular, and adopted the gestures of marketplace *jongleurs*. Their mission was to emulate the lives of Christ and the Apostles, and to evangelize that their peers should do likewise.

The impact of friars on the architectural identity of cities was enormous. Their approach to monuments was radical. The first generation of friars simply did not build. St. Francis forbade his followers to erect churches, instructing them instead to request permission from local priests and bishops to use existing churches and piazzas. As a result, friars began to transform the entirety of Italy's merchant cities, filling streets and marketplaces with their cries to penance and their captivating parables, or *exempla*. The most banal secular places became potentially sacred precincts, no longer only the areas within or immediately fronting church portals.

The dispersion of sacred space initiated by the mendicant orders is evident in their settlement patterns, as at Florence (p. 23). Each order located itself by the only remaining open areas not occupied by major churches, the piazzas and open markets near or outside the main city gates, accommodating themselves in modest houses. In most communities mendicant settlements grew gradually with the numbers of their initiates and with the flow of gifts, leading to the construction of more traditional churches and cloisters of ever-increasing dimensions. The ability of the mendicants to win the support of both the Church establishment and the new urban classes was nonetheless clear from quite early on, in the 1220s, with the construction of the mother churches of the two major orders, San Domenico in Bologna and the Basilica of St. Francis in Assisi. Both structures surpassed the previously dominant churches in their cities not only in scale but also in the sophistication of their construction, which in both cases employed recent innovations of Gothic architecture imported from France, where both mendicant orders had won much papal support due to their successful battles against heresy. Eventually this monumentality was copied at local mendicant churches.

The gestation of mendicant settlements from humble origins to large-scale monuments is exemplified at Santa Maria Novella in Florence (p. 23). Today's church was begun in 1279, using the nave of the earlier 1246 church as its transept. Its reorientation led to the unusual frontage of the church on two piazzas, linked to one another by a sequence of *avelli*. Only the *avelli* and the lower portion of the main façade of the church were clad in marble until the erection of the Alberti façade in 1470, giving the complex a more horizontal emphasis than it has now, with the monumentality of the church immediately at the street. This array of bichrome

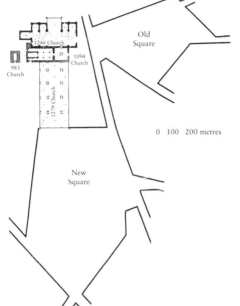

Santa Maria Novella
Florence

Old Square

New Square

0 100 200 metres

1246 Church
1094 Church
983 Church
1279 Church

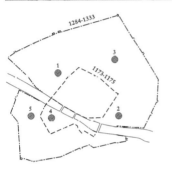

1284-1333
1173-1175

Plan of churches founded by orders of mendicants in Florence:
Dominicans: Santa Maria Novella, 1221 (1);
Franciscans: Santa Croce, 1226–8 (2);
Servites: Santissima Annunziata, 1248 (3);
Augustinians: Santo Spirito, 1250 (4);
Carmelites: Santa Maria degli Carmine, 1268 (5)

arches provided tombs for the church congregation, extending the image of burial at a sacred place to the urban periphery.

The interior chapels of Santa Maria Novella or of the Franciscan Santa Croce provided the same burial and memorial function as the *avelli* at yet grander scales. Two- and four-arched chapels flanked the taller central sanctuaries of Florence's Dominican and Franciscan churches respectively. The Gothic expression of these arches should not distract from their fundamentally classical imagery, of sequential arches triumphant, now over death. The families occupying these chapels were the new urban aristocracy, whose commercial wealth made them most capable of answering the friars' requests for alms. Santa Croce's chapels, for example, were patronized by the city's major banking families, such as the Bardi, Peruzzi and Baroncelli, who adorned their private sacred domains with some of the most important of Italy's early Renaissance paintings.

These opulent transept chapels were framed by the overall broad, spacious interiors of Santa Croce and other mendicant churches. While the openness of these structures recalls the original piazza settings for the friars, the overall magnificent effect of late 13th-century friaries was fundamentally at odds with the original principles and restrictive building ordinances of these orders. The success of the mendicants in drawing the artistic patronage of the new Italian urban cities away from older cathedrals and monasteries had the paradoxical effect of making them like the latter. Though

for a time they fragmented the once centralized religious urban identity of the communes, their monumental articulation eventually reinforced traditional symbols of universal rule, and set the stage for a new phase of architecture in Italy's communes, focussed on the cathedral and civic palace.

The Return to Monumentality at the Cathedral of Florence and Orsanmichele

The diffusion of religious spaces and patronage by the mendicant orders was only part of a larger revolution that was going on in Florence and other communes, where merchants, bankers and artisans were displacing the feudal classes as the dominant social force. While religion and economy contributed significantly to the transfer of power from noble *boni homines* to the leaders of the major guilds in Florence, most of this battle was waged and won in traditional warfare, which, between the death of Frederick II in 1250 and the battle of Benvenuto in 1266, turned Florence, Siena and all of Tuscany into fields of carnage. By the turn of the century most of the pro-imperial, largely noble Ghibellines or white Guelphs – such as Dante – had been killed or banished from their cities, and the newly dominant Guelphs, merchants, bankers and elite artisans set up oligarchies based upon professional, rather than clan, identity.

As in warfare, so in architecture: the major thrust of the building policy of the new political class in Florence followed traditional

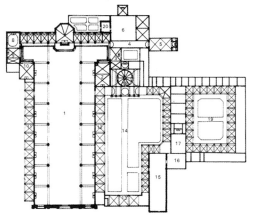

models, beginning with the Cathedral, and continuing with Orsanmichele and the monumental piazza and governing palace of the regime. In 1293, the same year when the commune passed the Ordinances of Justice, which sealed the fate of the Ghibellines and of overpowerful magnates, the oligarchy began to renovate the old cathedral of Santa Reparata, in front of the Baptistery. At the same time, the Arte di Calimala, one of the city's most powerful guilds, commissioned the polychrome piers on the exterior corners of the Baptistery. By the next year the commune had revealed more ambitious plans for their main church, introducing the possibility of constructing a new cathedral. In February of 1296 the city decreed that it would construct a church "of the greatest splendour." On 8 September the builders laid the foundation stone.

The architect responsible for the early planning of the cathedral was Arnolfo di Cambio, who had worked as a sculptor under Nicola Pisano in Siena, and on his own at Orvieto and Rome. He had also probably been engaged in other building projects in Florence, at the Badia in 1284, at the addition of the striped corner buttresses to the Baptistery in 1293, and at Santa Croce in 1294/5.

The Cathedral is the first of Arnolfo's architectural works in Florence that highlights his sculptural training, and with that the first of the city's churches to show strong influences from the expressive plastic tradition of Pisa, the home of Arnolfo's master. The initial project was constructed at, or more precisely, encircling the site of Santa Reparata, which continued to be used within the Cathedral rising around it. Arnolfo's work was the first of three phases in the church's construction. His project was the same width as the completed structure, and probably had the same tri-conch scheme and therefore domed crossing, though at the end of a shorter nave.

The evidence available suggests that Arnolfo's façade had a similar mix of Gothic, Romanesque and classical elements as at the Badia, at Santa Croce, and at his contemporary sculptural projects. The most certain aspect of the façade was its tripartite division, not only by three portals, but also reinforced by strong buttress divisions extending from the ground level to the roof. These strong vertical dividers recall similar divisions at the Badia and at the east end exterior and interior of Santa Croce. These vertical elements were counterbalanced by the same broad, square overall proportions that had been characteristic of Florentine church architecture since the Baptistery and San Miniato.

The façade of Santa Maria del Fiore is significant in uniting the tradition of mendicant funerary and chapel architecture and art with the earlier tradition of upper-storey representations of Christ, the Virgin and saints. The effect is of bringing the saints down to the level of the worshippers, which is consistent with the new narrative tendency, in sermons and art, established by the mendicants. However, as the ground-level arcades were occupied by saints, no place remained for private individuals to participate in the imagery

Arnolfo di Cambio's façade of Florence Cathedral
16th-century drawing
Florence, Museo dell' Opera del Duomo

Nave of Florence Cathedral (Santa Maria del Fiore)

of the church, as had been the case at the Dominican *avelli*. The focus of the sculptural programme and of its architectural setting, however direct its narrative presentation, is on the holiness of other, divine individuals – primarily the Madonna, as in Pisa – and not on the piety of contemporary Florentines.

The interior of Santa Maria del Fiore is consistent with this mixture of mendicant and traditional, Gothic and antique imagery and spatial sensibility. The Arnolfo nave had a wooden ceiling similar to that at Santa Croce. Only at the crossing would the imagery have transformed, with the transition from wooden to stone vaulting and from horizonal, linear space to vertical, rounded space at the tri-conch domes. Although the nave was vaulted later in the century, it retained this architectural denouement. The circular form dominates at the crossing, not only in scale but in its triplicate repetition, recalling less the single domes of the Florence and Pisa Baptisteries than the early triple-apse transepts of Tuscan Romanesque churches, including that of the still extant Santa Reparata.

Nearly half a century after Arnolfo's death circa 1310, Santa Maria del Fiore was enlarged, now under the direction of the city's powerful wool guild. Between 1351 and 1368 the Arte della Lana engaged a series of architects, including Francesco Talenti, Neri di Fioravante, Alberto Arnoldi, Giovanni di Lapo Ghini, and Talenti's son, Simone di Francesco. All were members of the main building committee and its various sub-committees, joining important painters and sculptors of the day, including Taddeo Gaddi, Andrea Orcagna, Andrea da Firenze, as well as members of powerful banking families, such as the Portinari and Albizzi. In the 1360s they settled after much debate and revision on the cathedral scheme visible today. It has a crossing actually wider than the nave – something unprecedented – 72 braccia wide, exactly half the height of the equally unprecedented dome, which was to await Brunelleschi for the resolution of its overwhelming technical challenges.

As the Cathedral grew, the city undertook the elaboration of its setting. In 1339 the commune passed an ordinance requiring that

Cathedral from the Via Proconsolo
Begun c. 1294, dome 1418-36
Florence

the pavement level be lowered in front of the partially constructed façade, in order to enhance its view and scale. In 1363 another ordinance stipulated that all houses built around the tri-conch apse of the church should correspond to its curved geometry. The ordinance furthermore required that these houses be constructed with arcading, which reflected the arcades applied to the apse elevations. The result is a remarkable correspondence between church design and piazza setting, with the only disruption occurring at the south-east corner of the space, when one first enters the Piazza del Duomo from today's via Proconsolo. This seemingly inconsistent right angle provides an ideal point for viewing the entire crossing, apse and dome ensemble (top).

The piazza setting for the Cathedral and its perceptual sophistication, like the interior spatial sequence of the Cathedral itself, were not completed for aesthetic reasons alone. The viewer of the church is provided with the same denouement upon arrival from the restricted Via Proconsolo at the angled corner of the piazza as he or she has upon arrival at the domed crossing of the church within. Such a view was most likely coordinated with civic processions, such as those of San Giovanni and Corpus Domini. Like the church interior during the liturgy of the Eucharist, the exterior space of the

city was becoming a theatrical space, now less for the preaching of friars than for the adoration of the church's divine patrons, and for the magnificent display of the clerical, confraternal and guildsman processions.

The religious and architectural affirmation of the ever-growing status of Florence's major guilds is clearest in the design of one of the last important religious monuments of the Trecento, Orsanmichele. The present structure in fact began not as a sanctuary but rather as a grain market hall, which in 1285 was constructed to replace a modest chapel built on the site over 40 years earlier. In 1292 an image of the Madonna began to perform wonders, which led to a gradual reversion of the site to its earlier sacred status. The lay confraternity of Orsanmichele, which had been founded the year before and was responsible for placing the image at the market, quickly grew in importance, soon becoming the most wealthy and prestigious confraternity of Florence. The confraternity's active presence and the development of the site into a place of pilgrimage made the grain loggia as much a holy place as one of commerce. After a fire and attempted repairs, it was rebuilt in its current form, between 1337 and the 1350s.

The new Orsanmichele was constructed in stone. This choice of material was justified in a document stating that stone was best suited for a building "in which the veneration of the glorious Virgin Mary could be more appropriately celebrated, and grain and meal better conserved" (*in quo veneratio gloriose Virginis Marie posset aptius clebrari, et granum et bladum melius conservari*). The piers supporting the vaulted six-bay space were ornamented on the outside with a series of deep niches, and on the inside with flatter inset areas for panels and, later, frescoes. Soon after the beginning of construction, a Communal ordinance decreed that these panels and frescoes were to be decorated with the various patron saints of the city's major guilds. The same guilds also populated the exterior niches with statues of their patron saints, many of which were to be sculpted by later generations of classicizing sculptors, ranging from Ghiberti to Donatello to Nanni di Banco to Verrocchio.

The next stage in the resacralization of Florence's grain loggia came in 1352, when the confraternity of Orsanmichele decided to replace an existing tabernacle to the Madonna with a new one by Andrea Orcagna. Orcagna's elaborate sculptural masterpiece takes up an entire bay, grazing the ceiling with its remarkable domed roof. The tabernacle establishes an altar-like focus on the series of bays aligned with the Bernardo Daddi *Madonna* panel, of 1346, that it houses (p. 80).

Orsanmichele ended its function as an open grain market in the 1360s, when its arches were sealed and the interior dedicated exclusively to the adoration of the Virgin. The one seemingly functional aspect of the enlarged structure, an added upper-storey grain warehouse, reveals the traditional hieratic role which the guilds were assuming in Florence. The enclosed grain reserves were

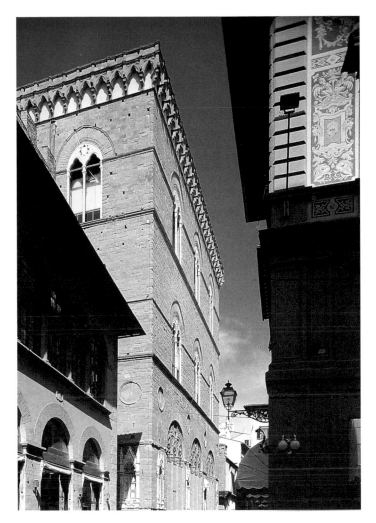

Orsanmichele, begun 1285
Florence

ready for distribution in case of the return of the famines and plagues that had beset the commune between 1330 and 1348. The saints depicted on the piers supporting these reserves therefore functioned like the ex voto Madonna at Pisa Cathedral, to ensure the material well-being of the commune. Since, however, the Orsanmichele saints were the patron saints for individual guilds, the guilds themselves were taking on the image of city patrons, the symbolic "pillars of the community," like so many apostles supporting the Heavenly Jerusalem described in Revelation. In place of the living communal officials who once regulated an active grain market at this location, these anthropomorphic piers were now offering munificence to a passive population, as well as a dignified setting where local and distant pilgrims could make their prayers for material and spiritual intercession to the Madonna, now with no disturbance save for the watchful eyes of the guilds' patron saints.

Late Mediaeval Siena

While the Guelphs, and soon the major guilds, were engaging in ever more sophisticated church-building campaigns in Florence, their counterparts in another important Tuscan centre of commerce and banking, Siena, were engaged in a yet more ambitious project. The Cathedral of Siena began with a substantial structure in the late 13th century. By the third decade of the 14th century it was developing into one of the largest cathedral designs of Latin Christendom, which extended and finally broke the resources and engineering skills of the commune.

The construction of Siena Cathedral began as early as 1226. The still extant portions of this earliest phase, at the nave interior, show the influence of Pisan Romanesque architecture in the bichrome banding above the arches, which extends down the composite piers. The heavy frieze above these piers probably originally supported a barrel vault. The strong horizontal emphasis of this frieze, together with the banding and broad bay spacing, redirects the vertical thrust of the piers, and focuses the view of those entering the church towards the crossing, which was articulated with a dome like that at Pisa Cathedral.

Comparisons with Pisa are consistent with Siena's political status as a pro-imperial, Ghibelline city, up to the end of the 1260s. The dedication of Siena Cathedral to the Virgin was a similar declaration of civic autonomy. This autonomy was most touted following the overwhelming victory of the Sienese and allied Tuscan Ghibellines over the Guelphs, led by Florence, at the Battle of Montaperti, on 4 September, 1260. Just as the Pisans had dedicated a mass to the Virgin before their victory over the Saracens in 1087, so the Sienese named the Virgin as Queen of the Commune before marching into battle against the declared allies of the Pope (see p. 40).

The defeat of the Sienese by the Florentines at the Battle of Benvenuto six years later and the rise to dominance of the Sienese Guelphs failed either to dampen the antagonism of the two cities or to break the strong cultural link between Siena and Pisa. The rivalry between Florence and Siena, as the two leading banking communities of the Latin west, became increasingly channelled into economic competition, and also into what has become known as *campanilismo*, literally, competition over whose bell towers, and public buildings in general, were larger and more magnificent. The Sienese were already in possession of a larger and more modern Cathedral than the 11th-12th century Santa Reparata of Florence. By 1285, one year after Arnolfo was engaged by the Florentines to build the Badia, the Sienese were ensuring their margin by employing another apprentice of Tuscany's greatest mid-13th century sculptor, Nicola Pisano – indeed, Nicola's own son, Giovanni.

The Gothic sensibility visible in Arnolfo's Florentine work is more pronounced in Giovanni Pisano's contribution to Siena Cathedral, though it never loses the classicism present in Nicola's work or in the earlier Romanesque portions of the structure. Giovanni's energies appear to have been concentrated on the lower half of the façade, above the triumphal arch base, which antedates

Cathedral, begun c. 1290
Orvieto

Giovanni's work. The triple portals leave no wall space for sculptural niches, which Giovanni could only insert above the level of the spring-points of their arches. As with Arnolfo's façade for Florence, the niches are Gothic in form, but in both cases the relation of the sculpture to the frame and to the entire structure is distinctly classical, with the entire façade serving as a stage set for the dramatic gestures of the saints, prophets and classical philosophers declaiming to one another and to onlookers below. Though the personages were taken from the Bible and classical antiquity, their rhetorical expressiveness is contemporary, drawing from the tradition of friar preachers. However, in all other ways Giovanni's façade catered to the pre-mendicant tradition of theocratic monumentality. The elevated setting and presence of these calcified *jongleurs* were an updated version of the San Miniato façade mosaic figures of Christ, the Virgin and Saint Minias, or, closer to Giovanni's home, of the sculptural figures on the façade of Pisa Cathedral or at the Pisa Baptistery, which Giovanni himself had carved with his father.

Work on Siena Cathedral later in the 14th century showed a continued tendency to distinguish it from the profane space of the city, as well as to compete with the achievements of the Florentines and with the other town with a great new cathedral in the region, Orvieto (above). One indication of the degrees to which the Sienese were willing to go is the peculiar upper façade of the church. Its framing piers sit uncomfortably above the structural void between the pediments of the portals below and their supporting pilasters.

The technical explanation for this disjunction is the heightening of the nave after the façade had already been elaborated by Giovanni Pisano and his predecessors. However, the new upper façade was extended beyond the actual width of the entire nave. In doing so, the designers maintained what was apparently more important to them than the appearance of structural logic: the proportions of the façade as a geometric and architectural-iconographic composition, of a square temple front situated above a triumphal arch entry. The perfect proportions of this temple front are now emphasized by the circular rose window, which it frames with its four equal sides, and by the equilateral triangles of the pediments.

The disjunction of the façade is indicative of a tendency, indeed an obsession, of the Sienese during the mid-Trecento to increase the magnitude and magnificence of their church without regard to certain architectural conventions. Between the end of Giovanni Pisano's tenure in 1297 and the completion of the upper façade after 1357, the Sienese had been engaged in one of the most remarkable extravagances of late mediaeval architecture, even exceeding the excesses of the impossible dome of Florence Cathedral or the disastrous verticality of Beauvais. In 1339, after already extending the choir two bays over a new Baptistery, communal authorities set in motion a design that would transform the existing nave and choir into the transept of a new nave, to be built perpendicular to them on a far larger scale, terminated at the current north transept with a huge radial choir similar in concept to Suger's choir at Saint Denis, and, in scale, to the choir of Paris's Notre Dame. Insurmountable structural and aesthetic problems in resolving this curved termination led the Sienese to adopt another scheme, almost as grandiose and more consistent with the cruciform plans of the region. The unfinished carcass of this final scheme can still be seen to the west of the existing transept, in the remarkably tall and curiously curved piers embedded into the brick and marble walls of the Museo del Opera del Duomo. The ominous twist of these piers at their upper extents is a testament to their folly as far too narrow and broadly spaced supports for a gargantuan vault, at the height of France's tallest cathedrals but at over one and a half times the span of the final Santa Maria del Fiore nave. All that saved the Sienese from an architectural catastrophe was a series of unrelated disasters that shifted their attention and sapped their resources – the same droughts, famines, bank failures and plague that beset Florence from the early forties on. In 1357 the Sienese accepted the advice of a Florentine consulting architect, Benci di Cione, and razed the unstable portions that were immediately threatening. All the Sienese were left with, beyond the empty portentous space cleared for the new nave, was the more reasonable alternative of extending the height of the existing nave and completing the façade with the purest geometry and most resonant hieratic forms they could create.

Cathedral, begun c. 1226
Siena

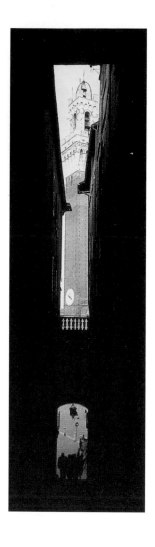

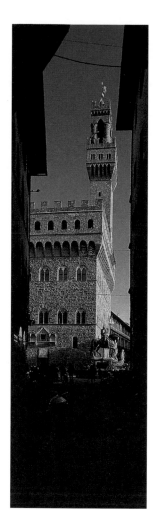

began, usually accompanied by real bloodshed. This situation became more complex the moment cities began to grow, and to lure artisans and serfs away from their feudal duties, often with explicit offers of freedom. In most cases, even the most powerful feudal lords could not compete with the lure of urban life.

The most politically and economically astute of these lords instead moved into the city themselves before losing their entire subject populations. They simply rebuilt their rural fortresses in urban tower-house complexes virtually sealed off from the rest of the city, and transplanted their subjects within their walls. As one might imagine, this situation became somewhat heated, the more such noblemen transferred to the cities. Each feudal group, known as a *consorteria*, vied against the other and against civic authorities to retain the fidelity – and economic and military support – of their subjects. Each built itself the tallest tower possible to assert its right and power over its claimed subjects. The result was the Manhattanization of Italy's communes, which bristled like pin-cushions with towers that would be the envy of many a modern corporate chairperson. Extreme examples are still visible in Bologna and San Gimignano (p. 31).

The tallest tower visible on the San Gimignano skyline is the tower of the Commune. The more elaborate towers of Florence and Siena began as similarly crude statements of forceful dominance, consistent with the frequent recourse to violence by civic governments as they sought to assert the jurisdiction of communal law over private oaths and vendettas, and, equally important, to maintain the right of the city to collect taxes from all residents. The tower of Florence's Palazzo Vecchio began as a private *consorteria* tower, the Torre Foraboschi, around which the Florentines built their asymmetrical public palace, starting in 1299. Only over the following 19 years did they finally develop the building to its present state, constructing a shell around the old tower and then crowning it with its remarkable four-column belfry. The final imposing form of the Palazzo Vecchio set off an inter-city scale of *campanilismos*, influencing the designs of the Volterra and Siena city halls, with the latter adding a tower between 1325 and 1348.

The design of the towers of Siena and Florence appear to have been carefully coordinated with their urban settings. The remarkable height of Siena's Torre della Mangia is partially of necessity, as the communal palace is situated at a low point not only at the Campo, its piazza, but also in the entire city, particularly in relation to the series of tower houses along the Via di Città and to the Duomo above. The curved shape of the Campo directs the views of onlookers towards the tower, as does each of the streets leading to the Piazza.

The Florentines developed similar perceptual effects at the Piazza della Signoria, but over a longer period of time and in a more piecemeal fashion. The piazza began as the rubble-covered site of the Casa Uberti, which the Florentine Guelphs destroyed and cursed

Architectural competition in secular architecture

There is another version of *campanilismo* that existed between Siena and Florence besides that of religious architecture. This is *campanilismo* in the true sense, namely, in the construction of bell towers. The bell tower was an architectural element shared by secular and religious buildings, and was used to regulate the daily activities of citizens, churchgoers, monks and friars. The relative height of these towers and the volume of their bells in comparison to other bell towers determined the status of one authority over another, with the highest and loudest symbolizing the licence and ability to control.

The effectiveness of these towers in encouraging obedience was not purely relative, however, due to another quality they had – as weapons for military defence and assault. Indeed, the recent architectural origin for the tower in mediaeval and Renaissance Italy was the fortified feudal enclave. The first stage of true *campanilismos*, therefore, began with the establishment of rural feudal towers well above the roofs of serfs or tradesmen. Escalations in height were only necessary when one feudal lord began to encroach on another's territory, at which point architectural war

never to be built on again, after having banished the over-powerful Uberti family. The city started to plan a palace beside this site as early as 1280 to replace the nearby Bargello. In its first gestation, according to the 1299 design, the Palazzo Vecchio faced only the void of the Uberti piazza to its north, with the remaining façades fronting narrower streets. Only over the following 82 years did the commune fully develop, execute and embellish the piazza that exists today, starting with a plan to open another space to the west of the tower, and then linking the two spaces with the missing void to the northwest. As soon as the full-size space was conceived, after 1306, it became necessary to increase the height of the palace and tower to provide a structure in scale with the dramatic 3/4 viewpoint at the mouth of today's Via Calzaiouli (p. 35).

As important as the perception of sheer height appears to have been to the Sienese and Florentines in constructing their towers and settings, it was not the only aesthetic paradigm driving their designs. Both towers are remarkably integrated into sophisticated public palace and piazza elevations, which have their roots in architectural traditions other than purely defensive fortification. The Sienese palace is a distillation of an earlier, fully evolved civic palace type

that may have originated in northern civic-palaces, such as at Bergamo, Como or Cremona, and had closer monumental expressions at Orvieto, Todi, and the Palazzo dei Papi in Viterbo. The common element in all of these schemes was the construction of the governing chambers and residence above an open loggia that often served as a marketplace. In most cases, excepting Orvieto and Siena, these palaces faced the principal churches of the Communes, and as such show their debt to the earlier palaces of municipal government before the evolution of lay communal governments, namely the bishops' palaces, to which the Viterbo Palazzo dei Papi is directly linked, and the even earlier seats of authority, the arcaded canon cloisters adjoining cathedrals.

The design of the Campo in Siena (p. 32) recalls these religious architectural origins. In 1297, the town passed an ordinance requiring that all private houses built on the Campo be articulated with triforate windows, explicitly to be modelled on the windows of the Palazzo Pubblico. These windows, in turn, were more elaborate versions of the biforate windows of the nave of the Cathedral, which stood in a similar relation to the biforate windows of the adjoining Sienese Bishop's palace as the Palazzo Pubblico did to the Sansedoni

Piazza del Campo, begun c. 1297
Siena

and other private palaces on the Campo. The sequence of these windows around the Campo provided a rhythmic unity to the space similar to that of an arcaded cloister.

The Palazzo Vecchio in Florence appears to be separate from this tradition in all of its aspects, excepting its ornate biforate windows, which are nonetheless set in the aggressively rusticated stone of its militaristic walls. It is completely closed on the ground level, indicating that even at the end of the 13th century, when it was begun, the city still had to compete with the tower houses of the urban consorterie, not only visually, but also literally, as a giant bastion within the city protecting the governing regime against unruly clans and mobs. The only precedent besides the tower house enclaves appears to be the Palazzo del Capitano del Popolo, or Bargello, built in the 1250s, which has a similarly rusticated base, crenellated roof and tower. What distinguishes both structures from most of the consorterie enclaves before them is their horizontal scale, their rectilinear plans with archiated courtyards, and the overall regularity and uniformity of their designs. Though their courtyards were quite probably influenced by monastic and canonical courtyards, one structure does exist in the region that appears to have been their direct prototype, built between 1238 and 1249, immediately before the Palazzo del Capitano del Popolo's construction was approved. This structure also shared with them their namesake, as the Palazzo del Imperatore in nearby Prato (p. 34). This palace was indeed one of the few etymologically legitimate *Palazzi* on the Italian peninsula, as the residence of the emperor, whose original home, in antiquity, was the Palatine hill. The Palazzo del Imperatore had begun as the seat of the feudal Alberti, then was converted by Emperor Frederick Barbarossa into his regional palace in the late 12th century, and finally expanded fourfold in scale by his successor, Frederick II. It was and remains one of the most imposing of Frederick II's structures in Italy, next to Capo del Monte and the Gate of Capua, but until now has been neglected by architectural historians as a prototype for the development of public and later private palace design in Florence. It has a plan that is crystalline in its purity of forms, with a symmetrical courtyard surrounded by battered and rusticated walls whose weight is alleviated only by their dazzling white stone and curved Ghibelline crenellation. Its dominant presence in the city and region was assured by a now truncated tower, dating from the Casa Alberti, upon which was placed a bell which continued to be used as the primary bell of the commune for years after the palace was taken over by the Guelph regime of Prato, after the Battle of Benvenuto.

The Palazzo del Imperatore and other structures by Frederick II provided alternative models to religious architecture or to the far cruder tower-house fortifications for magnificent civic architecture. By setting the antique forms commonly used in religious architecture within a fortified framework, Frederick II made them appear as direct references to the palatine architecture of Imperial Rome,

which was consistent with his overall policy of asserting his independence from papal temporal authority.

The architecture of Frederick II influenced equally cities that were pro-imperial and pro-papal. When the Florentines adopted this secular palatine typology at their Bargello and Palazzo Vecchio, they were taking a step in differentiating the temporal power of the commune from the established imagery of religious-based rule. This secular typology is consistent with the construction of the 13th- and 14th-century palaces of Florence and Siena in their own piazzas, separate from the cathedrals. This innovative approach to secular architecture does not necessarily imply, any secularization of communal authority however. The same governing and administrative bodies responsible for the construction of these public palaces and piazzas were investing equal if not larger quantities of their money and energies in the elaboration of their cathedrals and cathedrals piazzas, all of which had *campanile* that were as dominant as the palace belfries, if not more so. The simultaneous elaboration of magnificent civic and religious complexes in communes such as Florence and Siena is better understood in terms of the interrelation between civic and religious authority, rather than their disjunction.

The success of communal oligarchies in pacifying their single most dangerous threats, the urban consorteria clans, was in winning the allegiance of individual members of those clans. It did this by legislature, enforced by physical violence exercised by the Commune, by the threat of such violence embodied in civic *campanile*, and often by banishment from the city, temporarily or for life. The communes also won the allegiance and docility of their citizens through religion, first with threatening images of sacred authority, as at San Miniato, and then with the mendicants'

Palatium Imperatoris
Entrance and ground plan
Prato

evangelization of the apostolic life. The latter, however, threatened to topple not only the old, feudal consorterie, but also the new guild regimes of the communes, by undermining the very notion of hierarchical, centralized authority. By the beginning of the Trecento, most communal regimes were redirecting their patronage back to building projects that reinforced the centrality of their power and of the church authority behind them, namely at civic and Cathedral piazzas.

In rebuilding Rome within their communes, cities like Florence were staving off a process of religious, social and political change that threatened the very notion of concentrated, universal authority. So long as other states, such as seigniorial Milan, France, or later Spain, were less advanced in these developments and more sophisticated in their deployment of primitive military force, such a reversion by communes like Florence may have been seen as necessary for their sustained political independence. The first actual wave of social revolution nonetheless hit Florence, well into the Florentines' progress in building the Cathedral and civic piazza, but before the completion of either. This was the revolt of the Ciompi, or wool-carders, one of the lower-class worker groups that were denied by law the right either to form guilds or, consequentially to hold political office. In 1378 the Ciompi took over the city government. They or other non-major guild citizens retained control over the government up to 1382, when the upper guilds succeeded in organizing a bloody massacre of their usurpers. Ten months later the new guild oligarchy completed the triumphal-arch Loggia dei Lanzi, which even the conservative Matteo Villani described as "vainglorious." The regime quickly paved the Piazza della Signoria, lined it with the same arcading as around the rear of the Duomo, and then continued this arcading as far as the closed arches of Orsanmichele. By 1420 the Commune had set Brunelleschi to work on completing the cathedral cupola.

These structures helped to create the fiction of Florence as a paradigm of order, civic magnificence, and Republican values that was being promoted by the humanists as well as by Late Trecento and early Quattrocento artists. This image and variants of it were appropriate for the new role of Florence and the few other large cities on the peninsula that emerged victorious in the architectural and military wars for local and territorial dominion. Florence, Milan, Venice and Papal Rome, for example, were becoming more than cities – indeed, were becoming territorial states, where, for the first time on a sustained basis since the late empire, the tendency of temporal power was towards greater concentration in larger centres rather than dispersal to smaller fiefdoms and local communities and neighbours. Within these centres, however, the dispersion of the images of authority continued, shifting from mendicant enclaves, guild pantheons or civic monuments to the palaces of the powerful families, which were on their way to dominating the new oligarchic and despotic governments of Italy.

Alexander Perrig

Painting and Sculpture in the Late Middle Ages

Reviving the art of the age of Christ

The reform of sacred images at Assisi

Since the year 1260, the panel crucifix below (left) has hung in a side chapel at Santa Chiara in Assisi. During the lifetime of St. Francis of Assisi (1181/2–1226) it hung behind the altar in the little church of San Damiano. It closely resembles the panel crucifixes that were the distinctive legacy of Umbrian and Tuscan painters' workshops of the 12th century; however, the rigidity of the figure is said to have unfrozen at one notable moment in its history. One day between 1205 and 1208, when the future founder of the Franciscan order was kneeling before it asking for guidance, the figure of Christ moved and said: "Go and repair my house, which, as thou seest, is wholly fallen into ruin."

The incident is reported by Tommaso da Celano (who died c. 1260), friend and companion to St. Francis and his first biographer; though admittedly he did not include it until the second version of his life of Francis (1246–7). By the time the world learnt of the figure's miraculous speech, the days of the *Christus triumphans*, Christ triumphantly upright in His victory over suffering and death, were already over in Italy. A change had come over the making of crucifixes, a reform that came late in comparison with developments in France and Germany. This change owed much to the newly established Fransciscan order.

The reform was initiated by Elias of Cortona (c. 1180–1253), the first minister-general of the order, appointed by St. Francis himself as his vicar. Responsible for the building of the great basilica in Assisi, he had asked the renowned master Giunta Pisano to paint a

Panel crucifix from S. Damiano, c. 1200
Tempera on wood
Assisi, Santa Chiara

Giunta Pisano
Panel crucifix, c. 1240
Tempera on wood, 174 x 131 cm
Assisi, Santa Maria degli Angeli

panel cross that showed a dead Christ in the place of the traditional living Christ triumphant, an image that derived from the 5th century. This huge work (now lost) was completed in 1236 and installed on the original rood screen of the Lower Church as its most important adornment. It prompted not only pious feelings, however, but also misgivings, at least among the elder friars; and these misgivings were heightened by the presence of a kneeling Elias of Cortona at Christ's feet (p. 38, bottom). The minister-general was assuredly tiny in relation to the figure of Christ; nonetheless, this seems to have contributed to the feeling against him amongst the Franciscans, which led to his being deposed in 1239.

To judge by a later panel cross by Giunta Pisano that still survives (p. 36, bottom right), the controversial crucifix will have borne a resemblance, both in the figure of Christ and in the fundaments of style, to Byzantine icons. It was thus a novelty to the friars not only in its iconography but also in its formal idiom. And this implies that, in commissioning the Pisan painter, Elias of Cortona was aiming at more than a mere reform of the crucifix. In instructing the painter to model his gigantic cross on the tiny crucifix in an icon with scenic representations (in Byzantine art, there were extremely few crosses in isolation from a crucifixion context), he may well have had a reform of the artistic idiom *per se* in mind. Giunta's cross does not in fact appear to have been either the only or the first sacred image that the minister-general commissioned for the church (the building of which had been ordered by the Pope); a panel portraying St. Francis, for the high altar, was probably commissioned before it. Though no documentary evidence that this altar panel ever did exist now survives, its prior existence is implied by the increasing appearance of iconic pictures of St. Francis on the high altars of Franciscan churches from 1235 on, the date at which Bonaventura Berlinghieri's panel in San Francesco at Pescia (p. 38) was completed. These iconic pictures were not only the first high altar images of a saint but were also the first sacred panels to be painted in an imported rather than native Italian style.

The iconic style and the mendicant orders

Byzantine icons had always found their occasional way west. A number were venerated in Rome in the early Middle Ages. They were apparently valued as highly as the costliest relics, on the grounds that they were authentic works (it was believed) by the contemporaries of Christ and the Virgin Mary – Luke the evangelist; Nicodemus, the Pharisee who came to Christ and later helped to bury Him; or indeed an angel painting in secret in the early years of the Christian era.

Prior to the 13th century, this belief in the venerable authorship of iconic works had led to copies being made and motifs being borrowed. In terms of style, however, this process had no impact, aside from brief periods when the reception of icons was particularly

intense. This changed following the capture and looting of Constantinople by the Crusaders in April 1204. During the fifty years and more that the city was occupied, art treasures and relics from numerous churches and monasteries were transported west, together with word of the significance, miraculous powers, and manner of production of the images.

One of the first to bear such word was probably Elias of Cortona. In 1217 he was made provincial minister of the *Terra Sancta* by Francis of Assisi; the term covered Greece and Constantinople, Armenia, Syria, Palestine and Egypt. In the four years that preceded his appointment as minister-general, he acquired so thorough a knowledge of the eastern Church that he was constantly being consulted by the Pope and clergy. What he learnt and saw on the spot of Byzantine art and its production seems to have convinced him that in those venerable panels the true likenesses of Christ, of the Mother of God and of the saints, and the styles of the early Christian primitives, had genuinely been transmitted intact.

Bonaventura Berlinghieri
St. Francis with Scenes from his Life, 1235
Tempera on wood, 160 x 123 cm
Pescia, San Francesco

Master Jacob
Mosaic, begun 1225
Florence, Baptistery

Scarcely had Elias returned to Italy (1220) when the number of supposed originals by Luke or Nicodemus, and copies of these, began to grow significantly, as did the cults and legends that went with them. It was St. Dominic who opened the season, as it were. In 1221, when the Dominican nuns in Rome moved from Santa Maria in Tempulo to San Sisto, he himself carried their most precious possession, a pre-Carolingian icon of Mary, at the front of the procession. In 1225 a similar image, found in a Lucchese fort that the Pisans had overrun, was placed on display for veneration in the Cathedral at Pisa. By the end of the 13th century most towns of any size had not only a "Christian primitive" panel of there own but also a confraternity sworn to uphold its claims and tend the legends associated with it. Thus when a Dominican by the name of Fra Giordano da Rivalto (c. 1260–1310) turned to the subject of Byzantine icons in a sermon he preached in Florence in 1306, he was probably saying things that the people of Florence had heard countless times before: that "the first pictures of them [the Magi] that came from Greece ... were painted by saints"; that those portrayed in them "[are] shown exactly as they appeared and were in life"; that Nicodemus was the first to portray Christ as He looked on the cross, having been "present when Christ was crucified"; "that Luke left an authentic portrait of the Mother of God on a panel now revered in Rome" (that is, the Salus Populi Romani in Santa Maria Maggiore); and that images of this nature, imported from Greece, thus possessed "the highest authority ... and as much evidential value as Scripture".

Elias of Cortona had apparently considered it his duty to have the panel crucifix he had commissioned done in such a way that it would appear as the "true" image of the crucified Christ even to those who were accustomed to seeing Christ triumphant as the true likeness. Both the miniature of Elias himself and the words put into his mouth – *Jesu Christe pie miserere precantis Helie* (Jesus Christ, have mercy on the praying Elias) – were intended to reinforce that title to veracity. The picture and the petition alike attested the "truth" of the new crucifix by presenting it as the Almighty, present here and now and able to hear and answer prayer. The fact that the cross on the panel was painted an ultramarine shade rather than being left in its natural wood colour (to judge by subsequent works that survive), in contradistinction to earlier panel crucifixes and Byzantine crosses, was probably intended to inspire confidence. It was as if the cross partook of a heavenly substance, thus standing directly for entrance into the realm of immortality and triumph. The old had been incorporated into the new, and any potential objection that God was being portrayed in too human a manner had been anticipated. Within decades, every new panel cross, including those that were not made for Franciscan churches, followed the example set by the minister-general's.

Minister-general Elias of Cortona at the foot of Giunta Pisano's lost cross at Assisi (1236). Like a witness, the kneeling figure asserts the truth of the Christ he worships. Engraving, 17th century

Master of Tressa
Madonna with the Large
Eyes
Tempera on wood
Siena, Museo dell' Opera del
Duomo

Coppo di Maarcovaldo
Madonna del Bordone, 1261
Tempera on wood,
225 x 125 cm
Siena, Santa Maria dei Servi

The iconic style and the communes

In contrast to the churches of the new mendicant orders, the secular priesthood and monastic community seem largely not to have opened up to Byzantine art till the latter half of the 13th century. Venice and Pisa constituted exceptions to this rule, since it was in their ships that the Byzantine booty was transported; and so too did Florence. As early as 1225, mosaic work was begun on the vaulted ceiling of the Florence Baptistery (p. 39) – work that was to become, when completed, one of the most magisterial achievements of the primitive style in Italy. The Calimala merchants' guild, which had been responsible for the upkeep and decoration of the Baptistery since the 12th century, hired a Venetian mosaic maker, Master Jacob, to do the work – not only because Venice had the best mosaic artists but also because the choice of a Venetian guaranteed that the style of the mosaic would be of the desired kind.

The gigantic ceiling mosaics were already half finished before Byzantinism caught on in Siena. Its advent was less striking than in Florence; its impact was all the greater. Sienese Byzantinism (and this was the secret of its tenacious hold) was adopted and championed by the city state, as in Venice. The reason for this may be sought in the victory won by the Ghibelline Sienese over a superior army of Florentine Guelphs on 4 September 1260 at Montaperti – a victory of crucial importance for Siena. On the eve of the battle, Bonaguida Lucari, the head of the Sienese government, had enlisted the heavenly powers on the side of Siena by declaring the Virgin, to a crowd of citizens assembled in the Cathedral and in the presence of the bishop, to be Queen of the Commune. This ritual was performed before the high altar, probably adorned for the occasion with its festive frontal, the old wooden antependium. Once the *Madonna with the Large Eyes* (left, top) had taken the Sienese part on the following day, as required, the antependium was promoted to a permanent altar image.

The lost original of the Madonna icon of which this is a replica was in the home for the blind of the Guides (hodegoi). The Hodegetria icon was the most copied of all icons, and the replicas influenced Italian images of the Madonna in the 13th century.

Hodegetria icon
12th century
Athens, Byzantine Museum

It did not enjoy this new honour for long, however. The Queen – frozen in audience, attended by two angels, and holding her Child before her in the posture of a presiding judge – was presently challenged in her claim to be the "true" queen of Siena from two quarters: by the Nikopoia (victory-bringing) icon in Venice, and by the Hodegetria icon in Siena. Both images were Byzantine and supposed to be the work of St. Luke. Beside them, the *Madonna with the Large Eyes* seemed too modern, seemed to present a false picture of Siena's queen.

The Hodegetria icon in Siena was in the possession of the Servants of Blessed Mary, the Servites, an order established in 1233 in Florence. Its friars were largely exiled Florentine Ghibellines, and they played their own part in undermining the standing of the Cathedral Madonna. Immediately after the victory at Montaperti, they commissioned the Florentine painter Coppo di Marcovaldo, who had supposedly been taken captive in the battle, to paint a large panel (p. 40, bottom left); and the enthroned Madonna in this panel must have seemed like Life itself compared with the mummified Madonna of the old picture (p. 40, top). Both Virgins, iconographically speaking, are rendered in the same manner. Flanked by two angels on a gold ground, the Madonnas are looking out of their pictures; their shod feet are visible, resting on cushions; the right hand of each is touching the right foot of the Child, who is raising His right hand in blessing and holding a scroll in His left. In both panels the Virgin's halo, embellished with circular ornamental motifs, overlaps on the upper decorative frame; the feet of the thrones are carved to resemble vegetation; the seats of the thrones consist of three layers of cushions; and the Virgin's wimple has two layers of cloth. And yet it is as if this surface similarity were merely there to show the Sienese how the *Madonna with the Large Eyes* could become an authentic portrait of the Queen of Siena: by eliminating the symmetrical body posture and fabric folds, by accentuating the sense of spatial volume, by inclining the Madonna's head and giving her more delicate facial features, by the chrysographic use of gold – in short, by transforming the entire appearance into a Byzantine one.

And certainly Coppo's panel aspired to be the authentic portrait of the city state's Queen, as suggested by the non-Byzantine robes and the imperial eagle embroidered onto the wimple and framed with circles. The cloak, the close-fitting tunic, the wimple and the footwear were all (despite the earthy colouring of chestnut, buff and dark red) in line with the contemporary apparel of queens. This lady is thus shown to be a ruler in the secular realm. The imperial eagles are a reference to the eagle banner of Manfred, King of Sicily (1232–66), under whom the Sienese had won their victory at Montaperti. They betray the Madonna's Ghibelline "cast of mind". Her divine status is suggested merely by the angels, her halo, and the chrysography of her cloak and skirt. The demonstrative politicizing of the work's message was presumably intended to strengthen the

whom it owed the victory at Montaperti; her title to governance, however, was expressed solely in the flanking presence of the city's four patron saints, half-figures that no longer survive. The Madonna together with these flanking portraits, with arcade columns between, constituted a frieze with a focal point in the middle.

This iconic frieze, inspired by Byzantine iconostatic trabeations, served the prime purpose of gathering into a visibly present community the saints whose relics were kept in the Cathedral. The painted images of the saints would be shown during mass, as if, from a position beyond the wall of a celestial loggia, they were in conversation with the celebrant priest. This afforded so persuasive a visual underscoring of the priest's intermediary role that the Cathedral's new image was soon being copied for the retables of many another high altar (cf. p. 41, bottom). This resulted in a paradoxical situation. The altars in private side chapels, or those used by lay bodies, featured full-figure panels of ever-increasing dimensions (pp. 42 and 43), and these made their appeal primarily to the faithful, not the priest, whereas the images on the high altars were more understated half-figures that did not take the congregation of the faithful into account. The most important place in the church, though it had been ideologically consolidated, seemed aesthetically down-graded.

In Siena – and from 1260 to 1300 it was Sienese workshops that produced most of the Madonna panels for side altars in Tuscan churches – people seem gradually to have wearied of their *Madonna del voto* as a result. In 1308 the Opera of the Duomo resolved to replace the small retable with a very large one that would be visible

Sienese in their belief that the Queen of Heaven was on the side of the commune, despite the interdict imposed on the city by the Pope on 18 November 1260.

Coppo's panel had a considerable impact. It was immediately imitated, in apolitical copies commissioned by other confraternities. And it also seems to have led to the *Madonna with the Large Eyes,* so recently placed on the Cathedral high altar, being removed once more. The image that took its place bore no resemblance to Coppo's Queen, however: it was a half-figure Hodegetria (p. 41, top), possibly the very one that had previously been venerated by the Servites. It was known as the *Madonna del voto*, and thus as the authentic image of the Queen in whose service the city state avowedly stood, and to

Duccio di Buoninsegna
Maestà, 1311
Tempera on wood, 214 x 412
(original dimensions of the whole altarpiece: c. 500 x 468 cm)
Siena, Museo dell' Opera del Duomo

throughout to the entire congregation. Duccio di Buoninsegna (c. 1255–c. 1318) was commissioned to create a high altarpiece with predella panels. The front side was to feature an enthroned Madonna in large format, surrounded by adoring saints and angels. This was Duccio's *Maestà* (top).

The great Maestà was the first official portrait, as it were, of the Sienese city state's patron and queen. It lacks the explicit political affiliation of Coppo's Madonna; but it possesses in a high degree the openness to the commune and congregation that the image which previously occupied that high-altar position, the *Madonna del voto*, had not had. Gold striations, the transcendent status symbol, have been reduced in it: in contrast to most Byzantine-style Madonnas, including earlier works by Duccio himself, the gold is absent from the cloak and merely appears on the undergarment which is almost concealed by it. This cloaking of the celestial brings the Queen of Heaven closer to her earthly subjects, and thus has the effect of stressing the secular aspect of her role, as patron of the city. She is seated on an inlaid marble throne that recalls Siena's romanesque Cathedral in its colours and spatial weight. The Child, clad in imperial purple, is turned like a spokesman to an audience beyond the painting. The Madonna too seems open to the fore, and this attitude of Mother and Child appears in some sense a response to

the petitioning of the four kneeling patron saints of Siena in the foreground to right and left, who are presented in the style of ambassadors to a royal court. The presence and manner of these four kneeling figures introduces a historical element into the picture: it is as if the Sienese, through its advocates, enjoy a permanent audience with the Madonna and Child.

In this new Madonna the people of Sienese were unreservedly happy to see their queen, and demonstrated as much, after its completion, on 9 June 1311, when the *Maestà* was ceremonially collected from Duccio's workshop by the clergy, government and people and carried in triumphal procession, to the sound of bells and music, to the Cathedral – for all the world as if it were a real, living queen. Shortly after, she made her entry into the Council Chamber of the Palazzo Pubblico too, thus to preside officially over the city's government proceedings (p. 45). This fresco, completed in June 1316 by Duccio's pupil Simone Martini (c. 1284–1344), uses an ornamental frame to suggest a window in the west wall of the old town hall, through which, on a dais positioned before a deep blue sky, the heavenly hosts are seen thronging about the Virgin and Child.

Simone Martini's picture differs from the Cathedral "audience" Madonna in having a reduced number of angels (six, not ten) but an

Simone Martini
Maestà, completed 1316
Fresco
Siena, Palazzo Pubblico, Sala del Mappamondo

increased number of saints (ten, not six). To show that the Virgin is outside her residence, she is seen seated beneath a canopy of the kind held over kings and queens in processions. On this canopy are the arms of Siena. In place of her ultramarine cloak in Duccio's *Maestà*, the Virgin is wearing a brown robe with gold striations here, not dissimilar to the brown garb in Coppo's Ghibelline Madonna (p. 40, bottom left). Her throne seems a light, transportable thing, with tracery like that of a Gothic choir and wings that look as if they might be folded together. As in Duccio's painting, the four patron saints of Siena are kneeling to either side of the steps before the throne, though now an angel kneels in front of either pair, bearing flowers as a gift from the commune.

The Madonna and Child are gazing out towards where the Council, beyond the "window", must be sitting. It is to the Council that the Child's blessing, and Solomon's admonition that those who judge should love justice, are directed. In the eyes of the Council, however, this blessing and admonition will hardly have been the main thing. Positioning the fresco on an end wall implies that it was meant to be associated with the images of the Sienese commune's territories on the end wall directly opposite. These images served a purpose comparable to title deeds: they gave a "truthful" record of what territories were owned and how they were come by. The

Madonna's relation to them was that of a queen who, paying regular visits to her lands, both underlines her continuing concern for law and order and emphasizes her proprietorial claims.

The minor Renaissance of the Christian primitive style in sculpture

The fact that the Byzantine iconic style could so readily be thought Christian primitive and copied, following the conquest of Constantinople in 1204, was symptomatic of a crisis for which St. Francis of Assisi and his earliest followers must bear part of the responsibility. Franciscan sermons were different from what had previously been preached. They were simple, rich in images, and referred to everyday life. They imperceptibly quickened their congregations' perceptions, and unwittingly changed their attitude to native art. Italian art, compared with Byzantine, had become rigid, unemotional, formulaic, and it was becoming obvious that an urban society now growing more aware and sophisticated demanded more. True, native art seemed to be of the selfsame Christian origin as Greek; but it had degenerated in the course of time, and become a mere caricature of "true" art.

It was relatively straightforward to reform the central genre, painted sacred images. There was no shortage of models to copy, nor was it difficult to learn the new styles. To reform sculpture

45

The Franciscans liked to use illustrative material in their sermons and even took pictures into the pulpit with them, as a 13th-century poem satirizing the mendicant orders' new sermon style suggests. It became increasingly important to have pictorial scenes on the pulpits themselves.

features stripped from Roman ruins had been incorporated into its exterior walls; and their position at that sacred place seemed to confer a certain sanctity on them, too. Their reception followed a similar pattern to that of Greek painting, mosaics and ivory carving. Ancient reliefs had always served as intermittent sources of inspiration, especially in the 12th century. The borrowings were confined to motifs, however. It was not until the formal modes of contemporary sculpture came to appear remote from an original "truth" that it seemed possible to take the style of Roman antiquity and use it as a vehicle for Christian content.

Nicola Pisano had previously been active in Apulia, possibly as one of the sculptors who created classicizing art to please the imperial tastes of Emperor Frederick II (1220–50). Working *all' antica* was nothing new to him, in other words. Narrating Biblical tales in a Roman relief style was nonetheless a novel departure, different from chiselling copies of ancient busts and triumphant reliefs. The difficulties of the new challenge are apparent from the unsystematic way in which Nicola met it. He filled his visual spaces with substantial figures positioned in condensed spatial strata and wearing classical garments, hair styles and beards, even with classical features. This was his idea of an ancient style; but in reality, if we leave aside the three lions that bear the columns of the pulpit and the six Biblical figures standing over the capitals, the only work that genuinely has a note of classical antiquity is the reliefs of the *Nativity*, the *Adoration of the Magi* and the *Presentation in the Temple*. In the *Adoration of the Magi* (p. 47, top) the Virgin in her priestess vestments was essentially copied by Nicola from the Phaedra seated on a Roman sarcophagus in Pisa (p. 47, bottom). The small gable behind her head is intended to show that she personifies the Church. She seems altogether conscious of her mission on earth, and her presence in this ritual adoration is a commanding one. The two bearded magi are like Roman senators kneeling to an image of Juno. Only the Child Christ, reaching out impatiently for the gift being offered to Him, breaks the rather solemn emotionality of the ceremony.

Compared with the first three reliefs, the *Crucifixion* and *Last Judgement* seem born of a quite different stylistic persuasion. Given the nature of the affects implied in these dramatic scenes, the ancient remains available in Pisa could serve as models only for one or two minor figures; essentially, Nicola had recourse to Byzantine models for these panels, a fact which suggests that icons and Roman marble reliefs were to some extent considered interchangeable.

In addition to these two sources in what was considered "Christian primitive" art, Nicola drew upon a third style, the Gothic, in his work on the pulpit. As if to forestall any comparison of his arches with pagan triumphal arches (and the reliefs of prophets filled into the spandrels do indeed recall the Victory spandrels of the Arch of Constantine), he added trefoil cusping to them – in other words, a tracery motif. This defamiliarization of his

proved more problematic, though. The attempt was not made until mid-century, first in Pisa, in a pulpit (top). The use of pulpit sides as surfaces for reliefs had become more important in the wake of the Franciscan habit of illustrating their sermons with pictures. The reliefs done by Nicola Pisano (c. 1205–80) for the marble pulpit of the Pisan Baptistery (which was also a parish church) established – practically overnight – a style whose classicism seems almost polemical in its antithetical difference to the reliefs of the Cathedral pulpit, done in an unbending, geometrical manner about a century earlier.

Nicola drew particularly upon Roman reliefs for inspiration. Sarcophagi were heaped around the Cathedral, while decorative

classical manner is interesting not least because, at that date, Gothic tracery was as unknown in Tuscany as the figure of Christ nailed to the cross with three rather than four nails was (in the *Crucifixion* panel). Both features point to the Ile de France, the home and origin of tracery and one of the first areas where the three-nail cross became common. In the second quarter of the century, sculpture there had gone through a brief period of classicism inspired by ancient statuary; the most famous product of this phase is the Visitation group at the west entrance of Reims Cathedral. Whoever prescribed the programme of Nicola's panels may well have been a theologian who studied in Paris, as did Federigo Visconti, Archbishop of Pisa from 1254 to 1277, who commissioned the pulpit; and he presumably belonged to the Dominican friary of Santa Caterina, for the Pisan pulpit was scarcely finished (1259/60) when Nicola was commissioned to make the shrine of St. Dominic in the Dominican mother church, San Domenico, in Bologna. He was assisted in his work by Arnolfo di Cambio and the Pisan friar Guglielmo.

Curiously, Nicola's classicism appears to have been approved without reservation by the Dominicans; this is suggested not only by his being commissioned to make the shrine of St. Dominic but also by the enthroned Madonna, imitated from a Roman statue of Juno and adorned with classical ornament, that Arnolfo di Cambio made after 1282 for the tomb of Cardinal Guillaume de Braye in the Dominican church at Orvieto. In contrast, the Opera of the Duomo in Siena did not wish Nicola to repeat his Pisan approach when, on 29 September 1265, they commissioned him to make a similar pulpit for Siena Cathedral (p. 48). Instead, they required him to change stylistic course completely, and follow French models. Possibly the Pisan reliefs of the young Christ had sparked controversy; but it is equally possible that the Sienese had detected the weakness in them, their lack of expressive flexibility. At all events, a new subtlety, both physical and emotional, is apparent when we compare the Siena pulpit with the Pisan. To achieve this subtlety, indeed, the diminished monumentality that resulted from taking French sculptural miniatures (such as ivory or silver reliefs) as models was apparently accepted as inevitable.

Using the Gothic style in sculpture introduced a new vividness and vitality that went far beyond what was achieved in contemporary painting with its Byzantine influences. The microcosms of Nicola Pisano, his son Giovanni, and his other pupils, as seen on the Sienese pulpit, the shrines and ciboria, the tombs, fountains and façades, exerted a compelling hold on visual conceptions until well into the Trecento, among painters too. Yet it was the very conviction of their figures, a vitality independent of dogmatic rules, that helped undermine the concepts of "truth" and "authenticity" in art that were so inseparable from Byzantinism, and so made manifest the covert crisis that art in central Italy had slipped into in the years after 1204.

Phaedra
sarcophagus
Pisa, Camposanto

Nicola and Giovanni Pisano
Pulpit, 1265–68
Marble, 460 cm
Siena, Cathedral

Roger Bacon and the birth of the natural style

Roger Bacon's reform proposal

No one in the 13th century seems to have perceived as clearly as the Franciscan Roger Bacon (c. 1214–94) that something was wrong with an art so ill-matched to the requirements of society. Bacon, a scientific mind who studied colour and light, doubtless realized long before he became a Franciscan (in 1257) that visual images were of great importance not only for congregations but also for their favourite preachers. He will have realized, too, the limits of the uses of images, in his own life as a Franciscan. The conclusions he came to in his encyclopaedic *Opus majus* (1266–68), written expressly for the Pope, make that work one of the most illuminating and important documents produced in the Middle Ages.

Bacon felt that, in his day, images had failed in their function as aids to understanding. They were not vivid and evocative enough. Instead of presenting the content of Scripture in so palpable a way that its literal and its allegorical, moral and mystical meanings were clear, he asserted, images were deceitful both in sum and in detail. Bacon blamed theologians, since they commissioned works and designed the programmes of their contents. They had no notion of geometry, perspective and optics, he said – though if they consulted Euclid's *Elements* and other available books on geometry (as their predecessors in the late classical period had done, using images to clarify and make vivid the truth and meaning of the Word), all would be clear. Divine wisdom would be apparent to all, he believed, if only the things mentioned in Scripture were set before human kind in palpable form. Biblical tales would seem present reality; one might see Solomon's Temple, and indeed the New Jerusalem, with one's own eyes! For this reason, argued Bacon, nothing was worthier of the attention of those learned in the ways of God than to have three-dimensional works made to this end; and he urged the Pope to give the necessary command, adding that there were three or four men who had the necessary abilities.

The men Bacon had in mind were not the Giottos but rather such as himself, theologians with an interest in science and optics, such as his English countryman John Peckham (c. 1240–92) or another from Silesia, named Witelo, who was probably a Franciscan lay brother. In Bacon's view, they alone possessed the know-how required to conceive images in three dimensions; only they, therefore, were properly suited to design visual presentations of the true content of Holy Writ. Bacon did not need to point out that the painters of the age could not apply this skill because they had lost it in the course of the centuries. The proof was readily available, in the frescos of the nave in the Lower Church of San Francesco at Assisi. The left initial picture (p. 50) represents only what the bare account of Tommaso da Celano offers, and not a jot more: a naked Francis, calling unto God in heaven, being taken into the protection of a pious bishop of the town and given a cloak by him, and the many people who hear

Francis cry out, at their head (now no longer distinguishable) Francis's father, Bernardone, wrathful and holding the clothes that his son has given back to him. The picture has neither space nor locality nor palpable, physical bodies – nothing that might convey to the beholder a sense of having witnessed an event that remains relevant. Whether the faithful could visualize the reality that was behind the words, and behind their translation into paint, or could follow the interpretations to be placed upon them, depended entirely on the imaginative powers and rhetorical skills of preachers.

Roger Bacon was the first since the time of Pope Gregory the Great (590–604) to define the expectations that needed to be made of art, and in doing so he identified the gap between that ideal condition and the actual state of affairs, which Bacon found unsatisfactory. Those who commissioned works and drew up the

programmes, and the artists themselves, still proceeded as if pictures were necessary in churches so that (as Gregory had said) those who could not read might at least learn what they were debarred from in books by contemplating the walls. They still proceeded, claimed Bacon, as if their task remained what it had been in the first millennium: to provide a substitute for the written word, to inform the illiterate of what was written in the Bible, the Apocrypha, and the lives of the saints. Not that art had ignored the growing need for space and time contextualization that began in the universities and extended to urban communities which, by the year 1200, were already becoming more literate. But even the Siena Cathedral pulpit (p. 48), as late as the 1260s, attempted to provide this ampler interpretation purely by increasing the number of figures and giving them individual characteristics. All spaces and all times were treated as one. The *Dream of Joseph* appeared to take place right behind the back of the high priest in the *Presentation in the Temple*, the *Flight to Egypt* at Joseph's back, and all of these were immediately under a row (double in places) of figures gathered together by no more than a principle of addition. The didactic purpose consisted solely in encouraging the faithful to recognize and love the figures and stories they were already familiar with. The task of placing what had been recognised in its context of space and time, and of

commenting accordingly, fell to the preachers, since the common people were not permitted to read the Bible. Small wonder that the clergy felt overtaxed, and privately wished for more eloquent pictures.

The birth of the natural style

Bacon proposed his reform of images in a conspicuous place, the introduction to the fourth and most important part of the *Opus majus*, which dealt with geometry and *perspectiva* (optics). He sent his manuscript, completed in 1268, to the Pope at Viterbo, as instructed. But Clement IV (1265–68), in whom Bacon had placed his hope, died that same year. The Papal See was vacant for three years following his death, a circumstance hardly conducive to keeping interest in Bacon's work alive. It was left to Pope Nicholas III (1277-80) to grasp its significance. Formerly the protector of the Franciscan order, Nicholas had scarcely been elected Pope but he summoned John Peckham to the Papal University of Viterbo (where Witelo was already active). Nicholas had the chapel of Sancta Sanctorum in Rome renovated and frescos painted there that look like first attempts to exemplify Bacon's new concept of the pictorial image (cf. p. 51). Compared with the frescos in the nave of the Lower Church at Assisi, the martyrdoms portrayed at Sancta

Martyrdom of St. Peter and St. Paul
Fresco, c. 1278–80
Rome, Scala Santa, Chapel of St. Laurence
(Sancta Sanctorum), south wall

Sanctorum might as well be eye-witness accounts. The space has real depth. The figures do not look as if they can simply be moved to right or left like cut-outs, but seem able to move to and fro, to exist in space, to act, see and communicate.

The *Martyrdom of St. Peter* takes place on the outskirts of a city, with a hill and the city itself in the background. The walls, gates, towers and buildings lend the city an imposing air of size and grandeur by the mere circumstance of being placed at different spatial levels. The landmark monuments of the Obelisk and the Mausoleum of Hadrian identify the city as Rome as seen from the elevation of the Vatican. The four women appear to have emerged onto a space before the city walls, and their position in contrast with the three men suggests that they are relative latecomers, a suggestion which in turn marks the passing of time – that very time during which St. Peter, bleeding to death on his inverted cross, is said to have delivered his last sermon to the passing people of Rome.

This crucifixion, with its counterpart to the right of the lancet window in Sancta Sanctorum, the *Decapitation of St. Paul*, constitutes part of a pictorial, decorative ensemble in which the martyrdom images seem to exist in suspension. They are framed by narrow tapestry borders and capped by a segment of the heavens, seeming as thin and lightweight as parchment. It is as if the martyrdom pictures had been hung against a rich red ground, fastened solely by the delicate acanthus tendrils that coil at the top of the frames, with doves attending. On the lunette cornice, as if to attest their weightlessness and lack of a fixed place, there is on either side a beaten gold amphora of striking size, between the paintings and the lower part of the substantial lunette frame, containing verdant vegetation.

Amphoras, vegetation and tendrils, segments of sky, doves, and additionally cross-bearing angels in flight pointing down to the historical pictures from a blue area at the zenith, together with the rosetted framing of the lancet window – these constitute the repertoire. Their symbolic significance and their inner relation to the paintings are palpable, and in this sense the frescos in this papal chapel were the first to offer visual material apt to preacherly purposes, as Bacon desired. The images in the complete pictorial ensemble make clear the literal, textual meanings, illuminating historical reality, which is both of value in itself and important for the deeper meanings it points towards. It would be idle to nail down those deeper meanings; identifying them was the task of theologians, and their deliberations came to various conclusions at various times. What counts here is that the framing ensemble provides visual cues for interpretation. The two martyrdoms are presented as an eternal legacy to prompt meditation. The two golden vessels, sources of life, suggest an allegorical view of the meaning of martyrdom. And in its solemn arrangement around a source of light, the ensemble also draws attention to the Light that gave the martyrs their common faith and strength.

OPPOSITE:
The Creation, Noah and the Ark
below: Scenes of the Life of St. Francis, c. 1290
Frescoes on the nave of the Upper Church
Assisi, San Francesco

Putting Bacon's proposal into practice had tremendous implications for the history of western art in the post-classical age. The reform achieved a revival of objective means of gauging the internal "correctness" of a picture. The measure applied was God's own Creation, the world that anyone could see about him. To follow that Creation in art meant taking the things of the world as the image of Truth and the vehicle of the timeless, infallible style of the Deity.

Jacopo Torriti's work at Assisi

The frescos of Sancta Sanctorum marked what might be called a test period in the Baconian reform. After they were completed, two monumental cycles on similar subject matter followed. One, of which only two apostles' heads remain, is in the narthex of Old St. Peter's in Rome; the other, poorly preserved, is in the choir and transept of the Upper Church of San Francesco (officially a papal chapel) at Assisi. They had scarcely been begun when the Pope, who had commissioned them, died (in 1280). The reform of sacred images seemed destined for the doldrums; but Nicholas IV (1288–92), himself a Franciscan and from 1274 to 1279 the minister-general of the order, saw to it that the work was continued at Assisi, and carried out as his revered predecessor, Nicholas III, had intended. The nave, at that point not yet decorated, became the home for a whole new generation of reformed-style history paintings – scenes from the Old and New Testaments, and a twenty-eight-part cycle depicting the life of St. Francis.

Jacopo Torriti was apparently first entrusted with the conception of these. Posterity knows his name because he and his assistant Jacopo da Camerino twice broke through the anonymity behind which Franciscan artists normally conceal their work. They did so, doubtless on the orders of the Pope, by recording both their names and their likenesses in the apsidal mosaics of two of Rome's greatest basilicas. The importance of these portraits is comparable with that of the minister-general Elias of Cortona in Giunta's panel cross of 1236 (p. 38, bottom). They not only show how Bacon's proposed reform was being put into practice but also illuminate the role of artists in the Franciscan order. In the mosaic completed first (1292) in the Lateran Basilica, Torriti and his assistant appear with the apostles, kneeling dwarfs amid standing giants. Torriti is kneeling on the left, in the mosaic's field of honour. With his left foot on a piece of parchment, symbolizing the foundation of his work, he presents himself as the designer of the work, dedicating his instruments to his patron saint, St. James. These instruments are the rule and compasses. Hitherto they had been the tools of the architect; at times they had been emblems associated with the Creator. The fact that they are in Torriti's hands shows that he had designed his mosaic on geometrical principles, in accordance with Bacon's ideas. They are proof that the work is a true image of the real, and their bearer an artist of the new scientific kind. The artist who designed the frescos of Sancta Sanctorum had been of the same type; and any artist who was responsible for the making of new pictures at that time – such as Jacopo da Camerino, seen beating a panel on the other side of the mosaic – will surely also have been of like persuasion.

After the decorations for the ceiling vaulting, the first pictures to be conceived were the Biblical scenes in the window area. They were arranged in two registers (p. 53) – Old Testament scenes on the right, New Testament on the left, with the lower scene serving as continuation of the scene above it. The choice of scenes was an achievement in itself. It had to be made with two different readings in mind, the natural (horizontal narrative) and the artificial (vertical, to follow the wall). The latter was of greater importance; as the next bay in the nave shows, the aim was to lead the beholder onward to deeper levels of meaning.

This bay shows the Creation of the universe at the top, and, below, God's command to Noah to build the Ark, together with Noah's building of it. Both pictures, in order to establish sources in Early Christian art, drew upon the famous cycle of frescos in San Paolo fuori le mura in Rome, then freshly restored; 17th-century drawings recorded its appearance in former times. Both pictures brought their models up to date in line with the latest in science and Biblical exegesis. In the Creation scene, the concentric circles appear not as a window onto a starry sky but as a repository of cosmic energies. The centre, a glowing fiery vacuum, is occupied by the one authentic God in the form of Christ. The heavenly bodies are in a sphere of their own that revolves around the divine sphere. Emerald green in colour, it marks the transition from the white boundary of the divine sphere to the colourful earthly realm. There, clouds drift through a blue sky above lands and waters rich in vegetation, animals and fish. Light, personified as a youth, and Darkness, as a woman, rule over this realm in equal measure. It may seem paradoxical that the divine sphere is fire-red while God's vestments are ultramarine or purple, but the effect is intended to show God emerging from His realm to take an active part in earthly affairs. The God of Creation seems able to reach out from His vacant space into the spaces of His Creation, and to withdraw again; He is distinct and separate from Creation even as He plays an active part in it. This is the visual representation of a new interpretation of Creation as described in Genesis.

The scene in the lower area serves as a kind of gloss on this new interpretation. It shows Noah at work on the Ark that God has commanded him to build, giving orders to his three sons, busy with saws and hammers. This Noah, too, was prompted by a figure in a San Paolo scene from Genesis, not by the two standing Noahs in that presentation of the building of the Ark, however, but rather, by the seated God of Creation in one of the San Paolo Creation pictures. Noah's "divine" posture – seated, giving instructions – and his "divine" apparel of white tunic and red pallium imply that he is

St. Francis Preaching to the Birds, c. 1295
Fresco in the portico of the Upper Church
Assisi, San Francesco

comparable with God, being the creator of an Ark that did not previously exist, but at the same time utterly different from Him, in that he required materials from God's prior Creation (raw materials, numbers and measures, tools and men to use them, and above all the Word as instrument of planning) in order to make his Ark at all. Noah is thus a go-between. He is not in possession of the divine Word (unlike the Creator of Adam in San Paolo, holding a scroll). And this was the paradigm, for Torriti and others, of the new artist: giving instruction to his assistant in order to achieve the work he has designed in accordance with the command of God's vicar.

The new St. Francis cycle

The conception of a Biblical cycle had a tradition of visual imagery to draw upon. The painter of the St. Francis Cycle had at best the rudiments of a tradition to work with: essentially, he was making new skins for a new wine. The only apt comparison is with the Early Christian painters of cycles. The trompe l'oeil architecture that encloses the pictures is itself eloquently suggestive of the skill that went into this new making. It has almost no depth, yet it makes the impression of a substantial construction. Viewed sideways, down the length of the nave (p. 49), there appears to be a gallery running along the sides behind the real pillars, but seen from the front (p. 53) the bays with their pictures look like separate framed recesses; the former reading reflects the underlying continuity, the latter the actual discontinuity of the cycle of scenes.

Those for whom the St. Francis Cycle was painted could be expected to value the meditative contemplation of pictures in a single bay at a time over a rapid walk-past of bay after bay. Hence the flanking frame effect of the real pillars was not "touched out" by trompe l'oeil but emphasized, by placing the spirals of the inner and outer painted colonnettes (which run in contrary directions), and the trompe l'oeil consoles and coffers, in a perspective relation with the axes of the windows. Most of the window axes are out of alignment with the centre axes of the bays, so the perspective relation to them has the effect of highlighting the content unity of the base and wall areas in the individual bays. These areas suggest the façade of a church raised above the ground, behind the mysteriously gleaming windows and the doorless entrance of which there may be a hall of light – a metaphor, this, for the realms which are invisible to the human eye but to which those who grasp the meanings of the pictures, in their hearts and minds, can achieve access.

To achieve entry into that hall of light is the aim in contemplating the pictures, as they themselves remind us. The two first bays are of signal importance in attuning the beholder to the message, and the three scenes at their bases are compositionally focussed inward to the central and most important one (cf. the three scenes at the bottom of p. 53). The central picture derives its full meaning from those to either side of it, and in turn endows the flanking pictures

St. Francis Praying before the Crucifix at San Damiano, c. 1295
Fresco in the nave of the Upper Church
Assisi, San Francesco

The Stigmatization of St. Francis, c. 1295
Fresco in the nave of the Upper Church
Assisi, San Francesco

PAGE 56:
St. Francis Renouncing his Worldly Goods, c. 1295
Assisi, San Francesco, nave of the Upper Church

PAGE 57:
The Dream of Innocent III, c. 1295
Assisi, San Francesco, nave of the Upper Church

with greater meaning. In each of the first two bays, mountain or city settings are split and the spatial area defined as a place of decisive moment. In *St. Francis Giving His Cloak to the Beggar* the centre axis runs through the saint himself. Pictured in an altogether ordinary wayside location, Francis has, as it were, come off his high horse and is giving his cloak to a man who (a caption informs us), though poor and ill clad, is in fact a knight, noble of spirit. The architecture of the side pictures elaborates on the meaning of this gesture. In one we see a pagan temple decorated with winged Victories and flanked by municipal buildings; the temple is in use as a prison. In the other, Francis, in a dream, is being shown the Palace of Heaven by Christ. This juxtaposition leaves no doubt that a choice must be made between fame in one's home town on earth

and fame in one's heavenly home, and that Francis, in sharing what he has, has taken the latter course. In *St. Francis Renouncing His Worldly Goods* (p. 56) the choice is an absolute either-or. St. Francis has uncompromisingly put possessions and the prosperity of his father behind him. Again, it is the pictures to either side that amplify and clarify the meaning of this moment. *St. Francis Praying Before the Crucifix at San Damiano* (p. 55) is to the left, *The Dream of Innocent III* (p. 57) to the right. The former shows Francis receiving his mission, and realizing that he must decide against his father on this earth and for his Father in heaven, while in the latter he is upholding a church identifiable as San Giovanni in Laterano, or, in other words, has become an indispensable pillar of the Roman Church.

The dissemination of the natural style

The impact of the Assisi frescos and the role of Giotto

The frescos in the Upper Church at Assisi were probably completed by about 1295. They hit the needs and nerve of the age so precisely that, within decades, painting in the west was following the natural style exemplified in them. They supplied the learned with everything that the intellect required for profound exegesis, while to the common people they showed things in immediate, palpable form that had seemed incomprehensible and unreal in earlier art. As for artists, they took the unity and rhetorical force of the frescos as an occasion to rethink the fundaments of their own thinking on art, and to replace the old approaches and workshop methods with a new manner that promised profit and reputation.

A number of artists had enjoyed the privilege of working on the frescos, following the process of conception very closely and acquiring and extending the expertise involved in establishing natural visual spaces. These artists naturally played the key role in disseminating the new style. It is all the more regrettable, therefore, that the contemporary sources are silent about their names and numbers and places of origin. The only one of the painters whom we know by name and who can be assumed to have been one of the fresco artists was Giotto (1266/7–1337), a pupil of Cimabue, to whom the frescos in the transept are ascribed. Giotto had an advantage over any Fransciscan who practised an art, in so far as he was under no requirement to hide his light under a bushel.

Giotto's career seems to have begun when the Franciscan mother monastery, pleased with his work, recommended him to daughter institutions elsewhere, such as San Antonio in Padua. The frescos in the chapter house there, destroyed all but for two fragments, were scenes depicting the life of St. Francis and the early history of the order. They were the first venture into the new style in northern Italy, and, despite the fact that the artist applied the Assisi manner with a certain stiffness, they must have caused a sensation. A wealthy Paduan merchant, Enrico Scrovegni, desired something similar, first for a private chapel in the ambulatory of the Santo and then for the Arena Chapel.

This chapel, built in 1303, had not technically been endowed by the Scrovegni family; rather, it was the work of the Paduan chapter of the order of Cavalieri Gaudenti, founded in Parma, probably in 1261. Enrico Scrovegni was a *coniugato*, or lay member. Tainted by the fact that his father had been a notorious usurer, he co-funded the chapel in hopes of atonement. He subsequently took a quarrel with the council of the order as an occasion to acquire the sole title to the chapel from the Pope; and at this point he commissioned the paintings for its interior without further consultation with the order. In every respect, then, the background to Giotto's commission was unusual. The sheer contrast between the official description of the Arena Chapel as a private chapel and its actual size and pomp

prompted amazed public comment and indignation. Given human nature, it was inevitable that the artist who carried out the commission, the most significant ever given by a private person, should become famous, quite regardless of the quality of his work.

Today it is next to impossible to assess Giotto's achievement accurately. Our view of things is compromised by two factors. On the one hand, Florentine chauvinism has made a mythic hero of Giotto, who was born in a nearby village; on the other hand, the Romantic cult of genius later abetted Giotto's elevation. Giotto, who is not mentioned in any source before 1309, was declared by Florentine myth to be the founder of modern painting, while later ideas of genius saw Giotto as well-nigh infallible. In reality, things were more prosaic. A list of Giotto's known works would show that they are largely variations on pictorial types developed in Assisi. In the *Prayer of the Suitors* (p. 61, top right) and other scenes from the Life of the Virgin, the use of a choir space and the placing of the four colours – blue for the calotte, green for the coffered ceiling, red for the cornice and ochre for the rest of the architecture – is borrowed from the *Vision of the Throne* scene in the St. Francis Cycle. The only difference is the change of side to frontal view and the addition of side aisles.

These and other scenes suggest that Giotto was confident in his handling of the architectural element in his models; but his figures sometimes show him in difficulty. For the young couple following the donkey in the *Flight into Egypt* (p. 61, bottom left), he borrowed the two boys in the Assisi *St. Francis Renouncing His Worldly Goods* (p. 56). However, his success in integrating them into their new setting is doubtful. The limping male figure to the fore seems to be combing the donkey's tail, while the woman, also walking on the spot, is bunching up folds of her cloak in her left hand. Between the two is a hand which ought (if the Assisi picture is indeed the model) to be the left hand of the man, but here it has become the right of the woman. In the Assisi fresco, the body language is perfectly clear: the elder boy is plainly telling the younger not to throw the stones at St. Francis that he is holding in his raised outer garment.

The proliferation of characters in Giotto's *Flight into Egypt* is not authorized by any Biblical or apocryphal text. In all probability, Scrovegni had wanted the journey of the Holy Family to resemble a merchant's business trip. It seems that the artist had a number of such wishes to respect. Enrico was not only the son of a man whom Dante had placed in the seventh circle of hell but also a Cavaliere Gaudente who had stolen the limelight from the Paduan branch of the order; and he therefore had a twofold interest in presenting an image. The chapel's iconography was to be Marian, anti-usurist, and sexually chaste, and was to make Scrovegni's personal commitment

FAR LEFT:
Giotto
The Last Judgement (detail)
Hell

LEFT:
Giotto
The Last Judgement (detail)
Enrico Scrovegni offering the model of the Arena Chapel to the Virgin Mary

to these Gaudenti ideals manifest. In the Life of the Virgin, this implied emphasizing not only the chaste husbands associated with Mary (Joachim, John, indeed Joseph) but also scenes that showed the corrupting nature of usury and money: Jesus driving the moneychangers out of the temple, the pact of Judas, and Judas hanging himself. The artist also had to take care that the allegories of virtue and vice, to be done in the base areas, did not call forth undesired associations. This would undoubtedly have been the case if, for instance, the traditional polar opposite of charity had been represented in its apt location – avarice. Instead, envy was put in its place – a neat twist, since this returned the accusation upon those who envied the wealthy owner of the chapel his millions.

Enrico Scrovegni's need to see to his image bore fruit in other, structural ways too. In the *Last Judgement* (p. 59), Scrovegni the model of charity and chastity appears in person, immediately above the door of the chapel, where none could miss him. This pious figure is presenting the chapel to the Virgin, who, flanked by St. John and an angel, is symbolically standing between him and the infernal torments that await the usurer or the Judas. Scrovegni is offering the chapel together with a grey-robed monk of the order, a diplomatic and necessary gesture, since the people of the city were well aware that the Arena Chapel had begun as the work of the Gaudenti. The monk seems Scrovegni's factotum in the picture, however, merely doing the hard work for his master, who is in business with the Queen of Heaven.

Enrico Scrovegni probably drew on the services of a theologian from the Paduan Franciscan monastery to design the programme of the cycle. Whoever this was, he must have possessed great mental flexibility and imagination to have incorporated Scrovegni's wishes without offending against theological decorum. The number of written sources he drew upon is itself testimony to his judiciousness: as well as the Bible and Apocrypha, he consulted the *Legenda aurea* of Jacobus da Voragine and two Franciscan devotional tracts, the *Meditationes vitae Christi* (c. 1300) and Ubertino di Casale's *Arbor vitae crucifixae Jesu* (1305). The programme he devised seems to have detailed not only the subjects and personae of the scenes but also such aspects as colour and gesture. We see this in the fact that, for the first time, the clothing of Mary, Christ, and the twelve apostles is consistently given the same colours in the Arena Chapel, to facilitate recognition; and attitudes and gestures that had hitherto been canonical have been altered according to the latest exegetical writings. In the *Adoration of the Magi* (p. 61, top left), for example, Mary is not gazing into the distance, as had been usual in earlier art, but has lowered her gaze in accordance with an observation in the *Meditationes,* to the effect that a lowered gaze was the sign of modesty in a virgin. In *The Wedding Feast at Cana*, the bridegroom is St. John – in flat contradiction of the Biblical account, but in accordance with the *Meditationes,* in which Christ takes His favourite disciple aside at the end of the feast and urges him to leave

Giotto
Adoration of the Magi (top left)
The Flight into Egypt (bottom left)
The Prayer of the Suitors (top right)
Christ Purging the Temple (bottom right)
Frescoes, 1304–06
Padua, Arena Chapel

The Examination of the Stigmata, c. 1295
Fresco in the nave of the Upper Church
Assisi, San Francesco

his wife and follow Him. In the *Ascension,* Mary and the disciples are not standing, as in the Assisi version, but kneeling around the point of Christ's departure, with radiant expressions. Choirs of angels are appearing in the heavens to welcome Christ in.

These few examples suggest the subtle resourcefulness of the programme Giotto worked from. It seems to have been so detailed that it could hardly have given the artist a more specific plan without being done in actual sketch form. (For the craft of drawing among the laity in the Middle Ages, see pp. 416–40.) The scope of the iconographic innovation in the Arena Chapel frescos is indeed great, and reflects the intellectual vigour of the monastic orders, furthered in Padua by the presence of its famed university, rather than the thought or imagination of a lay artist. To present that innovative vigour as the achievement of Giotto would amount – quite apart from the fact that (as always) the written sources tell us nothing of the person who designed the programme – to historical misrepresentation.

Dethroning the Byzantine image

The work done in the nave of San Francesco at Assisi in the final years of the 13th century constituted a challenge to the mythic supremacy of Byzantinism. The Byzantine manner is still apparent in the Biblical cycle – for example, in the face of the Creator and the gold striations of his garb (p. 53) – but in the St. Francis Cycle it is even absent from the three (fictitious) sacred panels in the scene showing the examination of the stigmata (p. 62). The panel cross in this picture no longer has anything of the formulaic style of a Nicodemus crucifix (cf. p. 36, right). The Christ nailed to the blue (celestial) cross with three nails, in what was then the modern fashion, looks quite slack, like a real corpse. The enthroned Madonna in the left panel is seen frontally, head held up, as in earlier Romanesque Madonnas; her bearing and physical presence are so full of life, however, that her grieving sideways glance at her crucified Son, and the loving care with which she touches the shoulder and foot of the Child, seem almost a response to real events outside the picture.

The three panels are like the images on a rood screen of the time. We might readily take them to be copies of such, not least because the figures portrayed – the Madonna, the crucified Christ, and the Archangel Michael – were particular objects of St. Francis's veneration. Be that as it may, in the years ahead the natural-style cross became the norm, just as the Byzantine cross institutionalized in 1236 by Elias of Cortona had previously been; similarly, the Madonna in the left panel, though she did not become canonical, inaugurated an endless series of "natural" Madonnas. Giotto adopted both, and was one of the first to disseminate the new style. He reproduced the cross for the small altar crucifix in the Arena Chapel, for instance, and in the monumental panel crucifix that was once on the rood screen of the Franciscan church in Rimini. The

Madonna type, together with Duccio's *Rucellai Madonna* of 1285 (p. 42, bottom), provided Giotto's principal inspiration for his Ognissanti Madonna (p. 63), which itself was originally on a rood screen, together with a panel cross and a panel showing the death of the Virgin. When Girdano da Rivalto asserted the high authority of icons by Luke and Nicodemus in 1306 (cf. p. 38 above), their age had in fact already passed. Within years of his sermon in Florence, the "natural" crucifix and Madonna had largely supplanted their Byzantine forerunners, even in Dominican churches (p.67, bottom).

The example of Duccio

In Siena, Byzantinism had been tantamount to the official art of the city state ever since the installation of the *Madonna del voto* (p. 41), so the change in style was attended with difficulties. If Duccio's *Maestà* (p. 44) had been done in the new style of Giotto's *Ognissanti Madonna* rather than the "Christian primitive" style, it would have struck most Sienese as "false", for all its beauty, when it was carried in procession to the Cathedral in 1311. But Duccio had found a way of harmonizing the old and the new in such a way that his Madonna

could be seen as a new creation by St. Luke while at the same time eroding the authority and claim to authenticity of the Luke style.

Duccio respected what probably appeared to him as the specifics of the Christian primitive style: elongated bodies, delicate limbs, oval faces with long noses and small mouths, pale flesh colour, a canonical repertoire of gestures complete with stock attitudes of walking or standing, and a concern with flowing robes and with landscape. But he also tried his utmost to loosen up what was visually formulaic and make it more natural. In the *Maestà*, though the figures are crowded like a royal court, each has individual breathing space established by the spacing of the throne and the ranks of saints, and further spatiality is asserted by the subtly managed folds of their robes. Duccio's delicate figures have so many hair styles (wavy, curly, straight or bushy) and are wearing so many carefully differentiated materials that it almost seems he had been out to demonstrate the superiority of his figures over the rather wooden ones in Giotto's *Ognissanti Madonna*.

Duccio had greater opportunity to naturalize the Christian primitive manner in the pictures for the Marian predella (some of which are lost) and the twenty-six scenes of the Passion which he painted on the back of the *Maestà* (p. 64). The crucified Christ in the centre picture, and the two thieves, are painted in the same way as the panel-within-a-fresco at Assisi. The delicate halls and loggias that serve as setting for the action, with their coffered ceilings or groin vaulting and their several doors, seem to derive directly from the frontal and side-angle views in the Assisi nave cycles.

Unlike Giotto's, Duccio's mastery of spatial values was very likely a self-taught thing, acquired by studying what he saw in Rome or Assisi. Even so, his perspective constructions sometimes go far beyond those of Giotto's Arena Chapel. The *Crucifixion* extends over two levels of the panel, like the *Entry into Jerusalem* (p. 64, top left) which begins the cycle. This latter picture was the first to present the scene as one happening in a fairly confined space and witnessed by crowds – which include us as onlookers, looking down as if from a tree. Another picture on two levels shows Christ being questioned by the high priest, Caiaphas, and Peter denying Christ (p. 64, top right); it was the first to reflect the fact that these two Biblical scenes were happening simultaneously in different parts of one and the same palace. We see a two-storey building, the lower part suggesting both a façade and an inner courtyard, with steps leading up to the interrogation room. In this lower half, a number of men are sitting talking, warming their hands and feet, killing time. One of them, identified as Peter by his halo, is marked out from the rest by his green robes. The maid standing at the left is accusing him of being a follower of Christ; Duccio shows that Peter's denial is a lie by aligning his axis with Christ's and relating his gesture of denial and posture to the steps in such a way as to imply that, in his thoughts at least, Peter is with his Lord. The steps, and the landing that links the two levels, might easily be thought ad hoc inventions.

OPPOSITE:
Simone Martini
Guido Riccio da Fogliano
Fresco, 340 x 968 cm
Siena, Palazzo Pubblico,
Sala del Mappamondo

FAR LEFT:
Duccio di Buoninsegna
Reverse of the Maestà
panel: 100 x 57 cm
The Entry into Jerusalem
Siena, Museo dell' Opera del Duomo

LEFT:
Duccio di Buoninsegna
Reverse of the Maestà
panel: 99 x 53.3 cm
Christ before Caiaphas and St. Peter
Denying Christ
Siena, Museo dell' Opera del Duomo

Duccio di Buoninsegna
Reverse of the Maestà
with 26 scenes of the Passion, 1311
Tempera on wood, 214 x 412 cm
Siena, Museo dell' Opera del Duomo

In fact they seem to derive from the roofed outside steps in the Assisi fresco of *St. Francis Renouncing His Worldly Goods* (p. 56), visible behind the saint's angry father.

Scenarios such as these, or the dizzyingly panoramic landscape that Duccio painted to convey the reality of Christ's third temptation, can scarcely be explained purely by Duccio's immense ability. They seem to owe something at least to having been commissioned as a simple showing-forth of the literal meaning of the gospels. They need no ambiguous concepts or visual cues as keys to hidden meanings, nor do they presuppose the specialized knowledge that only a theologian would have. The painter, guided by what may have been no more than a list of subjects or Bible verses, was able to concentrate fully on the actions and settings that the texts suggested to his imagination, and in this respect Duccio's Passion cycle on the back of the *Maestà* is a more personal creation than Giotto's work in the Arena Chapel.

Duccio's *Maestà* as quarry

Duccio's *Maestà* was not only used for the Sienese city state's propaganda purposes; it also served as a miniature Assisi. Both the main picture on the front of the retable and most of the twenty-six scenes on the back provided text-book examples of how to develop the Byzantine qualities of the original model towards a more natural style. From the *Entry into Jerusalem*, for example, Pietro Lorenzetti (died 1348) took the idea for his fresco on the same subject in Assisi. From the street and piazza setting of *Christ Healing the Blind*, and from the palace setting of *Christ before Caiaphas*, Simone Martini drew the inspiration for some of his settings in the Agostino Novello retable. These settings in turn were the seedbed for pictures of the ideal city, such as Ambrogio Lorenzetti's fresco *Allegory of Good Government* (pp. 66/67) in the Palazzo Pubblico in Siena.

In Duccio's history scenes an enigmatic painter appears, dubbed Barna by Ghiberti and Vasari, who did the largest New Testament cycle of the century on the right side-aisle wall of the Collegiate Church of San Gimignano, around 1340. Unlike Simone Martini or the brothers Lorenzetti, Barna da Siena retained the Byzantine elongation of figures. His *Last Supper* (p. 78) is enclosed in the same kind of grid frame as the *Maestà* reverse pictures, with console beams and the walls recessed in upright rectangular shapes, and even some of the personae (compare Christ, Judas and John) are in the same positions as in Duccio. This might be seen as a text-book case of imitation, were it not that Barna's cycle as a whole keeps a critical distance from Duccio, implying a quite different view of Biblical events (cf. below pp. 73–8).

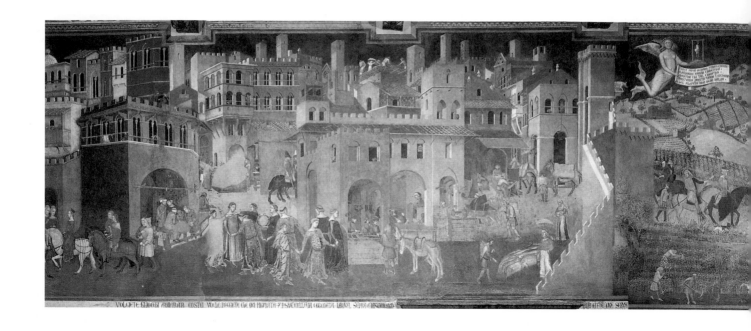

OPPOSITE:
Ambrogio Lorenzetti
Madonna Giving Suck
Tempera on wood, 90 x 48 cm
(Archbishop's palace)
Siena, Museo del Seminario

Pietro Lorenzetti
Birth of the Virgin, 1342
Tempera on wood, 187 x 182 cm
Siena, Museo dell' Opera del
Duomo

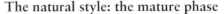

Ambrogio Lorenzetti
Allegory of Good Government: Effects of Good Government
in the City and the Country, 1337–40
Fresco in the Sala della Pace
Siena, Palazzo Pubblico

The natural style: the mature phase

The paintings in the Lower Church of San Francesco at Assisi

The Fransciscan mother church did not initiate the reform advocated by Roger Bacon, but for three decades – from 1290 until the monastery was looted in September 1319 – it was the foremost engine of change. Barely was the painting of the Upper Church complete but it became increasingly necessary for the Lower Church to be painted anew. Prominent ecclesiastics were expressing a wish to be interred near St. Francis, so a number of chapels were built near his remains; and each of these chapels tore a hole in the existing walls and the frescos on them. These new chapels required interior painting of their own; but, furthermore, it became essential to redecorate at least the west transept.

The first chapel, broken into the end wall of the right (north) transept, was endowed by Cardinal Napoleone Orsini (died 1342) and consecrated to St. Nicholas. It appears to have been painted in the early years of the Trecento. Though these paintings were done in all probability before the frescos of the Arena Chapel (pp. 58–61), they are in some respects superior to these. The master who did them (reputedly a pupil of Giotto) seems to have had a better grasp of situation, milieu, and the ways in which a figure can be brought to life than Giotto himself. Giotto's Christ purging the temple of the moneychangers (p. 61, bottom right) seems a prisoner of his own cloak, while a comparable figure in the Orsini chapel – a robbed Jew raging at a sacred image that failed to prevent the theft (p. 68) – is angry from head to foot rather than merely above the waist. His rage is expressed in the position of the legs, in the flapping of his robe, and in the use of material folds to convey the agitation of the arm that holds the whip.

After the painting of the St. Nicholas chapel was finished, another artist known to us as a pupil of Giotto painted the next chapel, the Magdalene chapel, endowed by Bishop Teobaldo da Pontano (died 1329). The movement of figures was not his strength, but he excelled at landscape. The Master of the Magdalene contrived to include an entire legend in a single landscape (p. 69). At its centre, catching the eye, is the unwieldy ship, rudderless and without sails, appearing to drift from the forbidding rocky coastline at left towards the harbour at the right, in the wake of two angels flying ahead. According to legend, the Magdalene and her companions had been forced to sea in such a vessel, from the coast of Asia Minor, and by the will of God had reached Marseilles. The two angels above the lighthouse, celestial pilots, are beginning a complex manoeuvre: the rearward angel is flying towards the city, while the angel to the fore is about to fly a broad curve which, to judge by the direction of its gaze, will bring it round to the small rocky island in the left foreground. This manoeuvre, begun directly above the harbour, is visually echoed by the parting of the lines of the harbour quay. The curving line of the rearward mole, and the

lines of the small vessels that echo it, draw our gaze towards the city; the outlying edges of the harbour bar to the fore lead away towards that same rocky islet at bottom left. This twofold divergence of lines reflects the two principal strands of the legend. The main strand ends in Marseilles, where the Magdalene settles, preaches, and converts the Governor; the eyes of the haloed Magdalene seated in the ship are accordingly fixed on the city. In a secondary plot, the near-converted Governor and his pregnant wife embark on a journey to Rome (to hear what St. Peter has to say concerning the Magdalene): the Governor's wife gives birth and dies on the outward voyage, and is buried with the baby on an island, where her husband finds her miraculously awakening from the dead when he stops there on his return voyage. Since this isle of the dead plays a part on the outward and return legs, the fresco offers not only a reading starting at the city (along the lines we have noted) but also a second, in the reverse direction, coming from the bottom left corner. This secondary material is treated in an altogether understated way. We are not likely to notice that another vessel, sails furled, has touched land at the islet, or that a man is disembarking, until our attention has moved from the main action to that corner. This man is the Governor, and the child, now two years old, is running away from his outstretched arm to its mother (as the legend says), while the mother herself seems at once a shrouded corpse and a woman awaking from sleep.

The fresco is an excellent example of learned painting. Based on material that could have fuelled a cycle for an entire chapel, it skilfully deploys a minimum of markers of location and action to

convey the key stations in a whole narrative, and at the same time implies that these toings and froings image forth the mysterious ways by which God works through His saints. Painting the picture presupposed an intellectual endeavour at once philological and visual. The philological level required condensation of the narrative – by a monk, undoubtedly. The visual level of design work was inseparable from this, since whoever prepared the digest of the legend had to do so with the form and function of the proposed painting in mind. Drawing up an iconographic programme and designing a visual form were practically one and the same thing, and so, as in any case that called for more than a mere presentation of simple meanings, the tasks will have been given to one and the same artistically gifted and scholarly member of the order. It is no wonder that the cycles in the Lower Church are anonymous. Indeed, signed frescos prior to the Quattrocento – by no means uncommon in parish or diocesan churches – are unknown in the churches of the mendicant orders.

The St. Martin Cycle, in the nave chapel of that saint, and the Passion Cycle in the south transept, only escape from this anonymity on the surface of it. Some of the frescos are now ascribed to leading lay artists such as Simone Martini or Pietro Lorenzetti, but these attributions are based on evaluations of style, not on archive evidence. They differ from other attributions of San Francesco frescos merely in being more plausible. The St. Martin and Passion Cycles, each in its own way, are palpably different in style from all the other mural work in the church, work that is normally ascribed to the Isaac Master, Giotto, the school of Giotto, or some other convenient name. Both recall the painting of Duccio in some way. The one impresses us by the subtle, tactile materials and the sensitive accounts of spiritual states that are characteristic of Simone; the other is spectacularly stagey, dramatic and colourful, qualities that put us in mind of Pietro Lorenzetti.

Pietro probably did his work between 1315 and 1319 – that is to say, not long after the "school of Giotto" had done the cycle of pictures in the north transept telling the childhood and youth of Christ. He was familiar, needless to say, with the pictures his teacher Duccio had painted on the back of the *Maestà* (p. 64). None of them, however, with the exception of the *Entry into Jerusalem*, appears to have influenced his work. As the fresco of the *Last Supper* (p. 70) shows, the cycle was conceived with new ideas taken from theology in mind. Even the architectural settings of the action were unparalleled in art in Siena or elsewhere. The hexagonal supper hall looks for all the world like the lower part of a Nicola or Giovanni Pisano pulpit (cf. pp. 46 and 48), with trefoil arcades, mitred imposts, and statuettes on the abutments of the capitals. On the left (to the right of Christ) is a rectangular kitchen area that extends into the close foreground of the picture, and here, to the crackle of a blazing fire, the washing-up is being done, while a dog licks the plates and a cat sits snugly purring.

There was a point to this unique architecture. The idea was to draw attention to the essential meaning of the Last Supper. The form and the functions as well as the lighting and the numbers all serve as pointers. The columns, the three-dimensionality of the interior and the hexagonal ground-plan give this supper room, lit by an unseen source, the perfection of a temple. In the kitchen, lit by the fire, the staff are using Jewish prayer stoles as napkins or to dry plates; this area represents a superseded Old Testament realm of the past which serves to prepare what takes place in the present New Testament realm. The triplication of walls and arcades is a reminder that this space open to eternity (the starry night sky) is under the sign of the Trinity, while the number six that recurs throughout (the hexagon, the ceiling beams, the inlaid faces of the marble seats) points to the sixth day of the Jewish week – Friday – on which the death of the Redeemer assured the perfection that is so radiant in Pietro's painting. In sum, the work contains a parable of the history of the Christian church and an alert presentation of the duality of Christ, at once divine and human, one with the Father and the Holy Spirit yet at the same time completing His work on earth with a new Passover meal.

Unlike Pietro Lorenzetti, Simone Martini was not required to paint the multiple meanings of Biblical history. In painting scenes from the life of St. Martin (p. 71) in the chapel consecrated to that saint and endowed by the Franciscan Cardinal Gentile da Montefiore (died 1312), what mattered – as in Duccio's scenes on the back of the *Maestà* (p. 64) – was to convey content in simple pictures. Although they deal with different subject matter, whereas Pietro's deal with the same, they owe a greater debt to Duccio; Simone, paradoxically, appears to have had the greater freedom. What made his task problematic was the need to paint ten scenes on fairly small wall spaces, which meant relatively small, profile rectangle formats. In order to achieve monumentality despite the circumscribed space, Simone had to use over half the height for an average figure, and had to make do with reduced space around his figures as a result. In the deathbed scene (p. 71), which plainly inspired the *Ascension of St. John the Evangelist* in the Peruzzi Chapel of Santa Croce, we do not experience the disproportionate relations of the figures to the architectural setting as a blemish: indeed, this low hall in a bishop's palace, its rearward apartments in darkness, the rhythms of its arcades dissonant, and the left (in

BOTTOM, AND DETAIL LEFT:
Pietro Lorenzetti
The Last Supper, before 1319
Fresco, 244 x 310 cm
Assisi, San Francesco, Lower Church

of Martin's soul heavenward, above the roof of the hall. The Franciscan beside him, bent over in grief and clasping his hands, seems to be weeping freely, while the nobleman whose hands are concealed in a smock is casting his moist-eyed gaze upward.

The funeral scene is not as demonstrative in its grief. The mourners are clearly silent, presumably listening to a *Dies irae* sung by the two monks holding candles. These monks, it is true, have originals in the Christmas carol singers in the St. Francis Cycle, yet they still seem especially created for the *Funeral of St. Martin*. By making simple changes to their heads, mouths, foreheads and eyes, Simone has changed the key, as it were, from a forcefully optimistic C major to a muted and mournful minor to suit the context; and the unconscious gesture of sorrow with which one monk is clenching his habit underpins a sense that their song is as much a sigh as a chant.

In about 1319, once the paintings in the Lower Church were complete, San Francesco at Assisi might rightfully have claimed to contain the most modern repertoire of artistic strategies in the west. It had everything an artist needed in order to paint representational pictures that did justice to the real world: archetypes of individual and group behaviour and gestures, all manner of terrains, interior and exterior architecture, furniture and equipment, clothing (and the folds in draped robes), and, by no means least, a range of new decorative features, framing devices, colour combinations and surface textures. The gestures taken from the everyday idiom and adopted for the high register of art were in themselves a considerable visual resource. They must have compelled the interest of contemporaries for a variety of reasons, one being that the class distinctions that

shadow) contrasting with the right (lit up), seems a wholly apt place for the small gathering to experience their mixed feelings of grief and hope. The hall is a place of this world, the tower soars to the ultramarine heavens as if to highlight the journey of the saint's soul to the next. It is no accident that the grief-stricken, twilit, asymmetrical nature of this deathbed scene is turned around in the funeral picture, which shows an airy, evenly lit church interior, altogether consoling in its symmetry and the radiant blue of the catafalque, tracery windows and vaulting.

Just as the setting is profoundly apt to the action, so too is the carefully nuanced repertoire of body language, which outdoes anything that art had hitherto seen. The death scene alone features almost as many new attitudes of grief as people. The priest with his black stole, flanked by two servers of different ages, is gravely reading the prayers. Two kneeling deacons in gold brocade are trying to ease Martin's final moments, the one (to the fore) by adjusting his pillow, the other, bowed over him and sobbing, tenderly holding the bishop's left hand in his own. One of the servers kneeling at Martin's feet is wringing his hands, while the other, in the fervour of prayer, is apparently witnessing the transport

Simone Martini
The Death of St. Martin, before 1319
Fresco, 284 x 230 cm
Assisi, San Francesco, Lower Church, Chapel of St. Martin

prevailed on earth were so irrelevant to them. Vulgar mannerisms such as the crooking of fingers, or propping a hand on a hip, served to express celestial solidarity with the poor and were first painted on jubilant angels (p. 71) in a fresco showing the apotheosis of St. Francis, in the Lower Church. The thumbs-up gesture was similarly made respectable (as if in defiance of Quintilian's classical book on rhetoric, which asserts it to be unworthy of a public speaker) by having St. Francis make it in the scene that shows him preaching to Pope Honorius III. Subsequently, before it disappeared from the artists' repertoire around the year 1365, at least three holy persons – among them the Madonna in a Sacra Conversazione, and a Christ having His feet washed – were allowed to make this plebeian gesture; but only one genuine plebeian, the servant in Pietro Lorenzetti's *Last Supper* (p. 70), who is jerking his thumb to indicate that the people next door need fresh plates.

Illusionism on the defensive

Following the looting of Assisi in September 1319, when the city and its predatory ruler suffered the consequences of the papal interdict (not lifted till 1352), San Francesco ceased to be the source of artistic energy in the west. Its role as pioneer was assumed by Florence and Siena. In Florence, the choir chapels of the new Franciscan Church of Santa Croce, under construction since 1295, were the crucibles of artistic innovation in the 1320s and 1330s. In Siena, beside the Franciscan monastery (where the Lorenzetti frescos are almost completely lost), the Palazzo Pubblico and the side altars in the Cathedral were the main sites of activity (pp. 65–7). In both

Angel
Detail from The Apotheosis of St. Francis, before 1319
Fresco
Assisi, San Francesco, Lower Church

places a conjunction of capital, learning and artistic virtuosity bore fruit in achievements that Ghiberti (1377/8–1455) was to praise as great works of art of the post-classical era.

Of the Santa Croce frescos, those painted by Giotto's pupil Taddeo Gaddi in the Baroncelli Chapel appear to have long been the most renowned. They were probably done in the late 1320s, at a time when opposition to the prevalent illusionism was growing in Dominican monasteries (cf. the next chapter). Their main feature, the five-part Life of Mary on the east wall of the chapel (p. 72), was thus in part an apology for the Franciscan natural style. The cycle must have struck contemporaries as the height of verism, with a number of new trompe l'oeil effects (complex side views, the temple buildings proportioned according to their position, additional lighting from above in *Joachim and the Shepherds*, from the angel) added to the tried and tested (mock architecture, mock cupboards with still lifes in the panels below, the apparent use of lighting sources outside the picture). But all these means of establishing verist effects were means to the end of teaching. The sham architecture, for instance, unlike that in the St. Francis Cycle (p. 53), looks not like a construction one might enter, but rather like a three-dimensional frame to

Taddeo Gaddi
Scenes from the Life of Mary, c. 1328–30
Fresco
Florence, Santa Croce,
east wall of the Baroncelli Chapel
(left: state prior to the most recent restoration)

accommodate the pictures. The most striking features are the spiral colonnettes. The fact that there are only four of them suggests that we should associate them with the temples, which curiously enough have only four columns per aisle. This association would have gone further with contemporaries, who would have been reminded of the four spiral marble columns that supported the baldachin in St. Peter's in Rome and were then revered as remains of the Temple of Solomon. Giving four of the six colonnettes this spiral form was a statement symbolic of the Church, the new Temple, the flesh and blood vessel of which was the Virgin Mary.

The positioning of the four "Solomonic" colonnettes is odd, however. Instead of being paired on the two levels, there are three of them at the bottom, while the fourth stands alone between the *Meeting at the Golden Gate* and the *Birth of Mary*, marking a sharp divide. And not only did the fourth stand alone, it was also (as old photographs show) incomplete, without a capital or impost block – indeed, not even long enough to meet the entablature. (The last restorer but one painted the missing part in, but at the last restoration this was again removed, to leave the relevant area blank.) The colonnette stands in for the conception that occurs between the meeting of Mary's parents and her birth, and thus also stands symbolically for the conception of the new Temple, the Church. Thus the three colonnettes (a trinity) in the lower register indicate that, when the Virgin was brought before the high priest

and married, the Temple was complete, and ready to receive the Son.

The sham architecture, like the historical frame of reference, declares the meaning of the events to lie in their heralding a new era. Of this new era the pictures show us nothing; but they do tell us what it signifies. The angled placing of the temples in the two bottom scenes is the clue. Though they are not positioned to the very fore of the pictures they appear in, both buildings overlap the tops of the frames (in contrast to the foregrounded temple in the topmost, lunette scene, which – correctly – is cropped by the frame). This trick is meant symbolically. The temples are emerging from the dead past of their pictured realities and becoming part of the present, living reality of the new Temple. The Jewish religion is superseded by the Christian, the high priest and his residence by the Pope and his.

The Dominican counter-position

The years of affliction

The innovative energies that revolutionized painting in central Italy
between 1280 and 1345, and placed a region which previously had
been an extra into the centre-stage limelight of art history, derived
neither from a chance accumulation of regional talent nor from the
miraculous powers of one great genius. Rather, it was prompted by
the fact that Bacon's proposal for a reform of painting had not fallen
on deaf ears at the papal court; far more, it had led to fruitful
collaboration between scholars versed in *perspectiva* and painters
quick and ready to learn. The painters gradually and impercetibly
slipped into the role of exegetes on meaning, interpreting in a
fashion that had previously been the prerogative of the clergy. They
also rose in social status. Simone Martini enjoyed the friendship of
Petrarch; Giotto was appointed director of public works in Florence
in 1334. Both cases, historically speaking, marked the vital first step
towards emancipating the fine arts from a context of mechanical
craft. The question is: what prevented the generation of Giotto's,
Martini's and Lorenzetti's pupils from already achieving the position
that painting and the plastic arts enjoyed by 1420 in Florence?

An important factor was the troubles that afflicted the 1340s.
The plague of 1340 was followed by the collapse of the Florentine
and Sienese banks. In May 1342, in Florence, Walter de Brienne,
titular Duke of Athens, was made dictator for life, in an attempt to
avert worse things; but all he achieved in his endeavour to establish
more equitable taxation was his expulsion from office and from the
city, in July 1343. The crafts guilds took advantage of the vacuum
his departure left to break the power of the magnates, which had
endured for almost half a century. A more democratic new
constitution had barely come into force but the series of disasters
began to seem truly apocalytic. In 1346, those trading associations
that were still in business in Florence found themselves facing the
highest deficit in the history of the city. The Tuscan harvests were
eaten by plagues of locusts (as had already happened elsewhere in
Europe); the following year they were ruined by hail showers. In
vain did the communes organize processions and pray; in the spring
of 1348, the Black Death hit the starving populations, beginning in
Pisa. It raged for a year; by the time the worst was over, the social
fabric of the semi-depopulated towns was at sixes and sevens. The
streets were full of newcomers who had fled poverty or the
marauding mercenaries who roamed the countryside, and had
occupied empty houses; of those who had remained, some were
ordinary citizens who had rapidly become wealthy and acquired the
new manners that went with their riches. Society had become
volatile, an explosive mixture. Insurrections routinely let off steam.
Intellectuals either took refuge in irony and sensuality, as in
Boccaccio's *Decameron* (1348–53), or reached for their morality.
Repentance was the order of the day. Public penitence was a good

begged him to abandon his secular studies and burn his own books. By no means every intellectual had the fibre to resist appeals of this nature. Many emulated St. Jerome in feeling their very learning to be sinful; led by a Pisan, Pietro Gambacorta (died 1392), they joined together to establish the Hermits of St. Jerome – one of the many confraternities of penitents created at that time.

Was the new style a fruit of affliction?

Behind the boom in morality and repentance, and its escapist tendencies, lay the desire to return to an original state of innocence, the loss of which was supposed to have incited the anger of God. This desire, dominating all thought of the past, also crippled initiative in art. Those sculptors and painters who survived the plague were neither less gifted nor worse trained than their deceased fellows (among whom were the Lorenzettis in Siena and, in Florence, Maso di Banco, Bernardo Daddi and Andrea Pisano); but most of them treated their inheritance as a fool treats a treasure, living off it and spending without increasing it. As if to justify their fixation on the past, the guild of painters in Siena began their statutes of 1355 with a statement that appealed directly to the age of Pope Gregory the Great (590–604), an age when the need for pictorial images could be legitimated by the illiteracy of the common people: "Since we are able, by the grace of God, to reveal to the uncouth people who cannot read the miraculous things wrought by and through the power of holy faith..."

This changed state of affairs was encouraged by the more circumscribed means available for commissions. In the plague years, the average sums fell; from 1349 to 1363, the money spent on commissioned religious paintings dropped to a fifth. Only the institutions, which received considerable legacies during the plague years, still commissioned on any scale – Santa Maria Novella in Florence, and the fraternities of Orsanmichele and Bigallo; in Siena, the hospital of Santa Maria della Scala (though it preferred investment in relics to art). If commissions had been few in the 1340s, things did not improve for artists as the century wore on, and many shared workshops or reached agreements on cooperation, to divide commissions between them. Even the highly regarded Bartolo di Fredi (c. 1330–1410), who was sharing his workshop in Siena with Andrea Vanni as early as 1353, largely depended on work for churches outside the city, which had not yet caught up on modern painting.

This only explains the decline in innovation; it does not account for the specific nature of the art that was produced. As *Moses and Aaron's Rod* (p. 74) illustrates, in the Old Testament Cycle at San Gimignano, signed by Bartolo and dated 1367, that specific quality resides not so much in the massive use of allusion as in the manner of allusion. Pharaoh's throne room has resulted from a recasting of the papal audience chamber in a fresco by Ambrogio Lorenzetti. The arcades have been removed from their original architectural context

way of safeguarding one's reputation. In July 1355, two months after the magnate government had fallen in Siena, one of those who had been toppled, a merchant named Giovanni Colombini (1304–67), gave away his fortune in order to lead a life of humility and self-castigation and to preach against privilege and wealth. Attempts by the ruling classes to banish him failed, since his followers were growing so quickly in number. In 1367, the year of his death, the Gesuati way of life – for so his followers were known, who by then were numerous in Umbria and Tuscany – was approved by the Pope.

If Colombini and the Gesuato went in for a modern, urban form of penitence, others preferred the hermit way of life practised by some of the early Church Fathers and revived in pictures since the 1320s. Giovanni delle Celle (c. 1310–96), abbot of the Vallombrosan monastery of Santa Trinità in Florence, retired to the forests of Vallombrosa in 1356, tormented by his conscience on account of his necromantic leanings. Dozens followed his example. Even Petrarch toyed at times with the thought of a hermit's life. Boccaccio, though he had little time for such things, was embarrassed in 1362 when a Carthusian monk visited him and

Lippo Memmi
The Apotheosis of St. Thomas of Aquinas, c. 1323
Wood, 375 x 258 cm
Pisa, Santa Caterina

Buffalmacco, and others. Then Taddeo Gaddi intervenes in the discussion. True, he says, all of these artists painted in such a way that one thinks their achievement next to impossible. But their art has faded away, he says, and is fading still. No one contradicts him. Plainly there was a tacit agreement among the artists present that the fault could not lie with the artistic community of the present – otherwise the losses would be the fault of those now at table, including Taddeo and Orcagna. Both of them had been numbered among the finest living painters in Florence at the time of the Black Death. But the illusionism in their art at that date had faded away just as palpably as that of Lorenzetti had under the brush of Bartolo. The blame lay elsewhere, with new aims in the designing of programmes.

The role of the Dominicans before 1348

It was the Dominicans, above all, who set these new aims. They were accustomed to detecting heresies in all innovation, and appear to have felt that the new style of art that had been entrancing congregations in Franciscan churches and elsewhere since the late 13th century constituted a danger – that religious content might be gradually secularized. At first they were unable to tackle the problem, since the Dominican order had its own problems in the years between 1285 and 1310. But as soon as the crisis was past, and the Dominicans had acquired an ally in their aversion to the Franciscans, in the person of Pope John XXII (1316–34), they began a systematic opposition to illusionism, advocating a conceptual form of art that drew on the tradition of the 13th century, a tradition which ideally did without any concrete reference to the here and now.

One of the first examples of this new tendency was the enormous panel showing *The Apotheosis of St. Thomas of Aquinas* (p. 75) in Santa Caterina at Pisa. Thomas of Aquinas (1224/5–74) was canonized in 1323, and the picture was presumably painted to mark the occasion. It presents him as a god-like master of the spirit and foe of heresy, presiding over the cosmos. All the light of divine, God-given and earthly wisdom is gathered in his Dominican mind and conveyed onward to the community of Christian scholars in his writings. If this painting, more two-dimensional the higher up we look, claiming absolute values for Thomist doctrine, is compared with Giotto's great St. Francis panel then on the high altar of the Franciscan church in Pisa, the effect is of night and day. The Giotto must have seemed a dire provocation to the Dominicans, since the main picture – rather than isolating the stigmatized St. Francis from localized contexts, and treating individual scenes as subsidiary (as in Berlinghieri's panel, p. 38, top) – focussed full attention on stigmatization happening in the here and now. Giotto's painting had taken a controversial miracle and given it dogmatic form in an image of perfection, likening St. Francis to Christ, even in this world; so the rival order inevitably felt called upon to make a response.

like building blocks and put back together again purely for purposes of symmetry, with no regard to spatial or functional logic. The rear wall of the new hall thus created is like a theatrical backdrop, folds and all, with an arcade to the fore, while the floor is like a skating rink on which the figures seem able to stand only by adopting extremely stiff postures.

The two-dimensionality that results is more than a mere side-product of an assembly procedure. It also reminds us that anti-illusionism was the new order of the day. Tuscan art in general was of this kind in the period following the Black Death. It is as if the new artists had singled out the most remarkable achievements of their predecessors as wrong-headed.

They had not, in fact, as the writer Franco Sacchetti (c. 1330-1400) tells us. In one of his tales (number 136), a group of painters and other masters leaves Florence one day, some time between 1352 and 1366, and goes up to San Miniato al Monte to work on a difficult commission in the church there. After they have eaten and drunk with the abbot, the painter Andrea di Cione, called Orcagna (c. 1308-68), asks at large which painter was the greatest master, after Giotto. Cimabue is named, Stefano, Bernardo Daddi,

Andrea Orcagna
The Triumph of Death (fragment), before 1348
Fresco
Florence, Museo dell' Opera di Santa Croce

of judgement and the need to turn away from vice, lust and the things of this world. Conceived by a magister at the Dominican college, these masterpieces can be ascribed to the Florentine master Bonamico di Martino, known as Buffalmacco. Their closeness to the Santa Caterina *Apotheosis of St. Thomas* can be seen in the extensive use of writing, among other things. *The Triumph of Death* (bottom) is like a devotional tract told in illustrations. The first image (detail, p. 77) derives from a 13th-century French text describing an encounter with death. A group of aristocrats out hunting suddenly come across three corpses, and the sight and stench of the bodies, in various states of decay, bring home to them the meaninglessness of a life spent hunting things that are themselves nothing. They can choose either to retrace their path into a ravine that ends in hell or to ascend a difficult mountain that leads to renunciation.

The ascent leads over the roof of the cave in which the three bodies are lying. That roof marks a turning point in the path, and serves as a pulpit from which an aged hermit is preaching against pride. Those who heed his words cannot be destroyed by Death or the Devil. Those who do not, those who opt to remain in the garden of delights (the right side of the fresco), will have no time to repent when Death descends upon them and annihilates all their pleasures with his scythe. The garden is no more than a mass grave. From it, devils are snatching the fatted souls and cramming them into the fiery clefts of the mountain of hell; and only a few can still be saved at the last moment by angels. At the left of the mass grave, backs to the hunting party and half separated from it by a spur of rock, are those who have nothing to lose: outcasts, beggars and cripples. For them, this world is in any case an antechamber of hell. They are the compositional and intellectual pivot on which the two halves of the painting hinge. Their beseeching cry for death, aimed towards the garden, is a cry of accusation and an appeal to conscience; but it goes unheard, leaving us in no doubt that those enjoying themselves in the garden are the future prey of the devils.

Up to the mid-14th century, the Dominicans seem rarely to have been able to influence art outside their own monasteries in a conceptual direction; but in Pisa they enjoyed a signal success. Between 1332 and 1336 a remarkable set of frescos was painted at the Camposanto there. Three colossal pictures – *The Triumph of Death*, *The Last Judgement* and the *Thebaid* – preached the terrors

Buffalmacco (Bonamico di Martino)
The Triumph of Death, 1334/42
Fresco
Pisa, Camposanto

This dismal painting, which for the first time placed hell at the centre of a universal diabolical empire (the Last Judgement takes place beside the mountain of hell), touched the nerve of the age so precisely that even the Franciscans, who were not normally attracted to pessimistic moralities presented in black and white, wanted something similar themselves. They commissioned Andrea Orcagna to paint a trilogy of frescos inspired by the Pisan paintings on the wall of the right side-aisle at Santa Croce in Florence. And it was no accident that this concession to Dominican ideas occurred in the 1340s, at a time when the Inquisitor in Florence was a Franciscan and the two major orders were for once working very closely together.

Barna da Siena's New Testament Cycle in the Collegiate Church of San Gimignano (p. 78) is related to the Pisan paintings and to Orcagna's in its scale and its doomful emotionalism. Its anti-illusionism is already apparent in the two-dimensionality of the framing of the twenty-six scenes. True, in *Christ's Entry into Jerusalem* the upright bar of the frame cuts between the two parts of a single scene like the post of a window; but the spatial effect created in this way is intended to distract attention from the composition's violation of perspective. The towers of the city look as if they were there to prop up the horizontal frame at the top. Christ's destination seems isolated from space and time, and Christ Himself an equestrian statue mysteriously drifting towards it.

The reason why the visual space is thus reductively approached as a vehicle for signs is apparent in *The Pact of Judas*, in the bottom left compartment (p. 78). The architectural box is no more than an incidental adumbration of a historical location. It is primarily intended as a commentary on the whispering conspiracy; placed in the abstract emptiness of the picture in this way, it emphasizes the secrecy, away from the world, of the pact. It also suggests, by its resemblance to a church portico with an open portal to the rear, that even if the conspiracy is not witnessed by this world, it is most certainly witnessed by the eye of the All-Seeing. The heavily emphasized architectural symmetry, which we may take as analogous to the created symmetry of the human form, implies a reminder – since the action is displaced out of the centre – of the inhumanity of the pact, which is wrecking the ordained, stable harmony of Creation.

Seen like this, it is only logical that the architectural setting in the adjacent *Last Supper*, unlike its model on Duccio's retable (p. 64), lacks side walls. Open to the whole world, it proclaims that the

action taking place in it has no need whatsoever of secrecy. The symmetry of the composition underlines the perfection and purity of those gathered at supper and their purpose, while the triplication of the windows and ceiling compartments points to the Trinity, and so to the divine nature of Christ's role. Not only in these works but throughout the cycle, non-rational spatial structures are used as means of morally placing the action.

Florence and the supremacy of Dominican aesthetics

The afflictions of the 1340s affected the fortunes of the monastic orders, too. While the Franciscans stagnated and lost standing in the eyes of society, the Dominicans emerged both morally and financially fortified. Tightly disciplined by their General, Jean de Moulins (1349–50), and his successors, the Dominicans felt the time had come to impose not only their view of the world but also their ideas concerning the nature and tasks of sacred art on society. Orsanmichele in Florence probably provided them with the first opportunity. The Compagnia (confraternity) of Orsanmichele had been founded in 1291 with the special purpose of venerating the miraculous image of the Virgin on a pillar of the loggia at the corn market. In 1304 the image was destroyed in a fire, whereupon the Compagnia put up a newly-painted picture modelled on Giotto's *Ognissanti Madonna* (p. 63), with a tabernacle. Forty years later – the Commune having meanwhile begun the building of a new market hall in 1336, the one that still stands today – the Compagnia's thoughts again turned to the destroyed image, and in 1346 they commissioned Bernardo Daddi (died 1348) to reconstruct that image, using copies, and replace the modern picture with the reconstruction of the old (cf. p. 80, top). After the Black Death, the Compagnia used 86,000 of the 350,000 gold florins left to it by members who had succumbed for a new tabernacle. The painter Andrea Orcagna was commissioned to make it.

Orcagna conceived it as a two-sided retable (pp. 80–1). That the whole is a domed construction on a square ground-plan becomes apparent only when one walks around it. Even the octagonal towers are made to seem two-dimensional by means of sophisticated gilding and colour incrustations. A marble surround 162.5 centimetres high was added in 1366, further diminishing the solid presence of the huge tabernacle; the base of the tabernacle cannot be clearly seen through the bronzework of this surround. The surround separated the tabernacle from the profane loggia area (the arcades opening onto the street were walled up in or after 1367) and gave it something of the appearance of a mirage for those who visited it on Sundays or feast days, when the entire front would be ashimmer with lighted candles. It was a glittering, fairy-tale church portal, rich in gold and gems, mysteriously arisen from the depths and opening onto the painted beyond in Daddi's picture.

Where the front is open, the rear is closed, the portal sealed off with a relief (p. 81) that has something of the appearance of a large

Andrea Pisano
Painting (top)
Sculpture (bottom)
Marble reliefs from the campanile, 83 x 69 cm
Florence, Museo dell' Opera del Duomo

carved gem in a golden setting. The relief shows the death of Mary at the bottom and her Assumption at the top, two scenes which had previously been related but nonetheless presented in separate pictures. The stepped effect of two undefinable zones is similar to that in the earthly realm in the Pisan *Apotheosis of St. Thomas of Aquinas* (p. 75). The scene of the Virgin's death appears almost to be happening in a semi-subterranean area, with the cave-like canopy over the heads of the mourners touching the spiral columns at the sides. The Assumption, by contrast, seems to be set against a coloured, tiled wall, somewhat recessed and with the arcading overlapping like the tassels of a curtain. The contrast between the lower and upper regions is enormous, and doubtless expresses the difference between the worldly vale of tears and the infinite spaces of Paradise. The upper region does indeed seem to represent the Garden from which Adam and Eve were once expelled and which mediaeval cosmographers asserted to be in the highest, easternmost regions of the earth, as the posture and position of St. Thomas suggests. This eye-witness of the Assumption of Mary into heaven is kneeling in mid-air – to indicate that he has not entered that verdant upper realm in the flesh but has merely been transported there in the spirit; from the New Eve he is receiving nothing, a nothingness (to be equated with the Virgin's girdle) that stands for the mental vision of faith.

This metaphysical version of the girdle, which appears in legends though not in the Bible, comes as a surprise, since the Commune of Florence had since 1350 possessed the key to the reliquary of the "true" girdle of the Madonna in the Prato, and one of the hymns that the Compagnia sang in honour of the sacred image was about the odyssey of the girdle. But the Assumption itself is even more surprising. The mandorla in which the Virgin is sitting, held by four angels, touches the top of the arched frame, conveying the impression that she has come to a premature standstill. There is a point to this, as the red and gold patterning inside the mandorla suggests. The perspective of the patterning points to a magical undertow drawing the Virgin and her throne into the depths of the pictorial area. The resulting imprecision of locality stands for the unknown place at which Mary passed from this world to the beyond. It is like a sacred version of the magic doors which (as Florentine readers knew from French courtly romances, for which they had recently developed a taste) could only be seen and passed through by those who possessed supernatural powers.

This immense relief is like a corrective of the Assunta pictures of the first half of the Trecento, which showed Mary being taken upward in a three-dimensional space no different from earthly spaces, and handing St. Thomas her girdle. In other words, it perfectly suits a programmatic desire to make the tabernacle a manifesto of correct belief – and thus gives away its Dominican origins. That desire is chiefly apparent in the facts that statues of the twelve apostles stand on the corner columns of the tabernacle, their

opened gospels or scrolls inscribed with the verses of the Latin Creed (the opening words, *CREDO IN UNUM DEUM*, are held by St. Peter); that the corner columns on the surround, with their angel candlesticks, are each guarded by four Guelphic lions; and that, atop the gable that crowns the front, there stands the Archangel Michael with drawn sword, the protector of the Church. But the reliefs on the base, which can only be seen by squatting down and peering through the bronzework, were also conceived as orthodox instruction. They constitute a rosary running around the base, consisting of eight main sections (marked by scenes from the Life of Mary; cf. p. 80, bottom) and twenty-three linking sections, eight of which feature prophets and fifteen allegories of virtues. These last follow the classifications in Thomas of Aquinas's *Summa theologica*. The numbers match the prayers (fifteen Our Fathers, fifteen times ten Hail Maries, and fifteen Glory be to Gods) that make up a rosary; the Dominicans claimed that the founder of their order had introduced it.

Scarcely had Orcagna's tabernacle been completed by the addition of the surround, and the hall at the corn market officially consecrated as a church (in 1366), but the monastery of Santa Maria Novella commissioned the most opulent creation that had ever yet been conceived to glorify a monastic order. Yet again, it was a layman's fears for his immortal soul that provided the money. Buonamico di Lapo Guidalotti (died 1355), a merchant who served as treasurer to the Duke of Athens during his short-lived dictatorship, was so seized by fear of God during the plague years (which robbed him of his wife) that he endowed a new chapter house, suitable for use as a council chamber and Inquisition tribunal as well, and furthermore left 417 gold florins for its decoration.

Given the size and shape of the surfaces to be painted, designing the frescos must have been one of the trickiest conceptual tasks of the century. Probably begun by Guidalotti's friend and executor Fra Jacopo Passavanti (died 1357), it appears to have engaged the monastery's scholars for a full decade. The design was not ready for work till 1365. On 30 December that year, the prior of Santa Maria Novella agreed a contract with the painter Andrea da Firenze (Andrea Bonaiuti, died ?1378) to paint the required pictures on the walls and rib vault of the huge, approximately square room within the space of two years.

The chief aim of the paintings was to present the Dominican order in general, and St. Thomas of Aquinas and St. Peter Martyr in particular, as those appointed by Providence to complete Christ's work of redemption. This aim was explicitly satisfied by the fresco on the right (east) wall, the *Triumph of the Church* (p. 82). (Above it on the vaulted ceiling is the *Navicella*, showing the ship of the Church surviving every peril at sea.) The *Triumph of the Church* describes the indoctrination, and persecution of heretics, which were being practised in the name of the Pope and of the salvation of souls. Those who do this work are presented as the most important

Andrea da Firenze (Andrea Bonaiuti)
The Triumph of the Church, c. 1365–67
Fresco
Florence, Santa Maria Novella, Spanish Chapel

Andrea da Firenze (Andrea Bonaiuti)
Christian Wisdom in the Spirit of St. Thomas of Aquinas, c. 1365–67
Fresco
Florence, Santa Maria Novella, Spanish Chapel

persons on earth, after the Pope. In the group in front of the domed church at left (symbolic of the *ecclesia universalis*), which represents the community of the faithful presided over by their ecclesiastical and secular leaders, a Cardinal in the habit of a Dominican is the second highest personage. He is seated on the same level as the Emperor, and on the right hand of the Pope, the only one who sits higher. The book he is holding declares him to be the custodian of official doctrine. He personifies the Dominican order's claims to power. The nature of that power is indicated by the black and white dogs – *domini canes*, Dominicans, dogs of the Lord – at the bottom of the picture. Two of them are watching over four sheep at the feet of the Pope and Emperor, an image of the Christian flock. To show that they are alert to danger from any quarter, one of the dogs is turned towards the clergy, the other to the laity. The pack of dogs racing to the right, urged on by St. Dominic, represents the zeal of the order in saving lost sheep and destroying wolves – the task of the Inquisition. This bloody business is only intended as a metaphor of the Dominicans' commitment to doctrinal work, however, as the two groups at bottom right, near the pack of dogs, show. In one, twelve false apostles are having the fallacies in their teachings proved to them by the Inquisitor, St. Peter Martyr (counting off point after point on his fingers). The other, of indeterminate size, is being impressed by the *Summa contra gentiles* of St. Thomas of Aquinas, which the saint is holding up to them in black and white.

The fresco's composition follows the same paratactic approach as Giotto's *Last Judgement* (p. 59) in the Arena Chapel, sixty years earlier, or the Pisan *Triumph of Death* (p. 76) done in the 1330s. The size and disposition of individual figures disregard the spatial contexts of the composition as a whole; they are placed according to the hierarchical ranking of a system of belief. Combining the domed church with scenes portraying the Christian community does result in a distinct impression of depth, but this has as little impact on proportional considerations as the angled position of the Gateway of Paradise has on spatial values in Paradise. Given the absence of spatial distance, the fact that the church dome overlaps some of those we can see in Paradise must be taken as a theological metaphor meaning that the Paradise of the Blessèd is "behind" the Church on earth. Indeed, the use of foreground and background, of upper and lower, seems generally only to make sense if taken metaphorically – to express the relation of the present to the future, or of the desirable permanence of Paradise to the transient here and now, with its unresting greed for the garden of delights, from which one should turn away. The sheer size of the figures militates against any other way of reading. Those who are in Paradise are the same size as the figures in the cross-section of society at the bottom – except, perhaps, for the prominent persons seated on the dais, who provide the template for other figures of importance, such as St. Peter or the four sainted Dominicans going about their work spurring on dogs, combating heretics, converting the heathen, or

paving the way to heaven. These are giants compared with the dancing girls in the pleasure garden at right, or the souls being admitted by Peter through the celestial gate; only Christ Himself and the Virgin (a lone white giantess among the hosts of angels) are bigger – exactly the same height as the Gateway of Paradise.

The west wall facing it (top) reads like a logical vindication of the east wall fresco's claim to power. With the Holy Spirit on the vault above, it images forth the comprehensiveness of Dominican wisdom as personified in St. Thomas of Aquinas. There are two rows of figures, one on top of the other. The lower, on two levels, represents the twice-sevenfold system of the sacred and profane sciences, personified by a congress of aristocratic damsels at each of whose feet a specialist is engaged upon the relevant business. The upper row, seen against heavens featuring the seven cardinal virtues, numbers twice five receivers of divine inspiration, presided over by Aquinas. The ten are Job, David, Paul, Mark, John the Evangelist, Matthew, Luke, Moses, Isaiah, and Solomon.

Given the schematic perspective, this picture has a two-dimensionality comparable to that of the Pisan altarpiece of Aquinas (p. 75). The shallow stepping makes hardly any aesthetic impact. Quite the contrary, it is contradicted both by the increasing size of the figures from bottom to top and by the fact that the top level, far from being overlaid by the tops of the choir stools, the pinnacles and gables, in the bottom row, is independent of it, in suspension above it. The Biblical persons seated above the personifications of the sciences, together with the presiding Aquinas, might just as well be in the foreground as in the background. One might even say that they possess the divine ability to be at once everywhere and nowhere.

Only the architecture of Aquinas's throne makes a different impression in this unreally two-dimensional picture. Seen from the front and foreshortened, it is like a fragment of palpable reality transposed to a conceptual realm, a literal embodiment of the non-literal throne of the sciences. The dais before the throne – on which the tiny figures of the heretics Sabellius, Averroes and Arius are crouching – seems almost to be emerging through the foreground limit of the picture, reaching its heretical crew into the chapter house. This seeming intrusion into real space is a reminder that heretics must be excommunicated from the intellectual community of the saints and of the sciences, and that their thinking, divorced as it is from the cardinal virtues (the gift of the Holy Spirit) and thus purely of this earth, places them on the edge of the abyss.

The capitulation of Franciscan aesthetics

In about 1366, when the frescos of the new Dominican chapter house were being begun, a comparatively modest series of frescos for the Franciscans was nearing completion. Endowed by one Lapo di Lizio Guidalotti (died c. 1350), it was painted in the Rinuccini Chapel in the Sacristy of Santa Croce, the very Sacristy whose size may have prompted the Dominicans' wish for a larger chapter house. The frescos were commissioned from Giovanni da Milano, a painter from Lombardy who had settled in Florence, some time after 1360. The work he did unwittingly reflected the intellectual stagnation that then prevailed in the Franciscan order in Tuscany.

He painted five scenes apiece on the lives of the Virgin and of the Magdalene on the side walls (p. 85). These were largely recycled versions of scenes from the Baroncelli Chapel (p. 72) or the Magdalene Chapel in Assisi (p. 69). The quotations from the Baroncelli even included the main components of the sham architectural frame. Since they had to be used on both walls, for the sake of symmetry, their metaphorical implications no longer applied. Both the smooth and the spiral sham colonnettes became merely decorative. They are supporting not beams but borders, the horizontal linked to the vertical and creating a flat, decorative frame.

While the Dominicans were concerned to intellectualize the visual arts and make them the mouthpiece of their dogmatic view of the world, the Santa Croce frescos retreated into narrative pure and simple. The paradoxical angles of vision on buildings which gave Taddeo Gaddi's Baroncelli work such subtle ambiguity (cf. p. 72) were put right. The Baroncelli's three-aisle, three-bay basilicas acquired an extra bay in one case, or became a five-aisled church viewed frontally in another. It is hardly to be expected that the corresponding diminution of content was actually desired; rather, it seems to have happened of its own accord, as a result of lack of cooperation between the artist and the Franciscan theologians. In his instructions, the friar and curator who designed the programme, Ludovico di Giovanni, seems to have confined himself to the bare essentials – the subjects of the scenes, the persons who were to appear in them, and a few general principles of style. This gave the painter a free hand to pursue his own aims in points of detail and to highlight his own virtuosity in the perspective construction of buildings; and so internal contradictions were inevitable. Thus the spatial depths established in Giovanni's settings in the centre frescos are offset by figures painted too large. In *The Marriage of Mary* the spatiality is defeated by Giovanni's overdone angle. The rooms entrap the people like corsets. The frontal five-aisle church in the lunette scene of the expulsion of Joachim, a deft reworking of Giotto's picture of Christ driving the moneychangers out of the temple (p. 61, bottom right), seems to be there solely to express the unbending rigours of Church authority and the power of the high priest over the paralyzed community from which Mary's father-to-be is expelled. Though none of the pictures conveys an explicit moral message, they all seem steeped in morality and bent on exemplifying proper conduct, be it in church, between married couples, or in the presence of a miracle. In *Jesus in the House of Simon*, the lunette scene in the Magdalene frescos, the meal at which Mary Magdalene anointed Christ's feet has become an exorcism scene: the flock of devils flapping away through the roof of the dining hall suggest that the penitent woman's sins were indeed great (as chapter 7 of Luke's gospel tells). This visual emphasis on devils in a scene that is far from diabolic, though, suggests how greatly the Franciscans and their painter had now been affected by the either-or doctrines of the Dominicans.

Giovanni da Milano
Scenes from the Life of Mary, 1365
Fresco
Florence, Santa Croce, Rinuccini Chapel

Giovanni da Milano
Scenes from the Life of Mary, 1365
Fresco
Florence, Santa Croce, Rinuccini Chapel

The challenge to the courts

Stagnation in Florence (1368–1400)

After the Black Death it seemed for a time as if art was set to enjoy a new boom period in Florence. From 1349 to 1368, works were created that numbered among the most elaborate and demanding of the century, works which – though conceived in a spirit different from that of the illusionist masterpieces – were in no way inferior to them, in profundity of content or in artistry. Barely had this enviable state been attained, however, when Florence entered a period of Sienese-style troubles. A war with Pisa, then one with the Pope; inner disturbances; and a new economic depression – all of these stifled the commissioning instinct and once again brought building work on the Cathedral to a standstill. When the money at last began to flow again in the 1380s, it was only a trickle. In the mean time, the gentry, amongst whom anti-clerical feeling had been rife since 1343, had got into the habit of investing their surplus in state loans, lavish weddings and funerals, and beautifying their homes.

Santa Maria Novella was particularly hard hit by this reluctance to give money to the Church. Suddenly the Dominicans were forced to realize what it was to be *domini canes*, the watchdogs of the Lord, at a time when God's vicar, Pope Gregory XI (1370–78), was making war on the city and the excommunicated population revered as saints the eight members of the government commission charged with confiscating Church property. The loss of status seemed irreparable; in the year of the Ciompi rebellion, 1378, when the war was ended, the Great Schism began, spelling the end of Church authority. Artists were now largely compelled to share jobs as their counterparts in Siena did. Even Niccolò di Pietro Gerini (died before 1416), who had one of the most active painting workshops of the time, was routinely obliged to carry out the more remunerative commissions, such as frescos or altarpieces, in association with other masters (Pietro Nelli, Jacopo di Cione, Doffo, Ambrogio di Baldese, Lorenzo di Niccolò, Spinello Aretino).

The beginning of this period of stagnation saw an important changeover of the generations. In 1366, Nardo di Cione and Taddeo Gaddi died; two years later they were followed by Nardo's brother Orcagna. In 1369 Giovanni da Milano makes his last appearance in the documents. There is even no mention of Andrea Bonaiuti (da Firenze) after 1368 in Florence, though to judge by his will, dated 1379, he outlived these others. This generation that was passing had acquired its mastery under the virtuoso artists of the Franciscan natural style. Though they fell into line with the new conceptual style by about 1350 at the latest, it was their successors who properly fell victim to the discrimination against illusionism. In so far as they were still taught to create "realistic" visual spaces at all, they soon lost the skill, since there was no demand for it. Taddeo Gaddi's sons Agnolo (died 1396) and Giovanni, Stefano's pupil Giottino, and three painters who emerged from the Orcagna workshop – Giovanni del Biondo (died 1398), Spinello Aretino (c. 1350–1410) and Niccolò di Pietro Gerini – all largely tended to be content with the patchwork of pictorial resources that had supplied the standard method for centuries before Roger Bacon's theoretical reform. True, their approach was subtler than that of their spatially flat predecessors. They retained the desire to play variations on their original models, and give them the greatest similitude (cf. p. 420, left). But this aim no longer related to a more natural rendering of spatial values within paintings, or of the relation of figures to their spatial settings. The implications for history painting can be seen in the fresco cycle of the Legend of the True Cross, painted in the choir of Santa Croce between 1388 and 1392. It was endowed by the Albertis, the most powerful of the merchant families who were calling the shots in the Commune once more, following the coup of 1382.

The artist commissioned to do the frescos was Taddeo's son, Agnolo Gaddi. He scarcely suffered from lack of imagination. But faced with this job, the biggest assigned to any painter in Florence in the half century from 1370 to 1420, he went to work as if all he had to do in order to construct his narrative was to consult his patron's wishes and a card index. He worked from a programme that aimed to present the legend as fully as possible, and Agnolo accordingly had to fit at least three episodes into each of the eight spaces at his disposal. In the second picture from the bottom on the left side wall (p. 87) he had to show the adoration of the Persian king, Chosroes, who had removed the True Cross from Jerusalem and was being worshipped as God the Father by his subjects; the dream of Emperor Heraclius on the eve of his duel with the son of Chosroes; and, third, the duel itself (on a bridge). Agnolo rose to the occasion by borrowing his father's temple approach (cf. p. 72) for Chosroes and his worshippers, placing the open tent of Heraclius next to it, with guards outside, and then filling the rest of his space with landscape and the figure of Heraclius riding out on horseback.

The fact that the adoration episode is actually a narrative in its own right is apparent solely from the circumstance that the two worshippers of Chosroes who are kneeling before the right aisle have their backs to the guards in the centre (dream) portion, while Heraclius is turned towards an angel appearing from the top right and screened from the Persian sanctum. And the time that elapses between the three episodes is indicated merely by the successive diminution of the locations – temple, tent, bridge. While this reduction in size makes a sort of sense in terms of the increasingly dynamic action as the sequence goes on, it does not relate to any differentiation of spatial levels. Though the tent of Heraclius is set back in relation to the temple of Chosroes, it seems proportionally larger, its centre pole thicker than the temple columns, and Heraclius more substantial than the enthroned Persian. Much the same applies to the proportional relations of the mounted to the reclining Heraclius. Were it not for the rock that appears to be leaning against

Agnolo Gaddi
The Adoration of Chosroes, The Dream of Heraclius,
The Duel of Heraclius, between 1388 and 1392
Fresco
Florence, Santa Croce, choir chapel

the tent, we might be forgiven for thinking the horse and rider were thundering out of the tent itself, strangely enlarged. The rocks, trees, bridge and stream (meant to be the Danube) complete the pile-up of inconsistencies. Juxtaposed with no regard for proportion, they look like a mere inventory of props.

It may have cost Taddeo Gaddi and other artists of his generation a wrench to paint contrary to their knowledge of perspective, when required; but Agnolo Gaddi, by contrast, seems to have had difficulty creating anything remotely resembling a visually coherent space. The juxtaposition method took over, and quite drove out the carefully thought-out compositional methods of his teachers. Indeed, it became so automatic a process that Agnolo seems quite to have forgotten to teach his apprentices; when his pupil of many years, Cennino Cennini, published his *Libro dell'Arte* near the end of the century, his compendium of the master's teachings included not a

word on methods of composition. What his master had taught him apparently ran to no more than an instruction to use string to mark the most important horizontals and verticals of a proposed fresco on the plaster.

Nor does *perspectiva* seem to have been much taught in Agnolo's workshop. The word does not occur in Cennini's treatise; he seems only to have learned what Agnolo recalled of his own father Taddeo's rules of thumb (presumably): "the moulding which you paint at the top of the building must slope downwards towards the background" while that at the bottom "must appear to rise" and that "halfway up the façade must be quite even and level". He recommended darker colours for distant mountains and lighter for landscape that was closer; and, since mountains in Agnolo's art were simply props interchangeable with trees, buildings, tents or bridges, the prescription was simple: "take some large stones, sharp-edged

Giovanni d'Ambrogio (from a design by Agnolo Gaddi)
Justitia, 1383-86, marble and enamelled tiles
Florence, Loggia dei Lanzi

Simone Talenti and Benci di Ciona
Loggia dei Lanzi, 1376–82
Florence

and not smooth, and copy them from nature".

The horizon of artists was shrinking, as Agnolo's Legend of the True Cross frescos and Cennini's *Libro* suggest; and this affected the sculptor's craft even more than the painter's. In the 1350s there already appears to have been no sculptor to whom the plastic work on cabinet constructions such as the Loggia del Bigallo or the new tabernacle of Orsanmichele could be entrusted; in both cases a painter (Orcagna) had to do the job. Similarly, in 1383–86, when the spandrels of the Loggia dei Lanzi (left, bottom) required plastic filling, the Cathedral stonemasons' lodge and its architects Benci di Ciona and Simone Talenti, who had been commissioned by the Commune to plan and construct the hall (for use in state festivities, receptions and swearing-in ceremonies), were unable to come up with appropriate suggestions themselves. In the event they were designed by Agnolo Gaddi, who presumably conceived the seven relief allegories of the Virtues, in trefoil frames, much as he was used to conceiving figures in paintings. The sculptors followed his instructions to the letter, and the relief figures that resulted (left, top) look anything but tactile or physically present in consequence. They seem to be flowing out sideways, and even in close-up it is hard to make out anything of the bodies smothered in these landscapes of fabric folds.

The team of architects also surrendered the design of the architectural sculptures for the Cathedral itself to painters, as a document dated 5 September 1387 records. It notes payment for a drawing of an apostle done by Lorenzo di Bicci (c. 1350–1427), from which Piero di Giovanni Tedesco was to carve a statue. We do not know what the final product was like, but if it resembled the late Trecento sculptures for the façade and side portals that still survive, its sole merit will have lain in its solid craftsmanship. Only in the years from 1391 to 1397 was there a glimmer of a spirit to combat formalism. A sculptor with classical ambitions made the reliefs on the Porta della Mandorla (p. 89) at that period; the curls of vegetation and the energetic figures need not fear comparison with the work of Arnolfo di Cambio or Andrea Pisano (pp. 46–48 and 79).

Just as the artistic standard fell, so too did the esteem in which artists were held. We cannot be sure whether payment was poorer too, or if that was the reason why Agnolo Gaddi, the most commissioned painter of his day in Florence, was unable to pay a fine of 600 lire imposed when he beat up a tax collector, Miniato Tufi, in 1392. But there is no doubt that the readiness of clients to pay up was at a low ebb. Giovanni del Ponte (1380–1437/42) was a hardworking painter of altarpieces and *cassone* (chests); when he was sent to gaol in 1424, it was through no fault of his own, but because the Strozzis, Tornabuonis and Rucellais had failed to pay him for painted chests. He was ruined; and his fate makes terribly clear how wide a gap the new moneyed aristocracy had opened between themselves and the middle classes, to satisfy their status

Porta della Mandorla, 1391–1421
Florence, Cathedral

Hercules
Sculpture on the Porta della Mandorla

consciousness. To those who stood on their dignity, intent on status, even spontaneous hospitality could seem an offence against propriety. In November 1410, when Monna Margherita, the patrician-born wife of a nouveau riche wholesale trader, Francesco di Marco Datini (1335–1410), condescended to dine with painters (among them Niccolò di Pietro Gerini) newly arrived from Florence to decorate the exterior of the Palazzo Datini in Prato, the agents of the master of the house, who was away, affected to be outraged. It wasn't a wedding feast, nor were the men starving, wrote one man who feared he would be blamed for the scandal to a colleague.

Francesco Datini himself was convinced that his contempt for artists was well founded. When he was presented with a request for payment by the three painters who had decorated the loggia of his Palazzo in 1392 (among them Agnolo Gaddi and Niccolò Gerini), he first threw the threesome out of the house and then followed up with a steaming letter: "If Giotto were still alive, I believe he would be cheaper. You have found the soil loose, and so suppose you can dig your spades into me as deep as the handle. God protect me from others of this breed." The miserly Datini, needless to say, would have raged at a Giotto's demands as well. But in behaving to the three painters as he did, he felt that he was in the right not least because (in his eyes) they were no Giottos. It took months of argument, and special pleading by his notary, before he paid out, not the 60 florins ordered by a commission, but 55 – better than nothing.

The view that contemporary artists were no Giottos was a common one in Datini's day. Neither the second part of Filippo Villani's *De origine civitatis Florentiae et eiusdem famosi civibus* (c. 1381/2), which deals with famous Florentines, nor Cino Rinuccini's *Responsiva* (1397), makes even a passing reference to living artists. Later, too, a Lorenzo Ghiberti or a Cristoforo Landino (1424–1504), author of a celebrated commentary on Dante, thought only artists who lived before 1368 worthy of mention. And in a poem (1487) devoted to the monuments of the Camposanto in Pisa, by Michelangelo di Cristofano, a trumpeter from Volterra, the only painters referred to apart from Benozzo Gozzoli (1420–97) are those who were active in the first half of the Trecento (Stefano, Taddeo Gaddi and Buffalmacco), although a notable number of the Camposanto frescos were done between 1370 and 1392 (by Andrea Bonaiuti, Piero di Puccio and Spinello Aretino, among others). It took a new sense of historical continuity to rescue names such as Agnolo Gaddi, Antonio Veneziano or Starnina from oblivion, and the care and diligence of a Vasari (1511–74) to pen remotely fitting obituaries for such artists. Still, the memory of the artists of an era so long regarded as a negligible quantity had faded so greatly that

Tommaso da Modena
detail of a fresco cycle:
Forty Dominican scholars, 1352
Treviso, S. Nicolo, chapter house
of the Dominican monastery

Palazzo Davanzati
c. 1330–mid-14th century
Florence

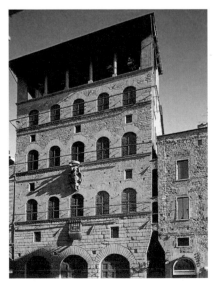

LEFT:
Frescoes in the Sala dei Pavoni,
1395–1400
Florence, Palazzo Davanzati

even Vasari himself sometimes failed to discover the names of artists who had painted works as spectacular as the frescos in the chapter house of Santa Maria Novella (pp. 82–83), for example. For centuries, Andrea Bonaiuti (Andrea da Firenze) was unknown – like his younger contemporaries Giovanni del Biondo, Niccolò di Pietro Gerini, Mariotto di Nardo and Lorenzo Monaco.

Given that the loss of artists' prestige went hand in hand with a drop in quality, it is tempting to think the latter responsible for the former, and to blame the painters and sculptors themselves for their social slide. But the situation was more complex, as a comparison with the Sienese experience shows. There, more artists held public office between 1360 and 1420 than ever before (including the painters Lippo and Andrea Vanni, Bartolo di Fredi and his son Andrea di Bartolo, Paolo di Giovanni Fei, and the sculptor Jacopo della Quercia). In the same period in Florence, not one of their fellow artists there achieved a comparable honour. Political involvement on the part of artists was tantamount to subversion in the eyes of the Florentine *hautbourgeoisie*, to judge by the fate of Giovanni di Pietro, the goldsmith. At some public occasion in 1393 he called out, from the ranks of the fourteen lower guilds, *viva il popolo e gli Arti!* – whereupon he was decapitated for disturbing the peace.

The social slide had political reasons and was the cause rather than a result of the decline in artistic quality. The fact was that artists had never ceased to do what was required of them. What they lacked, from the late 1360s on, was that support on the part of the intelligentsia that had spurred their creativity in the past. Even when they had chapels to decorate, the vital preparatory phases of their work now seem to have been as rudimentary as in the case of the exterior decoration of the Palazzo Datini in Prato. "Signor Torello, Ser Lapo [Mazzei, the notary and companion of the owner] and I," wrote one of Francesco Datini's agents in 1410, "met these painters, and after much debate we agreed that they should draw an outline according to their ideas on the matter, and that we shall then refer to the drawing and proceed together from there." Nothing in this statement suggests the remotest personal interest in the proposed work, much less a concept that might have been put before the artists for consideration. The only mental effort the three agents were willing to make was to see whether the outline drawing appealed to them when the time came. Clearly no inspiration could be expected in such an approach.

In this case, Datini's agents were playing (as unpaid amateurs) the parts of the (paid) *buffoni, giullari* or *uomini di corte* who were sometimes consulted before painting on or in a house was begun, and were probably sent to negotiate with artists at times. Unlike these entertaining characters, though, they had no ideas of their own; and this suggests that the artists were simply expected to paint whatever was in fashion. The Palazzo Davanzati in Florence (p. 91) – the only Tuscan Trecento palace to survive, more or less, the desire of subsequent owners for redecoration – was painted inside between 1395 and 1400, and affords an object lesson in the concerns of a society bent on aping the ways of the aristocracy. Several of the rooms had half-length tapestries painted on the walls, and above them a sham gallery with perspective arcades opening onto an arboretum. This gallery will presumably have given the occupants of the Palazzo the exalted feeling of living in a fairytale residence, a royal court – though one which the coats of arms in the arcade spandrels proclaimed to be their very own property. In the Camera della Castellana the "courtier" occupants were furthermore given to understand that they were in a nobleman's castle witnessing a tragic love affair behind the wall of the loggia, involving the beautiful lady of Vergy Castle (the *castellana*), the valiant knight Guglielmo, and the jealous and vengeful wife of Duke Guernieri – characters in a tale written in France in 1285 and familiar to the Florentines in an abridged translation.

Even when its gesticulating figures told whole stories, this kind of mural painting required no particular sensitivity in the artist. It could be commissioned from any of a multitude of artists who had shifted their professional attentions, given the shortage of public commissions, to decorating private interiors for the affluent. These *pittori di camera*, like wallpaper decorators today, probably showed potential clients a catalogue of decorative motifs to choose from. In the case of the Palazzo Davanzati, the criterion for selection will presumably have been suitability to a court image. At all events, Francesco di Tomasso Davizzi (died 1400) and his wife Catelana degli Alberti, the couple who commissioned the work, were not in the slightest disturbed to find that the gallery motif not only sat ill with the sham tapestries of the interior but was also incompatible with the garden setting beyond.

The origin and original function of the gallery motif are obscure.

If we disregard the unpeopled sham galleries in the conclave hall at the papal palace in Avignon and in the great hall of Castello Pandino near Cremona (painted c. 1338–40 and 1370 respectively), only the frescos done in 1351–52 by Tommaso da Modena for the chapter house of the Dominican monastery at Treviso (p. 91) are at all comparable. The main work, beginning 212 cm above floor level, shows whole batteries of studies, in each of which a Dominican saint, Pope or Cardinal, identified by inscription and individualized, is at work. Like the sham gallery of the Palazzo Davanzati, painted four and a half decades later, this frieze of sham architecture was meant to engender a sense of community by making the occupant feel part of an ideal world, in this case a world of pious scholarship. When they looked up, the monks could feel they were the youngest scholars in a universal university, the distinguished members of which, different though they might be in their persons and fields of activity, were all working towards the same goal in their spirits, each helping the other's efforts onward by his own. Given that the sequence of studies divides above the entrance into one set facing left and one facing right, and that both sets run up to the fresco in the centre of the end wall (painted around 1250) of a crucifixion with Saints Peter and Paul, it must even have looked as if – in the Dominican view – changes of direction only served to bring out an inner symmetry and an unswerving devotion to the sufferings and the legacy of Christ.

A row of juxtaposed, perspective-drawn compartments was an effective, accessible and easily transferable means of establishing simple continuity. This may have been why painters of interiors were so ready to adopt the approach. However the idea of painting the architecturally misconstructed gallery arcades in the Palazzo Davanzati came to be adopted, though, it remained a formula. And there was no response in Florence to the distinctive realism of the Treviso characters. Even the fourteen scholarly figures in Andrea Bonaiuti's fresco of St. Thomas of Aquinas (p. 83) seem unbending and schematic compared with Tommaso's portrait figures, which ring forty changes on the simple subject of Dominican scholars at work, deploying pen and ink, paper and books, different attitudes of concentration or meditation, and carefully individualized characters (gentle or mean, cheerful or sour, with good sight or poor, lean or plump, shaven or not) to establish a real variety. In retrospect, Tommaso's work seems symptomatic of a change in the cultural leadership.

The great contrast: Padua and courtly art in northern Italy

That changeover occurred in the last third of the Trecento. While central Italy was becoming artistically provincial, the north was girding its loins. The most powerful of the condottieri who had arrogated communal power to themselves in the past decades – the Viscontis in Milan, the Scaligers in Verona, the Carraras in Padua – were very well aware of the importance of architecture, poetry and the visual arts in asserting an ideological foundation for their rule. They sought out not only outstanding scholars and panegyrists but also the finest architects and artists. Their courts, linked by marriages, became the seedbeds of a new culture.

The most attractive was the court of the Carraras. It benefited from the university founded by Frederick II in 1222, a magnet that drew many to Padua, and from the no less famous Sant'Antonio. A centre of the new humanism in the mid-13th century, Padua expressed the pride it took in its past by putting up a monumental tomb to the mythic founder of the city, Antenor, in 1274, and expressed its confidence in the construction of the Palazzo Ragione in 1306, which contained an assembly hall which at that time was the largest in the western world. In Padua, where the historian Titus Livius (59 BC-AD 17) was revered like a saint, a poet was crowned in the ancient Roman style, in 1315, the first time this had been done since antiquity. It was in Padua that Francesco Petrarca (1304–74), the universally respected humanist, spent the last years of his life. A number of painters quit Florence for Padua, too, such as Giusto de'Menabuoi (recorded in Padua from 1370) and Agnolo Gaddi's pupil Cennino Cennini (recorded there in 1398). Padua assimilated the natural style of Assisi before any other city in upper Italy, and neither the conceptual art of the Dominicans nor the Byzantine style favoured in nearby Venice had any chance of striking roots. Under the enlightened rule of Francesco I (1355–88), illusionism, by then obsolete in Tuscany, was once again sounded in all of its registers. When political ambition, intellectual acumen and artistic powers of expression joined forces, the results could be impressive, as is shown by the Chapel of St. James, which Bonifacio Lupi di Soragna, a courtier, had built on to the right transept of Sant'Antonio in 1372–76 and painted by Altichiero da Zevio (c. 1330–after 1390) and his workshop (pp. 94 and 95).

Built by the Venetian sculptor and architect Andriolo de'Santi, who, like Altichiero, had previously worked at the court of the Scaligers in Verona and was thus well versed in the art of anticipating rulers' dreams, the chapel is exceptional even in its shape. Seen from the nave, it looks like a smaller and simpler version of the new Palazzo Ducale in Venice, then still unfinished. The *piano nobile*, patterned in red and white and with gables above, has five Gothic marble tabernacles in place of windows, each with a statue of a saint and two coats of arms. The ground floor (as it were) looks like an open hall the rearward arcades of which originally looked partly blocked by tombs (make-believe entrances to crypts, with real graves above them) and partly open to the pictorial world of the *Crucifixion* fresco.

Today the illusionist effect is negated by the two unlit oculi (which have been walled up from the outside). The impact they make is that of real architectural features, an impact they probably did not have as long as pale northern light was entering by their dark panes. Their oval shape and intrados, and the distance that is apparently between them and the pointed arches, suggest that these oculi were intended as part of the pictorial effect – pale, mysteriously glimmering discs, brighter at the edges, reminiscent of the eclipse of the sun and moon that occurred at the death of Christ. In other words, the *Crucifixion* fresco was the first painting to be a theatre using natural exterior light for a more brightly or a more dimly lit scene, according to conditions.

The scene, painted largely in earthy colours (ochre, brown and rose), can in fact be seen as a precursor of panoramic pictures. The bottom portion is painted to look like a balustrade running between the red columns across the chapel floor; in the centre bay its place is taken by the front of a genuine sarcophagus. Unlike the functional barriers that separate modern audiences from panoramic illusions, keeping them at the correct distance for the trick to work, here the balustrade is itself the key to the visual effect. It establishes a point of view that could not have been conveyed by perspective alone, by suggesting that we are witnessing the crucifixion from the hall of Pilate's residence, say, or from the Jewish town hall. The crucifixion is happening on our own level, in our own world.

The panoramic effect was not aimed at for its own sake; it was especially intended to tempt the congregation forward at mass and make communion a rich experience. To this end, the altar was placed in the centre of the "hall", so that the cross in the fresco would effectively be an altar crucifix from the point of view of the congregation, and the fresco as a whole look like a triptych – an altarpiece to end all altarpieces, since the visual world it presented seemed very reality.

Behind this ingeniously theatrical presentation there was a strategy to achieve the real aim of the endowment (to glorify a courtier's family) by indirect means. This strategy is apparent in the frescos on the vaulting and the end walls of the chapel, too. These frescos only appear to give a faithful account of the life and posthumous miracles of St. James. In fact they all tend towards an apotheosis of Bonifacio Lupi, using as vehicle the story of King Ramirez of Asturia. In a dream, Ramirez was urged by St. James to fight the Moors, whereupon, after consulting his council, he defeated the infidels at Clavijo, in 844, with the help of the saint. This story is presented in three continuous scenes on the left (west) end wall, above the choir stalls (p. 94). The central scene showing the council assembly is the oldest surviving group portrait of a court. The king, enthroned beneath a baldachin adorned with lilies of Anjou, has the features and beard of Louis I (the Great) of Hungary (1342–82), who took Padua's part against Venice, thanks chiefly to the diplomatic skills of Bonifacio Lupi. The latter, viewed from the perspective of the king, seems to have taken a modest place on the edge of the left half of the group; seen from our point of view, thowever, his profile is not only in the foreground but is also on the centre axis of the chapel wall. Wearing a splendid helmet inscribed with the word "Amor", pointed out by the gestures of two

Altichiero da Zevio and others
The Dream of King Ramirez, The Council Assembly, The Battle of Clavijo
Fresco, 1376–79
Padua, S. Antonio, Cappela di S. Giacomo

Altichiero da Zevio and others
Crucifixion, 1376–79
Fresco, c. 840 x 280 cm
Padua, S. Antonio, Cappela di S. Giacomo

nearby councillors and by the look of the neighbour to his left and his wife, half turned towards him, to his right, he has the presence of an *éminence grise*, carefully monitoring what is said in the assembly. His gaze seems fixed not only on the king but also on his own ruler, Francesco I, seen in profile in a commanding position on the other side of thc throne room.

Another person in Lupi's line of vision is Francesco's friend Petrarch. Of all the councillors, he is the only one seen full face and with a book. Seated at the right of the king and addressed by him, he is presented as the counsellor *par excellence*. Beside him sits Lombardo della Seta, the learned jurist and connoisseur of antiquity, who had dealt with the legal side of building the chapel for Bonifacio Lupi. The presence and prominence of the great poet and his friend the jurist, together with the word "Amor" on Lupi's helmet, transforms this council of war (as it was in the legend) into a council of peace in the humanist spirit, debating diplomatic ways of avoiding war rather than strategies of victory. The presence of the two men also seems to suggest that they played an important part in the conception of the chapel decoration.

This recasting of the council of war as a council of peace warned contemporaries not to take the final scene showing the Battle of Clavijo at face value. The fighting is only peripheral; what is being shown could in reality be titled "The Power of the Prayer of Louis the Great". The king, kneeling and gazing down a line cleared towards the city by his officers, seems to have gathered his army about him in order to call upon the saint to intervene. The left body of troops, apparently reinforced continually, is in reverent mood, while the right seems to be employed in quietening the disturbing noise of the enemy's weapons. The prayer is heard, unnoticed by most of the army, and the walls of the mighty enemy city are laid low by the saint, who, according to Jacobus da Voragine, was dubbed "the son of thunder". The meaning is clear: as long as Louis the Great can bring down walls for Padua by the force of prayer, there is no need to take up arms and fight for independence.

This hijacking of the legend of St. James is in itself proof of the extensive influence that the programme designer had on the frescos. The close cooperation of the designer and the painter seems to have been one of the main reasons why Altichiero's Ramirez frescos were so superior in quality to the three-part picture of Chosroes and Heraclius painted by Agnolo Gaddi only a few years later (p. 87). The story of Ramirez was presented like a three-act play, in illusionist manner, its changing locations interlinked to create a seamless continuity. The bedroom and throne room are parts of one and the same great palace. The foreground level connecting them, beginning at steps on the left and ending in the open on the right, creates a phenomenal twofold effect. On the one hand, it requires us imaginatively to fill in the interval between the dream and the council assembly – the king's awakening, leaving his private chambers with the image of the Madonna, emerging into the palace courtyard, and entering the crowded hall. On the other hand, it invites us to think that the king kneeling in the third scene went straight out from the throne room to his waiting army: in this respect, the third scene feels like the logical continuation of the first and second. In context, the effect is of a metaphor, for the profound effect that hidden causes can have upon the world.

We cannot determine whether the Chapel of St. James was built and painted to outclass Enrico Scrovegni's famed Arena Chapel. It does seem, however, that the next chapel, the Oratory of St. George, built on the square before Sant'Antonio in 1377–78 and frescoed by Altichiero, did pursue this end. Endowed by Raimondino Lupi di Soragna (died 1379), a relative of Bonifacio, it was made so similar to the Arena Chapel that no one who sees the scenes of Christ, St. George, St. Catherine and St. Lucia can help being reminded of Giotto's pictures (pp. 58–61), or realizing how great was the progress that had been made in the paintings done seventy years later. The comparison reveals Altichiero's work as something of a manifesto of the new era. Its arresting realism, bravura perspective, and subtle use of colour and form, gave it a subsequent importance for art in upper Italy comparable to that of Masaccio for Florence and Tuscany two generations later. It set new standards and was a model for artists such as Pisanello, Jacopo Bellini, Mantegna, Foppa and others. It may even have influenced those who knew the Chapels of St. James and St. George only by hearsay – such as the enigmatic (Bohemian?) painter who, around 1400, painted frescos of the months of the year (p. 97) in a room in the Bishop of Trent's Eagle Tower. The only reason he failed to achieve the panoramic effect of Altichiero's *Crucifixion* was that he apparently did not care to give the poles that separate his months the look of actual columns.

It is understandable that the demand for a rebirth of art, and the quest for a scientific form of spatial representation (linear perspective), and indeed the entire revival that we now associate with the term Early Renaissance, originated in Florence and not in Padua. None of the artists who were embarking on careers in Padua around 1400 had occasion to see the art of their fathers as a decline from previous achievement. Quite the contrary: the danger in Padua was that the previous generation might be seen as a standard never again to be attained.

From a fresco cycle of the months of the year, before April 1407
October
Fresco
Trent, Castello del Buonconsiglio, Eagle Tower

Alick McLean

Renaissance Architecture in Florence and Central Italy

The architecture of territorial states, tyrannies and powerful families
By the end of the 14th century, when Coluccio Salutati wrote the above praise of Florence, most of Italy's cities had completed their major civic building complexes, paved their streets and built their last ring of city walls. Even the new territorial states, such as Florence, Milan, Venice and Rome, were beginning to shift their public building activities from initiating new projects to refining and expanding existing structures. This shift from new construction to refinement, expansion or reconstruction in the public sphere can be attributed to a variety of factors. The large scale projects of the 11th to 14th centuries had been largely driven and entirely financed by the expanding populations and economies of Italy. The peak in population and wealth was around 1300, when Florence, for instance, had a population of 100,000. By 1400, the famines, bank failures and plagues of the previous century had cut this population almost in half. The wealth that had been accumulated in the cities still largely existed, but was concentrated in fewer hands, and was less capable of being augmented through local investment due to the drastic cut in the work force, which had itself become more expensive.

New public projects therefore became more rare, and were generally tied to the gestation of new institutions or to significant changes in existing ones – such as the replacement of communal regimes by tyrannies or the return of the papacy to Rome. One consistent exception to the decrease in public expenditure on architecture was in fortifications. While cities were generally not building new city walls, most circuits being already too large for the decreased populations they enclosed, the invention of the cannon led cities to reinforce their existing walls. They added thick battered sections and polygonal or curved bastions, whose raked or curved surfaces could better deflect artillery and whose projecting ramparts could provide vantage points for firing on attackers scaling the

"Let us climb the hill dedicated to the holy blood of the Blessed Miniato on the left bank of the Arno, or the two-peaked mountain of ancient Fiesole, or any of the surrounding ridges from which every cranny of our city of Florence can be fully seen. Let us climb up, pray, and look down on the city walls jutting upwards to the heavens, on the splendid towers, on the vast churches, and the splendid palaces. It is difficult to believe these could have been completed even at public expense, let alone built out of private men's wealth, as is the case."
– *Coluccio Salutati, De seculo et religione (quoted from Michael Baxendall, Giotto and the Orators, Oxford, 1971, p. 67)*

"I think no prudent man in building his private house should willingly differ too much from his neighbours, or raise their envy by his too great expense and ostentation; neither, on the other hand, should he suffer himself to be out-done by any one whatsoever in the ingenuity of contrivance, or elegance of taste, to which the whole Beauty of the composition, and harmony of the several members must be owing, which is indeed the highest and principal ornament in all building."
– *Alberti, De Re Aedificatoria, IX, I (translation James Leoni's edition, first printed in 1726, reprinted from the 1755 edition by Dover: Mineola, N.Y., 1986)*

Town plan of Florence in the 15th century, engraving, Paris, Bibliothèque Nationale

Rocca Roveresca, c. 1483–1490
Mondavio

intervening wall sections. The simultaneous rise of expanding territorial states, of tyrannies and of more sophisticated military technology and fortifications was not coincidental, as the concentration of wealth in larger centres allowed their rulers to finance large armies and expensive machines of offense and defense in order to expand and defend their territories and to pacify internal dissent.

The shift in the focus of public architecture from primarily new public monuments and spaces to renovations, occasional new institutions, and fortifications did not undermine the continuous tradition of monumental architecture dating back to the 11th century. Architects were challenged to concentrate their energies on developing and refining decorative schemes applicable to old or new public structures. They turned increasingly to what they considered accurate applications of the classical orders, which allowed them to express the same notions of *Romanitas* and empire of their predecessors more articulately. Nor were the opportunities for applying this revived *all'antica* style limited to public structures. The new concentration of wealth in the hands of a few families, individuals, and – in the case of new tyrannies – despots, gave these patrons the means to build monuments to their own growing political and social aspirations. While private chapels and palaces had existed in the 14th century and earlier, their display of wealth and power had been constrained by sumptuary laws and by public-building ordinances regulating church, piazza and street construction. Though many of these ordinances remained in force throughout the 16th century, opportunities for magnificent individual expression grew. By the end of the 15th century, many families had constructed for themselves residences that stood out as dramatically in the cityscape as the tower houses of the 11th and 12th centuries, but now they expressed family power through the sophistication of their plans and the elaboration of their architectural symbolism, rather than through their raw height.

The rise of new state and private patrons led to changes in the ways architects did business. An architect in the period from the late 12th to the end of the 14th centuries might have expected to spend most of his career working on a few public projects in one or perhaps two communes. His counterpart in the 15th and 16th centuries needed to work on a series of smaller-scale projects for a number of public and especially private patrons. Architects had therefore to sell themselves more often, and they developed more sophisticated means for doing so. Architects probably took the lead from the experience that most of them had as sculptors, goldsmiths or painters, who had for over a century been managing their careers with many smaller commissions from multiple public and private patrons. Unlike architects, who in the 13th and 14th century engaged in their major projects as members or leaders of the Cathedral workshops, other artists had their own workshops. As can be seen in the painting sections of this survey, artists were

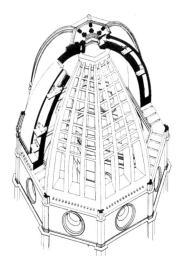

and Orsanmichele, as well of even more distant mediaeval structures, from as far afield as the Veneto. Their innovations were in the critical approach to borrowing from the past, and in their innovative compositional schemes. Rather than assimilating traditional elements directly, they did so through the matrix of what they considered the antique to be, either adopting only what corresponded to their notions, or correcting local practices according to them. However, their actual faithfulness to the antique was, limited by a number of factors. First of all, they continued to retain, whether consciously or unconsciously, specifically mediaeval building techniques and, particularly, geometric proportioning systems. Furthermore, they depended on antique models that were in fact Romanesque, most notably the Baptistery in Florence. Last of all, the one antique architectural treatise to which all referred, Vitruvius, presented considerable difficulties in its interpretation. Nonetheless, what the architects of this period developed and then passed on to later generations of architects in Italy and then throughout the world was a critical approach to tradition that eventually led to a rethinking of all aspects of building design.

Filippo Brunelleschi was the first to adopt this critical approach to design. His ability to distance himself from local building traditions can be explained by various factors. He was by training not an architect, but a goldsmith, and therefore was a member not of the stonemason's guild but rather of the silk guild, which extended its membership to goldsmiths. It was due to his renown as a craftsman, not as an architect, that Brunelleschi was solicited to compete for the project to build the most ambitious project of recent history, the cupola of Santa Maria del Fiore (p. 101). The challenge of winning this commission led Brunelleschi to depart from local traditions in order to devise a technique for constructing this unprecedented span. It also led him to enlist the assistance of two of the most innovative sculptors of the day, Donatello and Nanni di Banco, not for their knowledge of structural design but for their ability to produce, together with Brunelleschi, a convincing model of the proposed cupola.

The model that Brunelleschi, Donatello and Nanni di Banco constructed was indeed so innovative and so convincing that it appears to have won the commission for Brunelleschi before it was even completed. Though Brunelleschi was working on his design as early as 1417, the competition for the cupola was officially decreed on 19 August 1418. Less than two weeks later, well before the 12 December deadline, members of the commission came to watch the production of only one of the models, that of Brunelleschi. The explanation for this visit is that Brunelleschi was alone among the competitors in insisting on building the project without the traditional centering. While other competitors built their models with scale versions of the scaffolding supporting and centring the cupola from the ground, Brunelleschi developed a system for making it self-supporting.

capable of responding extremely quickly to changes in taste, and even of precipitating these changes, which more than anything else guaranteed them a continuous flow of commissions from a limited clientele. Architectural styles had generally changed more slowly due to the expense and duration of projects, and, perhaps most importantly, due to the greater conservativeness of patrons in expressing their taste in monuments displayed permanently before the public.

While architects continued to seek and find large-scale commissions, they succeeded in the 15th century in freeing themselves from these commissions as their primary means of experimentation, innovation, and self-promotion. Architects adopted various media that had previously been primarily technical or non-existent, architectural models, drawings and treatises, as their new means for exploring quickly and inexpensively new architectural styles, and for presenting them directly to potential clients. The advent of these media and the success architects met with in winning significant commissions precipitated a transformation of architectural culture, which now became equal to the culture of painting in its ability to change style, refine expression and reach new patrons. It also changed the status of the architect, whose fame became based as much on his ability to represent his ideas in words and images as on his capacity to build them.

The Rediscovery of the Antique in Fifteenth-Century Florence

Recent studies have stressed that the rediscovery of the antique in 15th-century Florence was based at least as much on a rediscovery of the local building traditions of the proto-Renaissance and even Trecento as on close empirical observation of the ancient monuments of Rome. Brunelleschi, Michelozzo and Alberti adopted the geometric schemes, proportions and ornamentation of buildings such as the Florence Baptistery, San Miniato, the Palazzo Vecchio,

Filippo Brunelleschi
Ospedale degli Innocenti (Foundling Hospital), begun c. 1419
Façade (above), loggia (below)
Florence

Brunelleschi's system consisted of four parts. First of all, Brunelleschi made the octagonal cupola out of a double shell, the inner of which was to be strong enough to support the outer but lighter shell. Brunelleschi stiffened each of the eight faces of the cupola with a system of stone chains and exposed ribs, the vertical curvature of which he maintained with a series of curvature control templates. He then made both of the shells thick enough that, though octagonal, a circle could be inscribed in their walls. Brunelleschi's study of historical domed structures showed him that the presence of a circular shape within a polygonal dome gave such a vault the same properties as a circular vault: that every inward force was counterbalanced, rendering the structure self-supporting, aside from the outward thrusts at its base. Brunelleschi then applied this same concept on a smaller scale, that of the brick coursing itself, which he devised as a series of perfect circles laid upon one another. He used the strength of each completed course to support the next under construction by inserting vertical bricks at discrete intervals into each course. These intervals were short enough for the vertical bricks to sustain the weight of the bricks laid horizontally between them, up to the point that this next course, with its own corresponding vertical bricks, was complete and self-supporting. The visual result of this bricklaying technique was what has erroneously been called a herring-bone pattern, as the juxtaposition of horizontal and vertical bricks only occurs periodically, and not at every other brick. The practical result was the elimination of the enormous expense, delay, and obstacle of wood scaffolding and centring. All of these techniques were present in the scale model of the project, which Brunelleschi made with full-sized bricks. The very process of making the model, therefore, was critical in convincing the *operai* of the Wool Guild of Florence, who were sponsoring the project, that the final version of Brunelleschi's cupola could be built not only as the model appeared, but also as it was made.

Brunelleschi began construction work on the cupola in 1420. Despite the input of Ghiberti and other competitors, almost the entire project, up to its completion and consecration in 1436, followed the specifications that Brunelleschi had drafted with Donatello and Nanni di Banco when preparing their model in 1418. The overwhelming success of his cupola was probably one reason why Brunelleschi won first place in a new competition, in 1436, for the lantern capping the entire composition. The wording of the judges makes it clear, however, that Brunelleschi had also succeeded in developing a design that not only resolved the structural problems presented by the lantern, but also appealed to the mixture of traditional and novel architectural fashions popular in early 15th-century Florentine society: "...Filippo di ser Brunelleschi's model has the better form ... and is comprised of better parts (for the) perfection of said lantern..." The notion of the perfect whole as only achievable through its composition by perfect parts is a distinctly

Filippo Brunelleschi
Santa Croce, Pazzi Chapel, 1429– c. 1461
Florence

Filippo Brunelleschi
San Lorenzo, old sacristy
1419/21–1428
Florence

BOTTOM LEFT:
Filippo Brunelleschi
San Lorenzo, nave
begun c. 1419
Florence

scholastic notion, and had often appeared in similar form in the 14th century. However, the criterion of "perfection" for the parts had changed dramatically since the beginning of the cupola project, largely through the offices of Brunelleschi himself: the model was now the antique.

Brunelleschi's first project manifesting the mixture of traditional and original style praised by the judges in 1436 was neither the lantern nor the cupola, whose major visual attributes, including its pointed Gothic form, had been established well before Brunelleschi, in 1367. Rather, it was his foundling hospital, the Hospital of the Innocents (p. 102), begun in August 1419, a year after Brunelleschi began his collaboration with Donatello and Nanni di Banco on the final model for the cupola. The one classical lesson incorporated into both buildings was the perfect circle, whose form determined both the thickness of the cupola's octagonal shells and the curvature of the arches of the hospital arcade. While round – as opposed to pointed – arches had long been present in Florentine buildings, and even in recent hospital projects in the area, they were seldom designed to be perfectly consistent in their curvature, width, spring–points and apex height. As with the cupola, Brunelleschi took over an established prototype, in this case the Florentine arcaded hospital type, and then rigorously refined its design and simplified its execution.

A clear idea of the novel architectural theory behind Brunelleschi's design is expressed in a contemporary comparison between Brunelleschi's original project drawing of the Hospital and the scheme as completed by Brunelleschi's successors, after the master left the project in 1426 to devote himself exclusively to the cupola. The author is Brunelleschi's biographer, Antonio Manetti. Among other things, he faults the final scheme for distorting Brunelleschi's proportions of the entire façade, for failing to frame the upper-storey windows at either end with pilasters, and finally for turning down the architrave at the end of the south-western extension of the elevation. As revealing as the idea of "correctness" in this critique is Manetti's description of Brunelleschi's drawing itself. It is "precisely measured in small-scale braccia," and only shows the loggia elevation, not the plan of the complex. The latter was not necessary, as it was laid out strictly according to the traditional geometric proportioning system of a square inscribed in a rotated square ($1:\sqrt{2}$). Since Brunelleschi was departing from local practice in using the modular proportioning system of the classical orders for the columns and pilasters of the façade, however, a "precisely measured" drawing was essential for its execution. The precision of the drawing also indicates how important a similarly accurate execution of the project was to Brunelleschi: his new aesthetic depended on an utter consistency in all of the parts, right down to the width of individual columns and the standardization of the simplified Corinthian capitals, all parts of which were

Filippo Brunelleschi
Santo Spirito, begun c. 1434
Round arches in the nave and transept
Florence

harmonically related to one another and to the dimensions of the arcade bays, and, in turn, to the entire façade.

Brunelleschi's concentration of his ingenuity on developing a systematic *all'antica* vocabulary at the Foundling Hospital was consistent with the needs of his patrons, the Florentine Silk Guild. Unlike the Wool Guild sponsoring the Cupola, who encouraged Brunelleschi's structural ingenuity to complete a long-term, expensive project whose impact was primarily in its unprecedented scale, the Silk Guild appears to have been interested from the outset in demonstrating their philanthropy as quickly as possible with the minimum expense, and therefore in the aesthetic, rather than scalar, impact of the one public face of their hospital, its façade. Given the standardized plan of the complex and its consequently standardized entry arcade, Brunelleschi chose to articulate the individual parts in an *all'antica* style, the beauty of which could be achieved less through elaborate and varied ornamentation than through the consistency, harmony and simplicity of its execution.

One of the most remarkable aspects of Brunelleschi's work at the Foundling Hospital is that he gave this fundamentally civic structure, run and patronized by lay persons, the architectural guise of a church. It substitutes one face of a cloister for the traditional urban-arcade type, encouraging its eventual completion as an formal outdoor religious space. Brunelleschi did not distinguish between religious and lay architectural styles when designing monumental buildings. The naves of San Lorenzo (begun 1419; p. 104) and Santo Spirito (begun 1436; right) share the arcading, frieze and fenestration rhythm of the Foundling Hospital, only with more elaborate capitals, with ornamented impost blocks inserted beneath the abacuses. The more vertical proportions of the resulting arches give a more staccato rhythm to the nave, directing movement along them rather than through them in a way recalling early Christian and Byzantine naves such as at Santa Sabina in Rome (422–32) and S. Apollinare in Classe, Ravenna (534–49).

Brunelleschi further adapted his use of column and arch in his centrally planned religious structures. In the Old Sacristy (1419/21–1428) of San Lorenzo, Brunelleschi subdivided the walls with pilasters supporting a broad frieze, cornice and arches, and then inserted into the resulting framed spaces of the lower level order-less arches and pedimented doors. The repetition of the arch in this and in his more refined Pazzi Chapel (1429–c.1461) at Santa Croce (p. 103) is neither to direct movement through nor along, but upwards, towards the pendentive roundels and the cupola they support. He even applies his ordering pilasters to the cupola, where they become ribs emphasizing surface and its parts rather than entire enclosed volume. The effect of his applied ordering scheme is to redirect the upward thrust of the arches and dome into a fugue of curves, lines and planes.

Only within the remarkable loggia of the Pazzi Chapel, with its coffered barrel vault and dome, does Brunelleschi achieve interior

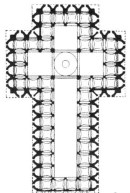

Santo Spirito, ground plan

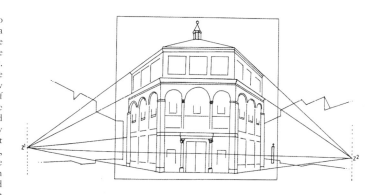

Diagrammatic reconstruction of Brunelleschi's demonstration of perspective using the Florentine Baptistery as an example

Brunelleschi and Perspective

Philosophers and painters had already explored the problem of perspective long before the time of Brunelleschi and Alberti, but the fact that their interests were of a different nature isolated them from one another. Euclid, Roger Bacon and Robert Grosseteste had examined perspective in relation to their studies of optics. They were interested in ascertaining the mechanisms with which we perceive the visible world, not, however, in developing a convincing representational tool. It was with this second end in mind, that, starting with Duccio and Giotto, painters began their own studies on perspective. Giotto's works in the Arena Chapel in Padua or the Bardi Chapel in Florence, for example, show how important it was for him to represent spatial relationships and volumes, both in order to create a framework for his narrative paintings and to make the figures and objects more convincing representations of reality, rather than rendering them merely as signs. Behind both the scholastic and these artistic approaches however, lay a common goal: to describe as precisely as possible the relationship of the individual viewer to the objects observed by him or her at a given moment, and to determine, either in theory or in representation, to what extent this relationship would change as soon as there was a shift in the distance or in the angle of vision. This common interest in the dynamic relationship between subject and observed object was ultimately based on the religious scepticism felt by both sides: the time-honoured traditions of humanistic or biblical erudition, the works of the Early Fathers, monastic scribes, illustrators or traditional mosaicists, did not provide sufficient information to enable the world to be understood and described. Instead of relying on existing formulas and pictures, both sides strove to trust only that which they saw with their own eyes.

The first artist of the Renaissance who proved to have acquired an exact understanding of the principles of vision was Brunelleschi. He did this in a way that every philosopher, excepting the purely empirical thinker, would have disapproved of deeply – without the help of a theory and without even using abstract geometry. He simply provided his field of vision with a grid and subsequently sketched the contents of this grid with the greatest accuracy. He is reported to have given a public de-

monstration of this method on two occasions; once on the Piazza della Signoria in Florence and once on the Piazza del Duomo in the same city. The latter occasion is easier to describe. Brunelleschi placed himself in the middle of the main entrance of the new cathedral and looked in the direction of the Baptistery, which was on the same axis as the Cathedral nave. This resulted in his field of vision being precisely framed by the entrance. Alberti, the first theoretician to describe the process, supplied a few suggestions as to the manner in which he could have then captured this framed view. Alberti called Brunelleschi's "door level", and what today in studies of perspective is termed the "picture plane", the "window". It is most likely that a grid was then superimposed upon the "window". Brunelleschi could have used the door frame in order to create such a grid, either by marking each of the four sides with orientation points at equal distances from each other or by stretching threads between these points. Whatever the manner in which Brunelleschi divided up his "window", he guaranteed the accuracy of the picture by remaining at an absolutely fixed distance to it while working. This can also be seen in the method which he used in order to show the viewers the completed picture, a method which is as strange as it is brilliant. He cut a small peep-hole at eye-level in the painted canvas and then positioned a mirror in front of it. In this way he laid down the exact distance between the eye of the beholder and the reflected picture, thereby enabling it to be seen true to scale.

Brunelleschi's breakthrough consisted in the fact that he contrived a method with which it was possible to reproduce accurately a particular view. The precision of the method enabled rapid progress in this field, since it provided artists and theoreticians who attempted to construct such a view geometrically with a two-dimensional pattern, comparable to that of a photograph. Alberti supplied the theoretical and practical skill which was needed in order subsequently to define these geometrical rules of perspective, as described in his treatise *Della Pittura*. This treatise resulted in a great increase in the use of perspective construction. Alberti was therefore the first who succeeded in uniting the interests of philosophers and painters. A whole range of practical exponents and theoreticians in the field of perspective, for example Paolo

Albrecht Dürer
Device for the construction of a drawing in perspective

Uccello, Piero della Francesca and Leonardo da Vinci, supplemented those things which he had failed to recognise or explain. Today, architects and painters still consider the method of perspective construction as refined by Leonardo to be a valid one, and use it themselves accordingly.

At the same time, Leonardo was one of the first artists who attempted to free himself from the bonds of perspective. Similar to its modern equivalent, photography – whose absolute precision renders it, paradoxically enough, imprecise – perspective allows the object to be viewed from only a single viewpoint. It therefore dissociates the observer from the object, a problem which was exacerbated by its frequent application in individual, two-dimensional panel paintings. Interestingly enough, this format first became popular shortly after the discovery of perspective, which was largely due to Alberti and his opinion that a painting should be seen as a "window". The viewers looking through this window as defined by Alberti are

reduced to the level of voyeurs. They leave it up to the artist to take up the challenge of collecting detailed information on the observed object. Leonardo attempted to get around the problem by experimenting with depicting an object from several viewpoints or by reducing it to a number of detail drawings, or even by repeating objects or figures in varied poses, implying the temporal sequence of motion.

volumetric effects resembling his classical precedents, such as the Pantheon and Temple of Minerva Medica. Brunelleschi's reason for departing from the bichrome linearity of the Tuscan Romanesque tradition may have been a visit to Rome, mentioned by his biographer Manetti. Another project of this period, the uncompleted Santa Maria degli Angeli (begun 1434), shows a similar plasticity and *Romanitas*, with its highly articulated sixteen-sided plan, giant order columns, and Pantheon-style dome. The idea behind this project, if not the project itself, was to exert a powerful influence on later Italian architects: it is an independent, centrally planned temple, essentially a cupola on its own, now classicized, and thereby the ideal form to symbolize the perfection of God on earth.

Brunelleschi's classicism determined to a large degree the style of the man who took over the completion of some of his projects, including the lantern of the cupola, Michelozzo. Michelozzo applied the loggia of the Foundling Hospital to the nearby library of the Dominican San Marco (right), although initially with less technical success – a row of columns displaced from a load-bearing wall beneath led the first structure to collapse. Michelozzo's training was as a sculptor, and his ingenuity remained concentrated in the brilliance of his ornament and in the precious, reliquary quality of his smaller structures, such as the elegant classicizing frames for many of Donatello's works, or the San Miniato Cappella del Crocefisso. One of his more distant works, the Portinari chapel at Milan's Sant'Eustorgio (1462), transmits Brunelleschi's linear classicism within a centrally planned structure. Here Michelozzo fuses Brunelleschi's style with the Early Christian and Lombard history of the site, something that was soon to be adopted by the city's next great architect, Bramante.

Manetti's comments on Brunelleschi's Foundling Hospital project and on his work in general were not the only firsthand accounts of the impact of this new classical style. In his 1435–6 treatise on painting, *Della Pittura*, Leon Battista Alberti praised Brunelleschi's achievements at the cupola and elsewhere as "equalling and exceeding" those of the ancients. Alberti also singles out Donatello and Masacchio for their roles in restoring the antique style to Florence in sculpture and painting respectively. Alberti's judgement of recent Florentine achievements and the instructions and examples he gives to painters reveals his fascination with classical practices. Alberti's taste for classicism had a different source than that of the artists he praises, however, though a similar one to the patrons of these artists. Alberti was trained as a humanist, and had spent his early career analyzing classical Roman poetry and treatises and then composing his own, such as his 1424 *Filodoxeos,* which he successfully passed off as a lost classical play, and his 1429 *De commodis et incommodis litterarum.* By 1432 he had left his civil and canon law studies in Bologna, and began to ply his philological and legal skills in the papal Curia in Rome, under Pope Eugenius IV. His first sign of interest in architecture is his 1433 *Descriptio Urbis*

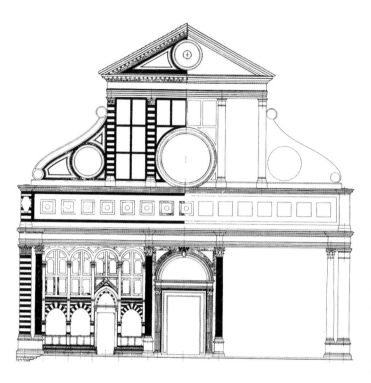

Leon Battista Alberti
Santa Maria Novella, begun 1458
Geometric design of the façade
Florence

thinkers, capable of composing narrative scenes convincingly. At a moment of feudal recalcitrance in Rome and of nervous anticipation for the reunification of the eastern and western churches, Alberti's emphasis on the unity of diverse parts and their harmonic interrelation seems to be programmatic. Though all evidence is circumstantial, one fact remains: nearly all artists commissioned by Eugenius IV's successor, Nicholas V, were those who followed the Florentine style codified by the pope's classmate from Bologna, Alberti. The new-style *all'antica* was thereby spread from Florence to the place of its inspiration, Rome, and from there throughout the Italian peninsula and eventually western Christendom.

Alberti did not begin to show the same critical engagement in architecture as he did in painting and sculpture until during a short visit to Ferrara, in 1442, when he offered a design for the base of an equestrian statue for his friend and the city's prince, Lionello d'Este, and possibly another design for the campanile of Ferrara Cathedral. By the next year Alberti is considered to have begun work on his rewriting of Vitruvius' *10 books of Architecture*, in his *De re aedificatoria*, which he composed up to 1452. In the meantime, possibly as early as 1446, he began work on his first architectural commission, discussed later, the Palazzo Rucellai in Florence (1446–51). His first church commission, for the completion of the façade of Santa Maria Novella (1448–1470; pp. 110–11, and drawing above), came from the same patron, Giovanni Rucellai, whose name is inscribed in large Latin letters across the structure's attic temple front. Although he argues against polychrome architecture in his treatise, Alberti fuses his polychrome design almost invisibly with the existing 13th and 14th-century façade of Santa Maria Novella. He thereby compromises secondary rules in order to achieve his fundamental law of design: harmonic unity, with all the parts composed so tightly that the alteration of any one would ruin the whole. This law must be quite familiar to the reader by now, recurring in reference to Siena Cathedral and Brunelleschi's lantern. It is a scholastic one, whose abstraction saves it from an explicit rigidity, allowing variation according to type and style as long as a building remains internally consistent. However, the love with which Alberti patterns the polychrome marble façade and adopts motifs from his favourite building, San Miniato al Monte (p. 17), suggests that he was attracted to the overt expression of order possible through polychromy – something he may also have learned from Brunelleschi's palette of pietra sirena against white plaster. Yet another, later, Rucellai commission, the reconstruction of the Holy Sepulchre (p. 109) according to exact measurements from Jerusalem (1467), is further proof for Alberti's acceptance – and mastery – of Florentine polychrome design. The jewel-like perfection of this structure recalls Michelozzo's tabernacle in San Miniato. It stands as a textbook example of another of the precepts from Alberti's treatise: that the most exalted of all commissions are sacred buildings.

Romae. Here Alberti described and napped the classical remains in the city using sophisticated surveying techniques.

A critical turning point in Alberti's life and possibly in the course of the arts in the 15th century, was reached in 1434. During this year Alberti left Rome, following Eugenius IV to Florence during a period of conflict both with the Roman nobility and with the eastern Council of Basle. Eugenius IV's difficulty in reasserting his hegemony in Rome and his choice of Florence as a place of refuge recalls similar events during the Investiture Controversy of the 11th century. Alberti's overt delight in seeing the "equalling and exceeding" of the ancient masters by the Florentines may have taken on a new urgency, because a year after his arrival he completed *De Pictura*, and then translated it into the vulgar *Della Pittura* for publication a year later, now with the above-mentioned dedication to Brunelleschi. Alberti advocated the same mixture of *latinitas* and innovation in painting that he had seen in Brunelleschi, Donatello and Masaccio's work, and developed explanations for their techniques that could be adopted by other artists and diffused. Alberti never alluded to this new style as one in the interests of the papacy. He merely emphasized single-point perspective, harmony and order, as well as a status for artists above that of craftsmen – as

PAGES 110/111:
Leon Battista Alberti
Santa Maria Novella
Detail of the upper part of the façade

Santa Maria Novella
Marble inlay, façade
Florence

Alberti's other major church commissions, at San Francesco in Rimini (1450–1468; p. 113), San Sebastiano in Mantua (begun 1459), and Sant' Andrea (begun 1471; p. 112) in the same city, all show qualities that extend beyond the more narrow definition of the orders, harmony and proportion in his treatise. As at Santa Maria Novella, where Alberti fused motifs from the earlier structure and from the older San Miniato, the humanist architect added onto an existing Gothic structure at San Francesco in such a way that complimented the established plan and forms, while incorporating references to another earlier monument in the city. The older monument was Rimini's Arch of Augustus, which Alberti freely adapted with elements of Rome's Arch of Constantine, establishing what would prove to be a continued preoccupation in his work: the fusion of the classical triumphal arch with the basilical section. A medal of the church by Matteo de'Pasti, the local architect in charge, shows how Alberti intended to reconcile these two, with the same curved half gables that flank the temple front of Santa Maria Novella. The medal also reveals another of Alberti's formal obsessions: it shows a gigantic – and probably unbuildable – semicircular dome spanning the entire nave.

Alberti continued his church design under the patronage of another tyrant family, the Gonzagas of Mantua. His first project for them was San Sebastiano, where he adopted a centrally planned Greek cross. This plan and its resulting simple section allowed him to develop a façade primarily as a temple front, overlaid with a

Leon Battista Alberti
Tempietto del Santo Sepolcro
1467
Florence, San Pancrazio
Rucellai Chapel

broken pediment and dropped window, arguably adopted from the distant triumphal arch at Orange, France. Following Rudolph Wittkower's reconstruction, a broad stairway extended across the entire façade, as in Vitruvius' or his own version of the classical temple, and as recently used in such church structures as the Romanesque and Gothic Cathedral of Massa Maritima in Tuscany.

The last of Alberti's major commissions brought him to his most compelling combination of classical building forms with contemporary traditions. This was Sant'Andrea in Mantua (p. 112). The layout is an adapted basilical plan, with a series of chapels in place of the customary side-aisles of the nave. The church is located at the termination of a series of important streets at the centre of the city, and is flanked by a market square. The elaboration of the church is only on the interior and façade, however, the latter of which is nonetheless so plastic as to appear free-standing. It is indeed more than a façade, an extraordinary hybrid of narthex, porch, triumphal arch and temple front, all capped by a mysterious, looming barrel vaulted projection that disappears upon approaching the entry. The entry is a round arch poised on top of orthodox Albertian Corinthian piers, which are in turn flanked by three tiers of windows and outer-corner Corinthian piers. The arch is capped by a wide frieze and broad pediment. The intrados of the arch simply continues within the depth of the façade as a barrel vault, with the piers similarly extending inward, only to be broken by a smaller-scale repetition of the main arch running transversely. A low doorway breaks a large expanse of unarticulated wall terminating the central façade barrel vault, and leads the viewer into a space that explodes in a height well beyond the pediment of the façade. The painted coffering of the barrel-vaulted nave echoes the coffering of

109

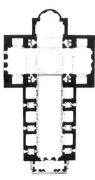

Ground plan
Entrance façade (left)
Nave and choir (right)

the façade vaults, and resonates through the side chapels, each of which repeats the triumphal arch and barrel-vault motif of the façade. Only at the end of the nave is the linear geometry of the barrel vault changed into its purely symmetrical variant. Here a huge cupola extends one's vista up to another unexpected leap in scale, and provides the centralized, ideal form of the early Renaissance, pinioned between the massive supporting structures of nave, chapel and transept triumphal-arch vaults.

The explorations of Brunelleschi and Alberti with the classical orders, centrally planned spaces, and either temple-front or triumphal-arch forms, were adopted by members of the next generation of Tuscan architects, such as Francesco di Giorgio and Giuliano da Sangallo. In his S. Maria delle Grazie al Calcinaio in Cortona (p. 114), perched upon the hillside leading up to the Etruscan citadel town, the Sienese Francesco di Giorgio executed one of a number of his extended Greek-cross structures, between 1484 and 1490. The open siting of the church allowed him to develop all of the elevations with classical pilasters and pedimented windows, which he repeats around all eight sides of the octagonal dome drum. As at Brunelleschi's cupola, the drum of S. Maria delle Grazie al Calcinaio assured the reading of the cupola from great distances, with its windows establishing it as a third-storey harmonic in scale and articulation with the stories below. The façade has a contained verticality similar to that of the dome, terminating its simple nave plan with an extended temple front divided by the same ground-storey frieze and corner piers that run around the entire church, and punctuated at the centre of the upper

storey, below the pediment, by the same round window that terminates the other axes of the cross plan. Within, the church follows the scheme developed by Brunelleschi of *pietra sirena* pilasters against white walls supporting a broad frieze capped by generous semicircular arches. In extending these pilasters across the barrel vault of the nave, Francesco di Giorgio shows a tendency to emphasize discrete spatial subdivisions closer in spirit to Brunelleschi than to his apparent source for the barrel vault itself, Alberti.

A compressed version of this increasingly prevalent small domed church type appears for the first time as a purely centralized structure at Giuliano da Sangallo's Santa Maria delle Carceri in Prato (1485), facing Frederick II's classicizing Castello del Imperatore (1236–49) (see p. 34). The history of Santa Maria delle Carceri (p. 114) stands in rude defiance of any tendency on the part of some historians to see the Renaissance as a period of secularization and rationalization. One day a young child saw tears in the eyes of the painting of the Madonna at a small tabernacle at the future church's sight, located by the town prisons, or *carceri*. She ran to tell her story, which was corroborated by witnesses including the bell ringer of the church. The town agreed that a church should be built to honour this miraculous painting, its architect to be chosen in a competition.

The local architect who won this competition never succeeded in building his project however. The reason lies in the extended reach of the Florentine Medici, the same family that had patronized the later works of Brunelleschi and many of the works of Michelozzo.

Lorenzo de Medici either questioned the quality of the competition design or simply was looking out for the best interests of his favourite architect, Giuliano da Sangallo, to whom he summarily granted the commission.

The simple liturgical needs of a small pilgrimage church in an area of Prato that was already well served by churches provided the ideal opportunity for Giuliano da Sangallo to fulfil what had become the *Kunstwollen* of his era, a centrally planned, free-standing classical church. The completed building shows once again the enduring influence of Brunelleschi, with the interior subdivided by pilasters and arches, and with a cupola drum punctured by round windows almost identical to the design of the Pazzi Chapel at Santa Croce. The whole composition is capped by a lantern reproducing in miniature an effect somewhere between Brunelleschi's at the Florentine Cathedral and the early mediaeval lantern of the Florentine Baptistery. In this and other ways this structure brings the history of Tuscan architecture full circle to its first centrally planned structure, the Baptistery of San Giovanni. The white marble walls of Santa Maria delle Carceri are subdivided by similar bands of green Pratese marble common to the Baptistery as well as to Pratese structures from the 11th to 14th century. The pedimented doors and upper-storey windows above them, beneath the planned but unexecuted pediments, recall the upper level temple front of San Miniato al Monte. Nonetheless, the imprint of hundreds of years of intervening history is still present, whether in the crossed plan that had developed to provide for congregations' liturgical needs, albeit modest, or in the stepped plinth supporting the structure like that of one of the only preceding, and less perfectly symmetrical, centrally planned structures of the 15th century, Alberti's San Sebastiano.

The diffusion and development of the centrally-planned church type *all'antica* was nonetheless hindered, at least in Tuscany. The argument generally advanced for this, by both modern architectural historians and critics of the 15th century, is the form's limited compatibility with contemporary liturgical needs. The centralized plan, particularly in its most radical, circular form, reduced the useful space available within the church, and undermined hierarchic distinctions between celebrants, choir and congregation. The Florentine Giovanni Aldobrandini, for example, criticized the circular tribune of Santissima Annunziata (c. 1444–77), a project initiated by Michelozzo and elaborated by Manetti and Alberti with nine chapels around a central choir. Aldobrandini complains that the plan was impractical, as the sixty-odd Servite friars for whom it was to be made would not be able continually to sing their chants without disturbing the masses in the individual chapels. Furthermore, the small size of the chapels would lead congregations to overflow into the choir itself, in turn interrupting the chanting of the friars. Aldobrandini continues with both typological and moral critiques: such central structures with satellite chapels, however laudable for their antique origins, were designed to function as

Francesco di Giorgio
Santa Maria delle Grazie al Calcinaio, 1484–90
Cortona

seldom built in Tuscany until after the fall of the Republic. Similar restraint is visible in the monumental architecture of that other great Republic, Venice, whose classicism remained tempered by its Byzantine and Gothic heritage until after 1527, when the Roman-trained architect Jacopo Sansovino arrived in Rome, followed two years later by another Roman-trained architect, Michele Sanmicheli. This was, not coincidentally, just the time when the Venetian Republic was aggressively expanding its inland empire more than halfway across the Italian peninsula. For Tuscan artists such as Alberti wishing to engage in more elaborate – and expensive – classical experiments, they had no choice but to seek patrons in cities such as Mantua, Ferrara, Milan or Rome, where despots and popes had greater prospects of securing unchallenged autonomy, and less difficulty overriding the will of bickering elected assemblies in appropriating scarce funds for personal and state aggrandizement.

The arrival in a princely court was no guarantee of unfettered classical experimentation, however, no matter how powerful the monarch. The local workforce would have to be converted instantly from generations of Gothic and pre-Gothic traditions, something that required the full support of the patron himself. A useful tool for enlisting this support was the architectural treatise, something with which Alberti achieved some success with Nicholas V, and even more with Ludovico Gonzaga, who, incidentally, brilliantly mixed financial and political pressure on the Florentines to force them to build Santissima Annunziata's tribune according to Alberti's design. This may explain the proliferation of Renaissance treatises (see insert, pp. 116–7), such as those by Filarete, Francesco di Giorgio, Sebastiano Serlio, or Andrea Palladio.

mausolea for Emperors, and not to serve "convents like this one". Furthermore, the presence of lay women in the chapels so close to the chanting friars was bound to cause the latter "turbatione". It should be added, however, that when first asked their opinion, the Servite friars were themselves "most affectionate" of the design.

However dubious his functional and typological critiques, Aldobrandini was right in inferring that the primary motive of the architects and their patron, in this case Mantua's Ludovico Gonzaga, was to commemorate the latter with the same magnificence accorded Roman Emperors. This assessment could only have pleased Gonzaga as much as it disturbed the Republican Florentines and drew the envy of their own implicit tyrants, the Medici, whose unofficial status prevented them from overt expressions of their own quasi-imperial aspirations. The political exigencies of Florentine patrons such as the Medici, who were insinuating themselves into most of the city's and region's monumental building projects, may be the reason why the more extravagant classicizing experiments imagined as early as Brunelleschi's own near-circular Santa Maria degli Angeli were

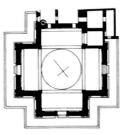

Giuliano da Sangallo
Santa Maria delle Carceri
begun 1485
Prato

The first of these architect-theorists, Filarete, travelled from Florence to Milan in 1451 upon the recommendation of Piero de' Medici, who had close political and banking ties to the new rulers (1450) of the northern city, the Sforzas. After a temporary stay, he settled in the city in the 1460s, concurrently beginning work on his treatise and on one of his most elaborate projects, the Ospedale Maggiore. Filarete's drawings for this northern version of Brunelleschi's Foundling Hospital show an extravagance in scale and ornament unimaginable in the Florentine context, though his additive composition of classical elements gives it a distinctly Gothic character. This may have been a response to the firmly established Lombard and Gothic traditions of the city, although Filarete shows nothing but contempt for this "barbarous modern style" when he discusses it in his architectural treatise, the *Trattato d'architettura* of the 1460s. The built courtyard of the Ospedale Maggiore (1461–5) is more restrained than the version drawn in his treatise. Despite its congestion of ornament, the arcade has the proportions and elegance of form of the Foundling Hospital, and indeed succeeds in producing the unified cloister effect only implied by Brunelleschi's colonnade.

Another foreign architect, Bramante, adopted a similar mixture of local and classical styles in his work in the city. Bramante arrived in Milan between 1477 and 1482, when he began work on one of the most remarkable Greek-cross churches of the Renaissance, Santa Maria presso San Satiro, which was in fact a renovation of a centralized Early Christian monument. The fourth, choir arm appears as long as the three-bay transept wings due to a mixture of architecture and scenography: it is in fact less than one bay deep. Bramante had trained as architect and painter under some of the greatest perspectivists of his time, Piero della Francesca and Francesco di Giorgio, both of whom worked in his native Urbino. His gift for scenography made his paintings and drawings powerful persuasive tools for advancing his architectural ideas, allowing his clients to imagine themselves in a Bramantesque setting. Nonetheless, even his more elaborate Santa Maria delle Grazie (right) in Milan shows either his respect for the local tradition or the latter's intransigence. Its linear demarcation of parts goes far beyond anything imagined by Brunelleschi, producing on its exterior a dizzying effect closer to the 14th-century panelling of Florence Cathedral. It is on the interior that Bramante begins to break with the linearity of either his Tuscan predecessors in Milan or the city's tradition. The circle predominates, occupying all scales of decoration, plan and section, which are drawn together by the climax of the cupola itself. This geometric play is transformed in the coffering of the nave arches and, most markedly, at the apses, into a powerful, very Roman means of spatial definition that shifts the circular motif from planar ornament to massive, sculptural volume. These elements of Santa Maria delle Grazie show Bramante's preoccupation with more explicit Roman forms, which he would

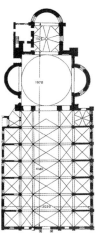

Santa Maria delle Grazie
Interior and ground plan

115

Many and varied were the forms in which architectural theory was committed to paper in the late Middle Ages. Abbot Suger of Saint-Denis has supplied

Leon Battista Alberti
De re aedificatoria, frontispiece of
the 1550 Italian edition

us with a description of the decisions he made on inventing the first Gothic architecture for his famous abbey. In his exposition, two themes are accorded special significance: the powerful effect of such magnificent architecture on the observer, awaking a sense of awe and therefore also of religious belief, and the honour, or rather the dimension of true greatness, such a building bestows not only on its owner and patron, the King of France, for whom the abbey was intended to be both shrine and tomb, but also on its architect. The latter was namely himself, Suger, a fact which he was not slow to point out. Neither of these two aspects of displays of architectural splendour were at all new, but originated from Vitruvius and had been integral to Christian ecclesiastical architectural theory since Constantine the Great. Even up to our present time, they have remained leitmotivs of architectural theory. The only significant changes with respect to these concern the methods with which people have attempted to achieve this awe-inspiring effect and self-aggrandisement.

Even the harshest critic of the Abbot of Saint-Denis, Bernard of Clairvaux, had to acknowledge the powerful aura which Suger had imparted to his church. Bernard was of the opinion, however, that the vertiginous shapes and especially the distorted forms of the gargoyles and bizarre beasts which were an integral part of late Romantic and early Gothic

architecture distracted the poor monk in the most abominable manner from concentrating his soul upon God. He himself was the proponent of an architecture of a more modest beauty, of a style capable of provoking contemplation and of instilling the love of God. In his own Cistercian abbeys, Bernard himself developed an architectural style in which the architecture itself was the decorative element, expressed by its proportion and harmony. In order to allow this architecture to achieve its full impact, he advocated lighting effects similar to those invented by Suger – this time, however, using windows made of transparent glass, which were intended to emphasize the architectural structures rather than disguising them, and which immersed the harmonious forms of the building's interior in a light as pure and radiant as the new white habits of the Cistercian monks.

Bernard's emphasis on architectural form and design, which were to be valued more highly than the decoration, became the basis of the first building regulations in Italy of the late Middle Ages to deal explicitly with aesthetics drafted by the Franciscans. The modest locations and the simple message of that carefully proportioned architecture, to which narrative decorations were now also added, contributed considerably to the remarkable success which the friars experienced in winning the support of the devout inhabitants of Italy's cities. Cathedral-building societies such as the Opera del Duomo in Florence felt obliged to adopt a similar approach in order to compete with the settlements of the mendicant friars in the outlying areas of the city. The Florentine Opera borrowed from these ideas during the construction of their

Filarete, Trattata d'architettura, ca. 1465, classical column order

cathedral, whereby they adopted the wide proportions of Santa Croce, applying them to the cathedral façade, the belfry and to Orsanmichele.

In this manner, therefore, a clear and harmonious architecture came into being in the late 14th century which dissociated itself from narrative figures and depictions while simultaneously presenting them with an effective framework. It formed the definitive foundation for the artistic and architectural theories of the 15th century.

Leon Battista Alberti laid down the principles of these theories, firstly in his treatise *On Painting*, which he wrote in 1435–36. In this he advocated two important points. First, one must create a framework of strict proportions, in

order to show the figures represented in perspective. Secondly, one must arrange and execute these figures in such a way that they correspond with the narrative content, thus forming a dramatic whole. The dramatic unity of a painting was not simply to serve the purpose of bringing its moral content to the fore. It was also intended to demonstrate the genius of the painter. Alberti was of the opinion that the struggle to achieve fame was as practical as it was praiseworthy – but only as long as the artist, in pursuing this aim, was concerned with mastering the theory and practice of painting and did not resort to superficial solutions.

Alberti based his architectural theory on the intellectual content of his treatise on painting. He linked these ideas to a thorough analysis of the writings of Vitruvius and extensive commentaries on certain types of building and architectural practices. In his treatise *De re aedificatoria* (c. 1442–52) he explained, among other things, how to determine the most favourable and appropriate site for a building and how to apply the classical orders in an appropriate manner, in order to express its character, status or

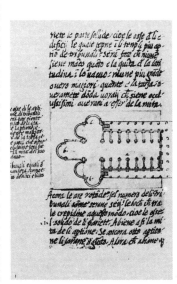

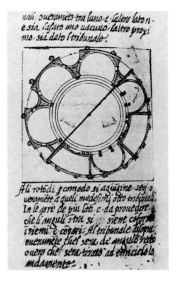

Leon Battista Alberti
De re aedificatoria
Church floor plan with transept (left)
Centralised building floor plan with
circular apses (right)

intended use. Many people have interpreted Alberti's opinions concerning what is appropriate in such a way as to give the impression that he wished to emphasize hierarchical decorum only. However, they equally express his idea of narrative structures and the associated dramatic effect.

Despite the intellectual connection between his writings on painting and those on architecture, Alberti never combined these into a single work. If he had done so, he could have developed a theory for an all-embracing work of art, in which painting and architecture achieve a completely new effect by means of their interaction. After all, his architectural writings and letters are interspersed with remarks which indicate that he accorded both the figurative and abstract decoration of buildings a significant role in some designs. Since he tended to speak rather from the viewpoint of the theoretician than that of a practising artist, he did not add any illustrations to his text. He adopted another viewpoint only when he himself became a practising artist, after which he continued his studies in the buildings themselves.

While none of the later writings of the 15th century displayed such versatility or

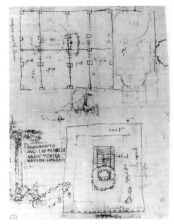

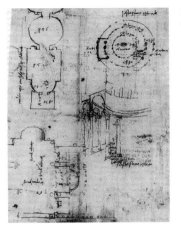

Francesco di Giorgio
classical mausolea and temple in Rome
(left)

Late classical and early Christian
monuments (right)

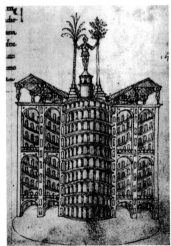

Filarete
Trattata d'architettura

the ability to theorize in abstract terms as Alberti's treatise, theorists did begin to combine words with pictures. Drawings were incorporated into numerous architectural writings of the Renaissance. The first of this type was Filarete's treatise *Trattato d'architettura* from the year 1460. There then followed Francesco di Giorgio's *Trattato di architettura civile e militare* (c. 1482), *L'Architettura* by

Serlio (1537–75), and Palladio's *Quattro Libri dell'Architettur*, from the year 1570. This new type of representation can be partly attributed to the fact that all these artists, in contrast to Alberti, had had a professional education in painting and drawing. This means of representation also enabled the authors to develop and convey architectural ideas in an extremely effective manner, even making it possible at quite an abstract level, as can be seen in the work of Francesco di Giorgio. In this, he discussed the idea that the church is based on the shape and the hierarchical relationships of the human body, and created a drawing based on the ideas of Vitruvius (and those of Plutarch), which were essentially similar to his own and which permeated the whole of architectural theory and practice of the Middle Ages and the early Renaissance, whether in John of Salisbury's treatise *The Body Public*, from the 12th century, in Alberti's own writings, or in the sculptures, pilasters and frescoes of the facade of Orsanmichele. Serlio's depictive strategies in his discourse on tragic, comic and rustic scenes in architecture are equally subtle, as evinced not only by his drawings, but also by the design of the actual text. The general tendency of all writings after Alberti, however, is to deviate from his balanced mixture of abstract theory and practical applications, and to increasingly lean towards the exposition of formal ideas. While Alberti discussed the classical orders and buildings of antiquity in depth, his successors committed detailed drawings and reconstructions of the remains of classical buildings to paper. In addition, they interpolated drawings of their own completed, planned or imaginary buildings, in which they presented their proficiency in redesigning the classical orders and models to its best advantage.

The *Quattro Libri* of Palladio are an especially extreme example of this tendency to illustrate treatises. In this text, Palladio intersperses drawings of the antique and representations of his own

buildings, leaving relatively little space for text, however. Drawings replace words, albeit at a less theoretical level. In the final analysis, however, he was trying to achieve an exalting effect, similar to that advocated by Alberti and Suger. By Palladio's time, treatises not only had become a work of art but also enabled specific architectural ideas to be communicated with a previously unheard-of precision. Palladio succeeded in achieving this by applying the technique of orthographic projection for the first time in a systematic manner, showing the floor plan, cross-section and elevation of a building in different illustrations. The

disadvantage of such a drawing technique was, however, that no space remained for the representation of a building in its actual or planned environment. Only the appearance and the plan of the building itself were shown, isolated from any context whatever. This concentration on the building alone is understandable if one considers the type of building with which he was primarily concerned: basilicas, which are isolated objects at the centre of a piazza, palaces in streets empty of any shops, and, most revealing of all, villas set within country gardens or uncultivated fields.

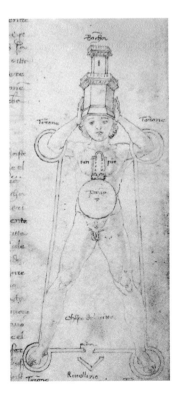

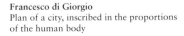

Francesco di Giorgio
Plan of a city, inscribed in the proportions
of the human body

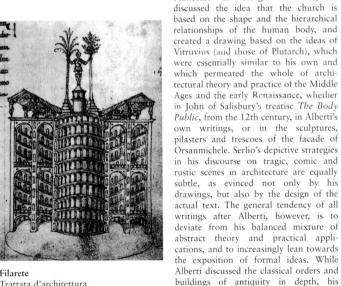

Floor plan of the cathedral,
the Palazzo Piccolomini and
the Palazzo Comunale
Pienza, Piazza Pio II

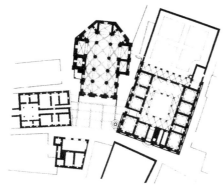

Filarete
Trattato d'architettura
Plan of the ideal city
Sforzinda

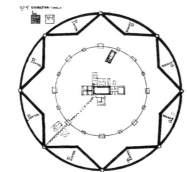

Ludovico Sforza
Donato Bramante
Vigevano, designed
before 1499

Unknown artist
Ideal city, 15th century
Urbino, Palazzo Ducale

The image of the ideal city in Western Europe was sustained during a large part of the Middle Ages in the monastic environment. It occurred in two different forms: on the one hand, in manuscripts, to illustrate the biblical descriptions of the heavenly Jerusalem given in the Revelation of St. John; and, on the other hand, in buildings corresponding to the ideal type, particularly monastic cloisters, which were based on the principles laid down in the Carolingian ideal plan of St. Gall (circa 820). These ideal city representations showed a biaxial symmetry, and their absolute purity differentiated them from the nature of those random real structures which were forced to adapt to the manifold requirements of hectic city life. At the plan of St. Gall, the biaxial ideal was even extended to the pig-sties and chicken-coops.

The ideal image of the city, alienated from reality, continued to be of great influence on the architecture of monasteries and churches during the whole of the high and late Middle Ages. It can be seen, for example, in the continued tradition of the peristyle monastery quadrangle and the gallery of Romanesque churches. Despite this ideal's apparent limitations, it was used as model for redesigning existing cities and designing new ones. This occurred as soon as the municipal authorities or the despots in Italy's urban centres succeeded in extending the sphere of their authority to include urban legislation and planning. An early example of this was the new settlements in the territory of Florence, which were all constructed on a symmetrical grid and grouped around a square in the centre. At least one or even both of the most important buildings in the city, the church and the town hall, were inevitably to be found at this square, which was sometimes linked with an arcade. These new towns were surrounded by equally regular defensive walls. Matters became more interesting where the ideal form and the existing situation collided with one another. In such cases, legislators and town planners proved to be remarkably inventive and imaginative. They tended to deviate from the standardized geometric form of the ideal, while nevertheless retaining a symbolic layout. The inhabitants of Siena planned their Campo on a precipitous and uneven site, transforming it into a theatre-like, semicircular piazza, and surrounded it with galleries in the Piano nobile which were reminiscent not only of the arcades on the façade of the Palazzo Pubblico on the other side, but also of the front and dome of their cathedral. In Prato, a half-ruined piazza in front of the church was transformed into a generous square surrounded by arcades, with an indentation in the centre, thus reflecting along a straight axis the floor plan of the transept, which was on the projection of this axis. The Florentines used a similar design incorporating arcades for the piazza in front of their cathedral and reflected in its shape the elaborate, undulating movement of the radial crossing of the church. In Florence, however, it was the loggia of Brunelleschi's orphanage which came closest to realizing the ideal of a biaxial symmetry in a space similar to that of a monastery.

Only those having the power to buy or expropriate sites from their private owners were able to do with them as they wished. With the growth of territorial states and principalities in the late 14th and 15th century, oligarchies and tyrants in possession of such power grew in numbers, which led in turn to the spread of idealized planning throughout the whole of Italy. Perhaps the earliest example of this was the Pienza of Pope Pius II, where the classical façades of the church and those of the adjoining palace on the cathedral square complemented

each other. The Sforza family rebuilt the centre of Vigevano, allegedly with the help of Bramante and Leonardo, and lined the elongated square in the city centre with a continuous colonnade, above which arose the classically designed façades of the houses.

This idealization in architecture was accompanied by legislation which took upon itself the task of restricting the use of these squares and others similar to them within the city, particularly those across which religious and political processions traditionally made their way. When the Piazza della Signoria in Florence was finished around 1380, it was one of the few city squares in Italy not intended for use as a market-place. Towards the end of the next century,

laws were passed in Rome and other cities which were intended to impose similar restrictions on the use of distinguished squares and streets. The Popes, starting with Nicholas V, drew up plans to redesign the Vatican with wide, level streets, and passed laws to regulate their use. These laws permitted anyone who wished, and who possessed the necessary means, to build a magnificent palace and buy up the adjoining property of less wealthy landowners, even against a poorer neighbour's will.

The next logical step in the direction of a perfect, ideal city required a type of tabula rasa, like that which had existed in the form of the colonial settlements around Florence. The first plan of this type was designed by Filarete, com-

missioned by the Sforza for a city which was to be called Sforzinda. One of the most remarkable projects of this kind, and one which was actually realized, was the city of Sabbionetta, commissioned in the late 16th century by the Gonzagas. The painting shown opposite of an ideal city from the 15th century vividly depicts the qualities these ideal squares and cities were supposed to possess upon their completion. The city is laid out on a perspective grid and the elevation of each building is segmented by means of classical forms such as arcades or an entablature. The most idealized element is the circular church in the centre. The absolute regularity of the rationalized design and the architectural structure make it impossible to add something to

this design or remove anything from it. Similar to depictions of the heavenly Jerusalem from the early Middle Ages, the piazza remains undesecrated by commercial hustle and bustle, and is completely empty of people.

119

explore further in the city that was to prove the most conducive to innovations in the antique style, late 15th- and early 16th-century Rome itself, under the encouragement and patronage of the institution claiming to be the legitimate heir of the ancient Roman Empire, the papacy.

The Renaissance palace

Though Brunelleschi's Foundling Hospital was the first building to be articulated with the new antique style, it had few followers in secular architecture until later in the century. Brunelleschi was responsible for one other, the Palazzo di Parte Guelfa in Florence (begun 1415), to which he applied pilasters articulating the corners of each façade. Its pure rectangular plan, tall volume and generous windows recall the sanctuary of all the guilds, Orsanmichele, and finally that building's prototypes, the Palazzo Vecchio and Bargello. These structures, together with the civic palaces discussed in the last section, show a far more restrained application of ornamental forms and rigorous plan geometries than in the religious architectural tradition. The structures that most explicitly adopted ecclesiastical and classical ornament were the residences of the two institutions claiming the title of their Imperial Roman predecessors. These were the palace of the Popes in Viterbo, and the castles of the Holy Roman Emperor, specifically of Frederick II, whether at Capo di Monte, with its perfect octagonal plan, elaborate portal and graded rustication, or at Tuscany's own Palazzo del Imperatore in Prato (p. 34), with its crystalline form, temple-front portal framed by Corinthian pilasters, bichrome ornament and graded rustication, and, in the most extravagant way, the Doges' Palace in Venice. Though these structures exerted a significant influence on civic architecture, their

example was never followed in domestic structures except in the increasingly frequent adoption of their name, *palazzo,* which derives from the original dwelling-place of Roman Emperors on the Palatine hill in Rome. As early as the 13th century in Prato powerful citizens of the commune applied this august name to their residences, but none showed any concerted attempt to adopt the ornament or plan of papal or imperial palaces, except in rare applications of polychromy or the more frequent use of polyfoil windows. The exception to this rule is Venice, where from a very early time the protected nature of the lagoon and stable character of the Republic afforded the city's patriciate the possibility of building elaborately decorated, symmetrical compositions that often derived from the Doges' Palace itself, but never competed with it.

It should not be surprising that the first structures in Tuscany where the forms of church and imperial architecture began to be applied in a monumental fashion were the houses of powerful merchant and banking families. They had the funds at their disposal to engage in elaborate building projects, and their businesses could only benefit from architectural representation of the stability and lofty character of their mercantile or banking houses. Some early examples are in the palaces of Italy's most precocious banking cities, Lucca and Siena, such as the latter's Palazzo Tolmei, Palazzo Chigi-Saraceni, and, at the most sophisticated level, Palazzo Sansedoni, although the latter's triforate windows were required by ordinance and are subsumed into the unified design of the Campo and facing the Palazzo Communale.

The tendency to emulate the major civic government palaces in domestic palace design was maintained in the first monumental private residence in Florence of the 15th century, the Palazzo Medici (p. 122), begun by Michelozzo in 1444. Like its predecessors in Venice, Lucca and Siena, it remains more restrained than its civic prototype, the Palazzo Vecchio. This is not to say that something more ostentatious had not been imagined. Had the Medici adopted the project that Brunelleschi is reputed to have designed, they would have situated a more elaborate Medici Palace at a site recalling the original all-powerful bishop rulers of Italian cities, directly across from their church, in this case San Lorenzo, the parish church of the Medici – which Brunelleschi was redesigning, replete with a Sacristy for the Medici family tomb. Michelozzo's palazzo design produces its own magnificent effect despite its greater restraint. It is a near symmetrical plan with a generous arcaded courtyard. Michelozzo articulated the exterior on the ground floor with similar rustication as at the Palazzo Vecchio. He then reduced this rustication in two stages on the upper floors, imitating the graded masonry of Frederick II's Palazzo del Imperatore. The semicircular arches of the windows, mouldings and cornice are the only explicitly classical elements on this façade; the rounded bifore windows within the larger semicircular frames makes the overall effect, when combined with the rustication, closer to that of Tuscan bishops' palaces, the

Luciano Laurana, Francesco di Giorgio
Palazzo Ducale, begun c. 1454
Urbino

Bargello or the Palazzo Vecchio, than of the recent experiments in classicism by Brunelleschi or Michelozzo himself.

The inner courtyard of the Medici Palace is quite another matter (p. 122, bottom). Here Michelozzo shows his debt to Brunelleschi, essentially wrapping the arcade of the Foundling Hospital around its four walls. The fact that Michelozzo completed a more elaborate version of this same classicizing courtyard within the Palazzo Vecchio indicates that the historical linkages between the Medici Palace and the city's governing palace were more than coincidence. The Medici Palace was a *de facto* extension of the Palazzo Vecchio, not only because of the Medici's powerful influence, but also because it did indeed provide the only suitable quarters in the city for accommodating visiting ambassadors and dignitaries. The layout and elaborate decoration of the interior rooms ideally served such a function, something that could only add prestige to the Medici's original source of power, as a bank, a term that indeed derives from the long bench lining the façade of this and other banking residences. Here clients awaited their chance to meet with the powerful family, in order to arrange their financial affairs, joined by citizens from all levels of society seeking favours from the Medici court. Depending on their status, these proto-courtiers would arrive at various depths within the semi-public, semi-private space of the palace, most arriving no further than the Sala Grande, decorated with classicizing paintings by artists such as Uccello, Pesellino, and the Pollaiuolo brothers. Only the most august guests would penetrate into the more private domains.

The application of explicitly classical forms on the exterior, entirely public façade of a palace was quite rare in 15th-century Tuscany. The first example generally goes unmentioned, namely the Palazzo Datini in Prato, built by one of Tuscany's most successful international merchant bankers in the late 14th century. Shortly after Datini's death, in the first decades of the 15th century, classical columns and bichrome window frames recalling the nearby Palazzo del Imperatore were painted onto the façade. It was not until after 1446, however, when Alberti began work on a palace for Giovanni Rucellai, that classical orders were to be applied in the actual masonry of the façade, and here only as pilasters. As with the Medici Palace, which was expanded by the Riccardi family in the 17th century, the structure visible today is more extended than the original. In the case of the Palazzo Rucellai (p. 123), it was the patron himself who went beyond the original design. The difference between the two projects reveals the difference in goals of architect and patron. Alberti compensated for the constrained setting and limited breadth of the palace's ground plan by elaborating a façade with the same close attention to proportion, harmony and symmetry that he advocated in his *De re aedeficatoria*. He not only applies to the façade the orders that Michelozzo reserved for the interior of the Palazzo Medici, but also superimposes them on three levels. He varies them according to Vitruvian laws of progressive refinement, moving from the Doric

Michelozzo di Bartolomeo
Palazzo Medici-Riccardi, begun c. 1444
Exterior façade (left)
Inner courtyard and ground plan (below)
Florence

order at the ground level to modified Ionic and Corinthian orders above, separating each by friezes decorated with the same private emblem of Giovanni Rucellai that appears on the façade of Santa Maria Novella: a sail filled with the winds of Fortune. Within this ordering matrix Alberti deftly underlays upper-storey semi-circular biforate windows and lower-storey square windows similar to those at the Palazzo Medici and Palazzo Vecchio. He separates the former from the classical orders by their rustication, while linking the latter to these same orders with classicizing mouldings that compensate for the greater distance between them and the framing pilasters. The five bays of the design are arrayed in a perfect symmetry centred on the single central portal. The entire composition is supported by a basement level of diamond-shaped, archaeologically correct *opus reticulatum* masonry, which is itself underscored by the requisite bench for Rucellai's banking clients.

The variations of smooth and scored masonry and subtle gradations of relief in the classicizing pilasters, friezes, window frames and door prevent any appearance of crowding or confusion on this densely elaborated façade. All is controlled by Alberti's proportions and symmetry. This remarkably tight composition lived up so thoroughly to Alberti's stated ideal that nothing more could be added or taken away – indeed, it proved incapable of sustaining the later elaborations ordered by Alberti's ambitious patron. At some point after Alberti ended his involvement in the project, Rucellai enlisted the assistance of another architect, perhaps the same one who oversaw the technical aspects of Alberti's original scheme, Bernardo Rossellino. Having succeeded in purchasing property to one side of the original site and expecting to purchase yet more, he ordered the extension of the façade from its symmetrical, square, five-bay format to an eight-bay design. Even had he succeeded in

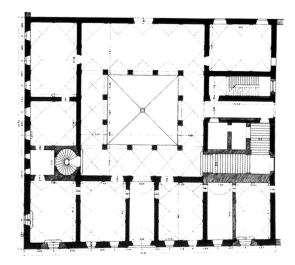

obtaining the property to complete the final, eighth bay, the resulting composition would have broken with Alberti's classical sensibilities by centring the elevation not only on a blank wall, but also on a pilaster. But Rucellai, despite all his banking wealth and political connections with the Medici, was never able to buy out the modest house of his neighbour, with the result that the final bay of the building remains pathetically incomplete, betraying in its fragments of arches and rustication the paper-thin veneer of architecture with which Alberti sought to transform a series of simple dwellings into Florence's most beautiful palace. The ruse would have worked had the patron respected Alberti's project, which made up for the site's deficiencies with magnificent, classical design. However, Rucellai was tied more to the local taste in magnificence, whether at the Medici Palace or its predecessors, where scale was the final sign of power, not aesthetic elaboration. In seeking to fill the entire face of the triangular piazza that his palace faced with his own presence, and then failing by less than a bay, Rucellai shattered the magic of Alberti's ideal composition while making a parody of his own ambitions.

As with his church designs, Alberti's one Florentine palace had no followers until the next century. Though the city became congested with grand palaces over the next fifty years, they were all based on the Palazzo Medici's model, of a generally aggressively rusticated Tuscan Gothic exterior, with classical orders only appearing in the courtyard and interior decoration. The palaces of Giuliano da Sangallo were typical, and show how great a gap existed between local tastes for houses versus churches. It would be almost impossible to detect the same hand in the bombastic Palazzo Strozzi exterior (1489–1504; p. 124) that applied elegant classical pilasters and polychrome decoration to Santa Maria delle Carceri (p. 114). The only tell-tales are the symmetrical composition, classicizing basement window frames and friezes, and the exploitation of the freestanding site with a powerfully cubic volume. There is indeed some question as to Sangallo's authorship of the palace. Though he is documented as having built its remarkable wooden model, the design itself may be by Benedetto da Maiano, and the heavy cornice by Il Cronaca.

As with innovations in church design, only sites outside republican Florence proved fertile for classical experiments in palace design. Even in the palaces of princes, however, architects met resistance to purely classical schemes. The palace in Urbino (p. 121) of Alberti's great humanist friend and warrior prince, Federico di Montefeltro, is a case in point. The structure is too vast in scale on too irregular a site to admit anything beyond local symmetries in plan. The architects, Francesco di Giorgio and Luciano Laurana, tried to tame its endless, bending façade on the city's main square with classicizing doors and windows, but the overall effect remains that of a bastion bristling with the chambers of the prince and the offices of his bureaucracy. This encastlated effect is even more pronounced on the façade looking across the territory of Urbino, with its central portion framed by two round towers. As mediaeval as these appear now and probably at the time, these towers delimit one of the most remarkable classical references in castle design, with precedents not only in Laurana's triumphal arch of Alfonso of Aragon in Naples, but also in the entries of Frederick II's palaces, with classical portals and sometimes galleries sandwiched between two towers. The motif may well derive from the Imperial Roman palace type, which was diffused particularly in the Eastern Mediterranean during the final centuries of the empire. Its imperial origins are underlined in the Palazzo Ducale version with the imaginatively superimposed Corinthian columns and coffered arches, the upper storey achieving its refinement through the fluting of the columns and floral bosses centred in the coffer squares. The effect is to open to the prince *qua* Emperor the view over his citizens and countryside, beginning with the formal garden before the loggia, and extending to the furthest visible Apennines. The prince, in turn, is both visible to and distanced from his subjects. The classical arches enshrining him also provide a hint of the elaborate classical treatment of his private quarters within the palace, most elaborate in his remarkable studiolo. At the same time, he is protected by the turrets framing these arches. This view from Montefeltro's gallery, as well as the imperial status he sought to convey, are both documented in the remarkable portraits of him and his wife by Piero della Francesca (p. 272).

Benedetto da Maiano, Giuliano da Sangallo, Il Cronaca
Palazzo Strozzi, 1489-1504
Florence

Leon Battista Alberti?, Giuliano da Sangallo
Palazzo Venezia, 1469–74
Rome

contemporary Latin prose to its Ciceronian origins, only with an unmistakably religious twist that indicates that the source is the Early Christian Rome of Constantine and his successors, not the Rome of the first Caesars. The loggia literally bridges the would-be world religion's mother church with the quasi-imperial residence of the papacy initiated only decades earlier. It thereby provides the ideal vantage point for the Pope to bestow his blessing on his worshipful subjects in both of his personae, as the spiritual heir to St. Peter and therefore to Christ, and as the temporal heir of the ancient Roman emperors, underlined in the Pope's title – *pontifex maximus* – as in his architecture.

The papacy thereby infused Alberti's forms with the ideological power it had been waiting to receive. They were quickly adopted and elaborated in the residences of cardinals, first in the courtyard of Cardinal Barbo's (later Paul II) Palazzo Venezia (below), again attributed to Alberti, though worked on by Giuliano da Sangallo between 1469–74. They next appear in the elevations and courtyards of Cardinal Raffaele Riario's Cancelleria (before 1489–1517) and its nearby look-alike, the Palazzo Corneto-Giraud-Torlonia. Both of the latter buildings show the hand of a master profoundly influenced by Alberti. The remarkable resolution of the interior corners of the Cancelleria courtyard with double corner piers, and the similarity of this design to the courtyard of Santa Maria delle Pace (p. 132), suggest some involvement of the latter's architect, Bramante, freshly arrived in Rome from Milan. The formal convergence of palace courtyard with church cloister indicates how far classical architecture had begun to penetrate domestic design, albeit for the house of a cardinal. This was just the beginning, however. Through these Roman residential monuments, whose theocratic aura was constantly being reinforced by the innovations in classical religious architecture, the style of *all'antica* began to be diffused back to the north, where it met success in direct

The full convergence of classical church and classical palace design only occurred in the city of their origins, Rome, under the patronage of the city's powerful cardinals and the Pope himself. By the time of Nicholas V, the papacy was beginning to strengthen its hold over the Roman republic and the city's powerful families. One of the first documented applications of the classical orders to a Roman palace was at the Benediction Loggia of Old St. Peter's, attributed to Alberti himself and completed before 1464, probably under Pius II. This three-storey loggia comes down to us in a drawing by Maerten van Heemskerck, showing what appear to be the first truly superimposed classical columns (not pilasters) of the century, possibly excepting those directly attributable to Pius II, at the cathedral of Pienza and the loggia – again overlooking the landscape – of his adjoining palace (see insert on the ideal city, pp. 118–9), both attributed to Bernardo Rossellino, the same sculptor and architect who assisted in and expanded Alberti's Palazzo Rucellai. The Benediction Loggia restored this arcaded-gallery type to its imperial origins as accurately as Alberti sought to restore

Palazzo Cancelleria, c. 1489-1517
Inner courtyard
Rome

proportion with the recasting of civic institutions from the mediaeval republic to the Renaissance Empire.

The Palace, the Villa, and the Interiorization of Private Life

The gradual assimilation of classical forms to residential structures in 15th-century Italy was accompanied by a transformation of the domestic life of those dwelling in them. The Palazzo Rucellai, for instance, was built upon a site that had previously housed a series of residences. The price of such magnificence in scale was the cost of furnishing the extra rooms – and learning how to take advantage of them. Previous generations of Florence's powerful families had conducted much of their business in ground-storey arcaded openings of their residences and in market streets and squares, and had celebrated weddings, funerals and festivities at corner loggias, such as the Loggia degli Alberti or Rucellai's own loggia. Now the banks lining the street of Florence's major palaces provided only waiting room for entry into the more private confines of palace courtyards and office chambers. The families themselves retreated increasingly within these same courtyards, interior halls, and hidden gardens for their once semi-public festivities, a trend that was accompanied by the privatization of family life itself, with the focus increasingly on the individual family unit, not the vast extended family of the mediaeval *consorterie* and their magnate successors. This parallel interiorization of domestic architecture and family life transformed the character of the late mediaeval city from arcaded streets congested with business activity, family celebrations and traffic into arteries of traffic alone, with the tall rusticated walls of palaces only entertaining a public beyond immediate family and clientele when religious and civic processions passed by their dignified façades.

The interiorization of family life took one step further with the development of two related building types in 15th-century Florence, namely the garden and the villa. The former began to develop at structures like Michelozzo's Medici Palace and the Pitti Palace, based on simpler gardens at the first Medici Palace, near San Marco, and in turn on the cloisters and more extensive green precincts of the numerous mendicant foundations filling the circumference of many cities' walled areas. The more such gardens became popular with the urban patriciate, the more the demand grew for newer, more elaborate gardens, which first began to be built around fortified family strongholds in the Tuscan countryside. The Villas Medici at Careggi (p. 126) and Castello (p. 127) were both such cases, with Michelozzo elaborating the former with a loggia that barely tamed its castle-like design. Castello and the Villa Medici at Fiesole were more refined versions of this evolving type, with regularized fenestration and restrained classical ornament reflecting an increasingly formal approach to the facing gardens, but now derivative from the emerging palace type, with little accommodation to their rural settings. What they did introduce, however, was places from which to enjoy distant views of the countryside, which was no

Michelozzo di Bartolomeo and others
Villa Medicea di Careggi, 1457
Careggi/Florence

longer just to be country explicitly owned by the Medici, but – especially at Fiesole – entire panoramas of Florence and the Arno valley.

The codification of the villa as a monumental architectural form, if such types can ever be defined in so hard and fast, a manner awaited the regularization of their plans into symmetrical arrangements and the fusing of explicitly classical forms to their exteriors. The first tendencies in this direction were two of the palaces mentioned above, namely the palace of Federico di Montefeltro at Urbino and that of Pius II at Pienza, with their monumental classical loggias overlooking their domains. It was the achievement of the Medici, perhaps the most prolific builders of the type in western history, to crystallize a model that would influence all later villas, from papal villas to Palladian villas to Versailles to Jefferson's Monticello. In 1480, Giuliano da Sangallo started work on the Villa Medici at Poggio a Caiano. He began with an arcaded plinth supporting a perfectly symmetrical plan, bisected laterally with a remarkable barrel-vaulted space terminated with oculus windows more recalling church interiors than any secular spaces built to date. His crowning achievement, however, was the entryway providing access perpendicular to this barrel-vaulted space. Fresh from work on Santa Maria delle Carceri, where he was concurrently engaged, he took the radical step of adopting the temple front of the facing Palazzo del Imperatore, and applying it to the portal of his patrons' villa, now with six columns rather than the two pilasters of Frederick II's Tuscan residence, and with a frieze within the pediment recalling ancient Greek architecture as the architecture as much of ancient or recent Emperors. All the restraint that the Medici demonstrated in selecting Michelozzo over Brunelleschi's design for their urban palace was here cast aside. As so often the case in the history of the villa, such as the antique Villa Adriana or the 16th-century Villa d'Este, this structure was a private statement of the imperial ambitions of its patrons, ambitions that were to be at first dashed, and then fully realized, in the following decades.

Villa Medicea di Castello
after 1465, bought by the Medici family in 1480
Florence

Giusto Utens
Veduta of the Villa Medicea di Castello
Florence, Museo di Firenze comera

127

Giuliano da Sangallo
Villa Medicea di Poggio a Caiano, 1480–85
Poggio a Caiano, Florence

OPPOSITE:
Villa Medicea di Poggio a Caiano
Great Hall of Leo X, with frescoes
by Andrea del Sarto, Pontormo and others
begun c. 1521
Florence

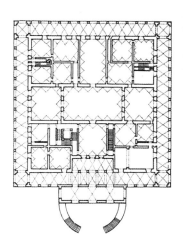

Wolfgang Jung

Architecture of the High Renaissance and Mannerism in Rome and Central Italy

"Great was the part that the papacy played in the culture of the Renaissance, that radiant flower of an era, after which the feverishly overtaxed spirit of Italy naturally collapsed in exhaustion."

Gregorovius, *History of the City of Rome in the Middle Ages*

Towards the Golden Age

In the late 15th century and particularly in the 16th century, the Church and papacy laid claim to supreme rule both in the religious and in the secular realm. Pope Nicholas V promoted the use of visual images to enforce this claim; it was not enough for the liturgy to symbolize Christian faith – what was needed was *spettacoli grandiosi* to lead the uncertain back to the fold of the faith. In like manner, architecture must express the *auctoritas ecclesiae* through majestic, monumental buildings like those of classical antiquity. But the claims and those who put forward those claims prompted widespread dissent. Around the turn of the century, the Borgia Pope's unbounded greed for power and his ruinously wasteful taste for splendour precipitated the first profound crisis in the Church and provoked calls for fundamental ecclesiastical reform. Notwithstanding, the demands of Nicholas V set the agenda for the Popes who followed him in the century of reform.

In 1503, Giuliano della Rovere ascended St. Peter's Chair as Pope Julius II. He was determined to take a new broom to the Church, in every department. His first concern was to restore the authority of the Church – and the first step towards this had to be an overhaul of Vatican budgeting. In Rome he aimed to reinforce the Vatican's power over the citizenry, while at the same time he defended the Vatican State against the Venetians. On 21 December 1507, Egidio da Viterbo proclaimed that Julius II saw the arrival of an era of imperial, universal Church hegemony. This was the Golden Age. And Julius II called upon Bramante, Michelangelo and Raphael to give visible form to the *ecclesia militans et triumphans* (the Church militant and triumphant).

As the Cinquecento began, Bramante's plan for the Tempietto of San Pietro in Montorio (p. 131), done around 1502, fundamentally rethought the centrally-built votive church. It immediately became the very definition of the dawning High Renaissance. Bramante was commissioned by the Spanish monarchy to build a memorial chapel on the site where tradition had it that St. Peter had been crucified. Above a crypt, and raised on a stepped base, is an extremely small centrally-planned room, and above this in turn is a tambour with many openings; the building is surrounded by a Tuscan (Roman Doric) order of columns and crowned by a dome and lantern – though these have been altered over the course of time. Serlio's architectural treatise informs us that the building was originally meant to be framed by a circular court with a portico. It was the new understanding of architecture as both ancient and modern that gives this design its exceptional monumental character. The sculptural decoration of the walls, together with the use of the correct order, create the impression of a Roman temple. At the same time, Bramante was seeking to reconstruct the model of the round temple. He used Vitruvius, as well as the Temple of Hercules Victor and the Vesta, as sources for his model. The classical age was therefore the formative principle behind this design. The reference to

St. Peter's martyrdom, and beyond it to the birth of the *ecclesiae romanae*, meant that the design was at the same time seeking to use history to legitimize the Church's religious and secular claims.

Similar considerations determined the plans for St. Peter's, which were started a few years later (1505/06). Pope Nicholas V had started restoring and extending Old St. Peter's about half a century previously, but the work soon came to a standstill. Julius II, however, who considered himself to be a great innovator in the Church on a par with its founder, St. Peter himself, decided not to proceed with the partial extensions, but instead to tear down Christianity's time-honoured central church. Bramante was chosen as the architect of the new building. His first suggestion, in collaboration with Giuliano da Sangallo, was probably a centrally-planned building, though the sketches do not make this entirely clear. Bramante was making use of what the 15th and early 16th centuries were convinced was the most frequently used, and indeed the definitive, form of classical sacred building. The most important reference points for humanist architects were the Baptistry in Florence, which, though Romanesque, was thought to be antique; the Temple of Minerva Medici and Bacchus (Santa Costanza); and, above all, the Pantheon and the centrally-built Church of the Holy Sepulchre in Jerusalem, which, like St. Peter's, had also been founded by Constantine and was the second most important shrine of Christianity.

Donato Bramante
Tempietto San Pietro in Montorio, 1502
Rome

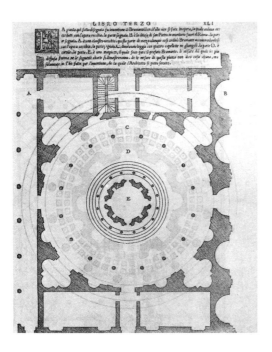

Donato Bramante
Plan of the Tempietto and porticoed courtyard
San Pietro in Montorio (after Serlio)

131

Donato Bramante
Cloisters of Santa Maria della Pace, completed in 1504
Rome

Bramante's very first plan was already a major step forward from the designs of centrally-planned buildings formulated in the Quattrocento by such architects as Francesco di Giorgio and Leonardo, for he placed the piers that supported the central dome at a slight angle in relation to it and the lateral domes. This meant that he was able to determine the diameter of the central dome without being affected by the width of the naves, and was able to surround it with a corona of lateral domes of hitherto unimaginably large proportions. However, the piers of this early quincunx solution were totally inadequate to support the weight of the originally planned roof (a dome similar to those used by Serlio). The solution to this problem, suggested by Giuliano, was to rework the ground plan on a more massive scale, enlarging the piers. The plan made by Peruzzi, who was Bramante's assistant, outlines its essential features.

The eventual shape of the Church (begun in 1506) was a Latin-cross type, however, and not centrally-planned. One is forced to the conclusion that the Pope himself must have demanded this alteration, probably because this placed his own mausoleum at the end of the building, right behind St. Peter's grave. However, Julius II did temporarily shelve plans for Michelangelo to build his tomb. Though Pope and architect disagreed about the form of the new building, they both had the same goal in mind: this most important of humanist buildings was to be the architectural symbol of the *ecclesia militans et triumphans*. The reference to the Rome of the Caesars was an essential aspect of this. Despite this – or perhaps because of it – more and more believers began to doubt the truth and absoluteness of Christian teachings, and in particular the guidance of the Church itself, shown by the dissent of Erasmus of

Rotterdam and by the Lateran Council, which was eventually convened in 1512.

Meanwhile, Bramante's idea of a sacred building that combined ancient and modern elements was to serve as a model for the next generation. He himself went on to produce a plan for Santa Maria della Consolazione (p. 135) in Todi, probably about 1508. Above a square flanked by four semi-circular apses sits a mighty domed tambour. There is a striking similarity to some of the early studies by Leonardo, who often conversed with Bramante when they were both working in Milan. Raphael, Bramante's most famous pupil, was to develop the basic plan for St. Peter's to new levels of excellence in Rome, in the Chigi burial chapel in Santa Maria del Popolo and the monastic church of Sant'Eglio degli Orefici. Antonio da Sangallo the Younger was to use the quincunx solution as a starting point for his design of Sant'Egidio in Cellere, outside the city gates. Finally, in 1518, four years after Bramante's death, Antonio da Sangallo the Elder started on Madonna di San Biagio at Montepulciano (p. 134), a church of monumental simple forms. In contrast with Bramante's early designs for St. Peter's (bottom right), however, this architect adapted the cross plan by extending one side into an apsidal form, which also solved the more fundamental liturgical problems. Bramante's model acquired a wider circulation when it was published in Serlio and Palladio's architectural treatises.

Julius II sought to translate a *renovatio romae* into action, to run parallel to the *renovatio ecclesiae* (renewal of the Church). He introduced a new currency, in conflict with the independently-minded Commune; raised taxes; and attempted to bring the legal system under his control. Most significantly, however, he intervened directly in Rome's urban development (p. 136).

On the side of the Pope's Castel San Angelo that faced the city, Giuliano da Sangallo extended the apartment of Julius II by means

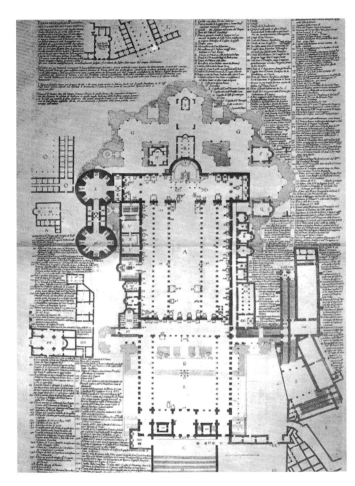

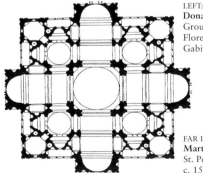

LEFT:
Donato Bramante
Ground plan of St. Peter's, 1505/06
Florence, Galleria degli Uffizi
Gabinetto Disegni e Stampe

FAR LEFT:
Marten van Heemskerck
St. Peter's, view from the north-east
c. 1535
Pen drawing, 12.8 x 20 cm
Berlin, Staatliche Museen zu Berlin-
Preußischer Kulturbesitz,
Kupferstichkabinett

Antonio da Sangallo the Elder
Madonna di San Biagio, 1518–45
Montepulciano

Leonardo da Vinci
Sketches of centrally-planned buildings,
c. 1498 or later

OPPOSITE:
Based on a design by **Donato
Bramante** (?)
Built by **Cola da Caprarola and others**
Santa Maria della Consolazione, 1508
Todi

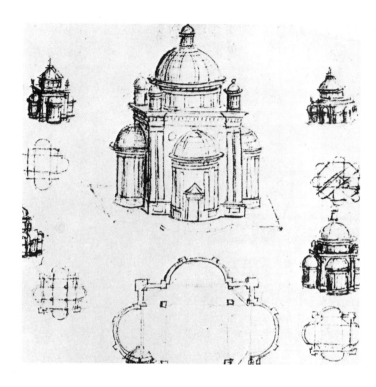

of a loggia bearing a tympanum. A few years later (c. 1509), a square was created on the side of the Tiber opposite the Castel, and the street leading from it to the Papal Mint was widened (marked as J on the plan). The Loggia all'antica became the optical vanishing point of the Via Papalis (A), the Via Sistina (C), and the Via Recta (D), thus visually reinforcing the Pope's presence in the city. At the same time, the Loggia was the ideal platform from which the Pope could symbolically overlook the city – in particular the banking quarter along the Via Giulia (H), which even then was already a centre of power. Around 1508, Bramante planned a palace (P) to be built there, which was to house not only the city notaries, but all the other officials needed to take care of the innumerable economic transactions that took place in this part of the city. Placing the jurisdiction under the complete authority of the Pope in this way would have lessened the importance of the Commune in the same degree as the imposing building and the piazza in front of it, the Platea Nova, would have outdone the Capitoline mediaeval palaces of the Senators and Conservators on the Campidoglio. Extending the visual axis from Castel San Angelo to the Platea Nova would have made this the most majestic platform imaginable for papal supremacy in the heart of the new Rome. But the project came to nothing: in 1511, the Commune succeeded in persuading Julius II, in

a moment of notable papal weakness, to give it up of his own accord.

Just as Raphael's fresco of Justice, in the library of Julius II, programmatically stated the Pope's claim to dispense justice in general and in particular heralded the project of the Palace of Justice, so too the Parnaso fresco both represents Poetry and presents a design for the Belvedere Court (p. 137). Not long after he became Pope, Julius II commissioned Bramante to link his private apartments with the Quattrocento Villa of Innocent VIII, about a thousand Roman feet away. The series of courtyards, which were flanked by two narrow buildings originally three, then finally one storey high, were reserved for theatrical performances and competitions, as well as leisurely walks under orange trees and the study of classical sculptures; despite this, the main purpose of the design was – as it had been in the Palace of Justice – to represent the all-encompassing power of the Pope. He wanted both to evoke the ancient grandeur of classical buildings and to outdo the residences of the most important royal courts and ruling families. The fundamental model was the axial series of courts of the Temple of Fortuna in Palestrina, which at that time was associated with the Pope's namesake, Julius Caesar. Bramante arranged the series of courtyards in accordance with the Pope's line of vision from his

Reconstruction of the building work of
Julius II and Bramante (1503–13), on
the map of Rome by Nolli (after Tafuri)

The major streets in 15th-century Rome
A Via Papalis
B Via Floreta and Campo de Fiori

Work during the papacy of Sixtus IV
(1471–84)
C Via Sistina
D Via Recta
E Ponte Sisto

Work during the papacy of Alexander VI
(1492–1503)
F Via Alessandrina

Work carried out by Pope Julius II
(1503–13) and Bramante
G Via della Lungara
H Via Giulia
I Piazza and Canale di Ponte

L Via di Ripetta
M Apse of Santa Maria del Popolo
N Belvedere
O Vatican loggias

Works planned but not carried out
P Palace of Justice
Q Extension of the old Cancelleria
R St. Peter's

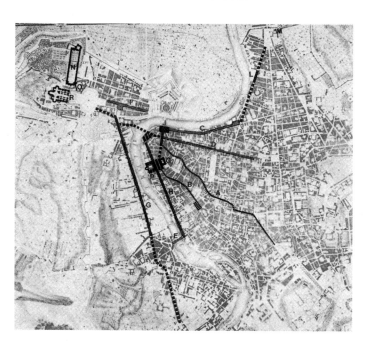

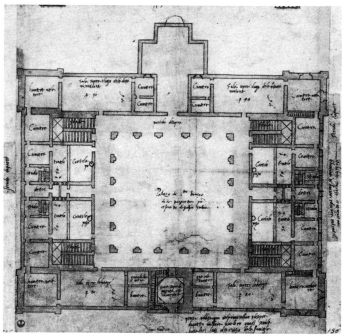

Donato Bramante
Plan of the Palazzo dei Tribunali in the Via Giulia in Rome
Florence, Galleria degli Uffizi, Gabinetto Disegni e Stampe

apartments. He thus inclined the more distant and higher of the courtyards, like a stage, towards the horizon. No less scenographic are the staircases which contain the theatre steps, and the slightly lower arcades of the upper courtyard; they were intended to distract attention from the unsolved problem of the changes in height, making the second courtyard look lower and all the more monumental. The vanishing point is located at the inverse-exverse circular stair made famous by Serlio. Raphael was to respond to this theatrical arrangement in a study for *The School of Athens* (p. 332).

The Palazzo Caprini and the Villa Farnesina, though on a much smaller scale than the Palace of Justice or the Belvedere Court, were similarly inspired by the idea of a *renovatio romae*. In the Palazzo Caprini (after 1501; p. 138, top), known as the House of Raphael because Raphael later lived in it, Bramante combined the ideal of classical architecture and high utility (the ground floor was a row of shops) with modern comfort and low construction costs. The façade is a thing of classical majesty. The ground floor is heavily rusticated, while the *piano nobile* features a Doric order. The origin in the Roman *insula* prototype is apparent in the design of the shops, at street level; renting these out could recover a large proportion of the construction costs and subsequently contribute to the maintenance. A familiarity with Vitruvius is apparent in the overall disposition of the rooms, but the building nonetheless clearly bears in mind the more limited means of a middle class with an eye on the residences of Cardinals and the wealthy. The vestibule is followed by an inner courtyard and spacious stairs, reception hall and private apartments, with a study, heated bathroom and chapel; there are kitchens and store-rooms at street level. The House of Raphael, and other buildings derived from it, made a distinctive contribution to the restoration of imperial Rome. But it was not till Bramante rediscovered the classical technique of cladding brickwork in stucco that wealthy employers were able to have façades of a monumental character built. Bramante conceded in clear terms that the Doric order and rustication were sham by the simple device of splitting the keystones above the shopfronts down the middle – contrary to the logic of statics.

Peruzzi built the Villa Farnesina (after 1508) for Agostino Chigi, a leading Sienese banker to the Pope, on the bank of the Tiber opposite the banking district, below the Gianicolo lauded by the classical poets (pp. 138, bottom, and 139, top). The austere building was meticulously related to the geometrical terraces and gardens around it. Set back as it is from the Via Lungara, which had been broadened under Julius II, the Farnesina is not particularly visible, and thus played only a modest part in the restoration of Rome's glory, to the anger of the Pope. The humanist discussions, banquets and dramatic performances given at the Farnesina delighted Leo X, however. Pindar and Theocritus were translated there; Bembo, Bibbiena and Giovio were frequent visitors; Sebastiano del Piombo and Piero Aretino were permanent guests. The entrance loggia, for which Raphael and his pupils did a series of frescoes of Cupid and Psyche, was used as a stage for classical theatre, while the gardens served for satyr plays. Frescoes by Peruzzi offered illusionist views, furthermore, which transported the beholder to ancient Rome – and indeed even deceived Titian.

Times of euphoria and crisis

Pope Leo X (1513–21), the son of Lorenzo the Magnificent, made his entry onto the political stage as an innovator and peacemaker. As a Medici, he always endeavoured to maintain and extend the power of his Florentine family, but, in contrast with his predecessor, who was always keen for conflict, he sought a stable relationship with the invaders of Italy, France and Spain. In the mean time, Rome under Leo was seeing a flowering of the highest order – one which ruined the Vatican banks. Leo X was a declared patron and lover of the arts, and a great deal was expected of any architectural projects, even if they were not actually carried out. If the age of Julius II was the age of Bramante, upon his death all the important impetus came from Raphael and his colleague Antonio da Sangallo. They continued work on Bramante's designs, though with some alterations, and developed his ideas and models.

Raphael, who had been suggested by Bramante for the office of "First Architect of St. Peter's", was confirmed in this position by Leo X without delay. He worked on his first design together with Fra Giocondo, who was at the time the most important expert on classical architecture; they were joined in 1516 by Antonio da Sangallo, who was the staunchest advocate of academic Vitruvianism. A wood engraving by Serlio shows Raphael's first design for St. Peter's (p. 139, bottom). He fundamentally reworked the Latin-cross design with a closed-off choir that had been demanded by Julius II. He broke through the choir, which had

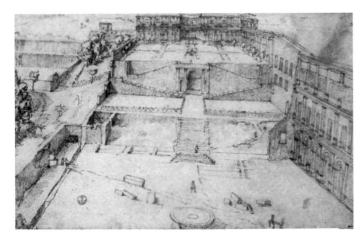

already been completed, and surrounded it and the apses with ambulatories. This enabled him to compensate for the disproportionate sizes of the side aisles and choir. Above all, however, it allowed him to surround the main dome with four lateral domes, just as Bramante's original plan had suggested. He designed the façade as a portico with a gigantic order of columns. In contrast with this, Antonio at first adopted a suggestion of Fra Giocondo's and put a dome-shaped roof along the entire length of the nave; eventually he evolved a design with just two domes on the long axis. The architects principally collaborated on the façade. Instead of a columned portico, they finally decided on a Colossal order, adjusting the order on either side as appropriate. Alberti's Sant'Andrea in Mantua (p. 112) was the main influence. In addition, the motif of the triumphal arch gives the Loggia della Benedizione an imperial note.

In contrast to Julius, Leo at first appeared to be striving for peace and harmony, especially with the Roman Commune. His claim to temporal power was no less than that of his predecessor, however. This is clearly shown by the preparations for the ceremonial conferment of the freedom of the City of Rome upon Leo's brother Giuliano and his nephew Lorenzo in September 1513. The Commune had agreed to this after a series of concessions. Classical theatrical productions and opulent banquets were ordered, as were poetry readings and masses. A wooden theatre was built for this purpose on the Capitol, directly in front of the palaces of the Senators and Conservators; it was designed by Rosselli, probably based on a plan by Giuliano da Sangallo. A celebration involving the Pope's family was used – however symbolically – to take possession of the Commune's most sacred place. What was probably the first sketch even planned to surround the theatre with a stone wall. Such a structure, however, would have become a permanent sign of the Pope's triumph over the citizens.

It was not just the political centre of the Roman Commune that the Pope attempted to occupy symbolically; he was also interested in the centre of ancient Rome. It was at the beginning of his rule, furthermore, that the Medici Pope commissioned Giuliano da Sangallo, and then in 1515 Antonio da Sangallo, to design an enormous family palace in the centre of the city, between the Piazza Navona, the Roman university and the Pantheon. This residence, which was probably meant for the Pope's brother, was of considerable political importance, for Giuliano da Medici had married a relative of the French king in 1515. The new palace, and the French church of San Luigi dei Francesi, which was planned to be built in the immediate vicinity, would have been impressive signs of the friendship between these two ruling houses, especially in the wake of the Peace of Bologna and the Concordat of 1516. At the same time, the intended site was a focal point of ancient Rome. The Piazza Navona would have become its forecourt and the Pantheon – figuratively – part of the building.

These two papal architectural commissions – the temporary theatre on the Capitol and the plans for the area adjacent to the Piazza Navona – were based on a further concept: they were to express the association of the Arno and the Tiber, of Florence and Rome. The Medici Pope was attempting to restore the former power of his family in Florence, which had been lost when they were banished from that city in 1494. There are parallels for both projects, in the wooden façade of the Cathedral that was erected for Leo's triumphal entry into Florence, and in the family palace in the Via Laura, which was also planned by Giuliano da Sangallo.

Two projects in particular enable us to understand the Medici family's architectural policy. Both were designed for the Medici family church, San Lorenzo. While the wooden façade of the Cathedral would last just a short time, the façade of St. Lorenzo, started in 1516, was to be both a triumphant and an enduring sign of the presence of the Medicis in Florence. It was intended that the façade should incorporate a lavish series of sculptures, and Giuliano da Sangallo started by submitting several designs. However, neither the first designs, which were probably copied from ones made for Santa Maria di Loreto, nor the later ones, which, though on a gigantic scale, were less impressive, were convincing. Jacopo Sansovino, the architect who designed the wooden façade for the Cathedral, had just as little success. Another innovative proposal, which was probably made by Raphael, also failed, probably because its author had designed a Roman, not a Florentine, building; one need only recall the Gonzagas' sharp rejection of the SS. Annunziata rotunda or the Palazzo Salviati, designs which they had commissioned. It was not until late 1516 that the commission was secured, by Michelangelo (p. 141, top). Michelangelo aimed to make the architecture and sculpture of the work a mirror of all Italy. But in the following two years he made only slow progress in developing its architectural structure, instead devoting his attentions chiefly to the sculptural work. Suddenly, from one day to the next, the whole project was abandoned in 1519. The reason for this, though not expressed in so many words, was probably the death of Lorenzo de' Medici, and the substantial weakening of the dynastic pretensions of the family that went hand in hand with this. At this point, if not earlier, the Medicis must have realized that occupying the city, in however symbolic a manner, was a risk too great for even a Medici Pope to take in republican Florence. The Pope's Chancellor promptly suggested that the representation of the family should be moved from its urban context into the inside of the church.

Michelangelo was straightaway commissioned to plan and build the New Sacristy, which was the burial chapel of four Medicis (p. 141, bottom). Thus, after his work on the tomb of Julius II, death was once again his theme. The artist began once again, as he had years before, with the idea of a free-standing tomb, which he intended to place in the centre of a space whose shape imitated Brunelleschi's cubicular Old Sacristy. In subsequent reworkings he extended the Old Sacristy by a further section, added windows that tapered optically, replaced the ridged dome with an illusionistically striking version of the dome of the Pantheon, and finally moved the tombs against the walls. The defamiliarisation of traditional elements – both the orders and the design of the sarcophagi – lends the design its fundamentally irrational character. At the same time, this design of Michelangelo's was a major contribution towards the formulation of an anti-classical early Mannerism, which negated the ideals and norms of the classical Renaissance; Vasari touched upon this in his life of Michelangelo. The artist removed classical forms

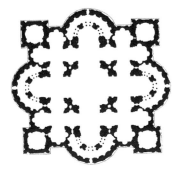

Bramante/Peruzzi
Ground plan of St. Peter's, pre-1513

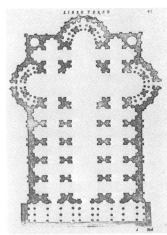

Raphael
Ground plan of St. Peter's, 1514

Reconstruction of the building work during the papacy of Leo X (1513–21), on the map of Rome by Nolli (after Tafuri)

Reconstruction of the Capitoline Theatre in 1513, axonometric projection – based on Bruschi

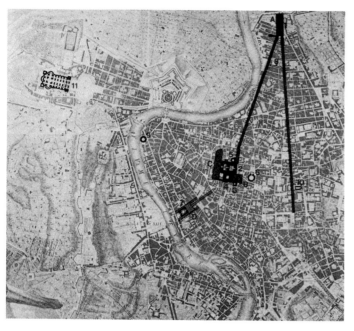

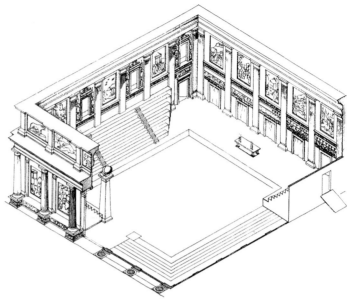

1 The obelisk planned by Raphael and Antonio da Sangallo, c. 1519
2 Plan by Antonio da Sangallo the Younger for a Medici palace, c. 1515
3 Palazzo Medici (later Lante) by Giuliano da Sangallo, 1514 onwards
4 University
5 San Luigi dei Francesi, centrally-planned by Jean de Chenevières, 1518
6 Pantheon
7 Palace of Cardinal Alessandro Farnese by Antonio Sangallo the Younger, 1514 onwards

8 Ospedale degli Incurabili
9 San Giovanni dei Fiorentini (competition 1519 onwards)
10 San Marcello al Corso (1519 onwards)
11 Raphael's plan of St. Peter's

A Piazza del Popolo, based on plans by Raphael and Antonio da Sangallo the Younger
B Piazza Medicea, on a plan by Antonio da Sangallo the Younger
C Piazza Navona
D Piazza Farnese

from their normal context, in order to rework the idiom as something new. The sole decisive factor in this was his own artistic will. In the place of traditional norms and models there now appeared virtuoso effects. His labours were not finished, however, because of republican revolts; the Medicis were once again driven out of Florence (1527) and Michelangelo stopped work on the New Sacristy. Once the Medicis had returned, he refused to complete it.

In the years ahead it was the architecture of palaces, in particular, that contributed to the development of Mannerist concepts of architecture. Raphael's plans for the Villa Madama marked the point of departure; his palaces for his friend Branconio d'Aquila and Guilio Romano's Villa Lante were the landmark achievements in this development in Rome. Raphael received the commission to design the Villa Madama (p. 142) in 1517/18. This villa, probably the most important of the High Renaissance (which can be said to have ended with its construction), proved a unique expression of the Age of Humanism, with its archaeological studies of ancient monuments and their descriptions, the adoption of classical ways of life and the performance of classical plays. The villa was planned to accommodate guests of the government on their way to meet the Pope; the functional programme, which was directly borrowed from Pliny, included a vestibule and *anditio*, reception courtyards and gardens shaded by orange trees, a hippodrome, a secret garden and fish ponds, terraces for celebrations, baths and a nymphæum, a collection of antiquities, and an "almost" Vitruvian theatre. As in its

Michelangelo Buonarroti
S. Lorenzo, design of the façade,
1516/17–19
Florence, Casa Buonarroti

BOTTOM:
Michelangelo Buonarroti
S. Lorenzo, New Sacristy, 1519–27
Florence

most important model, the Belvedere Court, the rooms were arranged along optical axes. Instead of the stage-like opposites of the Belvedere, however, this design offered a wide range of theatrically arranged views. The requisite presentation of papal power was achieved in various ways: for instance, in the valley façade and the balcony, which was centrally-planned and covered with a triumphal arch reminiscent of the Loggia della Benedizione in the Vatican. In the theatre, as in the Belvedere Court, the Pope was, in a figurative sense, the main actor as well as the principal member of the audience. Once again *otium*, leisure, had the same political importance as it had in Bramante's design.

Raphael went one step further with his plans for the Palazzo Branconio dell'Aquila (p. 143, top), reinterpreting the *renovatio romae* at a fundamental level. Raphael's transformation of the traditional models and rules of the classical Renaissance was radically different from Michelangelo's (also around 1518/19), though it had a similarly significant long-term impact. Bramante himself had occasionally applied Vitruvius' rules in a rather less than orthodox fashion; Raphael, however, considered both Vitruvius and Bramante to lack the wealth of decorative features that characterized the late classical age. His own design thus emphasized lightness and grace as well as material luxury and complexity of composition. The shop floor of the palace (which was destroyed in the 17th century in the course of architectural work on St. Peter's) featured an arrangement of five arches flanked by three-quarter columns that remained close to the style of Bramante. This structural arrangement was taken to extremes in the *piano nobile*, however. Convex niches appeared to extend the visual impact of concave columns. The rather too small columns of the window frames made no contribution to the overal structure. The first order on the intermediate storey was lost in over-extravagant stucco-work, while on the top floor the façade finally became entirely decorative and abstract. The horizontal disposition was no less idiosyncratic. While the façade at the level of the shops was still clearly framed by three-quarter columns, the niches on the *piano nobile* were a weak feature, and the pictorial panels on the top floor contributed little. The vertical axes established by the massive Doric columns on the ground floor were displaced on the first, and this displacement continued on the second. It was not functionality but decoration that was the point: the façade was of an unparalleled opulence (coloured marble, painted stucco, grisaille, statuettes in the niches). The Palazzo Branconio was a unique expression of the luxurious style of Pope Leo X's Rome and, as the 1520s began, an unmistakable precursor of Mannerism.

Much in the manner of Raphael in the Palazzo Branconio, his most important pupil, Giulio Romano, violated the norm in the Villa Lante (p. 154), one of his early works in Rome, by his use of variety, contrariety and surprise, by dissonant rhythms and a deliberate discontinuity. Indeed, contrariety in juxtaposition was his

Raphael
Villa Madama, begun 1518
Rome

Raphael
Villa Madama, garden façade

Raphael
Villa Madama, loggia

rule. His point of departure in planning the villa was the legend that the home of Martial, the Roman poet, had stood on this Gianicolo site. The hope was to see it rise again above the ruins, thus uniting the ancient and the modern. But the design shows how very much of its time this notion of classical antiquity was. The interplay of the regular (dictated by the cubic exterior) with the asymmetry of rooms of different sizes gives an idiosyncratic ground plan to the villa, while the constantly changing nature of the façades lends it an experimental appearance. In the teeth of all structural logic, the three broad Venetian windows cut across the cornices. Nor is any attempt made to restore a visual sense of order on the next floor, so that the windows above seem detached, disoriented. As in the Palazzo Branconio, the peripheral areas of the façades are again weakened by the displacement of columnar axes and other moves.

The Villa Lante marked a caesura in this development. The death of Raphael in 1520, and the great public mourning that marked his passing, denoted the end of the classical Renaissance; and with the death of Leo X in 1521, the age of boundless optimism was over. The Lateran Council, concluded in 1517, had had no impact; though Leo X had at times brought Erasmus of Rotterdam round to his way of thinking, the resistance of those who wished to reform the Church continued to grow. A profound religious and political crisis now threatened the Church.

The Age of Reformation and Counter-Reformation
The Protestant Reformation forced the Church to undertake a fundamental rethinking of its organization. The strong rejection of the Pope's authority north of the Alps was reflected – in the Italy of Clement VII and his successors – in the foundation of numerous orders such as the Theatines (1524), Barnabites (1533) and Jesuits

142

Giovan Battista Naldini
Façade of the Palazzo Branconio
dell'Aquila
Pen drawing
Florence, Galleria degli Uffizi
Gabinetto Disegni e Stampe

BOTTOM:
Palazzo Spada
based on the Palazzo Branconio
dell'Aquila
mid-16th century

(1540). The religious crisis triggered by the Reformation and Counter-Reformation soon engulfed the entire peninsula. The political crisis was no less intense and far-reaching. Clement VII attempted to fight the French and Spanish invaders; but the forces of Charles V succeeded in sacking, pillaging and burning Rome. The Church was to remain politically helpless for a long time to come. The all-powerful Charles V conquered Florence in 1529, and was crowned Emperor in Bologna in 1530. Almost all of Italy either owed allegiance or was directly subject to him. Pope Paul III (1534–49) pursued a policy intended to re-establish the stability of the Church, though he himself was an admirer of Erasmus, a friend of the new orders, and not in any fundamental disagreement with the reforms. He authorized the Inquisition in 1542, followed a year later by Church censorship. It was not until the Council of Trent (1546) that the Church began to show signs of revising its view of itself.

During the crisis sparked off by the Reformation, public display of the humanist culture and political power of the Popes was, if anything, an argument against the papacy, however much it might be justified, in the name of *magnificenza*, as a way of achieving the city's *renovatio*. For a short time the Church made the security of its own state its prime concern, and placed extravagant works of self-glorification on a back burner. It was not until the Church had consolidated its position that the Popes were able once again to devote their attention to *magnificenza*. At the same time, the Reformation presently put an end to the humanist idea that classical antiquity and Christianity might be reconciled in a new unity. The new (Protestant) ideal was modest dignity, avoiding all ornamentation. The classical repertoire of forms was steadily abstracted, codified, and enlisted in the service of communication. At the same time life at the courts of France and Spain, who had invaded Italy, was enormously attractive. High and Late Renaissance forms continued to be used, but the main artistic idiom throughout Europe was the diverse and at times contradictory range of forms known as Mannerism.

In the years following the Sacco di Roma (the Sack of Rome carried out by Emperor Charles V's Spanish and German mercenaries in 1527/28), the architectural activity of the Vatican state reached an all-time low. St. Peter's was particularly affected by this. Though taxes had been raised yet again, the German-speaking countries, in particular, refused to pay them. The progress of the work on St. Peter's, which was directed for a long period by Antonio da Sangallo, was correspondingly slow, and largely restricted mainly to raising the central area underneath the dome. A sketch drawn by Marten van Heemskerck in 1535 shows that the building site of St. Peter's was effectively a ruin (p. 144). The real problem of the design was revealed by the wooden model which Antonio produced between 1539 and 1546, which was even big enough to walk on. The building, though gigantic, was neither simple nor monumental – neither in its ground plan, nor in the shape of the building, no or in

Giulio Romano and G. F. Penni
View of the Villa Madama from the south-
east, detail from the *Battle of Constantine*
Vatican, Sala di Constantino

the design of the façades. Michelangelo, who had returned to Rome in 1534 but did not work as an architect until after Antonio's death in 1546, was biting in his criticism of Antonio and his model.

Work on the Villa Madama proceeded just as slowly after the death of Raphael. Most of the efforts were devoted to painting the few rooms that had been built, and constructing more terraces. The building itself, which had been started just a few years before in the expectation that it would become the supreme symbol of humanist culture, turned into a mere classical backdrop for antique sculptures, if Heemskerck's sketches are to be believed. Above all, however, Serlio and Palladio reduced and amended the virtuoso diversity of the design in their treatises.

Antonio da Sangallo started building the Farnese family palace (right) between the Via Giulia and the Campo de Fiori while Leo X was still alive (c. 1514). An important model for the first design, which was rather block-shaped compared to what was eventually built, was Bramante's plan for the nearby Palace of Justice. When he became Pope, however, Sangallo's client discarded the original design. Pope Paul III's family palace was enlarged to such an extent that it was soon wider and taller than any other building in the city. In addition, a square was laid out in front of the fortress-like residence, and the Via Baullari, which met it at an angle, was straightened, broadened and extended through to the Via Papalis. Though Vitruvius' description of Roman houses was a starting point for Antonio, this massive building was not meant to be a reflection of ideal classical values, but was intended rather as an ostentatious display of the power which the Farnese family had gained through the papacy. This interpretation is supported by the fact that the family spent far less on ecclesiastical buildings and charitable causes during this time than they did on their palace. Michelangelo, who was asked to continue Antonio's work, made a few radical alterations. For example, he framed and raised the central window in the *piano nobile* of the façade facing the piazza, and also distinctly enlarged the main cornice. The new, monumental proportions and the lily and acanthus friezes bearing the family crest owed nothing to Vitruvius. Michelangelo's most radical innovation was never realized, however. Vasari informs us that the artist wanted to create a line of vision from the piazza, leading through the courtyard and gardens, over a bridge that was to be built over the Tiber, to Trastevere, which would have been dominated by an ancient statue of Hercules. This would have been an extraordinarily dynamic effect, a striking counter to the static character of the palace.

In the same period, between 1532 and 1536, Peruzzi built a palace for the Massimo family (p. 146). His approach was altogether different from Antonio's. He chose not so much to dominate the urban context as to continue it by other, sophisticated means, by echoing the curve of the Via Papalis in the curve of the façade and placing the entrance portico on the Via del Paradiso. With its portico frescoes and the block rustication of the façade, the building makes

144

Antonio da Sangallo the Younger and Michelangelo Buonarroti
Palazzo Farnese, begun c. 1514
Detail (below) of the façade (bottom)
Rome

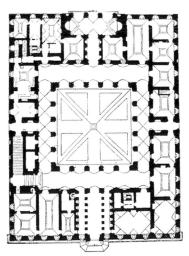

Palazzo Farnese
Ground plan

Baldassare Peruzzi
Palazzo Massimi alle Colonne, 1532–36
View from the Via Papalis (top)
Inner courtyard (bottom)
Rome

an extremely elegant impression in changing light. And, where Antonio had drawn up his plan with a Vitruvian regularity, Peruzzi came up with an admittedly unorthodox but extremely diverse range of rooms, variously planned and lit. Visiting the palace, what we find is not so much a palpable logic as a movement, as if beyond theatrical backdrops, to ever new prospects. Peruzzi was not only a master illusionist but also the leading stage-set designer of the time, and the palace profited from his experience. Furthermore, as his sketches demonstrate, Peruzzi had studied not only Vitruvian, imperial Rome, but also the anti-classical period that followed it, with a meticulous, archaeological attention. Peruzzi planned to classify the very real diversity of types in a treatise on architecture, a major undertaking full of contradictions which in the event he never completed; it was left to his pupil Serlio to build on the master's work, and codify and disseminate the language of architecture.

Giulio Romano, who had followed Federico Gonzaga's call to Mantua in 1524, was commissioned by him to build a *villa suburbana*, the Palazzo del Té (p. 147). The layout of the flat building and its various façades, open loggias and broad courtyards, as well as the exedras which opened out to reveal landscape like a backdrop, created a sum effect at once simple and theatrical. There are numerous violations of the rules of the orthodox view of the classical era, which Vasari calls "capricious inventions", and these were intended for the delectation of the few who would have understood and appreciated them. These illusory, virtuoso effects include tying the Tuscan rusticated order to the rhythmically divided bay of the Belvedere, and the Doric triglyphs, which look as if they

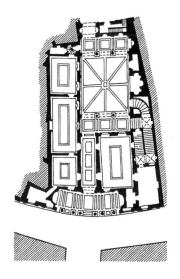

Palazzo Massimi alle Colonne
Ground plan

are about to fall into the area below the entablature. In this way Giulio created both a classical and an entertaining setting for courtly life; Bramante and Raphael, meanwhile, were trying to use classical forms to create a new golden age in the modern age.

In autumn 1546, after a successful career at the court of Mantua, Giulio was chosen as the architect of St. Peter's. He accepted the position, but died just a few months later; and so, contrary to all expectations, the 72-year-old Michelangelo was commissioned to continue the work on St. Peter's. Michelangelo used Bramante's first plan (p. 133, bottom) as a starting point. It was clear, simple, well-lit and not muddled, but the main thing was that it was of a classical size. Michelangelo drastically reduced Antonio's ground plan (p. 150, bottom), both in terms of size and with regard to the layout of the interior. At the same time, he tautened and monumentalized the exterior; the staircases between the apses, in particular, strikingly illustrate the sculptural tensions that he introduced. For the next eighteen years, the construction work proceeded at high speed, if for no other reason than that the financial means were readily available; the Spanish had contributed a large part of the treasure which they had looted in America. The outside of the building was raised to the height where the dome rises above the tambour. Michelangelo had asked for the plans of Brunelleschi's dome on Santa Maria del Fiore soon after the work was started, to help him plan the dome for St.

Peter's. Using this as a starting point, he worked out many different solutions, and finally decided on a relatively flat curve with a tall lantern, establishing a subtle interplay of dynamic and gravitationally weighted forces which he hoped would continue in the lantern. And if, as Alberti stressed, the dome of Florence Cathedral covered "all the people of Tuscany", Michelangelo's dome would surely have covered "all of Christianity". However, his successor, Giacomo della Porta, built the dome somewhat steeper than Michelangelo envisaged, and reduced the height of the lantern.

Nine years after the Sacco by his armies, Charles V of Spain entered Rome in a triumphal procession. The target of this procession was the Capitol. Walls of wood and canvas were designed to serve as theatrical backdrops for the occasion. In direct response to this, Paul III decided in 1537 to move the statue of Marcus Aurelius to this site. Throughout the Middle Ages, this bronze equestrian statue, which was probably the most important of the classical age, was a symbol of law and government. As a result, the Capitol figures of the wolf and the lioness, which had until then always been considered to possess an analogous significance, were moved to a different position. The equestrian statue had been identified for a long time with Constantine, the builder of the Basilica of St. Peter's, and this made it possible to re-emphasize the close connection between imperial rule and Christianity. By doing

Michelangelo Buonarroti
St. Peter's, western apse
Rome

Michelangelo Buonarroti
St. Peter's, Colossal order of the
cubicular exterior of the building
Rome

**Michelangelo Buonarroti and Giacomo
della Porta**
St. Peter's, tambour, dome and lantern
seen from the north-west
Rome

Michelangelo Buonarroti
Interior view of the dome (left)
Exterior view of the choir and apses seen from the west (below)
Rome

this, the Pope was continuing the measures of Julius and Leo, and this is particularly underlined by the figure of Jupiter. It was the Pope's wish to leave his own, and the Church's, mark on this most sacred of secular places. The image he had chosen was that of reviver of the city's fame. Michelangelo interpreted this requirement sympathetically. The oval square is shaped according to the visual axis of the spectators (pp. 152 and 153), and stretches between palace walls of great tectonic power. Every detail, whether it be the horizontally covered porticos, the shape of the base of the statue, or the baldachin (which was not built) above Jupiter, contributes to this staged effect. The affinity of this "reverse perspective" to theatrical sets has often been commented on. Michelangelo was indeed creating a stage. And though it was to become the model of innumerable town houses and squares, it was never surpassed.

This design for the Capitol was the first time that a Pope had been able to give an area of Rome a completely uniform appearance. Completing the work did, it is true, take more than a century. The Via Pia, the street which Pope Pius IV planned (c. 1562) to lead from San Marco to the Quirinal and from there to the Roman bridge over the Aniene, was the scenographic king-pin, as it were. This utterly straight road began at the sculpture of the Dioscuri, and its vanishing point was at the Porta Pia, Michelangelo's design for the façade of Rome's city gates (right). Just as the Aurelian walls had not been built to withstand modern artillery, the façade, which was just a few bricks deep, was not intended as a means of defence. Above all, however, Michelangelo's design faced not outwards, but in towards the city. Nor was the new street intended to be functional. Rather, the Via Pia was a stage and the Porta Pia the wings. An immediate model for this showpiece was the tradition of classical theatre, which had a

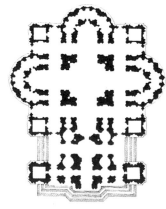

Antonio da Sangallo the Younger
Ground plan of St. Peter's, 1539

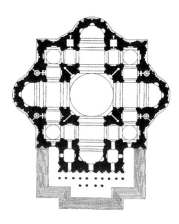

Michelangelo Buonarroti
Ground plan of St. Peter's, 1546–64

150

Michelangelo Buonarroti
Porta Pia, begun 1562
Rome

View of Via and Porta Pia
Fresco in Lateran Palace, Sala all Coneistoro
Rome

festivities and courtly leisure. Vignola, the Villa Giulia's first architect, designed the exterior along the lines of the Palazzo del Tè: heavily tectonic but less theatrical, with a rusticated order framing the central entrance; the central semi-circular porticoed courtyard, which faced a nymphæum, was a development of the circular courtyard of the Villa Madama. Though it is also designed around a curved – albeit oval – inner courtyard, the Casino, which was the work of Pirro Logorio, is in an entirely different idiom. While it is the order that holds the numerous decorative features of Vignola's design together, the façades of the Casino do not have any order whatsoever. Instead, statues, reliefs, inscriptions, mosaics, marble inlays and shining plaster determine its appearance. In 1562, Vignola published a treatise about architectural orders which, thanks to its classifications, soon became the standard reference book for following generations. Ligorio, a famous expert on antiquity, archaeologist and collector, for his part published a book in 1533 on the *Antichità di Roma*, which suggested that the classical era should be recreated in a "scientifically correct" new form. Though they were fundamentally different in approach, both villas were subsequently taken as models during the Baroque period, when a villa became an absolute must.

The first home of Ignazio di Loyola and the order of the Jesuits was in the immediate vicinity of the Palazzo Venezia on the Via Papalis. With the support of Francesco Borgia, Ignazio was able to start planning the order's church and monastery, around 1550, but Cardinal Alessandro Farnese soon became interested in the prestigious project (p. 155, bottom). He shortly took control of the project, and suggested that Vignola should be the architect. The reason for this was that he wanted not a merely functional solution

considerable influence on the conceptual world of the 16th century. The tragic stage drawn by Serlio, dominated by a monumental city gate, and also the stage preferred for comedies, with a villa surround, seem to have been an inspiration. In like manner, the artist articulated the elements of his façade design entirely according to their visual impact. The façade contained nothing of the interplay of dynamic and gravitationally weighty forces already familiar; rather, it had an air of playful, festive decoration. In this sense, Michelangelo's Via and Porta Pia were direct precursors of early Baroque city planning in the Rome of Sixtus V.

While the Counter-Reformation was attempting to draw up the theoretical programme of a new spiritual experience, courtly society, which had for a long time also included the Popes, was developing a culture of refined elegance. The Villa Giulia (begun 1551, p. 154) and the Casino Pio (begun 1559, p. 154, bottom), the latter started by Paul IV and continued by Pius IV, are both equally fascinating. The Villa and the Casino, within the Aurelian walls and in the gardens of the Vatican respectively, afforded the settings for papal

Etienne Dupérac
The Campidoglio after the plan by Michelangelo, 1569

but a modern building in honour of his family. There was a long delay between the placing of the foundation stone (1554) and the start of actual building (1568), and during this time the Council of Trent formulated its requirements of sacred buildings. It decided, amongst other things, that tombs and chancel screens should not be placed in the main nave, that wide hall-like areas should be created so that large congregations might hear the sermons, and that numerous chapels should be built. At the same time, all distracting decorative features were to be avoided. Vignola's single-aisle ground plan, with clearly separate chapels, met these requirements perfectly. However, he was not able to convince his employer of the merits of his façade design, which, though demandingly complex, lacked coherence. And just as the Farnese had replaced Antonio da Sangallo with Michelangelo in 1546, they now discharged Vignola, in order to employ Michelangelo's assistant Giacomo della Porta in his place. He lifted the façade in a rhythmic crescendo towards the centre, in order to give dramatic life to the entrance – above which was the unusual motif of a tympanum within a tympanum.

The building, which was completed in 1577, became both the finest expression of the Roman Late Renaissance and the symbol of a Church which had left the crisis of the Reformation behind and was looking for a new departure, even though the century of Reformation would not end symbolically until the age of Baroque, with the canonization of Ignatius Loyola, Fillipo Neri, Teresa of Avila and Francis Xavier on 22 May 1622. While the Tempietto in San Pietro in Montorio (p. 133) and the first plan for St. Peter's (p. 133) had been symbols of a macrocosm that was still in harmony, Il Gesù became an allegory of the path which humanity had to tread in order to attain salvation. During the High Baroque, Bernini's pupil Gaulli would express this idea in a fresco which creates the illusion that the vault above the nave has been pierced, uniting the architecture of the church with the dome of Heaven.

The triumph of antiquity?

If there is one *complexio oppositorum*, one irreconcilable set of contradictions, that characterizes the Renaissance, then the Cinquecento in Rome probably affords the most striking example.

The Golden Age which Julius II had proclaimed saw the overhaul of the Vatican's finances but also great deficits; great military victories, and the serious consequences of the division of the peninsula between France and Spain; and the first reformatory resistance, along with the division of the Church. When it ended, an age in which imperial greatness and power on a par with the Caesars' could be articulated was eclipsed, and the conviction that there could be a revival of the classical era in the modern age was lost. The age of the Reformation and Counter-Reformation was characterized both by a new religious spirituality and by the often exaggerated intellectualism of courtly society. At the same time, the classical age was classified, and reduced to a few, easily applied elements.

Michelangelo Buonarroti
River god on the staircase of the Senators' Palace

Michelangelo Buonarroti
Detail of the façade order of the Conservators' Palace

**Giacomo Barozzi, called Il Vignola,
Bartolomeo Ammannati and others**
Villa Giulia, 1551–55, entrance
Rome

Giacomo Barozzi, called Il Vignola
Villa Lante, 1568–78
Aerial view of the entire complex
Bagneia

Pirro Ligorio
The Casino of Pius IV in the Vatican, begun 1559
Entrance (below) and ground plan (right)

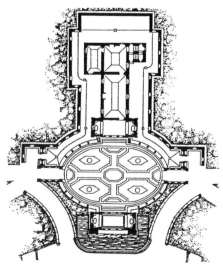

154

BOTTOM:
Giacomo della Porta
The façade of the Church of Il Gesù,
1572–74
Rome

Giacomo della Porta
Villa Aldobrandini, 1598–1603
View from the garden
Frascati

In the Quattrocento, the view of antiquity was considerably different. The Early Renaissance was founded upon a conceptual principle essentially conducive to uniformity. It applied equally to historical events and the shape of buildings. The depiction of history in centrally-planned buildings was the highest expression of this principle. The classical age proved to be non-uniform, however, if one attempted to reduce it to a single basic model. Vitruvius' treatise, in particular, was difficult to understand, and the multiplicity of ancient models contradicted what he said. Leon Battista Alberti reformulated the principles of art in response to this. At the centre of art stood antiquity, the perfect model, integrated into all areas of life. This basic principle continued to apply even though each artist interpreted antiquity in his own individual way, even though Early Christian and mediaeval forms continued alongside classical ones, and even though classical airs were used to establish political images.

At the beginning of the Cinquecento, however, there was a distinct change of emphasis. Julius II and Leo X commissioned Bramante and Raphael to present the legitimacy of their power in a new way. The power of the Popes had become greater, and had to be reflected in more magnificent classical forms. The evocation of classical Rome was to give a historical basis and legitimacy to the *ecclesia militians et triumphans*. The classical age created by Bramante and Raphael, however much it was conceived as part of some timeless Golden Age, became the image of a highly unstable political situation. Nevertheless, the classical age remained the formative principle behind the works of Bramante and Raphael, even when the younger of the two artists extended the classical language, towards the end of the second decade of the Cinquecento, by adding forms from Late Classical architecture.

Subsequently, as the free interpretation of antiquity warred with its rigorous codification, this principle was misplaced. Both the Church and secular society required an architectural idiom at once evocative and subjective. Classical forms were divorced from their contexts, changed, and juxtaposed in new combinations; and they were also put before a wider public. At the same time, the number of treatises attempting to express a theory of antiquity grew; rather than indicating the new contexts in which antiquity might still play a relevant part, these treatises preferred to classify and to lay down rules. The larger the repertoire of classical forms became, the greater grew the potential for new combinations. These stereotypes, initially conceived as a response to the countless interpretations of antiquity, themselves led to constant reinterpretation.

Thus the changing view of antiquity reflected the shifting phases of the Renaissance in the 16th century. Various though the Golden Age was, the triumph of antiquity was a short-lived one; and, lively though the irreconcilable positions of the Reformation and Counter-Reformation were, the one great casualty was the loss of thinking attuned to the classical world.

155

Jeanette Kohl

Architecture of the Late Renaissance in Venice and the Veneto

The background

During the years of 1527–28, numerous ambitious artists and architects fled from the confusion of the Sacco di Roma, and from the papal States, which until then had been a lucrative domain for them. Many of them headed for Venice. Amongst the Venetian immigrants of the late 1520s were three artists whose presence was to trigger a historical development that came late in the day: the 16th-century Venetian architectural Renaissance. This trio of renovators in the spirit of Roman architecture comprised Sebastiano Serlio (1475–1554), Michele Sanmicheli (1484–1559) and Jacopo Sansovino (1486–1570). About a decade later they were joined by Andrea di Piero, the son of a Paduan miller, who had been trained as a stonemason; a generation younger than the others, he brought the twin influences of the classical age and the Roman High Renaissance to perfection in Northern Italy's architecture. Around 1540, alluding to Pallas Athene, his patron Giangiorgio Trissino gave him the resounding name "Palladio".

When Serlio, Sanmicheli and Sansovino arrived in Venice, they found a city-like conurbation of about 125,000 people. Contemporary Florence had only half that number of inhabitants, and Rome barely 50,000. Nonetheless, the three of them had left the cultural centre of Europe for what was, by their standards, and despite its urban character, an architectural development area.

Venetian Traditionalism

A characteristic of the 15th century in Venice was the city's persistent, even dogged grip on architectural forms from its past history. The west wing of the Doges' Palace, which had been under construction since 1340, was built in 1424 in the Gothic style, and as late as 1484 the Grand Council of Venice decided, following a devastating fire in the government building, to rebuild it in the no longer fashionable *maniera tedesca*. Even in 1581, the Venetian chronicler Francesco Sansovino wrote angrily about the dominance of Gothic buildings in his home town. A second, decisive characteristic of Venetian architecture was the use of local traditional forms of buildings. Venice was not founded by Rome and as such did not see Roman classicism as a paradigm for expressing its own identity as a city. Its individual history, and the special political and geographical position of the city, was embodied in an

exemplary manner by two great buildings, which were considered worthy models right into the 16th century: the Basilica of St. Mark and the Doges' Palace. St. Mark's was the prototype of a Byzantinism whose influence on ecclesiastical buildings reached right into the Renaissance; the ducal palace, which dated back to the 12th century and was a symbol of the Republic's independence, served for some centuries as a model for secular buildings.

Venetian traditionalism was closely tied up with the specific social and political structure of that city and its system of government, the Serenissima Signoria. Ever since the Serrata, when the Great Council was closed to non-aristocratic representatives in 1297, a small caste of old-established patrician families had ruled the island state. Just under 3.5% of the entire population in 1540 were *nobili*. The stratum of *cittadini* was about the same size; these were mostly wealthy entrepreneurs who were nevertheless unable to attain the highest government offices, such as Procurator and Doge. All other inhabitants – except for the clerics – formed the lower layer of the population.

The main feature of Venice's oligarchical system was a strict hierarchical structure that all but eliminated the possibility of social movement. Amazingly, this system continued for over five hundred years without ever being seriously shaken. The conservatism and

homogeneity of the *nobili*, and their desire to preserve their traditions, were expressed in architecture. This involved a largely unified basic position that cited and paraphrased types of architecture from their own history, whether Venetian-Byzantine or Venetian Gothic; this can be seen particularly clearly in Venice's private palaces.

Building in Venice before 1530

Around 1500 Venice was a mass of densely-packed buildings. The sharp rise in population during the 13th century (to over 100,000 inhabitants before the Black Death in 1348) had led to a building boom and rapid urban development to which Venice had difficulty putting a stop. During the 14th and 15th centuries, as a result of dispossessions and state purchases, clearings known as *campi*, which had their own wells, were laid out amongst the sea of houses that, due to the shortage of space, were growing skywards. A working system of bridges and roads was also developed and social housing developments were started. In contrast, the jewel in the city's crown, the *admiranda urbis Venetiae*, St. Mark's Square, appears to have left much to be desired at that time. It was not until the first decade of the 16th century that a start was made on redesigning it.

The re-building of the Old Procuratie in St. Mark's Square

Venice's procurators decided shortly before 1500 to tear down their old, dilapidated administration building on the north side of the square, which dated back to 1204. The *Procuratori* were the nine highest-ranking executive officers of the city; three of them, the *Procuratori de Supra*, were responsible for the administration of the district around St. Mark's. The three-storey Procuratie Nuove (above) was planned – like its predecessor – as a multi-purpose building: there were shops on the ground floor, and apartments for the procurators above. After a fire destroyed part of the building site in 1512, the contract to continue it was given to Bartolomeo Buon (born 1440), who had in the mean time been promoted to the post of "proto", a sort of chief architect for the procurators. Buon died in 1529, and his successor was Jacopo Sansovino, who had just arrived from Rome. He was not left with much to do apart from finishing the never-ending building's west wing by 1538.

The rebuilding of the Procuratie Vecchie vividly exemplifies fundamental characteristics of the tradition-bound Venetian architecture of the early Cinquecento: it is *architettura aerea*, the building is as open to light and air as possible, and there is a blurring of the boundaries between public, commercial and private areas. The typical Venetian motif of arcades creates a

certain monotony and disguises the actual division of the building into nine separate procurators' palaces, each with its own entrance at the back. At the same time, this standardization pointedly demonstrates the equality and unanimity of these top government officials, and the solidarity of the state. The dominance of columns and arches in a double row of arcades, and the relationship of one arcade in the ground floor to two in the floors above, recurs on the façade of the Doges' Palace, as does the acroteria at the top of the building. A Gothic stylistic idiom is avoided, but not at the price of giving up Venetian building forms: the new Procuratie Vecchie is quite simply a new version, one storey higher, of the previous, Venetian-Byzantine building. It was only when his own designs for the new layout of St. Mark's Square were carried out, starting from 1537, that Jacopo Sansovino was able to bring about an epoch-making modernization of Venetian architecture.

Verona and Vicenza
In addition to the rather ambitious Sansovino, Venice secured the services of a further Roman specialist: in 1528, Michele Sanmicheli, who had been trained in the circle of Bramante and Giuliano da Sangallo, was appointed the republic's architect for fortifications.

He was active mainly on the Venetian mainland and in his home town of Verona, which had been under the control of Venice since 1405; he left traces as lasting there as Sansovino did in Venice. Sanmicheli gained fame through his new concept of defensive buildings. A report made in 1536 by the general commander of Venice, Francesco Maria della Rovere, concerning fortifications at the entrance to the lagoon, shows what special symbolic and representative importance was apportioned to this rather coarse architectural task. The report makes the criticism that the architectural appearance of these fortifications as strongholds ran counter to the republican character and tradition of the city, as they were an expression of authoritarian types of government. Fortresses should therefore be built strong, but should also bear witness to the openness and desire for peace of Venice. The Porta Palio (above), one of Sanmicheli's numerous fortified gateways, was designed with this double purpose in mind. It is both a stately and a defensive building: the dominant rustication and extensive unity of the external façade suggest impregnability, and at the same time the classical order of the columns, and the way the ornamentation imitates the classical style, clearly proclaim republican Venice.

Vicenza, the third centre of the Venetian Renaissance, was dominated by the architecture of Andrea Palladio (1508–1580). His

158

buildings included the Basilica Palladiana (p. 165), the Palazzo Thiene, the Villa Rotonda (p. 175) and the Teatro Olimpico (below). This theatre, the first built definitely after the classical age, was brought into being in 1580 by the "Olympian Society", of which Palladio was a founder member, and it is considered to be his last work. The solution he arrived at for this task was to design a theatre *all'antica*, half-elliptical with tiers of stepped seats and a stage façade, the *scenae frons*. This design was the result of two things: Palladio's previous experiences with the temporary, wooden "half-theatres" of the time, and also his intensive studies of the descriptions of ancient theatres in Vitruvius' architectural treatise. The ancient theatres of Rome, Pula and Verona, as well as the ruined Teatro Berga in Vicenza, were known to him personally. The Teatro Olimpico, however, born of the spirit of the ancients, is not merely the showplace of humanistic theatrical ambitions, but also their memorial. The Olympic athletes of Vicenza's theatrical circles evidently could not resist the temptation, offered by this cultural *pièce de résistance*, to literally play to the gallery themselves: the statuettes in the niches, and on the entablatures of the colonnade behind the auditorium, are portraits of the members in the attire of ancient heroes.

In 1570, the first edition of Palladio's historical and influential treatise *I Quattro Libri dell'architettura* (above) was published in Venice; in it he commented on individual buildings and their underlying principles. At this time Serlio, himself the author of a comprehensive pattern book on ancient architecture, was already dead, as were Sanmicheli and Sansovino. Without their theoretical and practical preliminary work, however, Palladio's change of paradigm from traditional Venetian forms to the use of ancient norms would – at least in practice – have been unthinkable.

Church architecture of the Venetian Early Renaissance

The first consistent attempts to outgrow the use of Gothic forms in Venetian church architecture did not occur until 1460. Typically enough, however, these efforts were accompanied by an appeal to the local Byzantine style. From the early Middle Ages to the 13th century, Venice had been under the control of the Byzantine Exarch of Ravenna. The influence of Byzantine culture is evident in St. Mark's, a domed cross-type church built in 1063 that was to become the typological archetype of Venetian sacred buildings: it was copied in the 11th and 12th centuries, and the domed cross-type scheme was adapted in numerous Early Renaissance churches. Even the hall and basilica-like churches of the Early Renaissance, which were so common in Venice and the Veneto, did not entirely manage to avoid being similar to St. Mark's. The foundation of the church of San Zaccaria (p. 161) dates back to a donation from the Doge Pasquale Malpiero in 1457, and was the Easter church of the Signoria and Doges. From 1458 Antonio Gambello was entrusted with the planning and building of the church; after his death, the task was passed to Mauro Codussi, who had already made a name for himself by building the church of San Michele in Isola (from 1469). Codussa (circa 1440–1504) is considered the pioneer of Venetian Renaissance church architecture. The change in style that he introduced can be clearly seen on the façade of San Zaccaria: he placed an open, most rhythmic building onto the rather weighty and closed ground floor built by his predecessor. Its structural elements – free-standing pairs of columns, pilasters and clearly spaced circular windows – take on the character of a relief the further upwards one looks, and culminate in the upper storey in a two-column colonnade

Pietro Lombardo
Façade of the Church of Santa Maria dei Miracoli, 1481–89
Venice

Pietro Lombardo
Interior of the Church of Santa
Maria dei Miracoli, 1481–89
Venice

placed in front of arcades. The spiritual connection of the Easter church to the Doge and his private church of St. Mark's was given a formal means of expression by means of paraphrases and quotations of parts of St. Mark's Basilica.

The most beautiful and important church of the Early Renaissance in Venice is without doubt the votive church of Santa Maria dci Miracoli (left), which was built by Pietro Lombardo and his craftsmen between 1481 and 1489 in honour of a miraculous picture of Mary. This relatively small, compact building comprises simple, stereometrical basic forms – cuboid, hemisphere and cylinder – and its structural clarity is captivating. A barrel-vaulted hall-like church had in the past been Leon Battista Alberti's preferred scheme (Rucellai Chapel, S. Andrea in Mantua, p. 112), and in this case a domed choir was connected to the nave; this form reminds one of models such as the Arena Chapel in Padua (p. 58) or the Cappella dei Mascoli in San Masco. Though there are some traditional architectural elements, such as the round pediments, the domed choir and the multi-coloured encrustation of the interior, that remind us of St. Mark's, these features nonetheless combine as an individual and united architectural concept whose distinction lies in the extensive agreement between the interior and the exterior. The façade corresponds to a cross-section through the building: the semi-circular pediment marks the barrel-vaulting, while the two floors reflect the entrance and the nuns' gallery above it. A feature of this two-storey, compact building that was unusual in Venice until that time is the way the building is lavishly encrusted with green-white-red marble and round slabs of porphyry, this emphasising the composition and size of the building. Alberti considered the colourful marble dressing to be an antique element. The attempt to come closer to ancient Roman architecture is also made clear by the classical motifs of the choir pilasters, capitals and decorated friezes of the interior. The interior features a simple and impressive connection of the nave to the choir: fourteen steps, an allusion to Mary's visit to the temple, lead up to the triumphal arch over the choir, behind which is the domed sanctuary. The architecture dictates the way the light falls and stresses certain features; the nave is lit diffusely, from the side, whereas the sanctuary is lit brightly through the windows in the tambour and proclaims itself to be the spiritual centrepoint of the building.

Palladio's Christian temples

A basic change of paradigms in Venetian sacred architecture did not take place for another hundred years, when Andrea Palladio started building his churches. The façade of San Francesco della Vigna, and the churches of San Giorgio Maggiore (p. 161) and Il Redentore (p. 163), herald a fundamental new definition of traditional Venetian architectural forms and demonstrate Palladio's preference of elements from ancient temples. His attempt to achieve an architectural unity of ancient temple and modern place of worship

was by no means as unproblematic as is suggested at first glance by the buildings themselves, however. "The most perfect and outstanding form for a church is the round one [...]; as all its parts are, after all, equally distant from the centre, it is most suited to testifying to the unity, eternal nature, uniformity and justice of God," he writes in Book IV of his *Quattro Libri*; nevertheless, none of his Venetian churches were built in this style. There was a huge gap between ideal and reality. Apart from liturgical and functional considerations, the conclusions of the Council of Trent (1545–63) were decisive in this matter. The Counter-Reformation philosopher Carlo Borromeo rejected the form of the Ritonda (or round temple) which Palladio favoured, saying that it was heathen, and insisted that it must be possible to trace the ground plan of a church back to the crucifix, the symbol of Christ's suffering. Palladio keeps to this when describing the ground plan of San Giorgio Maggiore in Book IV, saying that "its cruciform helps the beholder visualize the cross that our Saviour hung from."

The Venetian Senate decided on 4 September 1576, in the face of a devastating outbreak of the plague, to build a votive church in honour of the Redeemer, Nostro Redentore; in 1577, it entrusted this important task to Andrea Palladio, who had already distinguished himself with the monastery church of San Giorgio, which was started in 1566. They wanted two provisional models to be submitted, based on two different ground plan concepts: a centrally-planned and a cross-type design. There were controversies at subsequent meetings of the Grand Council, and at the end those in favour of a centrally-planned church, led by Palladio's friend Marcantonio Barbaro, were defeated. Palladio was faced in consequence with the difficult task, when producing his ground

plan, of having to take into consideration the triple function of the church as well as producing an architecturally pleasing result. For Il Redentore was, primarily, a votive church, built to express gratitude for the mercy shown by the Redeemer; secondly, it was a processional church, as the Senate had vowed to hold an annual procession (on 21 July) to the church; and finally, it had to fulfil the requirements of a monastery church, because it was under the control of Capuchin monks. Palladio's solution was to create three separate and structurally different spaces, placed one behind the other, which open out in turn as one walks through the church (p. 162). The barrel-vaulted nave, flanked by evenly-spaced columns, marks the last part of the processional path and the destination of those taking part. Connected to it is the centrally-planned presbytery, covered by a tambour and dome, and closed off at either side by almost semi-circular tribunes. Here Palladio returns to the ideas behind the Ritonda to express the endless nature of God in the area around the altar, and uses this architectural form to express the votive character of the church. Finally, the monks' choir is placed

Andrea Palladio
Interior of the Church of Il Redentore,
1577–92
Venice

OPPOSITE:
Façade of the Church of Il Redentore

Stately city architecture

When, in 1529, following the peace brought about by the Treaty of Bologna, the Serenissima decided to have St. Mark's Square and the adjacent Piazzetta of the Palazzo Ducale rebuilt, it assigned the task of producing a plan for the development to its Proto Sansovino. His ambitious plan included tearing down the Old Procuratie, which was still under construction, and flanking both squares with the same style of building. The Old Procuratie was not pulled down and the south side of the Square was not built until Vincenzo Scamozzi started it in 1583; however, Sansovino did produce three new stately buildings next to the Piazzetta: the Mint (Zecca), the Libreria, and, as an annex, the Loggetta (p. 164). The Mint was commissioned in 1535 by the Provveditori della Zecca; this solid piece of Doric rusticated architecture on the waterfront by St. Mark's was finished in 1545 (p. 164). The originally two-storey building has overtones of fortress architecture, and suggests stability and impregnability. In this sense, the façade of the Zecca is not simply Mannerist playfulness, but also constitutes a symbolic monument to the crisis-proof Venetian currency, the Zecchino, and to the state itself.

The Libreria, started in 1537, is right next to the city treasury, and is its ideational counterpoint. Venice, which had been the capital of European printing since about 1490, had inherited the valuable and comprehensive manuscripts collection of Cardinal Bessarione, and now wanted to house these together with its own rapidly growing stock. It was also intended that the Libreria should contain rooms for an elite school and new offices for the procuratori. The size, fittings and position of the Libreria are all remarkable: it was a scientific and educational institute, a structural counterpart to the political centre of power of the Doges' Palace, twenty-one arcades long and covered lavishly with sculptures, so lavishly that Palladio called it "probably the most richly decorated building erected since antiquity". In order that this humanistically imposing building, which became the prototype of Venetian classicism, did not completely steal the show from the Doges' Palace, Sansovino kept the total height of the Libreria noticeably

behind the presbytery – as it was in San Giorgio – and is optically separated from the first two sections by means of an exedra. All elements fit in with the longitudinal scheme without losing their independent characters. Palladio used sketches of the ancient Diocletian and Titus baths as authorities for his structuring of the nave. The façade of Il Redentore is also determinedly classical: the motif of two classical temple fronts placed one before the other, with the foremost one marking the nave – just like a temple *in antis* – is a device which Palladio borrowed from the classical era. The function of the façade as the setting of the liturgical end of the procession is strengthened by the raised position, along the lines of ancient podium temples, and by the triumphal-arch motifs of the portal and central section. In San Giorgio Maggiore and Il Redentore, Palladio returned to a domed central section connected to a long nave, which was exemplified in the form of Santa Maria dei Miracoli. He connected this form with a monks' choir connected to the rear of the presbytery, a solution which was codified at the Council of Trent and was propagated by Carlo Borromeo in his *Instructiones Fabricae et Supellectilis Ecclesiasticae*. Palladio's tightrope walk between the architectural norms of the heathens and the contemporary demands of the Counter-Reformation led to what was basically a hybrid of a centrally-planned building, a pilaster church and a temple front. He nonetheless succeeded in harmoniously connecting all the sections by standardizing the proportions, the structure of the walls and the arches of the individual sections. His use of colour contributed to the effect: the traditional, sensuous colourfulness of Venetian churches gives way to an abstract white, an expression of the purity of the Divine Spirit.

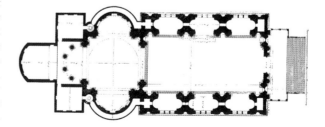

Il Redentore, ground plan

Jacopo Sansovino
The Mint (La Zecca), 1535–45 (additional storey c. 1570)
Venice

BOTTOM:
Jacopo Sansovino
Libreria (left) and Loggetta (right) on the Piazzetta, begun c. 1537
Venice, San Marco

either side of the serliana, and these – together with the lavish decoration of the mezzanine and the abundant use of reliefs on the entire façade – create a picturesque chiaroscuro effect. The idea of a town forum on the ground floor derives from classical times, and it had already been put into effect by Bramante on the Piazza Ducale in Vigevano and in the Loggia della Benedizione in Rome; the Libreria took this idea and added to it the representational requirements of a palace of humanistic science and art, one moreover, which had been built as a monument by the city's aristocrats in the most outstanding position.

The contrast between Sansovino's classicism, which derived from the Roman High Renaissance and relied heavily on plastic effects, and Palladio's strict classicism, is at its clearest when comparing the Libreria and the Palazzo della Ragione (p. 165) in Vicenza. In 1546, Palladio, together with his master Giovanni da Pedemuro, presented a wooden model to the Grand Council of Vicenza, showing the somewhat dilapidated government palace, which dated from the fifteenth century, with a new livery. According to this model, the old palace would be surrounded by a double arcade, behind which buttresses would support the dangerously heavy weight of the inner, increasingly unstable walls. The basic idea for the design went back to Sansovino's Libreria, but simplified the latter's opulent appearance. Palladio increased the intervals between the arcades, widened the serliana, and used it as a continuous motif on both the ground floor and the *piano nobile*. Ornament was reduced to a minimum; instead, simple, circular oculi were used in the spandrels – a motif adopted from the Palazzo della Ragione in Padua. The columns of the serliana, which are placed one behind the other and thus create a sense of depth, remind one strongly of Sansovino, but Palladio has an altogether more elegant solution for the classical problem at the

lower than that of the Palace – though a sense of rivalry does come through in the double-arcade scheme, a variation on the ancient Theatre of Marcellus in Rome. The ground floor, designed as an arcade of pilasters with demi-columns embedded in them supporting the entablature above, is carried out in the Doric order; in the upper floor, which is Ionic, a variation on this arcade motif is accomplished by narrowing the serliana – a central, wide arch on columns is flanked by two narrow openings, which reach up as far as the columns' imposts, where they meet an entablature. A characteristic device of Sansovino is the use of two small columns on

corners of the Doric order. Instead of the huge pilasters at the corners of the Libreria, he uses a second column, optically correcting the effect of the wider corner sections by narrowing the sides of the relevant serliana. The Palazzo della Ragione launched Palladio's rapid rise to success. It was a monument of prosperity and of the stronger position of Vicenza's aristocracy in the wake of the new peace with Venice. The preservation of the old nucleus of the building, together with its new classical apparel, attest both the strong sense of tradition of these clients and their need to identify with a new, humanist era.

Private building projects

Venice is famous for its many Palazzi, private residential palaces, the earliest of which date back to the 12th century. No other type of commission expressed Venetian conservatism as clearly as that to build palaces. It was a conservatism that must have driven the most innovative minds of the Renaissance, including Palladio and Serlio, to distraction – with the result that neither of them, despite constant employment in this area, built a single palace in Venice.

There are two main reasons for the unusually large number of impressive town palaces in Venice. Firstly, there were a large number of clients, businessmen who had made their fortunes in sea trade, including wealthy *cittadini* and *nobili*; secondly, the city itself enjoyed a remarkably steady level of prosperity right up until the end of the 18th century. In addition, the fairly-going attitude of the *Magistrato alle pompe* who was responsible for enforcing the laws on luxuries meant easy access to the means for architectural pomp. This makes the uniformity of palaces built between the 12th and 18th centuries, and the way clients kept to these compulsory standards, all the more remarkable; this, too, demonstrates the solidarity and equality of Venice's upper class.

The typical Venetian Palazzo until well into the 16th century was a mixture of *casa* and *fondaca*, a residence with a warehouse and office. As a position directly adjacent to a canal was necessary for transporting goods, almost all the palaces were jostled closely together. This meant that light only entered from two directions, from the front and through the courtyard at the rear. This in turn determined the typical three-part ground plan covering three storeys, which is a feature of almost all these palaces. Downstairs there is an *androne*, a central corridor leading to the courtyard; next to it the warehouse and office; on the upper floors there is a central *sala*, flanked by two rows of rooms leading from front to back. The façade mirrors the layout of the rooms by means of a central window arcade designed to light the sala, which is separated from the windows to either side (p. 169, bottom). The Venetians kept loyally to this scheme for many centuries. It is not just the delicacy of the Gothic façades, so prevalent right into the 16th century, that is striking, but also the openness of their fenestration through the ages. While the first Renaissance palaces in Florence were built in

165

OPPOSITE:
Giovanni Condi
Spiral staircase of the Palazzo Contarini
dal Bovolo, 1497–99
Venice

Michele Sanmicheli, Giangiacomo Grigi
Palazzo Grimani, 1540–62
Venice, Grand Canal

the 15th century as well-fortified, solid cubes, Venice's residences did not require this defensible character. Venice's stable political and economic situation, combined with its strategically advantageous position in the lagoon, and also the climactic conditions, positively encouraged the charming and airy innocence of its palaces, a fact further underlined by the customarily colourful and sometimes illusionistic façade paintings.

Inside, admittedly, and especially towards the back, the Palazzi were usually very dark; they were boxed in between their neighbours, often had hardly any or even no space for an inner courtyard, and the stairways and ground floors in particular left much to be desired in the way of light and air. But the representational requirements of these buildings rose steadily, and in the early 16th century there was a re-evaluation of both these areas. One spectacular result of these efforts is the staircase that was added to the Palazzo Contarini on the Rio di San Luca (p. 166) by Giovanni Condi between 1497 and 1499. This cylindrical staircase, added at the rear of a Gothic palace, twists upwards with a sweeping motion, an effect which is caused by the rising shape of the arched column arcades, dissected by a balustrade, which imitate the movement of the spiral staircase. The Venetian principle of transparency and openness in its arcades is applied here to both the staircase and the five-storey loggia, in order to defy the notorious shortage of light and air at the rear of buildings.

Sixteenth-century Renaissance palaces

There are three buildings on the Grand Canal that stand out from amidst the mass of Palazzi that, even in the 16th century, were still locked into traditional approaches. These three buildings employ a classical architectural idiom. The earliest example is the Palazzo Vendramin Calergi (p. 168), which was built in the first decade of the 16th century by Mauro Codussi. It was commissioned by Andrea Loredan, an influential and wealthy aristocrat. He employed the best-known architect of Venice's Early Renaissance, to create a residential monument to his, and his family's, power and nobility. This individualistic endeavour, which is expressed both in stylistic novelties and in the unusual height and size of the palace, differs significantly from the general attitude amongst the *nobili* until then, which was to see themselves and their fellow aristocrats as equals. This building has had an eventful history; Richard Wagner died in the mezzanine in 1883, which in its turn was a motif in Thomas Mann's *Death in Venice*. It is a skilful fusion of traditional Venetian forms and classical elements. In contrast to Gothic palaces, the façade of the Vendramin Calergi palace is wider than the wall behind it. The windows in the upper floor are of a uniform height and form, and their biforate shape is united by an arch with a central oculus. The window arcades have a classical column motif placed in front of them, and this bears a strong, unbroken

entablature that emphasizes horizontal values and optically connects the regularly spaced sequence of windows; the fluted columns of the upper storeys correspond to pilasters on the ground floor, the *pianterreno*.

Although this is a radical break with Gothic tradition, Codussi still retained traditional elements in the ground plan and façade. These include the division of the façade into a central group of windows in front of the *sala*, which are separated from the narrower sections to either side; the minimizing of walls in favour of window arcades; and the balconies in the *piano nobile*. This suggests that the client's traditional values were being respected, and the result is a basically traditional palazzo dressed up as an Early Renaissance building.

Codussi's attempt at a classical interpretation of Venetian palace façades was not emulated until nearly thirty years later, when the Palazzo Corner della Ca' Grande (p. 169) was built between 1537 and 1561 according to plans by Jacopo Sansovino. The wealth of the Corner family, also known as Cornaro, was legendary, and, like some other influential Venetian families, they had good connections to the papal Court in Rome. Giovanni Cornaro, who was the nephew of the King of Cyprus, commissioned Sansovino in the hope that his experiences in Rome would lead to the creation of a palazzo *alla romana*; this would adapt the ambitiousness and majesty of Roman

architecture to his own representational purposes. It is questionable whether this concealed a political allegiance to Rome, as is sometimes suggested in research. The Palazzo Corner della Ca' Grande originally had a two-storey façade (Scamozzi added the third storey after 1556). The name Ca' Grande is entirely justified: the neighbouring buildings, some of them five storeys high, do not even reach up to the top of its *piano nobile*. Behind this monumental façade, not visible from the outside, are concealed very high double storeys. Sansovino varied Bramante's façade scheme of the House of Raphael (p. 138) in his own two-storey design, and combined it with plastic elements borrowed from Michelangelo. The rusticated entrance floor, which contrasts clearly with the upper storey's colonnades of coupled

columns, was not a usual feature in Venice before that date. The reference to Michelangelo was made quite consciously in the ground floor: both the arrangement of the windows in the full and half-storey, and the use of voluted consoles, are a paraphrase of the structure of the wall of the Bibliotheca Laurenziana's entrance hall in Rome. Sansovino took the combination of the three-part, traditional façade with a regular sequence of axes even further than Codussi; the walls of the two side-window axes are almost imperceptibly wider than those of the *sala*, and the axial pattern is strengthened by the coupled columns in front of the walls. The Palazzo Corner set the standards – especially in terms of the contrast between the ground and upper storeys – for the Venetian baroque.

Mauro Codussi, Tullio Lombardo (?)
Palazzo Vendramin Calergi, before 1500–09
Venice, Grand Canal

Jacopo Sansovino, Vincenzo Scamozzi
Palazzo Corner della Ca' Grande, begun c. 1537 (additional storey after 1556)
Venice, Grand Canal

The palace of the procurator Girolamo Grimani was also planned as a two-storey building. It was started by Michele Sanmicheli circa 1540, and a further storey was added after his death in 1546 by Giangiacomo Grigi (p. 167). Here, too, the architect was obviously attempting to reinterpret the Venetian three-part façade scheme along the lines of a classically uniform, regular sequence of window axes – but the result is quite different. Though arcade and colonnade motifs are combined here also, the total effect of the proportions and shaping of the walls is more hefty and stocky than the Ca' Grande. In addition, Sanmicheli, whose experience as a fortress builder is reflected in the powerful and serious character of the Palazzo Grimani, took up the idea of the serliana which Sebastiano Serlio had suggested for use in Venetian palaces; here he used it to vary the central three window axes. The order of all the storeys is alike and completely unites the façade in a system of horizontal and vertical values. The two Renaissance palaces of Ca' Grande and Grimani had very little effect on the palace architecture of the next few decades, and for that reason there is little mention of a Roman phase in private Venetian architecture; the majority of designs in the late 16th century continued to use traditional paradigms such as emphasizing the surface of the wall and a three-part ground plan with a central loggia-arcade.

Palladio's Palaces in Vicenza
Palladio succeeded in building a classical town palace – a pleasure denied him in conservative Venice – in nearby Vicenza in the 1550s and 1560s. There he was able to bring to life his ideals of *grazia* and *bellezza*, aspects that he himself claimed to miss in Venetian palaces. Palladio, who travelled to Rome several times between 1541 and 1551, took his inspiration for the Palazzo Chiericati, begun in 1551, as well as the Palazzo Valmarana, begun fifteen years earlier, from Michelangelo's plans for the Roman Capitol (c. 1546) – though his results are entirely individual.

Palazzo Corner-Loredan (Venetian-Byzantine style)
13th century
Venice, Riva del Ferro

The Palazzo Chiericati, which was situated on the Piazza Matteotti in Vicenza (p. 170) and belonged to the wealthy Girolamo Chiericati, and whose complex construction history cannot be recounted in detail here, is generally found to be remarkable. It reverses the principle of many Palladian villas, that of a close cube with a central, open columned portico: instead, there is an open, two-storey colonnade of columns, whose central part, on the upper floor, is closed. The intuitive feeling of unease that overcomes one when looking at the façade proves to be justified: a copy of the ground plan in Palladio's *Quattro Libri* shows the palace as the architect himself wished to build it, as a completely open double colonnade facing onto the piazza. Palladio was forced to compromise by his client: while Chiericati was quite in favour of an open and public portico, along

Andrea Palladio
Palazzo Valmarana, 1566–1582
Vicenza

Andrea Palladio
Palazzo Chiericati, begun c. 1551
(completed 1746)
Vicenza

of pilasters in a secular building – the motif had appeared twenty years previously in Michelangelo's plans for the Capitol. He optically emphasized the pilasters and entablature, thereby systematizing the surface of the wall and bringing about the classical and monumental appearance of the façade. In order to avoid clashes between the Colossal order and neighbouring buildings, however, and in order to integrate the building as well as possible into the street, Palladio omitted the colossal pilasters from the outer axes, instead placing an atlas at the height of the *piano nobile*, standing on a pilaster in the ground floor. As in his country villas, Palladio showed himself to be a master at integrating architecture and surroundings.

Villas in the Veneto

In the early 15th century, Venice owned extensive parts of the Upper Italian mainland, though a century later this had shrunk to the areas around Verona, Padua and Vicenza. After the Peace of Bologna in 1529, a wave of settlement by Venice's nobility took place in the remaining *terraferma* possessions. There were a number of causes of this utilization and development of undeveloped mainland territory, a process known as *villegiatura*. Venice wanted to exert greater influence and make its presence felt where it counted, in order to tie its remaining possessions closer to itself and compensate for the continuing loss of numerous territories in the Aegean. An outbreak of the plague in the 1520s, and the resulting shortage of provisions, had clearly revealed the reliance of this city trading and metropolis on imports of food. In order to improve the self-sufficiency of the city, it was necessary systematically to extend and intensify its own mainland farming operations. And finally, Vasco da Gama had

the lines of a classical forum, that would be a feature of the town that everyone could use, he also wanted to be able to overlook the square from a central *salone* on the first floor. It was Leon Battista Alberti who had suggested in his architectural treatise that there should be "columned halls running right around the squares, as in classical times"; this idea has left its mark on this semi-public palace, which is structured around a courtyard and has a typically Palladian, strictly symmetrical ground plan. The motif of the open, slightly raised ground-floor colonnade, whose columns bear an entablature in the place of arches, probably dates back to Michelangelo's designs for the Palazzo Capitolino, but was also suggested by Alberti as being suitable for the porticos of houses belonging to important citizens; the sculptures were added at a later date.

Palladio's Palazzo Valmarana in Vicenza (above) had little in common with contemporary palaces in Venice. According to a commemorative coin, the building, which was begun in 1566, was commissioned by the widow of Giovanni Alvise Valmarana, who was a friend of the architect's. Palladio published the whole plan in his treatise, but only the front part of it was completed as envisaged; the strict symmetry of the axes of the ground plan and façade had to be adapted to the slanting direction of the road. The traditional three-part scheme of the façade was dropped in favour of a subtly differentiated five-part division, which reflects the layout of the interior. This was the first time that Palladio used a Colossal order

Jacopo Sansovino
Villa Garzoni, 1547–50
near Ponte Casale

discovered a direct sea route to India in 1498. This caused a commercial crisis in Venice, which had until then been the crucial centre for trade with the Far East; a committee convened to deal with the crisis made the urgent recommendation that greater investment needed to be made in agriculture. State aid for *villegiatura* development will have come at just the right moment for many wealthy Venetians, who seized the opportunity to escape the restrictions and stress of city life – for a while at least – and combine a pastoral way of life with growing food, a profitable and useful business that provided a lucrative alternative source of income. The discovery of beautiful landscapes as an aesthetic source of pleasure went hand in hand with putting country and agricultural work on a philosophical footing; the enthusiastic concept of *santa agricoltura*, holy agriculture, reached its high point with Alvise Cornaro.

The first villas in the Veneto to be built along classical lines, both in the 1530s, were Alvise Cornaro's Casinò near Padua, and the Villa Trissino near Vicenza, which was re-modelled on Rome's Villa Madama (p. 142). In the following decade, Roman models mostly retained their determining influence, as can be seen in Sanmicheli's Villa Soranza near Padua, and the Villa Garzoni near Ponte Casale (above), which was designed by Sansovino circa 1540, finished in 1550, and whose ground plan is modelled on Giulio Romano's Villa Farnesina.

Palladio – a master of villa architecture

Palladio's first villas date back to the early 1540s. Some of his designs, such as the Villa Pisani near Vicenza, which was built in 1544, still kept to the traditional local style of castle-like villas with sturdy towers. Even here, however, Palladio eliminated the usual T-shaped *sala* in favour of a cross-shaped salon, which marked the centre of the building. Palladio introduced this principle of centralization, together with the both useful and decorative connection of the residential and agricultural buildings by means of columned walkways, called *barchesse*, in his plans for the Villa Pisani; these features soon became his trademarks, and appear, in full glory, in his two best-known villas, the Villa Barbaro in Maser and the Villa Rotonda near Vicenza.

Marcantonio Barbaro, a Venetian procurator, and his brother Daniele, the Patriarch of Aquileia and in consequence a high-ranking Church official, built their model estate between 1556 and 1558 on the slopes of a wooded hill (p. 173). It was the intention of these two educated humanists to realize the ideal connection of beauty and usefulness on their own estate. Their friendship with Alvise Cornaro may also have decided them to involve themselves in the planning and construction of the villa, for Cornaro particularly recommended humanist clients to influence designs. Their interference must have caused Palladio some grief. It is hard to imagine

Andrea Palladio
Sequence of rooms in the Villa Barbaro, 1556–58
Maser, near Treviso

OPPOSITE:
Andrea Palladio
Exterior view of the Villa Barbaro

that he would have been enchanted by the nymphaeum and its rather shapeless sculptures, designed by Marcantonio Barbaro, which was added to the rear of the building; it is also known that Palladio considered the illusionistic decoration of the interior, by Paolo Veronese (p. 172), to be an eyesore. The result, nonetheless, was one of the most exceptional villas in the history of architecture, which brought the related concepts of the *vita activa* and *vita contemplativa*, active and contemplative life, into accord. The most important goal of Palladio and the Barbaros was to reconstruct an idealised, classical villa complex, as described by Pliny and Vitrivius, that blended harmoniously with the natural surroundings. The central axis of the middle building is a cross-shaped *sala*, and from

its centre the view extends to all four points of the compass; the shapes of the rooms extend outwards, as if right into Nature. This rectangular central building joins onto a row of rooms, which runs at right angles to it, and together they form a T-shaped ground plan. The cross-arms, which are fronted by an arcade, lead to agricultural buildings on either side. The concept of *santa agricoltura* is lived up to by the sacral theme of the façade: the four Ionic columns, which support a pediment, can be traced back to Palladio's studies of the Fortuna Virili temple in his *Quattro Libri*.

About ten years after the Barbaros' ideal *villa rustica* with its excessive sacral overtones, probably the best-known and most momentous villa suburbana in the history of architecture was built.

173

Andrea Palladio
Central dome of the Villa Rotonda, begun c. 1566 (?)
near Vicenza

"It may well be that architecture has never been more extravagant, " was the remark an impressed Johann Wolfgang von Goethe made in 1786 of the Villa Rotonda (p. 175); it was built, standing freely on a hilltop, purely as a stately building for the canon Paolo Almerico. Goethe's second impression, "Within it can be called habitable, but not homely," is entirely comprehensible. The lack of homeliness resulted from architectural elements that were borrowed from sacral architecture, and from the strict geometric shape of the property, which was planned according to precise mathematical proportions. It is not just the four identical temple fronts, in the style of classical podium temples and placed against each of the four sides of the square building, that are sacral elements; the very shape of a residence as a centrally-planned building with a rotunda and dome derives from ideal notions of church architecture. Finally, the entire building, including its porticos, is in the shape of a Greek cross. The central domed hall (left), almost the "Holy of Holies" of this residential temple, is remarkably dark, and its only source of light is the four corridors that lead to it; they make it possible to see directly into the open, as in the Villa Barbaro. This pronounced sacral motif of the Rotonda is surely connected to its function as the status symbol of a rich cleric. Palladio should, generally speaking, nonetheless take credit for having applied elements from classical temples to secular architecture – a crucial achievement in the ennobling and enhancement of villa architecture.

Andrea Palladio
Villa Foscari (Malcontenta), 1559–60
near Venice

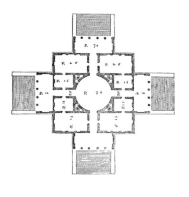

Villa Rotonda, ground plan

Andrea Palladio
Exterior view of the Villa Rotonda

Uwe Geese

Italian Renaissance Sculpture

Early-Renaissance Architectural Sculpture in Florence

Nicola Pisano and antiquity

When Nicola Pisano (c. 1220–1278/84) completed his pulpit in the Baptistery at Pisa (p. 46) in 1260, he was ahead of his time, in so far as he had created sculptural forms that would only become staple principles of the Renaissance decades later. In the amiable war between architecture and sculpture, Pisano's Baptistery pulpit struck a blow for the autonomy of sculpture. Thus the personification of *fortitudo* as Hercules, in particular, was not merely the first heroic nude anywhere in the centuries since antiquity; it also featured elements of figural moulding that separated the figure from the stiffer architectural background and gave it a presence accountable wholly in terms of the organic movement of the body. The verisimilitude of this naked human body, complete with the skeletal frame, muscles and sinews, was as indebted to classical originals, however, as it was to any study of the actual weighting and interplay of a leg tensed for standing and a leg relaxed, at ease. For the first time, the classical principles that had governed figure composition in antiquity were being applied to post-classical sculpture. Nicola's immediate observation of organic fact was not as important for his work on the sculpture as the study of antique models which he saw on sarcophagi in Pisa.

Whatever the case, this earliest Renaissance sculpture remained an isolated achievement. It was not until around 1400 that significant sculptural work had an occasion to rise to: the famous competition to make the second bronze door of the Baptistery in Florence.

The Florence Baptistery Doors

As early as 1330, the sculptor Andrea Pisano (c. 1290–1348) was recorded at work on the south, city-side door of the Baptistery (p. 178, top), having been commissioned by the city of Florence to replace the old wooden door with a new one with gilded bronze reliefs. These reliefs, fourteen to each wing of the door, were framed with quatrefoils. The upper ten on each side presented scenes from the life of John the Baptist, while the remaining reliefs showed prophets.

In the winter of 1400, the Arte dei Mercanti di Calimala, the leading merchants' guild in Florence (and responsible for the maintenance and decoration of the Baptistery), decided to have the next of the remaining two wooden doors replaced by a bronze door, and to find the best artist for the task through a public competition. Every sculptor was required to submit a trial bronze relief showing the sacrifice of Isaac within twelve months. This trial piece was to meet certain requirements in addition to the subject matter: the quatrefoil framing of Andrea Pisano's door panels was to be retained, and the sculptors were to demonstrate that they could give a precision rendering of a Biblical passage, and portray people

Filippo Brunelleschi
The Sacrifice of Isaac, 1401–02
Bronze with gilding, height: 45 cm, breadth: 38 cm
Florence, Museo Nazionale del Bargello

(clothed or naked), animals, landscape and vegetation. The seven finalist sculptors chosen from the larger number who applied were offered payment for their trial pieces. These seven, besides the Florentine artists Filippo Brunelleschi and Lorenzo Ghiberti, were Jacopo della Quercia, Simone di Colle Val d'Elsa, Niccolò di Pietro Lamberti, Niccolò d'Arezzo and Francesco di Valambrino.

The decision appears to have been taken in summer 1402. The trial pieces by Brunelleschi (top right) and Ghiberti (bottom right) found particular favour, and are the only ones to have survived. Both had satisfied all the circumstantial requirements of size and shape, and the figures were fixed by the Bible; so the experts decided according to other criteria. The financial viability of the whole project was of course a consideration, despite the fact that a decision to go ahead had been taken in principle: Ghiberti's trial piece, weighing seven kilograms less than Brunelleschi's, was preferable in this respect, since it implied a saving of over two hundredweight of bronze for the whole door. Furthermore, Ghiberti's was cast in one piece, bar a very few extras, whereas Brunelleschi's consisted of figures mounted on a based panel, an extremely labour-intensive method. These different casting methods were not without implications for the aesthetic impact of the two works.

The trial pieces

In Brunelleschi's trial piece, the victim, Isaac, is in the centre of the composition, on an altar. The altar and the rocks on which Abraham and the ram are standing mark a horizontal, though on different levels; the other figures seem merely to have been placed about these three main ones without any compelling logic. The logic of the composition derives solely from the Biblical account. An odd side effect of this is that the dramatic focus of the scene, Abraham's attempt to sacrifice Isaac and the intervention of the angel, seems an almost secondary thing.

Brunelleschi was nonetheless making a new departure. His scenic, dramatic manner of composition was largely unknown to the Gothic visual universe of the preceding age. Moreover, in Brunelleschi's relief there are echoes of classical sculpture – the nakedness of Isaac, for instance. The boy seated behind the ass is modelled on the Capitoline figure of a youth extracting a thorn. And the other youth, fetching water, is presented in a complex physical posture – his attention on the impending sacrifice – that has something of the dynamics of classical statuary. The emphasis on horizontals and verticals constitutes Brunelleschi's nod to Pisano, and remains within the Calimala's conservative brief; and yet, by placing the sacrifice at the centre of his scene, Brunelleschi does seem to have anticipated a way of seeing that was to be codified by the discovery of linear perspective only a few years later.

In contrast, Ghiberti (1378/81–1455) used a diagonal compositional grid. The rock formation that extends from the top left to the bottom right bays of the quatrefoil splits the narrative

Lorenzo Ghiberti
The Sacrifice of Isaac, 1401–02
Bronze with gilding, height: 45 cm, breadth: 38 cm
Florence, Museo Nazionale del Bargello

177

Andrea Pisano
South Door, 1330–36
Bronze, partially gilded
Florence, Baptistery

Lorenzo Ghiberti
North Door, 1404–24
Bronze, partially gilded
Florence, Baptistery

content into two separate parts, but also has the effect of linking the altar to the subsequent sacrificial victim, the ram. This in turn confirms the place of the figures in the landscape. The robes and posture of Abraham have something of Gothic tradition to them, but the naked body of Isaac, altogether in line with classical ideals, affords an arresting contrast.

The two trial pieces also differed in their rendering of the Old Testament passage in question (Genesis 22, 1–19). Unlike Ghiberti, Brunelleschi was free in his interpretation, and indeed arguably wrong. The Biblical narrative says that the attendants were left behind, some distance from the place of sacrifice, but on Brunelleschi's rocky terrace there is not even any sense that the attendants are unable to *see* what is happening. Some sense that the two locations were rather more separate was required by the Bible, however; the boys were expected neither to see nor to hear the sacrifice. Ghiberti solves this problem by placing his attendants behind a rock spur, which we must suppose puts them out of earshot and sight of the altar, and so satisfies the account in Genesis.

Brunelleschi is also free in his treatment of the sacrifice itself. In the Bible, the angel speaks to Abraham; Brunelleschi shows him preventing the sacrifice by seizing Abraham's arm. In Ghiberti's version, Abraham has raised the knife to strike, his eyes fixed on Isaac. This is the very moment at which the angel must free Abraham from his tormenting conflict between fear of God and love of the son he must kill; and in Ghiberti's rendering it is Isaac, looking up, who first becomes aware of the angel.

A group of thirty-four judges proved unanimous in their choice of Ghiberti's piece, by the artist's own account; and that same year the Calimala had his relief gilded. Brunelleschi's was bought by Cosimo de' Medici, who also had it gilded. Both are now in the Bargello in Florence.

On 23 November 1403, the contract for the second door of the Baptistery was agreed. The Calimala, however, had meanwhile decided that the east door of the Baptistery, facing the Cathedral of Santa Maria del Fiore, should be the next to be replaced, rather than the north one. This meant changing the programme, since it was impossible, for iconographic reasons, to have Old Testament subjects on the east door of a Christian church building. The relief Ghiberti had made was thus useless for the present purposes. The Calimala made no changes in their prescriptions of form, though, continuing to abide by the overall design adopted by Pisano seventy years previously. The contract envisaged a working period of nine and a half years for the twenty-eight reliefs required; in the event, they took twenty, and it was not until 19 April 1424 that the two wings of the door were mounted in the east portal of the Baptistery.

The third Baptistery door
On 2 January 1425, less than a year after Ghiberti's first door was installed in the east portal of the Baptistery, the artist and the

Andrea Pisano
Detail from the South Door: John Baptizes Christ
Bronze, partially gilded, 39 x 39 cm
Florence, Baptistery

Lorenzo Ghiberti
Detail from the North Door: The Last Supper
Bronze, partially gilded, 39 x 39 cm
Florence, Baptistery

Calimala agreed a further contract. Ghiberti's status had fundamentally changed in the mean time. He had been involved in the architectural problems of Cathedral construction, and had thus advanced from craftsman to architect, and an expert on geometry. On 16 April 1420, together with Brunelleschi and the Cathedral's master-builder, Battista d'Agnolo, he had been appointed by the Arte della Lana (the wool and cloth merchants' guild) to oversee the construction of the dome of Florence Cathedral. In social terms, this placed Ghiberti on a par with scholars.

The Calimala was now dealing with a master who not only tackled the technical solution and execution of commissioned work with a degree of independence that had previously been unknown but had also assumed responsibility for the content design. Ghiberti had accomplished, for the first time, an act of emancipation from those who commissioned work, and their intentions; and this was in itself an achievement, a turning point in the social history of European art. It had implications for the third of the Baptistery doors. When the work was begun, in 1428 or 1429, the number of reliefs appears to have been reduced from twenty-eight to twenty-four; but this was not enough for Ghiberti. Partly with the bronze reliefs on the baptismal font of the Siena Baptistery in mind (cf. p. 198), he cut the number once again, to a mere ten, and came up with an entirely new framing design. He replaced Pisano's superannuated quatrefoil framing with a grid resembling a ladder, enclosed in its turn by strips of reliefs. Each relief panel was now flanked by two niche figurines, and at the sides of the rungs of the ladder, as well as on either side of the reclining figures at the top and bottom of the ladders, there were rings containing portrait busts. This gave the reliefs a substantial, interlinked unity. The figures in the frame were distinctly larger than those in the reliefs, like small architectural sculptures reaching out from the space defined in the reliefs. Even the space that encloses the beholder is meticulously defined by the door frame, the frame around a real architectural space. This addition of different spatial levels is matched by the spatial depths within each relief. Every one of the reliefs has its own independent artistic value within the overall scheme, to an extent hitherto unknown.

It is the distinctive working of the reliefs that makes this possible. In Pisano's Gothic panels, and indeed in Ghiberti's first door, all the figures had to be of equal size, with no perspective differentiation; the priority was to fill the area available, rather than to suggest spatial depth. But Ghiberti aimed to show closer figures as appearing larger, and figures further off as appearing smaller, as figures do in the real world; and so he adopted the new perspective approach in the third door, which made possible the transformation of a flat surface into the semblance of three-dimensional space.

Lorenzo Ghiberti
Detail from The Gates of
Paradise (East Door):
The story of Joseph
Bronze with gilding, 80 x 80 cm

Lorenzo Ghiberti
The Gates of Paradise (East
Door), 1425–1452
Bronze with gilding, frame height
506 cm, width 287 cm
Florence, Baptistery

SCHEME BELOW:
Topics covered by The Gates of
Paradise (after Krautheimer)

	Eve			Adam	
Ezekiel (?)	*Adam and Eve* Creation of Adam Creation of Eve The Fall Expulsion from Paradise	Jeremiah (?)	Prophetess	*Cain and Abel* Adam and Eve outside their shelter Abel tending the flocks The sacrifices of Cain and Abel Cain kills Abel God the Father banishes Cain	Joab (?)
Elias (?)	Noah Leaving the Ark Noah's sacrifice Noah's drunkenness	Jonah	Hannah (?)	*Abraham* Abraham and the three angels The sacrifice of Isaac	Samson
Prophet	*Jacob and Esau* Rebecca praying to God Rebecca's confinement Esau selling his birthright to Jacob Isaac sending Esau out to hunt Jacob with a kid Isaac blessing Jacob	Rachel (?)	Prophet	*Joseph* Joseph is sold by his brothers Collecting the grain The discovery of the silver cup Joseph reveals himself to his brothers	Prophet
Miriam	*Moses* Moses receiving the tablets of the Law The people at Mount Sinai	Aaron	Joshua	*Joshua* The Israelites crossing the Jordan Erecting the stone memorial The fall of Jericho	Gideon (?)
Judith	*David* David kills Goliath The entry into Jerusalem	Nathan (?)	Daniel (?)	Solomon and the Queen of Sheba	Balaam (?)
	Noah			Puarphara	

Ghiberti's interest in the spatial dimensions made available by perspective went hand in hand with an interest in truth of content. It was now possible to present different phases of a narrative on different spatial levels, and to relate them internally according to the contextual requirements of the story. Thus the ten reliefs of the Gates of Paradise, in presenting their Old Testament subjects, include a varying number of scenes within each relief.

The Calimala was delighted with Ghiberti's new door, to say the least; and the artist himself said later that it was the finest of all his works. Indeed, the guild was so impressed that they decided on an unprecedented move. Because Ghiberti's door was so superlatively beautiful, they decided to install it not in the place it was intended for (and to which the iconographic programme was apt) but in place of the east door. This meant removing the present east door, with its Life of Christ, Church Fathers and other Christian material, to the north portal, and hanging the new door in the east in its stead. This was a radical departure, in so far as Christ was having to quit the preferred east side of the Baptistery, to make way for an Old Testament cycle; this flew in the face of traditional priorities. But Lorenzo Ghiberti's magisterial artistry had persuaded the guild to abandon their preconceptions. It was the first time that a work of art was placed in its position for aesthetic reasons rather than on grounds of content.

Lorenzo Ghiberti
Detail from The Gates of Paradise (East Door):
The Creation, the Fall, the Expulsion of Adam and Eve from Paradise
Bronze with gilding, 80 x 80 cm
Florence, Baptistery

Lorenzo Ghiberti
Detail from The Gates of Paradise (East Door):
Cain and Abel
Bronze with gilding, 80 x 80 cm
Florence, Baptistery

Lorenzo Ghiberti
Detail from The Gates of Paradise (East Door):
Self-portrait, aged about 70, on the frame, c. 1447
Bronze
Florence, Baptistery

The Cathedral of Santa Maria del Fiore

The sculptures for the pier buttresses of the north choir apse

The stonemasons' lodge of Florence Cathedral decided to have twelve larger-than-life prophets to cap the pier buttresses in the north choir. Early in 1408, Nanni di Banco was commissioned to do a marble figure of Isaiah (p. 185). Since the last payment to the artist was made that December, it seems the statue was completed within the year. We do not know whether it was ever installed in the position it was originally intended for, however; the prophets programme was never carried out. The statue is now in the right-hand side aisle of the Cathedral.

This early sculpture by Nanni is torn between a traditional Gothic approach to the figure and the new style based on classical antiquity. The body's weight is on the right leg, according to the Gothic ideal; the folds of the cloak, and the scroll held in Isaiah's left hand, are likewise in line with that ideal. On the other hand, the emphasis on the body's physical presence, almost palpable through the robes, is as much a product of the early Quattrocento's sense of antiquity as the bare arms, the facial features, and the classically styled hair.

A brief month after Nanni, Donatello was commissioned to do another marble figure, a David (p. 185), for a pier buttress in the choir. His last payment was made in June 1409, so it is safe to assume that the statue had been completed by that date. Again, we have no record of whether it was placed in its intended position. First it was in the Opera del Duomo, until 1416, and then, after Donatello had done some further work on it, it was placed in the Palazzo Vecchio. Donatello's David, presented as the youthful and triumphant vanquisher of Goliath, was excellently suited to symbolise the Commune's victories over its enemies in a public, official place. The head of Goliath between his feet, the laurel-wreathed hero's weight is on his left leg, the bareness of which is emphasised rather than cloaked by the fall of his robe. His torso is clad in a tight-fitting leather tunic that gives even highlighting to all of his physique. Again, the thin fabric over his shoulders, hips and right leg are revealing rather than concealing.

David is holding his right hand in front of him because at one time it held the sling from which he fired his stone at Goliath; this is now lost. The statue freezes him at a particular moment, lifting him out of the atemporal, mythologized continuum of Old Testament narrative in a manner new to sculpture at that time, as new as the stress on the physicality of the body. This early marble David of Donatello's is widely seen as the sculptor's first known work (though this is disputed) – and it already anticipates the figurative and innovative richness of Early Renaissance sculpture in Florence.

In summer 1410, Donatello was paid for work on a colossal terracotta statue of Joshua which he appears to have placed on the cornice of a pier buttress. Apart from a little documentary evidence

Nanni di Banco
Isaiah, 1408
Marble, height: 193 cm
Florence, Cathedral

Donatello
David, 1408–09
Marble, height: 191 cm
Florence, Museo Nazionale del Bargello

concerning payments, we know next to nothing else. There is merely a view of the Cathedral in 1684 that shows two immense figures on the buttresses in the north choir apse, from which position they were removed not long after. The *Joshua* may have been one of these two figures that Vasari refers to in his life of Donatello, as being positioned outside the church at the corners of the chapels. Figures of such colossal proportions, though not unknown in antiquity, were quite new in the Florentine Early Renaissance. Matching the sculpture's proportions to those of the architecture, on the one hand, and taking into account the effect on a viewer at a distance, on the other, must have presented as signal a challenge to Donatello as the technical problem of mounting the pieces in position. Vasari reports that the two large statues were made of brick and plaster, and if Donatello worked on the spot with these materials the difficulty of transport would of course not have arisen. To what extent these lost figures satisfied the expectations of those who commissioned them, or those of the artist, cannot now be said.

The Evangelists on the façade
In December 1408, the Opera del Duomo commissioned both Nanni di Banco and Donatello to sculpt a monumental seated figure of an Evangelist to flank the main entrance on the west front. Nanni was assigned St. Luke, while Donatello was asked to do St. John. A statue of St. Mark was commissioned from the somewhat older sculptor Niccolò di Pietro Lamberti. The original intention was to commission the fourth Evangelist from the sculptor who did the best work on his first, but in the event, in May 1410, none of the first three being finished, St. Matthew was commissioned from Bernardo Ciuffagni. Nanni received his final payment in February 1413, but the other statues were not completed until 1415. They remained in their intended positions until the Cathedral façade was torn down in 1587, after which they were placed inside the Cathedral; since 1936 they have been in the Museo dell' Opera del Duomo.

Nanni di Banco's *St. Luke* (p. 186) is wearing a garment that is belted around his waist, and over it a wide cloak that is draped over his left shoulder, right arm, back and legs. He is holding a book in his left hand, and his right hand is resting on his thigh. This figure shows many of the influences of Donatello upon Nanni's work. The elongated neck and bent head and the length of the fingers are inspired by Donatello's marble David; the stilted position of the right hand and rather exaggerated anatomic bend of the left hand, together with the oval shape of his face, are equally clearly derived from Donatello's *David*. Both the figures of *Isaiah* and *St. Luke*, and the way St. Luke's cloak is draped over his legs, show how much International Gothic had influenced Nanni's style. Though he was also clearly influenced by Donatello, features such as the frontal view of the legs and the heavy folds in the garments show that he lacked the former's artistic certainty.

Donatello's *St. John* (p. 186) is also clad in a belted garment which is covered by a cloak that falls in very extensive folds around his legs. While his arms appear quite relaxed, there is still a tension in the figure, caused by the fact that his head and legs are pointing in different directions. This *contrapposto* composition of a seated figure is a characteristic of Donatello's early work. If the figure is viewed at eye level, the unusual elongation of the upper torso and head as well as the gentle angle of his thighs are all quite noticeable. These apparent imbalances are corrected if one looks at the figure from below, however. At the same time, the three-dimensional and monumental effect of the figure is increased. Donatello was creating a precise optical relationship between the high position of the statue in a niche on the façade and the position of the beholder.

The niche figures of the Campanile
It was not until 1415 that the Opera del Duomo decided to fill the empty niches on the second floor of the north and east façades of the Campanile with marble figures. The more visible west and south sides had already been filled with eight Old Testament figures that Andrea Pisano and his workshop had completed in the 14th century. Donatello was commissioned to produce the new statues. He completed two figures by 1420; due to their lack of iconographic attributes, they cannot be identified and have, for lack of a better

Nanni di Banco
St. Luke, 1408–13
Marble, height: 208 cm
Florence, Museo dell'Opera del Duomo

Donatello
St. John, 1408–15
Marble, height: 215 cm
Florence, Museo dell'Opera del Duomo

Donatello
St. George, c. 1416–17
Marble, height: 209 cm
Florence, Museo dell'Opera del Duomo

idea, been called the *Beardless Prophet* (1416–18) and *Pensieroso* (The Thinker, 1418–20). In 1421, he and his assistant Nanni di Bartolo were commissioned to create *Abraham and Isaac*. All three sculptures were placed on the east façade. Donatello was paid for two other prophets between 1423 and 1436. One of them was *Jeremiah*, and the other was described in contemporary sources as *Habbakuk*. Both figures were first placed on the north side, but in 1464 Kings Solomon and David, by Andrea Pisano, were moved to make way for them on the north side.

Donatello omitted iconographic attributes, evidently trusting that his prophets' individual physiognomies would make it possible to tell the difference between them. How they were interpreted can be seen from the writings of Vasari, who believed that at least two of the prophets were modelled on contemporary people. Because of his

bald head, the Florentines rather disrespectfully called Habbakuk (p. 187) "Il Zuccone", the pumpkin. It is true that there is an aspect of portraiture in the extraordinarily naturalistic, almost ugly shape of the heads, creating an individuality that had never before been seen in sculptures of prophets. This development was part of an overall increase in the expressiveness in Florentine sculpture of the Early Quattrocento.

Abraham stands out from amongst this series of prophets, if for no other reason than that he and *Isaac* form a group. The reason for this is that Abraham is famous in the Old Testament less for what he said than what he did. Abraham is shown about to sacrifice his son, whereas the other prophets look appropriately philosophical. Their robes, which are derived from portraits of Ancient Roman senators, are full to a degree that contrasts with

186

Donatello
Habbakuk ('Lo Zuccone'), 1423–26
Marble, height: 195 cm
Florence, Museo dell'Opera del Duomo

the corporeality of the figures. But it is not the case that the garments are emphasizing the bodies. Rather, the bodies assert their individual dimensions, such as the anatomically correct right arms of Jeremiah and Habbakuk, underneath the robes. Due to the high position of the statues, the garments form heavy masses of material which do not detract from the bodies emerging from underneath them as much as give them expression and meaning. The generous folds that are falling diagonally from the left shoulder of *Habbakuk* convey a strong and impressive sense of the prophet's air of pathos.

The niche figures of Orsanmichele

All but four of the total of fourteen niches on the outer sides of Orsanmichele's arcade pillars had been filled with sculptures in the first third of the Quattrocento. One of these was Lorenzo Ghiberti's *John the Baptist* (p. 188), which was commissioned by the Arte dei Mercanti di Calimala; Ghiberti created it between 1413 and 1416, and it was the first ever life-size statue to be made out of bronze. The casting of the figure, which was done in one piece, was such a complicated and chancy process that the goldsmith had to carry it out at his own risk. The statue is leaning forward a little, and the body is almost completely surrounded by a heavy garment. A long piece of material connects the foot of the right leg with the left hip, which, due to the position the figure is standing in, is bent slightly. Both this and the heavy cascades of folds are elements of International Gothic, and show how greatly Ghiberti's work on this figure was influenced by it.

The four crowned patron saints (p. 189) of the Arte dei Maestri di Pietra e Legname, the guild of Florentine stone masons, were conceived along more classical lines. The relief on the pedestal shows the various professions that were united in this guild, namely builder, stonemason, architect, and sculptor. This group of four statues, called the *Santi Quattro Coronati*, was created by Nanni di Banco c. 1414–16 and needed a particularly wide tabernacle. The four saints are portrayed standing closely together in a semi-circle, wearing classical dress and deep in conversation. This latter scene-setting device enabled Nanni to successfully fit all four figures in one niche. The two patron saints on the right are placed so closely together because they have been fashioned out of a single block of marble. Vasari suggested that Donatello must have helped Nanni complete this difficult commission.

Donatello countered both Ghiberti's Gothic and Nanni's classical style with a series of stylistic ideas which were incorporated into the statue of St. Mark (p. 188) which he was commissioned in 1411 to produce for the Arte dei Linaiouli, the guild of linen merchants. It was a *contrapposto* composition, and is a figure that communicates the various functions of the different parts of the statue with unusual clarity. For instance, the right leg, which carries the body's weight, is surrounded with such strictly vertical folds that one is reminded of

Donatello
St. Mark, 1411–13
Marble, height: 236 cm
Florence, Orsanmichele

Lorenzo Ghiberti
St. John the Baptist, 1413–16
Bronze, height: 255 cm
Florence, Orsanmichele

Nanni di Banco
Four Crowned Martyrs, c. 1414–16
Marble, height: 183 cm
Florence, Orsanmichele

the fluted columns of classical temples. The free leg contrasts with it for two reasons: firstly, the robe is draped around it in a very Gothic manner; secondly, unlike the right leg, the shape of the left leg can be clearly made out underneath the cloth. In accordance with the compositional style, the right shoulder is turned towards the interior of the niche, whereas the left shoulder is bent forwards in a very normal human position. Finally, the *contrapposto* position of St. Mark's head, and the way he is looking far into the distance, appear to free the statue from its confinement within the niche; indeed, the figure has clearly been conceived with this effect in mind.

St. George (p. 186) appears as a youthful hero wearing classical armour and holding a shield that is resting on the ground. Of particular interest in this figure is the way its relationship to its niche differs from that of the figure of St. Mark; it is a relationship of contrasts, giving the figure an appearance of isolation. The main explanation for this is the fact that the figure of St. Mark was only completed at the front, whereas St. George was very nearly a sculpture in the round.

Donatello

The most important and influential sculptor of the Early Renaissance was undoubtedly Donato di Niccolò di Betto Bardi, or Donatello. He was probably born in Florence in 1386, the son of a carder, and has been shown to have worked as an assistant in Ghiberti's workshop while the latter was occupied with his first Baptistery door. The earliest work that can be ascribed to Donatello is the marble David dating from 1408/09, which was placed on the Cathedral's pier buttress. During the following years he produced numerous sculptures made of marble, clay, bronze and wood, mainly for clients in Florence, though also for others in Pisa, Siena and Prato. Donatello did most of his work from 1444 to 1453 in Padua, and probably moved there in 1446/47. The main work he produced there was the equestrian monument to Gattamelatta. It was probably after it was put up in 1453 that he returned to Florence, but evidently received ever fewer commissions there. Four years later, when he was more than seventy years old, he attempted to gain the commission to produce bronze doors for the Cathedral, but these never got further than the planning stage. It was possibly a commission from Cosimo de' Medici to work on the bronze pulpits in S. Lorenzo that caused him to return to Florence in 1459. Donatello died while working on this project, on 13 December 1466.

Rilievo schiacciato

It is not only in the large-scale sculptures Donatello produced that his innovative powers are evident. His inventions in relief sculpture were just as pioneering and decisive in the development of European

Donatello
Pazzi Madonna, c. 1417–18
Marble, 74.5 x 69.5 cm
Berlin, Staatliche Museen zu Berlin–Preußischer Kulturbesitz

art. It started with the relief on the pedestal of his figure of St. George for Or San Michele (p. 186). Compared with the relief on the pedestal of Nanni di Banco's *Quattro Santi Coronati* (p. 189), which was created just a year earlier, it is a radical break with traditional approaches to relief. While Nanni portrayed his four stonemasons and tools in high relief and lacking spatial qualities, Donatello managed for the first time to create a sense of depth within the plane of the relief. The scene of the action, St. George's fight against the dragon, appears to have been foreshortened on both sides. This area, which opens out into a landscape, gives the scene a sense of depth. The new relief technique that was able to create this optical effect was called *rilievo schiacciato*, "squashed" or "flattened relief", a technique that also enhanced the dramatic effect of the event being narrated. In the case of St. George's fight against the dragon, the battle has intensified to the moment when St. George has gathered all his strength to deliver the deathblow from his rearing horse.

The marble relief of the Pazzi Madonna
Donatello was able to modify this *rilievo schiacciato* when necessary, as is shown by the marble relief of the Pazzi Madonna (top), which was created c. 1417–18 and named after the Palazzo

Pazzi in Florence, where it was presumably displayed. The Madonna is holding her son in a close loving embrace, and this is shown within an optically foreshortened frame. The very slight sense that one is viewing this scene from below adds to the monumental nature of the half-length figure without detracting from the close relationship of mother and child. Donatello uses the subtle changes of height of *relievo schiacciato* to give the garments a soft and almost silk-like quality, in keeping with the delicacy of the bodies. With this portrayal, Donatello managed to refine half-length reliefs of the Madonna, which were intended for private meditation and were increasingly popular throughout the Quattrocento.

The Feast of Herod
The high point of Donatello's new relief technique was the *Feast of Herod* (p. 191), which was created, c. 1425, for the font in Siena's Baptistery. There is a great deal of subtlety in the way he relates the central scene in the foreground, the presentation of the head of John the Baptist. At the very moment that the kneeling soldier passes the head of the Baptist to Herod, the guests are seized with horror. Salome leads the group on the right, whose appearance is classical, and the figure in the centre has turned imploringly towards Herod, who has also shrunk back in dismay. This compressed scene is balanced by the classical arcades, which are depicted according to the laws of perspective and create a sense of depth on an unprecedented scale. This relief offers the most arresting use of linear perspective, a discovery of Brunelleschi's, in the Early Renaissance.

The Cantoria in Florence Cathedral
Luca della Robbia (1399/1400–1482) had been working since about 1431 on an organ loft for Florence Cathedral. Two years later Donatello was commissioned to produce a counterpart for the singers and musicians. The differences between the two *Cantorias* (pp. 192 and 193) once again display Donatello's innovative powers. Both galleries were supported by five powerful brackets, and the four spaces between them were filled with reliefs. Luca della Robbia created a balustrade in front of which were four self-contained reliefs which were flanked, or separated, by classical fluted paired pilasters. One more relief was added on each side, so that the *cantoria* was decorated by a total of ten reliefs. All of them show boys and girls dancing and making music, the very picture of the words of Psalm 150, part of which is inscribed in the three entablatures. Luca della Robbia's gallery is dominated by architectural elements. His paired pilasters are placed directly above the brackets supporting the entire structure, separated only by a line of inscription. The content of the reliefs themselves was entirely in accordance with the contract and the function of the gallery as an organ loft. In contrast, the way they are incorporated into the surrounding architecture makes them look like visual set pieces that had been added on later.

Donatello
Feast of Herod, c. 1425
Bronze with gilding, 60 x 60 cm
Siena, Baptistery, panel on the baptismal font

Luca della Robbia
Cantoria, 1431/2–38
Marble, height: 328 cm, breadth: 560 cm
Details
Florence, Museo dell'Opera del Duomo

Donatello chose a wholly new approach to the combination of architecture and reliefs for his gallery. It is true that the architecture is the dominant force here also, if only because of its function. The wall brackets carry an entablature that forms the lower part of the composition. Its upper projecting section supports the balustrade. While Luca della Robbia broke the vertical lines with a horizontal entablature, Donatello continued his vertical lines above the wall brackets by means of corbels. These corbels on the upper part of the entablature in turn supported paired columns which reflected the system of paired pilasters on Luca's gallery; the columns carry a projecting ledge with an alternating acanthus and vase pattern. Behind the columns, which are placed slightly apart, is a frieze of reliefs that continues around the entire gallery. It depicts putti that are dancing wildly and singing; the front row is moving to the left, and the row behind is dancing in the opposite direction. Their movement in opposite directions creates a kind of shifting play amongst the figures, and this impression is strengthened by the pairs of columns standing in front of them. Because only sections of the relief are visible, it appears to come to life when one moves along it. Donatello achieved this by using a further technique which was designed entirely for the purpose of creating an optical effect. The columns are decorated with the same rather indifferent mosaic as the background of the relief. This means that although they remain objects with distinct architectural functions that both block and frame our view of the relief, the fact that they are similar to the background reduces their normal visual dominance of the scene. There are no clear models for this in art history; Donatello's *Cantoria* is an unprecedented interplay of architectural spatial qualities and the movement of human figures. In addition, the way this frieze of figures is freed from its architectural frame shows how keen Donatello was to create completely three-dimensional, free-standing sculpture.

The bronze David

Donatello's figure of David is one of the most important sculptures of the Early Renaissance; recent research has suggested that it was cast in bronze in the mid-forties of the Quattrocento. This was the first time since classical antiquity that a European artist had dared to produce a life-size, completely three-dimensional nude. It was the figure with which Donatello finally crowned his long-lasting ambition to free sculpture from its functional architectural role.

The graceful appearance of the youthful hero, who is naked except for a hat and leather leggings, is due in part to the balanced harmony of the position he is standing in. He is standing firmly on his right leg, and his left foot is resting on the head of Goliath, which is lying on the ground, in a casual gesture of victory. The

Donatello
Cantoria, details, 1433–38
Marble and mosaic
Florence, Museo dell'Opera del
Duomo

bend in his hips which this causes is countered by his thorax, which is almost completely upright. In keeping with the casual nature of his position, however, his head is turned slightly to the left and he is looking down on the trophy of his battle. The bend of his free leg which is caused by its position on Goliath's head is reflected in his left arm, which is resting on his hip; his right arm, resting on his sword, mirrors the position of the right leg. It is the treatment of his skin, as a most finely polished, almost black bronze surface whose reflections emphasise the naturalness of his body, that convey the sensuousness of his youthful figure. It has an androgynous beauty that has sometimes been used to support the theory that Donatello was homosexual. Vasari suggested that this bronze figure had many of the qualities of a cast made using a living model: "... this figure is so natural, lifelike and gentle that artists believe it must have been formed over a living body."

The only reference in this figure to the classical age is Donatello's revival of the life-size, three-dimensional nude. The way the figure has been shaped can hardly be said to be based on classical ideals, and there are not even appropriate Early Renaissance models. There are various features that are treated in a naturalistic way, including the folds of his throat, left shoulder and bottom; the somewhat feminine curves of the latter are the first suggestion of the Renaissance ideal of the imitation of nature, which was to shape Vasari's views as an artist of the Late Renaissance.

There are no documents to show why the figure of David was created. All that is known is the place where it was probably originally intended to be set up. Placed in the middle of the Palazzo Medici's courtyard, the victory of this Old Testament hero against his opponent would have been interpreted as an allusion to the political and military resolution of the Commune under the rule of the Medicis to thwart the desire of Naples and Milan to become great powers.

The Penitent Magdalene

This wooden sculpture of the reformed prostitute who washed the feet of Jesus in the house of a Pharisee, dried them with her hair and rubbed them with oil, was created between 1453 and 1455 in Donatello's late period after his stay in Padua. The mediaeval *Legenda aurea*, by Jacobus da Voragine, had a considerable influence on art; in it Mary Magdalene, the chief witness of Christ's resurrection (John 20, 1–18), sought her salvation in the loneliness of a wilderness which some sources considered to be southern France.

The penitent is clad in a shaggy fur robe and is leaning on her left leg, with the right leg slightly to the back. She is holding her hands in prayer in front of her chest. Her sunken eyes, broken teeth and bony hands all emphasise the exhausted ascetic appearance that Donatello wanted to produce. Her skin, which has been tanned and dried by the elements, together with her high cheekbones and long

Donatello
The Penitent Magdalene, c. 1453–55
Wood with polychromy and gold,
height: 188 cm
Florence, Museo dell'Opera del Duomo

Donatello
Judith and Holofernes, c. 1456–57
Bronze, partially gilded,
height:
236 cm
Florence, Palazzo Vecchio

had a remarkable taste for the blood thirsty horror of the decapitation itself, but Donatello concentrated on the moment between the drunk man's loss of dignity and the woman's gaining of dignity – she had, after all, been willing to break the commandment against killing in order to save her town.

It was mainly the patriotism of this scene that caused the group to be placed in the Palazzo Medici. When the Medicis fled the city in 1495, it was set up on the Piazza della Signoria in front of the Palazzo Vecchio as a symbol of the republican Commune; later it was moved to make way for Michelangelo's *David*.

The equestrian monument of Gattamelata in Padua
Donatello stayed in Padua after 1444, working on a bronze crucifix for the Basilica del Santo. Although this work was not completed until 1449, it surely cannot have been the only reason for his move to Padua. The commission to produce an equestrian monument to the Paduan Erasmo da Narni, called Gattamelata, was a major new challenge to his artistic and technical abilities that could only be answered in Padua itself (p. 197).

hair, suggest her once legendary beauty and sensuousness. Her hair is also a symbol of her reverence for Christ and her penitence, and its loose, unbrushed appearance shows that she has renounced all worldly vanity. Many pictures on this theme in Quattrocento Florentine art were influenced by Donatello's sculpture.

The figure used to be in the Baptistery in Florence, although it is not certain if that was also its original position. After the Arno flooded in 1966, it was necessary to do some restoration work, and this exposed the original colour; it also gave her back the former aesthetic appearance of her body.

Judith and Holofernes
When Donatello returned from Padua c. 1456–57, he created a major work to be placed next to his bronze David, the first sculpture in the round in the Florentine Early Renaissance; the new work was the bronze group *Judith and Holofernes* (far right). The appearance of the group varies greatly according to which side it is seen from. Donatello portrayed the moment at which Judith beheaded Holofernes, the wine-sodden military commander of the Babylonian ruler Nebuchadnezzar, a deed which saved her people from destruction. After Holofernes' banquet, she pretended to be submissive, then took her sword and "twice she struck at the nape of his neck with all her strength and cut off his head" (Judith 13,8).

The exceptional naturalism of some of the eleven separately cast pieces which comprise the group has led some critics to wonder whether Donatello might have cast certain sections such as the cushion and Holofernes' legs from real models. Renaissance painting

Donatello
Equestrian monument of Gattamelata, 1444–53
Bronze on marble plinth, height of statue: 340 cm
Padua, Piazza del Santo

Gattamelata ("honeyed cat") was the *condottiere* (mercenary commander) of the Venetian army. The statue was probably commissioned and paid for by his family, with the agreement of the Serenissima, after he died in January 1443. It is hardly likely that his record of mainly unsuccessful battles led to an equestrian monument being dedicated to him; rather, it was because of his famous loyalty, which also explains his nickname. Indeed, a contemporary satire made fun of the Venetians for doing something quite un-Roman in portraying their military leader on the very horse on which he fled.

It has not been possible to ascertain whether the monument was meant to be a tomb or a memorial. The first possibility is supported by the height of the base, also designed by Donatello and included tall blind marble doors which were based on classical sarcophagi and representing the gates to Hades. It was not until 1456, after the monument was completed, that a proper tomb was set up in the Basilica. On the other hand, Vasari describes it as a memorial.

Although honorary paintings of commanders on horseback had been a feature of Italian art since the 14th century, Donatello revived an imposing form of ancient sculpture with his equestrian statue. Donatello's bronze statue draws on various models, without really copying any of them. A starting point for his work was probably the statue of Marcus Aurelius which stood in front of the church of San Giovanni in Laterano. Other models could include Roman coins featuring equestrian statues. Other elements, such as the horse's near fore hoof, which is placed on a cannon ball for the sake of stability, seem to refer to the posture of the horses of San Marco in Venice, which ruled Padua at that time.

In contrast to classical equestrian statues, Donatello's *Gallamelata* is wearing a lavish uniform, though it is decorated with motifs from the armour of Roman emperors and his contemporaries probably interpreted it as such. However, many 15th century pieces of armour, such as the arm and leg guards and the long sword, show that the important aspect of Donatello's *condottiere* was not that it should be an exact copy of classical armour, but rather that the commissioners should be able to express their contemporary claims by using ancient symbols of power. With this in mind, Gattamelata's physiognomy should perhaps be re-evaluated in order to establish to what degree the statue actually is a portrait.

The statue was placed on the Piazza del Santo in front of the façade of the Basilica of St. Anthony, which the Paduans call "Il Santo"; due to the height of its base, it conveys the sense of monumental size which has been a feature of most equestrian statues ever since, such as that of Louis XIV. The *condottiere* dominates the entire square with the command staff of a Roman officer, which he was awarded by Venice in 1438.

Jacopo della Quercia
The Archangel Gabriel appears to Zacharias, 1428–30
Bronze with gilding, 60 x 60 cm
Siena, Baptistery, detail from the baptismal font

Various sculptors
Baptismal font, 1416–c. 1429
Marble, bronze with gilding
Siena, Baptistery

Sculpture in the second half of the Quattrocento – the influence of Donatello

Jacopo della Quercia

Jacopo di Pietro, who was called Jacopo della Quercia (c. 1374–1438), came from Siena; he was older than Donatello and was one of the participants in the 1401 competition for Florence's Baptistery door. Until that year there is little reliable information about his artistic work, apart from a few attempts at attribution. One of his main works is the Fonte Gaia, a complex fountain for the Piazza del Campo in Siena; little remains of it apart from a few pieces of figures, though there are various contemporary drawings in London and New York, and photographs of an attempt to reconstruct it that was made in the 19th century. The programme of the fountain, which consisted mainly of reliefs and a few sculptures in the round, referred to Siena's Roman history and various Christian virtues. In the middle was the Madonna and Child (the former the patron saint of Siena, which was called the *Civitas Virginis*), echoing the ethos of good government in the frescos inside Siena's town hall. The sculptor earned the nickname 'Jacopo della Fonte' for his work on the fountain.

Lucca della Robbia
Ceiling of the Chapel of the
Cardinal of Portugal,
1461–62
Terracotta, painted and enamelled
Florence, San Miniato al Monte

He was originally supposed to deliver two reliefs for the baptismal font in Siena's Baptistery, but he only completed one of them. Donatello was commissioned to produce the other. Quercia kept very closely to the text in his interpretation of the annunciation of the birth of John the Baptist to Zacharias (p. 198), which is narrated in Luke (1, 8–20). He depicts the sanctuary with the angel Gabriel approaching the altar from the right. The altar is placed in front of the arcade-like central projecting arch of the temple which frames the scene, together with the platform, separating it from the people praying to either side. In the New Testament account the people were praying outside; by placing them inside, as witnesses of the appearance, Quercia produced a dramatic effect by having them share Zacharias's astonishment, much as happened in Donatello's *Feast of Herod*. The sense of perspective created by the architecture is also clearly borrowed from Donatello.

The baptismal font in Siena's Baptistery is one of the most important Early Renaissance works to be produced by a group of artists. Quercia completed the upper marble ciborium and the figure of St. John the Baptist that it bears between 1429 and 1430.

Luca della Robbia and his workshop

Luca della Robbia was born in Florence c. 1400, the third son of the wool merchant Simone di Marco della Robbia; he was probably taught by Ghiberti or Nanni di Banco. His earliest documented work was the singing gallery in Florence's Cathedral (p. 192), to which Donatello created a counterpart. He produced some further marble works, some of them with Donatello, and then, from 1441-42, worked on the *Tabernacle for the Sacrament* in the hospital church of Santa Maria Nuova in Florence, which is now in the church of Santa Maria in Peretola. This work is his first datable, though still restricted, use of enamelled terracotta, which was later to become the hallmark of his workshop. It is not the invention of enamelled terracotta as such, but its use in large-scale sculpture, which is considered to be Luca's important innovation.

workshop's distinctive techniques and using casting moulds, he contributed greatly to the popularity of enamelled terracotta. Great favourites were the peaceful pictures for which Luca had already produced moulds of the Madonna and Child in white glaze on a blue background. Andrea's later works tend to be more colourful and decorative, and in the *Madonna of the Stonemasons* (p. 201) this led to the close relationship between mother and child being related to the lavishly decorated frame.

Andrea's eldest son, Giovanni (1469– after 1525), continued the family tradition in their Florence workshop, while the younger son Girolamo (1488–1566), exported this technique to Paris, where he did decorative work in various buildings including Fontainebleau, under the direction of Francesco Primaticcio (1504/05–1570).

Bernardo Rossellino

Bernardo Rossellino (1407/10–1464) was one of three sculptors who came from Settignano and who would have a considerable influence on Florentine sculpture until the 1470s. He brought his younger brother, Antonio (1427/28–c.1479), and friend Desiderio da Settignano (c. 1430–1464) to Florence. All three sculptors worked on tombstones at some point in their careers.

Towards the end of the 1440s Bernardo produced his most important piece of sculpture, in Santa Croce, Florence. It was the tomb of the humanist and historian Leonardo Bruni (p. 202), who had been the Chancellor of the Republic of Florence and died in 1444. The classical style of the architectural frame points to the influence of Leon Battista Alberti. The tomb is framed by two Corinthian pilasters, which support imposts and a round arch; underneath the arch is a tondo showing the Madonna and Child, which is flanked by two angels. Over the arch are two putti holding a coat of arms; they were probably added at a later date and do not fit in very well with the overall composition. The rear wall is divided into three vertical spaces, and in front of them is the sarcophagus. On top of it is a sculpture of the dead Bruni, resting on a bier supported by two birds of prey. His head, which is crowned with laurels as a sign of his literary achievements, is turned towards us, and his right hand is resting on a book.

The colourfulness of the tomb, with its use of white, black and red marble as well as some gilding, underlines the detail of the design, which is based on the ancient triumphal arch. This was the first humanist tomb whose triumphal features are designed to honour the humanist rather than suggest salvation in death. It was a model for later Quattrocento tombs, including those made by his brother, Antonio Rossellino, and Desiderio da Settignano.

Agostino di Duccio

He was born in Florence in 1418, and it is not known who he was trained by. He was driven out of Florence in 1441 after being accused of stealing silver from SS. Annunziata, and reappeared a

He decorated the ceiling in the Cardinal of Portugal's chapel (p. 199) in San Miniato, Florence, between 1461 and 1462; it is basically a three-dimensional cubic pattern with five prominent relief tondi. The latter mirror motifs in Donatello's Old Sacristy in San Lorenzo. The central tondo contains a dove, representing the Holy Spirit. Around it are four tondi depicting the cardinal virtues of Temperance, Fortitude, Justice and Prudence. It was the most aesthetically pleasing ceiling decoration in the Early Renaissance, and influenced later designers.

Due to its careful modelling, the bust of a young woman, which was formerly attributed to his nephew Andrea, is now considered to be one of Luca della Robbia's later works. She is dressed according to the fashion of the time, and her hair is drawn away from her forehead and decorated with jewellery, giving her a most aristocratic appearance. The pale glaze of her head and strands of hair contrasts with the monochrome blue of the background. Her head is bent forward slightly, and she is looking down; this gives her a very natural appearance, which makes it difficult to decide whether the bust was a portrait or a depiction of contemporary ideals of feminine beauty. Andrea della Robbia (1435–1525), Luca's nephew, worked in the family workshop while his uncle was still alive, and ran it after Luca died in 1482. By keeping exclusively to the

Andrea della Robbia
Madonna of the Stonemasons, 1475–80
Enamelled terracotta, height: 134 cm,
breadth: 96 cm
Florence, Museo Nazionale del Bargello

Bernardo Rossellino
Tomb of Leonardo Bruni, c. 1448–50
Marble, partially gilded, height: 715 cm
Florence, Santa Croce

Agostino di Duccio
Luna, c. 1450–57
Marble, partially painted and gilded
Rimini, Tempio Malatestiano

Antonio Rosselino
Tomb of the Cardinal of Portugal, 1461–66
Marble, partially gilded, height: 400 cm
Florence, San Miniato al Monte

203

year later in Modena. He arrived in Venice with his brother in 1446, went to Rimini, where he was in 1449, and then went to Perugia and Bologna, in 1462. The first record of him working as a sculptor is in 1463, when he was back in Florence, working unsuccessfully on the same block of marble that Michelangelo would later transform into his *David*. As he was not having any success, even in his home town, he left Florence for Perugia at the beginning of the 1470s, when he was in his fifties, and died there c. 1481.

Although Agostino di Duccio produced sculptures in all the many towns he visited during his years of travel, one of his most remarkable works is the sculptural interior that he created for the church of San Francesco in Rimini, which is also called the Tempio Malatestiano. Most of the work consisted of decorating the piers that supported the arches over the side chapels; he directed the work, though it is not certain which sections he did himself.

Amongst his later works in the Tempio Malatestiano are the reliefs of the Capella dei Pianeti. They show the twelve signs of the Zodiac and the seven planets, which in his time included the sun and moon. The latter was personified as *Luna* (p. 203), who is clad in a billowing garment. She is being drawn across the clouds by two horses and is carrying a crescent moon.

Florentine portraits

If the terracotta bust of the person provisionally identified as Niccolò da Uzzano can indeed be attributed to Donatello, then it is probably the piece that led to the revival, c. 1430, of the classical traditional of portrait busts. The genre was at his notable best around the middle of the Quattrocento, as there was a greatly increased demand, particularly in Florence, for these prestigious busts. One of the earliest examples is the bust of Pietro de' Medici (p. 205 top left) by Mino da Fiesole (1429–1484); it dates from 1453, though there is some doubt about the inscription that provides us with that information.

Mino's main artistic model was Desiderio da Settignano. He started his career in Florence before moving to Rome and Naples. He returned to Florence between 1456 and 1461, and was back in Rome in 1463. A year later, after Desiderio's death, he returned to Florence in order to share the role of main sculptor with Antonio Rossellino, and he received numerous commissions. The bust of Pietro, the eldest son of Cosimo de' Medici and father of Lorenzo the Magnificent, shows him dressed in a valuable upper garment made of brocade. The vertical folds of the cloth over his chest are reduced to a simple uniformity. There also appears to be a degree of idealization about Pietro's individual features. Even the position of his head, which is turned to the left, and the way he is gazing into the distance, go beyond his importance as an individual and tell of his political significance; they also contribute to his rather stiff appearance.

Antonio Rossellino's bust of Giovanni Chellini (p. 205, bottom right) makes a rather more natural impression. Chellini was a teacher of philosophy and a famous doctor, and one of his patients was Donatello. This bust is the first work which we definitely know is by Antonio, and it is also one of the most interesting portraits of the age. A cast copy of the head was probably made while the doctor was still alive. The technique of making plaster masks was described by Pliny the Elder, and Cennino Cennini's description of it in the Quattrocento shows that this classical technique was in use c. 1400 and later. The bust is clad in an evenly folded coat whose collar sets the head off against the chest. His face shows all the features of the elderly doctor and philosopher at the height of his wisdom. There are bags underneath his eyes, which are set in hollows below strong eyebrows. His hollow cheeks and the folds of skin in his neck emphasize his nose and the firm chin underneath a tight-lipped smile.

Another bust of an elderly man is that of the Florentine merchant Pietro Mellini (p. 205, bottom left), which was made by Benedetto da Maiano (1442–1497) in 1474. It is likely that he was trained as a sculptor and portraitist in Antonio Rossellino's workshop. Benedetto travelled to Rome, and probably Naples, before returning to Florence to work for both Florentine and non-local clients. There are many works in wood, terracotta and marble that either were signed by him or have been attributed to him. The dated marble bust of Mellini, who is dressed in a similarly lavish brocade garment as Pietro de' Medici, is a portrait of a rich Florentine merchant whose choice of dress was designed to give him an air of nobility. His natural appearance and the high level of detail in his wrinkled face suggest that this was another portrait bust made using a plaster mask. However, it is also known that Benedetto made extensive use of terracotta models. Mellini's eyebrows are raised, wrinkling his forehead; his pursed lips and the wrinkles on his cheeks, which start at the sides of his nose, create a sense of bemusement. He is portrayed as a careful man who is aware of his status as an important Florentine merchant. Mellini's bust is unlike the others in its rounded base, allying it to ancient types.

The bust which has been provisionally identified as that of Marietta Strozzi (p. 205, top right) and is now in Berlin shows how difficult it is to determine the identity of female Quattrocento portraits and their creators. They are rarely dated, signed or inscribed with the name of the woman shown, and they present idealized youthful beauties before character moulds their faces. Marietta Strozzi is presented as a youthful woman, whose head is raised coquettishly.

Francesco Laurana

Francesco Laurana (c. 1430–1502) came from Vrana in Dalmatia and first appeared in Naples in 1453, where he worked on the *Triumphal Arch of Alfonso I* (p. 210), probably on the instigation of Pietro da Milano, with whom he worked. Alfonso of Aragon had

Mino da Fiesole
Piero de' Medici, c. 1455–60
Marble, height: 55 cm
Florence, Museo Nazionale del Bargello

Benedetto da Maiano
Pietro Mellini, 1474
Marble, height: 53 cm
Florence, Museo Nazionale del Bargello

Desiderio da Settignano
Portrait bust of Marietta Strozzi, c. 1455
Marble, height: 52.5 cm
Berlin, Staatliche Museen zu Berlin–Preußischer Kulturbesitz

Antonio Rossellino
Giovanni Chellini, 1456
Marble, height: 51.1 cm
London, Victoria and Albert Museum

Niccolò dell'Arca
Lamentation of the Dead Christ,
c. 1462–63 (or 1485)
Painted terracotta
Bologna, Pinacoteca Nazionale

Guido Mazzoni
Adoration of the Child, c. 1485–89
Painted terracotta
Modena, Cathedral crypt

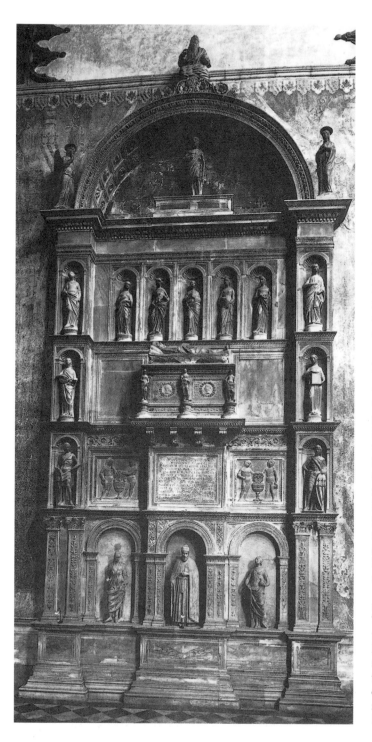

Antonio Rizzo
Monument of Niccolò Tron, 1476–79
Marble and Istrian stone, partially gilded and painted
Venice, Santa Maria Gloriosa dei Frari

captured Naples in 1442 and was an admirer of classical antiquity; he founded the first humanist academy in Italy. Under his rule, Naples developed into a centre of sculpture. He commissioned the classical arch in commemoration of his victory; it replaced the gateway to the mediaeval castle of Castelnuovo. The arch looks as if it has been squashed into the space between the tall and powerful round towers. It is a highly complex design that has three functions, those of entrance to the castle, triumphal arch and cenotaph.

Pietro da Milano, who had been working in Ragusa and was in close contact with Laurana, was given the task c. 1451 of realizing the design together with about thirty other sculptors. The work was far from complete when Alfonso died in 1458. The arch was not finished by Pietro da Milano until 1471.

The arch is a two-storey structure that is subdivided into six horizontal levels, and this is what makes its extraordinary slender height possible. Most of the sculptural decoration is on the high attics above the arches and on the cornice; motifs from classical triumphal arches are combined with Christian iconography and historical scenes. Although Laurana is now considered to be the most important sculptor working on this arch, it was not until the end of the 19th century that he gained proper recognition amongst art historians.

Adoration and lamentation ensembles in Emilia-Romagna
Together with the younger sculptor Guido Mazzoni (c. 1450–1518), who came from Modena, Niccolò dell'Arca (c. 1435–1494), who was from Apulia and whose real name was Niccolò d'Antonio, was the most important sculptor of the Quattrocento in the Emilia-Romagna region. His nickname derived from his most important work, on the shrine (arca) of St. Dominic in the church of San Domenico Maggiore in Bologna, and although his contemporaries recognised his experience as a sculptor, he was considered to be a rather difficult person. He was regarded as extremely stubborn and ill-mannered, and differed from his colleagues in that he was not prepared to teach students. However, it was probably precisely this strained imagination that enabled him to imbue his Lamentation of the Dead Christ (p. 206; detail p. 207), which is now in the Pinacoteca Nazionale in Bologna, with such an extraordinary degree of expressiveness.

The ensemble is made up of large terracotta figures which were originally painted, though most of the colour has worn off since. They have met around the body of Christ, which is lying on a bier in the foreground, and are lamenting his death. Niccolò archieved this high power of expression by choosing a material which was easy to shape and which he could use to convey grief in their faces and in the positions of their bodies and clothes. However, the very expressiveness of the two women rushing towards Christ from the right has led to problems both of date and of attribution. Though 1462/63 was long considered to be the period it was created in, a later date c. 1485 has also been suggested. There have even been recent suggestions that these two women were sculpted not by Niccolò at all but by a later artist.

However undecided art historians may be on these points, Niccolò's lamentation scene does appear to have served as a model for other large-scale terracotta lamentations, such as those of Guido Mazzoni. He was born in Modena and first achieved distinction as a stage designer. During his life he worked as a painter and goldsmith, but it was as a sculptor, and above all as a creator of adoration and lamentation ensembles, that he gained prominence. His earliest work was a group in Busseto, which is dated 1476/77. It was followed by lamentation groups in Ferrara (before 1485) and Modena (c. 1485). Mazzoni's scene of adoration (p. 206) in the Cathedral crypt in Modena was recently restored, and its colourfulness is particularly surprising. In keeping with the occasion, it is rather more subdued than Niccolò's lamentation scene. Niccolò dell'Arca's works in Bologna and Mazzoni's groups in Naples, Ferrara and Modena are the main works of Emilian Renaissance sculpture.

Venetian tombs

Pietro Lombardo (c. 1435–1515) and Antonio Rizzo (1430/40–c. 1500) are considered to be the main sculptors of the Venetian Early Renaissance, with Rizzo being the more important of the two. They both probably started work in the same year, 1476, on two tombs for Doges. Lombardo worked on the *Monument of Pietro Mocenigo* (right) in the church of SS. Giovanni e Paolo, while Rizzo worked on the *Monument of Niccolò Tron* (p. 208) in Santa Maria Gloriosa dei Frari. The Tron monument was finished in 1479, the Mocenigo tomb in 1481.

The unusually monumental size of the tomb that Rizzo designed owes little to Florentine models. The structure is four storeys high and is crowned at the top with a round arch, which implies that it has rather more in common with papal tombs in Rome, with a suggestion of classical triumphal arches. There is a protruding façade bay in the middle of the lower two storeys, and it supports the sarcophagus and the figure of the Doge on it. The Doge himself is standing in the central niche at the bottom, portrayed as he appeared in his later years. This statue is countered in the area underneath the arch by a figure of the resurrected Christ, the intention being to depict the Christian life of the Doge and the fate that awaited him in death.

Rizzo's career in Venice came to an abrupt end when he was forced to flee the city in 1489. He had been caught embezzling funds that were meant to be used to build the Palazzo Ducale. He is last recorded as staying in Cesana at the beginning of 1499, and in Ferrara a little later. It is not known where or when he died.

Pietro Lombardo and his two sons, Tullio and Antonio, came from Carona on Lake Lugano, and had a considerable influence on Venetian sculpture from the late Quattrocento until the 1530s.

Francesco Laurana
Triumphal arch of Alfonso I, c. 1452–71
Marble
Naples, Castelnuovo

victories in Cyprus, and on the pedestal of the tomb are four reliefs, depicting two Deeds of Hercules and captured arms. The inscription in the centre of the pedestal recounts the Doge's military trophies, and the six niches around the triumphal arch are filled with statues of warriors and emperors. The effigy of the Doge originally held a banner in triumph, an iconography which was echoed by the Christian theme at the top. There, above a relief of the three women at the tomb of Christ, is a figure of the Risen Christ accompanied by two angels.

Andrea del Verrocchio

Verrocchio's (c. 1435–1488) whole name was Andrea di Michele di Francesco de' Cioni, and he came from Florence. He had a background as a goldsmith, though he also worked with bronze, sculpted and painted, and Leonardo da Vinci was one of his pupils. He even had some reputation as a musician, though he is mainly known for his bronze sculptures. His work, in Florence, formed the high point of Quattrocento Italian sculpture.

One of his major works is the group of *Christ and Doubting Thomas* (p. 211) in the central niche of the façade of Orsanmichele that faces onto the Via dei Calzaiuoli. The niche had once belonged to the Parte Guelfa, but after the political defeat of this party, which was loyal to the Pope, it was sold to the Mercanzia, the merchant's court, who removed the figure of St. Louis of Toulouse by Donatello. Donatello and Michelozzo designed the architectural frame of the niche before 1422, and it is an early example of Renaissance architecture. Verrocchio was evidently first commissioned to produce a statue of St. Thomas, the patron saint of the Mercanzia, to appear on its own in the niche. However, to place the saint in a dramatic encounter with Christ went against all the traditional notions of the purpose of niche figures. There was nothing comparable elsewhere in the façade niches of Orsanmichele, and even Nanni di Banco's *Quattro Santi Coronati* was not really conceived as a dramatic event. This concept was probably a suggestion of Verrocchio's, and he was probably reflecting current ideas that favoured contrasting the frame and figures.

These cannot have been the only aesthetic reasons that swayed the Mercanzia to agree to Verrocchio's ideas. Indeed, there must have been more than just aesthetic reasons, especially in the Quattrocento, for relegating the patron saint to a rather unstately sideways position at the edge of the niche. It is the figure of Christ that has been placed in the centre of the niche; Thomas is approaching him from the left and appears to be about to touch the wound that Christ has revealed on his right side. Thomas is stepping from outside into the niche, and because he is turned away from us our gaze is drawn towards what he is doing. Christ has raised his right hand in blessing over the head of St. Thomas, which gives the impression that the latter has already lost his doubts and believes once more. Verrocchio's new interpretation of this theme greatly

Pietro's first known work, the tomb of the scholar Antonio Rosselli, which he worked on in 1467 in Padua, owes a lot to Desiderio da Settignano's Florentine tomb of Carlo Marsuppini, so that it is safe to assume that he either studied or worked for a while in Florence. He worked in Bologna c. 1462–63, moving on to Padua between 1464 and 1468 before arriving in Venice in 1471. He had established a business there by 1474, and his large workshop produced many architectural and sculptural works.

The monument of Doge Pietro Mocenigo (p. 209), who died in 1476, is considered to be Lombardo's masterpiece, though his sons may well also have worked on it. The tomb achieves a harmonious balance between architecture and sculpture. It is based more closely on classical triumphal arches than Rizzo's monument. Because the niches on either side are recessed, the arch is emphasized; the effect that is created is of three warriors carrying the sarcophagus underneath an arcade. This is the first time that a Doge was portrayed standing on his sarcophagus, in full armour beneath his state cloak. The monument was clearly intended to celebrate Mocenigo's fame and achievements, shown by the inscription on the sarcophagus, "EX HOSTIUM MANIBUS", "from the booty of the enemy", meaning that state funds were not used. In addition, the inscription is flanked by two reliefs showing the Doge's military

Andrea del Verrochio
Christ and Doubting Thomas, 1467–83
Bronze, height (Christ): 230 cm, (Thomas): 200 cm
Florence, Orsanmichele

extended the iconography of the Mercanzia by giving them the right to include the figure of Christ. Their patron saint was making Florence's citizens aware of the absolute religious legitimacy of the Mercanzia's activities. In that respect, the form of the group was probably less important to the Mercanzia when it made its decision than the way it could be interpreted. Verrocchio worked on the bronze group for over fifteen years, until it was finally put in position in 1483. At the beginning of the 1990s, the group was removed from the niche, thoroughly restored and exhibited in Florence and New York.

During the 1460s, Verrocchio worked on a traditional theme of Florentine iconography, the figure of David overcoming foreign tyranny. His bronze David is dated c. 1470, and although it is a three-dimensional sculpture that owed a great deal to Donatello, it does not manage to create such a sense of drama as the latter's versions of David. From 1479 until his death in 1488, Verrocchio worked on the terracotta model for an equestrian monument to another great Venetian military leader, Bartolomeo Colleoni. He borrowed from both classical models and Donatello's *Gattamelata*, and created a vigorous ensemble of horse and rider. The sense of power that is so obvious within the figures appears to have been frozen in place. In his will, Verrocchio suggested that his pupil Lorenzo di Credi should complete the Colleoni monument; instead, Alessandro Leopardi finally cast the work, and it was erected in 1496 on the square next to SS. Giovanni e Paolo.

Andrea del Verrochio
Tomb of Giovanni and Piero de' Medici, 1472
Marble, pietra serena, porphyry, bronze
Height: 450 cm, breadth: 241 cm
Florence, San Lorenzo

Small bronzes

A passion for collecting and knowledge

Small bronzes are an extremely delightful and fascinating feature of the classical taste that became popular during the Italian Renaissance; they were mainly intended for private collections. Princes, scholars and numerous church officials created collections of various objects, which varied according to the personal preferences of the collector and included both pieces of art and a range of objects that had been collected from all over the known world and its peoples. During the course of the Quattrocento, collectors steadily became more interested in classical antiquity and its occasionally rather fragmented sculptural legacy. Collectors were driven by the desire to find out more about the world and the way in which they fitted into it.

Special rooms were put aside to house the collections in residences and palaces. These were called *studiolo* and derived from the classical idea, which Petrarch had revived, that research and studying would only be successful if carried out at night, by candlelight, in a secluded room.

The courtyard of statues in the Vatican, and small bronzes

The *studioli* of Renaissance rulers and scholars and the objects that were meticulously gathered together there were meant to form a model of the world that would make it possible to comprehend the nature of the universe. There were no rules or obvious relationships governing the objects that were collected, and their role was quite different from the stately functions of public sculptures; instead, they were part of a contemporary intellectual philosophy of life. Towards the end of the Quattrocento, these collections were supplemented with "autonomous" small bronzes, which were designed especially for collectors. This new genre made wide sections of known classical sculptures accessible to *studioli*. The aesthetically formative impetuses behind this development were an expert knowledge of art and a passion for collecting.

The production of small bronzes was given new impulse when new techniques for casting bronze were developed (cf. pp. 216–7). This accounts for the many bronzes that are cast directly on natural models, such as lizards, frogs, crabs, mussels and birds' claws, which were used as the feet of oil lamps. A further important development was the collection of statues which Pope Julius II placed in the specially designed "Cortile delle Statue del Belvedere" in the Vatican when he became Pope in November 1503; it had a lasting effect both on the rise of private collections and on contemporary art. There were already a number of collections of classical artefacts in Quattrocento Italy, but what made the collection of Pope Julius II special was the fact that an interest in classical antiquity and its sculptures had penetrated the Vatican, the very sanctuary of Christianity. It was the climax of the influence of the classical era on Renaissance Italy. At the same time, the collection marked the dawn of a conscious interest in classical sculpture, because the courtyard was filled exclusively with original classical sculptures, in so far as one can call Roman copies of Greek sculptures original. This was yet another reason why the Belvedere collection was so important, because its statues were extremely well-known and their fame spread rapidly throughout the western world in the letters and reports of artists, travellers and ambassadors.

The discovery of Laocoön

On 14 January 1506, a sensational discovery was made in a Roman vineyard. The marble figure of a man and his two sons fighting two powerful snakes (p. 213) was discovered in a secret underground chamber. Julius II sent his court architect Giuliano da Sangallo to the scene on the very same day, accompanied by the young Michelangelo. Giuliano was well read in classical literature and realized immediately what he was looking at, because the Roman author Pliny had mentioned the group, which he saw between 70 and 79 A.D. in the palace of Emperor Titus in Rome, in his *Historia Naturalis*. The group shows the tragedy of the Trojan priest Laocoön, who had warned his people fervently against accepting the legendary Trojan Horse that the Greeks were presenting them with at the end of their ten-year siege in order to make the Trojans believe that they were withdrawing. In

Apollo Belvedere
c. AD 130–40
Roman copy of a Greek original
Marble, height: 224 cm
Rome, Vatican Museums

Laocoön group
First century AD
Roman copy of a Greek original
Marble, height (without the base): 242 cm
Rome, Vatican Museums

retribution, Athena, the Greek Goddess of War, sent two sea serpents to crush him and his two sons while they were making their sacrifices at the altar.

Laocoön, who met his death in an attempt to save his native city, brought the train of events that had been directed by the gods to an end; Troy was defeated, and the next stage would be the foundation of Rome by Aeneas. After losing a fight with Diomedes, Aeneas, who was the son of Anchises and Aphrodite, fled the burning city with his father and after criss-crossing the Mediterranean finally arrived in Italy and founded Rome.

The Laocoön group, which was discovered at the very time when Rome was striving towards a kind of rebirth based on its classical past and glorious history, immediately acquired a symbolic significance. Two months after it was found, Julius II bought it for his courtyard of statues, where it was seen by many artists. Pliny himself had preferred it to any other sculpture, and Michelangelo thought it to be the finest sculpture ever created. Bernini considered it the greatest achievement of classical art. Many small bronze copies of the Laocoön group and other sculptures in the Cortile ended up in the *studioli* of princes and scholars, as well as in artists' workshops. Small bronzes on classical themes were, however, popular even before the Cortile was created.

Belvedere torso
First century BC
Marble, height: 195 cm
Rome, Vatican Museums

213

Pier Jacopo Alari Bonacolsi, called Antico
Apollo Belvedere, late 15th century
Bronze, partially gilded, height: 45.5 cm
Frankfurt am Main, Städtische Galerie Liebieghaus

The Apollo Belvedere

Before the Laocoön group was found, the later *Apollo Belvedere* (p. 213) was considered to be the most famous classical sculpture. Owing to the relatively good condition it had been preserved in, together with Apollo's powerful and muscular frame, it took on the character of an idealized view of antiquity.

It was discovered on a piece of land belonging to Cardinal Giuliano della Rovere on the old road to Mariano; at first the statue was placed in the garden of the Cardinal's residence near SS. Apostoli, but between 1503 and 1509 it was moved to the Cortile delle Statue. The statue became so famous that Pier Jacopo Alari Bonacolsi (c. 1460?–1528), who specialized in classical antiquity and was aptly nicknamed "Antico", produced many bronze reductions of the statue. Antico invented the process of indirect casting to preserve his original moulds (cf. pp. 216–7).

Antico was born in Mantua and probably first worked in Bozzolo as a goldsmith and sculptor; he is first mentioned in 1487 in a sort of letter of recommendation to the court of the Gonzagas in Mantua. He was introduced as "lo Antixi", which suggests that he was already well-known for his small bronze copies of classical sculptures. The letter asked that he should be given work at the Mantuan court, and he was finally rewarded with the position of *familiaris*, a sort of courtier to the family, which gave him the right to life at the court, together with accommodation and other privileges. Four years later, in 1501, he rose up the hierarchy to the position of *cameriere,* or valet, which raised his income as well as bringing him into closer contact with the Prince, though it also meant that he owed a personal debt of allegiance to his sponsors.

It is probably in the same year that he first cast a bronze copy of *Apollo Belvedere* reduced to the size of a statuette. He had probably been working on the model since 1498, and three copies of the statuette have survived. They are now in the Galleria G. Franchetti alla Cà d'Oro in Venice, in the former collection of O. Beit in the Fitzwilliam Museum in Cambridge, and in the Städtische Galerie Liebieghaus's museum of classical sculpture in Frankfurt am Main (left). There are stylistic reasons for believing that the statuette in Frankfurt is the oldest of the three. The strap which holds the quiver up was signed "ANT" to show that it had been produced by the Mantuan court artist himself, and, of the three, the Frankfurt statuette keeps most closely to its classical model. Antico altered the original statue's position, however, by positioning the lower part of the right arm, which had broken off the original, closer to the body, and reducing the size of the step Apollo is taking. This creates a more peaceful appearance which, together with the more slender shape of his limbs, brings the statuette into lines with Renaissance ideals, which governed how classical sculptures were viewed. Further evidence of the early date and aesthetic quality of Antico's Frankfurt bronze reduction of Apollo is provided by his eyes, which are inlaid, and the gilding which covers his hair, sandals, cloak and quiver.

Antonio del Pollaiuolo
Hercules and Antaeus, c. 1470
Bronze, height: 45 cm
Florence, Museo Nazionale del Bargello

Hercules and Antaeus

Antico was not the only sculptor who created statuette-sized copies of *Apollo Belvedere*. A letter which he wrote in 1519 to Isabella d'Este, who was probably the first female Renaissance art collector, highlights the growing market for small-scale sculptures, which he himself had created with his new technique for casting bronze. He offered her copies of statuettes which he had produced for Bishop Ludovico Gonzaga. There were eight statuettes in the series, and he particularly recommended *Hercules and Antaeus* to the Marquise of Mantua, telling her that it was the most beautiful example of classical sculpture that he had ever seen. Isabella subsequently bought this very small bronze, and there is another copy of it in the Kunsthistorisches Museum in Vienna.

The scene that is portrayed is one of the Deeds of Hercules. When he was returning from the gardens of the Hesperides on the Atlantic coast of Africa, the hero travelled through Libya, which was ruled by the giant Antaeus, son of Poseidon and Gaia, the gods of the ocean and earth. He refused to let foreigners travel through the country unless they were prepared to fight with him. What they did not know, however, was that Antaeus drew his strength in battle from contact with his mother earth. Hercules quickly realized this and beat Antaeus by lifting him off the ground and crushing him to death. The allegorical message of this battle was that earthly desires could be conquered by the intellect.

One of the earliest Renaissance versions of this story, which was simultaneously one of the first small bronzes to use a mythological theme, was the *Hercules and Antaeus* (p. 215) produced by Antonio del Pollaioulo, which is usually dated c. 1470. He shows a considerable knowledge of anatomy in his daring portrayal of the two figures engaged in this deadly battle. Hercules' face shows that he is concentrating on winning the battle, while that of Antaeus shows the dismay he feels as he realizes that he is about to be beaten. The detail of both faces and bodies has a lot in common with large-scale sculptures. The figures are supported by the remarkably firm lionskin that Hercules is wearing. This is a convention that was used for figures made of marble, which were structurally more fragile, but is clearly completely unnecessary in a small bronze, as is demonstrated by Francesco da Sant'Agata's *Hercules and Antaeus*, which he produced during the first quarter of the 16th century, and which is now in the National Gallery of Art in Washington.

Small bronzes were not just a way of copying classical sculptures. Many sculptors used them as a way of tackling intellectual themes such as Nature, as is shown by the goat-like figures which populate both classical landscapes and collections of bronzes. Direct casts of natural subjects such as small animals, and the large sub-group of oil lamps, are further interesting aspects of this genre.

Dieter Blume
On the Techniques of Bronze Casting in the Renaissance[1]

Fig. 1 Demonstration model of bronze casting according to the technique of Antico, original model in wax

Fig. 2 Piece moulds made of plaster for the reproduction of the original model

Even though the autonomous bronze miniature was first rediscovered as a genre in the Renaissance, bronze casting had nevertheless been practised on a large scale throughout the whole of the Middle Ages. Its basic technique is, in principle, very simple. A freely moulded wax model is coated with a mixture of plaster and sand, or clay, channels being added for pouring in the metal and to permit air to escape. When this mould is fired, the wax melts out and the liquid metal is cast in the negative mould created in this manner. Since the mould must be smashed after cooling, only one cast is possible. If the casting proves unsuccessful, the mould is lost. This is therefore called the waste mould method.

In order to save metal and, more importantly, to prevent the cracks and flaws which can occur on the cooling of solid metal castings, it is better to make bronzes using the hollow casting technique. This method usually entails moulding the wax model over a pre-pared clay core.

On removal from the mould, the bronze has a very rough surface. As a result, it depends on technical ability and experience as to how clearly details, such as hair, can already be perceived in the unfinished casting. After casting, a certain amount of what is known as cold work is usually necessary. This includes smoothing the surface and working out the lines and details by means of en-graving. Examples of unfinished castings which have not been engraved are also extant, however.

The desire to retain the model, once finished, in order to be able to make more castings of it, led to a considerably more complicated procedure. Records show that it was used for the first time by Pier Jacopo Alari Bonacolsi, called Antico, who was a master of this technique from the 1580s onwards. The traces of work which have been retained on the inside of the statuettes can be observed on X-ray photographs of his bronzes, so that the individual phases of work of this artist can be accurately reconstructed.[2]

He probably moulded the original wax model on a wire framework (Fig. 1). From this design a negative mould was then made, which, due to the overlaps occurring at the arms and the legs, could only have been obtained from piece moulds made of plaster (Fig. 2). Using these plaster moulds, any number of models for the casting could

then be produced. To this end, Antico proceeded as follows. First, he put the piece moulds together in sections in such a way that the individual limbs, the torso and the head remained separate. Into the moistened, hollow moulds of these parts of the body he then poured molten wax, which immediately solid-ified on the cold mould. After a few moments, he turned the mould around again; the wax which had not yet solidified flowed out, leaving a layer of wax one millimetre thick (Fig. 3). He subsequently filled the remaining hollow space with a fluid mass of plaster and sand, which, upon solidification, formed the core of the bronze (Figs. 3,4). It was only after this plaster mass had dried that the piece moulds were removed, revealing the individual pieces of the figure moulded in wax (Figs. 3,5,6). They were then put together, and it was possible to vary the inclination of the arm or head or touch up details while doing so (Fig. 7).

The casting and air channels, which are also made of wax, must sub-sequently be attached to the casting model created in this manner. In add-ition to this, iron nails are driven into the core of plaster and sand, which hold it in the original position later, after the wax has been melted out (Fig. 8). Only then can a model be covered with the casing, which, in the Renaissance, pre-sumably also consisted of plaster and sand. It was probably built up carefully in layers, starting with a relatively liquid mixture in order to capture the details more precisely. This casing is fired after hardening, whereby the wax flows out through the prepared channels (Fig. 9 shows a casing sawn through the middle after the wax has been melted out). Only now can the molten metal be poured in, whereby the liquid bronze rises from the bottom to the top, slowly forcing out the air as it does so. The figure is standing on its head during this process. After being freed from the mould, the casting still requires a considerable amount of work. The channels and the iron pins must be removed, together with the ridges which are formed by the intrusion of the hot metal into the cracks and flaws in the mould (Figs. 10,11).

Antico's bronzes are distinguished by the intensive cold work, which smooths the surfaces to such an extent that they reflect the light. This is something which sets him considerably apart from his contemporaries. It took another 70 years before Giambologna in Florence aspired

Fig. 3 Production of the plaster model for the left leg in sections

Fig. 4 The negative mould for the individual parts of the figure after being put together and filled

Fig. 5 The head modelled in wax, with the accompanying negative moulds made of plaster

Fig. 6 The individual pieces of the model before being put together

Fig. 7 The finished model

Fig. 8 The model with the channels for pouring in the bronze and allowing air to escape

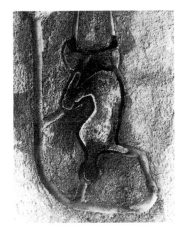

Fig. 9 The casing after the wax has been melted out, sawn through the middle

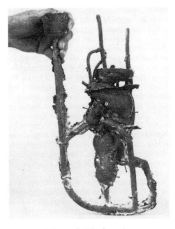

Fig. 10 The unfinished casting

Fig. 11 The bronze after completion of the first phase of cold work

to comparable surface effects, in the second half of the 16th century. In contrast to this, the Paduan and Florentine bronzes from the time around 1500 display structured surfaces which are achieved by means of careful working with hammers or embossing tools. In the best works of the Paduan sculptors Severo da Ravenna and Andrea Riccio, almost all the details of the wax model have been retained in the castings, which meant that very little cold work was required. The soft modelling in wax which was transferred to the metal conveys an extremely lifelike impression.

The reproduction of the model by means of piece moulds was also practised by Severo da Ravenna in Padua from the turn of the century onwards. He produced his bronzes in large numbers,[3] and, since most of the casting and finishing was done by assistants, there were considerable variations in the quality of the individual pieces. Miniature bronzes continued to be produced from the models made by the artist after his departure from Padua (1509) and even after his death. In comparison to the excellent quality of Severo's own works, however, the quality of these left much to be desired.

Antico, on the other hand, appeared to have produced only small numbers of his statuettes, and probably also supervised the finishing of the later castings, even though he did not actually do any finishing himself. There are recastings of his works in existence, however, whose surface treatment is so coarse that they were presumably executed after his death.

Andrea Riccio employed yet another technique in order to be able to re-use his designs. He modelled a clay core, which he shaped to such a degree as to define the attitude of the figure. This core could be cast relatively easily, and he modelled the figure in wax each time afresh on the clay core reproduced in this manner.[4] This also explains why the different versions of his bronzes always displayed a slight variation. Since he ran a large workshop and people continued to work from his models for a long time, stark discrepancies in the quality of the pieces associated with him can be perceived, similar to that observed for Severo's designs.

The castings taken from natural objects which were common in Padua at the time were based on a relatively simple procedure. The naturally found object, a lizard or a shell, was brought into the desired shape and painted with a relatively liquid clay mass so as to capture even fine details, then dried and fired at a high temperature. The animal or shell became charred and the ashes were flushed out with the molten bronze. Since models were available in nature in great numbers, an unsuccessful casting did not constitute an irretrievable loss.

[1] This article is a shortened version of one dealing with the same theme in the exhibition catalogue: *Natur und Antike in der Renaissance* (Nature and Classical Antiquity in the Renaissance), Exhibition in the Liebieghaus - Museum alter Plastik, Frankfurt am Main, 5 December 1985 to 2 March 1986, pp. 18 ff..

[2] R.E. Stone, 'Antico and the Development of Bronze Casting in Italy at the End of the Quattrocento'. In: *The Metropolitan Museum of Art Journal*, 16, 1982, pp. 94 ff.. Stone succeeded in elucidating numerous technical details with the help of X-ray analyses. He gives an excellent overview of the casting techniques of the Renaissance artists. The figures on this double page illustrating the procedure followed by Antico have been made using a demonstration model prepared by Lothar Brügel which was commissioned by the Liebieghaus.

[3] R.E. Stone, loc. cit., pp. 110 ff..

[4] R.E. Stone, ibid, pp. 111 ff..

Michelangelo
Battle, c. 1490–92
Marble, height: 80.5 cm, breadth: 88 cm
Florence, Casa Buonarroti

Michelangelo
Madonna of the Stairs, c. 1490
Marble, height: 55.5 cm, breadth: 40 cm
Florence, Casa Buonarroti

Michelangelo Buonarroti

Michelangelo Buonarroti (1475–1564) called himself Michelangiolo, and was the most remarkable artist of his age. He was an architect, painter and poet, though his main talent lay in sculpture. He started work at the workshop of the artist Domenico Ghirlandaio at the age of thirteen, and left after a year to go to Lorenzo de Medici's art school. The bronze sculptor Bertoldo di Giovanni (c. 1440–1491) became his mentor here, and probably acquainted him with classical sculptures. The story goes that Lorenzo the Magnificent's (p. 256) attention was drawn to him when he produced a faun's head - though the existence of the piece has not been proved; at any rate, Michelangelo lived in close contact with the Medici family in their Florence palace from 1490 to 1492.

The earliest extant work by Michelangelo, the small marble relief in the Casa Buonarroti in Florence, was created during this time, c. 1490, and is known as the *Madonna of the Stairs* (top right). Michelangelo was just fifteen years old, and he completed the popular Quattrocento scene of Madonna and Child using Donatello's technique of *rilievo schiacciato*; his Madonna is less smooth in appearance than Donatello's *Pazzi Madonna* (p. 190), but is carved in finer detail. Donatello's Madonna, as well as other models, presented the intimacy of the mother-and-child relationship by means of half-length portraits. Michelangelo, in contrast, showed the full length of the Madonna in profile sitting in the foreground, and this adds to the monumental nature of the work. It is unusual that the child, who is held by his mother on her lap, is turning away from us. He has fallen asleep at his mother's breast, and his rather

muscular right arm is hanging loosely at his side. His posture accords with the thoughtful appearance of his mother; she appears to have had a premonition of the fate awaiting her child. While sculptures on this theme by Michelangelo's predecessors concentrated on the relationship between mother and child, Michelangelo adds further impact to his scene by including children playing on the steps.

A short time later, c. 1490–92, Michelangelo produced the *Battle* relief (top left), his second piece and also his first unfinished one. It made considerable use of classical models, and within a very small area depicted a battle between humans and centaurs which was described in classical literature. Michelangelo sculpted entirely naked figures and omitted the spatial backdrop that was customary in the Quattrocento. The *nonfinito* (unfinished) condition of the work was not a matter of choice but was dictated by the circumstances of his clients. It appears that this young sculptor was already seeking the figures that he believed had a prior existence in the stone.

The shady Bacchus

A reasonable general understanding of art was becoming more widespread in urban centres towards the end of the Quattrocento, and this meant that collecting became even more popular. It was not just small bronzes but all sorts of rediscovered classical artefacts and contemporary *all'antica* sculptures that were avidly collected. And wherever there was trade there was also deception. Michelangelo produced a study of a sleeping Cupid in a classical style which was

Marten van Heemskerck
The gardens of Casa Galli, with Michelangelo's Bacchus
Berlin, Staatliche Museen zu Berlin–Preußischer Kulturbesitz
Kupferstichkabinett

Michelangelo
Bacchus, 1496–97
Marble, height (without the base): 184 cm
Florence, Museo Nazionale del Bargello

brought to Rome by a clever art dealer. He buried the figure for a while and then sold it to Cardinal Raffaello Riario as a genuine antique. When the latter discovered the fraud, he succeeded in getting his money back. The figure passed into the collection of Isabella d'Este in 1502, and eventually disappeared.

Michelangelo came to Rome on 25 June 1496, where the same Cardinal showed him around his collection of antiques and commissioned him to produce a figure of Bacchus (right). Michelangelo had finished it within a year, but Riario was not entirely satisfied with the result, meaning that he did not want to accept the figure, let alone pay for it. It eventually became part of the collection of the banker and humanist Jacopo Galli.

The figure shows the young God of Wine raising his cup with his right hand and looking at it drunkenly. His weight is on his left leg, though his right is touching the ground, and he looks as if he will fall over the moment he tries to walk. His left hand, which is hanging next to his thigh, is holding a piece of fur and a large bunch of grapes, which a young satyr behind him is eating. He is standing on a rocky plinth and is a three-dimensional life-size sculpture, and the *all'antica* treatment of a classical theme shows that it was meant to be viewed as a classical sculpture. The Dutchman Marten van Heemskerck (1498–1574) saw it in the garden of the Casa Galli between 1532 and 1535, amongst a group of other classical sculptures, and its appearance of age was increased because its right hand was missing. It has not been explained why Riario refused to pay for the statue, however, or indeed whether it was deliberately commissioned as a classical piece for fraudulent purposes.

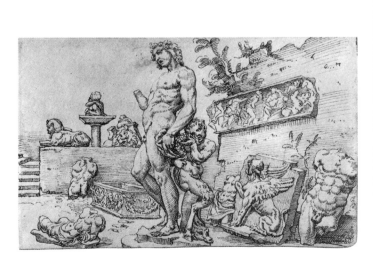

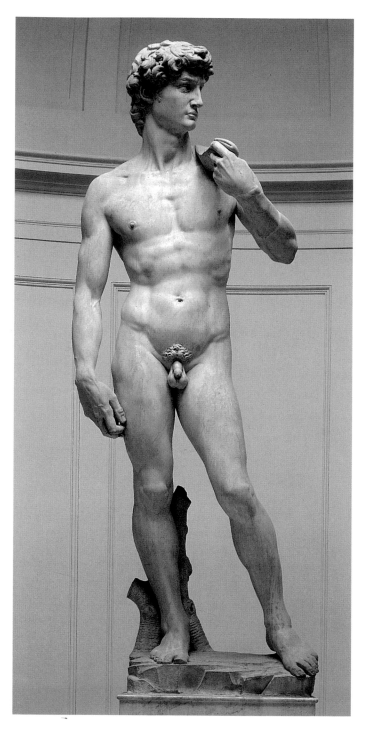

Michelangelo
David, 1501–04
Marble, height (with base): 434 cm
Florence, Galleria dell'Accademia

The colossal statue of David

David (left) was created between 1501 and 1504, and was one of Michelangelo's greatest sculptural achievements. It was the start of a new era of colossal statues in the Cinquecento. In addition, it joined Donatello's David, and Judith and Holofernes, as political symbols of Florence.

There are two reasons for the great size – over four metres – and lack of depth of the figure. First of all, the figure was meant to top the Cathedral's single unoccupied pier buttress, hence its colossal size. Secondly, Agostino di Duccio had made an earlier unsuccessful attempt to work at the piece of marble intended for the task. Much as Michelangelo may have wanted to turn the used stone into a masterpiece, he does not appear to have kept to the original specifications for the figure. Rather, he used his figure of David to create a new view of the human virtues as deriving from the relationship of the human spirit, personal courage and young athletic bodies. The biblical shepherd boy had turned into a heroic Renaissance man.

Elements such as the gigantic size of the figure, which was in keeping with classical colossal statues, its enlarged head and large hands were in keeping with the original contract; but the very masculine nudity of the figure argued against its use on an ecclesiastical site. A commission which included such famous artists as Botticelli and Leonardo was set up to decide what should happen to *David* once it was finished, and where it should be sited. After lengthy discussions which included aesthetic considerations, the decision was made to erect the statue in front of the Palazzo Vecchio, on the very site occupied by Donatello's *Judith and Holofernes*.

There were considerable problems concerning transport to be overcome before it was possible to move the figure there on 5 June 1504, and the process took five days. The statue was stoned, possibly because the citizens were offended by its nudity, and the private parts were covered with gilded leaves by 1545 at the latest. After the figure was brought within the Academy in 1873, a copy was placed on its original site.

The tomb of Julius II in Rome

Michelangelo was summoned from Florence to Rome by Pope Julius II, and was commissioned to produce a papal tomb (p. 222). He presented his first designs in March 1505, for a monumental free-standing tomb based on the mausoleums of classical rulers. The designs included a very complicated iconography with over forty sculptures and a series of bronze reliefs, all in praise of the life of Julius II, to be combined harmoniously with the architecture as a whole. Michelangelo was to work on the project for the next forty years. Constant obstacles and reductions in the scale of the commission caused by his papal client led him to describe it as the "tragedy of the tomb", and the tragedy of the obstruction of his

Michelangelo
David, 1501–04
Details
Florence, Galleria dell'Accademia

Michelangelo
Moses, c. 1513–16
Marble, height: 235 cm
Rome, San Pietro in Vincoli

Michelangelo
Tomb of Pope Julius II, completed 1542–45
Marble
Rome, San Pietro in Vincoli

Michelangelo
Victory, c. 1520–25
Marble, height: 261 cm
Florence, Palazzo Vecchio

Michelangelo
Dying Slave, c. 1513–16
Marble, height: 229 cm
Paris, Musée du Louvre

own life's work must surely have also been in his mind. Michelangelo started work with great enthusiasm. He spent the second half of 1505 in Carrara, acquiring the enormous amounts of marble that would be needed. But at the beginning of 1506 the Pope altered his plans, possibly influenced to do so by the architect Donato Bramante, and made the building of the new St. Peter's his priority. Michelangelo felt betrayed, and as the Pope neither made further funds available nor granted him an audience, he fled angrily to Florence. However, a chance meeting with Julius II in Bologna in 1507 led to the commission of a bronze statue of the Pope, and Michelangelo finally returned to Rome in 1508, at the Pope's urgent request, to paint the Sistine Chapel. Despite the size of this new task, characteristic of the Pope's ambitious plans, Michelangelo started work on his tomb again.

Work on the project did not resume properly until the Pope died at the end of February 1513 and it was necessary to carry out the terms of his will. A new contract was drawn up to mark the second phase of the work, and this time the commission was for a tomb that would be connected to the wall at one side. By 1516 Michelangelo had produced the Louvre *Slaves* (right) and Moses (p. 222). Just a year later, however, the plans were altered yet again and the scope of the tomb was reduced by half. It is uncertain whether the statue of *Victory* (right) was produced for the tomb. At the same time, Michelangelo had started work for Pope Leo X on plans for the façade of San Lorenzo in Florence. Further delay to his work on the Tomb of Pope Julius was occasioned by his work on tombs for the Medici family (pp. 224 and 225). This meant that Julius' successor was not impressed when he finally did produce new plans for the tomb. Work on the tomb was interrupted a short while later, when political events forced the Medicis to leave Florence in 1527. Yet another new design was produced in 1532; this was not carried out either, because Michelangelo had been commissioned by the Pope to carry out other work, such as the fresco of the *Last Judgement*, which he completed during the papacy of Paul III in 1541. Finally, a contract was signed in 1542 for a plan which included none of the sculptures which had been produced or planned previously apart from the figure of the sitting *Moses*. Instead of the *Slaves*, figures were to be included representing the *vita activa* and *vita contemplativa*, which Dante had personified as the biblical sisters *Leah* and *Rachel*.

The tomb was finally built in San Pietro in Vincoli in 1545, using the statue of *Moses* as the central figure. Older interpretations related Moses' appearance of barely concealed excitement to the situation immediately before the Tablets of the Law were broken, but a more recent suggestion is that Michelangelo had portrayed Moses at the moment when God told him that he would not see the Promised Land. This prophecy thwarted Moses' aim in life, and in that respect it has a similarity with the situation of Julius II, who had not succeeded in unifying Italy as a Church state. Even

Michelangelo had been hindered by the decades-long disaster from carrying out what he himself considered to be his life's work. As there was no use for the two *Slaves* on the final tomb, Michelangelo gave them to a former patron, and they are now in the Louvre.

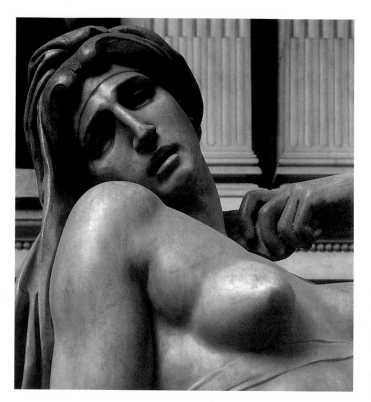

BOTTOM, AND DETAIL LEFT:
Michelangelo
Tomb of Lorenzo de' Medici, 1521–34
Marble, height (Lorenzo): 178 cm
Detail: Aurora
Florence, San Lorenzo, Medici Chapel

OPPOSITE:
Michelangelo
Tomb of Giuliano de' Medici,
1521–34
Marble, height (Giuliano): 178 cm
Florence, San Lorenzo, Medici
Chapel

The Medici tombs in Florence

Like his first plans for the Tomb of Pope Julius in Rome, Michelangelo at first thought of producing the Medici tombs in Florence, which he worked on from 1520 to 1534, as free-standing monuments in the New Sacristy which had been specially built in the north choir of San Lorenzo. The work was commissioned due to the early death of the designated Duke of Urbino, Lorenzo de' Medici (1492–1519). He was to be buried next to his uncle Giuliano (1478–1516), the Duke of Nemours. The death of these two men had a tremendous impact on the genealogy of the Medici family, as it meant that all the legitimate male heirs of Cosimo the elder (1389–1464) were now dead. For this reason, the decision was also taken to erect the tombs of Lorenzo the Magnificent (1449–92) and his brother Giuliano (1453–78) in the New Sacristy.

Michelangelo's original plan was for the four tombs to be placed at the side of the monument, an idea similar to his early plans for the Tomb of Pope Julius, which would have meant the actual tombs forming a sort of mausoleum and the sculptures taking on the iconographical role of façade ornamentation. However, the tombs were moved from the outer walls of the free-standing monument to the inner walls of the Medici Chapel, meaning that the Sacristy itself was now a mausoleum. A series of designs in the British Museum in London suggest that the decision to change to wall tombs was a gradual one, as double tombs on opposite sides of the chapel were also considered. The decision to use single tombs meant that all the wall space was taken up by the tombs.

The two tombs (left and p. 225) are positioned almost symmetrically, directly opposite each other. The walls above the bases are divided into three niches, which in turn are divided horizontally by an entablature and support segmental arches. The sarcophagi and allegorical figures are standing in front of the bases, and the Dukes themselves, rather idealized figures dressed in Roman armour, are sitting in the central niches above. The attributes of the allegorical figure on the tomb of Giuliano, which has a masculine body and female breasts, prove her to be a personification of Night. Her pose is derived from an ancient sarcophagus featuring Leda, which has since been lost. Her counterpart, who is turning away from us, is Day, a figure which draws heavily on the famous classical *Torso Belvedere*. Opposite these rather restrained figures on Giuliano's tomb are Dawn (female) and Dusk (male) on Lorenzo's tomb; they are resting in relaxed poses that dispel all sense of the weight of the material they are made of. The figure of Dawn even seems to anticipate the manner in which Baroque architectural sculpture relates to its space. The relationship of the two tombs across the chapel is fired not so much by the fact that they are placed opposite each other, but that both Dukes are looking towards, and meditating on, the Madonna and Child with saints on the entrance wall.

Michelangelo
Pietà, 1497–99
Marble, height: 174 cm
Rome, St. Peter's

Michelangelo
Pietà, c. 1547–55
Marble, height: 226 cm
Florence, Museo dell'Opera del Duomo

The Pietà sculptures

Michelangelo was just twenty-three years old when he signed the contract to produce a Pietà for the French Cardinal Jean Bilhères da Lagraulas (top). This makes it one of his early works. According to the contract, which still exists, Michelangelo was supposed to sculpt a Pietà that showed "a dressed Virgin Mary holding the dead Christ in her arms, both figures to be the size of normal people". It was to be finished within a year at a cost of 450 gold ducats. Michelangelo's chief client, Jacopo Galli, added: "that it will be the most beautiful marble sculpture now in Rome, and no other master nowadays would be able to do it better." There were many German pietàs north of the Alps, and it was a theme that French sculptors also occasionally depicted. But there was no precedent for the theme in contemporary Italian sculpture. This makes the artistic power with which Michelangelo contrived to unite his two figures in one composition all the more remarkable. The body of the dead Christ, lying almost horizontally across Mary's lap, is echoed by the wide folds of the cloak. The folds of cloth are both a framework and a support for the group. Michelangelo countered reproaches that he had made Mary an impossibly young mother by saying that this was the only effective way of displaying the virginity and eternal purity of the Mother of God. The group was frequently copied and served as a model for many sculptors; it was first erected in Santa Petronella, south of Old St. Peter's, probably because that was where the client was buried, and later, before 1519, it was moved to St. Peter's. It was carefully restored after being severely damaged by an art vandal in 1972.

The Florence Cathedral Pietà

Michelangelo's early pietà in St. Peter's was joined by two later reworkings of the same theme. One is now in the Museo dell'Opera del Duomo in Florence (p. 226, right). It was started in about 1547, and Michelangelo appears for a variety of reasons to have abandoned the work unfinished, around 1555. Stories abounded in art circles that he had destroyed his work in a fit of rage, though these should not be taken at face value. Christ's missing left leg later turned up as part of Daniele da Volterra's estate. It was not the first time that the tension between commissions and the artist's own demands had led him to leave statues unfinished. There was the notion that the very idea portrayed by a sculpture was in itself valuable, even if the statue itself was not completed. Art historians have coined the term *nonfinito* to cover this. The Duomo *Pietà* should be viewed as a *nonfinito* sculpture, because the idea of creating such a varied group of four figures from a single block of marble was far beyond anything that had been attempted previously, including the *Laocoön* group. Even later sculptors, working to Michelangelo's plans, were not able to complete the group. Michelangelo carved the face of Nicodemus in his own image, which suggests that he intended the group for his own tomb.

The Rondanini Pietà

Tradition has it that Michelangelo worked on a pietà just a few days before his death. This unfinished group (right) was kept in the Palazzo Rondanini until 1920; since 1952 it has been in the Castello Sforzesco in Milan. Mary is standing on a tall rocky base and is holding the body of Christ; this is the first time that Michelangelo, or any Italian sculptor, had presented Christ upright and in full length. Michelangelo started the work in 1552 or 1553 and returned to it later, and the stone shows traces of an earlier version. The small amount of stone that was left was not enough to produce the traditional satisfying type of pietà. The solution was to depict the two figures upright and united, as in a resurrection, and this aspect communicates some of the religious beliefs of Michelangelo's later years.

Sculptors during the age of Michelangelo and the Late Renaissance

Tullio Lombardo

We are not sure exactly when Tullio (c. 1455–1532) and his brother Antonio Lombardo (c. 1458–c.1516) were born, but they grew up in their father Pietro's Venetian workshop to become famous sculptors. Tullio's fame was to prove longer-lasting than his brother's. Pomponius Gauricus praised him in 1504 as the greatest sculptor of all times who was resurrecting classical antiquity in his works. Examples of his works are such Venetian monuments as that of Doge Andrea Vendramin (the figure of *Adam* in the Metropolitan Museum of Art in New York was originally part of this tomb), the unusually large altar relief showing the Coronation of Mary in San Giovanni Crisostomo in Venice, and such reliefs as the *Miracle of the Miser's Heart* and the *Miracle of the Repentant Youth* in the Santo in Padua.

The signed *Double Portrait* (top) in the Museum Ca' d'Oro in Venice was carved in high relief between 1490 and 1510. It shows a young couple; the style of the portrait seems to have been inspired by double portraits on classical monuments rather than by double portraits in northern European painting, as the latter did not favour classical expressions. The *all'antica* style is evident both in the shape of the bust and in the woman's nakedness, and places this couple in the realms of classical mythology. They have been identified as Bacchus and Ariadne, and there is a comparable work of Tullio's in Vienna's Kunsthistorisches Museum. On the other hand, a different interpretation would be that these are contemporary portraits disguised as classical ones. The double portrait in Venice is considered to be a self-portrait of Tullio with his wife. An entirely satisfactory explanation of the double portrait has yet to be given.

Jacopo Sansovino

The sculptor was born Jacopo d'Antonio Tatti (1468–1570) in Florence, and adopted the surname of his master Andrea Sansovino when he was apprenticed to him. The early models that he submitted in competition for large contracts were unsuccessful. He left for Rome in 1506 or 1507, and was one of four sculptors asked by Bramante to produce a wax copy of the *Laocoön*. Vasari reports that his version was approved by Raphael and a bronze cast of it was commissioned by Cardinal Domenico Grimani. The work has since been lost. Vasari continues that Sansovino produced a large number of wax models for Pietro Perugino, who lived in the same district of Rome.

Vasari was particularly impressed by a *Deposition* (p. 229) which was later acquired by Giovanni Gaddi and is now in the Victoria and Albert Museum in London. There are many figures in this lively crucifixion scene, which for the first time includes the deposition of the two thieves. There is a particular pathos in the contrast between the lifeless bodies of the crucified and their agitated helpers. Four of them are lowering the body of Christ from the cross, and two others are carrying the good thief away to the right. On the left, Mary Magdalene, John and another woman have come to the aid of Mary, who has fainted. At the bottom, isolated from the three groups around him, the body of the bad thief is hanging from the ladder. While Sansovino made use of classical models for his execution of individual figures, he was also creating a new type of deposition which influenced later artists.

Sansovino left for Florence in 1511, and produced a number of sculptures there that considerably raised his reputation, bevor returning to Rome between 1518 and 1527. From Rome he went to Venice, where he first worked as an architect; later he returned to sculptures in his workshop, and became the outstanding artist in Venice. It was during this time that he produced the reliefs and figures for the Loggetta del Campanile, which he had built between 1537 and 1540.

Jacopo Sansovino
Deposition, c. 1508–10
Wax, cloth and wood with gilding
Height (frame): 87.8 cm, breadth: 89.5 cm
London, Victoria and Albert Museum

Baccio Bandinelli
Hercules and Cacus, 1525–34
Marble, height about 496 cm
Florence, Piazza della Signoria

Baccio Bandinelli (1493–1560)

He was the son of the Florentine goldsmith Michelangelo Brandini and received his early training in his father's workshop. The latter's support and connections were especially useful to him in his relations with the Medicis, who were his patrons throughout his life. Bandinelli showed talent as a painter at an early age, but did not gain recognition as a painter. In addition, contemporaries of his such as Vasari and Cellini described him as a difficult person, given to jealousy, resentfulness and arrogance where other people's works were concerned. According to Vasari, hatred of his rival Michelangelo led him to cut up the preliminary cartoon drawing of the *Battle of Cascina* that was exhibited in the town hall. When Italy was negotiating for peace with the French king Francis I in 1515, the latter demanded that he be given the *Laocoön* group in the Belvedere. Leo X was able to change his mind by promising him a copy. The Pope gave the commission to Bandinelli, who had claimed that his copy would be better than the classical original. The work was finished in 1525 (p. 231, top), but was never delivered to the French court. It is now in the Uffizi in Florence. Bandinelli's copy reconstructed the right arm of the father, which was still missing at that time, as well as an arm and leg belonging to his sons. However, he did not give Laocoön as powerful an upper body as in the original. The muscles appear rather superficial and have been slurred to a large extent, and there is a network of fine surface blood vessels right across his body. Laocoön's outstretched right arm and the overdone look of pain on his face contribute to the air of pathos about the group which led contemporaries to consider the tragic death of the Trojan priest a reflection of what was happening to Rome at the time. That this interpretation is an accurate reflection of the tastes of the age is proven by the addition to the original classical Laocoön which was carried out by Michelangelo's pupil Giovanni Angelo Montorsoli at the order of Clement VII. He gave the father an arm that was stretched even higher than Bandinelli's, and added even further to the deadly drama of the battle. This was the form in which the art world knew *Laocoön* until 1957, when the missing original piece of the arm, which had been found in 1904, was reattached. This arm contrasts with the Renaissance versions, for it is bent at a much sharper angle; it has largely restored the classical appearance of the sculpture.

The Florentine Signoria decided in 1508 to commission Michelangelo to carve a colossal statue as a pendant to his *David*. The prolonged history of this project was closely connected to the changing political fortunes of the time. Finally, Bandinelli was commissioned to produce a Hercules beating Cacus (left). But even the transportation of the block of marble from Carrara to Florence led to stories making fun of Bandinelli's sculptural talents. When the marble block fell off the transport into the River Arno not far from Florence, it was said that the stone had thrown itself into the river in desperation when it heard that it was to be mutilated by Bandinelli.

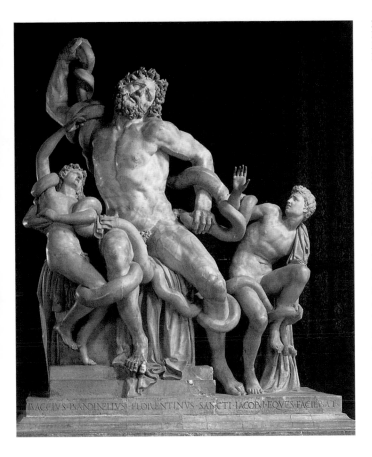

Baccio Bandinelli
Laocoön, copy of the Belvedere group
Marble
Florence, Galleria degli Uffizi

BELOW:
Giovanni Angiolo Montorsoli
Drunken satyr, c. 1532/3
Marble, height: 65 cm, breadth: 135 cm
St. Louis, The St. Louis Art Museum

The completed work suffered a similar fate, after it was finally erected on 1 May 1534 on the intervention of the Pope. Cellini remembered "more than a thousand sonnets on the disgrace of this bad piece of work" being attached to the figure. Vasari reports that the ridicule went so far that Duke Alessandro even had some of the lampooners arrested. After all, the triumph of Hercules over the son of Vulcan was an important part of Florentine political emblematics.

Bandinelli had produced a wax model in 1525, immediately after being given the commission by Pope Clement VII, and this has now been identified as the wax bozzetto in Berlin's collection of sculptures (bottom left). The block of marble was not the right shape for this composition, however, so he was given permission by the Pope to produce another model. Other artists considered this model to lack the power and vitality of the first one, and the final sculpture does indeed lack any sense of movement and animation. Bandinelli's Hercules is subjecting his opponent to a symbolical rather than physical beating. Though he is standing over the defeated Cacus, he is gazing into the distance and is quite removed from what is happening. The events seem to have been reduced to a mere political statement.

Baccio Bandinelli
Hercules and Cacus
Wax model
Berlin, Staatliche Museen zu Berlin –
Preußischer Kulturbesitz

Sculptors during the Counter-Reformation and the dawn of Mannerism

Bartolomeo Ammanati

Ammanati (1511–1592) came from Settignano, near Florence, and studied under Bandinelli and Jacopo Sansovino in Venice. He worked as an assistant to the Florentine sculptor Montorsoli on the Sannazaro monument in Naples. Later, he worked with Sansovino on the Libreria di San Marco in Venice. After working in Padua – where he produced a colossal figure of *Hercules* – and Vicenza, he returned to Rome towards the end of 1548 and dedicated himself to a study of classical antiquity; he got to know Michelangelo and Vasari, and married the poetess Laura Battiferri in 1550. Five years later he returned to Florence, and worked on a fountain and some bronzes. In 1560 he won the contract for the planned *Fountain of Neptune* (p. 234) on the Piazza della Signoria. Cellini and Bandinelli also took part in the project, though the latter died in February 1560 bevor starting carving the central figure on the fountain out of the block of marble he had been given. He had already planned a statue of Neptune, however, and Ammanati started work on it in 1561. The immediate model for this type of fountain with a colossal central figure was the *Fountain of Neptune* which had been made in 1557 by Montorsoli in Messina, and which was the earliest of its kind in Italy. Ammanati's gigantic *Hercules* in Padua and *Neptune* in Florence were the largest colossal statues produced in the Cinquecento. Soon after completing the Florentine fountain, in 1575, he experienced a religious crisis prompted by the Counter-Reformation which led him to damn all his earlier works, including the Fountain of Neptune, because of all the naked figures. He left all his property to the Jesuits.

Benvenuto Cellini

Benvenuto (1500–1571) was born in Florence, the son of the engineer and craftsman Giovanni Cellini. At the age of thirteen he became an apprentice goldsmith working for Michelangelo Brandini, the father of his later enemy Baccio Bandinelli. Giovanni was employed at the Medici court as a musician, and would have liked his son to be a musician as well. But Benvenuto preferred to work as a goldsmith, and later as a sculptor. He led a very interesting life and wrote a famous autobiography about it. He also wrote sonnets and treatises about sculpture and the goldsmith's art. He spent most of his time in Rome from 1519 to 1540, and ended up being imprisoned by the Pope. He was released on the recommendation of Cardinal Ippolito d'Este, and began work on planning and modelling the famous *Salt Cellar* (p. 233), which is his only remaining piece of gold work. The piece was originally meant for the Cardinal, but he shied away from its high cost. Cellini managed to show his model to King Francis I of France, who finally commissioned him to carry it out.

Benvenuto Cellini
Salt Cellar, 1540–43
Ebony and gold, partially enamelled, height: 26 cm, breadth: 33.5 cm
Vienna, Kunsthistorisches Museum

Bartolomeo Ammanati
Fountain of Neptune, 1560–75
Marble and bronze, height about 560 cm
Florence, Piazza della Signoria

Bartolomeo Ammanati
Allegory of winter, 1563–65
Castello, Villa Medicea, garden

Bartolomeo Ammanati
Fountain of Neptune, detail

Cellini combined the function of this ornamental vessel, which was to make salt and pepper available at the table, with the relevant gods, thereby developing an iconography similar to that of a sculptural ensemble. He also used aspects of monumental sculpture on small-scale gold work. Over an ebony base is a diagonally divided composition. On one side is the ocean and sea creatures, the realm of Neptune, and on the other is the earth. Enthroned opposite each other, on ocean and earth respectively, are Neptune and Terra, their poses derived from the figures in Michelangelo's Medici Chapel. On Neptune's side, the actual salt cellar is a boat, and on the earth side the pepper dish is flanked by a triumphal arch. Its lid is a female figure posing on the arch. The work was going to be melted down in 1562, but was rescued and presented in 1570 to Archduke Ferdinand of Tyrol to form part of his famous art collection; it is now in Vienna.

After Cellini returned from France in 1545, he was sent for by Cosimo I and made the request that he should be allowed to produce a large marble or bronze statue for the Piazza della Signoria. The Duke had wanted a figure of Perseus for a long time, and Cellini promptly produced a wax model. It found favour with the Duke and Cellini started work on the casting moulds in a specially prepared workshop. The Medusa was cast in summer 1548, and the figure of *Perseus* (p. 232) was cast in December of the following year. Cellini made a change from the original plans in that he quite considerably increased the size of the statue, evidently out of a desire to compete successfully with the other statues on the Piazza, such as Donatello's *Judith and Holofernes* group and the two colossal marble statues by Michelangelo and Bandinelli. Cellini placed his Perseus on a tall, square and extremely ornate marble pedestal with niches which he filled with small bronzes. He also carved the corners of the pedestal, in reference to his belief that one should be able to see a statue from eight sides. In this sense Perseus is a free-standing three-dimensional figure. The most effective side to see it from is the right, as this particularly emphasizes the sword which he is holding almost horizontally in his right hand, the head of the Medusa which he is holding up in his left hand, and the bend in his left leg. This is hardly a typical Mannerist composition, rather one which keeps to the classical notion that there should be just one effective viewing point for a statue.

Giovanni da Bologna, or Giambologna

Giambologna (1529–1608) was actually born Jean de Boulogne in Douai in Flanders. He was trained by Jacques Dubroeucq in Antwerp, and left for Rome around 1550 in order to study classical sculpture and Michelangelo's works. He decided to stay in Florence on his way home, in order to familiarize himself with Michelangelo's Florentine works. While he was there the art patron Bernardo Vecchietti persuaded him to stay. Finally he entered the service of the Medici family. Taking his aesthetic bearings from Michelangelo and

Giambologna
Rape of the Sabines, 1581–83
Marble, height: 410 cm
Florence, Loggia dei Lanzi

Cellini, Giambologna developed a new concept that finally overcame the strong influence of classical antiquity on the Renaissance. Its most exceptional feature was the *figura serpentinata*, a spiral upward movement through a figure or group of figures which countered the force of gravity. The bronze figure of *Mercury* (p. 236) was the product of over twenty years of work, during which Giambologna was seeking new forms of expression. Mercury, the Roman messenger of the gods, overcomes the force of gravity as he is supported by nothing more substantial than the breath of the God of Wind; he is rising into the air on winged heels, with a winged helmet and a herald's staff. Though the nakedness and *contrapposto* position of the figure show the influence of classical antiquity, the movement of the figure has little in common with classical statues. In contrast, all sense of weight is dissolved by the figure's spiral movement around its own axis, which even appears to extend into his index finger.

The *figura serpentinata* took on a new form in Giambologna's sculpture *Rape of the Sabines* (right), which was inspired by Michelangelo and his *Victory* group (p. 223). The main figure in the group is Romulus, who dominates the scene as he climbs over the Sabine man cowering on the ground in order to seize his wife. She is trying to fight him off and is looking desperately to her husband for help. The triad of struggling figures is a completely three-dimensional ensemble; the appearance of the group changes constantly as one walks around it, but the figures that make up this extremely complex sculpture always retain a sense of unity. This was one of his main works for the Medicis, yet it is quite different from Michelangelo's model. Though it is often said that Michelangelo's *Victory* was the first Mannerist figure, Joachim Poeschke has quite rightly pointed out that Michelangelo's use of the *figura serpentinata* was a direct consequence of the theme. In contrast, the Mannerist *serpentinata* was used as a formal end in itself, irrespective of the theme, and became a piece of "virtuoso" art. Mannerism was one of the most important developments in the history of sculpture, and not just in Italy. It was an age of increased enthusiasm for artistic beauty and elegance, which finally gave way to the Baroque as Italy underwent a religious revival. Giambologna was the most important Italian sculptor of his era, and influenced European sculpture during the late 16th and early 17th centuries. In this respect, his sculptures are already part of the next artistic age.

Barbara Deimling

Early Renaissance Art in Florence and Central Italy

International Gothic in Florence c. 1400

Florentine art at the beginning of the 15th century was dominated by a late Gothic form, what art historians refer to as International Gothic. This term was coined in the 19th century by the French historian Louis Courajod, in an effort to reduce the stylistic features of early 15th-century art, which were remarkably similar throughout most of Europe, to a common denominator. Tendencies towards a magnificent and richly ornamented art can be traced to an equal extent in the Franco-Flemish area, in the northern, southern and Westphalian areas of Germany, and in Bohemia, Spain and northern Italy. This art was often characterized by a high level of realistic detail, and in its ideal form was exceptionally elegant in line and clever in the use of fine materials. The starting point of this development was the Franco-Flemish area and its courts in Burgundy, Paris and Dijon; these late Gothic artistic ideals quickly spread throughout Europe, aided by the preference for small pieces of art, which were easy to transport. Much-travelled artists such as Starnina, Pisanello and Gentile da Fabriano carried this wealth of elegant courtly forms as far as central Italy. In doing so they helped the late Gothic form achieve a swift and decisive success, even in towns such as Florence which had at first turned their backs on this trend.

Gentile da Fabriano's Adoration of the Magi

One of the most important representatives of the late Gothic in Florence was Gentile da Fabriano (c. 1370–1427); his paintings were firmly rooted in reality, which makes it possible to view him as a pioneer of Renaissance art. As the second part of Gentile's name indicates, he came from Fabriano in Umbria. Before coming to Florence in 1420, he had already gained recognition as a painter in Venice and Brescia. The artistic experiences which Gentile gained in Northern Italy, a stronghold of International Gothic, are reflected in his altar painting, the *Adoration of the Magi*, which he created over a period of three years for the Florentine merchant banker Palla Strozzi, and which, to go by the date on the base, was completed in 1423 (p. 239). The exceptional display of splendour, the diversity of techniques, the great variety of treatments of the surface, and the rendition of natural phenomena all added up to a novelty which had a strong influence on his artistic colleagues in Florence.

The painting's frame contributes to our experience of the adoration of the three kings as a coherent event. The three arches do not extend all the way to the bottom, so that the appearance of a triptych, a picture made up of three panels, remains a mere suggestion. This means that the arches mark breaks that essentially divide the Holy Family, the Three Kings and their entourage from each other, without interrupting the action. Gentile made use of the area within the three arches in order to narrate the events before the Adoration. Top left, the Three Kings are standing in golden garments on a hilltop above an ocean. They are gazing at the star

TOP, AND DETAIL BELOW:
Gentile da Fabriano
Adoration of the Magi, completed 1423
Tempera on wood, 303 x 282 cm
Florence, Galleria degli Uffizi

that has announced the birth of a new King. In the central arch, we can see the three oriental kings and their retinue riding towards Jerusalem, where they intend to ask Herod about the new-born child. Finally, in the right arch, the kings arrive in Bethlehem, and the climax of their journey, the Adoration of Christ, is shown in the main section of the painting. The stable is on the left, with Mary seated in front of it; the kings are kneeling in front of her, and their retinue, including a dog, horses and exotic animals, is pressing forward from the right. Two maids stand behind Mary and Joseph, and they are inquisitively looking at the golden goblet that the oldest king has brought, eager to know what presents Jesus has received.

We unfortunately have only a vague idea nowadays what effect the painting would originally have had; it is now lit evenly and artificially in a museum, whereas candles and torches would have produced an uneven, flickering source of light and would have emphasized various parts of the painting in turn. Gentile strengthened this changing effect by treating the surface of the painting in a number of different ways. In some parts he placed a layer of gold or silver underneath the paint of an individual feature, which he then exposed again by engraving. The objects depicted in relief are of particular interest. Relief was a technique for enlivening flat surfaces, used mainly in Venice and the Paduan plain, which the artist introduced in a somewhat reduced form in Florence. Examples include the crowns of the middle and youngest kings, and the collar worn by the dog lying in the foreground; Gentile made them out of pastiglia, a mixture of plaster and glue, and these elements extrude from the surface of the picture.

Despite this markedly decorative treatment of the subject, one can also detect a tendency to record reality, which, on this scale, was a new departure in Florence. In the scene, in the right arch, showing the kings' arrival in Bethlehem, the kings are riding up a steep hill – the first king's horse is just about to cross the drawbridge – and they are lit by the golden rays of the star (or is it the afternoon sun?), casting long shadows. Further shadows are cast by olive trees onto the town walls. These studies of lighting done by Gentile can be regarded as the first to be carried out with such rigour in Florence. While shadows did appear in paintings before this, they can only be considered isolated experimental phenomena. Here, for the first time, one can feel an artist's desire to capture the play of light and shadow as it really is.

Gentile was commissioned to paint his magnificent *Adoration* by the banker Palla di Nofri Strozzi, for his family chapel in the Sacristy of Santa Trinità in Florence. We can see him and his son Lorenzo in the centre of the painting, immediately behind the youngest king. While Lorenzo, wearing a red fur hat, is gazing out of the painting towards us, Palla, wearing a fur-trimmed, richly decorated garment, is concentrating on the adoration. A falcon, his personal emblem, is sitting on his hand. This is the first time in Florentine art that a client is painted in equal size immediately

239

behind the kings, and it is an idea that was adopted some time later, though in a different form, by the Medici family (p. 255), the Strozzis' great rivals. Such a close connection of the person commissioning the painting with the events depicted therein tell of a new self-confidence, contrasting with the humble subordination of earlier patrons. The splendour with which Palla Strozzi is surrounded in the picture is also a significant feature. It reflects the pride and wealth of this successful banker, who, according to a 1427 entry in the land registry, was the richest citizen in the town.

The Brancacci Chapel

Two years after Gentile da Fabriano's *Adoration of the Magi*, Masaccio (1401–c.1428) painted the frescos of the Brancacci Chapel in Santa Maria del Carmine in Florence; these are considered to be incunabula of Renaissance painting and, thanks to their innovative power, served as a source of inspiration to artists for over a century. The painting of the chapel showing the Life of St. Peter was begun in 1424 by Masolino da Panicale (1383–c.1440), a painter whose method of depicting figures was still completely rooted in International Gothic, but whose technique for giving a sense of perspective to his subjects means that he must be considered one of the heralds of Renaissance art. As was the practice at the time, Masolino first painted the ceiling and lunettes, which were later destroyed by renovation. Masaccio joined him in 1425, and together they painted the upper wall panels. Masolino left town in the summer of 1425, and Masaccio continued working on the lower panels on his own, but left them unfinished in 1428, when he left for Rome, where he was to die in the same year at the early age of twenty-six. The chapel's frescos were not completed until nearly sixty years later, between 1481 and 1485, by Filippino Lippi.

The work was commissioned by the rich silk merchant Felice Brancacci, who fell out of favour with the Medici family, who were just beginning their rise to power, and was exiled by them in 1436. This explains the late completion of the chapel, which was probably undertaken after the rehabilitation of Felice's heirs.

Masaccio and Giotto

The theme of the cycle of frescos is the life of St. Peter, which reveals mankind's *historia salutis*; Peter as the first Pope underlines the function of the Church as the mediator between mankind and Christ the Saviour. This interpretation of history stressing God's saving grace starts with the Fall of Man and the banishment of Adam and Eve from Paradise, their violation of God's law having made a reconciliation between God and Man necessary. Both scenes are depicted on the entrance columns to the chapel, the *Temptation of Adam* by Masolino on the right and Masaccio's *Expulsion* on the left (p. 242).

The fact that these two frescos are directly opposite each other, as well as their similar theme, invites comparison; it also demonstrates

the different ideals of the Late Gothic and Early Renaissance. The distinguishing feature of Masolino's *Temptation* is the precise and courtly elegance of its execution, which can be seen in the sharpness of the contours, the fine detail, gentle modelling, and length of the bodies. Masaccio's powerful, true-to-life figures, whose bodies are shaped realistically, contrast with this. While Masolino's human protagonists show no sign of emotion, Masaccio leaves us in no doubt as to the human drama that is unfolding in front of our eyes: despair, shame, regret, sadness and plaintive cries set the tenor. Adam and Eve are driven by the angel out into the barren world, through the extremely narrow Gateway to Paradise, which shows graphically how impossible it will be to return to the Garden of Eden. Eve's head is raised in despair, her mouth opened to give voice to her sorrow, and her slightly stooped position communicates the burden of her guilt. Adam, full of shame and regret, has covered his eyes with both hands and is weeping bitter tears. Masaccio has encapsulated all mankind's pain in this fresco.

Masaccio's *St. Peter Baptizing the Neophytes* (p. 246) is similarly rooted in reality. Peter is standing at the edge of a river and is pouring water from a bowl onto the head of the convert kneeling in front of him, whose knees are being washed by the waters of the river. His hair is hanging in wet strands, dripping water. Of special interest in this painting are Masaccio's true-to-life observations, such as the convert waiting to be baptized, who is clasping his arms

Masolino
Healing of the Cripple and the Raising of Tabitha, c. 1425
Fresco, 255 x 588 cm
Florence, Santa Maria del Carmine, Brancacci Chapel

Masolino
Healing of the Cripple and the Raising of Tabitha, c. 1425
Fresco, 255 x 588 cm
Florence, Santa Maria del Carmine, Brancacci Chapel

around his chest and shivering with cold, or the young man in the centre, who is just getting undressed.

The realism with which Masaccio's divine characters were painted, and their expressive emotionality, is evidence that the thoughts of the painter were naturally coloured by this world. The spatial and temporal abstraction of Late Gothic painting has been dissolved. Celestial events are humanized and brought up to date in order to help the faithful understand them. The roots of this realism can be found in Giotto's art, and artists at the beginning of the Quattrocento consistently continued and perfected it. Giorgio Vasari (1511–74), the pioneering art historian, called Giotto the first and the beginning of the Quattrocento the second step of a *rinascità*, a rebirth of art, which was pervaded by a desire for realism, or, as Vasari put it, for truth. The *rinascità,* therefore, was not so much a rebirth of ancient forms; rather, it was a sense that human beings were worthy of being portrayed, to an extent unknown since classical times.

Massacio's Rendering of the Tribute Money

These new ideals can be seen most clearly in Masaccio's famous fresco of the *Rendering of the Tribute Money* (pp. 244/45). Masaccio took this story, told Matthew 17, 24–27, and produced a dramatic event. In the centre of the fresco is Christ, surrounded by His disciples; a tax collector is stepping towards Him to demand the temple tax, which was state revenue. Jesus asks Peter to catch a fish,

saying that he will find a coin in its mouth. His arm is outstretched as He gives this order, and Peter, who is hesitating and suppressing his disquiet about the tax collector, is also indignantly pointing to the right. Following their gestures, we come to an apostle at the left edge of the picture, who has crouched down at the edge of the sea in order to take the coin out of the fish's mouth. Next, our gaze is directed by the tax collector's hand, which is pointing to the right side of the picture, to the scene where Peter gives the coin to the tax collector.

Masaccio's success in capturing reality in this picture is arresting: within the centralized perspective, the powerful, very individual and lifelike figures move freely and confidently; we admire Masaccio's conversion of spiritual matters into images, the close observation, patient questioning, impatient demands, indignation and suppressed reluctance, and the further realism in the authentic range of mountains, reminiscent of the Apennines, and in the recording of atmospheric phenomena, such as the clouds drifting across the sky, and the long shadows. In contrast to Gentile da Fabriano, Masaccio did not limit his use of realism to individual scenes. Instead, it determined the entire character of his painting.

The rendering of the tribute money had only rarely been used in the history of Italian art, and Felice Brancacci appears to have had a particular purpose in making this extraordinary choice of iconography. At the time, Florence was engaged in an expensive war with Milan, and the government had been forced to increase taxes. This

Masaccio
Expulsion of Adam and Eve, c. 1425
Fresco, 208 x 88 cm
Florence, Santa Maria del Carmine, Brancacci Chapel

Masolino
The Temptation of Adam, c. 1425
Fresco, 214 x 90 cm
Florence, Santa Maria del Carmine, Brancacci Chapel

Masolino
Healing of the Cripple and
the Raising of Tabitha, detail (p. 241)

was to be controlled by means of a land register, which would give a precise listing of the property belonging to every single citizen. Naturally, this plan stirred the emotions of the more well-to-do citizens. In this fresco, Felice Brancacci was taking the side of those wanting to introduce the land register, for it shows, in exemplary manner, the duty of every inhabitant to conscientiously pay those taxes due the state. It is not known how Florentines reacted to the fresco, but we do know that a land register actually came into force in 1427.

Masolino's Healing of the Cripple and the Raising of Tabitha
There is one further particularly important fresco in the Brancacci Chapel: it is *Healing of the Cripple and the Raising of Tabitha* (p. 241). Masolino united two events, which are narrated separately in the New Testament, on one fresco. The healing of the lame man (Acts 3, 1–10) takes place on the left side of the picture, in front of a loggia, and the raising of Tabitha (Acts 9, 36–41) occurs on the opposite side, in the ground floor of a house. Masolino linked both scenes by means of the piazza to the rear, and the two fashionably dressed young men are the point of transition. Their elegant posture, their courtly dress and the careful, gentle modelling of their faces

shows Masolino's love of the Late Gothic's formal idiom. At the same time, he proves open to the new ideals of the Renaissance. He was one of the few painters of his time to master perspective: our eyes are drawn towards a single point, to the right above the heads of the two strollers, and the piazza displays a realism, freshness and spontaneity scarcely different from the way a modern Italian square looks. We can see washing which has been hung up to dry at the windows, bird-cages, plant pots, two neighbours who are leaning right out of their windows in order to discuss the day's events, and monkeys, which were evidently kept as pets.

Masaccio's Trinity
Masaccio's fresco of the Trinity, which he painted between 1425 and 1428, is one of the first pictures to show the use of linear perspective, according to which all lines of perspective converge on a single vanishing point at eye-level (p. 247). Masaccio probably learned the mathematical construction of perspective from the architect Filippo Brunelleschi, who is considered to have discovered the use of perspective (see p. 106). The sequence of work can be reconstructed along the following lines. First of all, Masaccio would have produced a rough drawing of the composition and perspective

Masaccio
Rendering of the Tribute Money, c. 1425
Fresco, 247 x 597 cm
Florence, Santa Maria del Carmine, Brancacci Chapel

lines on the roughcast wall. He then had to cover this with fresh plaster while making the actual fresco. In order to ensure that the lines of perspective were transferred precisely from the sketch onto the fresh plaster, Masaccio knocked a nail in at the vanishing point under the base of the cross and attached strings to it, which he pressed into the plaster or carved in using a ruler and slate pencil. The marks of this preparatory work can clearly be seen on the fresco to this day. Because fresh plaster dried quickly, work started on a section had to be finished on the same day; Masaccio painted this fresco in daily sections, stage by stage, and it took him about a month to finish the *Trinity*.

The perspective construction of the picture makes the impression that the wall really opens up into a space which the holy figures occupy. Two mighty fluted pilasters with Composite capitals flank the arched arcade, which is borne by columns with Ionic capitals. These classical architectural elements also confirm the influence of Brunelleschi, especially when this fresco is compared to his Loggia degli Innocenti, begun in 1419 (p.102).

The scene is dominated by the huge shape of God the Father, who is standing on a base and is supporting the crossbeam of the crucifix with both hands, presenting His Son with a countenance that demands deep respect. Mary and St. John are standing underneath the cross. Mary is gesturing towards her crucified son with her right hand, and is gazing out of the picture, but in the depth of her grief, which seems to have turned her to stone, she is

FAR LEFT:
Giotto
St. John the Evangelist, detail from:
St. John the Evangelist recalls Drusiana to
Life, c. 1326–30
Florence, Santa Croce, Peruzzi Chapel

LEFT:
Michelangelo
Study from Masaccio's Rendering of the
Tribute Money, c. 1489–90
Pen with red chalk on paper, 31.8 x 18.6 cm
Munich, Alte Pinakothek, Staatliche
Graphische Sammlung

we can see the cross standing on a small hill, Golgotha, with Adam's decayed corpse resting underneath. As has already been pointed out in the first chapter on architecture, it was not unusual in the Middle Ages for the holy sites of Jerusalem to be copied, the intention being to transfer the holiness of these places to one's own town (pp. 20 ff.). This example shows that the world view of the Renaissance was not really shaped by a secularization of the world and art – people during the Renaissance were just as concerned about the salvation of their souls in the life to come as people during the Middle Ages –, though there was an endeavour to illustrate God's order by those means that were available so as to make it an even more intense experience for the faithful.

The position of Fra Angelico in Early Renaissance painting

The history of the reception of Fra Angelico (c. 1400–1455) makes it clear just how much opinion of his works has changed during the course of time. While Fra Angelico's art was still considered to be the "last flowering of the dying Middle Ages" at the beginning of this century, research during the last few decades has stressed his connection with Florence's Early Renaissance. A picture has now emerged of an artist who could pick up old and new trends and translate them into his own visual language. Fra Angelico's work is permeated by a lyrical feeling for form which is founded on the ideals of International Gothic. At the same time, the three-dimensional modelling and sense of space show the influence of Masaccio and the sculptor Lorenzo Ghiberti.

The stylistic ambivalence of Fra Angelico's works shows that the development of art from Giotto to Michelangelo was not a rigidly organized development of artistic powers bent on "progress". All artists occasionally used old forms; they might be required by the function of the picture, the artist's experience, or the taste of the client. In the case of Fra Angelico, his orientation towards mediaeval philosophical thinking reveals the influence of the Dominicans, to which he himself belonged from about 1418 onwards. This order supported the general reform movement amongst monastic orders, whose goals were a return to the original rules of poverty, chastity and obedience, and a particular requirement was spiritual contemplation, which would enable the believer to achieve a more intimate understanding of the sufferings of Christ.

not looking at us but is staring vaguely into empty space. Below them are the patrons, kneeling on a lower step, and the bottom part of the fresco is taken up by a skeleton, which is resting on a sarcophagus. In the niche above it is the following inscription: "I was what you are, you will be what I am."

The iconography of this picture, its combination of trinity, death and decay, is unusual, but can be interpreted as a transposition of the Golgotha chapel in Jerusalem. The Golgotha chapel was built on the point where the cross was raised, which according to tradition was the same place where Adam was buried. In Masaccio's painting

Fra Angelico's early work

Fra Angelico's early work shows that the young painter examined and studied Masaccio's achievements thoroughly, resulting in a greater desire to create a sense of depth and a clear structure in his pictures. In his painting *The Last Judgement* (p. 249), the graves disappear into the distance and lead the beholder's eye right to the horizon, where a white stripe under the dark sky heralds the rising sun, a symbolic allusion to the arrival of the Supreme Judge.

Architecture is also an important element of the composition of the Cortona *Annunciation* (p. 251), which was created shortly afterwards, c. 1432–33. The loggia arcades, which lead into the distance on the left, act as a compositional connecting line between the annunciation and the banishment of Adam and Eve from Paradise, which takes place in the background on the left. The row of arcades indicates the causal relationship between the two events. Due to the Fall of Man, there was need of a reconciliation between God and Man, and the annunciation to Mary is the first indication that this is about to happen.

While the sense of perspective and space shows the influence of Masaccio, the expressive root of the annunciation is founded in Late Gothic and expressed by the gentle movements of the angel and Mary. Mary is leaning forward carefully, in order to listen to the angel's words; he is gently moving towards her and is proclaiming God's message with clear gestures. The peacefulness of this scene suggests that this picture is meant not

Fra Angelico
The Last Judgement, c. 1431
Tempera on wood, 105 x 210 cm
Florence, Museo di S. Marco

as a public expression of complicated theological or political beliefs, but rather as an invitation to the faithful for quiet contemplation.

The same expressive gentleness can be seen in Fra Angelico's *Descent from the Cross* (p. 252), which dates from the early 1530s. The painting was started by Lorenzo Monaco for the Strozzi Chapel in Santa Trinità – he painted the areas within the pediments – and finished by Fra Angelico. The figures in the main panel seem to have turned to stone, and the scene appears to have been reduced to no more than a presentation of Jesus' body, which we are invited to approach meditatively. Jesus' body crosses over the vertical lines of the composition: his legs, torso and arms form an X, which is continued in the figures standing on the ladders and kneeling nearby. This composition can be interpreted as an indirect reference to Christ, as the letter X was a traditional symbol for the Lord.

Fra Angelico and San Marco
After Cosimo de' Medici returned from exile in 1434, he instigated the allocation of the monastery of San Marco in Florence, which now belongs to the Sylvestrians, to the Dominicans. In 1437, the architect Michelozzo started to renovate the rather dilapidated

monastery (see p. 107); meanwhile, Fra Angelico was entrusted with painting the frescos, which were to cover the cloister, chapter, refectory, corridors and forty-five cells occupied by the monks. Fra Angelico worked intermittently at this extensive task, helped by his assistants, until 1450.

The *Annunciation* (p. 250) is an excellent example of the function of the cell frescos and their aesthetic effect. The simplicity and restraint of the picture are captivating. If one compares this painting with the Cortona *Annunciation* (p. 251), its plainness becomes even more apparent. In both cases the setting is a loggia, but the figures in the fresco are placed in front of a bare wall. The viewpoint means that the garden is scarcely visible. Every architectural ornamentation is avoided; even the capitals are out of sight, covered by the angel's wings. The garments stand out because of their plainness, and Mary's brocade-upholstered throne is replaced by a wooden stool on which the Virgin is humbly kneeling. Even the extremely gentle approach of the angel in the Cortona painting has given way to a complete lack of motion, similar to the figures in the *Descent from the Cross* (p. 252).

A comparison of the two shows that Fra Angelico avoided adding any invented details to the scene, in order not to distract the

Fra Angelico
The Annunciation, c. 1440–41
Fresco, 187 x 157 cm
Florence, Museo di San Marco

BOTTOM:
Fra Angelico
Madonna and Child with Saints and
Angels (main altarpiece of San
Marco), c. 1438–43
Tempera on wood, 220 x 227 cm
Florence, Museo di San Marco

cells' inhabitants in any way. This shows clearly just how much the aesthetic appearance of the pictures was shaped by their function, the wishes of the patron and the spiritual attitude of the artist. The cell frescos were intended to help the monks immerse themselves mystically in the life of Christ. The Dominican saint Peter the Martyr, who is deep in prayer, is standing to the left of the annunciation, and his meditative observation of the events unfolding before him was intended to serve as an example for the monks.

The main altarpiece of San Marco
The painting of the Madonna and Child with angels and eight saints (bottom left), which was created between 1438 and 1443 for the high altar of San Marco, is one of Fra Angelico's most important works; unfortunately it was "cleaned" with acid during the 19th century, which caused it to lose its former lustre. Fra Angelico's mastery is most apparent in the amount of space within the painting; a strong sense of depth is derived from the foreshortening of the magnificent Anatolian carpet. This picture is also one of the first panel paintings to have been conceived according to the rules of perspective. Fra Angelico was even suggesting new avenues of exploration by using a rectangular shape for the painting. It is one of the first of the Renaissance *palas*, a rectangular form originally framed by pilasters bearing an architrave, which took the place of multi-panelled altarpieces. Even the apparently uncomplicated iconography of Madonna and Child, surrounded by angels and saints, proves to be a carefully thought out theme, which both complied with the demands of the donator, Cosimo de' Medici, who was the patron of the main altar, and suited the Dominicans, to whose order the church of San Marco belonged.

All eight saints were special guardian and patron saints of Cosimo and his family. The red circles woven into the braid trimming around the carpet are a reference to the red spheres on the Medici coat of arms, and the Zodiac signs of Pisces and Cancer in the carpet possibly allude to the beginning and end of the Council of Union of the Orthodox and Western churches, which was held in Florence in 1439; Cosimo personally supported the change of venue from Ferrara to Florence.

These personal references to the clients are broadened into a general theological statement. The picture of the crucifixion, which appears in the foreground of the painting, and the predella of the *Mourning of Christ*, which was originally underneath it and is now in the Alte Pinakothek in Munich, point to the eucharistic function of the altar on which the painting was placed and which was used every day by the Dominicans to celebrate Mass. The Gospel according to St. Mark is open at a passage in which Jesus tells His disciples to set out to spread His Christian teachings, but not to take any possessions with them. This can be interpreted as a reference to the Dominicans, who were extremely successful preachers and followed Christ's injunction of poverty with great zeal.

Fra Angelico
The Annunciation, c. 1432–33
Tempera on wood, 175 x 180 cm
Cortona, Museo Diocesano

OPPOSITE, AND DETAIL BELOW:
Fra Angelico
Descent from the Cross, c. 1430–35
Tempera on wood, 176 x 185 cm
Florence, Museo di San Marco

The Magi Chapel in the Palazzo Medici

Fra Angelico's pupils Benozzo Gozzoli, started painting the palace chapel of the Medici family, which was built between 1446 and 1449, in the summer of 1459. The journey of the Magi to Bethlehem (pp. 254/55) unfolds in fairytale splendour on the three walls of the chapel. The fourth wall opens into a rectangular sanctuary, on whose altar the painting of the *Madonna Adoring her Child* by Filippo Lippi used to stand (p. 259). It has now been replaced by a modern copy, and the original is in Berlin. The procession of the Magi is moving towards this scene of adoration. The sequence is completed by the hosts of angels depicted on the side walls of the altar area, who have already begun to praise the new-born child.

Benzozzo's first fresco shows the youngest king with his retinue. The train of riders, pages and noble squires is snaking its way on winding roads. The painter has filled the scene with a wealth of variation and an incomparable degree of magnificence. There are gleaming materials woven with gold thread, various brocades, pearl-embroidered garments and velvet and silk cloths, jewel-studded belts and gilded, richly decorated bridles. This sumptuous display of wealth and splendour could not be a more tasteless contrast to Fra Angelico's San Marco frescos, which were also financed by the Medicis and which Benozzo Gozzoli helped Fra Angelico to paint. What explanation can there be for the discrepancy between the deliberate simplicity and magnificent richness of these pieces of Medici art? One answer is that, while Cosimo de' Medici oversaw the first stage of the decorations, an exchange of correspondence between his son Piero and the painter Benozzo Gozzoli informs us that Piero was responsible for the frescos. This change of generation also shows a clear change in the artistic taste of the clients. Piero preferred a sumptuous, stately display of magnificence of a type that was foreign to his father. The function of the room also played a role in the stylistic execution of the frescos, however. We know from contemporary documents that the chapel was not merely intended as a place of prayer; it was also a reception room for delegations and rulers. This explains the magnificently stately character of the frescos, which make direct reference to the Medici family and give the fairy-tale biblical procession a contemporary, political significance. The youngest king is an idealized portrait of Lorenzo, Piero's son and Cosimo's grandson, who was later given the name "Il Magnifico" (the Magnificent). His grey's bridle is decorated with the coat-of-arms of the Medicis, and behind him is a laurel tree, a broad play on his name, Lorenzo, suggested by the similarity of the Latin names Lauro (= laurel) and Laurentius (= Lorenzo). In the first row of his retinue ride his father, Piero, and Cosimo, his grandfather and the founder of the great family of Florentine rulers. The inclusion of members of the Medici family turns these frescos into a proud manifestation of the financial and political might of this family, which was just beginning its rise to power. This must also be the explanation for Benozzo Gozzoli's many borrowings of motifs

from Gentile da Fabriano's Strozzi altar painting (p. 239), as he cannot simply have done it for aesthetic reasons. The great rivalry between the Medici and Strozzi families – the latter were to lose the struggle for power in Florence – was being mirrored in art: the rivals' artistic motifs were borrowed, but then developed on a more lavish scale. In addition, the Medici were not merely members of the train, as Palla Strozzi was, but were portrayed as kings themselves, the youngest king being Lorenzo, on whom all the hopes of the family rested. He was to secure and extend the power of the House of Medici.

Power and patronage of the Medici in Florence

The Medici were the rulers of Florence for almost 300 years, and it was during the period of their rule that the great works of the Florentine artists of the Renaissance came into being. From Donatello and Brunelleschi to Paolo Uccello, Botticelli, Fra Filippo Lippi and Leonardo da Vinci, not to mention Michelangelo, Andrea del Sarto and Pontormo, the list of artists whose works were created under the protection of the Medici and commissioned by

aristocracy, who endeavoured to preserve their power using all the legal means at their disposal, and often illegal ones as well. The first Medici to obtain access to this oligarchy was Giovanni di Bicci de' Medici, born in 1360. Little is known of his father, Averardo, who died only three years after the birth of his son. Giovanni took over the banking house, founded by his uncle in 1348 in Florence, at an early age and built it into a flourishing enterprise. The wealth of the family was a crucial factor in their rise to power, and essential to maintaining that position. At the same time, this

wealth was the cornerstone of a patronage to which the city of Florence owes a major portion of its magnificent buildings, sculptures and paintings.

Giovanni was the first in the line of patrons in the Medici family. Not only did he finance the rebuilding by Brunelleschi of a chapel of the church of San Lorenzo, he also made available to the artist the means with which to build the Sacristy, the first centralized building of the Renaissance. This was to be Giovanni's final resting place.

When Giovanni died in 1429, his eldest son, Cosimo, had already been managing the banking house for a number of years. Under his skilful leadership, the company grew into an enterprise whose fame extended far beyond the borders of Tuscany. At the same time, Cosimo, who was later given the nickname "Il Vecchio" (the Old One), succeeded in taking power in Florence. His rise to fame after having first been imprisoned and banished to Venice for one year is one of the most fascinating episodes in the turbulent history of the Medici family. As early as 1434, Cosimo was recalled from exile and appointed Gonfaloniere. He filled this executive post for three decades until his death in the year 1464. Pontormo captured the noble features of Cosimo in a portrait which depicts him as having a pensive appearance, and radiating intell-

Jacopo Pontormo
Cosimo il Vecchio, c. 1518–19
Panel, 86 x 65 cm
Florence, Galleria degli Uffizi

them is long indeed. Even today, the Medici coat of arms is prominently displayed on many buildings, and their tombs and gravestones, created by the greatest artists of this period, are stone witnesses of their former power and greatness.

The Florence of the 15th century was supposedly a republic. This republic, however, was ruled by an oligarchy consisting primarily of members of the

Ottavio Vannini
Michelangelo presents Lorenzo il Magnifico with the bust of a faun made by himself, Fresco, 1635
Florence, Palazzo Pitti
Museo degli Argenti

Family tree of the Medici family, from its beginnings to the early 16th century

Averardo detto Bicci
|
Giovanni di Bicci
1360 – 1429
∞ Piccarda Bueri

Innominata — Cosimo il Vecchio (1389 – 1464, ∞ Contessina Bardi) — Lorenzo (1395 – 1440)

Piero il Gottoso (1416 – 1469, ∞ Lucrezia Tornabuoni) — Giovanni (1421 – 1463) — Carlo (1430 – 1492) — Francesco — Pierfrancesco il Vecchio (1430 – 1476)

Lorenzo il Magnifico (1449 – 1492, ∞ Clarice Orsini) — Giuliano (1453 – 1478) — Maria — Bianca (? – 1488) — Nannina (? – 1493) — Lorenzo il Popolano (1463 – 1503) — Giovanni Il Popolano (1467 – 1498)

Giulio (Clemente VII) 1478 – 1534

Alessandro (1511 – 1537, ∞ Margherita d'Austria)

Pierfrancesco il Giovane 1478 – 1525

Lorenzino 1514 – 1548

Giovanni delle Bande Nere 1498 – 1526

Lucrezia 1470 – ? — Piero Il Fatuo (1472 – 1503, ∞ Alfonsina Orsini) — Maddalena (1473 – 1519) — Giovanni (Leone X) (1475 – 1521) — Luisa (1477 – 1488) — Contessina (1478 – 1515) — Giuliano (Duca di Nemours) (1479 – 1516) — Cosimo I (1519 – 1574, ∞ Eleonora di Toledo, ∞ Camilla Martelli)

Maria 1499 – 1543 — Lorenzo (Duca di Urbino) (1492 – 1519, ∞ Maddalena de la Tour d'Auvergne) — Clarice (1493 – 1528) — Ippolito (1511 – 1535)

Caterina 1519 – 1589

Maria (1540 – 1557) — Francesco I (1541 – 1587, ∞ Giovanni d'Austria, ∞ Bianca Cappello) — Isabella (1542 – 1576) — Giovanni (1543 – 1562) — Lucrezia (1545 – 1561) — Don Pedricco (1546 – 1547) — Grazia (1547 – 1562) — Don Antonio (? – 1548) — Ferdinando I (1549 – 1609, ∞ Cristina di Lorena) — Don Pietro (1554 – 1604) — Don Giovanni (1567 – 1621) — Virginia

256

igence and determination. This portrait today hangs in the Uffizi (p. 256).

In the year 1444, Cosimo commissioned the architect Michelozzo to build the Palazzo Medici which, with its monumental, three-storey façade, served as a model for Florentine palace architecture from then on (p. 257). It was Cosimo's wish that Donatello also work on the project; not only did this artist produce the medallions, but he also created several important bronzes for the palace. Cosimo similarly financed with enormous sums the rebuilding of the monastery of San Marco, the interior of which was designed by Fra Angelico (see p. 250), while Paolo Uccello and the young Fra Filippo Lippi were numbered among the eminently personal discoveries of this artistic Medici. When Cosimo died in 1464, Florence honoured its most eminent citizen by burying him beneath a column in the church of San Lorenzo.

Cosimo's successor, Piero, to whom the people had given the nickname "Il Gottoso" (the Gouty) because he suffered from that illness, was to enjoy only a brief term of office. This Medici, who led a secluded life due to his illness and who was successful both as a politician and a businessman, died only five years after his father. Piero was an exceptionally enthusiastic collector of old coins and medals, although his main passion was for books and mediaeval manuscripts, with which he laid the foundations for the magnificent library of the Medici. Piero was also active as a patron

Palazzo Medici-Riccardi
Florence
commenced in 1444 by Michelozzo

of the visual arts, however. For example, he commissioned Benozzo Gozzoli to create the frescos in the chapel of the Palazzo Medici (pp. 254 and 255).

Piero's son Lorenzo took over the political leadership of the city at the tender age of twenty, and the period of his rule constituted the magnificent high point in the history of the Medici. However, it was also during his lifetime that the banking house began its gradual decline. The failing economy of the Italian cities on the one hand, and a less than optimal management of the family business on the other, led to the latter getting into difficulties. This did not restrain Lorenzo, however, who was interested in philosophy and a lover of the arts, from continuing to play the role of the generous patron, as had his father and his grandfather before him. Lorenzo, who loved luxury and the show of wealth, and who was given the nickname "Il Magnifico" (the Magnificent) because of his public extravaganzas, turned the gardens in the area surrounding San Marco (which are now built over) into a meeting place for the philosophers and poets of Florence, including the Neo-Platonic philosopher Marsilio Ficino and the poet Angelo Poliziano. Moreover, architects, sculptors and painters also participated in these gatherings. One of the most important artists he entertained at his house was the young Michelangelo. A painting by Ottavio Vannini shows Michelangelo presenting Lorenzo, who is sitting on a throne in the centre of the picture, with the bust of a faun (see p. 256 left). Lorenzo de' Medici also proved to be an outstanding figure in politics. He survived the assassination attempt instigated by the Pazzi family in Florence Cathedral, in which his brother, Giuliano, was murdered. Lorenzo commanded the assassins to be hung from the windows of the Palazzo Vecchio. Il Magnifico brought the war started by the Pope against Florence to a close through his great negotiating skill and courage. He also withstood the dramatic intensification of the feud with the preacher Savonarola. His early death – he died in 1492 at the age of 42 – signalled the end of the golden era of the Medici.

The eldest son, Piero, who was called "Il Fatuo" (the Unhappy), now became the new ruler of Florence. In the year 1494, the Florentines drove the politically and economically incompetent Piero into exile, together with the whole family, after he had made peace with the French king Charles VIII without consulting anyone and on terms humiliating to the city. One of the driving forces behind the exile of the Medici was the celebrated Savonarola, who denounced the wealth of the family, with its opulent city palace and its grand, capacious country villas (see left), and stirred up hatred against them. At the end of the 15th century, however, the Florentines turned against the fanatical monk, and burned him at the stake in 1498 (see right). The Medici were not to become rulers of Florence again until the year 1512. Of Lorenzo's three sons, only Giovanni had inherited the political talent of his father. He was destined early in life for a career in the church, and succeeded in gaining admission to the Holy See in 1513. As Pope Leo X he led a dissipated life, one, which was however, also dedicated to the arts. Raphael, for example, was one of the artists he patronized, and he commissioned Michelangelo to build the façade for San Lorenzo in Florence. When Leo X died in 1521, the curtain fell on the last successful representative of this branch of the Medici family to dominate the stage of Italian history.

The star of the Medici shone but once more in the person of Cosimo I, a fifth-generation direct descendant of the younger brother of the founder of the family, Giovanni di Bicci. Cosimo ruled his Florence in dictatorial style, though he nevertheless succeeded in bringing prosperity back to a Tuscany which had been on the brink of poverty. He saw his patronage as a political act which brought him prestige and a high reputation. Cosimo founded the famous picture gallery in the Palazzo Pitti, and

Unknown artist
Detail from:
Savonarola being burnt at the stake on the Piazza della Signoria, 1498
Tempera on wood
Florence, Museo di San Marco

the Uffizi, built by Vasari, can also be traced back to him. Once again, Florence under a Medici became the cultural centre of Italy. The history of the successfully ruling Medici came to an end with the death of Cosimo I in the year 1574, shortly after he was crowned Grand Duke. The following generations were unable to contribute further to the fame of the family.

Giusto Utens, Cafaciolo, the country villa of the Medici (detail), 1499
Tempera on canvas, 140 x 241 cm, Florence, Museo di Firenze com'era

Filippo Lippi
The Annunciation, c. 1440
Wood, 175 x 183 cm
Florence, San Lorenzo, Martelli Chapel

Filippo Lippi
Madonna and Child with Angels, St. Frediano and St.
Augustine (Barbadori altarpiece), 1437–38
Wood, 208 x 244 cm, Paris, Musée du Louvre

Filippo Lippi (c. 1406–1469)

When Filippo Lippi painted his *Madonna Adoring her Child* (p. 259) around 1459 for the Medici palace chapel, he was at the height of his fame. Next to Fra Angelico, he was the most respected painter in Florence. This high regard for Filippo as a painter continued, even though he turned out to be of an exceptionally difficult and eccentric disposition. An example is when, in 1450, he had to appear before court for forging a certificate. He was accused of entrusting paintings to his assistants rather than painting them himself, as he was obliged to do by contract. However, the most sensational scandal, given that he was a monk, was his love affair with the nun Lucrezia Buti. She bore him two children, a son, Filippino, who followed his father's profession (see p. 291), and a daughter. These scandals did not do the high artistic regard in which Filippo was held any harm, however: Cosimo de' Medici, Filippo's most important client, considered the painter's genius an ample excuse for the weaknesses of the man's flesh.

Filippo Lippi's early works

The extent of Filippo Lippi's early works has yet to be settled by research; both the dates and the attribution of individual pieces are disputed. Filippo Lippi began his career as a painter in the Carmelite monastery of Santa Maria del Carmine in Florence, where he made his vows, probably aged fifteen, on 18 June 1421 – the youngest age for novices. Just four years later Masaccio started painting the Brancacci chapel (pp. 240 ff.) in the church that belonged to the monastery. It is easy to imagine what a deep impression Masaccio's innovative and revolutionary work made on the young painter, who was still at the very beginning of his artistic development. Indeed, his works dating from the end of the 1420s show just how deep Filippo's admiration for Masaccio's artistic innovations was. The protagonists in the pictures are full of power and solemn weight, and their appearance is moulded by a traditional and sometimes coarse simplicity. Right from the start Filippo was clearly interested in greater realism, and this was to be the leitmotif of his paintings.

In 1428, Fra Filippo was made the sub prior of the Carmelite monastery in Siena. This one-year stay in Siena enabled him to study the elegant art of Siena's courts, which also influenced his own work. His paintings dating from the beginning of the 1430s show that the generous idiom of his earlier paintings, so reminiscent of Masaccio, had been toned down in favour of clearer contours.

Filippo Lippi and Flanders

The year 1437 was a turning point in Filippo's artistic development. It was the year when he started painting the Barbadori altarpiece (bottom left), in which the heavenly court appears in earthly, realistic surroundings; in the same year Filippo painted the *Tarquinia Madonna*, a tempera panel whose iconographic innovations show the painter's interest in new forms and content (p.

259). At first glance the picture seems to differ little from the already familiar depictions of the Madonna and Child. Mary is sitting on a semi-circular throne and is holding the baby Jesus in a gentle, motherly embrace; He is pressing against her energetically, trying to put His arms around her neck. The actual novelty in this is not so much the expressively emotional meeting of mother and child as the nature of the surroundings. Behind Mary there is a view of a bedchamber with a bed standing in an alcove. On the left we can see out through a window onto a landscape, and the door in the background is open, making it possible to see into the yard. This is the first time in Italian art that the enthroned Madonna and Child appear in homely, intimate surroundings. These surroundings underline the humanity of Mary and Christ and place them within our own field of experience. The humanization of these heavenly personages is emphasized by a further innovation that Filippo introduced to Italian painting: Mary and Christ are shown without haloes. They have become human, and appear in their everyday surroundings and in their roles as mother and child. In doing this, Filippo Lippi was taking the growing realism which could be seen in Giotto, and to a greater extent in Gentile da Fabriano and Masaccio, one step further. But what explanation is there for the change in Lippi's own artistic development? Even though the realism observed here is anchored in his early work, these radical innovations cannot simply be explained as a development from that. In fact, Lippi got his ideas from contemporary Dutch art. Its influence can be seen both in the imitation of individual motifs and

Filippo Lippi
Madonna and Child (Tarquinia Madonna), 1437
Tempera on wood, 114 x 65 cm
Rome, Galleria Nazionale, Palazzo Barberini

above all in the fundamental principle of giving the narrative a strictly earthly quality. Artists such as Jan van Eyck, Robert Campin and Rogier van der Weyden had been working in Bruges, Ghent and Brussels since the beginning of the 15th century on paintings that showed heavenly beings in domestic surroundings and carrying out everyday tasks. It is possible that Filippo came into contact with Dutch art in Padua, where he stayed in 1434. Flemish paintings tended to be present in the Veneto before they appeared in Florence, and Filippo was probably able to study northern art at first hand there.

The Annunciation of San Lorenzo
Shortly after the *Tarquinia Madonna*, in about 1440, Fra Filippo painted the *Annunciation* in the church of San Lorenzo in Florence (p. 258). This painting is also exceptional in its iconography. The events unfold under a double-arched loggia; the annunciation of Mary is taking place on the right side of the picture, and on the left are two angels. A garden surrounded by buildings borders the loggia and leads our gaze into the distance, where two towers form the backdrop. This view is not merely an artistic background, but is also

BOTTOM, AND DETAIL LEFT:
Filippo Lippi
The Feast of Herod, c. 1461–65
Fresco
Prato Cathedral, main choir

halves were probably the side panels of an organ or reliquary. In order for the Annunciation to retain a narrative unity when the doors were open, Filippo painted it on just one panel, and added the angels on another so that when the wings were shut they would balance the scene on the right.

The frescos of Santa Stefano in Prato

In 1452, Filippo Lippi started painting the choir of the parish church, now the Cathedral, of Santo Stefano in Prato. The frescos depicted stories from the life of St. Stephen, the church patron, and John the Baptist, the patron saint of Florence; the reason for this is that since 1351 Prato had been part of Florence's territory. One fresco, the *Feast of Herod* (bottom), will be considered in some detail here from the point of view of *grazia*, which contemporaries of Lippi considered to be a characteristic of his art. Philological research has shown that, in the Quattrocento, *grazia* was used to mean *varietà*, diversity, and *ornato*, decoration of the scene. In his treatise on painting of 1435, Alberti recommended diversity in pictures and related this to the great variety of gestures, positions, poses and emotions of figures that could give pleasure to the beholder. If one looks at Filippo's fresco, it is easy to understand the *varietà* aspect. The narrative of the painting begins in the centre, slightly to the left of which Salome is dancing. The guests at the banquet are watching her graceful movements admiringly. The events are continued on the left side, where Salome is averting her face in revulsion as she is given the head of John the Baptist; she presents it to her mother, Herodias, on the right side of the picture. Here we can observe a great variety of reactions to this event. While Herodias is looking with cruel coldness at the severed head of the Baptist, most of the guests are seized with revulsion and dismay. The couple in the foreground are holding each other tightly, daring a quick look, and someone else is hiding behind the chimney breast, while the woman at the end of the table is leaning right forward in her eagerness to get a quick look.

Here, *ornato* refers mainly to the posture and movement of the figures. Salome is the embodiment of a figure full of *ornato*: her

full of Christian and Marian symbolism. The closed-off garden, the *hortus conclusus*, is an allusion to Mary's purity; the fountain can be interpreted as a reference to the Water of Life; and the vine alludes to Christ's words, "I am the true vine" (John 15,1). Even the prominently placed glass vase in the niche in the foreground, a motif which Filippo Lippi borrowed from Flemish painting, is a way of praising Mary. In hymns, the Mother of God was praised as the *vas honorabile* or *vasello ornato*, an honourable or decorated vase, and the transparency of the glass further underlined her purity.

The presence of the two angels on the left side of the painting is surprising, as they are not mentioned in the New Testament. Their presence could be explained for compositional reasons, for they act as a counterweight to the annunciation; however, this does not explain why Filippo compresses the annunciation into the right half of the picture instead of giving it a more generous amount of space. This would mean, after all, that the angels would not be needed as a compositional balance. There is an explanation. Technical examinations have shown that the painting originally consisted of two sections. If one looks closely at the picture, one can see the dividing line down the middle. This means that the painting was not conceived as an altar painting, as we see it today; instead, the two

body is following the rhythm of the dance with elegant, agile movements, her dress, decorated with ribbons, is fluttering in the breeze, and a curl of her hair has come loose and is swaying gently.

Paolo Uccello: "O what a lovely thing this perspective is!"

"Paolo Uccello ... found pleasure only in exploring certain difficult, or rather impossible, problems of perspective, which, although fanciful and attractive, hindered him ... when he came to paint figures." Vasari crowned this unusually sharp criticism, which he wrote in 1568 in his Life of Uccello, with an anecdote which relates that Uccello preferred studying perspective to being together with his wife. When she pleaded with him finally to come to bed, he would simply reply, "O what a lovely thing this perspective is!" This negative evaluation of Uccello has continued right into our own century. Because of his concentration on the challenges of perspective theory, he has even been dismissed as merely second-rate. While Uccello may have had few successors, he was still a highly regarded artist in his own time, and no less an individual than Cosimo de' Medici was one of his most important clients.

This consistently dismissive evaluation of Uccello appears to be the reason why he has been largely neglected by art critics and historians. Until now, there has been no study of the artist's place in Early Renaissance art, and there are hardly any studies of his early works. We do know that Uccello (1397–1475) worked with Lorenzo Ghiberti in his workshop and was one of the artists who worked on the first Baptistery doors, started in 1407. After a lengthy stay in Venice from 1425–30, Uccello was commissioned, in 1435 or 1436, to paint the Ascension chapel in the parish church, later the Cathedral, of Santo Stefano in Prato. This work was finished by one of his employees, Andrea di Gusto, for Uccello was interrupted by a more important task: he was to paint the Sir John Hawkwood Memorial fresco (right).

The Sir John Hawkwood Memorial fresco

On 30 May 1436, Paolo Uccello was given the important commission, by Florence's Opera del Duomo, to paint the equestrian statue of the English mercenary leader John Hawkwood, who had served the city of Florence loyally for eighteen years until his death in 1394. Uccello completed the fresco (right) on the north wall of the Cathedral nave in the exceptionally short time of three months. The quick completion of the fresco appears all the more remarkable if one considers that the Opera del Duomo made Uccello destroy the fresco on 28 June, and to start again, as he "had not painted it satisfactorily". This has led art historians to speculate repeatedly on the extent of the erased sections, and the motivation behind the decision.

Uccello's portrayal is particularly remarkable, given that the perspectives of the views of the horse and rider, and the stone monument comprising sarcophagus and pedestal, differ. The

architectural base is seen from beneath (a position about two metres below its present one, as the fresco, which was transferred to canvas, was re-hung lower), while horse and rider are painted at eye-level. This discrepancy is especially surprising in light of the fact that Uccello was not one to shy away from attempting complicated perspectives. It is therefore quite possible that Uccello originally painted the horse and rider as seen from below, and that it was this that aroused the disapproval of the Opera del Duomo.

Paolo Uccello's contract specified that the fresco should be produced in monochrome using *terra verde*, in order to create the impression of a bronze monument. Bronze equestrian statues were popular in classical times as statues in honour of emperors and military commanders. This painting was indeed an allusion to a specific classical figure, Fabius Maximus, who defeated Hannibal, and to whom a bronze equestrian statue was raised on the Capitol in Rome as saviour of the Roman Republic. The last sentence of the inscription on Hawkwood's sarcophagus, praising this experienced and clever commander, is a quotation from a hymn to Fabius Maximus, which was engraved on an ancient stone which is now in Florence's Archaeological Museum. It is clear that parallels are being drawn between these two commanders. Florence is celebrating John Hawkwood, the loyal and glorious protector of the Florentine Republic, as a second Fabius Maximus, and is lauding itself as a second Rome, by erecting bronze monuments to its famous military commanders.

The fresco of the Deluge in Santa Maria Novella

Paolo Uccello painted his vivid picture of the *Deluge* (pp. 262/63) in the fourth bay of the east wing of the Chiostro Verde, the first cloister of the Dominican monastery of Santa Maria Novella in Florence, shortly after 1439. On the left, the fresco shows the destruction of humanity. The scene is dominated by the fight for survival against the floods of water, which are overcoming and destroying everything; somebody is desperately trying to hold on to the planks of the Ark, while others have found temporary safety on an island, or are swimming in the steadily rising waters, spitting out the water they have swallowed. A dog has sought refuge on a plank, and in the foreground two giants, who according to the Bible still lived on Earth before the Flood (Genesis 6,4), are threatening each other with wooden clubs. On the right side of the fresco the floods have already receded, and the Earth is covered with the gruesome spectacle of death. A raven is picking at the eyes of a corpse, and behind it to the left lies a child with a bloated stomach full of water.

Uccello illustrated the chronological interval between the two stages of the Flood by painting the Ark twice. The two scenes are connected by the enigmatic figure of a man standing staring to the right into empty space. Above him, Noah is leaning out of the Ark to receive the olive branch symbolizing peace between God and Man from the dove. Although this man is standing on a thin wooden plank and a drowning man is clinging to his feet, he conveys an impression of unshakable stability and security amidst the deadly chaos, and appears to be seeing a vision of a new future. Recent research has shown that this figure was probably Cosimo de' Medici, and his portrait, which appears on medallions, matches the features of this man. This reveals the message of the fresco. The dove, which is hovering immediately above Cosimo's head, is an allusion to his role as peacemaker in Florence. Once it was Noah who got people and animals to safety on the Ark; now it was Cosimo who, under the protection of God, would lead the city from the confusion of internal and external politics into a new age of wealth and peace.

In order to achieve a deeper understanding of this fresco, it is necessary to consider the two Arks. Since the Middle Ages the Ark had been considered a symbol of the Church, and Pope Boniface VIII (c. 1235–1303) interpreted the Ark as a symbol of the unification of the Western and Orthodox Churches. The Council of Union of the two Churches met in 1439 in the monastery buildings of Santa Maria Novella, and the high point was the signing of the treaty of union on 5 July of the same year. Cosimo had strongly supported the change of venue for the Council from Ferrara to Florence, and had been its main source of finance. By including his portrait in the fresco alluding to the unification of the two Churches, Cosimo was stressing the importance of his own person to the Council and was interpreting the success of the Church conference as a success of the House of Medici.

Paolo Uccello
The Deluge, c. 1439–40
Fresco (transferred to canvas), 212 x 510 cm
Florence, Santa Maria Novella, Chiostro Verde

The Battle of San Romano

The intention of the Medici rulers to depict and glorify themselves in art comes through particularly clearly in the last work of Uccello's that will be discussed here. *The Battle of San Romano* (p. 264) belongs to a three-part cycle of pictures that depicts the victorious battle of the Florentines, led by the mercenary Niccolò da Tolentino, against the allied forces of Lucca, Siena and Milan, in 1432. While the two other panels, which are now in the National Gallery in London and in the Louvre in Paris, narrate the deployment of the forces under the command of Niccolò da Tolentino, the painting which originally hung between the two, and which is now in the Uffizi, tells the actual story of the battle. The foreground is arranged according to the rules of centralised perspective, and the spears lying on the ground act as foreshortened lines of perspective. The force of this sense of depth is countered by the flat triangular composition of the two horses lying on the ground and the grey which is rearing in the centre. The weaving together of flatness and depth creates complicated relations between the figures in the picture, producing a sense of chaos and disorder in the beholder, which in turn further emphasizes the raging battle. The battling armies circle the centre of the painting. The Florentines are storming from the left, and the allied armies are fleeing to the right. The sequence of movement is fascinating: the Florentines galloping up on the left appear to be riding straight towards us, but then wheel around to continue in pursuit of the enemy. On the right only the rears of fleeing horses are visible.

Although Florence was victorious, the battle of San Romano was of little military significance, and would today be as good as forgotten had Cosimo de' Medici not commissioned this battle cycle; it was originally commissioned for the old family palace, and was finally displayed in the ground-floor *sala* of the new Palazzo Medici. However, this does not explain Cosimo's interest in this theme and his purpose in commissioning these historical paintings.

After the victorious battle of San Romano, ending the war against Lucca which had been in progress since 1429, the leader of the conservative government party, Rinaldo degli Albizzi, seized upon the opportunity to eliminate his political opponent, Cosimo de' Medici. Rinaldo accused Cosimo of having planned the overthrow of the government with the mercenary leader Niccolò da Tolentino in order to rule Florence as a dictatorship. Cosimo was arrested on 7 September 1433 and was banished from Florence for ten years. But the tide soon turned and the newly-elected Signoria, which was well disposed towards the Medicis, recalled Cosimo a year later from his exile in Venice. On 5 October 1434 Cosimo returned victoriously to Florence, where he was able to restore and consolidate his power, and laid the foundations of the dominance of the House of Medici in Florence, which was to last almost three hundred years.

During the time when the Medicis were substantiating their supremacy, Cosimo developed into an extraordinarily active patron, who saw art as an opportunity to visualize his political ambitions

Paolo Uccello
The Battle of San Romano, c. 1440–1450
Tempera on wood, 182 x 323 cm
Florence, Galleria degli Uffizi

and bring them subtly to the attention of the public. The picture cycle *The Battle of San Romano* by Paolo Uccello was intended to remind people of the Medicis' achievements in battle against Lucca, because it was their support of the mercenary leader Niccolò da Tolentino that had led to victory in the battle at San Romano. These historical pictures were not just Cosimo's way of presenting himself as an undoubted patriot; they were also the proof of his friendship for the mercenary. The latter had surrounded Florence with his troops after Cosimo was arrested, but soon gave up the siege, as it was endangering the life of his lord and friend. When Niccolò da Tolentino died in 1435, he was buried with all honours in Florence Cathedral. In 1456, the Opera del Duomo commissioned the artist Andrea del Castagno to paint an equestrian portrait in honour of the mercenary on the north wall of the Cathedral next to Uccello's *John Hawkwood*. In this way Niccolò da Tolentino found a place of honour next to Florence's other great military commander.

Domenico Veneziano, "la pittura di luce" and Leon Battista Alberti
Domenico Veneziano (c. 1400/10–1461) wrote a letter to Piero de'

Medici, Cosimo's son, on 1 April 1438, offering his services to produce an altar painting which he had heard Piero intended to commission. He added that the other two painters being considered, Fra Filippo Lippi and Fra Angelico, would not be able to carry out this task, as they were working on other projects. This letter shows that Domenico, who came from Venice, was very well informed about Florence's artistic circle. It is safe to assume that he must already have spent some time in Florence. This is borne out by his art, such as the St. Lucy altarpiece which was painted around 1445 (p. 265). Further research will be needed to decide whether Domenico was actually trained in Florence, as has recently been suggested, or whether he received his formative impressions at the hands of Gentile da Fabriano and Pisanello in Upper Italy; they would have taught him the elegant forms of International Gothic.

Domenico Veneziano painted the St. Lucy altarpiece for the Uzzano family chapel in Santa Lucia de' Magnoli. The main panel is now in the Uffizi, and the five predella panels are dispersed amongst various museums throughout the world. The light and clear character of the painting is created by its gentle brightness and delicate pastel

colours. The impression conveyed is that these holy figures are enjoying a wonderfully warm spring day. The sun is shining from the top right into the loggia, and Mary and Christ are enthroned in the central, slightly shaded niche. The brightness of the scene is in harmony with the light palette, consisting mainly of pastel shades. The colour scheme is dominated by pink and bottle green, and these colours harmonise with the pearl-coloured robes of St. Francis and St. Zenobius and the Madonna's sky-blue robe; more lively notes are set by the strong reds of John the Baptist's cloak and St. Lucy's shoes.

The bright colours and light atmosphere of this picture would be inconceivable without the influence of Leon Battista Alberti's treatise on painting, *Della Pittura*, which was published in 1435. Alberti came from a Florentine family that was living in exile and, after finishing his training in canon law, he entered the service of Pope Eugenius IV and accompanied him to Florence in 1434. Alberti was deeply impressed by the artistic innovations which were taking place in Florence and wrote three separate treatises, on art, sculpture and architecture. In his writings he backed up and legitimized these new achievements with references to classical and contemporary art theoreticians and artists.

Alberti considered light and colour to be inextricably linked with each other. He preferred "open and clear" colours: "Philosophers say that nothing is visible that is not endowed with light and colour. There is, then, a very close relationship between colours and lights in the function of sight; and the extent of this can be observed in the fact that as the light disappears, so also do the colours, and when it returns, the colours come back along with the strength of the light."

The light colours and brightness of Domenico Veneziano's altarpiece suggest that he was acquainted with Alberti's theories. Its style is typical of a movement which can be observed in Florentine art between 1440 and 1465; it has come to be called *pittura di luce*, "light painting", and Fra Angelico's later works, as well as those of Paolo Uccello and Andrea del Castagno, are numbered amongst its proponents. The term *pittura di luce* is somewhat unfortunate, as it only stresses the way that light and colour were treated, without taking into account the artists' efforts where perspective is concerned. These painters were equally fascinated by the foreshortening effect of linear perspective; Alberti included this in his treatise on painting.

Andrea del Castagno's artistic beginnings
The first biographers of Andrea del Castagno (1423–1457) imagined the artist to have started his career as follows: a young shepherd boy passed the time in the hills of Tuscany drawing and painting from nature, until Bernardetto de' Medici, a cousin twice removed of old Cosimo's, discovered the boy's talent and provided him with a proper education in Florence. Though one should not dismiss all of this as legend, it is likely that Andrea's artistic development was rather less romantic.

Andrea del Castagno
The Last Supper, c. 1447–49
Fresco
Florence, Cenacolo di Sant' Apollonia

As indicated by the second half of his name, Andrea came from the village of Castagno in the northern part of Tuscany. He probably received his basic training at the hands of the provincial painter Paolo Schiavo. This is suggested by the frescos in a chapel in the hamlet of San Piero a Sieve, halfway between Castagno and Florence, which critics consider to be the result of collaboration between these two artists. The frescos were probably commissioned by Bernardetto de' Medici, in turn suggested by the depiction of the two patron saints of medicine, Cosma and Damian, who were also patron saints of the Medici family. In addition, we know that Bernardetto owned several properties around Piero a Sieve. So there appears to be some truth in Castagno's biographers' statements that Bernardetto de' Medici was the young painter's sponsor, and he may well have introduced him to Florence's artistic circles towards the end of the 1430s.

The cycle of famous men and women
During the course of the fourth decade of the 15th century, Andrea del Castagno gradually developed into a respected Florentine painter of frescos. It was probably in the summer of 1448 that he painted his cycle of famous men and women in the loggia of the Villa Carducci in Soffiano, near Florence. The decorations were commissioned by the respected merchant Giovanni Carducci, who may have employed Castagno on the recommendation of Bernardetto de' Medici; Carducci had close connections with this

powerful family due to his business and political activities.

Pictures of famous men and women from the past are a feature of Italian art from the Middle Ages onwards. They were used as exemplary models to decorate the walls of palaces and town halls. This tradition and its didactic intentions remained popular right into the Quattrocento. Alberti recommended displaying famous people, so that "later generations, driven by their own search for fame, should desire to imitate their virtues."

Military commanders and poets who had contributed through their deeds and works to the fame and honour of Florence appear in Castagno's cycle, together with women from biblical history. The three poets Dante, Petrarch and Boccaccio are juxtaposed with three army commanders, Pippo Spano, Farinata degli Uberti (p. 267) and Niccolò Acciaiuoli. The three women are Christian protagonists, the Old Testament queens Esther and Tomyris together with the Sibyl of Cumae, who foretold the coming of Christ. The cycle is introduced by a painting of the Madonna and Child on the end wall, which is flanked by Adam and Eve. This combination of characters is surely not just a result of their function as models; the thought of heavenly salvation must have played a part, and the enhancement of ethical and humanist ideals and the honouring of famous Florentine citizens was probably an important consideration. So far it has not been possible to explain the iconographical programme of the fresco except in these general terms. The deeper meaning of the cycle is still hidden from us.

Andrea del Castagno
The Vision of St. Jerome, c. 1455
Fresco, 300 x 179 cm
Florence, Santissima Annunziata

St. Jerome: scholar and penitent

The increase in humanist studies led to a growing demand for paintings portraying St. Jerome as the main figure, for his translation of the Bible from Greek into Latin had led to his being considered the prototype of the humanistically educated scholar. As a result, pictures of St. Jerome in his study were one of the favourite themes of the Quattrocento (cf. p. 278). Concurrently with this, around 1400, a new iconography emerged which showed Jerome as a penitent atoning for his sins in the wilderness. This iconographical innovation was made in response to the lay brotherhood of Hieronymites, which was founded towards the end of the 14th century and recognized by the Pope in 1406; they considered themselves to be the penitent Jerome's successors.

The saint appears as a penitent in the wilderness in Andrea del Castagno's fresco of *St. Jerome*, which he painted c. 1455 for the family chapel of Girolamo Corboli in Santissima Annunziata in Florence. It is possible that Girolamo Corboli was a member of the Hieronymites, who had a branch of their order very near to Santissima Annunziata.

St. Jerome is shown standing on stony ground, and his emaciated, heavily creased face, together with the loss of his front teeth, attest to the terrible privations that he has had to endure in the lonely wilderness. The emphatic realism with which Castagno showed the asceticism that had shaped the saint's face would have been unthinkable if Donatello's *Magdalen* did not already exist as a

Andrea del Castagno
Farinata degli Uberti
From the cycle of Famous Men and Women, c. 1448
Fresco (transferred to canvas), 245 x 165 cm
Florence, Galleria degli Uffizi

model (p. 196). His head is leaning back slightly and his mouth is half open as the vision of the Holy Trinity reveals itself to him. The lion also appears to have noticed part of this vision, for it is crouching, roaring with fear, behind the saint's legs. Jerome is flanked by two female saints, probably Paula and Eustochium, the mother and daughter who followed Jerome to Bethlehem in order to hear his teachings.

The bright colours and light atmosphere, as well as the bold foreshortening of God the Father and Christ, show how close the artist had come to the ideals of *pittura di luce*. The extreme foreshortening obviously caused Castagno some difficulties, however, for he later covered the not entirely successful body of Christ with red cherubs, which he painted *a secco* on the fine plaster which had already dried out. In contrast to fresco paintings, paints that are applied *a secco* peel off over the course of time, and the

spaciously airy landscapes and the sensory depiction of expensive, heavy materials. The idealized geometry and consequently perspective structure of the pictures can be explained primarily by Piero's passion for mathematics; towards the end of his life he wrote three theoretical treatises, on geometry, perspective and the abacus. The detail of the background landscapes, on the other hand, and the tactile nature of the materials, show a knowledge of Flemish painting. Piero first came into contact with Flemish art in Ferrara – one of the d'Este possessions was a *Descent from the Cross* by Rogier van der Weyden – and he continued his studies later on, mainly in Urbino, for Federico da Montefeltro particularly liked northern art. Finally, the atmosphere of Piero's early works, which appear to be flooded with light, shows the influence of *pittura di luce*, such a feature of Florentine art. He learned about *pittura di luce* when he worked for Domenico Veneziano in Florence in 1439.

Early works

The *Baptism of Christ* (left) is considered to be one of Piero della Francesca's earliest works; he painted it during the early 1440s, shortly after his stay in Florence. Though there is some debate about giving it such an early date – some art historians think the painting should be dated a decade later – the richness of the light, the clear atmosphere and the light colours are all reminiscent of Domenico Veneziano's *St. Lucy altarpiece*. If it is compared with Piero's own *Resurrection*, which the painter produced for the reception hall of the town hall in Sansepolcro (right), the case for the early dating becomes even stronger. While the main characteristic of the modelling of the figures in the *Baptism of Christ* is gentleness, the fresco is dominated by strong layers of

result is that we can now see more of the original picture than Castagno intended. One can guess what technical difficulties the painter was faced with when foreshortening this figure.

Piero della Francesca – the nonconformist

Piero della Francesca's special position within the art of the Italian Early Renaissance has been stressed repeatedly by research. For example, Piero (c. 1415/20–1492) produced his main works not in the art capital of Florence, but in remote towns such as Sansepolcro, his home town on the border with Umbria, or nearby Arezzo. Piero worked for the provincial principalities that were slowly establishing themselves, such as the d'Este in Ferrara (c. 1450), Sigismondo Malatesta in Rimini (1451), and the rulers of Montefeltro in Urbino (from around 1460); but he never worked for the Medicis in Florence.

Away from the artistic centres, Piero developed a highly individual style of painting. The invariably serious and elevated tone of his paintings was determined by his stylized idiom, which was reduced to basic geometric shapes; its crystalline abstraction stimulated the Cubists at the beginning of this century, and even today it is still considered to be surprisingly modern. The measured solemnity of his scenes harmonizes well with his lyrical and

dark and light, which give the contours of the figures a robust firmness. The basic geometrical structures of the painting are outlined more clearly, and this is a stylistic characteristic of Piero's which was to become ever more pronounced during the course of his artistic development.

The cycle of frescos in Arezzo

After a journey to Romagna, where Piero worked at the courts of Ancona, Ferrara and Rimini, he returned to Tuscany at the beginning of the 1450s. In Arezzo, he continued the frescos in the main choir chapel of San Francesco (pp. 270–1) when Bicci di Lorenzo, who had started the work, died. The theme of the cycle of frescos is the story of the True Cross told by Jacobus de Voragine in the *Legenda Aurea*, from its beginnings at the time of Genesis through to the return of the stolen Cross to Jerusalem in the year 615.

The sequence of scenes had been carefully planned, as a result of which the events on the two walls of the chapel balance each other: the eventful history of the Cross at the time of the Old Testament is the typological precursor of the history of the Cross in the New Testament. In the lunettes are pictures showing the planting of the tree upon the death of Adam – the same tree from which Christ's cross would be fashioned – and the erection of the Cross, which had been brought back to Jerusalem by the Christian Emperor Heraclius. The central part of the wall is given over to Queen Helen and the Queen of Sheba, who are worshipping the Cross. In the lower part of the wall, the victorious battle that Constantine fought in the name of the Cross against the barbarians is matched by the defeat of the infidel Emperor Chosroes, who had stolen the Cross from Jerusalem. The course of political events led to the iconography of the frescos being altered by the addition of new scenes, however. These include the *Meeting of Solomon and the Queen of Sheba* (p. 270) and the *Battle of Constantine against the Barbarians*, two scenes that can be explained by reference to contemporary politics.

Art as propaganda for the Crusades

Any hope of a continuation of the union of the Western and Orthodox Churches, which was signed in 1436 in Florence, was destroyed by the conquest of Constantinople in 1453 by the Ottoman Turks. Popes Nicholas V, Calixtus II and Pius II all responded to requests for help by the Eastern Christians by enthusiastically promoting a crusade against the Turks to liberate Constantinople and the Holy Sites, an idea, however, that was never realized.

The meeting of the Queen of Sheba and Solomon had been cited by participants in the Council of Union as the typological forerunner of the meeting of the Byzantine and Western Churches. The conquest of Constantinople charged this scene with a rather

different meaning, however. This encounter of East and West was no longer the proud representation of a united Church; it now represented the pilgrimage made by the Byzantine Church – the Queen of Sheba – to request the help of the West. In the fresco we can see the Queen bowing humbly to representatives of the West standing on the left, probably important citizens of Arezzo. Solomon, who has been identified with Cardinal Bessarion, is acting as mediator between the two groups. Bessarion, who was named Protector of the Order of St. Francis in 1458, was one of the most enthusiastic supporters of the Crusade. Having been born in Greece, and being a Western cardinal, he was the most important mediator between the two sides. This allusion is continued in the fresco of the *Battle of Constantine*. Recent research has proved that this picture was referring to a particular battle: in 1456, a handful of crusaders had managed to prevent the Turks from crossing the Danube, just as once Emperor Constantine, who during Piero's time was constantly cited as a good example, had won against the barbarians in the name of the Cross – significantly, also at the Danube.

The Franciscans were among the most fervent supporters of the Crusade, mainly at the suggestion of their new Protector, Cardinal

Piero della Francesca
Discovery of the Wood of the True Cross and Meeting of Solomon
and the Queen of Sheba, after 1458
Fresco, 336 x 747 cm
Arezzo, San Francesco, main choir

OPPOSITE:
Details from: Discovery of the
Wood of the True Cross

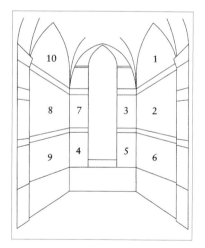

Piero della Francesca
The Legend of the True Cross
Schematic plan of the scenes
showing the narrative sequence
Fresco
Arezzo, San Francesco
Main choir

1 The Death of Adam and the Planting of the Tree
2 Discovery of the Wood of the True Cross and Meeting
   of Solomon and the Queen of Sheba
3 The Concealment of the True Cross
4 The Annunciation
5 The Dream of Constantine
6 The Battle of Constantine and Maxentius
7 The Torturing of Judas the Jew
8 The Invention of the True Cross and Recognition of the True Cross
9 Battle of Heraclius and Chosroes
10 Return of the True Cross to Jerusalem by Emperor Heraclius

Bessarion. They were the guardians of many relics in the Holy Land, which needed defending. So the Franciscans had special interests in using teachings and pictures in their churches to promote the possibility of a crusade against the Turks.

The Flagellation of Christ – the flagellation of Christianity

Piero produced the *Flagellation* (p. 268) around 1460, after a stay in Rome from 1458 to 1459. In the 18th century, the picture was in Urbino Cathedral; more is not known about the origins of this painting or who commissioned it. The action in the picture is split into two parts; on the right, in the foreground, are three men in contemporary dress, who are standing together in a square; the actual theme of the picture, the flagellation of Christ, is taking place further back in the painting. Both these scenes are combined in one painting, and yet they are actually peculiarly isolated from each other. The three men are taking no notice of the biblical events which are framed by the loggia, taking on the appearance of a picture within a picture; this aspect is reminiscent of the crucifixion panel in Fra Angelico's San Marco altarpiece (p. 250). The two scenes are separated by space – note the change in the pattern of the marble floor – and time. The sun is shining onto the square from the left, as is made plain by the shadows, but the figures in the flagellation are lit from the right.

The dichotomy of these two scenes is removed if one considers the flagellation of Christ to be a symbol. One can tell by their dress that the two men standing opposite each other in the foreground are a Byzantine (left) and a Western (right) ruler. This confrontation of

Piero della Francesca
Double portrait of Battista
Sforza and Federico da
Montefeltro, after 1472
Oil on wood, 47 x 33 cm
Florence, Galleria degli
Uffizi

Piero della Francesca
Rear of the double portrait
Triumph of Battista Sforza
and Triumph of Federico
da Montefeltro

CLARVS INSIGNI VEHITVR TRIVMPHO ·
QVEM PAREM SVMMIS DVCIBVS PERHENNIS ·
FAMA VIRTVTVM CELEBRAT DECENTER ·
SCEPTRA TENENTEM ·

QVE MODVM REBVS TENVIT SECVNDIS ·
CONIVGIS MAGNI DECORATA RERVM ·
LAVDE GESTARVM VOLITAT PER ORA ·
CVNCTA VIRORVM ·

Piero della Francesca
Madonna and Child with Angels and six Saints, adored by
Federigo da Montefeltro (Brera Altarpiece), c. 1472–74
Oil on wood, 248 x 170 cm
Milan, Pinacoteca di Brera

East and West is a reminder of the *Meeting of the Queen of Sheba and Solomon* in the Arezzo cycle of frescos (p. 270). Indeed, researchers are generally agreed that this painting should be interpreted as a call to join the Crusade against the Turks. The gesturing Greek is warning the prince to help fight the Turks, who are "flagellating" the Christian Church. The Byzantine Emperor appears in the role of Pilate – he can be recognized by his peaked hat and crimson shoes – and is helplessly watching what the heathens are doing; his hands are lying impotently in his lap.

The identity of the men standing in the foreground has prompted a flood of speculation from art historians. This is not the place to deal critically with individual suggestions. However, the enigmatic figure in the centre deserves further mention; he stands out from the other two because of his antique clothing, naked feet and faraway gaze. Like the flagellation scene, this figure also belongs on a different plane of reality. The suggestion that he is an angel seems most likely, as he matches the iconography of Piero's pictures of angels. In each case, the subjects are idealized youths, whose faces are framed by blonde curly hair like a halo. They are always barefoot and wear simple garments gathered at the waist. They are occasionally depicted without wings, such as the angel in the *Nativity* in the National Gallery in London. The role of the angel in the *Flagellation* may be as the mediator between the two sides, or possibly even as the guardian angel of tortured Constantinople.

Piero della Francesca and Federico da Montefeltro of Urbino

From about 1460, Piero was in regular contact with Duke Federico da Montefeltro of Urbino, who was fêted as one of the most successful army commanders of his era. His military activities did not prevent the Duke from pursuing the arts and sciences with equal energy. He commissioned the magnificent Palazzo Ducale in Urbino, which was started in 1455 (p. 121), employed numerous artists at his court, including the Fleming Justus van Gent, and in 1465 founded a famous library. Two of the paintings that Piero produced for the Duke have survived: the diptych with the double portrait of the *Duke and Duchess of Urbino* (p. 272), and the painting, now in Milan, of the *Madonna* (top), which includes Federico da Montefeltro wearing shining armour. Both paintings show that Piero must have come into close contact with Flemish art at Federico's court. In the Milan painting, the brilliant painting of the shining metal armour bears witness to the Flemish passion for reflecting surfaces; the idea of placing the portraits of the Duke and Duchess in front of a wide landscape also came from northern art. In addition, Piero painted both pictures using oil paints, not tempera, as was the custom until then. Mixing pigments and oil was a widespread technique in the Netherlands, as it made it possible to paint in greater detail. It was introduced into Italy in the middle of the Quattrocento, possibly by Domenico Veneziano.

Both paintings were painted after the death of Battista Sforza, Federico's wife, who died suddenly in 1472, aged twenty-six. In the Milan *Madonna*, her place opposite the kneeling Federico remains vacant, and the inscription on the back gives an account of her life that sings her praises and is phrased in the past tense. The black-clad Virtue Caritas, who is sitting on Battista's triumphal carriage and whose symbol is a pelican which she is holding in her hand (p. 272), can also be interpreted as a reference to the death of the young woman. Tradition, which liked to identify the bird with Christ, had it that the pelican tore its breast open with its beak in order to feed its young with its own blood. This self-sacrifice has its parallels in the life of the Duchess, as she died giving birth to her son.

According to Vasari, Piero became blind when he was old. Indeed, from the 1480s onwards no more paintings of his can be traced. But Piero appears to have turned away from painting even before he became blind in order to devote himself to his theoretical treatises, which he dictated towards the end of his life. He wrote *De Prospectiva Pingendi* and *De Corporibus Regularibus*, in which he researched the mathematical principles of perspective and proportion which had been so important in his own art. Piero della Francesca died, more than eighty years old, on 12 October 1492.

Andrea del Verrocchio (1435/36–1488) – the sculptor-painter

Though Andrea del Verrocchio's work as a painter cannot match his reputation as a sculptor (cf. pp. 210 ff.), he possessed one of the most important workshops in Florence, from which some of the most important painters – not sculptors – of his age came, a fact that has yet to be explained. Verrocchio's pupils and assistants included no less than Leonardo da Vinci, Pietro Perugino, Domenico Ghirlandaio, Lorenzo di Crei and Francesco Botticini. There are few paintings by Verrocchio, though recent research has attributed more paintings to

the artist and his workshop than forty years ago, when a mere five works were considered to have been painted by Verrocchio.

Verrocchio's most important painting is *The Baptism of Christ* (left), which owes its fame not least to the fact that the the young Leonardo completed the unfinished panel. Technical and stylistic examinations have shown that the painting was produced in two main stages. The first part was carried out by Verrocchio using tempera; he was probably prevented by other business from completing the painting, and it was given to his assistant Leonardo to finish, who used oil paints.

A comparison of the figure of John the Baptist, painted by Verrocchio, and the figure of Christ painted later by Leonardo using oils, shows the difference between their artistic ideals. The hand of the sculptor is clearly visible in the harsh treatment of the surface and the sharply contrasting light and dark shades, whereas the modelling of the body of Christ displays a gentleness which Leonardo achieved by means of gradual changes of colour. A similar procedure can be observed in the other parts of the painting that can be ascribed to Leonardo, such as the angel kneeling at the front, or the landscape behind it, whose contours become more blurred with increasing distance. This blurring of contours contrasts with Verrocchio's harsh emphasis of outlines, which border the body as clearly as if it was a statue, and set it off sharply from the background. It is this emphasis of line that distinguishes Verrocchio's painting, and which served as a model for the second generation of Early Renaissance painters, such as Botticelli and Filippino Lippi.

Antonio and Piero Pollaiuolo

The two brothers Antonio (1431/32–1498) and Piero Pollaiuolo (1443–1496) produced most of their paintings together. While Piero dedicated himself solely to painting, though, Antonio, who was the elder and more talented of the two brothers, was famous mainly as a goldsmith and sculptor in bronze. Vasari tells us that Antonio learnt to paint from his younger brother; he already knew how to design and draw groups of figures and compositions from his work as a goldsmith and sculptor. As a result, it is usually assumed that the designing of the compositions and figures in their paintings was done by Antonio, while Piero actually did the painting.

Antonio himself made the first reference to the brothers' work together. In a letter dating from 1494, he remembers that thirty-four years ago he painted pictures together with his brother for Piero de' Medici, which showed the Labours of Hercules and hung in the Great Hall of the Medicis' family palace. The Medici inventory of 1492 confirms Antonio's statement, because in that same hall, together with a picture of *John the Baptist* by Andrea del Castagno and a painting of *Lions in a Cage* by Pesellino, hung three large canvas paintings, which showed the hero battling the giant Antaeus, the Nemean Lion and the Hydra. Unfortunately, none of these

Antonio del Pollaiuolo
Battle of the Nude Men, c. 1470–75
Copperplate, 38.3 x 59.5 cm
New York, The Metropolitan Museum of Art,
Purchase, 1917, Joseph Pulitzer Bequest.
(17.50.99)

pictures have survived, though two smaller paintings remain, which are ascribed to Antonio and which are thought to be copies of the Pollaiuolo brothers' larger compositions. They show the defeat of Antaeus at the hands of Hercules (p. 275) and Hercules fighting the Hydra; the third picture of the Nemean Lion has been lost without trace. These remarkably small paintings would have decorated a casket or been kept as valuables in a leather wallet, to be presented to guests on special occasions.

It is not certain who these small panels belonged to, though it seems quite possible that they were also painted for the Medici family, because Hercules was a symbol of their powerful family.

The Medicis and Hercules
The figure of Hercules appears on the city seal of Florence from the 13th century on. Because of his power and courage, this classical hero was often used as an example of virtuous behaviour for Florentine citizens; he acted simultaneously as a warning to the enemies of republican Florence, because Hercules had been a famous killer of tyrants. The hero was thus both a moral example and an emblem of the republican attitude of the town; the Medicis appropriated this dual symbolism during the Quattrocento by applying the character of Hercules to themselves. By these means the family presented its moral and physical strength and assured

Antonio del Pollaiuolo
Hercules and Antaeus,
c. 1460–70
Oil on wood,
16 x 10.5 cm
Florence, Galleria degli
Uffizi

Antonio del Pollaiuolo
Martyrdom of St. Sebastian, c. 1475
Tempera on wood, 292 x 203 cm
London, The National Gallery

mythology and relates to the twelve labours which Hercules had to perform for King Eurystheus as a punishment for the terrible crime he committed of murdering his children. When Hercules set off, in order to fetch the King the apples of the Hesperides, he met the giant Antaeus on the way, who challenged him to a wrestling match. Antaeus was so strong that he was undefeatable as long as he touched the earth. Once Hercules knew this, he lifted the giant off the ground and crushed him with his hands up in the air. Antonio Pollaiuolo's remaining small panel shows the climax of this fight. The giant Antaeus has already lost his powers – his mouth is open to utter a desperate death cry, and he tries in vain to free himself from the iron vice of Hercules' embrace. We can see the sheer super-human effort made by Hercules, who is killing the giant with his arms. His muscles are straining with effort. He is leaning right back, so that Antaeus cannot touch the ground, and his face is distorted by the enormous feat of strength. The wild look on Hercules' face is reminiscent of the appearance of Andrea del Castagno's characters (cf. pp. 266–7), while the clearly anatomical drawing of his body shows the influence of Andrea del Verrocchio's art. Verrocchio, together with Antonio Pollaiuolo, introduced sculptural values to Florentine painting of the middle of the Quattrocento which would be definitive for the next generation of artists, including Sandro Botticelli.

The body as the prison of the soul

Between 1470 and 1480, Antonio Pollaiuolo created the famous copperplate of the *Battle of the Nude Men* (p. 275). This was the greatest engraving of the age, and it was the first in Italy whose artist can be identified. It has quite rightly been called the "most influential engraving that was ever published", because it was distributed as far away as northern Europe. Numerous copies of the whole composition have survived, together with individual groups of figures. The theme, the battle of ten naked young men, is unusual. Part of the surprise lies in the nakedness of the men, for up to that date nakedness was usually tied in with the theme of a scene; here, however, nakedness seems to have been an end in itself, to glorify the human body, as the ancients did. Antonio studied the anatomical composition of the human body in a way that few other artists of his era did. He dissected corpses, and also worked with living models. This interest in the human body, and the anatomical changes caused by adopting different positions, surely lie at the centre of this engraving. With this in mind, it has been suggested that Antonio created the engraving as a pattern to serve as a model for his workshop assistants and other colleagues. These could make use of the range of forms and copy groups of figures directly out of it. Such patterns and pattern books had been familiar since classical times, and they served as collections of motifs for types of figures, garments, body postures and compositions.

Florence's citizens of its republican beliefs, for which it, like Hercules, was willing to fight.

The Pollaiuolo brothers' painting of the three Labours of Hercules was therefore part of a well thought out decoration of the great hall in the Medici Palace which was, significantly, used as an audience room. The two other pictures in the room also kept to this political tenor, for they too presented city symbols: John the Baptist, who was the patron saint of Florence, and the lions, a reference to the Marzocco lions, an old symbol of the city which, like Hercules, was meant to illustrate the courage and strength of Florence.

Let us return to Antonio's panel, which shows the battle of Hercules with Antaeus (p. 275). Like the other two pictures that were produced for the Medicis, the theme derives from Greek

An unexplained feature, however, is the chain that the two warriors in the foreground are holding. The assumption has been that the abandoned battle has been caused by a quarrel about the chain, and various historical battles have been suggested as themes of the engraving; yet both warriors are holding the chain too loosely for one to be able to consider it the cause of the quarrel. Further evidence that this is not a real historical event is the fact that both the place of battle and the naked warriors themselves cannot be identified precisely. Recently the interesting suggestion has been made that the chain might be a symbol of the imprisonment in the body of the soul, which cannot be free until the person dies. The age-old theme of the dualism of the body and the soul was familiar to the Renaissance. It was taken up particularly enthusiastically by neo-Platonic philosophers, who were seeking to unite Plato's philosophy with the ideals of Christian religion. In this sense, the rows of vines and corn in the background could be an allusion to the Eucharist, and beyond it to the redemption of humanity through death. Antonio does not appear to have had any particular philosophical text in mind; these ideas were common property, and it was natural for them to be reflected in the art of the era.

Sandro Botticelli

Sandro Botticelli (1445–1510) approached his career as a painter by a very roundabout route. He first learnt the art of the goldsmith, and then became an apprentice of Fra Filippo Lippi's. After his training, c. 1470, the young painter founded his own workshop. The

first highlight of Botticelli's early period was the *Adoration of the Magi* (top), which he created in 1475. The painting was commissioned by Guasparre del Lama, who was a social upstart in Florence, having made his way up from very small beginnings by operating as a broker and moneychanger. In order to achieve respectability, he paid for a lavish chapel to be built in Santa Maria Novella, and he decorated it with Botticelli's altar painting. Del Lama's Christian name, Guasparre (= Caspar), determined the theme of the painting, as the first of the three Magi was his patron saint. We can see the sponsor standing in the group of people on the right, an elderly man, with white hair and a pale blue robe, looking towards us. Botticelli painted himself standing next to him, and this demonstrates how soon in his career he had gained artistic self-confidence (top); the most important members of the Medici family are also represented, though there is some debate as to their individual identities. Without doubt, however, the oldest king, kneeling in front of Mary and Christ, is Cosimo the Elder, who founded the family's rule over Florence at the beginning of the 15th century. But whatever led Guasparre del Lama to depict members of the Medici family, to whom he was not connected in any way, in his altar painting? It appears that he was trying to use this as a way of expressing his solidarity with that mighty family, whose goodwill he depended on in order to make successful business dealings.

Artistic self-confidence

The *Adoration* which was painted for Guasparre del Lama already shows the certainty and confidence the young artist felt when dealing with the theme of the painting. It is also apparent in the fresco of *St. Augustine* (p. 278), which Botticelli painted in 1480 for the Vespucci family. It spent most of its life in Ognissanti, the church of the order of Humiliates, where it was placed, together with the picture of *St. Jerome* by Domenico Ghirlandaio (p. 278), at the side of the entrance to the monks' choir. Ghirlandaio's fresco was on the left side, and Botticelli's picture was opposite it, so that

BOTTOM RIGHT, AND DETAIL LEFT:
Sandro Botticelli
St. Augustine, 1480
Fresco (transferred to canvas),
185 x 123 cm
Florence, Ognissanti

BOTTOM LEFT:
Domenico Ghirlandaio
St. Jerome, 1480
Fresco (transferred to canvas),
184 x 119 cm
Florence, Ognissanti

both saints faced each other. Indeed, both pictures form a narrative whole.

In Botticelli's picture, there is a clock on the right side above St. Augustine; its hand is between "I" and "XXIV", XXIV being the hour of sunset (detail, top left). The fact that Augustine is shown in his cell at a precise time of day, just before sunset, shows that this is not only a representative portrayal of the saint, but an account of a certain moment in his life. In an epistle ascribed to the saint and widely distributed during the Renaissance, Augustine writes that he was sitting in his cell one day during the last hour before sunset and was meditating on the fame and fortune of the saints. He was about to pick up his quill in order to inform Jerome of his reflections, when the saint appeared to him in a vision and explained to him that it was impossible to describe the sense of rapture if one had not experienced it oneself, as he had at that very moment – the hour of St. Jerome's death. Botticelli has captured St. Augustine's vision in his fresco. St. Jerome appears in the opposite fresco, by Ghirlandaio. Augustine is reaching for his inkwell and quill, in order to write down his thoughts for Jerome, and at that very moment he sees the vision. He is sitting up and looking upwards, and holding his right hand over his heart in a gesture of humility. His forehead is still creased by mental effort, and the light that is shining on him represents the rays of the vision, his "illumination". Botticelli has captured an instant in time between two successive moments in this painting, and by doing so has brought the narrative force of the picture to a climax.

A most illustrious commission

The rapid spread of Botticelli's fame was not confined to Florence. From the end of the seventies, the artist gained an increasing number of commissions from clients outside the city. The most famous of them was Pope Sixtus IV, who ordered Botticelli to come to Rome in 1481. Together with his Florentine colleagues Domenico Ghirlandaio and Cosimo Rosselli, as well as Perugino, who came from Perugia, Botticelli decorated the walls of the Pope's election chapel with frescos; the chapel was named the Sistine Chapel after its builder, Sixtus IV, and was to gain later fame chiefly through Michelangelo's frescos (pp. 316 ff.)

The pictures constitute an Old and a New Testament cycle of scenes from the lives of Moses and Christ, and above it is a painted gallery of pictures of Popes. Botticelli painted three scenes for the Moses cycle in the short space of eleven months. This included one of the most important pictures of the entire decorations, *The Punishment of Korah, Dathan, and Abiram* (p. 279). The fresco, which is in three parts, narrates episodes from the various risings of the Hebrews against Moses and Aaron, God's appointed leaders, as well as God's subsequent punishment of the agitators (numbers 16, 1–35). On the right side the story of the Israelites' revolt against Moses is told; they have become discontent in consequence of the

Sandro Botticelli
The Punishment of Korah, Dathan,
and Abiram, 1481–82
Fresco, 348.5 x 570 cm
Rome, Sistine Chapel

many privations they have suffered on their migrations, and want to stone Moses. In the centre is the revolt of Korah and Aaron's sons. They also want to offer incense, in competition with the authority of Aaron as high priest, who is solemnly swinging his censer in the background. The punishment of the agitators takes place on the left side of the picture, where they are swallowed up by the earth which has opened up beneath their feet.

The key to the meaning of the picture lies in the inscription in the centre of the triumphal arch. From St. Paul's Epistle to the Hebrews (5, 4), it reads, "And no man taketh this honour unto himself, but he that is called of God, as was Aaron"; it is thus a warning of the punishment that will be visited upon all who oppose God's appointed leaders. Aaron is wearing the papal tiara, consisting of three rings, which identifies him as the predecessor of the Popes, and this has a contemporary political significance. In Botticelli's time the supremacy of the Pope and his power over the Church were being increasingly questioned, and there were hopes of giving a general council wider authority. However, the Pope's right to lead was God-given, having its origins in the handing of the key from Christ to Peter. Perugino painted this central teaching of papal supremacy directly opposite Botticelli's fresco (p. 295). The immediate juxtaposition of the two pictures in the chapel underlines the connection between their content. No one should dare to attack the Pope's authority, which was given by God and legitimized by the passing of the key, and the charge, to Peter; otherwise he will be overtaken by God's punishment, just as Korah and his followers once were. This is a well thought out programme in which Sixtus IV illustrated the legitimacy of his papal authority, which had been passed from Moses, via Christ, to Peter; the supreme power given by God had then been passed to the Popes. The latters' pictures, above these narrative scenes, further stressed their divine authority.

The ideal of love

After Botticelli returned from Rome in spring 1482, he spent the rest of the decade working on the series of mythological paintings on which the present fame of the artist is based. Apart from the famous *Birth of Venus*, which shows the landing of the Goddess of Love on the island of Cythera and was probably painted for the Medici family (p. 283), the *Primavera* (p. 280, and detail p. 281) is probably one of the best known, as well as doubtless the most puzzling and disputed, of Botticelli's paintings, and its many layers of meaning still have not been satisfactorily explained.

The picture was intended for Lorenzo di Pierfrancesco, a cousin twice removed of Lorenzo the Magnificent. A recently discovered inventory dating from 1492 shows that the painting hung together with Botticelli's *Camilla and the Centaur* (p. 282) in Lorenzo di Pierfrancesco's palace in Florence.

BELOW, AND DETAIL OPPOSITE:
Sandro Botticelli
Primavera, c. 1482
Tempera on wood, 203 x 314 cm
Florence, Galleria degli Uffizi

Sandro Botticelli
Camilla and the Centaur, c. 1482
Tempera on canvas, 207 x 148 cm
Florence, Galleria degli Uffizi

Venus, the Goddess of Love, appears in the centre of an orange grove, on a meadow of flowers, and her blindfolded son Amor is above her, shooting his arrows of love. A probable model for the envisualization of the garden was the poetry of Angelo Poliziano, the Medici court poet, who lauded the Garden of Venus as a place of eternal spring and peace. In his poems, Poliziano tells how the gentle wind Zephyr is allowed entrance and bathes the meadows in dew, shrouds them in sweet scents, and clothes the earth with innumerable flowers. The God of Wind appears on the right of the picture as a blue-green winged being. He is puffing his cheeks mightily, in order to give off streams of warm air. But Zephyr's intentions turn out to be not so peaceful. He has forced his way into the garden, and the trees are swaying. He is following a nymph, who

is turning to look at him fearfully. Flowers are falling from her mouth, and mixing with those that already lavishly adorn the dress of the woman walking next to her. She in turn is reaching into her gathered dress, in order to strew the roses gathered there into the garden.

The key to this puzzling scene is an ancient written source, the *Fasti,* a poem of the Roman calendar by Ovid. In it, the poet describes the beginning of spring as the transformation of the nymph Chloris into Flora, the Goddess of Flowers. "Once I was Chloris, now I am called Flora", is the way the nymph begins her story, as flowers stream out of her mouth. Zephyr, she complains, flamed with passion when he set eyes on her, and took her forcibly before marrying her. He regretted his violence and transformed her into Flora, the Goddess of spring flowers (p. 281). The theme of this group of three figures is thus an allegorical portrayal of the coming of Spring, which is celebrated by the three Graces, companions of Venus who are gracefully dancing a roundel. They are led by Mercury, the messenger of the gods, and he is banishing the clouds that are threatening to force their way into the garden of Venus with his caduceus, a staff entwined with snakes. He is the guardian of the garden, in which, as Poliziano describes it, there are no clouds and there is eternal peace.

The painting does seem to conceal a further meaning, however, which goes beyond a mere depiction of the celebration of Spring and leads to a deeper understanding of the picture. The *Primavera* hung together with Botticelli's *Camilla and the Centaur* (p. 282) in a room in Lorenzo di Pierfrancesco's town palace. Until the inventory dating from 1492 was found, which named the young woman as Camilla, she had been identified as Pallas Athene, the Goddess of Wisdom, which explains the painting's alternative title, *Pallas and the Centaur.* Camilla, an Amazon-like heroine from Virgil's *Aeneid,* was known to the Quattrocento chiefly because of Boccaccio's book *Eligia di Madonna Fiammetta* ("Famous Women"), in which he presented Camilla as a model that prospective brides should imitate, because of her chastity and her modest behaviour. Camilla was a popular motif on the marriage chests in which the bride kept her dowry.

In Botticelli's painting, Camilla appears opposite a centaur. Centaurs were fabulous creatures of Greek mythology, half horse, half man, and were generally used as symbols of lust. In the painting he actually appears carrying a bow and arrows, as if he is about to set off on a hunt. Camilla, however, has just seized him by his hair in order to prevent him from doing this. The picture can therefore be interpreted as the victory of chastity over lust.

If we consider Botticelli's two paintings *Primavera* and *Camilla and the Centaur* as a pair, it seems likely that the idea of love as developed by the neo-Platonic philosopher Marsilio Ficino, who worked at the Medici court, was being illustrated in them. Ficino

Sandro Botticelli
The Birth of Venus, c. 1485
Tempera on canvas, 172.5 x 278.5 cm
Florence, Galleria degli Uffizi

saw love as a dual entity composed of physical and spiritual desires, which he viewed in terms of the polarities of sensuality and intellectuality, matter and spirit. Ficino described man's ideal journey through life as a striving away from sensual passions towards an intellectual desire for the illumination and wisdom of God. Ficino's idea of love seems to be reflected in both these paintings by Botticelli. Zephyr is the embodiment of unbridled desire, and this is renounced by the middle of the three Graces, who is wearing no ornaments and has turned her back on us; Cupid seems to be aiming blindly at her. She has turned away from her companions' game and is looking, lost in thought, towards Mercury, whose posture and gaze lead us out of the painting to the top left. He is not directing us into empty space, however, but across to the painting *Camilla and the Centaur*, which the inventory states was mounted over a door. So the change which is taking place in the Grace reaches its high point in

Camilla. While Zephyr gives free rein to his lust and desires of the flesh, these feelings are tamed in the centaur by Camilla. Mercury acts as the mediator between the middle Grace and Camilla. He catches the eyes of the Grace and leads them to Camilla, and this is also in accordance with his function as the messenger of the gods.

The theme of love, and in particular the presence of Camilla, who acted as a model for young brides, suggests that both paintings were produced as wedding pictures. It turns out that Lorenzo di Pierfrancesco married Semiramide d'Appiano in 1482; the style of the paintings suggests they date from that time, and they were probably intended for the young couple's wedding.

Religious paintings of the 1480s
It would be all too easy for the famous mythological paintings dating from the 1480s to obscure one's view of the religious works

283

Sandro Botticelli
The Annunciation, c. 1489–90
Tempera on wood, 150 x 156 cm
Florence, Galleria degli Uffizi

that Botticelli created at the same time; yet these were among the most beautiful altarpieces that the painter ever produced. One of them is the *Annunciation* (top). Mary and the angel meet in a room whose walls, consisting of grey *pietra serena*, contrast effectively with the vermilion floor tiles, which are set off against a pale background. Through the doorway, which is surrounded by a broad stone frame, we can see what looks like a northern landscape. The movement in the robes of the angel kneeling in front of Mary shows that he has just completed this motion, while Mary, who is standing, is bending towards the angel in a rather peculiar position. She is stretching her hands, which are slightly bent upwards, towards him, not to defend herself but in order to greet him. While Mary's right hand is reaching towards the angel's right hand, his hand remains at a seemingly immovable distance. Botticelli has captured the interplay of these hands in a quite fascinating manner, hands that want to touch each other and are yet held back as if spellbound. The angel's hand indicates the irreconcilable distance between the two halves of the painting, each of which contains one figure; it is placed precisely over the door frame, which draws a clear dividing line between Mary and the angel. It is this carefully considered and balanced composition that makes this picture one of the most beautiful of Botticelli's religious works of the 1480s.

Eschatological fears

The closer the end of the 15th century came, the greater were the fears which arose in anticipation that the end of the world and Judgement Day were imminent. The Dominican monk Girolamo Savonarola heralded its coming in fiery speeches, urging Florence's citizens to do penance and show regret for their disgraceful and all too worldly lives. Savonarola combated the luxurious way of life of the inhabitants, led by the Medici family, calling it a basic evil. On 7 February 1497 he built a "bonfire of the vanities" on the Piazza della Signoria, on which citizens were meant to burn their magnificent robes, valuable furniture, books, paintings and other luxury items. But Savonarola's fate soon took a different turn. His fanatical behaviour, which bordered on tyranny, unleashed a growing opposition against him, which extended right up to Rome's Curia. The Holy See responded to Savonarola's uncompromising criticism of the established Church by excommunicating him. Savonarola was taken prisoner, accused of heresy, and condemned to death by strangulation and burning. On 23 May 1498, Savonarola was publicly executed on the Piazza della Signoria and his body was surrendered to the flames (p. 257).

Botticelli was deeply affected by these events. This is shown by the paintings which the artist produced at the end of the 15th century. They are founded on a deeply religious feeling which shows evidence of great empathy and passion, and Botticelli showed that he considered the meaning of the pictures to be more important than correct proportions and aesthetically pleasing figures. One painting that deserves special mention in this context is *The Mystic Nativity*, which is one of the most important paintings dating from Botticelli's late period (p. 285). At first glance, it appears to be a straightforward representation of the Adoration by Mary and the shepherds. A closer examination of the lower part of the painting, however, shows that it differs from conventional depictions of the Adoration. We can see three pairs of angels and people on the piece of lawn at the front; they are embracing each other amicably, and there are also several demons lying on the ground tied to stakes. The humans are holding olive branches in their hands; these have ribbons tied to them on which are written passages from St. Luke's Gospel: "Glory to God in the Highest, and on earth peace and good will towards men."

The key to our understanding of this painting lies in the Greek inscription on the top edge of the picture:

"I, Alessandro, painted this picture at the end of the year 1500, in the troubles of Italy, in the half time after the time, at the time of the fulfilment of the 11th of St. John in the second woe of the Apocalypse, in the loosing of the Devil for three and a half years. Then shall he be chained according to the 12th, and we shall see him [trodden into the ground] as in this picture."

According to this, the painting envisualizes the arrival of the peaceful times that will come after the plagues described by St. John

Sandro Botticelli
The Mystic Nativity, 1500
Tempera on canvas, 108.5 x 75 cm
London, The National Gallery

in Revelation. Botticelli considered himself to be living in the age of the second "woe", in the eleventh chapter of Revelation, when the courtyard of the temple was left to heathens for three and a half years. It would be followed by the fulfilment of the prophecy made by John in the twelfth chapter (12, 1–5): the apocalyptic woman will appear, about to give birth and fleeing from the Devil. In exegetic writings, the apocalyptic woman was identified with Mary, and she was interpreted as a symbol of the Church. And this is also the theme of Botticelli's picture. Mary should be understood as a symbol of the Church; the birth of the Saviour heralds the rebirth of the Church. It is the dawning of a new day, as is shown by the morning light in the background of the picture. The Devil will be banished forever, and eternal peace will reign. Botticelli did not view this *renovatio* as a distant event; according to his calculations, it would take place in 1503.

Sandro Botticelli
Lamentation over the Dead Christ, c. 1495
Tempera on wood, 107 x 71 cm
Milan, Museo Poldi Pezzoli

Domenico Ghirlandaio

No other artist of the Quattrocento captured contemporary life as vividly and realistically as Domenico Ghirlandaio (1449–1494). He transposed biblical scenes to the streets and squares of Florence, allowing famous townspeople to take part in the events. This topical treatment of biblical events may well be the reason for Ghirlandaio's popularity, for he was the most famous painter of frescos of his time. Ghirlandaio produced his most important works in the 1480s. Before this, he worked together with Botticelli, Perugino and Rosselli in the Sistine Chapel in Rome; he painted two frescos there between 1481 and 1482, the *Calling of St. Peter* and the now destroyed *Resurrection*. The prestige connected with his work in Rome may well have contributed to Ghirlandaio's growing popularity, because once he had returned to his native city he was flooded with a conspicuously large number of commissions.

The frescos in the Sassetti Chapel

Ghirlandaio began painting the Sassetti family chapel, in Santa Trinità, before he left for Rome. The frescos show stories from the life of St. Francis, the patron saint of Francesco Sassetti, who commissioned the work. One of the most remarkable scenes in the cycle of frescos in the Sassetti Chapel is that showing the confirmation of the Order of St. Francis, in the lunette of the end wall (p. 288). In the centre, St. Francis is kneeling with his brothers in faith before Pope Honorius III, who is handing St. Francis a scroll confirming the Rule of the newly-founded Order of St. Francis. In

MO POMPEI FVLVIV
AVGVR
IT QVAE ME CONT

Domenico Ghirlandaio
The Confirmation of the Rule of the Order of St. Francis
by Pope Honorius III, c. 1480–85
Fresco
Florence, Santa Trinità, Sassetti Chapel

Domenico Ghirlandaio
Birth of Mary, c. 1485–90
Fresco
Florence, Santa Maria Novella, main choir

the foreground, important Florentine personalities are taking part in the historical events. On the right we can see Sassetti, who commissioned the paintings, with his young son Federigo. At his side is his employer, Lorenzo the Magnificent, followed by Antonio Pucci, a powerful and loyal friend of the Medici family. On the other side are three more of Sassetti's sons, and in the foreground Lorenzo the Magnificent's two young sons, his nephew and their teachers are climbing up the steps. The first to appear is the court poet Polizian with Giuliano, Lorenzo's nephew, followed by his sons Piero and Giovanni. The latter would later become Pope Leo X (cf. p. 257).

The extravagant architecture in the background is quite remarkable; it takes the form of a large arched hall which opens onto the Piazza della Signoria in Florence. The Loggia dei Lanzi with its three wide rounded arches, and the left side of the Palazzo Vecchio, are clearly recognizable in the distance. Even the arched hall further forwards can be identified. It is the Tempio della Pace, the Temple of Peace in Rome, which used to be attributed to Emperor Vespasian, but was in fact built by Maxentius and Constantine. The scene is therefore a mixture of buildings from Rome and Florence, just as the events in the foreground refer to both cities. The confirmation of the Rule of the Order took place in Rome, while the spectators came from contemporary Florence. By these means Florence is being glorified as the new Rome, as the new centre of the world. St. Francis once demonstrated his submission to the Pope as the head of the Church; a comparable action is now taking place with regard to Lorenzo the Magnificent, the ruler of Florence, on whom the attention of all those standing in the foreground is focused. There is no coincidence whatsoever in the fact that Ghirlandaio has placed the two events side by side.

The inclusion of the Roman Temple of Peace may, however, be an allusion to a particular event. Ever since the conspiracy of the Pazzi family in 1478, who were, with the knowledge of the Pope, planning the deposition of the Medici family and in the course of which Lorenzo's brother, Giuliano, was murdered, relations between Florence and Rome had been extremely tense. In 1480, however, with the help of Antonio Pucci, a peace treaty between the two parties was signed, and this is clearly what is being alluded to here. Why, however, was Francesco Sassetti interested in referring to this peace in his family chapel and honouring Lorenzo the Magnificent's important position as ruler of, and bringer of peace to, Florence? Francesco, who held one of the highest posts in the Medici bank, was placed in a very difficult position at the time that the chapel was painted, because his position had been subjected to numerous challenges and questioned repeatedly. Lorenzo backed Francesco despite all the difficulties, so that the latter felt very much in his patron's debt. This is borne out by a letter which he wrote to Lorenzo: "I would gladly give you my life, my children, and everything that I have in this world." And so, indeed, Francesco

Sassetti dedicated his family chapel not merely to his own memory, but also to the glory of Lorenzo the Magnificent.

The arrival of the Portinari Altar in Florence

The decoration of the Sassetti Chapel consisted not just of the cycle of frescos, but also of an altarpiece showing the *Adoration of the Shepherds* (p. 286, and detail p. 287). Mary is kneeling reverently in front of Christ, who is lying on the ground, and Joseph has just turned around in order to look out for the train of the Magi, who are approaching the stable on steeply winding roads. An important source for this painting was the triptych of the *Adoration* by Hugo van der Goes (p. 286). This painting was commissioned by Tommaso Portinari, a banker employed at the Medicis' bank in Bruges, and transported to Florence, where it was erected in 1483 in Sant'Egidio. The triptych was widely admired by Florentine artists such as Botticelli, Filippino Lippi and, above all, Ghirlandaio. They were fascinated by the realism of the scene, which was evident to a degree hitherto unknown in Florence, mainly in the rough simplicity of the shepherds. Ghirlandaio borrowed both the entire composition of the Adoration and the emphatic plainness of the shepherds from Hubert van der Goes, though he softened their coarseness in his own altarpiece (p. 287). A similar degree of northern realism can be observed in Ghirlandaio's *Old Man with a Young Boy* (p. 290), in which the artist is merciless in his portrayal of the unknown old man's face, which is disfigured by warts.

Ghirlandaio's contracts

Ghirlandaio received two further major commissions in the 1480s, and fortunately both of the contracts signed by the clients have

289

gold and ultramarine. This was an important addition, as paying for the paints was the responsibility of the artist and was already included in the price of the altarpiece. In order to guarantee compliance with individual points in the contract, such as the painting being done by Ghirlandaio alone and the use of high quality pigments, the painting was examined after it was completed and its value was estimated.

In the contract for the frescos in Santa Maria Novella, Giovanni Tuornabuoni stressed that Ghirlandaio should enrich the various scenes with "figures, buildings, castles, towns, mountains, hills, plains, rocks, costumes, birds and animals of all sorts". The frescos reflect this desire for narrative detail. In the *Birth of Mary* (p. 289), we see a room divided by pilasters, with a staircase leading down into it. A guest is being received at the top of the steps, and in the new mother's room there are already some ladies assembled to congratulate her. While Anna is sitting up in bed to receive her guests, a maid is pouring water into a bowl in order to bathe the new-born Mary. In the frieze along the top of the room there is a row of dancing putti that show the influence of Donatello's *Cantoria* in Florence (p. 193).

Because of their narrative wealth, the frescos in Santa Maria Novella are among Ghirlandaio's most important works, which not only praised God, but were, as Giovanni Tuornabuoni phrased it in his contract, also intended to add to the praise of the house of Tuornabuoni.

Filippino Lippi

The reputation of Filippino Lippi (c. 1457–1504) as one of the most important Florentine painters of the end of the 15th century was already assured before his death. He enjoyed the special favour of Lorenzo the Magnificent, who recommended him to other art patrons such as Cardinal Carafa in Rome, who in turn praised Filippino as a second Apelles. When Filippino died, at the comparatively young age of 46, all workshops in the Via de' Servi were closed during his funeral in the church of San Michele Visdomini, and Vasari relates this fact with a good deal of respect; it was an honour that was normally only accorded to princes on the day of their funeral.

Filippino was born c. 1457 in Prato, the son of the Carmelite monk and artist Fra Filippo Lippi and the nun Lucrezia Buti. He grew up in his father's house and learnt the art of painting from him. When Filippo went to Spoleto in 1467 in order to work on the frescos in the Cathedral, his son accompanied him as an assistant. After his father died in 1469, Filippino helped to finish the frescos, under the direction of the workshop assistant Fra Diamante. Three years later, the young painter started work at Botticelli's workshop in Florence. There he was exposed to the influences that were to shape his work. We do not know precisely how long his apprenticeship to Botticelli lasted, though he was certainly no longer

survived. The works in question are the cycle of frescos for Giovanni Tuornabuoni in Santa Maria Novella in Florence, and the altarpiece (p. 286) for the Church of the Ospedale degli Innocenti, a shelter for orphan children. The latter was produced in 1488. It shows the Adoration of the Magi, and two orphan children are kneeling in the front row, an allusion to the purpose of the hospital. The contract clearly stated that Ghirlandaio was to carry out the work on the painting entirely unassisted. This clause was evidently necessary, as Ghirlandaio employed many assistants – including the young Michelangelo – due to the large number of commissions he received, and these carried out a large proportion of the work. In addition, Ghirlandaio had produced a sketch for the painting which he was expected to keep to precisely, though it was left to him to decide the colouring. He was to use good quality paints, however, including

Filippino Lippi
St. Philip Exorcizing the Devil in the Temple of Mars, 1497–1502
Fresco
Florence, Santa Maria Novella, Strozzi Chapel

Filippino Lippi
The Vision of St. Bernard, c. 1485
Wood, 210 x 195 cm
Florence, Badia

working there when Botticelli accepted the commission, in 1481, to produce some frescos for the Sistine Chapel in Rome.

Filippino's early work clearly shows the influence of both his father, Filippo, and Botticelli. The paintings repeatedly display the transparent veils and valuable cloths that both these masters liked painting. In addition, the vivid and precise use of lines was adopted by Filippino from Filippo and Botticelli. Compositions which made a strong use of lines were to remain one of Filippino's most conspicuous stylistic hallmarks.

Filippino received three major commissions for frescos, each of which marked a decisive stage in his life. In the 1480s, he completed the cycle of frescos by Masaccio and Masolino in the Brancacci Chapel in Florence (cf. pp. 240 ff.); then from 1488 to 1493 he worked for Cardinal Carafa in Santa Maria sopra Minerva in Rome; and finally, at the turn of the century, he completed the paintings in the Strozzi Chapel in Santa Maria Novella, again in Florence.

The Vision of St. Bernard of Clairvaux

Filippino also gained fame as a painter of panels. One of his most important and influential paintings is the *Vision of St. Bernard* (right), which is now in the Badia in Florence. Filippino carried out the commission for the family chapel of the cloth merchant Francesco del Pugliese in the Convent delle Campora. Its precise date is not known, but it is safe to assume that it dates from the early 1480s. Filippino adapted the theme of the picture from the *legenda aurea*. St. Bernard of Clairvaux was the most exceptional

Cistercian monk of the 13th century; Mary is supposed to have given him the strength to complete his writings when he had been weakened by illness and was about to give up. This large-format picture has captured the instant when the Mother of God appeared, not from above, but walking from the left accompanied by four very curious and incredulous young angels; she is placing her right hand on the open manuscript as Bernard, sitting at the desk, looks up at her. The weariness on his face, and the prominence of the veins at his temples, shows how great his mental efforts have been, yet the eyes with which he is looking at her show the great astonishment and reverence that have filled him at the sight of the Mother of God. In the background of the painting are cliff-like towers of rock. In front of the monastery, in the top right corner of the painting, brothers of the order are pursuing their activities, and on the left we can see out onto a hilly landscape. In the bottom right corner, Piero di Francesco del Pugliese, patron and son of the donator of the family chapel, is praying.

Vasari was among the early admirers of the attention to detail of this picture; the saint's manuscripts are particularly noticeable, as Filippino has arranged and painted them almost like an independent still life. This again shows the influence of Hugo van der Goes,

Giovanni di Paolo
Madonna of Humility, c. 1442
Tempera on wood, 62 x 48.8 cm
Boston, courtesy of Museum of Fine Arts, Maria Antoinette Evans Funds

himself, were too expensive. The artist even finally went to court, which found in his favour, and the heirs were forced to pay Filippino an additional one hundred florins. Filippino did then complete the frescos, in accordance with his contract, between 1497 and 1502.

On the left side of the cycle are pictures from the life of St. John, to whom the chapel is dedicated, and the frescos to the right depict the *legenda aurea*, illustrating points in the life of St. Philip, the patron saint of Filippo Strozzi. On this side, on the lower part of the wall, is *St. Philip Exorcizing the Devil in the Temple of Mars* (p. 291). According to legend, St. Philip subdued a dragon which had killed the son of the priest of the Temple of Mars with its fiery breath. Filippino chose to paint the dramatic moment of the exorcism, which the saint carried out in front of the altar to Mars. The altar, with the statue of Mars in its centre, stands in front of a mighty, semi-circular temple complex. Herms and satyrs, armaments and weapons, incense and sacrificial containers as well as two triumphant Victories adorn the niches and ledges of the elaborate building. In front of this imposing backdrop, the figure of Philip, who has raised his arm to exorcise the dragon, the high statue of Mars, and the priest who is descending the steps of the shrine, filled with consternation and wringing his hands, all combine to form a tall triangle that is filled with tension.

The stylistic conception of the frescos was quite a novelty in Florence. The strength of the characters' expressions and drama of their movements, the agitation of the lines and the overloaded decorum of the classical architecture formed a clear contrast to previous efforts by Florentine artists to achieve clear lines and balanced, harmonic compositions. Filippino was even anticipating the stylistic content of Mannerism here, which made him one of the most advanced artists of his age. With his work pointing the way forward, Early Renaissance painting came to a conclusion in Florence.

whose Portinari Altar had been put up in Sant'Egidio not long before (p. 286).

The Strozzi Chapel frescos

In 1487, Filippino was commissioned by the wealthy banker Filippo Strozzi to paint the family chapel in the transept of Santa Maria Novella. According to the contract, the work was to be completed by 1 March 1490, yet there was a delay in its completion, for Filippino had accepted another, better-paid task in the mean time, namely to paint the frescos for Cardinal Carafa's chapel in Rome. But even after he finished these frescos in 1493, Filippino only worked slowly at the Florentine cycle of frescos, leading Strozzi's heirs – Filippo Strozzi died in 1491 – to complain about the artist's slowness. But Filippino had good cause to behave as he did: he demanded more money, as the paints, which he had to pay for

Domenico di Bartolo
Madonna of Humility, c. 1433
Tempera on wood, 93 x 59.5 cm
Siena, Pinacoteca Nazionale

Sienese painting of the Quattrocento

While the development of the Renaissance in the 15th century proceeded in most Italian cities along humanist or scientific lines, artistic development in Siena still retained a noticeable amount of religious moral concepts. It is significant that the earliest portrait we have that was painted by a Sienese artist dates from the 1490s. The reason for this late development is partly to do with the work of some prominent Sienese ecclesiastical figures. In the 14th century it was St. Catherine of Siena who set an example by living and acting according to her religious convictions; at the beginning of the 15th century it was St. Bernardine of Siena whose forceful preaching held the masses in thrall.

A further characteristic of Sienese painting of the 15th century was its orientation towards local tradition, which overwhelmingly favoured the forms of International Gothic, though the Lorenzetti brothers, with their monumental visual language and large-scale painting (see pp. 66–7), formed an important counterpoint to this development. Painters at the end of the century were still keeping to tradition; these include Francesco di Giorgio (1439–1501/02), whose *Coronation of the Virgin* (p. 294) shows the same elegance of form, rhythmical cadences of lines, and ornamentation and decoration of the scene that had fascinated his fellow artists more than a century before. Sienese painters were also fascinated by the most up-to-date achievements in Florence, though these were generally accepted with a degree of reserve, apparently reflecting the century of antagonism that had existed between Florence and Siena.

The diversity of Sienese art

The varying styles of Sienese art will be discussed with reference to two paintings (both p. 292) by Domenico di Bartolo (c. 1400/1410–1461) and Giovanni di Paolo (1403–1482). The pictures were painted in the 1430s and 1440s. In both cases the Virgin Mary is being depicted as the Madonna of Humility, who is sitting on the ground as a sign of her selflessness. Despite this similarity, it would be hard to imagine greater contrasts in the pictures themselves. While the effect of Giovanni's painting is determined by its elegant grace and gentle charm, Domenico's picture is dominated by a monumentality of form that is unique in Sienese painting. One might even call it Siena's "Florentine" painting of the Quattrocento, which reveals both Domenico's own studying of Masaccio's works – Masaccio's own *Madonna of Humility*, in the National Gallery in Washington, is a direct model – and the influence of the young Fra Filippo, Domenico Veneziano, Luca della Robbia and Donatello. The iconography of Domenico's painting is also remarkable. A complicated, foreshortened halo, in the form of a star, is above Mary's head, and beneath it is a winged banderole bearing the inscription "Maris Stella" (Star of the Sea). This extraordinary iconography can be explained by means of the ideas which St. Bernardine of Siena developed concerning the

Mother of God. For instance, he called Mary the *Maris Stella*, whose rays extend the mercy of the Holy Spirit. This was Bernardine's way of emphasizing the role of the Virgin as mediator between God and Man. The star-shaped halo was therefore an allusion to the epithet on the streamer, describing Mary as the *Maris Stella*, and the wings were symbols of the Holy Spirit, who was sent out by Mary.

Stefano Sassetta

One of the most important painters of the Sienese Quattrocento was Sassetta (1392–1450); his painting of *St. Francis in Ecstasy* (p. 293) is considered to be one of his masterpieces. The painting was the centre of an altarpiece which originally stood on the main altar of San Francesco in Borgo San Sepolcro. It was a polyptych, painted on both sides, and it has been reconstructed during the course of research lasting several years. It turns out that St. Francis was

Francesco di Giorgio
Coronation of the Virgin, 1472–73
Tempera on wood, 337 x 200 cm
Siena, Pinacoteca Nazionale

Pietro Perugino

In the case of Pietro Perugino (1448–1523), his name is once again a good source of information concerning his background. His real name was Pietro Vannucci, and he came from a small town called Città della Pieve, which was rather closer to Siena than to Perugia. He started his training with Piero della Francesca, and continued it with Verrocchio in Florence. There he got to know Botticelli, whom he came to hold in great respect, and together with him signed a contract in Rome in 1481, to collaborate on the frescos in the Vatican's Sistine Chapel for Pope Sixtus IV. As Michelangelo later painted over the altar wall with his Last Judgement (p. 328), not all the work has survived; two parts that remain are frescos showing the baptism of Christ and Moses' journey into Egypt, which Perugino painted together with Pinturicchio. There is a further fresco, which he probably painted on his own, the *Charge to Peter*.

The Charge to Peter

Of all the scenes from the lives of Moses and Christ depicted in the entire cycle of frescos, the *Charge to Peter* (p. 295) is surely the picture, seen from a conceptual and symbolic point of view, that did more than any other to uphold the power of Sixtus IV, for each Pope considered himself to be the successor of St. Peter. In accordance with this, Perugino made sure his fresco was easy to understand. The conferring of the highest priesthood on earth takes place right in the foreground. Peter is kneeling in front of Jesus and is accepting the key – the symbol of ecclesiastical power – with his right hand, while he holds his left hand to his chest in a gesture of affirmation. Immediately on either side of the protagonists are the rest of the apostles in ancient robes, and then some contemporary figures. The young man whose profile we see on the far left is Alfonso di Calabria, who happened to be staying in Rome when the picture was being painted, while the man to the far right, carrying an empty frame in his hand, is thought to be the architect of the Sistine Chapel, Giovannino de'Dolci. Another powerful male profile, which is framed by a bush of curly hair, leaps to the eye just to the left. This is a self-portrait of Perugino, whose self-confidence as an artist – similar to that of Botticelli in his *Adoration of the Magi* (p. 277) – was such that he felt able to portray himself in this company.

This was Perugino's first major commission, and it already displays his own unmistakable style. It was the first place where he used the motif of a robe draped over one shoulder and held up at the front, which he used in several paintings. It reappeared continuously in his works. It is a very three-dimensional movement, which refers back to Verrocchio's bronze group the *Christ and Doubting Thomas* in Florence's church of Orsanmichele (p. 211). Even the gestures of the hands, slightly raised or gently touching their hearts, and bare legs of some of the figures are highly characteristic of his paintings.

painted on the rear side, which faced the monks' choir, so that the Franciscans were always reminded of the good example set by the founder of their order.

The strictly frontal view and motionlessness of St. Francis are remarkable, as is the symmetry of the composition. It is safe to assume that Piero della Francesca (the painting was displayed in his home town of Sansepolcro) was inspired by this impressive altarpiece. His *Madonna of Mercy*, which was painted for the polyptych of the Misericordia brotherhood and is now in the Museo Civico in Sansepolcro, displays the same sternness and solemnity that characterizes Sassetta's picture.

Pietro Perugino
Charge to Peter (Christ Giving the Keys to St. Peter), 1481/82
Fresco, 340 x 550 cm
Rome, Vatican, Sistine Chapel

The entire composition positively radiates a clarity and unity that is not just caused by the straightforward grouping in twos and threes of the main characters at the front, but is founded primarily on the symmetrical layout of the square behind them, which is reminiscent of the sterile townscapes of Piero della Francesca's circle. A geometrically paved plain appears to stretch into infinity, and the Temple of Solomon rises up in its centre. Perugino recreated this biblical building as if it had been originally conceived as an idealized piece of Renaissance architecture: a harmonic centrally-planned building with an octagonal ground plan, a dome and four small porticos bearing pediments, such as any of Sangallo, Bramante or Palladio might have designed, though with some modifications.

Perugino the architect – or at any rate an expert on antiquity? There were centrally-planned temples and churches in ancient times, especially in Rome, where Perugino would be able to see them. Just three kilometres away from the Vatican, as the crow flies, was the Arch of Constantine, which was completed in 315; he would have been able to study it, and he used it as a model for his two triumphal arches which stand symmetrically to the right and left of the temple, on the edges of the square. The similarly symmetrical hilly landscape in the background bears the unmistakable hallmarks of Perugino. He, and later on his pupil Raphael, were the only ones to place trees so bizarrely in landscapes. Compared to their surroundings, they are unrealistically tall, and yet there does not

Pietro Perugino
Allegories of Strength and Moderation, c. 1500
Fresco, 291 x 400 cm
Perugia, Collegio di Cambio (top)

seem to be the slightest breath of air bending their delicate trunks. Perugino placed bushes and trees in grand isolation, much as they grew in his native Umbria, a stretch of country that was very green, but also quite mountainous, due to the Apennines.

The Virtues of the Guild of Money-Changers

Perugino was given his most important commission in Perugia, the heart of Umbria, c. 1500. In 1457, an audience chamber had been created for Perugia's guild of money-changers on the ground floor of the Prior's palace, and it now needed to be decorated in a suitable manner. The first stage of the work was carried out by the Florentine woodcarver Domenico del Tasso, who produced the Bench, seats, and elaborately carved wooden wall panels. Next came Perugino, whose task was to paint the remaining areas of the walls. But what themes were suited to the work and goals of a guild of money-changers? The most competent Perugian humanist, Francesco Maturanzio, gave the following reply to this question: he said that it should be a programme showing secular and Christian virtues on the walls and some planetary gods on the ceiling. Perugino rose to the challenge and produced a work which has subsequently been praised very highly (p. 296). "If the art of painting had been lost, he (Perugino) would have rediscovered it. If it had never been invented, he would have done so"; this is the inscription beneath a self-portrait which Perugino was allowed to add in his own honour at a later date. Perugino had to fill six large arched areas. He allotted a separate fresco to each of the three Christian virtues. The figure of God the Father in all His glory, which is on the right of the bench above six prophets and sibyls, is the embodiment of Hope; next to it the Adoration is Love; and the Transfiguration of Christ is Faith. The worldly virtues appear in pairs in the lunettes, where they take the form of female allegories sitting in the clouds with inscribed panels next to them. Figures from antiquity who were once particularly associated with the virtuous characteristics of wisdom or justice appear nearby. For example, two from the right underneath the personification of Moderation, who appears with her traditional jugs of wine and water, is no less a personage than Pericles, who guided Athens towards its political and cultural flowering in the fifth century before Christ.

Perugino can surely not have completed all the frescos, together with the small grotesques which cover the vaulted ceiling, on his own. He must have been helped with some of the figures by an employee from his workshop. But the earlier belief that the especially successful sections, such as the figure of Courage holding the sword and sceptre, must be by Raphael is no longer tenable. Although Perugino kept to his own style throughout, and his later work is repetitive rather than innovative, Raphael was still only an exceptionally talented seventeen-year-old pupil at this time, and the works that we know he produced at this time reveal the limitations of inexperience.

Pietro Perugino
The Vision of St. Bernardine
Wood, 173 x 160 cm
Munich, Alte Pinakothek

The Vision of St. Bernardine

Perugino's artistic qualities are brought to light particularly clearly in his atmospheric altarpiece, the *Vision of St. Bernardine* (right). In this painting he placed his figures in a room constructed according to the rules of perspective; he allowed landscape, which was only a background feature in the Collegio di Cambio, to become the central view and create the atmosphere of the picture. An unmistakably Peruginesque feature is the sight of delicate little trees with sparse foliage growing in the background, beyond which one can see a broad valley, a winding river and a little village. In front of this view Perugino has placed a building which is pure Quattrocento, and in this Mary appears to St. Bernard in a vision. She is accompanied by two angels, and surprises him at his desk; the two apostles Bartholomew and Philip appear at his side. It is in the treatment of the different materials that Perugino displays his mastery, these include Bernard's gently flowing habit, the hard, angular stone of the pilasters, the careful detail of the book (the writing almost appears to be legible), and the haloes, which in the case of Bernard looks like a delicate circlet, and on the other figures like a disc speckled with tiny light bulbs. This altarpiece, which was painted around 1498 for S. Maria Maddalena di Cestello, was widely admired and copied in Florence, for at that time religious, devotional art was enjoying an enormous upsurge of popularity. Lorenzo the Magnificent was dead, and the city was increasingly falling under the spell of the fanatical evangelist Savonarola. He preached the establishment of God's kingdom on earth and the moderation of its inhabitants. Many artists, including Botticelli, renounced heathen art and dedicated their lives to religious paintings. Perugino's paintings, such as the *Vision of St. Bernardine*

with its clearly peaceful character, were exactly what was required by the moral and religious feelings of the age.

Perugino the portrait painter

This is not to say that Perugino devoted himself entirely to commissions for religious paintings from then on. It was during these years that he produced his most famous portrait, that of *Francesco delle Opere* (left). But even here the influence of Savonarola can be seen. It was imperative, given his social position, that Francesco, who came from a family of rich Florentine cloth merchants who had been perfecting the production of valuable silk cloths for generations, should be portrayed as a devout, God-fearing person. He therefore holds a paper scroll in his right hand, and on the streamer at the end of it we can read the words "TIMETE DEUM". The expression on his face is nonetheless very self-confident. His piercing look suggests that he is an experienced businessman who is not that easy to intimidate. Perugino succeeded in producing a marvellous psychological study. He captured every single feature of Francesco's face with his brush: his slightly raised left eyebrow, the sceptical furrow at the base of his nose and the almost mocking twitch at the right corner of his mouth. It is a portrait of high quality and points the way towards Raphael's portraits.

Pietro Perugino
Portrait of Francesco delle Opere, 1494
Wood, 52 x 44 cm
Florence, Galleria degli Uffizi

Pinturicchio
Burial of St. Bernardine, c. 1484
Fresco
Rome, Santa Maria in Aracoeli, Bufalini Chapel

Pinturicchio, the "interior decorator"

Bernardino di Betto di Biagio (1454–1513), who was called Il Pinturicchio, at first kept very close to Perugino in style, especially as his fellow countryman, who was ten years his senior, had fetched him to work on the frescos in the Sistine Chapel in the Vatican and had worked on several scenes together with him. Once he had been initiated into the high art of fresco painting, Pinturicchio was no longer able to free himself from its spell. In the course of time he perfected a gossipy, pleasant manner of painting that appealed considerably to his clients – including several Popes from Sixtus IV and Alexander VI to Pius III. Though Vasari dismissed him as a "superficial interior decorator", the frescos, since destroyed, that he created in the Castle of the Angels in 1497 was one of the first modern cycles of histories, documenting and interpreting contemporary political events.

Pinturicchio's independent career began shortly after the Sistine Chapel was completed. He was commissioned by the jurist Niccolo di Manno Bufalini in 1484 to decorate his chapel in S. Maria in Aracoeli, which he intended to dedicate to St. Bernardine. The latter had once brought a long-lasting family feud between the Bufalinis and the Baglionis, who lived in Perugia, to a peaceful conclusion. Pinturicchio was to give new life to the Franciscan monk's miracles and healings on the chapel's walls. He portrayed St. Bernardine as he had been moulded by his life of strict abstinence: as a gaunt, beardless, and finally toothless monk, unshod and using a rope as a belt. In the fresco showing the burial of St. Bernardine (p. 298), it is not just his fellow monks and the invalids they cared for that are grieving – they are joined by members of the Bufalini family. But in stark contrast to the ascetic approach to life of the mendicant friars,

Pinturicchio
Departure of Aeneas Silvius Piccolomini for the Council of Basle, 1507
Fresco
Siena Cathedral, Piccolomini Library

the patron feels no embarrassment about paying his last respects to the saint wearing fur-trimmed gold brocade and accompanied by a page.

If one considers the composition of this fresco, it plainly differs little from Perugino's *Charge to Peter* (p. 295). As in that painting, a broad square opens out behind the row of people at the front, and the pattern of the paving slabs directs our vision far into the background to a temple, which is rather elongated. The only major alteration is that Pinturicchio replaced Perugino's strictly symmetrical triumphal arches with two Renaissance palaces. On the left he added a lavishly ornamented loggia, through which the funeral procession is approaching, and in the background on the right he just had room to include scenes from the life of the saint in the palace's double arcade. Above it, minuscule angels are carrying a mandorla with Bernardine's soul up to heaven.

Papal glorification

Pinturicchio was at the height of his artistic prowess when he was commissioned by Cardinal Francesco Todeschini-Piccolomini, in 1507, to decorate the Cathedral library in Siena with frescos. It was not the deeds of a saint that the cardinal wanted remembered by posterity, but those of his uncle, Aeneas Silvius Piccolomini, who had founded the valuable library and was better known as Pius II. Pinturicchio displayed the life of the Pope, starting with the departure of Aeneas Silvius Piccolomini for the Council of Basle and going up to his journey to Ancona, where he died in 1464, as a novel-like series of courtly processions through beautiful landscapes. One is almost reminded of Gentile da Fabriano's *Adoration of the Magi* (p. 239), though Pinturicchio's overall composition is more strongly inspired by northern European manuscripts which were richly illustrated, reflecting the desire for dukes, Popes and national heroes to be fittingly depicted and remembered. The smallness and decorative gilding of the frescos makes them look as if they are enlarged miniatures from a valuable codex.

Pinturicchio framed each individual scene in an illusory, vaulted building, a spatial motif that was first used by Masaccio in his fresco of the *Trinity* (p. 247). A conspicuous feature on the pilasters is the highly detailed grotesques, which also cover the entire ceiling of the library. Grotesques were highly fashionable. Since the painted grotto rooms of the classical Domus Aurea had been excavated in Rome in 1485, the complicated ornamentation which had been discovered there, which consisted of finely intertwining arabesques with putti, mythical creatures, candelabras and vases, had rapidly spread throughout Italy in the course of just ten years, mainly by means of pattern books. It was mainly Pinturicchio, who knew the originals, but also Perugino and Signorelli, who from then onwards integrated this type of ornamentation, so typical of the Renaissance, into their paintings.

Luca Signorelli
The Flagellation, c. 1475/80
Wood, 80 x 60 cm
Milan, Pinacoteca di Brera

The artistic beginnings of Luca Signorelli

The *Flagellation* (top) is the first painting known to us that was
signed with his own name by Luca Signorelli (c. 1445–1523), who
came from Cortona. *Opus luce cortonensis* is what it says on the
reddish-brown strip on the building in the background: the work
of Luca of Cortona. It is not without pride that Signorelli
announces that he has found a visual language which he considers
worth signing his name to. The influences of painters he modelled
himself on can still be seen, however. For example, this picture
reminds us of Piero della Francesca's painting on the same theme
(p. 226), where Christ is being tormented in a similar position. Yet
the powerful shapes of the flagellating soldiers suggest he studied
the works of Pollaiuolo, in particular his muscle-flaunting *Battle
of the Nude Men* (p. 273). The composition itself, with its closely-
packed wealth of detail – note the backdrop, an architectural
façade with classical reliefs – already displays Signorelli's sense of
balance and symmetry in his pictures. The blue robes of Pilate on
the left, whose high throne is positioned in an optically rather

unlikely position, are counterpointed at the bottom right in the
clothes worn by the soldier drawing his sword. The treatment of
light, which was later to become increasingly important to
Signorelli, is not very well developed in this picture. As a result,
though the bodies of the flagellators are lit in a way that displays
the plasticity of their bodies very clearly, their shadows on the
ground appear to scatter in all directions.

Signorelli painted a pendant to accompany the *Flagellation*, a
picture of Mary which was once hung on its back. These panels
were not altarpieces, but double-sided processional standards which
would lead processions around the town on important feast days.
Such processional banners had been known since the 13th century,
but were particularly widespread in Umbria and in the Marches
during the Quattrocento.

A picture within a picture

Signorelli was already a well-known artist when he painted his
Madonna of Humility, probably for the Medicis' country villa
Castello, outside the gates of Florence. In the picture, Mary is
turning towards Jesus, as if they were all alone on a meadow. She is
looking down at her little son lovingly, and He is stamping His right
foot in a display of childish defiance. Their immediate surroundings
are full of natural realism. Camomile is growing on both sides;
mallow, violets, chrysanthemums, poppies and many other flowers
are blooming around their feet. Behind Mary's back is a quite
different type of nature, namely a pagan one. Four shepherds, clad
only in loincloths, call the classical Arcadia to mind. They are so
engrossed in playing their pipes that they appear to be taking no
notice of what is happening in the foreground. They are grouped in
pairs, with one person playing his reed pipe while the other listens
thoughtfully. Included in this Arcadian, almost bucolic scene is a
ruined portal, on the left; a tree and smaller bushes have taken root
in its entablature. Nature has conquered all of Man's creations. The
same will happen one day to the classical round temple, which can
be seen on the right through the rock arch.

The question is why Signorelli placed this most human Mary and
Child in front of a backdrop that reminds one so strongly of Virgil's
Eclogues, a spring landscape filled with the songs of young
shepherds. This was surely not Signorelli's own scheme, a
supposition which is backed up by the information that the picture
was commissioned by one of the Medicis, either Lorenzo the
Magnificent or Lorenzo di Pierfrancesco. The circle of humanist
scholars which the Medicis had gathered around themselves in
Florence dealt principally with classical authors such as Plato,
Aristotle and Virgil. The background of the painting must therefore
be considered as an artistic interpretation of humanist thinking. In
addition, the use of classical motifs in religious pictures was by no
means a rarity. Classical reliefs on sarcophagi were a rich source of
inspiration for a wide range of Renaissance artists. They were also

the source of the youthful shepherds that appear in Signorelli's painting. As long as quotations from classical antiquity were not deliberately presented as pagan material, as in this case, they were automatically interpreted in a Christian sense. Small wonder that Virgil's fourth *Eclogue* was (erroneously) considered, even in the Middle Ages, to be a Messianic prophecy.

Michelangelo was later to create a comparable combination of religious and pagan motifs in his *Doni Tondo* (p. 315), in which he appears to have arbitrarily chosen ten naked young men as the background to a Holy Family. Like this, Signorelli's painting is also a tondo, or at least a circular painting that is mounted in a monochrome rectangular frame. It is therefore a picture within a picture, almost like a piece of painted architecture, which opens a window onto a broad landscape. In the upper part of the frame, the shape of the circle is repeated by the two smaller tondi, in which two prophets are writing down their prophecies on scrolls. On a shell between them is a bust of John the Baptist, and below it a simple panel bearing the inscription *Ecce Agnus Dei*. Both components, the painted frame and the round picture of Mary, were carefully co-ordinated by Signorelli so that the direction of light and tonal qualities were the same. As a result, a single source of light from the top left illuminates the entire painting. Another even stronger cohesive force is the greenish ochre colour of the frame, which reappears in the flesh tones, architecture and landscape of the circular painting.

The School of Pan

It was St. Augustine who said that the most beautiful symbolism was also the hardest to interpret. Had he lived 1100 years later, this

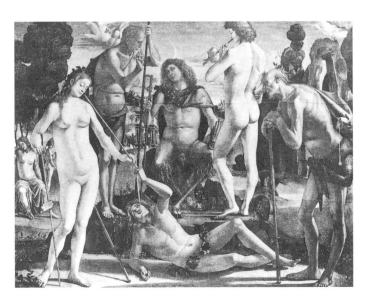

observation would almost certainly have sprung to mind when he saw Signorelli's *School of Pan* (left). The painting, which was destroyed during the Second World War, has repeatedly given researchers new food for thought. It is considered to be the oldest and most important Renaissance picture of the god Pan, who was later glorified, in Rome in particular, in connection with neo-Platonic pantheism. In Signorelli's picture, the God of Nature, son of Hermes and a nymph who bore him in the form of a goat, is sitting amidst several other inhabitants of Arcadia, but he does not appear to be aware of any of them. There are four shepherds, some of them making music, others lost in thought, and they represent the four ages of Man. The naked woman on the left together with the two female figures in the background have recently been interpreted as the moods of Woman, from self-satisfaction, to melancholy, to uncertainty. Like the *Madonna of Humility*, the *School of Pan* should also be considered in connection with the humanist Medici circle, who interpreted the figure of Pan, as Plutarch did, as the great god of Becoming and Passing.

Luca Signorelli
Resurrection of the Dead, 1499
Fresco
Orvieto Cathedral, San Brizio Chapel

OPPOSITE:
Luca Signorelli
Detail from: The Damned Consigned to Hell

302

Luca Signorelli
Detail from: The Damned Consigned to Hell

Luca Signorelli
The Damned Consigned to Hell, 1499
Fresco
Orvieto Cathedral, San Brizio Chapel

The Last Judgement in Orvieto Cathedral

Signorelli's frescos in the Cathedral of Orvieto are some of his most important works. It was here that he so dramatically captured the end of the world on the walls of the Cappella di San Brizio. He was awarded the commission in 1499 after prolonged negotiations, because neither Fra Angelico, who had started the frescos on the vault, nor Pietro Perugino, who had been the first choice to continue them in 1489, actually finished the work. The eventual decision to commission Signorelli to complete the paintings would not be a disappointment for the parish council. He stood on scaffolding for nearly five years and painted the *Antichrist*, the *Last Judgement*, the *Resurrection of the Dead*, *The Damned Consigned to Hell*, *The Blessed* and the *Coronation of the Chosen* onto wet plaster. What he was not able to complete during the course of a day on the prepared *al fresco* base, he had to add at a later stage *al secco*. These later additions – such as the putti floating in the heavens, or some of the skulls in the *Resurrection of the Dead* (p. 302) – have faded during the course of the centuries.

Of the scenes named above, it is the *Resurrection of the Dead* which always especially stirs one's emotions. Instead of keeping to the traditional approach of showing the dead rising from their graves, the resurrected, upon the trumpet blast of two large angels, are labouring to free themselves from an amorphous ground which does not appear to be made of any earthly material. Where the bodies are working their way up, it is glutinous and yielding, but changes instantly into a rock-hard, smooth substance as soon as it is needed as a support. We can see a mixture of vigorous young people and skeletons yet to re-acquire their flesh. For instance, the man sitting in the foreground still appears, despite his muscular frame, to be too exhausted to use it to get up. The process is also not yet complete in the resurrected man on the right side of the picture, though he is already engaged in a cheerful conversation with six skeletons, who appear from behind the painted coffered intrados like actors emerging from the wings. Not until the moment when the resurrected come fully back to life do they realize what is happening to them and gaze reverently up towards heaven.

There are few works in the Renaissance that contain such an abundance of nudes. Signorelli was clearly interested in displaying human anatomy. His work on the fresco was preceded by numerous studies of the structure of the human body. He repeatedly varied postures that he had worked out by painting them as seen from different angles of vision, or captured stages of motion like the freeze-frames of a film. While the skeleton in the centre of the front row has only just forced his shoulders up out of the ground, the entire torso, already turned to flesh, of the body to the right of it is already above ground. He in turn is propping his left hand on his knee and – in the next frame, i.e. the figure right behind him – pushes himself upright. Signorelli also worked some classical motifs into his picture. The two groups of three people in the background

were surely inspired by the marble *Three Graces*, which Signorelli may have known from the Libreria Piccolomini belonging to Siena Cathedral.

In the *Resurrection of the Dead*, it is not yet decided whether the resurrected will end up in Paradise or Hell. This decision has already been made in *The Damned Consigned to Hell* (pp. 303–4), the fresco which was painted diagonally opposite it. It is a scene full of pain and despair, with a pronounced cruelty far exceeding the not exactly squeamish depictions of Hell dating from the Middle Ages. Colourful shimmering demons – half-human, shaggy, goat-like beings – are forcing their way through the mass of people; each of them has grabbed one of the damned and is torturing him or her with excessive brutality. They are strangling their victims, throttling and tying them up, hurling them from the skies or throwing them to the mercy of the hellfire on the left. These events meet with the approval of three armed angels, who are standing on small cloud banks and covering the heaving masses beneath them with their heavenly swords. Signorelli has brought all his artistic ability to bear on this painting: there is an almost unending variety in the portrayed interactions, gestures and facial expressions and, not least, in the display of human anatomy – the fighting demons almost appear to be composed of bare muscle. This is the final and perhaps the finest hour of Quattrocento art, and at the same time a point of transition to High and Late Renaissance painting. The shimmering colours of the devils anticipate the metallic *intonaco* of Michelangelo's figures on the ceiling of the Sistine Chapel (pp. 316 ff.) and the Mannerist changes of colours of such artists as Pontormo (pp. 342–5).

Piero di Cosimo

Piero di Cosimo, whose real name was Piero di Lorenzo, was born in 1462 in Florence and also died there (1521). Despite this, his pictures have little in common with Florentine traditions of painting. While the main feature of the latter was a fine use of lines, Piero di Cosimo went for colourful harmonies. He was more of a painter than a draughtsman. His style was influenced, in consequence, by the atmospheric landscapes of early Leonardo. This is visible both in the hazy blue background of so many of his Madonna paintings and in his mythological and historical scenes. Piero was always inclined towards unusual themes. While other artists portrayed the creation of the world on canvas using scenes from Genesis, with Eve being created from Adam's rib, Piero di Cosimo preferred populating the dawn of the world in his pseudo-historical pictures with satyrs and centaurs going hunting for lions and bears, armed only with clubs.

It is still difficult to determine the precise extent of his works, as there is no signature, date or documentary evidence for any of his surviving paintings. The most important source for attribution is therefore Vasari's biography, which he wrote about thirty years after Piero died. Vasari, for example, mentions the "pretty head of a Cleopatra with an asp around her neck." This description matches a painting which later became known as *Simonetta Vespucci* (top). It shows the profile of a young lady, which stands out prominently against a dark cloud; her plaited hair is lavishly interwoven with pearls. Her cloak, which is slipping off her shoulders, reveals a snake which is winding itself around her golden necklace. It is this snake that led Vasari to identify her as Cleopatra, as it was well known that the Egyptian queen committed suicide using an asp. The modern title *Simonetta Vespucci*, in contrast, derives from the conspicuous inscription on the bottom edge of the painting, which was added later, presumably at the time when the painting passed into the ownership of the Vespucci family. This addition was probably an ambitious plan to create a posthumous artistic

Melozzo da Forlì
Christ in Glory, c. 1481–83
Fragment of the Ascension
Fresco (transferred to canvas)
Rome, Palazzo Quirinale

monument to the ancestress who had gained fame through Poliziano's poetry.

Owing to the appearance of the picture as a traditional profile in front of a broad landscape, the painting is normally dated as one of Piero di Cosimo's early works, from the time when he was still a pupil of Cosimo Roselli, who took him into his workshop like a son and after whom he was named "di Cosimo". As it was well known that all roads lead to Rome, he went there in 1481 with Roselli, at the bidding of Sixtus IV, to work on the frescos in the Vatican's Sistine Chapel.

Melozzo da Forlì

His contemporaries praised Melozzo da Forlì (1438–1494) as one of the best and most highly regarded painters of his age in Rome, yet his art soon fell into oblivion, overshadowed by the fame of the following generation of Cinquecento artists, including such painters as Raphael and Michelangelo. It was not until our own century that Melozzo's important and progressive position in Roman Early Renaissance art was recognized.

As good as nothing is known about the training and early works of Melozzo, but his later works show that the artist owed a great debt to the paintings of Piero della Francesca. It is possible that Melozzo had been able to study Piero's art in Ferrara, which was not far from Forlì, or he may have come into direct contact with Piero at the court of Federico da Montefeltro in Urbino, where Melozzo worked as a painter.

The first definite news of Melozzo's activities as an artist does not come until he is already working as a painter, or *pictor papalis*, for Pope Sixtus IV, for whom he painted frescos in the Vatican library. The superb fresco (p. 307), painted around 1480–81 and showing the Pope with four of his nephews and the librarian Platina, has survived. The picture is impressive because of the appearance of the unmoving, strangely isolated and heavily-robed figures, whose monumental character is reminiscent of the style of Piero della Francesca. The painting originally hung opposite the entrance to the Latin library, which had been rearranged by Sixtus. The Pope had opened it to the public, which meant the fresco was also a piece of representational art: it was a brilliant witness to the power and spirit of patronage of Sixtus II, whose public foundations were celebrated in the inscription composed by Platina.

After he had completed the work in the Vatican library, Melozzo painted the fresco in the apse of Santi Apostoli in Rome, also around 1480–81, which, despite the fragmentary state in which it has been preserved, must be considered one of his major works. The originally enormous fresco showing the *Ascension* has been passed down to us, on canvas, in sixteen separate fragments; the picture of *Christ in Glory* (left) is perhaps the most important of these. The illusionistic painting is singularly bold, with the figure of Christ seen from below and foreshortened. The masterly way in which Melozzo coped with these optical difficulties, as well as the illusion that the apse is open to the elements, make this fresco a milestone in the development of Roman ceiling paintings, and an achievement which would not be equalled until the 16th century.

Melozzo da Forlì
Pope Sixtus IV, his Nephews, and his Librarian, Platina, c. 1480–81
Fresco (transferred to canvas), 370 x 315 cm
Rome, Pinacoteca Vaticana

Alexander Rauch

Painting of the High Renaissance and Mannerism in Rome and Central Italy

However brief the period that we call the High Renaissance actually was, the four decades between *c.* 1490 and 1530 have always been regarded as the golden years of the Renaissance. Giorgio Vasari, the famous contemporary author of *Lives of the Artists*, certainly saw them as such, and so did the artists themselves, many of them combining the skills of painter, sculptor and architect in one. All were filled with the idea that they stood at the pinnacle of a new intellectual and artistic development which had begun in the Quattrocento. Baldassare Castiglione (1499–1529), the author and statesman of whom Raphael painted a portrait (p. 336), introduces us in his *Book of the Courtier* to a member of contemporary court society who is highly educated and cultured, and who strikes the modern reader as "mature" in the most comprehensive sense of the word. After the 14th century and the sublime cantos of poets such as Dante, the literature of the Quattrocento had produced only chivalric romances, lightweight novellas and, at best, philosophical treatises which sought to link Greek myth with Christian teachings. Now, however, Dante's verses were once again on everyone's lips; Michelangelo is said to have been able to recite whole sections of the *Divine Comedy*. Philosophical reflection, seriousness, meaningfulness and responsible action were the qualities increasingly expected of educated nobles and citizens. These expectations naturally filtered into Renaissance portraiture, in which the faces of the sitters reveal not simply their personal intellectual disposition – even to the extent of displaying a rather fashionable melancholy – but also the overall ripeness of the epoch. From a technical point of view, much has now become standard: perspective, for example, the device which the artists of the Quattrocento tried so hard to master, is now employed as a commonplace tool. The focus falls instead, from Leonardo onwards, upon the perspective of light and air, and upon a more accurate record and reproduction of psychological states. Understanding of the forms of classical antiquity, too, had reached such an advanced level that it was a question no longer of imitating the works of the past, but of creating new works in the spirit of these antique forebears, which were still considered a yardstick of artistic quality.

"High Renaissance" does not share the same connotations as "High Gothic" or "High Baroque". The High Renaissance signifies a distinct style which was the consummation and perfection of the preparatory stages of the Proto-Renaissance and Early Renaissance, and which – in principle – would tolerate no "successor". Hence Mannerism, which chronologically speaking followed directly on from the High Renaissance, cannot be seen as its continuation, from either a formal or an intellectual point of view. Instead, it was a questioning of seemingly irrefutable laws, as the artists of the day were indeed themselves conscious. Bearing in mind that stylistic divisions are always somewhat arbitrary and makeshift, and that they can also change – art historians around the turn of the century were still describing the Baroque as the "Late Renaissance" – I shall

Leonardo da Vinci
Annunciation, c. 1473–75
Oil on wood, 98 x 217.2 cm
Florence, Galleria degli Uffizi

BOTTOM:
Andrea del Verrocchio and Leonardo da Vinci
Detail from: The Baptism of Christ (cf. p. 274)

here adopt the conventional division of styles into Early Renaissance, High Renaissance, Mannerism, Baroque and Late Baroque.

Challenged to summarize the style of the High Renaissance in just a few words, we might identify a number of characteristics common to all three of its disciplines, painting, sculpture and architecture. In place of scenes and forms consisting of numerous components, and in place of filigree ornament, we find a reduction of form to simple but generous proportions. The multiple colours encountered in both the painting and the architecture of the Early Renaissance are replaced by an emphasis upon a small number of dominant hues, at times reduced even to monochrome. The new ideals are now the simple, large form and the striving towards a definitive solution in terms of both psychological expression and composition – a solution which admits neither addition nor subtraction. In painting, in particular, figures become noticeably larger. Groups of figures, and sometimes individual figures alone, often fill the entire pictorial plane – a development pioneered above all by Michelangelo. Through their use of linear perspective, the painters of the Early Renaissance were able to draw the viewer's eye into the picture, occasionally with the aid of figures in the foreground. In such works, however, the scene still remains distanced, as if seen in a peepshow. Any movement is entirely confined to within the picture; an outstretched arm never actually reaches beyond the pictorial plane to the viewer. Now, however, in the High Renaissance, figures appear to step or reach out of the picture. Michelangelo's *Libyan Sibyl* (p. 322) is a case in point: the length of the axis running through her outstretched arms and the open book is greater than the depth of the painted background niche – if we imagine her turned towards us, her arms and the book would reach forward in a manner found in no Early Renaissance painting. It is significant that it took a sculptor to develop this tangible forward projection in painting.

In contrast to the many artists of the Early Renaissance, each of whom made his own clearly definable contribution to the stylistic development of the era, the High Renaissance in Central Italy was dominated by just three outstanding names: Leonardo da Vinci, Michelangelo Buonarotti and Raffaelo Sanzio. (Their counterparts in northern Italy and Venice, Titian, Giorgione and Correggio, are discussed in the next chapter.) Even to their own contemporaries, such as the biographers Giorgio Vasari and Ascanio Condivi, Leonardo, Michelangelo and Raphael appeared to represent the consummation of the art of the Renaissance. The genius cult of the 19th and early 20th centuries did not fail to portray these three names as fixed stars in the firmament of art, and drew frequent comparisons with other giants of the past. Thus some saw a kinship between the genius of Michelangelo and the similarly brooding and pugnacious Beethoven; others compared the "divine facility" and harmony of the young Raphael with the music of Mozart, who died at a similarly early age. While this type of genius cult may hold little interest for us today, we can nevertheless agree with its conclusions in one particular point, namely the recognition that we are indeed dealing with three fundamentally different artist types. Leonardo, the scientific investigator and thinker, the inventor of war machines and technical equipment, the philosopher and analyst-cum-painter, who noted in his mirror writing that "The sun does not move" long before Copernicus, and whose oeuvre reflects his questioning and secretive nature. Michelangelo, the lone wolf, the dogged fighter, as his autobiography tells us, who earned himself a crooked nose in a fight as a young man, who strove after beauty, and whose oeuvre is hallmarked by struggle and challenge. And finally Raphael, the young and successful star, who appeared on his painter's scaffolding like an Apollonian youth on the stage, and who left behind an oeuvre ringing with the pure sounds of conciliatory harmony. Of course, our perceptions are also influenced by the interests and ideals of our own age and by our own personal preferences.

Returning to what we said earlier about the style of the High Renaissance, perhaps there was a reason why forms suddenly assumed such a generous scale, why formats became larger, why pictorial cycles became more direct in their didactic message, why forms became clearer and, finally, why pictorial messages became more generalized and generally more understandable. Whereas the Early Renaissance had spoken only to Italy, the High Renaissance addressed itself to the world. All Europe now looked towards Italy – not to Florence and the smaller centres of the Quattrocento, but to Rome. The artistic influence spreading from this city can only be described as epoch-making. There had certainly been art-loving popes during the Quattrocento, but it was only after the papacy had returned from its exile in Avignon and had built itself up into an centre of economic and political strength that, under Popes Julius II and Leo X, the Eternal City re-assumed its imperial character. But for the desire of the *pontifex maximus* to perpetuate the legacy of classical antiquity, such megalomaniacal monuments as Julius II's tomb, and such ambitious pictorial programmes as Michelangelo's cycle for the Sistine Chapel and Raphael's frescoes for the papal apartments, would have been unthinkable.

Within the spacious setting of Rome, where early Christian churches mingled freely with the colossal ruins of classical temples, and where aqueducts snaked their way between the Seven Hills, an equally free and far-reaching style found optimum room for development. The pictures of the High Renaissance were painted no longer to inflate the standing and pride of lesser or more powerful families of the feuding nobility in mediaeval Tuscan cities, but for a papacy that perceived itself as heir to Imperial Rome, and for a public that was streaming to the city from all corners of Europe. Michelangelo's last work, the design for the dome of St.Peter's which was only executed years after his death, is the logical conclusion of this global thinking, one which demanded the large form so characteristic of the High Renaissance.

Leonardo da Vinci

The eldest of the Leonardo–Michelangelo–Raphael triumvirate was Leonardo (1452–1519). Just a little younger than Botticelli, but 23 years older than Michelangelo, he towered – with his two colleagues – high above the other artists of his day. Leonardo was born in the citadel in the hilltop village of Vinci – or, as others argue, in the nearby village of Anciano – as the natural son of the Florentine notary Pier d'Antonio di Ser Piero and a servant girl called Caterina. He lived through the entire second half of the Quattrocento and during this time prepared the ground for the High Renaissance. Vasari was full of praise for the older artist: "Veramente mirabile e celeste era Leonardo...", he wrote in his *Lives of the Artists*: "This marvellously and divinely inspired Leonardo", "...who cultivated his genius so brilliantly that all the problems he studied he solved with ease. He possessed great strength and dexterity; he was a man of regal spirit and tremendous breadth of mind; and his name became so famous that not only was he esteemed during his lifetime but his reputation endured and became even greater after his death."

The young Leonardo outstripped the leading artists of his day even in his first works. As an apprentice in Andrea del Verrocchio's workshop, his earliest known painting is the young angel kneeling on the far left in Verrocchio's *Baptism of Christ*, begun in c. 1470 (detail, p. 309, bottom). When Verrocchio saw how greatly his pupil's figure surpassed his own, he is said to have put down his

Leonardo da Vinci
Adoration of the Magi (unfinished), c. 1482
Wood, 246 x 243 cm
Florence, Galleria degli Uffizi

profound emotion. While Verrocchio has attempted to achieve a similar effect by turning the eyes of the second angel upwards in reverence, the latter's gaze remains as vacant and artificial as that of an artist's model striking a pose. Leonardo's angel convinces us of his genuine involvement in the scene before him. Another striking feature is the way in which his body combines momentary stillness with movement – an indication of Leonardo's remarkable artistic powers even at this young age, and achieved through his treatment of material and composition. Leonardo's angel is robed in silk, falling in heavy, gleaming folds. The folds in the robes worn by Verrocchio's angel appear clumsy and shapeless by comparison; only his hands, in my opinion, betray the possible presence of Leonardo. Hands of this bony, cartilaginous type, with long fingers so emphatically pointing in a specific direction, are found in a number of other works by Leonardo, for example in the portrait of *Cecilia Gallerani* (p. 374) and in the angel in the *Virgin of the Rocks* (p. 373). They also appear in a painting which followed soon after Verrocchio's *Baptism of Christ*, namely Leonardo's *Annunciation* (p. 309).

The *Annunciation* was painted around 1473–75. It seems only logical that the young Leonardo should follow the great success of his earlier angel with a related motif. The panel was not exhibited in the Uffizi as an original Leonardo until 1867, since when it has been the subject of much debate. Incomprehensibly, there are still some who would like to attribute a smaller, unquestionably clumsy variation (Louvre) to the hand of Leonardo, while calling the present picture the work of another artist. It is true that the detailed precision of the ornamental stone table at which Mary is seated is untypical of Leonardo, and that the rustication on the building behind is alienating in its cold rectilinearity; these elements were probably executed by another hand, perhaps by Ghirlandaio or a pupil from Verrocchio's workshop. It may also be assumed that Leonardo – who left so many of his paintings unfinished – was happy to let others complete a picture as large as this one, measuring over two metres long. But the three most important elements, the angel, Mary, and the landscape background, are so characteristic of Leonardo's art and abiding style that they could only have been painted by him. Never before had an *Annunciation* been presented in this way. While the overall interpretation, the composition, and the striking linear perspective may belong firmly to the Quattrocento, the landscape background, the light, the poses of the figures and the expressions on their faces are all new. The golden light of late evening floods the scene, transforming the tall trees in the background into shadowy silhouettes. The angel also casts a shadow before him as he alights silently, with open wings, in the bed of flowers in front of Mary. Humbly bending his knee at a respectful distance, his tall, proud forehead is inclined forwards. With head lowered, he gazes at Mary from beneath slightly shaded eyes, with a look that is both penetrating and knowing. His soft lips are parted to announce the "glad tidings", but one senses that he will betray

paintbrush for good and from then on concentrated exclusively on sculpture. If this legend is true, then we can see the impact that Leonardo's painting must have had in his own time. If we lay the full picture (p. 274) in front of us and immerse ourselves in the scene, and if we then compare the interpretation of the figures and the treatment of the flesh, we can immediately understand why. The background is also attributed to Leonardo, since none of Verrocchio's other works feature an imaginary landscape in such typically Leonardesque style. In contrast to the rather set expressions on the faces of Verrocchio's figures, Leonardo's angel is animated by

Leonardo da Vinci
Mona Lisa (La Gioconda), 1503–05
Oil on wood, 77 x 53 cm
Paris, Musée du Louvre

Unlike his teacher Verrocchio or, later, Michelangelo, Leonardo art owed almost nothing to sculpture, as can be seen in the example of the next work, begun in Florence before Leonardo moved to Milan in 1482. In around 1481, Leonardo embarked upon a large *Adoration of the Magi* (p. 311) for the San Donato a Scopeto monastery, which lay not far from Florence. Although the picture never got past the stage of a wash drawing, the numerous figures peopling the panel nevertheless demonstrate how Leonardo uses a wide range of movements to bring his characters to life. These are not the permanent, statuary movements of a sculpture by Michelangelo, whose figures remain exquisitely frozen in the positions he gives them, but are movements in progress. The kneeling and bowing of the Magi thus simultaneously contains the seeds of motion in the opposite direction. These are fleeting moments, captured by Leonardo in dramatic gestures. Although recent research by J. Wasserman has shown that the two figures standing on the outside edges of the panel are taken from the Burial relief by Donatello on the Gospel pulpit of San Lorenzo in Florence, this fact only serves to underline Leonardo's emphatically painterly approach to the central scene. Only in the calming, statue-like figures framing his *Annunciation* does he look to sculpture for his model. What is most remarkable of all about his picture, however, is its entirely new organization: instead of presenting the arriving kings and shepherds one behind the other in a long horizontal line, as was the usual convention, Leonardo groups the figures around the Madonna as the central focal point. The apparently random arrangement in which the figures are distributed is offset by the perfect triangle formed by the main characters. The billowing turmoil which dominates the entire pictorial surface thereby appears to crystallize into clear forms in the centre of the composition.

Leonardo's life was as unsettled as his mind was restless. He left the *Annunciation*, for which he issued a bill for 300 florins, unfinished in Florence. In 1482 he wrote a long letter to Lodovico il Moro in Milan, offering his services as a military engineer, a designer of fortifications, an inventor of defensive and offensive war machines, a canal builder, a festival decorator, an arranger, a sculptor, a caster of bronzes, and – almost as an afterthought – a painter. In 1483 he started work in Milan on the *Virgin of the Rocks*. (His Milan works are discussed in the following chapter on painting in North Italy and Venice.) In 1502, Leonardo became General Engineer of the Romagna to Duke Valentino Cesare Borgia. One year later we find him back in Florence, where he was one of those consulted regarding the placement of Michelangelo's *David*. Leonardo's name appears in the records of the City of Florence Book of Painters for 18 October 1503, in conjunction with two works: the *Virgin and St.Anne* and the *Mona Lisa*. During this same period, he was also commissioned by Francesco Soderini to paint a scene from Florentine history, *The Battle of Anghiari*, in the council chamber in

nothing of his knowledge of the tragic outcome of events. The shape of his wings is taken up and echoed in his raised right arm and slightly bent fingers. The young Mary listens to his words attentively, with an expression more astonished than startled. The momentary suggestion of scepticism in her narrow, slightly slanting eyes seems to be giving way even as we look to a sensitive thoughtfulness. Her young face appears sweetly innocent and yet wise, like that of an intelligent and mature child. Even in this early work, Leonardo's masterly ability to fuse psyche and theme into a magnificent harmony is clearly apparent.

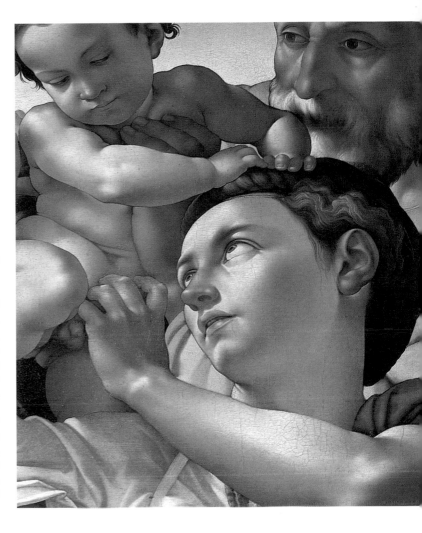

Michelangelo
Holy Family (Doni Tondo), c. 1503–04
Tempera on wood, Ø 120 cm
Florence, Galleria degli Uffizi

the Palazzo della Signoria. Leonardo's composition, which was to form a pendant to a similar fresco by Michelangelo, today only survives in drawings.

Leonardo treated the theme of the *Virgin and St. Anne* on several different occasions. The so-called *Burlington House Cartoon* (London), a charcoal drawing heightened with white (detail, p. 313), is dated to 1499–1501, whereas the oil version now in the Louvre was only completed in 1508–10 (p. 312). Some, however, may well agree with those who date the cartoon to around 1508, in view of the mature, uniform style of the figures and its cultivation of the large form. Both the cartoon and the oil painting reveal a kinship with the *Virgin of the Rocks* (p. 373), together with a new degree of maturity reached over the intervening years. Here, too, the triangle forms the basis of the taut, compact composition, and in the oil painting in particular, Leonardo clearly attempts to express in artistic terms the mystery of his subject – the coalescence of the three generations of St. Anne, the Virgin and the Infant Jesus. As in the *Mona Lisa*, the background is provided by an imaginary landscape, without place or time.

The *Virgin and St. Anne* was commissioned as an altarpiece by the Servite friars in Florence, and in 1501 Leonardo put his preliminary design on display in the Servite monastery. The response, according to Vasari, was huge: "for two days it attracted to the room where it was exhibited a crowd of men and women, young and old, who flocked there, as if they were attending a great festival, to gaze

in amazement at the marvels he had created." Does this not suggest a fundamental shift in the way people looked at art? It seems that it was becoming less a question of "what" than of "how": art was appreciated no longer in terms of its subject or its religious message, but for its showpiece character, its technical mastery and its virtuoso solution of artistic problems.

No painting in the history of the Renaissance has inspired so many interpretations and so much disagreement as the *Mona Lisa* (p. 314). Her smile, which has regularly been described as mysterious and unfathomable, has made her more famous than any other of Leonardo's works. There have been endless arguments as to whether the portrait shows a concubine of Giuliano de Medici or the wife of the Marchese del Giocondo, as Vasari would have us believe and as suggested by the painting's alternative title of *La Gioconda*. There has even been speculation as to whether the sitter is in fact a woman at all. The key to the mystery surrounding the painting and ensuring its lasting fascination can perhaps be found in Leonardo's own philosophy of art: "The moment is timeless. Time arises through the movement of the moment, and moments are end points of time." Perhaps Leonardo was the first to bring the phenomenon of Time into his pictures. Let us take a closer look: nothing in the

Mona Lisa's face, hands or posture expresses anything tangible or enduring. This is not simply a result of the *sfumato* technique, which dissolves the contours and robs the beautiful sitter of her substantiality. The smile flitting across her face appears to border between joy and reflection; her eyes seem both mild and searching, and her expression hovers between the questioning and the knowing. The longer you look at her face, the more you become aware that this smile could transform itself into another expression at any instant. No portrait by any other painter is so tantalizingly rich in possible interpretations. Leonardo, who recognized that "punto no è parte di linia" – the point is not part of the line – wrote the following words on beauty: "Look at the light and consider its beauty; shut your eyes for a moment and then look at it again: what you see of it now is not what you saw before, and what you saw of it before is no more." The beauty of the Mona Lisa is the beauty of intangibility, just as time is intangible. Time and motion are the phenomena which Leonardo introduces into painting in an entirely new way. Even the Mona Lisa's right hand, resting on top of her left arm, is not really firmly seated; it seems to have been placed there just an instant ago, but could equally well slip off again at any moment. Nor can we tell whether the index finger of her left hand is in the process of bending or unbending. The entire picture is suffused with ambivalence: are we seeing the beginnings of a smile, or is it already on the way to disappearing? Every time we close and re-open our eyes, as Leonardo suggests, we discover something new. Are her eyes slightly squinting, or is that just us? Might there even be a touch of cynical commiseration in her smile? Will her face look different to us tomorrow, when we are in a different mood? By capturing the

intangibility of the moment and of the passage of time, the transitory, Leonardo shows us the intangibility of the soul.

In 1507 Leonardo assisted the sculptor Rustici to complete a bronze group for the Baptistery in Florence. In 1508 he returned to Milan, where he completed the *Virgin and St. Anne*. In 1513 we find him in Rome, where he attracted no commissions of note. In 1514 he spent time in Parma and then in Bologna before returning to Milan. In 1516 the great Italian became court painter to Francis I of France, where painting commissions subsequently took second place to his role as universal Renaissance man at the royal table. In 1517 he took up residence in a château in Cloux, near Amboise, where he died two years later.

Michelangelo

To Pietro Aretino, the writer and art critic, friend of Titian and intimate of many leading personalities of the day, Michelangelo wrote "...that even kings and emperors consider it a great honour to be mentioned by your pen." In a letter dated 15 September 1537, the same Aretino wrote to Michelangelo: "To the divine Michelangelo. Just as those who do not reverence God bring disgrace upon their name ... so those who do not revere you bring shame upon themselves...". Further on, he continues: "I salute you with the greatest respect, for the world has many princes but only one Michelangelo!" Such was the veneration in which the artist was held in his own lifetime. Aretino's letter reached Michelangelo while he was working on the *Last Judegment*. Now aged over 60 years old, he had returned to the Vatican after a 25-year absence to complete the decoration of the Sistine Chapel with an enormous fresco on the end

wall above the altar. Once again, the sculptor had laid aside his chisel and taken up the paintbrush. But let us leave Michelangelo's last work in the Sistine Chapel and go back to the beginning. Michelangelo, who said himself that he had imbibed his love of stone with his nurse's milk in Settignano, who felt born to be a sculptor and whose magnificent last works – unfinished torsos – were also in stone, would probably never have become a painter of his own volition. It was only reluctantly that he addressed himself to painting, yet his first major commission in this field, the ceiling of the Sistine Chapel – named after Pope Sixtus IV, under whom it was built – would become one of the most important works in the entire history of painting. Michelangelo had done little to distinguish himself in painting up to this point: as an apprentice in Ghirlandaio's workshop, he received some technical instruction, but fresco and oils interested him less than the classical statues which, following a wave of excavations, had recently entered the Medici collections. He was also drawn to the works of sculptors who had dedicated themselves to the classical ideal, such as Donatello. Even in his very first painting, the tondo of the *Holy Family* (p. 315) which he completed in Florence in 1504, Michelangelo revealed himself as a painter whose formal vocabulary, use of line and, above all, vision of humankind stepped beyond the bounds of existing convention. His figures are muscular and powerful, almost athletic, and it must have been clear that this was an artist capable of taking the spirit of classical antiquity and breathing it into the Christian context of a Biblical scene. This becomes particularly apparent in a comparison with Luca Signorelli's somewhat earlier tondo of the same subject (p. 301 top). It is only after looking at Michelangelo's painting for a

Michelangelo
Details from the Sistine Chapel ceiling, 1508–12
The Creation of Adam (opposite page)
The Fall and The Expulsion from Paradise (above)
Fresco, each 280 x 570 cm
Rome, Vatican

while that you begin to wonder about the significance of the ephebes in the background, naked in the Greek fashion, and indeed about the background as a whole, in which Nazareth appears to have transformed itself into a palaestra. Here, already, Michelangelo is seeking to marry heroic antiquity with Judaeo-Christian concepts of salvation.

When Pope Julius II summoned Michelangelo to Rome in 1505 on the recommendation of Giuliano da Sangallo, it was as a sculptor, not a painter. Michelangelo was to create the most impressive tomb ever built for a pope. Three years later, however, with work on the tomb hardly begun, the Pope changed his mind: the sculptor was to paint the Sistine Chapel. According to rumour, this was a malicious scheme by Bramante to expose the great and experienced sculptor as a rather less talented painter. This is difficult to credit, however, when we consider that Michelangelo captured Bramante for posterity in the worthy figure of the Prophet Zechariah. Julius II's change of plan for Michelangelo was probably precipitated by the decision to build a new St. Peter's; it would now be some time before his tomb, originally planned for the old cathedral, could be erected. But there may have been another reason, too, one which would have a bearing on today's still far from satisfactory interpretations of the

317

Sistine Chapel frescoes. Might it have been that Julius II perceived the ceiling as an even more potent statement of his political achievements than the tomb which he had commissioned previously? The iconography behind Michelangelo's enormous pictorial cycle, with its 343 figures, has naturally long since been explained. We know who is depicted in each of the fields; we know the names of the seven Prophets and five Sibyls; we know that the four pendentives in the corners depict scenes from Judaic history, such as David's victory over Goliath, the story of Esther and the punishment of Haman. We understand the deeper symbolism behind the figures of Judith and Esther, David and Moses, all of whom turned around the fortunes of the Jewish people for the better. Naturally, the themes of the central frescoes, from the creation of the universe by the imperious figure of God to the creation of Man and the story of Noah, are instantly familiar to everyone. We even know that

Michelangelo portrayed the ancestors of Christ in the darker areas, unenlightened, as it were, about the coming salvation. These shadowy lunettes and spandrels are each assigned to main frescoes of particular brightness, a masterly device which heightens the contrast between them. From preliminary drawings, we also know that Michelangelo used male models for the female figures, including the Libyan Sibyl. What is not at all clear even today, however, is the iconography behind the scheme as a whole. It will take considerably more investigation to explain, for example, why themes from classical antiquity are woven into the programme of Christian theology and thereby accorded almost equal significance. How do we explain the role of the ancient Sibyls, who are granted the same physical scale and the same important status as the Prophets on either side of them? Why do the *ignudi*, the seated figures of naked youths who are sometimes – inaccurately – described as slaves,

occupy such a prominent position inside a church? And what is the significance of the gilded medallions which appear between the *ignudi*? These are questions that must still go unanswered; at best, we can establish that Pope Julius II wanted to secure for himself, by means of classical citations, the heritage of classical antiquity. The *pontifex maximus* in St. Peter's Basilica, supreme head of the Church foreseen by the Prophets, was also the ruler of a new Rome flourishing as in ancient times, a Rome whose destiny was contained in the ancient wisdom of the Sibyls. The Sistine ceiling might therefore be interpreted thus: the history of salvation, which promises "eternal life", has freed Rome from its heathenism and exalted it to an "eternal city". This Rome, resurrected by the mighty arm of the Pope, is now to assume the imperial role of carrying Christianity out into the world. The glorious days of Ancient Rome, corresponding more or less to the reign of Augustus, will return

under the rule of this Pope. It is thus my opinion that the programme says a great deal more about the political ambitions of the man who commissioned it than is generally considered to be the case, and, furthermore, that the programme was most certainly not devised by Michelangelo alone. In view of the fact that the artist's two favourite books were the Bible and Dante's *Divine Comedy*, the complex thematic programme, or *concetto*, of the ceiling is more likely to have been conceived on the instructions of the Pope by a *concettist* well-versed in theological philosophy and history. Such was the case, for example, with Raphael's Stanze. This would explain why Julius threatened Michelangelo on one occasion with the words: "...do you want me to throw you off the scaffolding?"; if the programme were indeed pre-planned, someone else could finish it. While the threat may not have been intended seriously, Michelangelo's writings reveal that he was nevertheless afraid that he would not be allowed to

complete his work. When the first section of the ceiling was unveiled to an astounded public on 1 November 1509, however, it must have been clear to all Rome, including Raphael, and above all to Julius, that this enormous work of art, bearing Michelangelo's unmistakable signature, could not possibly be finished by another hand.

Let us move now from the iconography of the Sistine ceiling, still not entirely explained, to its formal aspects. While those parts that are difficult to elucidate may belong to the "what" of the Pope and the *concetto*, the question of "how" is emphatically answered by Michelangelo alone. The artist is granted absolute freedom of design. It is striking that Michelangelo approached the seemingly insurmountable task of painting a ceiling of such vast proportions from his own distinctive angle: as a sculptor and an architect. This may have been the solution envisaged by the Pope and may explain why he chose his sculptor for the project. The lower walls of the chapel were already decorated with scenes from the lives of Moses and Christ, commissioned by Sixtus IV and executed by the Florentine and Umbrian artists Botticelli, Cosimo Rosselli, Piero di Cosimo, Ghirlandaio, Signorelli, Pinturicchio and Perugino. Above these frescoes, which occupied straightforward rectangular fields, Michelangelo now created a soaring barrel vault of painted architecture. The twelve existing windows along the lateral walls of the chapel were thereby integrated within the new scheme by means of twelve lunettes capped by twelve spandrels. Between these Michelangelo created attic storeys in which he placed the large seated figures of the Prophets and Sibyls. The entire central section of the vault appears to be spanned by arches, dividing the ceiling into nine separate pictorial fields. Between these arches, which are supported at either end by painted columns, the firmament is visible. Michelangelo skilfully grouped the nine central fields thus created into three triptychs: the Creation of the World, the Creation and Fall of Man, and the Story of Noah. He thereby organized the fields into a rhythmical sequence in which a large picture is flanked by two smaller ones, a device which dramatically emphasizes the four main scenes: *The Separation of Light and Darkness, The Creation of Adam, The Fall and The Expulsion from Paradise*, and *The Deluge*.

Those who look more closely at the formal composition of the ceiling will perhaps notice that the figures of both the seated Prophets and Sibyls and the ignudi grow increasingly bigger as they progress from the chapel entrance to the altar. Writers in the past have tended to ascribe this to the fact that Michelangelo's style grew increasingly free over the years. In 1926, for example, Paul Schubring wrote that when Michelangelo "removed the scaffolding after a year, he saw that the figures were too small for the viewer, and from now on his scale and composition swelled to an ever greater size..." Fritz Knapp, too, believed that from the "fine line and lean form" with which Michelangelo started, "he progresses with growing potency... One can see the increasing expressiveness of

his art." On closer inspection, however, it is possible to arrive at a quite different explanation: although, from a thematic point of view, the programme begins above the altar with the Creation of the Universe and ends at the entrance with the Story of Noah, it is not – as one might have expected in those days – designed to be read from the altar. Instead, the scenes are presented in such a way that they can only be viewed by those entering the chapel at the far end. This is of no mean significance. It shows that the entire ceiling was intended, in a new didactic thinking, to be read from the entrance and the area occupied by lay visitors. It follows, therefore, that the figures further away from the viewer, in other words closer to the altar, needed to be larger in order to be recognizable. By the same token, Michelangelo would have deliberately placed the crowded

continued on p. 329

The Libyan Sibyl
TOP: before its recent restoration
BOTTOM: after its recent restoration
Fresco, 395 x 380 cm

OPPOSITE:
Interior of the Sistine Chapel looking towards the altar

Restorer at work

The recent restoration of the Sistine Chapel ceiling

With the recent restoration of the ceiling, begun in 1980 under the supervision of Gianluigi Colalucci and completed in 1992, the original colours of Michelangelo's frescoes have been largely brought back to life. The restoration has also shed new light on the ways in which Michelangelo worked; it has been established, for example, that in the early stages he frequently made *a secco* corrections. After 1511, however, these virtually disappear. Whether the layer of dirt covering the frescoes would have been better left as a protective layer, and whether cleaning the ceiling will prevent the work from deteriorating further, are questions that must here remain unanswered. One fact is sure, however: the idea that the sculptor Michelangelo employed a moderate monochrome palette for his ceiling can no longer be upheld. While Michelangelo scholars in the past have spoken of "the dominant tone ... of the fictive stone of its architecture" (Freedberg), its "muted" colour scheme (Wöfflin), and its "sunset poeticism" (de Tolnay), the newly-restored ceiling today reveals Michelangelo employing a vibrant and luminous spectrum of colour. It is only now that we can see how, amidst the polychromatic richness of the enormous ceiling, two main colours stand out: green and violet. These are the liturgical colours of the Mass – however this is to be interpreted.

Michelangelo
Last Judgement, 1534–41
Fresco, 17 x 13.3 m (including base)
Rome, Vatican, Sistine Chapel

Michelangelo
The Crucifixion of St.Peter, 1545–50
Fresco, 625 x 661 cm
Rome, Vatican, Capella Paolina

scenes from the Story of Noah above the entrance, while assigning the pictures containing fewer – but significantly larger – figures to the other end of the chapel. Indeed, the number of figures in the central pictorial fields falls off as we move further away from the entrance: four in *The Fall*, three in *The Creation of Eve*, two in *The Creation of Adam*, and finally just one in the figure of God the Father racing through the universe. The logic of this argument becomes even more convincing when we draw two imaginary lines through the heads of the *ignudi* from the entrance to the altar: the resulting axes do not run parallel, but narrow symmetrically towards the altar. The size of the figures has been deliberately magnified in proportion to their increasing distance from the viewer, a calculated means of perspectival compensation which allows the ceiling to be read as a largely homogeneous and intelligible whole from the entrance area. For this reason, I cannot agree with Knapp, who believed that "As regards the whole, there is no indication of any intention to achieve a illusionistic, painterly effect", and felt there was "no question of any spatial coherence". On the contrary, Michelangelo appears to have anticipated the illusionistic devices which would subsequently become a standard feature of the ceiling painting of the Baroque.

It is notable, too, that almost all the figures are portrayed seated – not just the Prophets, Sibyls and *ignudi*, but also the ancestors of Christ in their shadowy lunettes. (Only the *putti* intended to represent statues on top of the pillars are standing.) At the same time, however, not one is seated in the same position as another; rather, Michelangelo offers us a multitude of different variations upon the same theme. The seated pose thereby becomes a vehicle for his grand-scale style: just as the mighty statue of *Moses*, carved in marble for Julius II's tomb, would appear even more gigantic if we were to imagine him standing up, so the figures in the Sistine Chapel can, in their seated positions, be portrayed as much larger than the limited ceiling space would otherwise allow.

On All Saints' Day in October 1512, the ceiling was unveiled. A few weeks earlier, in September, Michelangelo wrote to his brother Buonarroto in Florence: "I must tell you that I haven't got a penny and am having to go barefoot and naked, so to speak, and I can't have the rest of my fee until I've finished the job, and I'm having to put up with the greatest vexations and hardships ... as long as you can manage without, don't use any of my money ... at all events, I shall arrange it so that I can celebrate All Saints' with you, God willing. Michelangelo, sculptor in Rome." His letter is as distressing as it is sobering; it shows Michelangelo – painting the masterpiece of the century yet still modestly signing himself "sculptor" – made wretched by the burden of his commission. Lost in thought is also how he portrayed himself in the figure of the prophet *Jeremiah* (p. 321), pondering the Scriptures – or is his self-portrait to be found in the figure of Sadok, in one of the lunettes? Even if Julius II only went so far in exerting pressure on Michelangelo, unwilling to risk losing

him altogether, the position of the great artist under papal rule and protection can hardly be described as elevated. While Julius II wanted the Sistine ceiling to present the viewer with a coded programme which symbolically portrayed his rule as the equivalent or continuation of the supposedly felicitous years of the Roman Empire, Michelangelo held his own views on the purpose of his pictures: "For the principle of painting is this: Those who do not know their letters shall read from it – and again: The picture shall take the place of the book." At a personal level, Michelangelo's ambitions for his art cost him much struggle and hardship. As he expressed it in a letter to Francesco de Hollanda: "What you have to strive for with all your means, a great deal of hard work and a willingness to learn by the sweat of your brow, is to make the work that you produce with such great pains look as if it was dashed off easily, quickly, and virtually without effort – even if that is not the case" (after Condivi).

Through the hand of Michelangelo, Julius II succeeded in bequeathing his testament to posterity in an extraordinary work of art. His original plan for a tomb on an imperial scale would not be realized, however. One year after the completion of the Sistine ceiling, the Pope died.

For a long while Michelangelo was once again free to concentrate

upon sculpture. In 1535, however, Pope Paul III recalled him to Rome, this time to become senior architect, sculptor and painter to the Vatican. One year later, Michelangelo began work on the *Last Judgement* on the altar wall of the Sistine Chapel. In the twenty years since he had completed the ceiling, both his style and his approach had changed. It seems as if he wanted to prove that he could organize even the largest pictorial surface without the help of architectural divisions. Indeed, his pictorial surface could hardly be big enough: he went so far as to have the mouldings on the outlying edges of the altar wall chipped off in order to make use of every last inch of space. The *Last Judgement* is separated from the ceiling paintings by only a thin decorative strip, which traces the curve of

two arches at the top and thereby lends the composition, not inappropriately, the shape of the tablets bearing the Ten Commandments. A tremendous storm – the ascension of the Just and the fall of the Damned – is raging in a gigantic sea of human bodies. As the centralizing figure amidst the masses stands Christ in judgment, beardless in the classical manner, at once Apollonian and Herculean. His judgment is terrible; even Mary is recoiling in fear beneath his raised arm. Much has been said about this painting. In the tragedy of the *dies irae* it presents, perhaps there indeed lies something of a personal reckoning by the elderly Michelangelo, the brooding and tormented artist so rarely treated justly in his lifetime, and weighed down by the burden of his fate. Indeed, the artist portrays himself in the *Last Judgement* as a shed skin bearing his own features, dangling from the powerful hand of St.Bartholomew, who looks reproachfully and at the same time questioningly at Christ, asking whether he should save him or let him fall. This macabre self-portrait closely corresponds to the ageing artist's state of mind, as clearly revealed in his letters. He felt he had been exploited, even financially swindled by his employers, in particular by Julius II, who had treated the artist in such a cold-blooded, arrogant and domineering fashion. In one of his late sonnets, Michelangelo paints a bleak picture of his living situation: "Here I am poor and alone / enclosed like a pith in its rind, / or like a spirit holed up in a decanter; / and my dark tomb allows little flight... / About the exit are dung-heaps of giants, / as though all those who have taken of grapes or physic / do not go elsewhere to stool. / I have become well acquainted with urine... / Melancholy is my joy, and my repose / are these discomforts... / Anyone who might see me celebrating the Magi / would really be seeing something, or even more / if he saw my house here amidst such rich palaces... / I have a voice like a hornet in an oil jar, / coming from a leathern cask and a halter of bones; / My face has a shape which strikes terror.../ Precious art, in which for a while I enjoyed such renown, / has left me in this state; / Poor, old, and a slave in others' power. / I am undone if I do not die soon."

It is a noticeable fact, albeit one which has not previously been observed, that Michelangelo has positioned the cavernous entrance to the underworld at the very place where the eyes of the priest conducting Mass would be directed. In the effect created by the altar cross standing between the celebrant and the painted gateway to Hell, Michelangelo may have been engaging in a subtle form of symbolism. (We shall be discussing other instances of this interplay between altarpiece and altar function in the work of Fra Bartolommeo and Andrea del Sarto below.) The *Last Judgement* was completed in 1541, and despite its inclusion of numerous naked figures, it was received by Rome with acclaim. It was only later, upon the orders of Pope Paul IV, that Daniele da Volterra (from then on nicknamed "the breeches painter") and Girolamo da Fano covered the nudity with additional draperies. In this context, it is

Raphael
Sposalizio (Marriage of the
Virgin), 1504
Oil on wood, 170 x 117 cm
Milan, Pinacoteca di Brera

interesting to note how cleverly the writer Pietro Aretino sought to
defend the naked parts: he emphatically insisted that the "excessive
freedom in the portrayal of nudity [was] a source of particular
vexation to the Protestants."

It has repeatedly been said that the 60-year-old artist, whose own
experience of the world had led him to conclude that for many
rogues there are but few good souls, placed greater emphasis upon
the Damned tumbling into Hell than upon the joy of the Just
ascending into Heaven. The *Last Judgement* is undeniably influenced
by the poetry of Dante, and also by the myths of classical antiquity,
for example in the figure of Charon ferrying his bark across the
Acheron river. Towards the top, the few fixed points within the
enormous scene vanish and everything begins to flow. The viewer is
no longer presented with an ordered image, but is required to find
his own way through the composition. Here Michelangelo is already
anticipating the painting of the Baroque.

Michelangelo concluded his career as a painter with his frescos
for the Capella Paolina in the Vatican, the *Conversion of St. Paul* of
1545 and the *Crucifixion of St. Peter* of 1550 (p. 329), although it
would be another 15 years before he finally died (1564). In these
works, too, he was already thinking along Baroque lines, but his
mature Renaissance style was still unable to grasp the new principles
of organization which would be developed by Baroque painting.
Back in his world of stone, in his late Pietà groups and his designs
for the dome of the new St. Peter's, he continued even at an
advanced age to create masterpieces in the world history of art.

Raphael
Madonna with the Goldfinch,
c. 1507
Oil on wood, 107 x 77 cm
Florence, Galleria degli Uffizi

Raphael

Raffaelo Sanzio was the youngest of the three giants of the High
Renaissance. He was born in Urbino in 1483 and received his first
instruction in the techniques of painting from his father, Giovanni
Santi, a minor artist. Urbino, where Raphael spent his youth, was
also the seat of the warfaring but art-loving condottiere Federico II
da Montefeltro. At Federico's court, Raphael was introduced to the
works of such artists as Paolo Uccello, Luca Signorelli, Melozzo da
Forlì and Francesco di Giorgio, as well as the Flemish artists
Hieronymus Bosch and Joos van Gent. At the age of seventeen, his
father sent him to Perugia to become an apprentice under the highly-
regarded Perugino. In the four years he spent in Perugino's
workshop, Raphael learned all that his master could teach him, and
the period passed without problems or challenges. In his early
works, Raphael remained faithful to the Perugino School. This is
understandable, insofar as the stylistic characteristics which he had
acquired from his teacher, namely a clear organization of the
composition and the avoidance of excessive detail, also provided
useful means through which to express the new spirit of the High
Renaissance. In some works it is not easy to distinguish between the

hand of Perugino and that of the young Raphael. The idealizing beauty of Peruginesque women, with their calmly contemplative expressions and strikingly small mouths, lingers on for some time in the faces of Raphael's Madonnas (such as that in the Solly Collection and the *Madonna del Duca die Terranuova* in Berlin). Slowly and tentatively, however, Raphael began to modify the style he had learned, gradually assimilating the new techniques of Leonardo and Michelangelo. The conception, structure and style of his early, famous *Sposalizio* (*Marriage of the Virgin*) of 1504 (p. 331, top) correspond closely to those of the work of the same name by Perugino, and it is assumed that Raphael was here executing a repeat commission passed on to him by his teacher. But while the faces of the figures, such as that of the girl on the left, could have been painted by Perugino, Raphael can elsewhere be seen to introduce elements which reveal his interest in the achievements of the new age. The domed building in the semicircular upper half of the picture may be derived from Bramante's contemporary ideal of architecture, as expressed in his round tempietto at S. Pietro in Montorio in Rome. The scene is one of tranquility. Mary graciously receives the ring from Joseph, who is depicted barefoot in accordance with the custom of oath-taking ceremonies at that time. In contrast to the calm figures of the main group, one young man in the foreground is shown in motion; angered at his failure to win Mary, he is breaking a dead stick over his knee. Joseph's stick, on the other hand, has blossomed afresh in accordance with apocryphal legend, indicating that he has been chosen for Mary.

The School of Athens,
Detail: Plato and Aristotle

Raphael, Giulio Romano and others
The Burning of the Borgo, 1514
Fresco
Rome, Vatican, Stanza dell'Incendio di Borgo

In 1504 Raphael went to Florence, bearing a letter of recommendation from the Duchess of Montefeltro, Federico's daughter, to the gonfalonier Soderini. The intensive debates surrounding the new directions being taken in art at that time must have made a forceful impression on the young 21-year-old. It was a period in which Leonardo, just returned from Milan, was astounding the public with his *Mona Lisa*; Fra Bartolommeo was exhibiting his *Last Judgement*; and Michelangelo, who had come back to Florence from his first trip to Rome three years previously, had completed his *David* and was now working on the cartoon of the *Bathing Soldiers*, part of a series of historical and battle scenes planned for the Palazzo della Signoria. As we have seen, Leonardo also produced a design for another fresco in the same series, *The Battle of Anghiari*. As Benvenuto Cellini later recalled: "One of these cartoons was in the Medici palace, and the other in the Pope's hall: and while they remained intact they served as a school for all the world." Raphael responded to the artistic challenge posed by these cartoons in drawings in which he took up the theme of battle, such as his *Battle of the Lapiths and the Centaurs* sketch of around 1504.

Raphael's eagerness to assimilate the advances made by Leonardo is already apparent in his *Madonna with the Goldfinch* (p. 331) of 1506. The softness of the Virgin's face, the use of a blurring sfumato, and the sense of a transitory movement frozen in time – all these can be traced back to the older master. But whereas, in Leonardo, the contrast between the clear triangularity of the composition and the puzzling interlocking relationships of the figures often gives rise to an element of unease – a tension which Leonardo deliberately cultivated – Raphael never abandons the equilibrium of the equally-weighted composition and its self-contained components.

In autumn 1508, shortly after summoning Michelangelo to Rome, Julius II also sent for Raphael. If Vasari is to be believed, the Pope acted upon the recommendation of Bramante, the architect of St. Peter's, who was also originally from the Urbino area. A suite of papal rooms was to be decorated on the basis of a theologically-determined *concetto*. Some of the preliminary work had already been executed (perhaps not altogether to the Pope's satisfaction) by the artists Sodoma and Peruzzi. In contrast to the multiple small components typical of Early Renaissance frescoes, such as those by Fra Angelico in the Vatican and by Gentile da Fabriano in the Lateran (now lost), a freer, more generous style, appropriate to the might and breadth of the Roman papacy, was now the order of the day. It was an ambitious commission, and Raphael found himself obliged to recruit an increasing number of pupils and assistants for the task, so much so that in the later rooms, in particular, it is not always easy to distinguish between the various hands. In the case of the first Stanza, however, the Camera della Segnatura – so called, because it was here that the Pope signed acts of grace – the frescoes stem entirely from the hand of Raphael. He commenced work at the beginning of 1509, and from the very start broke away from the

passionate love of detail so characteristic of Florentine painting, and thus away from the style of Ghirlandaio, Botticelli and Piero della Francesco. He developed instead an expansive style of composition which presented itself as a homogeneous and easily intelligible whole. In large, arched frescoes Raphael brought to life the subjects he had been instructed to paint: the theological *Disputà* (*Disputation Concerning the Holy Sacrament*) and its pendant, *The School of Athens*, portraying the secular sciences of philosophy (p. 332). Aristotle and Plato (detail, p. 333) are seen in conversation at the centre of the picture. Just as one might imagine a scholarly discourse taking place in Ancient Greece, they are walking – in true Peripatetic manner – through a lofty lyceum. The gesture which Plato is making with his upward-pointing finger is symbolic in meaning: he is pointing to the source of higher inspiration, the realm of ideas. Aristotle, on the other hand, is gesturing downwards, towards the

335

starting-point of all the natural sciences. Like Michelangelo in the Sistine ceiling, Raphael also incorporates a number of his contemporaries into his fresco. Thus Plato is probably a portrait of Leonardo, while Archimedes, bending down to draw on a slate tablet with a pair of dividers, may be recognized as Bramante. The figure immediately behind and slightly above is that of Federico Gonzaga. In addition to these and many others whose identities are now lost to us, Raphael also included himself: together with Sodoma, he looks out towards the viewer from beside the pillar at the extreme right-hand edge of the picture.

The decoration of the Stanza della Segnatura continues with the *Three Cardinal Virtues* and *Parnassus*, whose underlying message proclaims Julius II as a new Apollo and his reign as the new, golden era for poetry and art. While a classical calm still reigns amongst the many figures populating the frescoes in this first room, the following Stanza d'Eliodoro shows Raphael – with the assistance of Guilio Romano – treating a highly dramatic event. In the *Expulsion of Heliodorus*, heavenly forces drive the desecrator Heliodorus out of the Jerusalem temple, their fury expressed through the dynamism of their poses as they hurtle through the air. While the consternated witnesses on the left react to the scene with horror, the high priest praying in the background is a statement of confident faith. Raphael here seeks to express inner feelings through bodily movement and posture, through the vehicles of line and composition. Despite all the momentum and drama in the picture, the composition remains controlled and self-contained, and is combined with a magnificent painted architectural setting reminiscent of Alberti's S. Andrea church in Mantua (p. 112). This would become an enduring principle of Raphael's art, and appears in the same Stanza in *The Release of St. Peter*, an artistic statement of light and dark which anticipates the chiaroscuro which we find cultivated later by Caravaggio.

The Triumph of Galatea (p. 335), which Raphael painted in 1512 in the palazzo owned by the banker Agostino Chigi (the later Villa Farnesina) is perhaps the supreme evocation of the glorious spirit of antiquity. Much of the beauty of Galatea's face lies in its hint of shyness and innocence, as if she were utterly unaware of her physical charms; the expression of devotion on her face is not unlike that of Leonardo's angel in Verrocchio's *Baptism of Christ* (detail, p. 309, bottom). The composition is clearly constructed upon the interplay of diagonals. The arrows strung in the bows of the putti establish directional lines which are taken up in the lower half of the picture. Thus the diagonal issuing from the arrow top left, for example, is continued in the dolphins' reins, while the arrow top right is restated in the body of the twisting sea nymph. Raphael positions the head of the beautiful Galatea subtly but clearly at the exact centre of the composition.

The above-mentioned works may be seen as high points of what we understand as High Renaissance painting in its most evolved

Raphael
Pope Leo X with Cardinals Giulio de'Medici and Luigi de'Rossi, 1518/19
Oil on wood, 154 x 119 cm
Florence, Galleria degli Uffizi

form. The transition to a new approach to art was complete. A painting was no longer to be the mere portrayal of an event, but was to translate and interpret its subject-matter in its composition. The movement of the body was now understood as an analogy for the animation of the spirit or the emotions; the external structure of a scene proclaimed its inner content. Everything in the picture was aimed at harmonious balance; each individual figure became an inseparable part of the whole. In this lies Raphael's significant contribution to the painting of the High Renaissance.

Raphael's style was by no means uninfluenced by Michelangelo's painting. Following the preliminary unveiling of the Sistine ceiling in 1509, the figures in Raphael's pictures acquire more voluminous bodies and more powerful arms, and there is a reduction in their numbers. The bold twisting position adopted by the young woman in the *Expulsion of Heliodorus* – a pose which reappears in reverse in Raphael's late work, the *Transfiguration* – would be inconceivable without the influence of Michelangelo. Any question as to the cause of the widely-acknowledged sudden change in Raphael's style after 1509 is removed for good, however, when we compare the Sibyls and Prophets executed by Raphael in the Capella Chigi in S. Maria della Pace (1512) with those by Michelangelo in the Sistine Chapel. In addition to the thematic kinship of these frescos with Michelangelo, Raphael's new approach to body volumes and twisting poses makes patently clear the enormous impact which the Sistine ceiling had made upon him.

The young painter from Urbino thus adopted the artistic innovations of his elder colleagues, in particular those of Leonardo and Michelangelo, and synthesized them with his own aims. This did not pass Michelangelo by; in 1541, long after Raphael's death, he was still complaining in a letter that "everything he knew about art he got from me."

After the death of Bramante in 1514, Raphael was appointed architect of St. Peter's. He also became increasingly involved with the excavations and surveys of ruins in Rome. He was adroit enough to leave the remaining frescos in the Papal apartments more and more to his assistants, including his important pupil Giulio Romano. Although he provided the designs for the *Burning of the Borgo* in the third Stanza and for the decoration of the loggias in the Vatican, and although he no doubt supervised their execution, they were largely painted by his pupils.

Raphael produced a number of other important works during his time in Rome. These included Madonna paintings such as the *Madonna della Sedia* (1513–14), and a series of famous portraits, including that of *Julius II* (1511–12), the *Donna Velata* (p. 336, top), *Baldassare Castiglione* (p. 336, bottom), and *Pope Leo X with Cardinals Giulio de'Medici and Luigi de'Rossi* (top right). He also provided the decorations for the upper zones of the lateral walls of the Sistine Chapel, which thus directly adjoined the works by his great rival Michelangelo. Instead of frescos, however, Raphael's

contribution took the form of a tapestry cycle depicting scenes from the lives of the Apostles. Raphael's cartoons for the cycle, which are today housed in London, were produced between 1515 and 1518. The tapestries were woven in Arras under Pieter van Aelst, and seven were hung in 1519.

One of the most frequently discussed and best-loved paintings of the Renaissance is Raphael's so-called *Sistine Madonna* (p. 338). For many people it remains the supreme example of western painting, and its popularity is virtually as great as that of the *Mona Lisa*. All who have written about this picture have acknowledged the strange and baffling expressions worn by Mary and the child Jesus, although attempts to decipher their meaning have frequently been evasive – "visionary pictorial composition" was one interpretation. Whole anthologies have been devoted to the problem. Famous painters and authors, including Goethe, Runge, Schlegel, C. G. Carus, Hebbel,

337

Raphael
Sistine Madonna, 1513/14
Canvas, 256 x 196 cm
Dresden, Gemäldegalerie Alte Meister

OPPOSITE:
Raphael
The Transfiguration of Christ, c. 1518
Oil on wood, 405 x 278 cm
Rome, Vatican, Pinacoteca Vaticana

of S. Sisto in Piacenza. The small town had become part of the Vatican state in 1512, and the picture arose shortly afterwards. Some see a portrait of Pope Julius II in the figure of St. Sixtus on the left, looking up at the Virgin and pointing out towards the viewer. Only recently have the questions surrounding this painting finally been resolved. As recent research by A. Prager has shown, the key to the mystery lies in the position in which the altarpiece originally stood. Taking again the intriguing question of what the Pope is pointing at and what the Mother and Child are looking at, the answer is as astonishing as it is persuasive. It has long been forgotten that, as in many churches, opposite the altarpiece in S. Sisto and above the rood screen at the far end of the chancel there stood a crucifix. The expressions of horror on the faces of Mother and Child are thus their reaction to the sight of death. It is interesting to note that, long before this successful interpretation, it was a writer, and not an art historian, who came closest to understanding the mystery: R. A. Schröder saw the "deepest horror" written in the face of the child, "before which even Death itself is frightened to death".

The device of linking a painted scene with other objects in the same room, for example by means of figures in the picture pointing to an object outside the painting, was by no means uncommon at that time. In addition to the research by Prater, I would like to suggest three other Madonnas in which a similar device may be present. In Bellini's *Madonna Lochis* (Bergamo, Accademia Carrara) and his Madonna for S. Maria dell'Orto in Venice, as well as in the Madonna attributed to Lazzaro Bastiani in Berlin (Staatliche Museen), the child Jesus is in each case portrayed in a frightened, bristling pose, for which the only explanation may again lie outside the picture. Here, too, establishing the setting in which these paintings orginally stood would greatly benefit our interpretation of their meaning. In his treatise on painting of 1436, Leon Battista Alberti observed: "I like there to be someone in the 'historia' who tells the spectators what is going on, and either beckons them with his hand to look, or ... challenges them not to come near... Everything the people in the painting do among themselves, or perform in relation to the spectators, must fit together to represent and explain the 'historia'."

Almost contemporaneously with Raphael's *Sistine Madonna*, Fra Bartolommeo executed the *Salvator Mundi* which today hangs in the Palazzo Pitti (p. 330), and which was originally conceived as the central panel of a triptych for the church of SS. Annunziata. Here, too, one of the Evangelists, who are grouped around the raised figure of the Saviour in the style of a Sacra Conversazione, points to an object outside the picture. In this case, his finger is directed towards the Host raised during the consecration by the priest officiating at the altar. At this moment in the Mass, the Host would have appeared at the centre of the round landscape held between two putti – the "world" above which the inscription "Salvator Mundi" (Saviour of the World) can be read. Fra Bartolommeo thus

Schopenhauer and R. A. Schröder (to name only German commentators), not to mention a host of art historians, have attempted to explain the painting, and others again have confessed, as Grillparzer did, how much they "would love to get the bottom of the matter". Schopenhauer spoke of the "terror-stricken" face of the boy Jesus; for the dramatist Hebbel, "The child is wild, teeth clenched, eyes blazing..." In the past, the pointing finger of the Holy Father was almost always interpreted as a gesture commending the worshipping viewer to the Madonna. It was also assumed that the Mother and Child were looking at the viewer. But it is precisely here that the puzzle arises. Why does Mary look so troubled? Why is the child, staring transfixedly out of the picture with his ruffled hair, appear to shrink back? Raphael painted the picture for the high altar

Andrea del Sarto
Lamentation of Christ, 1524
Oil on wood, 238 x 198 cm
Florence, Palazzo Pitti, Galleria Palatina

established a symbolic link between the picture and the Eucharist, and in so doing took up a theme treated by many artists during this period.

Fra Bartolommeo (1472–1517) was one of the painters who assimilated the methods of Leonardo, Michelangelo and Raphael with particular sensitivity. A stay in Venice in 1508 also enriched the spectrum of his palette. Torn in Girolamo Savonarola's day between the sacred and the secular life, he destroyed all his works of a secular nature and became a Dominican monk. He was unable, however, to completely sever his links with art. Although only his religious paintings survive, these testify to the calm, generous gestures and the solemn simplicity of composition that characterize the essence of High Renaissance painting. But while the content of his works may appear to be visible at a glance, we should not underestimate the deeper meaning of the gestures often demonstrated by his figures.

The pictorial device used by Raphael in his *Sistine Madonna* also directs our eyes towards another important representative of High Renaissance painting, Andrea del Sarto (1486–1531). He, too, was Florentine by birth. His figures are somewhat more sophisticated than those of Fra Bartolommeo and other contemporaries, and their expressions and gestures are more convincing. In at least one painting, he also created a similar link between the scene in the picture and its immediate context. In the *Lamentation of Christ* which he executed in 1524 for S. Pietro a Luco in Florence (p. 340), he incorporates the theme of the Eucharist directly into the picture by presenting the cup with the Host immediately beneath the body of Christ. At the same time, it should be noted that Mary Magdalene, kneeling in the right-hand foreground, is gazing intently not at the dead Christ – even though His foot is resting on her knee but at the Host floating above the goblet as if in a vision.

It is evident from this altarpiece that Andrea del Sarto drew as much upon Michelangelo as upon Raphael in his painting. But the picture also shows that the artist went far beyond his great predecessors in his portrayal of facial expressions, which reveal a greater individuality than before while losing nothing of the nobility of the classical ideal of the High Renaissance. Like the Venetian artist Lorenzo Lotto, Andrea del Sarto deserves far greater recognition than he has generally been accorded up until now.

In Raphael's last work, the *Transfiguration of Christ* (p. 339), Alberti's demands are met in an even richer fashion. Here again, the gestures employed by Raphael's characters are not simply intended to indicate another figure, for example, but point the viewer to a deeper significance. Indeed, in the case of this work, we find the presence of at least two entirely independent themes. On the one hand, this is a depiction of the transfigured Christ, brightly illuminated and with His hands raised, floating between Moses and Elijah in front of the disciples Peter, John and James. At the same time, however, the lower half of the picture portrays a scene in which the elderly Simeon's attention is drawn, by means of pointing gestures, to the blind boy, who is the only one able to "see" the Transfiguration as a vision, with his mind's eye. James, meanwhile, whom the people mistakenly think is the Saviour, is pointing with his outstretched left arm at the Christ, as if to say: "Not I, but He over there". The seated apostle in the foreground, grasping the Holy Scriptures in his hand, is also making an emphatic gesture – as if to stop the viewer from comprehending the scene too quickly, and to indicate to him to withdraw to a viewpoint further away, from where he will be able to take in the significance of the composition as a whole.

The *Transfiguration*, begun in 1519, was Raphael's last work. It was left unfinished when he died on Good Friday, 1520, his 37th birthday. While many of the paintings of his latter years were executed chiefly by assistants – albeit to his own designs – large parts of this last picture stem from Raphael's own hand. Thus the upper Transfiguration scene and landscape and a large part of the figural group on the left belong to Raphael, while the remaining figures can

Jacopo da Pontormo
St. Matthew, 1527/28
Ø 70 cm
Florence, Santa Felicità, Capponi Chapel

be attributed to his pupils Giulio Romano and Francesco Penni. Raphael's early death was followed by a gap of 13 years in the development of painting in Rome, until Michelangelo's return to the Vatican in 1535. Many have wondered what course Raphael's art would have taken had he lived longer. It is an acknowledged fact, however, that any further evolution of what we understand by the "classical" element of Renaissance painting would have been virtually impossible. Unlike Giorgione, whose similarly premature death seemed to interrupt an unfinished development, Raphael left no question marks. In not one of his paintings or drawings do we find anything to disconcert us. While Leonardo is often seen as "problematical" and Michelangelo as "highly individual", and while both developed certain elements in their work which look forward to Mannerism, Raphael never deviated from the classical path.

If we take a brief look at the generation which came after these three giants of the High Renaissance, it is striking that none of them produced a true heir. Although Raphael had numerous pupils, they may more accurately be described as assistants. Leonardo only had pupils during his years in Milan, and these did no more than copy their master's style. Michelangelo banned all his assistants from the scaffolding. Yet the impact which all three made on the painting of their day was so enormous that their presence can be felt in all the works of the subsequent period. The legacy of each artist may be briefly summarized as follows: from Leonardo the following generations took sfumato, the mysterious pose, and the art of capturing a transitory moment; from Michelangelo they acquired a new image of the body and of space, to the extent that it is possible to judge whether a painting belongs to the period before or after Michelangelo purely on the basis of the corporeality of its figures; finally, all those who have come after Raphael have sought to adopt from him composition in its most definitive form. Raphael's classical approach was taken up by the French schools in particular, and above all by Poussin, and the simple, magnificent clarity of his forms was also admired by the 19th century.

Mannerism

As the description of a style, the term High Renaissance, or indeed simply Renaissance, has never carried any pejorative or derogatory associations. Art critics have regularly found words of praise and encouragement for even the very first, tentative efforts by the Proto-Renaissance and Early Renaissance to create in a painting a pictorial reality corresponding to natural reality, even though such efforts were often far from satisfactory. Not so in the case of Mannerism, as we call the style that followed the High Renaissance. Like the terms Gothic, Baroque and Rococo, and more recently Pre-Raphaelite, Nazarene and indeed even Art Nouveau, Mannerism only began to receive a more sympathetic and even favourable press long after it was over (as late, in fact, as the middle of our own century). "Manic", "mania" and "mannered" – words all carrying negative

Jacopo da Pontormo
Annunciation (detail), c. 1527–28
Fresco
Florence, Santa Felicità, Capponi Chapel

Jacopo da Pontormo
Vertumnus and Pomona, c. 1519–21
Fresco
Florence, Villa Medici di Poggio a Caiano

connotations – were aspects of a characteristic that was seen in the art of the period between the Renaissance and the Baroque, i.e. approximately from the death of Raphael in 1520 to around 1600. Alois Riegl, an art historian of the Vienna School, was probably the first to see Mannerism not in the depreciating light cast upon it by Vasari, but as a style in its own right. Sir Ernst Gombrich aptly described the stylistic phenomenon as a "crisis in the conception of art". To complicate matters, E. R. Curtius, Dvorak, Panofsky, the Warburg Institute and G. R. Hocke have plausibly shown that "mannerist" tendencies follow on from virtually every "classical" era – as a "European constant", so to speak – thus rendering the use of the term "Mannerism" even more fraught. We shall not, however, be going further into the relationship between the original Mannerists and other "mannerisms", such as the "convoluted" Rococo style, the melancholy of Romanticism, or Dada and Surrealism – despite their inner kinship with works by such Italian artists as Pontormo, Bronzino, Tintoretto and Parmigianino.

Vasari, artists' biographer and himself a painter, was perhaps the first to introduce the concept in his *Lives*, when he described

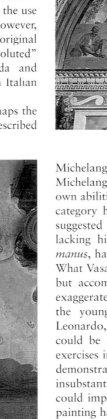

Michelangelo's successors and imitators as painting "alla maniera di Michelangelo". He clearly did not possess sufficient insight into his own abilities to recognize that, in many respects, he fell into this very category himself. The word *maniera* held derogatory overtones; it suggested that something was a poor imitation, as if the artist, lacking his own "manner" (i.e. style or method; from the Latin *manus*, hand), had simply copied that of Michelangelo or Leonardo. What Vasari meant was that many artists were reproducing the bold but accomplished movements typical of Michelangelo, but in an exaggerated fashion. Vasari failed to grasp, however, that the aims of the young generation had now fundamentally changed. What Leonardo, Michelangelo, Titian, and above all Raphael had achieved could be imitated but not surpassed. Even the most complicated exercises in perspective had long since been mastered. Leonardo had demonstrated how sfumato could be used to cloud a subject into insubstantiality and yet at the same time give it life, and no one could improve upon Raphael's compositional clarity. The goal that painting had followed doggedly for the past 200 years had now been reached. Leonardo may have said, "it is a poor student who does not surpass his master" – but the masters were unsurpassable in their field. Nothing remained for the younger artists but to seek out their own new and independent paths. These they arrived at in very different ways.

One of the masters of Mannerism was Federico Zuccari (1540?–1609), whose works include paintings in the Belvedere in the Vatican, in the Palazzo Vecchio in Florence, and in the dome of Florence Cathedral. He also designed his own house in Rome, the Palazzo Zuccari, a superlative example of Mannerist architecture. In

1607 Zuccari published a Mannerist treatise, *Idea de'pittori, scultori ed architetti*, in which he advocated the representation of events which are only to be seen in the imagination, and not in nature. His ideas contained the possibility of an alternative to conventional art. The focus now fell on the fantastical, often devoid of all correspondence to nature. In formal terms, this expressed itself in a number of typically Mannerist ways, such as a distortion of the "ideal" proportions of the human body, as seen in the overly long limbs of Parmigianino's figures (p. 387). The bravura execution of highly complex poses, demonstrated with such audacious ease by Michelangelo, was now carried to a "twisted" extreme in the *figura serpentinata*, one which Giambologna made all his own in sculpture (pp. 236 and 237). In the portrayal of rooms and settings, we find an increasing preference for the unreal and mysterious, as in the case of Tintoretto, who invented interiors which recede like tunnels into the sinister depths (pp. 408, bottom and 409, top). Others employed colour to heighten the mood of the picture, sometimes creating garishly bright, shimmering, almost dreamlike effects, as in the case

of Dosso Dossi (p. 382). El Greco, studying painting in Venice, took the Mannerist palette to the furthest extremes of what was then conceivable (p. 409, bottom). Naturally, the Mannerists threw overboard the smooth, easily intelligible composition perfected by Raphael; instead, they deliberately challenged accepted convention and captivated the viewer not through harmony but through confusion. *Stupore* – surprise – and *meraviglio* – the marvellous, astonishing, labyrinthine – were the new themes. If the viewer could no longer be impressed with truth to nature, then he would be captivated by amazement and stupefaction. The "idea" became an important concept amongst theoreticians of the day, and it was thus only natural that artists should seek innovation not just at a formal level, but first and foremost at an intellectual level. "One paints with the head, not with the hand", wrote Michelangelo, and in so doing provided the Mannerists with authorization for their often highly obscure paintings, many of which evade easy explanation. Instead, they present us with riddles.

The earliest examples of Mannerist painting are found in Florence, where its chief representatives were Pontormo (1494–1557), Rosso Fiorentino (1494–1540), and Bronzino (1503-1572). Pontormo, born Jacopo Carrucci but more familiarly known by the name of his birthplace outside Florence, started to move away from the contemporary High Renaissance style around 1520. Like many others, he profoundly admired Dürer's engravings, something Vasari disparaged. The originality of his art lies both in its composition and in its use of colour. Weightless figures feature in his art from an early stage, as for example in his fresco of the *Annunciation* of 1514–16 (Florence, SS. Annunziata). Thus the angel in the left half of the composition hovers suspended in the air, and even Mary, turning round in surprise on the right, is given no background setting (detail, p. 343). Emphatic colour is avoided in favour of an iridescent palette of pale pastel shades. There is a similar sense of weightlessness in his *Deposition* of 1523–30 in S. Felicità (p. 345). A turbulent cluster of bodies is rhythmically and harmoniously linked into a circle. The figures appear as if in a trance, lifted out of time and floating in space. The rise and fall of their movements seems to defy the laws of gravity, and luminous colours shimmer through their dematerialized bodies. Pontormo fundamentally avoids the pure classical palette in favour of a symphonic scale of chromatic hues. And whereas Raphael places the head of the beautiful Galatea at the very heart of his *Triumph of Galatea*, the centre of Pontormo's *Deposition* is given over to an utterly unimportant object – a raised piece of blue cloth. This was no doubt a deliberate affront to the sacred laws of classical composition.

In an altar painting of the same subject by Rosso Fiorentino in Volterra (p. 345), an early work of 1521, we find a similar example of bodies clinging together, with the figures at the top of the picture merging into a cluster. Here again, one of the figures looks out of the

Jacopo da Pontormo
Deposition, c. 1523–25
Wood, 313 x 193 cm
Florence, Santa Felicità, Capponi Chapel

Rosso Fiorentino
Deposition, 1521
Wood, 335 x 198 cm
Volterra, Pinacoteca

Rosso Fiorentino
Moses and the Daughters of Jethro, c. 1523
Oil on canvas, 160 x 117 cm
Florence, Galleria degli Uffizi

Agnolo Bronzino
Laura Battiferri, c. 1555/60
Oil on canvas, 83 x 60 cm
Florence, Palazzo Vecchio

picture at the viewer, as if seeking our sympathy for what is taking place. Rosso's colours, although sensitively gradated as in Pontormo, are less emphatically luminous. The chief focus of his attention is instead the complex construction of the composition. This is particularly clear in his painting *Moses and the Daughters of Jethro* of 1523 (p. 346). The confusion in the foreground of this scene of Michelangelesque turmoil is clevely planned and calculated. The frenzied atmosphere is intensified by the dramatic immediacy with which the scene is presented to the viewer – the way in which the limbs are deliberately cropped by the frame virtually makes the picture appear a cut-out! Moses lashes out in an explosive manner, while the young woman at upper right seems to freeze in horror. She is identified in the older Italian literature as a *manichino* (mannequin, dummy), frozen in mid-movement, a concession to the *bella maniera* demanded by Vasari. What Rosso is expressing here is the paralysis and stillness which follows the explosion of the fight. Here, too, Rosso flies in the face of Raphael's harmonious principles of composition: the point at the centre of the picture where the two diagonals intersect coincides with the naked sex of the battling Moses. This shocking emphasis is legitimized by the boldness of the composition. Rosso Fiorentino, whose proper name was Giovanni Battista di Jacopo di Guasparre, was a pupil under Michelangelo, Andrea del Sarto and Fra Bartolommeo. In 1530, probably following a recommendation by Michelangelo, he was summoned to the court of the French king, Francis I. The fresco cycle which he painted amidst the stuccoes in the gallery at Fontainebleau may be considered his finest achievement. Rosso died in Paris in 1540.

The youngest of this trio of Mannerists was Agnolo Bronzino, born in Monticelli, near Florence. Bronzino was a pupil and lifelong friend of Pontormo, and worked with him for many years, for example on the frescos in S. Felicità in Florence and in the Certosa in Galluzzo. Some of the details in works by his teacher also stem from his hand. Even at an early stage, however, Bronzino began to reject Pontormo's preference for the painting of northern Europe, returning instead to stricter rules of composition in line with a trend which has been associated with the Counter-Reformation. Bronzino refashioned the "unreality" of his Mannerist colleague Pontormo into a line and style of figural representation that was sharp-edged and crystal-clear. At the same time, however, he retained the sophisticated content of the Mannerist picture; indeed, he refined its cryptic subtleties even further. His *Allegory*, also known as *Venus, Cupid, Time and Folly* (p. 348), is a picture of highly complex symbolism: Love, represented by the two tenderly embracing main characters, is accompanied (as always) by Jealousy – in the shape of the howling figure pulling his hair on the left – and Deceit, the young girl looking out with a falsely innocent air from behind the boy holding the roses. In her hands, which are the wrong way round – the left hand on her right arm, the right hand on her left arm – she holds a honeycomb and a scorpion, and her body reveals itself to be

that of a chimera. This Love, we are thus informed, is no more than transitory. Only Folly – represented by a woman's face in the top left-hand corner, a mask without a brain – attempts to screen this love idyll from the eyes of Saturn, the god of Time. Saturn, however, tears her curtain aside with a powerful thrust of his arm. His hourglass warns of ending and death. On the ground lie two masks of appearances, just as everything in this picture is levelled at symbolism and instruction. Lasciviousness and an admonitory revelation of the evil of lust are presented side by side.

A certain psychological symbolism in Bronzini's portraits has also long been recognized. He portrays the poetess Laura Battiferri, wife of the sculptor Bartolommeo Ammannati (1511–1592), with an open book of poems and, like all his female sitters, head proudly raised (p. 347). The woman's stern figure radiates a sense of religious severity, something by which her husband was not unaffected. After the completion of his magnificent Neptune fountain in Florence (p. 234), Bartolommeo Ammannati suffered a religious life crisis which led him to damn his cheerfully pagan work and its numerous naked figures. The spirit of the Counter-Reformation permeated both the fine arts and literature in the second half of the Cinquecento. Bronzino was himself a poet, composing sonnets and comic poems, and it seems perfectly in character that wit, allusions and literary "images" should make up one of the fundamental characteristics of his art, and indeed of Mannerism as a whole.

The formal language of Italian Mannerism was transported to France by artists such as Rosso Fiorentino and Niccolò dell'Abbate (1512–1571), who came from Modena. Under the supervision of Francesco Primaticcio (1504–1570) from Bologna, they executed the paintings, sculptures and stuccowork for Francis I's palace at Fontainebleau. They subsequently became known as the School of Fontainebleau, and French artists such as Jean Cousin and Antoine Caron, Primaticcio's assistants, and Martin Fréminet were all influenced by their Mannerist style. Bronzino's *Allegory* also passed into the possession of the French king, probably as an instructional picture to assist the prince's education.

Bronzino is a prime example of how, in the later stages of Italian Mannerism, the earlier preference for formal exaggeration and compositional complexity gave way to a clearer style of representation. From now on, the enigmatic and sophisticated devices of Mannerist painting were played out at a deeper level, that of content. Increasingly, "understanding" a picture required an academic education. From here it was but a short step to the next stylistic development, the Baroque, which sought to combine both: a differentiated, symbolic message for the educated, and a formal simplicity which would make clear the full meaning of the picture even to the less educated.

Alexander Rauch

Renaissance Painting in Venice and Northern Italy

Regional Variations

In the broad countryside between the Alps and the Apennines, and from the mountains of Piedmont and Genoa across the Po valley to Venice, the artistic developments which took place during the Quattrocento were different from those seen in central Italy. While in the latter region Florence was *the* unrivalled focus in respect both of scholarship and of patronage, in northern Italy we look in vain for any comparable centre dominating the entire region where the artistic forces of the century are concentrated in a small number of major names: too great was still the political and thus, at first, the artistic isolation of its individual towns and cities such as Verona, Mantua, Padua, Ferrara, Bologna or Milan, and above all Venice; the Gothic survived here far longer. The connections of western Lombardy, for example, and Piedmont via Savoy with Burgundy, as well as the trade routes which led from Verona into the Tyrol, also meant that northern Italy was exposed for a longer period to the artistic influences of the north. A Giovanni Alamagno ("the German") was working alongside Antonio da Murano in Venice in the years around 1450, and later, if our records of his travels are correct, Dürer too visited the Queen of the Adriatic, but got no further. Conversely, what the artists of central Italy knew of the north at first was not the Dutch or German painters, but at the most just a few of their works, as we shall see.

An artistic map, if such a thing can be imagined, would show northern Italy throughout the 15th century as a patchwork quilt, covered by a whole variety of patterns developing with a rhythm of their own. Giorgio Vasari in his chapter on Giorgione wrote of northern Italy that "...the land between Tuscany and the mountains did not possess quite the abundance of artists of which Tuscany herself could boast since time immemorial, yet it was not totally unblessed in this respect"; a tendentious formulation on the part of an adoptive Florentine, to be sure, and less than fair to the artistic wealth of northern Italy. And yet one can understand Vasari's point of view when one considers that the influence of northern Italy and Venice did not reach central Italy until very much later, in other words not until after Florentine and Roman painting had passed its peak. Moreover, there was no dominant supraregional patronage in northern Italy to match that of the Medici in Florence. It was at most in the commissions of the ducal courts of the Gonzagas in Mantua, the Estes in Ferrara, and the Sforzas in Milan that there was any kind of regional promotion of the arts, but often it was only an individual artist – such as Mantegna – who in fact was able to transcend political boundaries and the confines of court-artist status. By contrast, it was artists from central Italy, where the foundation for the new art was after all laid, who, by accepting commissions from northern Italian cities, influenced the course art was to take there. Fra Filippo Lippi worked in Venice from 1434–37, as did Paolo Uccello prior to 1435 and Andrea del Castagno in 1442; the no longer extant library of the monastery of Santa Maria Maggiore was built by a Florentine, Michelozzo, in

1433/34; and the great sculptor Donatello was active in Padua between 1443 and 1452.

Similarly, Tuscans had been preparing the ground in Lombardy for the new style since the beginning of the century, if only in the field of architecture at first. Only in the second half of the 15th century did the northern Italian centres develop sufficient artistic autonomy: Padua and Mantua above all, in the person of Andrea Mantegna, and Venice, through the Bellini family. As a result, the "Renaissance" made its appearance here far later than in central Italy, but towards the end of the Quattrocento it was present in such strength and abundance that one is faced with an *embarras de choix* when trying to make a representative selection of artists and works.

The studios of northern Italy had struck out along far too isolated paths, then, for any early common features to be discerned. Furthermore, Venice had seen the forms of the 14th century maintain their vigour for a long time in her Byzantinesque devotional pictures against imposing gilt mosaic backgrounds which reflected her power and wealth. Full-frontal, in majestic dignity, the stern figures of the saints gazed out in admonishment from their gold panels; saints, who, still debarred from resembling any earthly human being, sought to appear holy and unapproachable. Nor should it be forgotten that in Milan, too, building on the cathedral had been going on for generations in the Gothic style. In numerous churches between Milan and Padua we find 15th-century frescoes, which, while still Gothic in style, are in no way inferior to the achievements of the Tuscan painters. And yet here too there is only one really outstanding personality, dating back to the previous century: Altichiero da Zevio (c. 1330–90), who worked in Padua (cf. pp. 94, 95). This late exponent of the Gothic seems to have seized on what Giotto had prepared; he ranks alongside Orcagna and the Florentines, in every way their peer. Like Altichiero, his Renaissance successor Pisanello was a far less skilful draughtsman than the Florentines, and yet the latter were surpassed by both painters in one very individual quality which was soon to become *the* characteristic feature of northern Italian and Venetian painting: the cultivation of colour.

Images of late-mediaeval life are already to be found in the painting of both Altichiero and Pisanello. The pomp of courtly society is reproduced in brilliant colour, wimples fluttering like butterflies round a pride of knights. But the case of these two painters, along with the terms essayed time and again in connection with the artists of this period – such as "mediaeval" and "early modern", "Gothic" and "Renaissance" – make it apparent that these traditional demarcations are hardly satisfactory, either in a temporal or in a formal sense. We have long known that the significant preconditions for what we call the "Renaissance" were already laid down during the 14th century. Many a "Gothic" form bears "Renaissance" ideas within it, and many an acme of the new style, or rather the new ideal, was not fully realized until the following century, the Cinquecento.

Vittorio Pisano, known as Pisanello (1395–1455), was trained in Verona. In about 1424 he went to Padua, where he was influenced by the Lombard Gothic of Giovanni de' Grassi. It is possible that the studios of Domenico Veneziano, Paolo Uccello and Donatello were also known to him. And yet we discover, for example in his painting *The Vision of St. Eustace* (p. 352), unmistakable features of the late Middle Ages, albeit with signs of a new, almost scientific view of the world of creation. And yet: the whole arrangement of the picture has less to do with composition than with a skilful distribution of the individual figures. And each of these figures is in itself a self-contained picture, which, separated out of the whole, would lose none of its beauty. The man on horseback in his modish turban, his mount bedecked in opulent harness, appears to the modern eye not so much a saint as a noble knight in the company of his hunting pack. Confronting him is the stag, the cross in its antlers looking more like a depiction of a carved crucifix than a "vision". The hounds, stags, rabbits and birds, while not lacking in symbolic content, are spread around the picture like the decorative elements of a tapestry. As for the elaborately coiled scroll at the bottom of the picture, it seems to belong entirely to the world of Gothic forms. The picture radiates devotion: Eustace sits there, calm and spellbound, albeit without any expression of emotion, his leg stiffly extended, and his horse adopts a similar attitude, as though it were taking a short step back before the cross. Yet this "apparition" is only mildly sacred in its depiction; there is no halo or radiance, and thus the whole scene has something of a secular atmosphere.

The starting point for the view of art we find in Pisanello and the contemporaries whose style is related is the International Gothic of around 1400. It is no coincidence that this little painting in London's National Gallery is no bigger than a miniature. Pisanello was merely continuing the tradition of Franco-Netherlandish book illumination with its aristocratic style, its calligraphic sign-language, and its elegance. It portrayed the courtly chivalrous community; what is on show here is a display not so much of machismo such as we find in Germany, but rather of rich and sumptuous costume; refinement, but with a hint of coquetry. The horseman is depicted as the representative of a social stratum whose importance was drawing to a close.

As we know, Pisanello drew on the Franco-Netherlandish books of hours of the Limburg brothers for his motifs. And like the illustrations in the books, his pictures too are often two-dimensional. Thus not only his landscapes, but also his portraits, are woven into a pictorial background conceived in ornamental terms. His *Portrait of a Young Girl* (p. 353) – whose identity is disputed – is conceived entirely thus. It dates from the time when Pisanello maintained close relations with the house of Este, making it probable that the girl in question is not Margherita Gonzaga, as has been suggested, but rather Ginevra d'Este, to whom Sigismondo Malatesta was betrothed in 1433. If this was the occasion for the picture, then the sitter is just

fifteen years old. The designs embroidered on her gown, such as the broom plants and the vase with the Este insignia, add weight to the possibility. Malatesta allegedly poisoned his young fiancée in 1440.

Here too, much of the effect of the picture is due to the austere profile view of the sitter, and the elaborate scattering of details in the background which act as a frame for the portrait itself. Pisanello seems to have been as little concerned about perspective here as in the picture of Eustace discussed above. The uncompromising profile draws attention to the head, in relation to which the bust appears too small to modern eyes, owing to the fact that there is no convincing illusion of depth in the shoulders. The flowers and butterflies of course conveyed additional clues to anyone who understood the language of columbine and carnation, regarded as symbolic of chastity. Perhaps the butterflies, as symbols of resurrection, hint at this being a posthumous portrait, which would necessitate re-dating it.

The fact that the vase on the sleeve is represented as broken gives this symbol of transitoriness an additional meaning, corresponding to the aphorism *homo quasi vas* – man is fragile like a vase. In view of the fact that Guarino, the humanist and poet at the Este court, had, in connection with painting, represented the extravagant costume of the time as the cultivation of vanity and demanded "verity", the symbol on this simple dress may already be seen as the consequence of a new perception, one that had turned its back on late Gothic ostentation.

Around mid-century Pisanello was already receiving commissions from all the courts of northern Italy: the Gonzagas, the Malatestas, the Estes and the Viscontis. Quite a number of literary sources, for

example the writings of Guarino, Strozzi or Basinio, mention works which have since been lost but for which preliminary sketches are in some cases still extant. In addition, Pisanello, who from 1438 devoted himself to the art of the medallion, left a series of portraits on bronze plates of rulers such as Gonzaga and Malatesta – miniature reliefs in which he, the greatest medallist of his age, succeeded in achieving a convincing illusion of depth. These were experiences on which he also drew in his painting.

"Paragone" – Art and Artists in Competition

In 1441 Pisanello painted a portrait of Lionello d'Este, which is now in Bergamo. The work was commissioned in connection with a competition among painters, in which immediately afterwards the Venetian artist Jacopo Bellini was required to meet the same challenge. This circumstance is of no small importance, showing as it does that for the painter it was no longer a question of demonstrating his craftsmanship, but rather that the "craftsman" now also had the social status of "artist". Like the humanistic philosopher, he had to be weighed in the balance of the *paragone*. It must be stressed that this was an honour for the artist: after all, during the Middle Ages measuring oneself against one's peers was a privilege reserved to the knightly class. While the task was not new, the solutions were, and it was not least thus that the new style was introduced. The new idea of the competition, implemented for the first time since classical antiquity for the Baptistery doors in Florence (cf. pp. 176ff.), was of great importance for the history of 15th-century art. The ground for this new status accorded to the artist had already been laid in the 14th century, however, when Dante had immortalized the two artists Giotto and Cimabue by naming them and comparing their achievements in his *Divina Commedia*.

Already in the case of the first artist whom I have chosen to represent the northern Italian region at this period, Pisanello, we can then discern at least three phenomena characteristic of the early stages of the Renaissance idea: a concern to master the technique of perspective; the fact that we have here an artist who, like many other Renaissance artists, was not just a painter but a talent in other art forms as well; and finally the *quasi*-ennoblement of the artist, as his status was raised from that of craftsman to a par with thinkers and philosophers.

The artefact produced by the artist also underwent a transformation which we see reinforced throughout the 15th century, a change from a ritual cult object to an aesthetic work of art. But did this change not lead to an aesthetic which served only its own ends? Of course art was to remain at the service of politics and religion, to fulfil the purpose of social information, of the natural desire for ornament and of the symbolic enrichment of theological and philosophical representations. But more than ever before, the work of art became a collector's piece, an example of the new task of uniting the imagination with the new discoveries of the natural world. Bible

Pisanello
Portrait of a Young Girl, c. 1433
Wood, 43 x 30 cm
Paris, Musée du Louvre

stories, for example, or legends, were to be illustrated naturalistically. The result was that artistic virtuosity, the talent to capture and aestheticize nature in a picture, itself became an object of admiration.

Perspective – or the Invention of Distance in Space and Time

No pictures by one of the central and universal personalities of the art world of this period have been preserved: the painter, sculptor, architect, theoretician and – above all – harbinger of the Renaissance, Leon Battista Alberti. Likewise a northern Italian, born shortly after Pisanello in Genoa (or perhaps Venice) in 1404, active in Florence from 1430 onwards, and then in Rome, he is now accessible to us only in his capacity as architect (see pp. 108ff.). Alongside his treatise on architecture, *De re aedificatoria*, he also left us the important *On Painting*, published in 1436. Here for the first time the basic concepts of proportion and perspective were set out as a guide to painters. From then on, both the design goals of the artist and the view of the beholder were to undergo a fundamental transformation.

It would be too simple to see this transformation as merely one of painting or design technique. Earlier representations had been no more than the pictorial reproduction on a plane of what was often a sacred subject; now, thanks to perspective techniques, a virtual space had been created, drawing the gaze of the beholder into it as if it were a hole; the picture had depth. The traditional Byzantine representation was a literally superficial, two-dimensional portrayal of God or the saints – depicted schematically, and with no individuality – against a gold background. The new style, however, sacrificed the act of redemption to the spatial interest of the beholder; and God is shown as working out His purpose on Earth, in all too human form, with the fragility of an earthly body, and vulnerable in the veracity of the depicted space. But how "veracious" is a Lombard or Venetian landscape or townscape as a context for a religious event in the Holy Land? Must it not be seen as an arrogance, to presume to look into heaven through the medium of perspective pictures? Also, important things were now often small because they were in the background; conversely, less important things, being in the foreground, were represented as large. Did perspective not create an illusion of reality, where previously only signs and symbols of the known verities of history or salvation were permitted? The vividness which perspective space or objects could convey became a new verity, created by and within the picture. The new verity of perspective was, in the broadest sense, still just another interpretation.

That the invention of perspective made possible the representation of spatial distances is clear enough. But the word "per-spective" means "see-through", and "distances" in perspective are to be understood in a twofold sense: namely, in space and in time. The beholder now no longer has the freedom of choice to consider a single part of the picture, but is drawn willy-nilly into the system of foreshortening which pervades the whole. While this leaves him in appearance united with the scene as depicted, and his gaze is also invited into this temporal scene, at the same time he is deprived of the objectivity provided by the freedom to consider whichever part he liked, as was still provided by the art of the late Middle Ages. The spatial effect generated by perspective also forced a temporal unity. The fact that distances in pictures could now be judged also made time, or a period of time, visible. Thus for example the duration of the procession in Gentile Bellini's *Procession in St. Mark's Square* (p. 355) can be estimated, whereas Pisanello's *St. Eustace* (p. 352) appears "timeless" in his perspective-free space, as if in endless prayer. It was, then, only the invention of perspective that finally made it possible for "movement" in a picture also to be perceived as flow of time – for figures floating in the heavens and for earthbound personages alike.

Jacopo Bellini
Madonna of the Cherubim, c. 1450
Wood, 94 x 66 cm
Venice, Accademia

their city on pillars sunk in the Lagoon, this barbican of Italy was at the same time the gateway to the Orient. As nowhere else in Italian painting, we find here images which document this relationship, and they become even more frequent following the capture of Constantinople by the Turks in 1453. Turbaned figures feature in the paintings of Gentile Bellini (p. 355), Carpaccio, and Lorenzo Costa (p. 377). The fantastical inscriptions, reminiscent of Arabic calligraphy, which we see in a number of paintings, are also indicative of an interest in the Orient; see for example the front of the sarcophagus and the hem of the garment in Cosimo Tura's *Pietà* (p. 364), or on the haloes of Jacopo Bellini's *Madonna*.

The Bellinis

Jacopo Bellini (1400–70/71) was the founder of the Venetian artist-dynasty, but very few oil paintings by him are known; all the more importance, then, attaches to his two extant sketch-books, one in the British Museum, the other in the Louvre, which provide a variety of information about the problems and goals of Venetian and northern Italian painting in the second half of the century. Carefully guarded by his sons as a collection of patterns, these drawings – even after their faded lines had been touched up – were already appreciated as works of art in their own right. At first sight they look like the illustrations to a text-book on perspective (pp. 354, 422), even though, in contrast to the Florentines, Bellini is far softer in his treatment of depth. It is above all his landscapes, which he has enlivened here with shading and hatching – genuinely pictorial means, in other words – whitch can be seen to be something lastingly Venetian.

It is clear that this left a number of theological and philosophical problems to be overcome. To represent the human appearance of God in the frailty of the human body, as for example in Mantegna's foreshortened *Dead Christ* (p. 370), did however impose a new obligation. To lend dignity to the depicted figure – irrespective of whether it was that of a saint or a ruler – became an additional requirement. As long as the portrait had to be no more than an idealized image, with likeness a secondary consideration, this had been no problem. Now, though, painters, medallists and sculptors had somehow to unite *similtà* with *dignità*. This became the content and problem of contemporary painting, and formed the theme of Pico della Mirandola's philosophical work *De dignitate hominis* ("On the Dignity of Man", 1496). A whole century later, Paolo Veronese was still having to defend himself against the charge of the Inquisition that in his *Feast in the House of Levi* he had depicted not only a person picking his teeth with a fork, but also dogs, fools and even Germans. In his response that "we painters claim the same licence enjoyed by poets and jesters", Veronese summed up the new awareness felt by artists of their position in society.

Venice in the 15th century

The Queen of the Adriatic had maintained close contact with Constantinople since time immemorial. From the moment in the 5th century when the inhabitants of Padua and Aquilea, fleeing from the Huns, had taken refuge on the Byzantine-occupied islands and built

Jacopo Bellini
Sermon of St. John the Baptist
Pen and ink drawing
Paris, Musée du Louvre, Cabinet
des Dessins

Gentile Bellini
Procession in St. Mark's Square, 1496
Oil on canvas, 367.5 x 746 cm
Venice, Accademia

Gentile Bellini
Sultan Mahomet II, 1480
Canvas, 70 x 52 cm
London, The National Gallery

Pictures in a style emancipated from Byzantine influences had been painted in Venice for a long time, but they were only the precursors of Venetian painting as such. While Altichiero and his Venetian contemporaries had still composed the space around their figures in a totally *ad hoc* manner, from now on the pictorial scenery seemed if anything an excuse to display spatial depth and clever architectonic spatial effects. Not for nothing is reference made to pre-Bellini and post-Bellini periods. Jacopo Bellini was active in Venice as early as 1424; a document dating from the previous year, in which he is mentioned as assistant to the Umbrian Gentile da Fabriano, refers to him as Jacopo Veneto. In 1441 he went to Ferrara, where he was victorious in the painting competition with Pisanello referred to above. In honour of his teacher, or so at any rate Vasari maintains, he gave his eldest son, born in 1429, the name of Gentile; in the following year his wife gave birth to a second son, Giovanni, whose legitimacy is in some doubt. In 1453 he married his daughter Nicolosia to the painter Andrea Mantegna, who was at that time still working in Padua.

This is just one example of the sort of family relationship one often encounters among artists, and when great artistic names come up in discussions of Venetian painting, they are – in marked contrast to the greater individualism of Florence – often the names of families in which more than one member made a name for himself: not just the Bellinis, but also the Vivarinis, the Palmas, the Tintorettos, the Bassanos, the Veroneses and the Tiepolos. Beyond doubt, the work of the Bellinis was the foundation of Venetian painting – it is with them that modern Venetian painting begins.

Too few pictures by Jacopo Bellini have survived for us to see them as representative of his work. A certain paradox has already been noted: the chance survival of his sketch-books has resulted in the founder of an important school of painters being remembered above

355

Gentile Bellini
The Recovery of the Relic of the Holy
Cross, 1500
Oil on canvas, 323 x 430 cm
Venice, Accademia

Giovanni Bellini
Doge Leonardo Loredan, 1501/05
Oil on canvas, 61.5 x 45 cm
London, The National Gallery

IOANNES BELLINVS

all as a draughtsman. His Madonnas best put across the style and skill of a master. It comes as a surprise that, although a pupil of the Tuscan painter Gentile da Fabriano, he brought very little of his Florentine experience with him, and, as we see in his *Madonna of the Cherubim* (p. 354), he largely followed the model of the leading Gothic masters, or, still more, the Byzantine tradition in Venice. This devotional picture looks altogether like an icon. The austere type of the half-length figure of the Madonna herself, the veil between the head and the hood, the face, seemingly isolated from its surroundings, the filigree calligraphy of the haloes, and above all the spaceless background ornamentally and exhaustively filled with angels' heads – all these features are reminiscent of an icon. And as with an icon, the whole is enclosed in a jewel-like arch-shaped frame.

The question has been asked time and again why Jacopo, in view of his Florentine training, preferred an older style to that of his "modern" teacher. Perhaps the real answer lies in the character of the artist, but it may also be that the importance of the conservative patrons who called the tune has been underestimated. One must bear in mind, after all, that the "modern" commissions were not always the lucrative ones: the conservative forces of the Most Serene Republic remained for a long time too proud, too rich, and too powerful.

Jacopo's eldest son Gentile Bellini (1429–1507) was already able to share in the harvest his father had sown. He too had no shortage of commissions, his talent as a portraitist having shown itself at an early age. And while the remuneration was meagre for each individual portrait in the large-scale prestige pictures which he painted, he must have earned himself a fortune in view of the great hordes of monks, noblemen, prelates and senators which populate them. See for example the *Procession in St. Mark's Square*, dating from 1496 (p. 355), or *The Recovery of the Relic of the Holy Cross* dating from 1500 (p. 356). Even though Gentile, still employing, as he did, largely Gothic forms, contributed little to the development of painting, and alongside portraiture concentrated his attention at most on the perspective in which his father had taken such great interest, his career was nonetheless spectacular. In 1469, he was appointed count palatine by Emperor Frederick III, and in 1479 – at the age of fifty, in other words – the Republic of Venice considered him worthy to be sent to Constantinople to paint the portrait of Sultan Mahomet II (p. 355). Mahomet "...could hardly understand," writes Vasari, "...how any mortal could possess the, as it were, divine skill of imitating nature so vividly." Bellini returned, a whole year later, piled high with gifts and honours, including the title of "bey".

Vasari also reports on the event which gave rise to the painting of *The Recovery of the Relic of the Holy Cross*: "By what chance I know not, the fragment had fallen from the Ponte della Paglia into the canal; and in their veneration for the holy wood of the Cross of Christ, numerous people plunged into the water; it was however the Will of God that none other than the Master of the Fraternity was found worthy to recover it..."

One thing is clearly apparent here: the inclusion of as many portraits as possible was just as important as the depiction of the miracle itself. "Miracles" – no matter how incredible from today's point of view – were, right up to the Enlightenment, fervently hoped for and not seldom contrived, sanctifying the site as they did and often enough making it a place of pilgrimage. After all, the miracle demonstrated God's willingness to meet local society. Bearing this in mind, the desire of the witnesses to be perpetuated on canvas should not be seen as mere vanity. They felt themselves, no less than their town or city – whose portrait, so to speak, was also being painted – to have shared in the miracle and the spiritual benefits it granted. The bridge, painted right across the middle of the picture, was indispensable for Bellini in order to assemble as large a crowd of eye-witnesses as possible. Catarina Cornaro, accompanied by the ladies of her court, is depicted, as if on a wooden apron stage, and so are the members of the Scuola, whose Masters dominate the right-hand side. Gentile has included himself in this group, along with his brother Giovanni (third and fourth from left). In fact, neither the canal nor the Ponte San Lorenzo ever became a place of pilgrimage, but the painting, as the documentary record of a miracle, has something of the aura of a votive picture, and preserves the memory of the ray of sanctity which shone down upon the city and her people. It goes without saying that this votive character restricts the potential for developing significant artistic aspects in the picture.

The Portrait

"His first works..." writes Vasari of Giovanni Bellini (c.1432–1516), "...were certain portraits, which met with great praise, in particular one which depicts Doge Leonardo Loredan." This picture (p. 357) was painted in 1501, when the Doge (who was proud of his Roman descent) took office, or shortly thereafter. It can indeed be considered one of the great achievements of Venetian painting, and not just in the field of portraiture. *Tutto spirito* was the verdict passed on it even by contemporaries. This is all the more remarkable in that it is by no means certain that our modern way of seeing things will necessarily always interpret a facial expression in the same way as it was perceived by earlier generations; and yet *tutto spirito* – "all intellect" – is how we perceive this image of the "humanist doge", as he was called, even today. There is no doubt about Bellini's technical virtuosity in the way in which he mastered the depiction of the brocade of the garment and the gold embroidery in the Doge's cap. But with what skill he played down the gold, in order to leave all the effect to be conveyed by the knowing eyes and the tightly closed, yet eloquent, mouth! Nor has Bellini attempted to camouflage the first signs of age – the wrinkles on the neck, visible in spite of the high collar – and the burden of care borne by the statesman, evinced by the shadows around the eyes. Only a generation before, all that had been required of a portrait was the reproduction of a type, with at most a few distinguishing features for ease of identification; this

Alvise Vivarini
Portrait of a Nobleman, 1497
Wood, 63 x 47 cm
London, The National Gallery

tone, darkening towards the top, of the intangible background. The man appears unapproachable as a result; he seems beyond the reach of everything, apart from a distant light which illuminates his eyes; and at the same time he appears engrossed, as if lost in thought about himself and his historic role.

The Doge is placed in the picture in such a way that he appears to be sitting or standing behind a balustrade. This schema appears time and again: it is based on the bust portrait pioneered by Florentine sculpture, and this in turn had its origin in the bust reliquaries of the Middle Ages. It may be that even at this period this was no longer such a conscious device, but it lent the form of depiction the additional suggestion of lasting dignity.

The *Portrait of a Nobleman* (1497) (lcft), the work of the Venetian painter Alvise Vivarini (c.1445–c.1505), follows the same schema. But Alvise, the youngest member of a family of artists from Murano, uses an oblique posture to put more movement into the man's shoulders, an impression enhanced by the hand reaching into the folds of his clothing; as a result, the austerity of the bust is largely mitigated.

From Tempera to Oils – Antonello da Messina

A transformation had taken place – and not just in mentality, which, as we see, was very different from Pisanello's, but also in style, and, not least, in the fact that we now encounter with much greater frequency the individual portrait, as opposed to the public and political image. From now on, pictures would evince a detailed, not to say meticulous, precision. The texture of fabrics is reproduced thread by thread; the embroideries, the eyelashes, the hair: all are punctiliously depicted. And once more it was an external influence which brought about this transformation. Netherlandish painting, represented by masters such as Jan van Eyck or Rogier van der Weyden, had long since prepared the ground for this kind of meticulousness. Jan van Eyck for example had connections with the court of the Dukes of Burgundy, and it was along such paths, which had been the conduits by which the influences of northern Europe had reached Italy once before, that the new mentality reached her now. Throughout the century, Netherlandish works were in extraordinary demand in Italy. They were not only a source of inspiration for artists, but they also unleashed discussions among scholars, for example the humanists Bartolomeo Fazio or Ciriacus of Ancona. We now know that the Portinari altar by Hugo van der Goes (p. 286) had been the subject of general admiration in a Florentine church since 1483, and its exemplary effect is thought not to have by-passed Leonardo. Jan van Eyck, Rogier van der Weyden or Hans Memling would after all also take portrait commissions from Italy: we have only to think of the famous marriage portrait of the merchant Giovanni Arnolfini, painted by van Eyck in Bruges in 1434, and now in the National Gallery in London.

portrait by contrast is characterized by totally different values: the sitter is not merely an individual, but even his emotional state is revealed. "Thin, tall of stature, of no great fortune, choleric, but as a ruler clever and wise", was how Leonardo Loredan (1438–1521) was described by one contemporary. He was Doge until 1521, and in the twelve or so years following the painting of this portrait, he was to guide the Republic through the War of Encirclement waged by the League of Cambrai.

Giovanni Bellini, who along with Verrocchio, Perugino and Ghirlandaio belonged to a generation whose pupils would be the great masters of the 16th century, has here given us a preview of a new style evident above all in the treatment of light and colour. A glowing shimmer of gold seems to join garment and countenance in a single magnificent unity, which is further enhanced by the cool blue

Antonello da Messina
Virgin Annunciate, c. 1475
Wood, 45 x 34.5 cm
Palermo, Galleria Nazionale della Sicilia

Antonello da Messina
St. Jerome in his Study, 1474
Wood, 46 x 36.5 cm
London, The National Gallery

Much in demand as this precision painting was, it could not be achieved using the tempera technique then usual in Italy. Only with the help of the secrets and techniques of oils, in which the Netherlandish painters were masters, could such fine colour transitions, transparent overglazing or the jewel-like brilliance of small details be attained. The Italian painter who concerned himself most intensively with the new technique of oils was Antonello, born c. 1430 in Messina. The fact that he stayed in Venice in 1475/76 signifies that he was able, from this date, to pass on his skills to the Venetians, and to Bellini in particular. It is not without significance that recent research has shown that Antonello da Messina did not, as Vasari reports, go to Flanders and there become "a friend of Johannes" (i.e. Jan van Eyck), and then return to "allow Italy a share in this useful, beautiful, and convenient secret." It is much more likely that he is in fact identical with one Antonello di Sicilia, who, at the beginning of 1456 in Milan, was in contact with the Netherlandish painter Petrus Christus, from whom he adopted the new method of painting.

The influence of Netherlandish painting, made known in the Venetian region by Antonello da Messina, was not, however, restricted to technique alone – a technique which, in addition to the differences in the treatment of rough and smooth texture had also made possible a more varied scale of light effects. Pictures now came to be characterized by a calmer expression and composition, as can be seen most clearly in portraiture. Bellini's portrait of Doge Loredan (p. 357) would perhaps be unthinkable without previous knowledge of the meditative calm already to be seen in all of Antonello's portraits. The fragmentation characteristic of pictures by Crivelli, Carpaccio or Cima da Conegliano, and the pleasure in detail also displayed by Mantegna and Cosimo Tura, and in central Italy by Pollaiuolo and even Botticelli, was avoided by Antonello. The gown of his *Virgin Annunciate* (p. 360), dating from as early as 1475, appears not with abundant folds, but with an austere monumentality we would not otherwise expect until the High Renaissance. Against a totally dark background, the lighting scheme not only gives the face volume, but also bestows on it something resembling mystical significance. Antonello well knew how to distinguish the psychological expressions on the faces of his aristocratic sitters from the unapproachable and un-individual idealized beauty of a Madonna. A comparison with Alvise Vivarini's *Nobleman* (p. 359) will make this clear enough.

The Consummation of Tradition
in the Work of Crivelli and Carpaccio

One could name a whole series of painters in this artistic region whose great achievement lay precisely not in the mere continuation of the contemporary style, but whose importance is manifested rather in the way they took the traditional style, into which their training had taken them, and brought it to a final perfection, each by adding an entirely personal touch of his own.

In a concern to give due weight to the new tendencies and their protagonists, it is often forgotten that society and patrons long clung to the older art, and did not by any means follow the new style at once. In the numerous monasteries, *scuole* (fraternities) and *fraglie* (guilds), in the institutionalized oligarchy of the powerful families, the demand for traditional prestige objects in particular was at times far stronger than any interest in novelty, albeit it was this variety of patrons in Venice which in itself was responsible for the way art developed there.

Among the many artists working in the traditional style, two stand out above all: Carlo Crivelli (1435/40–c. 1495) and, approximately twenty years his junior, Vittore Carpaccio (1455–1526). What they have in common could be demonstrated just as easily as what distinguishes them in respect of perception and execution. Both remained true to the Quattrocento, without any significant trace of a shift towards modernity. Their Gothic pleasure in narrative, their multi-faceted compositional style in which the actual motifs get lost,

361

Vittore Carpaccio
The Dream of St. Ursula, 1495
Oil on canvas, 274 x 267 cm
Venice, Accademia

BOTTOM:
Vittore Carpaccio
Two Courtesans, c.1510
Oil on wood, 94 x 64
Venice, Museo Correr

part in a political uprising, being made a knight in 1490, an honour which from then on he displayed in his signature. His somewhat stormy life stands in total contrast to the inward tranquillity which characterizes his pictures. He probably trained in Padua under Squarcione and Mantegna. From the latter, Crivelli derived a knowledge of classical buildings and a pleasure in inventing them (see p. 363). Otherwise, his style inclines towards the archaic. His almost Byzantine-Venetian traditionalism, which brings splendour and a wealth of detail into his pictures, displays revivalist features – a kind of neo-Gothic which we also find in Botticelli's later work. And in his Madonnas, which, surrounded by devout still-life props, have an icon-like serenity, he seems to want to revitalize the old style with the help of new techniques and experience. In so doing, he sometimes forgot the true function of painting: according to Alberti, the effect of gold was to be achieved by purely pictorial means; Crivelli, however, not only applied gold itself, but used plaster to achieve a relief of such

their sometimes schematic approach – all these are common to both, along with their perfectionism and a pleasure in the handling of texture.

In Carpaccio's case, the format often determines the simple composition. There is no ingenuity in the way the figures are juxtaposed, and in this he resembles Gentile Bellini, to whom he appears to have the closest relationship. But he never even approached the skill or reputation of Giovanni Bellini, especially in the treatment of figures and facial expression. It is even less possible to say whether the bored-looking ladies (right), waiting with somewhat vacuous expressions, really are courtesans, as the picture's title would have us believe. To be sure, the picture contains a number of symbolic allusions, which would first have to be decoded; but what makes Carpaccio's pictures attractive to modern eyes is precisely their naivety, into which one can read various secrets and which (with hindsight) can be related to 20th-century *pittura metafisica*. Carpaccio was less famous in his own day, and his patrons were the smaller ecclesiastical fraternities, the *scuole*, who, under state supervision, performed such humanitarian tasks as helping the poor and needy, or else represented the interests of the craft guilds. It was for the Scuola di Santa Ursula that he painted his major work, the large-scale cycle on the legend of their patron saint (top). His disregard of both geography and chronology, providing us instead with a loving inventory of the Venice of his own day, gives his pictures an additional value, especially where interiors are concerned. Whether he ever actually visited the Orient – as has been supposed – is an open question. His reputation did call him to distant provinces, however, for example to Istria and Dalmatia.

Crivelli also visited Dalmatia, albeit primarily because he had abducted the wife of a sailor, being sentenced in 1457. Ten years before his death, he drew attention to himself once more by taking

objects in the picture as garlands and baskets of fruit, to which he then applied the paint. His considerable, albeit traditional, skill, together with his love of old Venetian pomp and circumstance, brought him fame in the provinces, which no doubt also felt flattered, and especially in the Marches, where he was long active. Unlike Carpaccio, he was also a talented portraitist; also, and above all, he had the gift of bestowing on his female figures, such as his child-like Madonnas, a perfect beauty of countenance, achieved by the aestheticization of line and colour. It is this skill which puts him in the world class along with Antonello and Botticelli. The *Madonna della Candelletta*, painted around 1492, is one of his last great works of this kind (p. 364, right). The simplicity of the foreground may at a superficial glance deceive the beholder into overlooking the ingenuity with which the artist for example incorporates non-pictorial elements into the picture: the little candle is after all a votive offering, which would normally be set up by the faithful *in front of* the devotional picture. Here, Crivelli has painted it and included it *in* the picture.

Madonnas

If we juxtapose just five or six Madonnas (pp. 364–65) painted within the space of one artistic generation, in this case between 1468 and 1505, two of which belong to the type known as *Sacra Conversazione*, the different styles and characters of the artists become quite apparent. It is also evident, however, how difficult it is to judge these pictures by the criterion of their modernity. Is the *Madonna della Candelletta*, painted by Crivelli in 1492, more "old-fashioned" – on account of the Gothic splendour of the gown and its rigid symmetry – than Mantegna's earlier Madonna dating from 1485 (p. 370), for example, whose inclined head and bust display such unaccustomed movement? Are Crivelli's "neo-Gothic" features, or the dry expressivity of the *Pietà* painted by Cosimo Tura from Ferrara in 1469/70 (p. 364, bottom), not perhaps a foretaste of Mannerist sophistication?

An evolution can also be discerned in one central motif which, for more than a century, was significant in the *maestà* type of Madonna, namely the throne. In earlier styles, for example with Cimabue or Duccio (p. 42), the throne is usually represented as an armchair or often as a bench. What is always meant is the throne of heaven, with a canopy symbolizing the heavens. Right up to Giovanni Bellini, the representation of the throne canopy also underwent a transformation. The canopy for almost all of Bellini's Madonnas is simply a backcloth hung up and spread out behind the figure, replacing the back of the throne (p. 364, top). Crivelli has shown his Madonna against a length of gold brocaded cloth, which is inclined forward over her head, thus providing a canopy of a sort. The gold brocade, of course, represents heaven, the domain of the crowned Queen of Heaven. With Giovanni Bellini, it is often no more than a spread-out cloth, still showing the fold-marks. In his 1505 *Sacra Conversazione* Mary is depicted sitting on a marble throne (p. 365, bottom), with a brocade curtain still just

visible hanging from a rod behind it, and even Giorgione returns to this tradition in his Castelfranco Madonna (p. 388).

That this "backcloth" to the Madonna is symbolic, and no mere decoration, is shown by the changes in the way it is depicted in the various pictures. Providing the crowned Virgin with a throne and a heavenly canopy as marks of dignity, it represents not just a pictorial, but a religious and spiritual background.

In his Madonna, for example (p. 364, bottom), Cosimo Tura symbolically unites the theme of the *Pietà* with the throne motif, by taking for his "throne" the very tomb of the crucified Christ – a symbol of redemption, in other words. The background, which would otherwise be formed by the back of the throne, or by a canopy, here takes the form of the Hill of Calvary surmounted by the Cross.

Giovanni Bellini
Madonna and Child, c. 1468
Oil on canvas, 85 x 115 cm
Milan, Pinacoteca di Brera

Cosimo Tura
Pietà, 1469/70
Oil on wood, 48 x 33 cm
Venice, Museo Correr

Carlo Crivelli
Madonna della Candelletta, c.1492
formerly central panel of altarpiece
Milan, Pinacoteca di Brera

BOTTOM RIGHT:
Giovanni Bellini
Sacra Conversazione
(Enthroned Madonna, with Saints), 1505
Canvas, transferred from wood
(illustration cut off at top)
Venice, S.Zaccaria

RIGHT:
Giambattista Cima da Conegliano
Madonna with the Orange Tree and
SS. Louis of Toulouse and Jerome,
c. 1496
Wood, 212 x 139 cm
Venice, Accademia

Mary's throne, which uplifts and sanctifies her, is thus composed of the tomb (the seat) and Calvary (the back): her own special place is represented by the symbols of the death of her son.

In his *Madonna and Child*, painted in 1468 and now in the Pinacoteca di Brera (p. 364, top), Bellini also placed a hill in the centre of the background; the Madonna herself, however, is separated from the landscape by a thronecloth. In his *Madonna del latte* dating from c. 1490 (p. 371), the Milanese "painter-architect" Bramantino, whose real name was Bartolomeo Suardi (1465–1530), a follower of Bernardino Butinone from Ferrara where painting was concerned, also placed the Virgin against a striking background – in this case a rugged castle: this may be seen as symbolizing the God of the Old Testament, while to the left a new shoot emerging from a tree-stump represents the New Testament; here too, as with Bellini or Tura, the landscape elements are only legitimated by their symbolic values.

Giovanni Battista Cima (c. 1460–c. 1517/18), known by the name of his home town – da Conegliano – was active both there and in Vicenza, and was one of the most talented masters of the Venetian hinterland. In 1496 he painted a *Madonna with the Orange Tree* (top right), possibly one of the first Madonnas of this type, renouncing a closed background in favour of a – for him typical – free and open landscape. But here too, in what is no more than a seemingly naturalistic landscape, the central "background" is occupied by a symbolic motif: the orange-tree stands for Paradise, and thus Mary for the new Eve, with the focus on her virginity. The rock which forms the seat of her throne is an element of the natural landscape. Cima's devotional idea thus sanctifies his homeland, the countryside around Conegliano, which he has depicted here.

This picture is also an early example of the type known as *sacra conversazione*, developed in particular by Cima himself and by Bellini, but for which the ground had already been prepared by Domenico Veneziano and the young Bartolomeo Vivarini. How much this genre was influenced by Netherlandish painting is an open question, as is the issue of whether the whole concept of a *sacra conversazione*, as cultivated by 19th century art historians, actually means "holy conversation", or has to do with the Old Italian *conversare* ("turn towards"). In the earliest versions of this theme, prophets, saints or patrons were mostly paired in isolated juxtaposition, but later the figures are often turned towards each other in some kind of mental interaction, reminiscent of mediaeval mystery plays, or the then popular *theatrum sacrum* performances, which saw the appearance of the prophets for the first time.

Bellini and Mantegna

A glance at the work of Andrea Mantegna (1431–1506) will take us briefly back into the interior of the country. There is hardly any other painter of the period who demonstrates more clearly the striking differences between the atmospheric pictures painted in Venice and the harder, more plastic perception evinced by the schools of Ferrara,

Giovanni Bellini
The Agony in the Garden, 1459
Wood, 81 x 127 cm
London, The National Gallery

BOTTOM:
Andrea Mantegna
The Agony in the Garden, 1455
Tempera on wood, 63 x 80 cm
London, The National Gallery

Milan, or the university city of Padua. Born in Isola di Cartura, a small town between Padua and Vicenza, Mantegna was a contemporary of the Bellini brothers Giovanni and Gentile, whose sister he married. At the tender age of ten, he was apprenticed to Francesco Squarcione, a painter who had originally worked as a tailor and embroiderer, had been on a journey to Greece, and whose collection of antiquities was certainly more important than his art. From his pupils, to whom he entrusted the painting of the frescoes in the Church of the Eremitani in Padua, he expected an ability to paint very fine lines, a taste for the classical, and a plastic perception. Here, then, the foundations were laid for Mantegna's devotion to the world of classical forms, which he incorporated into his work only after Donatello and Brunelleschi, but with all the more determination. This was a pioneering achievement, in the sense that he was the model not only for contemporary Italians such as Bellini and Bramante, but also for his pupil Corregio, and, not least, for non-Italian artists of later generations, such as Dürer, Rubens and Poussin.

Mantegna's forms and colours are often harsh in their plasticity and crystalline in their hardness. The colours are clearly delineated, and many of the figures are so statuesque as to be almost holographic, seemingly chiselled out of the background. One needs to remind oneself of the great veneration then accorded to the stock of classical art-works still extant, and also of the fact that these then consisted exclusively of sculptures and reliefs; such classical painting as had been preserved was only re-discovered by the archaeologists of later generations. The classicized world of Mantegna's paintings often seems heroic and literally turned to stone, and while some of his contemporaries were still designing late-Gothic costumes, Mantegna's figures wear togas. The effect of his architecture is majestic, that of his perspectives imperious and inflexible.

One needs only to juxtapose two pictures on the same theme –

The Agony in the Garden by Mantegna (bottom) and by Giovanni Bellini (top) – to see the differences in the two perceptions. The very first glance shows us how much Bellini's picture is dominated by atmosphere. The light, the air, and the gentle outlines of the hills receding into the distance all merge into one, focusing on a single most distant point, which not by coincidence is at the centre of the picture. By contrast, Mantegna's version is characterized by a piling up of sharp-edged crystalline forms in the ice-cold clarity of the air. Moreover, there is an especially striking difference in the depiction of the main motif, the vision of Jesus: in the Bellini, an almost diaphanous angel just visible in the play of clouds and light; in the

Mantegna, children, opaque and almost three-dimensional in their plasticity, bearing the instruments of Christ's Passion.

While Mantegna's landscape seems to be chiselled in relief, and is dominated by the classical architecture of the centrally placed Jerusalem, Bellini has put the city well out of reach. A sleeping apostle in the Mantegna demonstrates the artist's mastery of geometric perspective; Bellini, in contrast, tones down the foreshortening effect by the way he has arranged the apostle's clothes, while developing the lighting perspective through colour gradation into the distance. And finally, Mantegna illuminates the clouds from above, despite the fact that the sun is below the horizon, giving them the plasticity one associates with a cold morning; Bellini, on the other hand, illuminates them only from below: the atmosphere thus becomes a statement about the time and the mood.

We come to similar conclusions when comparing two other pictures by the two painters: Mantegna's *Parnassus* (bottom right), painted in 1497 for the humanistic picture cycle in the *studiolo* of Isabella d'Este, and Bellini's *Feast of the Gods* (top right), commissioned by Isabella's brother, albeit not until 1514, and, moreover, revised by his pupil Titian. As if in competition with Mantegna, the Ferrarese artist Lorenzo Costa (c. 1460–1535) was required to paint *The Court of Isabella d'Este* (p. 377). Related in theme and structure, the content – allegorical and symbolic companies of deities in an imaginary landscape – is not always easy to decode. Certainly in Bellini's colour transitions, mild in the Venetian style, we have a foretaste of a Poussinesque Arcadian vision. Given that classical mythology only became one of the main themes in the 16th century, Mantegna's early allegory of gods and muses, antedating Raphael's *Parnassus* by thirteen years, takes on all the more importance.

From his early youth on, Mantegna was influenced by Tuscan painters, and above all by Donatello, who lived in Padua for some ten years up to 1453. Piero della Francesca may well have inspired Mantegna to find his style, and of course his later sojourns in Florence and Rome played their part. In 1459 he moved from Padua to Mantua, where he became the well-paid court painter to the Gonzagas. The decoration of the palace chapel in Mantua has been destroyed, but one of his most important commissions, the frescoes in the Camera picta (pp. 368–9), is still extant. The simple square room, illuminated only by two small windows, was formerly furnished with a bed, which quite certainly was employed as a show-bed in a kind of demonstrative ceremonial, such as we see later in the Chambre de Parade at Versailles. The precise meaning and ceremonial purpose of the room have not yet been given an exhaustive iconological explanation. However that may be, the bed must have had a certain importance in the scheme of things, and among other things the room was probably also intended as a place for the signing of contracts and the solemnization of marriages; hence its alternative name, Camera degli Sposi. The most important piece of evidence that the ceremonial room

Andrea Mantegna
Parnassus, 1497
Canvas, 160 x 192 cm
Paris, Musée du Louvre

Andrea Mantegna
Ceiling fresco in the Camera degli Sposi, completed 1474
Mantua, Palazzo Ducale

Andrea Mantegna
Ludovico Gonzaga, his Family, and Court, completed 1474
Fresco in the Camera degli Sposi
Mantua, Palazzo Ducale

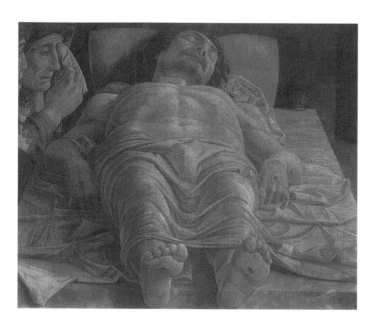

also had a legal significance is to be seen in the design of the ceiling. Painted as a *trompe l'œil*, it appears to give a view of the sky through an opening in the cupola, thus inviting divine witness to the ceremonial proceedings taking place in the room. The presence of heaven, often symbolized by a canopy, was, as we know, often required in numerous rites and cultic acts. Quite apart from the symbolic content, however, this ceiling by Mantegna is important in being the first in the whole history of art to give the pictorial illusion of being open to the sky. It represents the start of a process that came to dominate mural art by the time of the Baroque. Mantegna had completed these frescoes by 1474. He has individualized the human and historical situation of each of the figures in a lively and convincing manner, the scenes vividly recreating the life of the Gonzaga court.

Perhaps the most unusual picture we have by Mantegna seems also to require an unusual explanation: it is the *Dead Christ*, also known as *Cristo in scurto* (top right). The picture has been variously dated between Mantegna's time in Padua, around 1457, and as late as 1500, although the style of painting, with the soft folds of cloth and the heavy emphasis on perspective, do actually suggest as early a date as possible. In particular, however, observations made by recent scholarship cast a convincing light on the meaning of the picture.

The brusque foreshortening has not seldom been regarded as a slight, indeed as a provocation; nor has any explanation been forthcoming for the cramped confines of the picture, by which Mary and St. John are reduced to marginal figures. There is one small object, however, in the right background beside the pillow, which is the key to understanding the work: namely, a vessel of myrrh. The theme of the picture, then, is "anointing in the Jewish fashion", and the block of stone on which the corpse is laid out is the Anointing Stone of Christ, a major Christian relic which disappeared after the fall of Constantinople, where it was preserved, to the Turks in 1453. The relic, hallowed by the Body of Christ, is thus seen to be the real motif of the picture; it is the Christ figure which makes the relic speak. And more important than Mary are her tears, which, together with the Blood of Jesus, give the stone its speckled reddish-white coloration. No less provocative than the picture were the sermons being preached by the Pope at that time, calling for a crusade to liberate the Christian sites. Thus the provocation in the picture is not to be seen in the extreme perspective as such; at the time, this merely gave the picture its communicative impact.

The composition of the picture results in the eye of the beholder being drawn close up to the stone; standing at the foot end, he is personally involved in the scene of mourning which the painting depicts, as though he were on a level with the laid out Body of Christ. The wan light of the picture faithfully reflects the uncanny and moving atmosphere of the tomb, while – for all the directness of the provocative view – it nonetheless does supreme justice to the tragedy and grandeur of the sacred theme: these qualities have always been recognized, and point to the greatness of the painter.

Donato Bramante
Heraclitus and Democritus, 1477
Transferred to canvas
Milan, Pinacoteca di Brera

BOTTOM:
Bramantino (Bartolomeo Suardi)
Madonna del Latte, c. 1490
Oil and tempera on wood, 45.9 x 35.2 cm
Boston, courtesy of Museum of Fine Arts
Picture Fund

When Albrecht Dürer visited Italy for the second time in 1506, one of his reasons was to visit the now famous Mantegna, who, however, had died a short time before. That his importance transcended the bounds of the region where he worked had been recognized even during his lifetime. To be sure, the hardness of his lines and colours has not always found favour, and has given many the impression of his being less modern than in fact he was. We can gauge the distance by which Mantegna advanced the art of painting over a period of some thirty-five years by contrasting a Madonna by Jacopo Bellini, painted around 1450 (p. 354) with that painted by Mantegna in 1485 (p. 370). The idea behind the pictures is not dissimilar: the background is filled with the heads of angels. But whereas in the Bellini they form no more than a patterned backcloth, Mantegna has a choir of individual singing angels, while the infant Jesus seems to be listening in rapt attention to their heavenly song. Jacopo Bellini's Virgin looks as if she were immobile behind a plate of glass, while by contrast, the upper body of Mantegna's Mary, inclined slightly forward, creates a relationship which extends out of the picture towards the beholder, who is thus involved imperceptibly in the depicted scene.

Milan

Pisanello's early Renaissance forms also influenced the Milanese school, which had remained largely Gothic for a long time. We cannot describe the entire development here, but we shall at least mention Vincenzo Foppa, that pupil of Pisanello's to whom the painting of the Quattrocento here owes its beginnings. Starting with Foppa, and going on to Borgognone and almost all the Milanese artists up to the great architect Bramante, who was also active here as a painter, we can discern a common feature: a predilection for subdued, silvery colour effects verging on the monochrome. It is no coincidence that Mantegna's sense of colour went down well here, and the probability that Bramante studied under Mantegna is supported by the colour tradition which the painter-architect carried on. One might even ask whether precisely this initially subdued coloration in northern Italian painting did not exercise a general influence on what, following the mutual influences of the individual Venetian schools, we recognize as atmospheric use of colour.

Donato Bramante (c. 1444–1514) did not paint much, nor did his influence in this field extend beyond a very few individual artists, such as Zenale, or Bramantino, who, like Bramante, also came from Milan and also worked as an architect, and who, in his turn, exercised an influence on the work of Luini. Bramante came to Milan from Urbino in 1472 and stayed until the Duke was overthrown; very few of his pictures are still extant, among them the frescoes from the Casa Prinetti in Milan, now in the Brera, along with depictions of warriors, a singer, an orator and a philosopher. The quality of these pictures betrays Umbrian-Florentine and Paduan influences, and are reminiscent of the grace of form we associate with Melozzo da Forlì;

Leonardo da Vinci
Detail from Last Supper

venerability, by being depicted in a quasi-statuesque, sculptured manner. Castagno's figures, such as St. Apollonia, or Mantegna's St. Sebastian are painted thus, and in the drawing discussed above (p. 354), Jacopo Bellini has also placed the preaching St. John the Baptist upon a pedestal like a stone monument upon a plinth, lending him dignity and significance through his statuesque posture. As for Bramante, he has made the "scholars' colloquy" between a weeping philosopher (Heraclitus) and his laughing colleague (Democritus) his actual theme: they are disputing whether the world is round, this being the age of the discovery of unknown continents.

Leonardo da Vinci in Milan

As we see in this picture of philosophers by Bramante, but also in the many *sacra conversazione* altarpieces – and, incidentally, also in Raphael's *School of Athens* (p. 332) – painters had long been concerned to depict not merely actions, but also communication. Only now that artists understood how to achieve a differentiated representation of gestures and facial expressions could a well-known or significant subject of conversation be thematized in a painting. Having discussed Leonardo in the context of his work in Florence (pp. 310 ff.), we shall now follow him to Milan. His *Last Supper* (p. 372) in the refectory of Santa Maria della Grazie in Milan is also basically a "conversation", albeit one at the centre of the Christian faith. It is no coincidence that during the 15th century this theme in particular was taken up so often, and from various angles. As in a *paragone*, artists vied with each other to perfect a theme which, originating in the monastic refectories of Italy during the 14th century, was at this precise moment assuming a new function. Painters were seeing new opportunities of depicting human and

they also bear witness to an encounter with Leonardo da Vinci and Piero della Francesca. His picture of *Heraclitus and Democritus* (p. 371, top), by contrast, clearly owes much to what he learnt from Mantegna. The depiction in this painting is relief-like; the figures appear to be carved in stone, which gives them a monumental immobility, not to say rigidity. This picture is not perhaps in the same artistic class as those by Mantegna whitch we have discussed, but it is no less emphatic in the way it expresses what we find in so many other artists of the 15th century: major personalities of the past – saints, statesmen or philosophers – are often given a dignity, indeed

Leonardo da Vinci
Last Supper, 1495–98
Mural, 420 x 910 cm
Milan, Santa Maria delle Grazie, refectory
By kind permission of the Ministerio Beni
Culturali e Ambientali

emotional dilemmas in this motif of prophesied betrayal. Dignity of countenance, gesture, expression and the emotional reflection of varied temperaments were what artists were now seeking to reproduce. The *certa vivacità* demanded by Vasari, the enlivening of the whole of the picture, which only started to become articulate in the 16th century and is still lacking in the works of Mantegna, Ghirlandaio or Botticelli, has already been achieved by Leonardo in this picture.

The *Last Supper* was completed in 1498, and it was immediately recognized as the most perfect rendition of its theme, influencing all its successors to a greater or lesser degree. Ever since it was painted, it has been regarded as the major work of one of the most important artists of the Western world, not just on account of the masterly way in which the scene is constructed, but because here – in a manner immediately comprehensible for Leonardo's contemporaries and for later generations alike – the composition, coloration, expression, lighting and the attitudes of the individual figures are perfectly concentrated on the words: "One of you will betray me." And even at that early date, Vasari was already writing: "In all the faces one can read the fearful question: who will betray the Lord? And each expresses in his own way not only his love for Jesus, but also fear, anger and indeed sorrow, because they cannot understand his words." The Apostles, full of confusion and self-doubt, form small groups; they have been individualized, not to say psychologized. Only one, the traitor, compositionally and gesturally excluded from the community, constitutes the opposite pole to the dignity and serenity of the Lord, lonely in the consciousness of his message, whom Leonardo left unfinished. According to Vasari, he was unable to give his face the divine dignity he would have wished. The idea behind the pictorial motif and the maturity of its rendition complement each other. As Leonardo himself said: "The greatest evil is when the thought exceeds the work."

The mural today is badly damaged, gnawed by damp. One can only imagine its former beauty. There is something ominous about the dissolution of the contours and the invasion of the picture by damp patches on the wall, ominous because the artist saw these patches on the wall, these unsightly signs of the transitoriness of earthly things, as a stimulus to his imagination: after all, that which had become intangible on account of lost contours, that which was continually changing through new strength of its own, the unfinished – all this was at the centre of Leonardo's interest. And unfinished the most important of his works remained: the *Adoration of the Magi* (p. 311), the *Virgin of the Rocks* (p. 373), the *Battle of Anghiari* for the Palazzo Vecchio in Florence, of which only a fragment has been preserved, and also the *Portrait of a Musician* (p. 375) in Milan. If one asks why Leonardo left so many works unfinished, why so many drawings consist only of intimations, one can point to various reasons unconnected with his art: one is his alleged restlessness, which we can well believe in view of his moves from Florence to Milan, and then to

Parma and Bologna, thence to Rome and back to Milan. But there may have been an artistic reason too, namely this: Leonardo stopped at the point where continuation would have brought no further enhancement to the rendition, where, regarding an important problem as having been solved, without giving thought to completion, he proceeded to the next. We therefore possess perhaps fewer works than we do by artists of a more meticulous disposition, but the loss is not a loss of quality.

Let us look back: born in the Tuscan mountain village of Vinci, Leonardo joined Verrochio's studio at the age of fifteen, and was accepted as a member of the Florentine painters' guild in 1472. In 1481 he moved to Milan at the invitation of the Duke, to whom he had offered his services as sculptor, architect and engineer, and only incidentally as a painter. His main commission from the Sforzas at this time was not then a picture, but rather an equestrian monument of the founder of the dynasty, Francesco Sforza. He prepared drawings and a model of a boldly gigantic bronze sculpture, which was to stand more than five metres tall. However, the threat of

Leonardo da Vinci
Lady with an Ermine (Cecilia Gallerani), c. 1484
Oil on wood, 54 x 40 cm
Cracow, Muzeum Narodowe

imminent war meant that the metal destined for the statue was cast into cannon, and it is said that the model was shot to pieces by French soldiers. We are thus unable to experience the work of the universal artist in his capacity as sculptor.

The same applies to Leonardo's work as an architect. Numerous sketches, above all for centrally-planned buildings – such as were actually executed by Bramante and others – have been preserved (p. 134). We know that he worked as a military engineer, but there is no building attributable to him. Nor did he pursue to completion his great plan to collect and publish his scientific writings, for example on perspective and painting, taking up where Alberti left off, or on philosophy and anatomy. The *uomo universale* and all-round artist may well have recognized or feared that the complexity and abundance of the various problems in the individual fields were too great for a rounded solution ever to be found. Nevertheless, Leonardo did succeed in uniting what previously had been the preserve of individual disciplines such as philosophy, science, literature and art in isolation. He thus enjoyed the reputation of a great artist during his lifetime, and this at a period when artists had only recently liberated themselves from the status of craftsmen. While Vasari may have seen the importance of the role of the artist somewhat euphorically, he certainly did not overestimate it in this case. Leonardo in particular, who was on the closest of terms at the Sforza court with a poet like

Bernardo Bellincioni, a music theoretician like Gafurio or a mathematician like Pacioli, had already seen to it in the 1480s that an artist could become a household name, so to speak – a circumstance that did not become really general until the following century. If Michelangelo was the pride of the Pope in Rome, then Leonardo was the pride of the Duke of Milan, and later of the King of France.

Leonardo went to Rome in 1513, but the two years which he spent there were a disappointment. He got bogged down in experiments with varnishes, and unlike Michelangelo and Raphael, he received no commissions. In 1516 he went to France for good. He spent the remaining short years of his life in the little château of Cloux near Amboise, dying there in 1519.

A number of painters are counted among his pupils, including Boltraffio, Gianpetrino and Marco d'Oggiono, but I shall select only two of the most important, Giovanni Ambrogio de Predis (1455– after 1508) and Bernardino Luini, born c. 1475 and active until 1531/32. Neither these two, nor any of the others, can be considered successors in any real sense. They all adopted some elements of his technique and his style, or else created variations on his motifs. But none had great talent or a feeling for what was important. As is shown by a comparison of two pictures (p. 375), the imitators lacked one essential, namely emotional expression. The facial features of de Predis' *Nobleman* seem merely schematic, the mouth is weak;

compare this with the closed yet eloquent lips of the *Musician*, a portrait incidentally whose authenticity has been denied. But who else in this circle was able to paint this facial expression? Alongside Leonardo's *Lady with an Ermine* (p. 374), de Predis' *Girl with Cherries* looks like an intellectually challenged tart; likewise, the pupil's *Nobleman* seems a little short on the grey matter in comparison with the master's *Musician*. Leonardo's full-blooded and lively figures became mere dummies in the hands of his imitators.

Luini by contrast is quite a different matter; he summed up the Milan School, but in not one of his pictures did he make a serious attempt to imitate Leonardo, and this is doubtless the reason that he achieved a certain artistic autonomy – provincial perhaps, but all the more lively as a result. His *Girls Bathing* (top) evinces a style of painting totally independent of Leonardo's. Pastel-like, the scene has a refreshing lightness of touch, and had we not known the artist to have been a pupil of Leonardo, we would assume it to have been the work of a Venetian.

The Schools of Northern Italy
Verona, Genoa, Bologna and the other cities of northern Italy, with the exception of Venice, as we have seen, were provincial until well into the new century. Attention was focused either on Mantegna in Mantua, or on Venice, or on Leonardo in Milan. And yet a number of remarkable works from elsewhere do stand out, in particular from the intellectually sparkling ducal court in Ferrara. Here we find the mysterious and even today not fully explained murals painted by

Francesco del Cossa (1435/36–1477/78) and others in the Palazzo Schifanoia (pp. 380/1), with their astrologically inspired allegories. They betray an almost late-mediaeval breadth of esoteric knowledge of the movements of the spheres. Man continues to be seen – or maybe is seen once more – in terms of the cosmos. As so often, antiquity is conjured up through the medium of pseudo-classical cryptic symbols.

Perhaps the most extraordinary murals of this kind in northern Italy, likewise consisting of cosmic-astrological and classical mythological sequences, is the large-format cycle in the Palazzo del Tè in Mantua. They were created between 1526 and 1535 by the Roman artist Giulio Pippi (c. 1499–1546) – known after his birthplace as Giulio Romano. They were intended as the decorative climax of this extensive summer palace, of which he was also the architect. It was not as if there were no northern Italian artists available; there was, for example, the aforementioned studio of Francesco Cossa. But the Duke of Mantua expected of a Roman artist and pupil of Raphael a very special knowledge of classical Roman decorative art. And much later, Dominique Ingres claimed to have recognized that: "Jules Romain, c'est l'antique!"

A narrative series of pictures, humanistically encrypted allegories and mythologies accompanies the visitor through the halls. In the Sala delle Metamorfosi and in the niches of the Sala delle Aquile, Giulio has introduced sequences of motifs from ancient Roman painting. In the Sala degli Stucchi, he moulded friezes which were intended to correspond to the recently uncovered wall decorations in Roman ruins. *Grotti* was the term applied in Rome to the former imperial palace rooms which had sunk beneath ground level, and thus decorative schemes of this kind were called "grotesques". Giulio revived these too, in the Casino della Grotta. And of course his painting also reflected the influence of Correggio's *trompe l'œil* work, and fantasies of this sort were quite at home among the almost unreal decoration of the Palazzo del Tè.

The climax of the sequence is the *Fall of the Giants* (pp. 378–9) in the Sala dei Giganti, surely the most exciting thing Giulio ever created, and much praised and admired by his contemporaries, Vasari not excepted. Every inch of the walls and ceiling of the huge room, from the floor up, is painted in such a way as to make it appear that the building is collapsing. Enormous blocks of stone crash down to reduce the architecture to rubble, at the same time crushing and burying the bodies of the giants. This "disaster painting" makes it seem as though the building had been struck by an earthquake, and indeed, wearing his architect's hat, Giulio designed elements of the external structure with ready-made cracks and fissures, and with loose stones lying around, enhancing the effect of post-earthquake chaos on a giant scale. The total architectural effect of the Palazzo del Tè is one of ruination and breathtaking magnificence at the same time. Quite obviously we are dealing here with an example of Mannerism in its most unmistakable manifestation.

Lorenzo Costa
The Court of Isabella d'Este (allegory), post–1505
Canvas, 164 x 197 cm
Paris, Musée du Louvre

TOPAND OPPOSITE:
Giulio Romano et al.
Wall and ceiling frescoes
in the Sala dei Giganti, 1526–34
Mantua, Palazzo del Tè

Giovanni Francesco Caroto
Boy with a Drawing
Wood, 37 x 29 cm
Verona, Museo del Castelvecchio

Dosso Dossi (c. 1489/90–c. 1542) came from Ferrara, but also worked in Mantua from 1512 to 1516, before returning to his home city. While his painting is entirely different from that of Giulio Romano, he too evinces a Mannerist tendency, albeit less in his motifs than in his colours. Dosso's stylistic features are not altogether surprising, bearing in mind that important years during his training were spent in Venice studying the work of Giorgione and Titian, to whom he owes a very great deal. He also met Titian while he, Dosso, was court painter to the Este family in Ferrara. Unlike Titian, however, Dosso employed piercing, intense, almost phosphorescent colours: emerald green, for example, or mother-of-pearl white, like tempting lights, which he employed to place his – by contrast – entirely tranquil-seeming figures into curious, fairy-tale atmospheres. While Giorgione, as we shall see, uses colours in a classically balanced manner to draw the eye of the beholder to the meaning of a picture, Dosso veritably stages his pictures. *The Departure of the Argonauts* (p. 382, top) is one of his later works. A noteworthy feature is the proto-Impressionist way the colours begin to dissolve.

Quite different, profane, altogether human and without any trace of symbolism, allegory or religious background is the portrait of a child by the Veronese artist Giovanni Francesco Caroto (c. 1480–1546), known as the *Boy with a Drawing* (right). The lack of any kind of cryptic content suggests that those who see it simply as a

Francesco del Cossa
Pruning the Vines, detail from "March"
from the cycle of the Months, c. 1470
Fresco, complete picture 450 x 400 cm
Ferrara, Palazzo Schifanoia

portrait are correct. But that precisely as a portrait it is significant: for it is no longer the venerable, the classical, the historical or the allegorically important which alone is seen to be portrait-worthy, but the everyday as well. The boy, with loose red hair, rendered without any sign of noteworthy genealogy, is maybe the son of the artist known as Carotto or Caroto; or is it perhaps a retrospective self-portrait of himself as a talented child? Excited and pleased with himself, the young draughtsman shows us his very own work. Is it perhaps a mock competition? That would suggest the boy was competing with his portraitist. And who was the winner? Why the boy, of course; his open-eyed rascally smile forces us to this conclusion. The themes of this picture are the urge to create and the joy of creation. Wit is heralded for the new generation of 16th-century painters. Such optimism and clear simplicity show that the artist has long since crossed the threshold of the High Renaissance, a threshold which is as intangible and as fluent as Leonardo's contour-blurring *sfumato,* which, after all, appeared at just the same time.

Before we return to Venice, which was to take first place among all the Cinquecento schools, let us spend a while in Parma, one of the small towns of northern Italy. This was where Antonio Allegri worked, one of the very great painters. He is known as Correggio,

after the little town in Emilia where he was born in about 1489. By the time his major works were painted, Leonardo had been dead for several years. But Correggio must have been acquainted with some of his works, and Titian was already famous in Venice. In other words, he was in a position to borrow from both, but his work is so much his own that he appears as a master who has fallen from heaven. Vasari described Correggio as modest, reserved and indeed melancholic: "In his art too he was very serious, never sought to avoid effort, and indeed tended to make every task as difficult as possible – in witness whereof take the huge number of figures which he painted in fresco in the most perfect manner in the dome of Parma Cathedral, and so wonderfully foreshortened that the visitor ... never ceases to be amazed."

For a painter who was the first to invent an open heaven filled with floating figures and to perceive it as a grandiose phenomenon of light, it must have been demoralizing to hear such negative criticism of this work in particular: one canon complained that the accumulation of bodies was a "ragout of frogs' legs". In this "baroque" design Correggio was far ahead of his time; only someone who had perfect mastery both of physical bodies and of light could attempt such supreme tasks.

That Correggio had taken the new idea of an illusory open ceiling from Mantegna's Camera degli Sposi (pp. 368–9) is proved by the manner in which, as early as 1518, he approached a commission to paint the Camera di San Paulo in Parma. He treated the vault as a bower with oculi, through which putti gaze, just as in Mantegna's picture. But his first important trompe l'œil in a dome in which Mantegna's idea was brought to fruition was the Vision of St. John the Evangelist in the eponymous cathedral in Parma (p. 385). Never before had the art of foreshortening been so impressively mastered as here, especially in the floating figure of Christ. Never before either had light and colour been so effectively deployed as a counterweight to form. Vasari recognized already that Correggio had been the first to set a very dark colour against the light in order to enhance the effect of depth. Nor has the diffuse effect of clouds, haze or mist, a continuation of what Leonardo had pioneered with the sfumato technique, ever been executed more perfectly by any other master than Correggio.

The maturity of this mastery can be seen for example in the Abduction of Ganymede (right) or in the banks of clouds in the Ascension scenes in the domes of the churches in Parma. Correggio was the first to bring into dark church interiors a light which was simply painted. The painting of light must be seen as Correggio's chief interest – in many ways an anticipation of the effects to be achieved only later by Caravaggio with his chiaroscuro, and then by Rembrandt. One of Correggio's best-known paintings, The Holy Night (p. 384), presents the Nativity of Christ for the first time as a "miracle of light". The child Himself glows, illuminating the faces of the bystanders. Light alone is deployed here as a compositional

Correggio
Adoration of the Shepherds (The Holy Night), 1522
Wood, 285 x 190 cm
Dresden, Gemäldegalerie Alte Meister

Correggio
Zeus and Antiope, 1528
Canvas, 190 x 124 cm
Paris, Musée du Louvre

counterbalance to the shepherds standing to the left. A coup like this went well beyond anything being attempted with light by, for example, Titian in Venice.

The diffused glow, as of the late-afternoon sun, which lends such an intimate shimmer to the skin of the young Antiope as she reclines in anticipation is another first (p. 384). In pictures like this, Correggio presents us with a totally new concept of feminine beauty, one only rediscovered in the 18th century by such painters as Fragonard and Boucher. Here too, as with his anticipation of Baroque illusionism, Correggio was way ahead of his time. This is all the more astounding in that the barren soil around Parma from which Correggio sprang offers no hint that such a talent would emerge, and the same might be said of his teachers. Like Giulio Romano, Giorgione, Palma il Vecchio and Parmigianino, Correggio was not blessed with long life: he died of fever in 1534 aged 45.

Like Leonardo, Correggio had numerous pupils, but they paid paltry dividends on the huge investment. With one exception, none was a worthy successor; this exception was Francesco Mazzola, born in Parma and known as Parmigianino. Vasari tells of his precocious talent. And of the unusual *Self-Portrait* (p. 387), which allegedly found its way into his collection, he writes: "With the help of a convex barber's mirror he painted a self-portrait, without being deterred by the difficulty caused by the foreshortening of the beams, the doors and all the other objects, or the fact that many of the objects close to the mirror appeared enlarged, while others further away were reduced in size. Thus he painted a rather large hand in the foreground, so beautiful that the illusion seems perfect. The portrait itself was of divine beauty, for Francesco had more the face of an angel than of a human being." Parmigianino painted the picture on a wooden panel the shape of a skull-cap, corresponding in form to the convex mirror; the chosen shape thus draws attention to the fact that it is a self-portrait and cannot have been painted by another hand. A signature would have been totally redundant. When Parmigianino went to Rome in 1524, he presented the picture to Pope Clement VII, who was much taken by it, calling it a *meraviglia* (a "marvel") which aroused *stupore* ("astonishment"). The Pope gave the picture to the *enfant terrible* of the age, the writer Pietro Aretino, and via him it passed to the sculptor Alessandro Vittoria; then to the court of Emperor Rudolph II in Prague, where the Milanese Mannerist painter Giuseppe Arcimboldo (1527–93) was working.

From Correggio, Parmigianino had taken his conception of figures; but he did not adopt his teacher's intellectual attitude, nor the softness of his contours, and still less his light-imbued colourfulness. His pictures seem harder than those of his master; his style reflects the influence of Raphael and the experience of his sojourns in Rome and Bologna from 1527–31. Another characteristic of his work is a deeply Mannerist component. Like almost all the Mannerists, he provokes surprise, perturbation, astonishment, and indeed displeasure, through the cultivation of the "distorted" perception of the figure, the *figura*

Correggio
Vision of St John the Evangelist, 1520–24
Fresco in cathedral dome
Parma, San Giovanni Evangelista

Correggio
The Assumption of the Virgin (detail)
Fresco in dome
Parma, cathedral

Parmigianino (Francesco Mazzola)
Self-Portrait in a Convex Mirror, c. 1524
Wood, diameter 24 cm
Vienna, Kunsthistorisches Museum

Parmigianino
Madonna of the Long Neck, 1534
Oil on wood, 219 x 135 cm
Florence, Galleria degli Uffizi

serpentinata. Parts of the body are often elongated, a characteristic which gave the name to his *Madonna of the Long Neck* (right). A mystical adherent of alchemy, he invites the beholder to step into the elegant-seeming yet deep, complex and at times melancholic world of his pictorial invention, into the unreal enchanted rooms of his backgrounds, with their consciously illogical structure.

Venice in the 16th century

While Florence and Tuscany, and above all Rome, were forced into decline within a few decades as a result of looting by Imperial troops in 1527, Venice prospered, and during the 16th century became the most splendid city in Italy. Painting profited especially through the fact that from about the middle of the century, building needs were largely satisfied, and apart from individual churches, very little new construction took place. As a result, it was the turn of interiors to receive the attention of those with money to spend. The stylistic divide between the centres and the periphery of artistic activity grew narrower all the time. During the 15th century the studios of Mantegazza and Solari in Lombardy, the schools in Ferrara, and above all Mantegna's studios in Mantua and Padua had formed such centres, developing very local styles of their own; their influence, as in Mantegna's case, extended to Venice, and now it was the turn of the Queen of the Adriatic to repay in abundance what she had received during the previous century.

From the very beginning, colour – *poesia* – stood in contrast to the Florentine *storia*, and Venetian painting is far less narrative than lyrically contemplative. The foundations for this particular characteristic of Venetian painting had already been laid by Giovanni Bellini, as we have seen, but now two artists appeared who raised it to a new climax: Giorgione and Titian.

Giorgione

Now it is the appearance of things that stands in the foreground, and no longer their outline. It is obvious that Giorgione visualized his picture in colour from the outset; it was no longer a drawing subsequently coloured in. This was as revolutionary a development as the discovery of perspective, and also led to that sensuousness which is part of the essence of the Venetian perception.

Curiously, there is much about this initiator of Venetian Cinquecento painting which remains obscure to this day. None of his works bears his signature, and only very few attributions to him are totally unchallenged. A pupil of Bellini, his original name was Giorgio or Zorzo Barbarelli; he was born in Castelfranco in 1477 or 1478. He too was destined not to live long, dying in Venice in 1510. He was first referred to as "Giorgione" – "big Giorgio" – by Paolo Pino in 1548, "on account of his imposing appearance and greatness of soul". In his very earliest pictures he showed that for him, the landscape came first. Whenever one of his paintings features a landscape, it has liberated itself from the status of adjunct, and, as atmosphere, forms an important and integral part of the painting.

This can be seen in the *Sleeping Venus* (p. 397, top), which has rightly been described as one of the most perfect accomplishments of the Renaissance. The peace of the countryside and the slumber of a girl who seems unaware of her nakedness, the two linked by the late-afternoon sunlight which transfigures the scene: a poetic homage to beauty and nature in equal measure. We shall return to this picture once more in connection with Titian's *Venus of Urbino*. In the religious picture the *Enthroned Madonna* (top left), too, which he painted in 1505, the landscape occupies a primary position. This only becomes clear when we follow the lines of perspective of the raised throne and realize that the viewpoint of the beholder is envisaged to be well above the wall which separates us from the landscape. The attendant figures in this *sacra conversazione*, Saints Liberale and Francis, are placed lower, and thus the beauty of the Madonna is enthroned amidst the beauty of a landscape whose peacefulness reflects her expression.

The content of Giorgione's pictures, which often come across as lectures on classical myths, is no less enigmatic than the details of his life and work. His *Three Philosophers* (bottom left) is surrounded by all manner of interpretations. The picture is one of the few whose attribution to Giorgione is based on documentary sources, although the finishing touches are said to have been applied by his pupil Sebastiano del Piombo. Is it really the case, as X-ray pictures suggest, that the three figures characterized by their disparate ages were first intended to depict the Magi seeking to calculate the position of the star of Bethlehem, or are they astronomers, or – as a different interpretation would have us believe – are they Evander, Pallis and Aeneas? Or are they three great figures in philosophy – Virgil, Aristotle and Averroes? An attempt has even been made to read into this scene the story of the visit of Merlin the wizard to Blausius.

No less enigmatic is Giorgione's *Pastoral Scene* (p. 390), which probably dates from 1508. Two young men, one of them dressed in considerable splendour, are making music on the grass in an idyllic landscape, and have paused to talk. They have been joined by two naked girls, who in most descriptions have been represented as courtesans. Yet it is striking that there is no interaction between the men and the nude figures; it is as though the presence of the girls has not even been noticed. One of the girls is in the process of pouring water into a well, while the other is eavesdropping on the conversation, having removed her flute from her lips. Are these really intended as real girls who have accompanied the pair for a day in the country? Surely not! The nude figures are meant to be on a different plane of reality, for example the subject of the young men's conversation made visible, or perhaps nymphs, only visible to us the beholders, allegories of water and air and the audible sounds of nature which they engender: the splashing of water and the sound of the flute. For there is indeed a real wind instrument in the picture: the shepherd in the background is playing a shawm, but both he and his music have merged into one with the landscape. The concrete juxtaposition of figures from two levels of reality was after all a customary enough device: witness the inclusion in a *sacra conversazione* of saints from a quite different epoch. By analogy, I would regard this picture as an idyllic, secular *conversazione*. But this view may in the final analysis also prove unsatisfactory.

It is striking that none of Giorgione's pictures has ever had a valid interpretation – one that has been generally and lastingly accepted. Even shortly after the artist's death, Vasari was already writing apropos of the frescoes on the Fondaco dei Tedeschi: "For my part I have never understood the meaning of it all, nor have I found anyone who could explain it to me."

He could well have said the same about Giorgione's *Tempest* (p. 391), perhaps one of the most important paintings ever to be produced in Italy. One might ask whether this is a mere allegory of the opposition of man and woman and the two worlds to which they have respectively been assigned. The man has been equipped with a staff; the architecture and ruins behind him would then be symbols of construction and destruction. The woman, depicted cradling her child against the ravages of the tempest, is depicted against a background of houses, in other words symbols of shelter, and the two are separated by a river. Or do the contents of the picture in some cryptic fashion have something to do with the insignia on one of the painted houses, or with the Vendramin family, who commissioned the picture? The seated mother, suckling her child in the landscape, had long been an allegory for Mother Nature providing sustenance, *La Terra nutrice*. And as late as 1622, Mylius, in a copperplate engraving for his *Philosophia Reformata* (p. 392), was using the same pictorial image as Giorgione in his *Tempest:* on the right, the nursing Mother Nature, seated (*Allegoria della Terra*); on the left, the standing figure

Giorgione (Titian)
Pastoral Scene (Fête Champêtre), 1508
Canvas, 105 x 136 cm
Paris, Musée du Louvre

Giorgione
The Tempest, c. 1506
Oil on canvas, 82 x 73 cm
Venice, Accademia

of a man, watching and guarding her, albeit here depicted wearing armour and carrying a sword.

Whatever conclusion any particular interpretation may reach, Giorgione's pictures, throwing up insoluble problems as they do, and where even the seemingly plausible solutions lead *ad absurdum* once more, stand at the beginning of a painting tradition which no longer lends itself to "interpretation", because it no longer wishes to be interpreted – consider, for example, the later landscapes of the 18th century, or Monet's "Impressions". Giorgione's playing with hints that give rise to deeper expectations which then cannot be unravelled, with kaleidoscopic and arbitrarily assembled elements, suggests that he was concerned to maintain an everlasting scholars' colloquy, the *paragone* of intellectual disputation, rather than to provide satisfyingly logical but trivial answers.

The composition of the *Tempest* is courageous and inwardly strife-torn: a flash of lightning unexpectedly illuminates a chance section of landscape; it is as though the world were suddenly stripped naked and perpetuated thus on canvas. This naked coincidence and everything apparently lying around to be discovered are held together by the colour and the dreamy atmosphere of perfect harmony.

In spite of the paucity of his output, Giorgione's painting influenced the entire Venetian school. Hardly anyone remained completely untouched by him. Sebastiano del Piombo, to name but one, who studied under Cima, Bellini and Giorgione, attempted to continue Giorgione's style. And even his later work in Rome, where as a monk he was the Keeper of the Seal to the Pope (hence his nickname "del Piombo"), while influenced by Michelangelo, was still recognizably Venetian in its coloration.

Titian

It was granted to Tiziano Vecelli to consummate what Giorgione had started in epoch-making fashion, and not just in the sense that he was able to complete those unfinished works left behind by Giorgione after his early death, but also in the way that the style of Renaissance painting as a whole was to develop. That Titian's work became a secular phenomenon was not due to chance, but required a number of predisposing factors, which happened to come together in him: magnificent talent, untiring energy, and a long maturing process. If it is true that Titian was born in about 1477, which not everyone believes, then he was the same age as Giorgione, from whom, however, he had important things to learn. Unlike Giorgione, on the other hand, he had almost 100 years to bring his acquired skills to maturity, and thus put his mark upon the century, before dying in 1576.

Titian's work cannot be seen in isolation from his personality or – above all – from the social role which he played on the brightly lit art stage of wealthy 16th-century Venice. The uniqueness of his achievement becomes clearer when one realizes that this painter, who was born the son of a legal clerk in the Dolomite village of Pieve di Cadore, and was sent to Venice at the age of ten to study under Bellini, not only experienced a whole century, but also overstepped social barriers in a previously unheard-of way. Appointed painter to the Venetian Council in 1516, he was greatly sought-after and soon much fêted as a portraitist by all classes of society: the rich bourgeoisie, the Church, and the aristocracy. Eventually raised to the status of count palatine by Emperor Charles V, he retained the favour of the latter's son, King Philip II of Spain. His energy and the efficient organization of his extensive studio did not slacken even in his extreme old age. His rank and his age raised him to the status of "prince of painters", surely the first in the history of art, well before Rubens could allow himself similar airs, and long before 19th-century high society granted similar privileges to just a few selected artists, for example Makart in Vienna, or Lenbach and Stuck in Munich – and of course, Titian was the historical model.

The mosaic artist Sebastiano Zuccato, then Gentile, and above all Giovanni Bellini, were Titian's first teachers. In Bellini's studio, where he stayed until 1504, he was a fellow-pupil with Giorgione, and much of what he painted here was passed on to the respective client as the work of Bellini. Bellini's *Feast of the Gods* (p. 367, top) was altered by him, as has been mentioned. But even before this, in 1508, he worked alongside Giorgione on the frescoes in the Fondaco dei Tedeschi, the then much-respected "German Exchange"; of these frescoes only fragments, and engravings produced much later, remain to give us any idea of their pristine appearance. Around 1515 he was working in Giorgione's studio, being found worthy of finishing off the works of this master, too; thus, the naked nymph with the water-jug in Giorgione's *Pastoral Scene* (p. 390) may well be by his hand.

Titian soon came to outshine his teachers and, needless to say,

Palma il Vecchio
Nymphs Bathing, c. 1525
Transferred to canvas, 77.5 x 124 cm
Vienna, Kunsthistorisches Museum

Palma il Vecchio
The Three Sisters
Wood, 88 x 123 cm
Dresden, Gemäldegalerie Alte Meister

such pleasant younger painters as Jacopo Negreto, known as Palma il Vecchio (c. 1480–1525), who, a pupil of Bellini's, soon adopted Giorgione's style, and eventually even became something like a pupil of Titian himself. In religious painting, Palma remained true to the Quattrocento, doubtless following the wishes of his clients, but even so, he introduced a new type of picture, the horizontal-format *sacra conversazione*; where colour was concerned, however, he continued to cultivate the Venetian splendour, as shown by his unusual triple portrait, *The Three Sisters* (right). His training at the hands of Giorgione also induced a degree of softness in his work, as well as a certain enigmatic touch.

Titian, by contrast, did not continue with Giorgione's mysterious atmospheric effects or with his depth of meaning, as can be seen from a work such as *Heavenly and Earthly Love* (1514, Galleria Borghese, Rome). But in this first creative period, which we can date approximately to the years between 1500 and 1518, his closeness to Bellini and to Giorgione is still recognizable. The *Gypsy Madonna* and the *Madonna with the Cherries* are witnesses to this early style. Even if we follow the usual division of Titian's creative life into four phases, the second of which began powerfully with his best-known altarpiece, the *Assumption of the Virgin*, painted between 1516 and 1518 for the Frari church in Venice (p. 395), the fact cannot be overlooked that the *Andrian Bacchanal* of 1523-25 (p. 396) still contains major stylistic elements deriving from Giorgione and Bellini. This of course applies not to the totally novel, highly dynamic composition of the painting, which demonstrates something of a proto-Baroque vivacity, but rather to the still relatively distinct contours of the bodies, and the fine treatment of the landscape elements, particularly the foliage of the trees.

A comparison with Bellini's picture on a related theme (p. 367) shows not only the differences in perception – in Bellini's case almost moralizing, as through the artist would have allowed the Bacchantes

and the other participants at most a sherry-glass of communion wine; in Titian's version, by contrast, a full-blooded exhibition of human passions. A comparison of the figure in the right foreground of the two pictures makes the same point more succinctly. The juxtaposition and comparison of these two pictures has a long tradition, for both once adorned the study in the Palace of Duke Alfonso d'Este in Ferrara, and both have provided subject matter for scholarly disputation ever since they were painted. The *Venus Festival* of 1523 was painted in the same connection, after Titian had visited Ferrara and come away with commissions for pictures. And again it is no coincidence that it was precisely from Ferrara that commissions came for such classical themes as these, as well as for themes taken from Ariosto or Philostratos (cf. p. 380).

One of the most beautiful of the portraits painted for Ferrara is that of Laura de Dianti (p. 403). This beauty was the mistress, and later possibly the wife, of Alfonso d'Este; the picture was painted in about 1523, doubtless as a counterpart to a Titian portrait of the Duke. It was one of the first pictures to proclaim what was already at that date the artist's inimitable painting technique. The term "technique" is already going too far, however, if what we mean is the treatment and effect of colour. While with Giorgione, despite the softness of the transitions, a final trace of contour can still be sensed, this is totally absent from Titian's work. He applied the colours paste-like alongside each other, and thus achieved such an increasingly loose application that he already anticipates much of what we find in Velázquez, then in Rembrandt, and even more strongly in Franz Hals, and which on occasion – especially in respect of Titian's late work, for example the *Self-Portrait* now in Madrid, or his *Christ Crowned with Thorns* in Munich – has led to an unfortunate comparison with Impressionist painting techniques.

Titian
Pesaro Madonna, 1519–28
Canvas, 478 x 260 cm
Venice, S. Maria dei Frari

Titian
The Assumption of the Virgin, 1516/18
Wood, 690 x 360 cm
Venice, S. Maria dei Frari

Titian
Andrian Bacchanal, 1523-25 (some sources date as early as 1516/1518)
Canvas, 175 x 193 cm
Madrid, Museo Nacional del Prado

The effect of incredible vivacity arises precisely through the indeterminacy of the contours. No line can be identified any longer which could be understood as a precise demarcation of some form. In place of the careful modelling used by, for example, Leonardo when painting the *Mona Lisa*, we now have a lineless application of paint, which generates body, even though the deep boundaries are invisible. What Leonardo had achieved by means of *sfumato*, Titian achieves by means of a looseness of colour transitions, which brings out both light and colour in equal measure and at the same time.

If one wishes to understand in short steps the development of a hundred years of Renaissance painting in northern Italy in terms of brush-technique and application of paint, from Pisanello through to Titian, one need only look at one portrait by each of the various masters in succession, for example Pisanello's *Portrait of Ginerva d'Este* (p. 353), Antonello's *Virgin Annunciate* (p. 360), Bellini's *Loredan* (p. 357), Leonardo's *Mona Lisa* (p. 314), Lorenzo Lotto's *Lucrezia* (p. 398) and Titian's *Laura de Dianti* of 1523 (p. 403).

Titian painted the *Pesaro Madonna* (p. 394) in the same year as his *Laura*. It is noticeable that for a public commission such as this, the painting style is somewhat more conservative – something, however, which is not true of its epoch-making composition. The picture took its name from the man who commissioned it, Jacopo Pesaro, who is to be seen in the picture kneeling on the left in front

of the steps and looking towards the Virgin. Several years earlier he had achieved a decisive victory over the Turks while serving under the papal banner. For this reason it is St. Peter seen here recommending him to the Madonna. The key placed on the step beneath his feet makes him quite literally the key figure in this votive picture. The gradual raising of the figures right up to the Madonna herself places the emphasis on her as Queen of Heaven; but it is precisely this which is a new compositional technique: Titian has removed her from the centre of the picture and placed her at the upper vertex of a powerful diagonal. The columns assigned to her seem to stretch right up to Heaven. The way in which Pesaro's family are lined up in strict profile has something of the traditional about it, and yet Titian leavens the group by the trick of making the young boy look towards the beholder. This method of concentrating attention on the Madonna precisely by moving her to the edge of the picture, but at a higher level, would be imitated in many altarpieces in future years, as for example in the *Madonna with St. Nicholas* by Moretto di Brescia.

The Reclining Nude in Giorgione and Titian

If we compare the painting techniques of two reclining nudes, Giorgione's *Sleeping Venus* of 1508 and Titian's *Venus of Urbino* (p. 397) of about 1538, in other words from his third, compositionally calmer period, we shall come to a similar conclusion to that above in connection with the series of portraits. But over and above the painting technique, Titian's reclining nude addresses quite different sides of our emotions. The similarities are more immediately obvious than the differences, apart from the fact that Giorgione's untouched and silent landscape has become a private room. One thing the pictures obviously have in common is the pose of the two girls: the right leg held slightly bent at the knee, the shin beneath the outstretched left leg; the left arm following the contour of the body in a gentle arc; and the dark background framing and as it were cradling the head. And finally, there is a further correspondence in the right background of the two pictures, not obvious and only manifesting itself at a second glance: in his landscape, Giorgione has placed a fair-sized tree, with a smaller one to the left of it, and, between the two and further forward, a tree-stump; Titian repeats this compositional idea in his picture, only here the elements, shifted to the right, are no longer trees but a standing woman, a kneeling girl and a sleeping dog. It is the differences, however, which create an entirely new theme out of the same motif. The Urbino Venus is looking out of the picture at the beholder. The eyes appear somewhat dreamy, yet knowing. The head no longer rests in the crook of the right arm, as with Giorgione, but coquettishly on her shoulder and slightly raised, creating the impression that she has only just noticed the approach of the beholder. In contrast to Giorgione's picture, there is a whole series of elements here

Giorgione
Sleeping Venus, c. 1508
Oil on canvas, 108 x 175 cm
Dresden, Gemäldegalerie Alte
Meister

Titian
Venus of Urbino, 1538
Canvas, 119 x 165 cm
Florence, Galleria degli Uffizi

commissioned a nude from Titian, a *Danae*, which, according to a letter dating from 1544 and still extant, may well portray one Donna Olimpia, a well-known courtesan.

Titian's pupil Palma il Vecchio also painted a *Reclining Venus*, backed with a landscape as in the Giorgione, but with the same inviting expression as the Titian. We also know of a similar example by Lorenzo Lotto.

The Portrait

Lorenzo Lotto (c. 1480–1556) was an outstanding portrait painter, whose early work was influenced by Antonello da Messina and Alvise Vivarini; he had a superb ability to feel his way into the human soul, and in his work the facial expression takes on a particular depth of content. If one places his *Portrait of a Young Man* (bottom), now in Vienna, alongside Titian's so-called *Young Englishman* (p. 400, bottom), the differences are most obvious in the painting technique. Lotto proved his talent *inter alia* in fine brushwork which aimed at subtle reproduction of the material, whether it was brocade or hair, folds in the cloth or the casting of shadows. Titian, by contrast, painted with a lofty disregard for realistically fine renditions of texture. The famous master could afford to forego time-consuming details in favour of bold flourishes and almost impudent brush-strokes. His friend Pietro Aretino, the writer, who had at least two portraits of himself painted by Titian, wrote: "And if I had paid more *scudi*, then doubtless the cloth would have turned out as lustrous and soft as silk, or stiff as brocade." Titian, an important man in Venice, who took for granted his familiarity with the highest representatives of public life, knew how to give his sitters that lofty *grandezza* which

imperceptibly introduced and waiting to be discovered, which make Titian's Venus more seductive, her environment more tense, and the atmosphere more erotic. Thus this "Venus" has propped herself up not on a large cushion, but on a small, inviting pillow. She is showing her open hair flowing over her shoulder, emphasizing the look in her sensuously questioning eyes. To be sure, Giorgione too has arranged the folds of the sheet with great subtlety to focus the lines in the picture imperceptibly on the girl's lap. Titian, however, emphasizes this area, which is touched rather than covered by her hand, in a perhaps equally imperceptible but rather less subtle manner, using the straight line of the curtain behind her. While Giorgione's *Sleeping Venus*, perceived as a floating crescent moon, is unapproachable and to be understood allegorically – for who would wish to disturb the peace of this landscape and this slumber – Titian by contrast, by means of the curtain, with which he separates the reclining girl from the whispering activity of the servants beyond, integrates the beholder spatially and intimately into the picture, as if he had been invited to the bedside. No wonder, then, that Titian's "Venus" of Urbino has been traditionally regarded as a courtesan.

There are a number of indications, supported by documentary sources, that such nudes had the function of providing permanent mementoes of the erotic relationships enjoyed by aristocratic, or indeed ecclesiastical, clients. Titian's *Venus* hung in the Duke of Urbino's summer residence. Cardinal Alessandro Farnese also

lent them a dignity transcending mere likeness. It was precisely through the omission of decorative details, and by concentrating on the head and the look in the eyes, or the attitude of the hands, whose gestures he could make speak volumes, that the dignity of the sitter could be enhanced, while at the same time betraying a searching psychological observation.

It is a striking fact that such well-known portraitists as Lorenzo Lotto, who was probably a pupil of Alvise Vivarini, or Moretto da Brescia, or Giovanni Battista Moroni, took far more trouble than Titian over the rendition of texture and the pictorial accessories which raise the value of a painting. Above all, however, they sought to achieve an additional pictorial statement, in that they quite often portray the sitter along with objects connected with his professional or political life, and, over and beyond this, seek to make him more interesting through the use of cryptic symbolism – all of which implies a further individualization in the portrait. The last-named feature may have something to do with the fact that the 16th-century portrait artists still enjoyed nothing like the status of painters of narrative themes, for example, whose *opere d'invenzione*, whose imagination, was what made their pictures valuable. In the case of the portraitists mentioned here, we can see an attempt to enhance the portrait by means of *invenzione*.

Portrait and *invenzione*

Lotto was a master at this art. He painted one Andrea Odoni in the midst of his collection of antiques, not without symbolic references, and a young woman he painted as *Lucrezia* (p. 398), with emblems and additional statements, on a horizontal-format canvas. And thus the traditional small portrait became a large-format picture with a message and a certain entertainment value.

Even in the small *Portrait of a Young Man in Front of a White Curtain* (p. 398), which avoids any attempt at idealization, Lotto does not miss the opportunity to introduce, on the fringe, an *aperçu*, namely a burning oil-lamp in the top right-hand corner, in the pitch-dark room behind the curtain. The lamp is intended not just as a symbol of transitoriness, but also to draw attention to the dark

behind the bright curtain: an allusion to the artist's psychological perception of the young man. Does not the youth of the sitter similarly contrast with his joylessly dark clothing, and his critical, almost suspicious gaze?

Alessandro Bonvicino, (c. 1498–1554), known to us by the name of Moretto da Brescia on account of the fact that he spent his whole working life there, was another who, in addition to his altarpieces such as the famous *St. Justina*, painted quite a few portraits which bear witness to his great humanistic and intellectual breadth of interest. His *Portrait of a Young Man* (p. 399) sums up within itself all the possibilities of portraiture known to the age: quite apart from likeness, we have the mastery of texture, the capturing of the sitter's emotional state, and finally a theme which enriches the picture. The young nobleman is presented in a bold composition, as an almost cumbersome diagonal at an unusual angle from top left to bottom right. Gold brocade and a lynx fur stole, padded silk and gold coins proclaim both the wealth of the sitter and the skill of the painter. But Moretto also clearly understood how to introduce his "theme", namely the young sitter's melancholy, a fashionable complaint of the age by means both of the man's posture and of hidden details. Like *Melancholia* in Dürer's well-known engraving of 1514, the healthy, wealthy and handsome, yet melancholic young man is propping himself up on a cushion. Sewn on half-hidden to the underside of the brim of his hat is a label bearing the motto in Greek: "alack-a-day, I demand too much". Perhaps the inscription *iou-lian-posso* is a punning allusion to one Giulia Pozzo, who did not return his love. Such an assumption has been made, because otherwise the young man would appear to have everything: youth, wealth and good looks. Yet it is precisely because he is thus well-endowed that he represents the new, Mannerist, man: the melancholic, extravagant dandy who indeed outlived Mannerism to appear in the salons of Bohemia in centuries to come.

By contrast, such a searching emotional complication of the issue is totally absent in the work of Moretto's pupil, Giovanni Battista Moroni from Bergamo (1520/25–1578). Moroni painted his sitters just as they were – in their professional pose, or something analogous. It is precisely in this straightforward, indeed almost documentary, sense that the portrait of *The Tailor* (p. 399) should be understood.

It is not until we come to Titian, the most sought-after portraitist of the age, that the art of portraiture first came to enjoy parity of esteem with narrative painting. The numerous portraits he produced over a span of six decades show how little importance Titian attached to appurtenances and attributes, and by contrast how much he simplified wherever simplification was possible. It is this reductionism that turns persons into personalities and endows them with a significance that depends not on accidental props but on the timelessness of the attitude in which the sitter is depicted, and of course also on the coloration. Titian deploys colour in such a way that, dominating the picture, it characterizes the sitter. A red against a

magic dark from Titian's brush ennobles the sitter in a way never seen before, outstripping any textural variety whatever, or even gold.

The extent to which the composition, the pose of the figures, and of course the colour, together constitute a critical psychogram of the sitters was demonstrated by Titian in the triple portrait of *Pope Paul III and his Nephews* (right). Bent with age, but yet cunning, is how the Pope is depicted, sunk in his armchair, while his nephew Alessandro stands behind him indifferent and devoid of emotion. No genuflexion could be more ingratiating than that being performed by his other nephew, Ottavio, nor could any stare show more distrust than that on the old potentate's face. This Farnese family portrait was left unfinished, which is perhaps just as well, being quite revealing enough as it is.

In 1548 Emperor Charles V summoned Titian to the Diet of Augsburg. Although already 71 by then, the artist did not decline the honour, spending eight months in the Imperial city. The outcome of the laborious journey was two portraits of the Emperor. One of them hangs in Munich, and was, apart from the head, the hands, and the design of the whole, perhaps completed by another artist. The more important of the two pictures is undoubtedly the one now in the Prado: *Emperor Charles V after the Battle of Mühlberg* (bottom and detail p. 402). He is depicted here as the victorious ruler who had defeated the Protestant princes at the Battle of Mühlberg. The battle itself is not shown here, nor – contrary to advice given by Aretino – are any allegorical accessories, such as Fama or Victoria. The Emperor's armour and lance are all that point to his role as warlord; but it is above all the blood-red sky of the evening following the battle which symbolizes the event. Red is also the main colour in the

horse's saddlecloth, the Emperor's sash, and the plumes, both in his helmet and in the crownpiece of his horse's harness. The atmosphere of the picture creates a strange balance between the menace with which the horseman unexpectedly and suddenly emerges from the dark clump of trees, on the one hand, and the majestic calm of the dark shadows and the pregnant red tones which dominate the picture, on the other. The horse's head is lowered, the Emperor's is raised, vigilant, while his gaze, cold and emotionless, sizes up the situation. All this leaves no doubt about the active superiority of the victor even after the battle, and of the self-evidence of the historical role which is being fulfilled here. The tradition of the equestrian statue – such as Donatello's *Gattamelata* (p. 197) or Verrocchio's *Colleoni* – is here being continued in a different medium, that much is obvious enough; but it is also worth mentioning that this picture is in itself a monument to commemorate the special historical role of a Holy Roman Emperor who was always on the move. The oppressive glow of the sky, which can be understood as either sunrise or sunset, with its red, indigo, gold and leaden streaks, contributes an element of significance to the picture. Expression is being given here to a process of change: the struggle of the moods of the clouds victoriously broken

Titian
Emperor Charles V after the Battle of Mühlberg
(detail of illustration on p. 401)

Titian
Portrait of Laura de Dianti, c. 1523
Canvas, 118 x 93.4 cm
Heinz Kisters Collection

by the rising or the setting sun. Atmospheric horizons like this were to be a characteristic of many pictures produced by the Venetian school from now on. Veronese painted them, as did Bassano; and the invention long continued to be a source of inspiration for German painters such as Hans Rottenhammer, and, later, those of the 18th century.

The painting technique, which is in complete contrast to the clearly defined method typical of the Netherlands, has something inconclusive about it, something almost mysterious. How characteristic this is for Titian's later work is indicated by his final pictures, for example the *Pietà* in the Accademia, left unfinished at his death in 1577, and above all by the *Christ Crowned with Thorns*, now in Munich. These are paintings in which the question of completeness or incompleteness is no longer meaningful; the seemingly incomplete has attained such expressivity that its message cannot be further enhanced. However, there is not infrequently something sinister about these late works.

None of Titian's pupils, successors or contemporaries dared to take up or develop the brushtechnique or the perception characteristic of the master's later years – neither Paris Bordone from Treviso (1500–71), nor Palma il Vecchio, nor Giovanni Girolamo Savoldo (c. 1480–after 1548), who was influenced by Palma and whose chief interest was to cultivate the rendition of cloths and silks (cf. below), let alone Lorenzo Lotto with his fine brush technique. They all avoided both the sketch-like and the heavy components of Titian's palette.

Only in Tintoretto do we find anything comparable, with the result that he soon became famous for having mastered the rendition of night, thunderstorms, flashes of lightning and other barely paintable phenomena even better than his teacher Titian.

Tintoretto, Master of Mannerism

Jacopo Robusti – for that was his real name – was born in Venice in 1518, the son of a silk-dyer, or *tintore* (hence his own nickname, "little dyer"). He died here too, aged 76, almost at the end of the Cinquecento in 1594. In Venice with its love of legends, his biographer Carlo Ridolfi wrote that Titian had quickly broken off Tintoretto's apprenticeship out of jealousy, and also that the pupil had written on the walls of his studio the motto: *Il disegno di Michelangelo e il colorito di Tiziano* – Michelangelo's draughtsmanship and Titian's colours.

Tintoretto, however, was pursuing different aims from the predecessors and models we have named. The glowing tones, the many colours, and the fine gradations of luminous colour which we find in Titian he sacrificed in favour of a brusque alternation of light and shade, while his brush increasingly transformed the exquisiteness of luscious colours into subtlety of tone. And unlike Michelangelo, he developed an anti-classical manner of composition which aimed at extreme effects. It is possible that he was trained by Bonifazio de'

Tintoretto
The Rescue of Arsinoë, 1555/56
Canvas, 153 x 251 cm
Dresden, Gemäldegalerie Alte Meister

Pitati, Paris Bordone or Andrea Schiavone, but in any case he appears not to have left Venice. His early work up to 1548 reflects the influence of Parmigianino, and like him, he remained a Mannerist through and through. Thus, even the spaces in his pictures live by the tension of expressive deformation. His compositions are often dominated by eccentric features, above all the daring diagonals from bottom left to top right, which load the scenes with tension.

The Rescue of Arsinoë (top) is a typical example: the diagonal formed by the boat, which dominates the picture, has no counterbalance of any sort. On the contrary: the main characters, clinging to each other and somehow keeping upright in the swaying vessel only reinforce the drama of the theme. Particularly after 1560, the form and content of Tintoretto's pictures are marked by a visionary congruence which we only rediscover in El Greco, who owed it all to the influence of his Venetian training.

Titian's first securely dated picture – *Apollo and Marsyas*, now in London – was purchased by Pietro Aretino, the friend of the jealous Titian, which proves not only the high regard in which he was already held, but also his contact with scholarly circles. Like a man possessed, he is said to have struggled for commissions for poor rewards (*bassi trattimenti*), and to have carried out some of them, indeed, for no more than the cost of the materials.

In 1548 he painted *St. Mark Freeing a Christian Slave* (p. 406) for the Scuola Grande di San Marco. The picture tells the story of how a slave was to be tortured for having left his master in order to pray at St. Mark's tomb. The scene shows the instruments of torture being smashed by a miracle worked by the saint. The picture caused a sensation, perhaps less on account of the depiction of the crowd, whose perturbation is so convincingly rendered, than because Tintoretto succeeded in thematizing the event by means of the bold device of introducing the figure of the saint, depicted hovering above the scene, having made his potent intervention: the effect is almost theatrical in its total surprise.

After establishing a relationship with the Scuola di San Rocco in

OPPOSITE:
Tintoretto
Judith and Holofernes
(detail from illustration
on p. 408)

Tintoretto
St. Mark Freeing a Christian Slave, 1548
Canvas, 415 x 541 cm
Venice, Accademia

a particular room as this one is must be regarded already as a forerunner of the Baroque conception of picture and physical context as a single interacting unit.

The fixed scheme of Christ in the middle of the table, dating from Leonardo's *Last Supper* (p. 372), has not been abandoned here, geometrically speaking, yet the perception is very different. Classical proportions have given way to a Mannerism laden with tension. The theme too is different: what is depicted in this *Last Supper* is not the prophecy of betrayal, but the institution of the sacrament, and thus the doctrine of transubstantiation, which was being re-emphasized precisely at this time. The transformation of the bread into the Body of Christ is strictly speaking unpaintable. The same applies to the transformation of spirit into substance, and Tintoretto gives expression to this content not least through the hovering angels materializing into light. The agitation of the company, individually thematized by Leonardo, here extends to the whole. As the lamp overhead gutters, it seems as if the scene is being sucked into the depths. The servant on the right, depicted in the middle of a Mannerist turn, seems to be weightless and almost dancing. The dematerialized figures in the air come across like a whirlwind of spirits. This *Last Supper* was almost certainly Tintoretto's last major work, being completed in the year of his death. The drama, the eccentricity, the dissolution of the material aspect in favour of

1548, he received his first state commissions in 1551, working for the Doge's Palace, St. Mark's and other public buildings. His painting style at this time still bore the influence of Titian, his powerful bodies still have firm ground beneath their feet, as in *Judith and Holofernes* (top and detail p. 407), and his space still has a logical comprehensibility. After 1560, however, the breakthrough to a seemingly totally uninhibited dissolution of space was complete. In his *Discovery of the Body of St. Mark* (right) the room has been transformed into a spookily dark tunnel, the figures come across as ghosts, the backlit scene, as the corpse is hauled out of its tomb and slips out of its shroud, is positively creepy; surreal and nightmarish, it touches on the darkest fears of the soul.

The *Last Supper* in San Giorgio Maggiore (p. 409) was painted between 1592 and 1594. The space has by now become totally intangible; the many-figured scenery, plunged into darkness, has no background. The long table constitutes the diagonal which dominates the picture, receding as if into some nocturnal tunnel, among magically illuminated figures which grow smaller and smaller. Christ, in the centre of the table, already seems small in relation to the figures in the foreground, yet His radiant head is precisely at the geometric centre of the picture. Stooping, the Lord passes His disciple the bread, but in this pose, stooping to the left, He also turns towards the beholder, which is to say the congregation in the church of San Giorgio. For this picture, like its counterpart, *The Gathering of the Manna*, was painted to be hung, and thus to be seen, on the side wall of the church. In order to re-create the effect of this viewing position, one should look at the illustration obliquely from the left, thus foreshortening the table and the unreal space into which it recedes. A picture so closely attuned to the furnishings and viewing conditions of

Tintoretto
Last Supper, 1592–94
Canvas, 365 x 568 cm
Venice, San Giorgio Maggiore

El Greco (Domenikos Theotokopoulos)
The Dream of Philip II, 1579
Oil on canvas, 140 x 110 cm
Escorial, Real Monasterio

expressivity – these features were continued after his death by only one painter, the Greek-born, but Venetian-trained, Spaniard El Greco.

Right into his old age Tintoretto was still accepting such enormous commissions as the 22-metre-long *Paradise fresco* in the Council Chamber of the Doge's Palace. For all his immense output, he spared no effort to avoid repeating himself. His imagination was inexhaustible. Together with Veronese, he took over the leadership of Venetian painting which Titian had bequeathed. But although Tintoretto outlived the younger Veronese by six years, the development of genuinely Venetian painting after Titian was continued not by him, the Mannerist, but by the man from Verona.

Veronese, the Herald of the Baroque

It was Veronese who was to determine the course which painting was to take for the next century and up to Tiepolo. His work was not only the expression of a late Renaissance society drunk on a fullness of earthly life and festive splendour, but already displayed proto-Baroque and even Rococo features. Paolo Caliari was his name, born in Verona in 1528, the son of a stonemason, and universally known after his home town as "Veronese". He had already acquired a reputation even before he moved to Venice in 1555. He received his earliest training as a thirteen-year-old at the hands of his uncle, Antonio Badile, but soon joined the studio of the well-respected Giovanni Caroto. Along with Giambattista Farinati, alias Zelotti, he

Paolo Veronese
The Marriage at Cana
(detail from illustration opposite)

Leandro Bassano
Family Concert
Florence, Galleria degli Uffizi

set about painting murals in the villas and palaces in and around Treviso and Vicenza. That he oriented himself at first towards such models as Parmigianino, and above all the Mannerist frescos of Giulio Romano, is clear from his style, as is the fact that he later – 1560/61 – spent some time in Rome.

One would be justified in saying that these years spent in a world of pictures of the kind in demand in these villas – the summer residences of the wealthy Venetians – provided the precondition and the foundation for his later undiminished predilection for the cheerful and the festive. The painting of the murals in the Castello in Thiene, for example, gave Veronese an early opportunity to display his whole artistic temperament, showing his interest in the creation of a counterbalance to the everyday, world, a counterbalance that was both cheerfully carefree and pompous and noble. In contrast to the sinister earnestness and the dramatic tension in Tintoretto's dark colour tones, Veronese's colours became increasingly brighter and cheerful, and his *trompe l'œil* foreshortenings seem unburdened with heavy significance. If what his biographer Ridolfi reports is accurate, this was also true of his life, which laid everything at his feet: talent, success, fame and wealth. He had only to help himself.

His first Venetian commission was for a *Coronation of the Virgin Mary* for San Sebastiano, and even before the work was finished the senior members of the monastery were so thrilled that they pressed him to paint the ceiling as well. This too was a great success and much admired, keeping him busy with further work here until 1570. It was during pauses in the execution of these commissions that he painted his airy mythological and allegorical frescos in the Villa Barbaro (p. 172). In carrying out this work, he cheekily disregarded the structures of the architect Andrea Palladio by creating illusionistic paintings that ignored the room divisions. Palladio is known to have been annoyed by these *trompe l'œil* murals.

Now that his style had achieved full maturity, Veronese returned to Venice, the city which from now on clung on to him. The pictures which followed extended his high reputation to beyond the boundaries of the region, and led to commissions such as *The Marriage at Cana* (p. 411) and thus the chance to prove himself not only the unsurpassed master of ultra-large formats, and a painter of splendid festive fantasies, but also a virtuoso portraitist. For most, if not all, of the figures in *The Marriage at Cana*, with the exception of Christ, are portraits of real people: Don Alfonso d'Avalos is depicted as the bridegroom; Eleonore of Austria as the bride; Queen Mary of England is there, as are Francis I of France and Emperor Charles V; not excepting Suleiman I, all the potentates of the period are portrayed. He has even put a toothpick into the hand of the Marchesa di Pescara. The picture is more than an illustration of the story in the gospel, then: it is a political society portrait, and not only that, for with incredible self-confidence and courage, given the status of the artist, Veronese has used the large figures in the centrally placed musical ensemble in the foreground to perpetuate the memory of the Venetian painters of the day: Titian is playing the bass viol, the flautist is Bassano, and Veronese has put violas into the hands of both himself and Tintoretto. This chamber-music ensemble is more than an original idea. As a *concerto,* it literally stands for the harmony of Venetian painting and the co-operation of the painters in their mutual rivalry. It is correct to regard Titian on the bass as setting the tone, and Bassano's idyllic landscapes are properly reflected in his fluting.

Paolo Veronese
The Marriage at Cana, 1563
Canvas, 669 x 990 cm
Paris, Musée du Louvre

Incidentally, Leandro Bassano (1557–1622), the third son of the Jacopo who founded the large and prolific Bassano studio, also painted a music scene (p. 410). This picture too is a demonstration of more than just the interest of the family of painters in domestic music. Here too it is a parable of the harmonious co-operation of an artistic family in the production of pictures.

Leandro's *Susannah Bathing* (p. 413) clearly shows the influence of both Titian and Veronese. Bassano's painting, incidentally, is far less provincial than is generally assumed. This false impression may result from the "rural" element in what were admittedly almost mass-produced paintings. In truth, however, these paintings were both a domestic surrogate for the popular rural and pastoral motifs of Netherlandish painters, for example Pieter Aertsen, and also a

decorative counterpart of the *villegiatura*. Those who had no villa on the mainland could doubtless find a substitute in beholding Bassano's painted world.

But back to Veronese. He too painted "rural" scenes, above all in the villa frescoes mentioned above. However he was not concerned to produce good likenesses of the real Italian countryside: his "views", rather, are idealized landscapes, anticipating the inventions of the 17th and 18th centuries. Veronese's *Mars and Venus* (p. 412), with a temple ruin in the background complete with a live-looking satyr torso, is an eloquent example, quite apart from the "gallantry", already at this date, with which the myth is depicted. The same might be said of *The Rape of Europa* (p. 413, bottom). This "rape", which looks more like the willing departure of a bejewelled princess on an

411

Paolo Veronese
Mars and Venus, c. 1580
Canvas, 206 x 161 cm
New York, The Metropolitan Museum of Art
John Stewart Kennedy Fund, 1910 (10.189)

inviting mythological honeymoon, could quite easily have been painted by Boucher, were its style just a little more fluent.

The minutes of an Inquisition tribunal have been preserved at which Veronese had to answer for the liberties he took. He was asked, for example, why, in a painting of the Last Supper, he had depicted the Lord being waited on "by a servant whose nose happened to be bleeding". The interrogation went on: "Does it seem fitting to you to depict jesters, drunks, Germans [i.e. farmworkers], dwarfs and other frivolous figures at the Lord's final meal?" "No," Veronese replied, they were not in the immediate vicinity; they were there to indicate the wealth of the house. Whether Veronese convinced the tribunal is questionable; in any case, he was required to alter the picture within a few months. He did not in fact do so, for the Inquisition did not enjoy half the power in Venice which it had in Spain, and all Veronese did was give the picture a new title, namely *The Feast at the House of Levi*.

The *Triumph of Venice* (p. 415) on the ceiling of the Sala del Maggior Consiglio in the Doge's Palace was among the artist's major commissions in the last decade of his life. Veronese began it in 1580 and completed it in 1585, three years before his death. The approach of the Baroque can already be discerned in the abundance of floating figures and the bravura with which the illusionistic architecture scrapes the illusionistic sky. The intention here is to display the glory of Venice, the radiance of a centre of power to which subordinate peoples readily submit. Symbolic Victories, splendidly clad female figures on the balcony, ambassadors, among them Henry III of France as "Honor" – all pay homage to Venezia as she is crowned by Genius. The clouds are her throne, framed by the twisted columns which we recognize from Bernini's tabernacle in St Peter's in Rome, and which point yet further to the Temple of Solomon, signifying, in other words, the might and divine justice of the Venetian state. This ceiling painting is one of the last great homages of Cinquecento painting to the Most Serene Republic, whose most committed ambassador in this century was Veronese.

Alexander Perrig

Drawing and the Artist's Basic Training from the 13th to the 16th Century

Tablets, Paper and Parchment

The collections of European graphic material scattered throughout the world contain a mass of drawings whose number may well exceed that of all the paintings, sculptures and important buildings of the Christian era put together. It is so immense that one automatically assumes it to represent the totality of drawings created in Europe since antiquity. In reality, however, these collections tell us everything about the drawing practices of the last five hundred years, but almost nothing about those of the Middle Ages. This is due less to the fact that the stock of mediaeval drawings still extant represents a tiny fraction of the total, than to the absence, within this tiny fraction, of the very categories of drawing which are most important for our purposes. The drawings on pre-1425 paper and parchment sheets are almost exclusively autonomous: book illustrations, building plans, contract drawings (p. 422, left), figure patterns (pp. 418, 420), copies of paintings (p. 419, right). Draughts, studies, practice sketches and notes in drawing form are almost entirely wanting.

This absence is due to the same cause as explains the lack of literary "rough work" of mediaeval date (notes, writing practice sheets, draughts of letters, treatises, poems, romances etc.): such materials were only considered worthy of preservation if they had been produced with a view to long-term use (e.g. cathedral plans, pattern books). Logically enough, if this was not the case, expensive carriers such as paper and parchment were dispensed with in favour of continually re-usable wooden tablets coated with wax or powdered bone. The fact that such tablets were used as early as the late 7th century for both drawing and writing is documented by Adamnanus of Hy, the Abbot of Iona (c. 624–704). He had been told by the Gaulish Bishop Arculf, who had been shipwrecked on the coast of Scotland, of the latter's journey to the Holy Land; to give his listener a better idea of some of the churches he had visited there, the bishop had sketched their ground plans on wax tablets. Adamnanus subsequently made fair copies of his colleague's sketches, using them to illustrate his *De locis sanctis libri tres* ("Three Books on the Holy Places").

Artists had doubtless used treated wooden tablets, either loose or bound into some sort of codex, as vehicles for drawing from time immemorial. Apprentices, at least, were still doing so at a time when their masters had long since switched to paper for sketching – as witnessed by a number of drawings, dating from the second half of the 15th century, of boys sketching (p. 425 bottom). The impatient Michelangelo was perhaps the very first artist to use sheets of paper even as a beginner: needing no preparation, they were so very practical. Louvre Sheet no. 685 (p. 438) shows that he obtained his paper in his earliest years by tearing up old family ledgers. On the reverse of one we have the preface to one of his great-grandfather's account books.

Ambrogio Lorenzetti
Mary in an Annunciation scene
Sinopia, 240 x 172 cm
Montesiepi, San Galgano oratory

Sinopias and Preliminary Sketches

The most important of all graphic ephemera were, and are, preliminary sketches. By providing the first confirmation of the artist's subjective idea and giving him a means of judging the correctness of his own assessment, they form the basis and starting point for the realization of all painting, sculpture and architecture. It is all the more astonishing, then, that Cennino Cennini, who, in the 189 chapters of his *Libro dell'Arte*, deals with every aspect of the late-13th-century artist's workshop from facial make-up to the manufacture and preparation of wooden tablets, does not devote – even as late as c. 1400 – a single word to this species of drawing or to how it was actually done. What he describes instead, in Chapter 67, is a particular way of preparing a preliminary sketch, on the wall, for a fresco. It is presented as a four-stage process: 1. a preliminary outline in charcoal; 2. "brushing up" the contours and shading with a sharp-pointed brush and liquid ochre; 3. rubbing out the charcoal outline with a "bunch of feathers"; 4. drawing in the fine contours with a "thin, sharp-pointed brush" and "sinopia" (i.e. red ochre; in classical times exported from the town of Sinope). The end product was something resembling a giant watercolour.

The fact that Cennini, by ignoring the usual form of preliminary sketch, tacitly presented *this* laborious procedure as *the* act of preparing one, has given rise to some confusion among art-historians. His approach was seen in connection with the absence of any extant mobile sketches dating from before approximately 1425, and, notwithstanding the hundreds of instances in which the practice of drawing on tablets is documented, has been regarded as circumstantial evidence that "in the Middle Ages" artists painted directly, i.e. without a sketch, onto the final surface, namely the panel or the wall, in other words designed the picture as they went along. These preliminary mural sketches or "sinopias" – which often come to light beneath the fresco plaster when old frescoes are removed – are consequently seen as documents of an era-specific, i.e. "mediaeval", form of preliminary sketch, even though they are unknown before the middle of the 13th century, and continued beyond the end of the 15th right up until the early 17th century, when making preliminary sketches on paper had long been the practice throughout Europe.

However, what Cennini describes is merely the most time-consuming method of producing a full-scale mock-up of a fresco, but by no means the only one. As is proved by the sinopia for Ambrogio Lorenzetti's Annunciation fresco (right), the whole process can be carried out in a single stage rather than four. Indeed, of the sinopias known today, only a few are the product of Cennini's four-stage process. Most were produced quickly, like the Lorenzetti example, with the purpose of clarifying the main features of the composition and, of these, no more than the major outlines. Ironically, the "quick-and-easy" sinopia was used precisely for the monumental narrative frescoes with many figures, while the four-

stage process seems to have been confined to the mass-produced frescoes containing nothing beyond what could be found in any standard pattern-book: a single saint (Cennini refers to a Madonna), a Pietà, a crucifix between two saints etc. According to the logic implied by the identification of sinopias with preliminary sketches, artists created careful preliminary sketches with all the details only in those cases where it was least necessary. Conversely, e.g. in the case of Ambrogio's *Annunciation* or Buffalmacco's gigantic *Triumph of Death* (p. 76, bottom, and p. 77), this theory would imply that the subject was only finally conceived and composed during the actual painting process! Forced to explain this paradox, we would have to regard the numerous quick-and-easy sinopias as documents of an imaginative super-sense confined to just a few generations of

painters, and the few four-stage sinopias either as documents of a pointless waste of time and effort, or else as indications that assistants were at work. Such difficulties evaporate when we see the sinopia for what it clearly was: a mock-up, allowing the customer to assess the effect of the future fresco in its intended site, and before it was too late for modifications. Produced in the manner described by Cennini, it could take the place of a regular preliminary sketch, or *modello*, albeit it would then – and this would explain Cennini's one-sided interest in the four-stage sinopia – have to be paid for extra. Two such "giant watercolours", models of equestrian funerary monuments in pictorial form for the *condottieri* Piero Farnese (d. 1363) and John Hawkwood (d. 1393), were commissioned by the Florence Cathedral building supervisors on 2 December 1395 from Giuliano Arrighi, alias Pesellino, and Cennini's teacher Agnolo Gaddi, for the considerable sum of 30 florins each.

Painted on the wall of one of the Cathedral aisles on a scale of 1:1, they were intended, as was expressly stated in the decision to award the commission, to provide all those responsible with a means of assessing the project.

That a *modello* substitute of this kind only made sense with routine works requiring no programming is self-evident. If frescoes with a complicated subject, let alone narrative or allegorical cycles, were to be executed, four-stage sinopias would have been not only a pointless extravagance, but simply impossible to produce: no mural whose dimensions exceed, if only by a few metres, the field of vision of a painter standing on scaffolding in front of it can be designed ad hoc on the plastering without further ado. The substitute in such cases would be an enlarged reproduction, as it were, of the normal preliminary sketch, the production of which would require neither too much time nor particular care: how the end product would look

Taddeo Gaddi
Presentation of the Virgin Mary
Metalpoint, with white heightening, on paper primed olive-green 36.5 x 28.2 cm
Paris, Musée du Louvre

in detail would be clear enough from the portable *modello*. The painter would also have depended on this, or a revised final version, as the case might be, during the actual execution of the fresco. Only a portable *modello* of this kind could have supplied him with the – occasionally quite substantial – quantity of information which a sinopia would have provided either not at all or in a quite different form (i.e. the form rejected by the client). While the quick-and-easy sinopia could have served as no more than an abstract orientation aid to the painter, the portable sketch would have enabled him to determine his daily assignment (i.e. the area of wall he could cover with fresco in a day and which would receive the fresh plaster – which would cover any sinopia – on the morning in question), without regard to his own powers of memory, solely on the basis of his own desired working speed and the difficulty of the elements to be painted. Where the design had been sketched directly on the wall, there was no such possibility, thus necessitating each daily assignment to be kept as small as possible, since the painter otherwise ran the risk of forgetting what was in that part of the sinopia sketch now covered by the plaster. This is why Cennini illustrates a daily assignment painted over a four-stage sinopia by way of a "head of a madonna" – an example which would be quite incomprehensible, had he been thinking of a mural on the scale of Bonaiuti's *via veritatis* fresco (p. 82) or a fresco cycle by his teacher Agnolo Gaddi (p. 87), whose daily assignments often comprised several complete figures.

The appearance in the mid-13th century of wall drawings as preliminary sketches for frescoes may be connected with a more demanding attitude on the part of the client. It changed little as far the existing practice of preliminary sketches was concerned. Doubtless most of what was subsequently painted continued to be composed on a portable, i.e. small-format, carrier. Since the

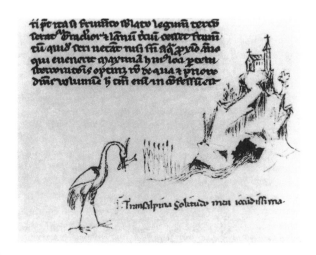

Francesco Petrarca
The Spring at Vaucluse, 1341
Pen and ink on parchment
Paris, Bibilothèque Nationale

419

implementation of Roger Bacon's picture reform under Pope Nicholas III (1277–80), this form of preliminary sketch had indeed come to have even more importance, in view of the fact that a spatialized pictorial world is more difficult to design than a two-dimensional one. Notwithstanding such considerations, however, Cennini pretends that this activity has nothing to do with the painter. Why? Could it be that he did not even consider it to be one of the painter's tasks?

The Dominance of ars liberalis: Programming and Design
Right into the 15th century, the design does indeed appear to have been the prerogative of the client or his programmers, as the case may be. Lorenzo Ghiberti (1378–1455), the sculptor, who proudly reports in his autobiography that after the completion of his first pair of Baptistery doors (1424) *"mi fu data la licenza"* ("I was given

the freedom") to realize the second pair on the basis of his own ideas, regarded the original concept as a design act of a special kind, more akin to theory than to practice. He accordingly gave it a corresponding name, teorica disegno, and assigned it to those disciplines in which, in his opinion, the modern artist should receive instruction: grammar, geometry, philosophy, medicine, astronomy, optics, history, anatomy and arithmetic. By implication, therefore, he was saying that the independent design of a picture had not hitherto been on the curriculum of an artistic apprenticeship. On the contrary, Ghiberti was putting it forward as a desirable addition – indeed, one of the preconditions which had to be fulfilled before painting and sculpture could rise out of their humble ars mechanica status to that of *artes liberales*, and before the "freedom" for the artist to work according to his own design could become the rule rather than the exception.

Ghiberti knew what he was writing about. Before he was accorded the privilege of designing the Gate of Paradise doors himself, the Calimala guild had had them programmed in the usual way. They seem to have taken it for granted that each of the humanists charged with the task (Ambrogio Traversari, Niccolò Niccoli and Lionardo Bruni) would, by dint of their education, make a better job of it than any mere artist could. Great was their astonishment, presumably, when the opposite proved to be the case. The fiasco could of course have been foreseen by anyone with any knowledge of the situation. For while Ghiberti devoted all his free time to extending his knowledge beyond the bounds of his own speciality, none of the programmers we have named considered it necessary to trouble himself with modern art, let alone with modern artists. Take Lionardo Bruni (c. 1370–1444): his substitute for his lack of specialist knowledge and of any pictorial concept of his own was arrogance pure and simple. On the evidence of the letter accompanying his programmatic proposals (the only ones to have been preserved), he seriously imagined he would be able to guarantee the Calimala success in the matter of the bronze doors by handing the artist a list of themes and explaining orally in each individual case what he, the artist, should bear in mind when executing the commission.

Bruni's abstract programming method (which probably did not differ in material respects from that of his colleagues) accords, it is true, with what art historians imagine under the heading of such a function. But it can hardly have accorded with that of his largely anonymous predecessors. To judge by the conspicuous intellectuality and contentual complexity of the major pictorial cycles of the 13th and 14th centuries, they took their task more seriously and fulfilled it more efficiently. Instead of compiling a mere list of themes, they evidently produced designs to a programme, in other words harmonized the iconographic programme with the pictorial design (cf. pp. 49, 52, 60, 67–69, 76 and 96 top). It is understandable that they are now no longer believed to have possessed the necessary expressivity of draughtsmanship. their degeneration to a monopoly of architects, artists and designers in the end determined the theory of their history, according to which it is a "fact that prior to 1500 no noteworthy draughtsmanship appears, or can appear, among amateurs..."

The Amateur Draughtsman

But clearly it could, and did. True, it is an open question whether Bishop Arculf and Abbot Adamnanus could use drawings to communicate anything more complicated than the ground plans of churches, or whether the Franciscan scholars Roger Bacon (c. 1220–92), John Peckham (c. 1240–92) and Witelo were just as competent in drawing figures as they were in the construction of diagrams designed to explain optical theses. Nor do we know how well or how badly Notker Labeo (c. 950–1022) could draw animals

a cycle of murals or stained-glass illustrations, or even a more than usually complicated individual picture.

From the early 14th century, as bourgeois foundations steadily grew in number and importance, non-clerical scholars also start to be recorded as draughtsmen. The first known to modern scholarship was the Florentine notary and poet Francesco da Barberino (1264–1348). He had presumably learnt to draw at one of the mathematical schools attended by those destined for mercantile professions, whose teaching staff was largely recruited from among merchants and surveyors, for both of which occupations a certain skill in draughtsmanship was essential. During a sojourn in Provence from 1309 to 1313, he composed an encyclopaedic didactic poem entitled 'Documenti d'Amore', which he decorated in his own hand with seventeen pen-wash drawings of allegorical content, and of which, on his return to Florence, he had four illuminated copies made. By his own account, Francesco also functioned on occasion as a programmer. It may be taken for granted that he prepared the preliminary sketches for the paintings he programmed in Florence and Treviso in the same meticulous way in which he designed the demanding miniatures which illustrate his didactic poem. This poem urges the "aristocracy" to practise the "art of drawing" for the very reason that they would then be able "more easily to convey their intentions to their artists".

No such statement, it is true, can be attributed to Francesco Petrarca (1304–74), who – like Ghiberti and Brunelleschi, both sons of notaries – also attended a mathematical school, his father having intended him for a mercantile career. But he certainly understood programming in terms of designing, and gave expression to his ideas for the pictures requested of him – e.g. at the Carrara court in Padua

on his tablets, or Dante Alighieri (1265–1321) angels on his, as neither saw fit to actually include a drawing of animals or angels in spite of having mentioned them in writing (the matter-of-factness of these references in the Boethius commentary and the *Vita Nuova* respectively indicates merely that Notker and Dante were accustomed to expressing themselves through drawing). Our astonishment is all the greater when we see the standard of draughtsmanship in the relatively few drawings that have been preserved. Those made, to illustrate their writings, by Adémar de Chabannes, the aristocratic monk of St Cybard d'Angoulême (c.988–1034), Giraldus Cambrensis, the Welsh scholar, archdeacon and canon lawyer (c. 1146–1223), Matthew Paris, the historiographer active in the Benedictine Abbey of St Albans (c. 1200–59), or the master of arts Konrad von Megenberg (1309–74) – to name only the best-known – stand comparison with any contemporary visual-art production by a professional. Since there is nothing to suggest that any of these scholars was particularly noted for his drawing talents, we can only assume they represent the tip of an iceberg. Until well into the 15th century, monasteries, cathedral chapters, parishes, guilds, fraternities and individual charitable benefactors doubtless had recourse to their like when they needed someone to design a programme of sculptures for a façade or pulpit,

– in the form of drawings, as is attested by the confident contours and the spatial persuasiveness of the little pen-and-ink sketch, accompanying a text by Pliny, with which he gave spontaneous expression to his mental image of the region of natural springs around Vaucluse (p. 419 bottom).

Until the beginning of the 15th century the main reason why non-artists practised the art of drawing was doubtless the opportunity it provided of giving a "graphic" description (in both senses) of what was difficult to describe in words. For many, this continued to be the main reason – Jean Bourré, for example, the Treasurer at the court of the King of France: when in 1481 the painter Colin d'Amiens was to execute the figure of Louis XI for the King's tomb, Bourré made it clear both in writing and in pictures how the royal effigy was to appear in respect of posture, physiognomy, coiffure and clothing. Others, however, appear to have discovered drawing additionally as a means towards inner enrichment. The tutor to the Carrara court at the beginning of the 15th century, Pier Paolo Vergerio (1370–1444), was of the opinion that even the ancient Greeks had practised it to this end. He urged one of his charges, Ubertino da Carrara, to follow the lofty example and to internalize the beauties of art and nature by drawing them. Vittorino da Feltre, the Pestalozzi among the humanists (1378–1446), urged a similar view. Appointed tutor to the Gonzaga court in Mantua in 1425, he established a school there for all social classes, at which drawing lessons were given by painters he paid out of his own pocket. Presumably Baldassare Castiglione (1478–1528) was only repeating what Vittorino's pupils had long known when, in chapter 49 of his 1528 bestseller *Il Cortegiano* (The Book of the Courtier), he attempted to explain why the perfect courtier of the title had, among other accomplishments, to master the art of drawing.

Drawing as ars mechanica

The mathematical schools were teaching the use of diagrams to solve such problems as calculating the volume of a ship's cargo space required for a particular consignment of wine-casks, thus providing young would-be merchants and scholars with the foundations of a possible future career or hobby in drawing. By contrast, apprentice painters, even in Vittorino's and Vergerio's day, were still being drilled mainly in the technique of optimizing other people's designs, making a definitive sketch, and converting the result into a painting. They learned drawing by copying numerous patterns for individual pictorial elements, first in metalpoint on a tablet, then with chalk, pen and brush on paper and parchment. The mastery of patterns was not a by-product of drawing lessons; it was the goal. It demanded hard work and patience, and nothing else, and literally made drawing an *ars mechanica*, especially in the first year, when the master's pattern-book had to be copied stroke by stroke. Cennini seems to have had such evil memories of this period

that, forgetting his own interests as a master, he advised the new generation of apprentices to copy only "a little each day" onto the tablet, "so that you don't lose all pleasure in it" (*Libro dell'Arte*, chapter VIII).

A sheet in the Pierpont Morgan Library in New York (p. 418) illustrates the terrifying reality: it was drawn in the first quarter of the 15th century, almost certainly by a Tuscan apprentice who had completed his first year and was using the initial stages of his familiarity with pen and brush, ink and parchment, to lay the foundation of a pattern-book of his own. When he started, he was still steeped in the habit – acquired during the "tablet" year – of drawing items as small as possible: this was to get as much on to the carrier (which measured approximately 20 x 20 cm) as he could,

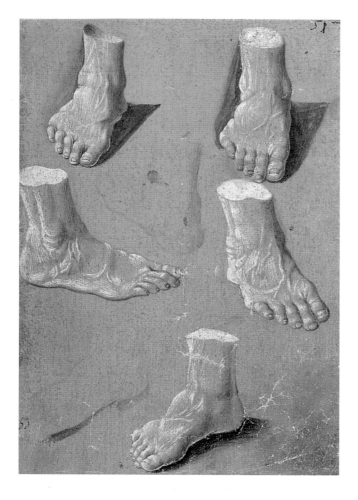

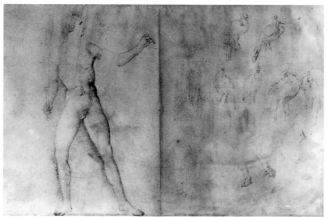

and thus put off the tedious task of re-priming it. Only after he had filled every available space in the top left-hand quarter did he overcome the *horror vacui* occasioned by the 30.5 x 76 cm parchment and allow himself to increase both the size of the figures and the amount of space between them. The drawings themselves attest to the trouble it cost to coax out of a pen moving forward in tiny steps the prescribed complete, and evenly sharp, contours, and out of a hesitant brush the obligatory not too hard and not too soft shading effects.

The crowded confusion doubtless simply reproduces parts of the master's pattern-book. It contains nothing but mini-patterns for the run-of-the-mill motifs of contemporary sacred and secular painting – in other words, what the clients asked for time and again: for example, a benefactor kneeling to the left and another kneeling to the right; a model townscape (as required by municipal patrons); a pelican appropriate to perch atop a crucifix; rudimentary figures from the calendar and zodiac, including peasants (depicted in the pose of both sowers and reapers), a peasant woman plucking a chicken, cripples, and a scorpion; a seated two-headed female figure, which could be incorporated into an artes or virtue cycle; a jumping horseman, who could be mobilized for battle, jousting or hunting scenes; two Gothic canopies to hang above saintly individuals; and a small miscellany made up of foliage, dog, bird of prey and monsters, which might come in useful as decorative elements for a page of a book. What this comprehensive card-index does not include is first of all any example of the art of composition, and secondly any drawing taken not from a pattern-book but from life or nature.

Composition Patterns and Pattern Compositions

This absence is typical. Complete compositions also appear only rarely in regular (i.e. masters') pattern-books prior to about 1425. Reproductions of paintings done by the owner of the pattern-book do not appear at all, a clear indication that the art of composition was not a concern of the artist's workshop, and thus not part of the curriculum. In fact, the few complete compositions to be found occasionally in pattern-books only reproduce works known to be in demand as copies of paintings or sculptures. They were seen not as illustrative material for a course in design or composition, however conceived, but as a stock-in-trade which would be useful if an order materialized, or indeed might clinch the order in the first place. For example, we find scattered throughout Europe many fresco imitations of the Navicella mosaics in the atrium of St. Peter's in Rome; now the benefactor who wanted to have one of these painted for his parish church in Milan, if he could himself not come up himself with a drawing based on the original or an already extant copy, would have no choice but to award the commission to a Milanese workshop which did have one in its pattern-book.

Even rarer than professionally drawn picture compositions in pattern-books are those on loose sheets. Before 1425, they seem to

Antonio Pollaiuolo
Three different aspects of standing male nude, two studies of arms
Pen and ink over metalpoint, watercolour, on white paper, 26.5 x 35 cm
Paris, Musée du Louvre

Maso Finiguerra
Seated painter's apprentice at drawing
Pen, watercolour, white heightening, on paper primed pale-pink,19.5 x 12 cm
Florence, Galleria degli Uffizi

have existed only in the form of those painting-like finished drawings of which that in the Louvre depicting *The Presentation of the Virgin Mary* (p. 419) is doubtless the best-known among those still extant. These quasi-paintings, executed with pedantic precision in at least three different media and colours, never having formed part of a pattern-book, are generally regarded as *modelli* intended for the client. But why coloured draughts, if clients – as appears from extant four-stage sinopias and contractual drawings (p. 422 above) – attached no importance to colour in preliminary sketches? Were there exceptional cases in which colours were required? If so, why do they not accord with those of the final frescoes (p. 72)? What was the point of the *modello* of an unframed individual scene, when one of the specific demands of the painted final product was that it should include a "frame" painted with a related motif?

Yet more telling than the exclusion of the framing context is, in the case of the Temple drawing (p. 419 top), the fact that the angles of inclination of the roof elements are markedly smaller than in the fresco itself. They correspond not to the actual content of the fresco, but rather to the apparent content as seen by a beholder looking from below. This proves the drawing to be a copy rather than a draught. Its complicated colouration can also be explained far better by seeing it as an examination piece rather than as a modello. After all, it provides information on matters that can only have been of interest to someone who wanted to know to what extent the draughtsman had understood, in Cennini's words, "the principle and gateway of colouration", and was in a position to prime and prepare the carrier as required for the task in hand, to make confident use of the brush and stylus, to employ colours properly, and to reproduce

Giuliano da Sangallo
Judith
Pencil, pen and bistre on paper, 37.7 x 27 cm
Vienna, Albertina

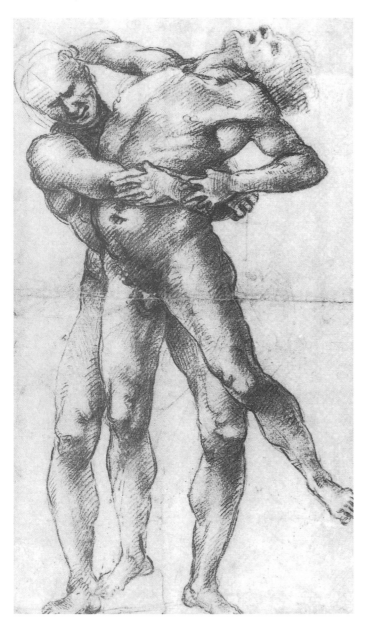

an existing picture of any given format: the head of the workshop, in other words, and not the customer (who might reasonably take it for granted that the commission was going to someone who knew his business). The head of the workshop must also have had a special interest in a perfect result: to all appearances, there was a market for these test pieces. For the buyer, they represented a cheap substitute for a painting, while for the workshop they were good publicity. They were for example the sort of art (later displaced by woodcuts and copperplate engravings) that the Paduan humanist Feliciano Feliciani, among others, could afford. According to his will, dated 1466, his house was hung with "drawings and paintings on paper by many excellent masters of drawing".

Before the 15th century, then, there was no workshop-internal picture-composition or design practice. Even in 1450, the existence of such was still far from being taken for granted, as is shown by the so-called sketch-books of Jacopo Bellini (c. 1400–70/71), two thick folio volumes with almost every page filled with black-and-white compositions of his own conception (p. 422). They are unique, and apart from the fact that they contain drawings, they have nothing in common with the *Liber veritatis* in which, from c. 1635, Claude Lorrain (1600–82) reproduced his own paintings in the form of pen wash drawings, for with few exceptions Jacopo Bellini's silverpoint and pen-and-ink drawings, by contrast, reproduce compositions that existed only in his own head, and not in painted reality. While all the important pictorial and monumental themes of the day are represented – from the Adoration of the Magi, and *St. Francis Receiving the Stigmata* (p. 422), to St. George and the Dragon – they seem understandable only as a demonstration of their creator's comprehensive imagination. They are doubtless rooted in experiences of ignorance and prejudice similar to what Ghiberti had encountered a generation earlier. A striking feature in any case is their penetrating intellectuality. The pattern-compositions seem to emphasize the learning of their author in precisely the disciplines which feature in Ghiberti's list of those he considered a necessary part of an artist's training (see p. 420 top). *St. Francis Receiving the Stigmata* gives expression to three, as it were heterogeneous, scholarly standpoints: firstly, that of the "historian" trying to understand the past on the basis of his own exegesis of written sources (which thus lead him to results diverging from the iconographic tradition!); secondly, that of the "opticist" versed in geometry, who, by virtue of his knowledge of the laws of perspective, reconstructs the facts as understood in terms of the visual reality perceived by the beholder; and thirdly, that of the "natural philosopher" versed not only in the appearance and behaviour of men and animals, but also in the history of the Earth. Jacopo's mountains, with their helical basic structure and the adamantine hardness of their material, reflect precisely what classical and mediaeval scholars conceived them to be: molten material thrown up by subterranean fires, petrified to hollow, flamelike formations.

Lorenzo di Credi
Drapery study for a personification of Astronomy
Pen over pencil, watercolour, white heightening, on white paper
39.5 x 26.1 cm
Florence, Galleria degli Uffizi

Filippo Lippi
Two studies of men's legs, draped kneeling figure,
and young man sitting on chair
Silverpoint, white heightening, on paper primed grey
19.4 x 25.9 cm
Florence, Galleria degli Uffizi

Studies from Nature in the Workshops

While the role played by the study of nature in the late-mediaeval workshop curriculum may appear to be more important than that played by the art of composition, the appearance is deceptive. It is true that Cennini praises the imitation of nature as "the triumphal arch" and the painter's "most perfect guide" (*Libro dell'Arte*, chapter 28). But what he understood by this "nature" which was to be imitated was the so-called "essence" of things, rather than their visible reality in the modern sense. Since Man's essence was considered to reside in his being made in God's image – a quality whose visible expression was thought to consist in a certain evenness of the limbs – Cennini regarded a knowledge of human anatomy as less important than familiarity with "correct" proportions, in which he saw the key to the lifelike depiction of human beings. And while he devoted a whole chapter – 70 – to these proportions, his anatomical instructions were limited to the casual remarks that man had one rib fewer than woman (namely the one which God took to create Eve), and that the penis must be "of the size which women prefer" and his testicles

"small, attractive and fresh". No wonder, then, that this passage through the "triumphal arch" make male and female nudes, which were becoming more and more frequent in the pattern-books of Cennini's time (p. 420, right), look like representatives of a thin-limbed, long-torsoed race with attenuated muscles – even when they were copied not from a painted or drawn pattern, but from a classical sculpture (p. 424 below).

A special case were the "dumb creatures" (*animali irrazionali*); since they evinced "no proportion whatever", Cennini recommended (chapter 70) that they be drawn or painted "as far as you can" direct from life (*"del naturale"*). That this had occasionally been done as early as the first sixty years of the 13th century is documented by, for example, certain capitals in Rheims Cathedral, the bird miniatures in Emperor Frederick II's book on falconry, and the elephant drawing by Matthew Paris, which dates from c. 1255. In Siena, this practice of painting from nature had already been extended to certain landscapes (p. 65), while in Cennini's day, such attention was concentrated largely on the inmates of the various court menageries in northern Italy. But from the outset, such studies from nature were excluded from the workshop curriculum. The apprentices can have benefited from the practice at best indirectly – insofar as from c.1390 they were faced, more frequently than in the past, with first-hand images, and perhaps were even allowed to draw from casts of small animals made from nature. Even their masters would seem to have drawn animals and plants direct from nature, if at all, only when they were concerned with the illustrations to a herbal or hunting manual, or the extension or modernization of a pattern-book. As soon as they were dealing with regular commissions which included the representation of animals (the creation of the animals, Noah's Ark, the procession of

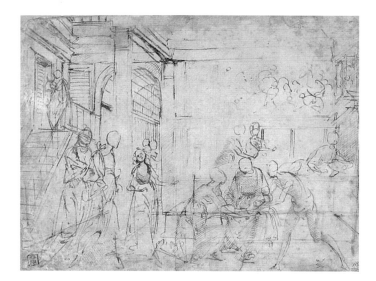

workshop was only indirectly determined by such study – through the intermediary of naturalized patterns – the pictorial world, in spite of attempts at linear perspective, came across only as more or less rigid and artificial. There was only one way to make it more natural, and that was by getting nature study into the workshops. This step, it seems, was first taken in Florence. There, as early as the first half of the 15th century, the practice began of having one's workshop colleagues pose for one – in the attitude of a thorn-remover, a horse-tamer from the Quirinal, a Donatello statue of David, a crucified Christ, of a kneeling saint, a bystander shepherd, or of an apprentice in various sleeping, day-dreaming, reading, writing or drawing poses (p. 425, bottom, and p. 429, top) etc., and, depending on the context, either nude or clothed in timeless, classical, contemporary, secular or monastic, ceremonial or everyday costume. At first the practice simply made a virtue out of local necessity. The local necessity was the virtual absence in Florence of any antiquities, and consequently of any opportunity for Florentine apprentices to study them, as Brunelleschi, Donatello or Ghiberti had been able to do while in Rome. The substitute, making studies from "living sculpture", seems also to have been accompanied from the outset by studies from "dead sculpture", i.e. plaster-casts of parts of the human body (p. 424, top). The two were mutually complementary in their beneficial effect. More than the study of Roman statuary and reliefs could ever have achieved, they honed the powers of observation not only of the articulation, surface structure and "language" of the human body, but also of the way in which different garment fabrics reacted to its individualities and its various postures (pp. 427, 429, bottom). The result was that generations of earlier nude, posture and drapery patterns lost their significance, and Florentine art felt the fresh breeze of verism.

Filippino Lippi
The Awakening of Drusiana
Fresco, Florence, Santa Maria Novella, Strozzi chapel

the Magi etc.), real-life nature was forgotten in favour of the clichés in the workshop books. And then even such a familiar domestic creature as the horse ran the risk of turning out like some merry-go-round steed – as for example in the works of Gentile da Fabriano, Pisanello, Jacopo Bellini or Uccello.

There was little point in including courtly costumes and coiffures (p. 421, top), classical sculpture, or even the reality of the human form under the heading of the "nature" that was to be studied directly. As long as the pictorial or sculptural output of a

Leonardo da Vinci
Various figure studies
Pen and ink on white paper, 27.8 x 20.8 cm
Paris, Musée du Louvre

Leonardo da Vinci
Study of the proportions of a head, eyes
Pen and ink on white paper, 19.7 x 16 cm
Turin, Biblioteca Reale

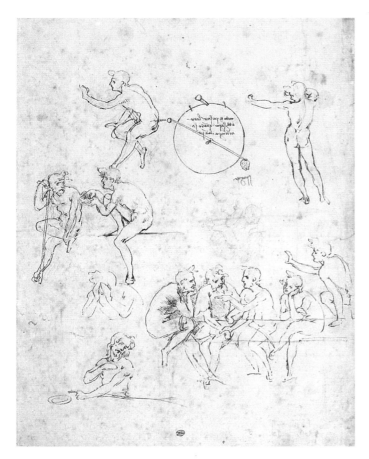

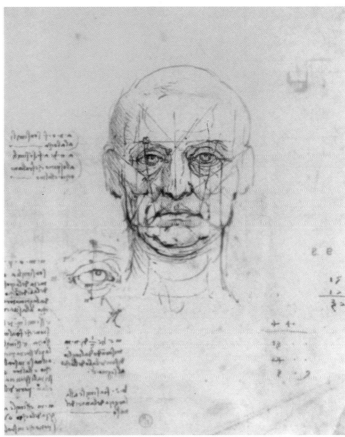

The Crisis in Basic Artistic Training

The study from life was a more efficient means of "naturalizing" the representation of the human figure than was the study from the classical sculpture, insofar as a pose adopted by a model, unlike that of a statue, can be adapted to current needs at any time. Even so, its efficiency was limited as soon as movement was involved. Movements such as stepping, running or dancing could only be represented by depicting the corresponding poses. Such poses (see p. 423) do not express movement, however, but are merely "stills", not essentially different from the representation of standing, sitting or reclining figures. To base on them a design of John striding through the wilderness, or Apollo pursuing Daphne, or Salome dancing (p. 260), thus meant that these figures were no less frozen in their tracks than Paolo Uccello's rearing horse (p. 264). Now that the standard of the correct representation of the human figure was the model posing in the workshop, there was no longer any possibility of suggesting dynamic effects by mediaeval techniques – in other words, by neglecting or distorting anatomical realities. The problem could only either be ignored altogether or else be seen as raising the question of whether studies from life and the internalization of patterns as hitherto practised could ever lead to the achievement of a dynamic art.

In principle, this question had already been answered in the negative even before the study from life had become the workshop norm, namely by Leon Battista Alberti (1404–72). The educated son of a merchant, he did not make himself explicit on the teaching practices he saw in painters' workshops. Indirectly, however, by recommending an alternative, he represented them as misguided. "I should like those who are just starting to devote themselves to the art of painting," he writes in the third book of his *Della Pittura* published in 1435, "to proceed as one does, as far as I can see, in the writing schools. Here they start off by teaching the forms of the individual

In a letter written around 1482, Leonardo da Vinci, who was approximately 30 years old at the time, introduced himself to Duke Ludovico Sforza, called Il Moro, in the hope of obtaining a position at the court in Milan: as the ideal adviser for the state of war then

Self-portrait, c. 1512–15
Red chalk, 33.3 x 21.3 cm
Turin, Biblioteca Reale

his time. However, driven by an insatiable curiosity and an unquenchable thirst for knowledge, he began to acquaint himself with all the branches of science then in existence. In every one of them, he improved the level of knowledge through his own research and used the results to develop new technologies. His mathematical, geometrical, mechanical, physical, hydrological, geological, cosmological, astrological, optical, botanical and anatomical findings and insights are still comprehensible today, since they are laid down in dozens of illustrated fragments of treatises and in thousands of scattered notes and sketches. When trying to clarify his own thoughts, Leonardo always bore in mind an audience to whom he had to explain them, one which demanded clarity and conspicuous proofs.

Since Leonardo's urge to experiment and perform research always aimed in different directions simultaneously, and, throughout his life, was stronger than the desire to systematize the results, none of his numerous book projects were continued up to the point of being suitable for publication, let alone actually published. The contents of his manuscripts remained hidden from the world for centuries. As a consequence, much of that which Leonardo had discovered had to be rediscovered again

Ornithogalum and plants (detail), c. 1505–08
Red chalk and quill, 19.4 x 16.2 cm
The Royal Collection,
© 1994 Her Majesty Queen Elizabeth II

prevailing, builder of self-invented transportable bridges and underground tunnels, expert in the field of conduit construction and diverting the course of rivers, fortress architect, and the inventor of new types of bombards, blunderbusses, slings and catapults. At the end of the letter he mentioned, rather casually, to what use he could be put during peacetime: as master builder, painter and sculptor, but also especially as the man who knew how to cast the bronze equestrian statue, the monument which the Duke wished to erect to his father, Francesco. The plan to erect this equestrian statue was, in fact, the main reason why Ludovico Sforza was scouring the ranks of the Medici protégés in the first place – he was looking for someone who would be skilled enough to undertake this very task.

The letter of application was successful. That same year, Leonardo took up his position with the Duke, as artist, engineer and master of ceremonies at the court in Milan. His official duties (development of fortification and drainage system projects, installation of bathing facilities, decoration of halls, making portraits, organisation of festivals and games, designing festival equipment, stage backdrops and costumes, construction of machines, etc.) occupied only a moderate proportion of

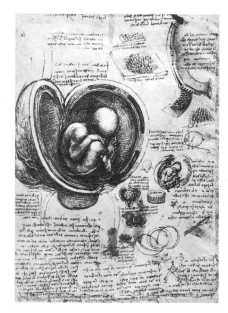

Drawings of embryos, c. 1510–13
Red chalk and quill, 30.1 x 21.3 cm
The Royal Collection,
© 1994 Her Majesty Queen Elizabeth II

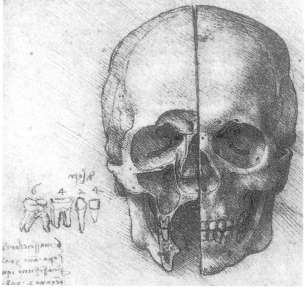

Two halves of a skull, c. 1490
Red chalk and quill on black chalk
19 x 13.7 cm
The Royal Collection,
© 1994 Her Majesty Queen Elizabeth II

later, and other researchers were to achieve fame by formulating laws of nature the workings of which he had already fathomed.

Leonardo's research, before taking on a life of its own, usually had its origins in something concrete. He probably started investigating the statics of arches and vaulted ceilings after a building collapsed, and became engrossed in hydraulics after becoming acquainted with the Lombardic practice of selling canal water and the methods thereby used to measure the water, which had their shortcomings. His preoccupation with the problem of optics and linear perspective, which began around 1482, may even have been rooted in his regret at having turned down an opportunity to teach perspective at the Verrochio workshop, which was to his own disadvantage (cf. incorrect use of perspective in the *Adoration of the Magi*, p. 311, and in the preliminary sketches for it). Yet Leonardo consistently succeeded in utilizing the results obtained in one field for research, experiments and constructions in other areas. As his knowledge and ability grew, so did the range of areas to be investigated, leading to a constantly increasing ramification of the research process. Leonardo's insights into the laws governing the flow of water not only influenced the direction of his anatomical studies (the issue of what governs the flow of the blood); they also determined the course of his investigations into aerodynamics and the flight of birds. Since Leonardo conducted his hydrodynamic studies parallel to his mechanical, topographical and geological ones and those on statics, and was able to make his ideas plausible to others in the best way possible (thanks to the know-how concerning linear perspective which he had acquired at the same time) he was, around the year 1500, the most sought-after expert on canal construction, river regulation, sluices and irrigation systems, reservoirs and bridges, amongst others. The Venetian government hoped to protect itself from the Turks (by damming the Isonzo river) with the help of his advice, and the Florentine government similarly hoped to force Pisa to submit to it (by diverting the Arno). People probably expected Leonardo also to help cut their costs, since he knew how to optimize human labour, even for the building of canals, for example, by designing a bucket excavator.

It is impossible to separate Leonardo's scientific activities or his role as an inventor from his artistic achievements. It was for the sake of art that he began to investigate his natural surroundings in Vinci, the village where he was born. Similarly, it was with the intention of perfecting the artistic portrayal of people that he embarked upon the scientific

dissection of corpses in Milan. How deeply he felt the faithful depiction of human behaviour to be dependent on a complete knowledge of that "inner life" which determines outward appearance is shown by the following little prayer: "Thus may it please our Creator that I am able to reveal the nature of humans and their morals in the same manner in which I describe their form." Leonardo could have said the same about the nature of the landscape. In order to be able to depict the latter, the artist felt that knowing that outward appearance which can be portrayed in sketches of nature was simply not enough. The bizarre, fantastic landscape backgrounds in Leonardo's paintings can be viewed as expressing macrocosmic "modes of behaviour" according to Leonardo's theory of the history of the earth. Microcosmic and macrocosmic body languages throw light upon each other during a soundless dialogue. The smile of the Mona Lisa cannot be explained without referring to the "story" told by the landscape.

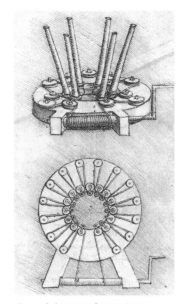

Plan and elevation of a weaving appliance
Codex Milan I

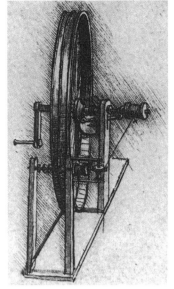

Thread-winder
Codex Milan I

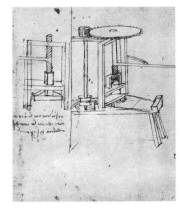

Printing press, c. 1490
Milan, Biblioteca Ambrosiana
Codex Atlanticus

Storm breaking over a valley, c. 1499
Red chalk on white paper,
29.2 x 14.9 cm
The Royal Collection,
© 1994 Her Majesty Queen Elizabeth II

Raphael
Two standing male nudes
Red chalk over metalpoint on white paper
41 x 28.1 cm
Vienna, Albertina

narrative picture. Nevertheless, his demand for an "ABC method" was not necessarily based on this realization. It may simply have derived from a desire to make art a learned profession right from the basic-training stage. It would indeed have to be so, should it turn out that the ABC method already formed the backbone of drawing classes in such elite schools as that run by Vittorino da Feltre. But however that may be, Alberti's demand was only taken up by artists when the fascination which had long been exercized by central perspective gave way to a sober assessment of its accompanying phenomenon, namely the freezing of the pictorial world, and when two great outsiders, Leonardo da Vinci and Michelangelo, had begun, through their work, to direct the attention of the entire Italian artistic community towards the problem of depicting movement.

The example of Leonardo and Michelangelo
Leonardo had already been confronted with this problem in the village of Vinci, where he spent the first seventeen years of his life. As he had learned drawing either from his father, the notary Ser Piero, or at the grammar school, he drew from patterns of his own choice, uninfluenced by the rules of urban workshop teaching. The potential range of patterns available in his "workshop", namely the parental home and its environment, doubtless consisted, however, of those interesting things which move around and refuse to keep still in frozen poses waiting to be drawn – peasants and livestock, cats and dogs, lizards, snakes, birds and insects. To capture these creatures on paper in such a way as to give them the appearance of continuing life demanded not only quick visual reactions but a no less nifty stylus. For this reason, Leonardo developed a shorthand technique at an early age that allowed him to note down very rapidly in graphic form, in metalpoint or chalk, whole sequences of movements, of a flying bird, for example, a farmhand at his digging, or a group of men conversing. These miniature notes he would take home and, with a pen, distil out the most appropriate attitude profiles (p. 431, left). By 1481, when he obtained the commission for *The Adoration of the Magi* (p. 311) in Florence, Leonardo, with his notebook method, was already way ahead of all the regularly-trained artists. While the protagonists in the composition sketches (p. 421) for a *Scourging of Christ* attributed to Ghiberti differ in almost nothing but the details of the poses (instead of free variations on particular pattern-book figures, they are recognizable as reflexes of a study of posing models), Leonardo's preliminary-sketch figures look like snapshot images caught in mid-action. Each of them evokes an instant taken from a lively short story.

Having moved to Milan in 1482, Leonardo soon realized that his shorthand method was no substitute for a detailed study of the body in motion. In order for the effect to be convincing even on a monumental scale, a knowledge of anatomy was needed. Anatomical knowledge had been already demanded of artists by Alberti and

letters, known to the ancients as 'elements'; then they go on to join these up into syllables, and finally into sentences. The same system should be followed by beginners in painting (and drawing). First they should learn by heart the surface outlines, the 'elements' of painting so to speak [by which he doubtless means straight and curved lines], then the joining of surfaces [i.e. cubes, pyramids, cones etc.], and finally every form of every organ and all the individual variations which the organs can assume. For these variations are not insignificant either in appearance or in fact. There are people with hooked noses, others with snub noses like monkeys; others have hanging lips..."

Alberti may have realized that the method of internalizing holistic or partly holistic patterns hindered rather than promoted the flexibility of imagination needed to create an internally coherent

Fra Bartolomeo
Draught composition for the lower section of the Carondelet Madonna
c. 1511
Black chalk, white heightening, on grey-primed paper
25.5 x 19.9 cm
Rotterdam, Museum Boymans-van Beuningen

Ghiberti, but they had meant something different from what Leonardo needed, namely mere knowledge of "the number of bones and muscles and visible blood-vessels", and "where beneath the skin each muscle is to be found" (Alberti). This knowledge, which corresponded in the main to what the medical faculties of the day were teaching their students, was doubtless important if artists were to be weaned away from the traditional, bible-based view of the human body (cf. p. 429). But it contributed next to nothing to a solution of the movement problem. Just how little is shown by the male nudes of that very artist who, according to Vasari, was the first to have the ambition to dissect himself (p. 275 and p. 425, top). The nudes by Antonio da Pollaiuolo (c. 1430–98) demonstrate with unparalleled clarity where a strong man's muscles are and what they look like, but nothing else. They give almost no insight into how these muscles are involved in the actions expressed by the bodily silhouette. No pivot-leg muscle is any more tense than a free-leg muscle, and no left biceps is any more in evidence than any right biceps. Even when the silhouette of head or torso indicates a bend or a turn, the symmetry of the bulges is nowhere questioned by any unilateral contraction or distension. Antonio's male nudes seem to consist of two wholes, each knowing nothing of the other: a silhouette miming energetic action and, beneath it, an immobile muscular corpse. It was representations like these which Leonardo, exaggerating somewhat disrespectfully, described as "sacks full of nuts".

The naturalization of the body and the naturalization of bodily movements were indeed two different problems. The first could be solved without anatomy (p. 429), while a definitive solution to the second could only be achieved with a study of anatomy which included a study of organic functions. Leonardo's anatomy thus proceeded from questions which even the medical schools of the time had not asked: for example, what happens beneath the skin when a man steps forward, kneels, stretches out his arm and grips a rod? Which muscles, tendons and bones are involved in such actions, and how? How do the facial organs, skull, teeth and jaws interconnect and interact (p. 432, bottom)? To what are due the differences in the shapes of the male and female abdomens, and how do their components function (p. 432, bottom)? Since Leonardo in his obsession for certainty sought to answer every such question by means of a section, and to illustrate every answer, the fruits of his labours consisted not just in the most comprehensive understanding of the external and internal structure and the mechanics of the human body that anyone had ever possessed, but also in an adequate means of conveying it. Just as he had the operation of military and industrial machines (p. 435), so Leonardo also brought the operation of the human organism into the public domain, by having his imaginary public take part in the dissection process, and this in turn by presenting them with all-round views, which, part by part and layer by layer, display the way the whole is put together.

Because the planned textbook on anatomy never came to fruition (the diagrams for it not being published until 1796), this new understanding of physical functions remained confined for the time being to the person of its author. Before the publication of a work of approximately equal value, namely Andreas Vesalius' *De humani corporis fabrica* in 1543, therefore, the acquisition of such understanding was reserved to the very few who, like Leonardo, had privileged access to the products of the dissecting room. The first such was Michelangelo (1475–1564). He had also taught himself to draw, albeit under the direction of a pupil of Ghirlandaio's, and therefore was more in conformity with workshop teaching practice than Leonardo. When, under the protection of the Medici (like Antonio del Pollaiuolo before him), he began to carry out his own dissections in the early 1490s, he did so without any ulterior didactic motives, but with the sole intention of understanding what was of direct benefit to his art, namely the mechanisms of bodily movement. He did

Leonardo da Vinci
Group of five grotesque heads, c. 1494
Pen and ink on paper, 26 x 20.5 cm
The Royal Collection
Reproduced by gracious permission of Her Majesty Queen
Elizabeth II © 1994

inventiveness, he would return to this question; he considered devoting a book to it, in order to set down in writing the ideas which had occurred to him regarding teaching methods and areas of the curriculum, or the thoughts he was currently entertaining on the ideal step-by-step approach. In about 1508, under the title "Study and its Ordering", he summarized the results of his reflexions to date in the Codex Atlanticus. "I say," he wrote, "that one should first learn about the limbs and their functions (*travagliamenti*, literally "burden of labour"); only when this knowledge has been acquired should one proceed to the motions which human beings undergo in different situations. And third, one should learn to compose narratives, whose study should proceed from the natural, chance, situationally-determined movements which can be observed in the streets, squares and fields, and which can be jotted down in shorthand contours (*con brieve discritione di liniamenti*), for example by drawing a circle for a head, and a crooked line for an arm, and similarly with the legs and the torso. These notes should then be filled out at home."

Writing these sentences, it seems the artist felt he could hear the traditionalists cursing about his proposals. He immediately went on the defensive. "An opponent will object that it is better, if one wishes to become a practitioner and create good works, to devote the first part of one's apprenticeship to the copying of various whole elements (*componimenti*), such as different masters have drawn on sheets of parchment or painted on walls, and that one thereby acquires speed in practice and good habits (*practica veloce e bono abito*). In reply, I would say that such habits would certainly be good if they could be acquired on the basis of works consisting of good elements and derived from learned [in the sense of familiar with theory] masters. But since such masters are so rare that one finds few of them, it is safer to go direct to nature, than to that which seeks to copy this nature – to the latter's great disadvantage – and thus leads to bad habits. He who has access to the spring does not go to the water pots."

According to Leonardo, then, the traditional "holistic method" should be replaced by his "ABC method", because it is simply a matter of chance whether the former allows a visualization of human movements or not. But, tellingly, in his eyes even the ABC method only made sense if it was backed up by an instruction in functions, in other words the teaching of the mechanics and physiology of movement. Only the two together made possible a profitable study of real moving bodies and a correspondingly realistic reconstruction of dynamic processes.

That Leonardo's basic training model met with opposition is understandable. And yet it came to be accepted with surprising rapidity, at least in Florence, where the unique opportunity existed of seeing, for about a decade (1506–c. 1515), works by Leonardo and Michelangelo alongside each other, namely the trial panel for the mural of the *Battle of Anghiari*, and the cartoon for the *Soldiers*

understand them; and not least thanks to his phenomenal memory for shapes, so quickly and thoroughly that his understanding of functions even began to influence his strokes when drawing. The outlines of even his earliest extant authentic works (pp. 438, 439 right) are composed of mobile linear single-celled units, which, simply through their expanding and contracting volumes, lend the contours the effect of "body", weight, and agile vitality. They represent lonely summits, not only in their subtle sophistication, but also in the way they harmonize the maximum economy of draughtsmanship with the optimum efficiency of expression.

The Reform of the Artist's Basic Training
While Michelangelo did not begin to think about transmitting his own artistic skills to younger artists until his maturity, and then only under force of circumstances, Leonardo was obsessed with the issue of training. Again and again, often in the midst of soaring scientific

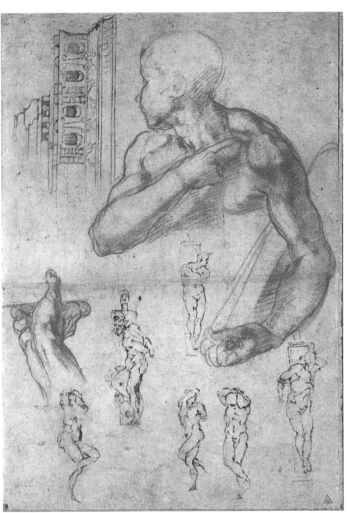

Bathing as part of the *Battle of Cascina* fresco. Precisely because the two compositions had nothing in common apart from the integral dynamics of their depiction of organism and action, they provided evidence of the efficiency of a method of design which visibly departed from the traditional foundations, and clearly proceeded from an understanding of anatomy different from that which had existed hitherto. They became the "School of the World", as the goldsmith and sculptor Benvenuto Cellini (1500–71) was to put it half a century later. On seeing them, more and more young artists doubtless began to regard the traditional ways of producing and teaching art as questionable, and reforms as inevitable.

As an apprentice, Cellini had the good fortune to be able to study the two sensational exhibits just in time before their removal. He perceived them through the eyes of a beneficiary of the reformed basic training. In about 1514, when he was starting his apprenticeship as a goldsmith in Florence, the traditional "holistic" method had already been displaced by Alberti's "ABC method". Cellini seems indeed to have already become acquainted with the latter in the formalized shape which it took in the first drawing textbooks of a few decades later. He had to learn the ABC of parts of the human body in a fixed order, beginning with the eye, which remained in force until the end of the 18th century.

Cellini found this order wrong. As the most beautiful parts of a human being – so he wrote in his unfinished treatise *On the Principles and Method of Learning the Art of Drawing* – the eyes were also the most difficult to draw. Consequently it was "greatly disadvantageous to art when the teacher, as far as I can see even now, sets those poor fellows his apprentices the task of drawing the human eye right at the outset. And as I myself experienced precisely

this in my tender years, I think that it must have happened to the others too. I am certain that ... the true and better method consists in requiring the easier tasks to be performed first." By these, Cellini meant the bones, and in particular, the easiest to copy, namely the shin-bone. One had to start here, and then progressively move on until one came to the noblest bone, the skull. Next, the bones should be measured to establish their proportions, and then fitted together to form a skeleton. This should then be depicted in various poses, in order to get to know how it worked. Only at the very end, after the drawing of the muscles, tendons and nerves had been mastered, was it the turn of the eye. If anyone desired the example of a great master who practised this method, then he should look at the works of Michelangelo, whose "noble style is so different from that of the other artists and from the style of the past precisely because this artist kept to the said order of the bones."

We may take it for granted that Michelangelo did not owe his style to any order either of flesh or of bones. Nor did he wish to turn his workshop into a charnel house when, in the 1520s, he taught his factotum Antonio Mini (1506–33) to draw. On the contrary – as is proved by a practice sheet now in Oxford (p. 439 left) – he had him begin with the same ABC as must have been forced upon Cellini. However, Michelangelo knew how to draw on the stimulating potential of alternating between analytical and synthesizing procedures far better than did Cellini's pedantic master. He apparently urged not only his good Antonio, but also the highly-talented Tomaso de'Cavalieri, whom he coached in drawing in 1532 – 33, at every stage to test the load, so to speak, of what had been learned; at the facial-organ and skull stage, for example, by head constructions on the pattern of the *teste divine* he had drawn himself (p. 437), or on autonomous variations thereof.

The new basic training was more than just a reform of an old one. It revolutionized the whole of art. It led to that internalization of the physical and motor properties of the organism which allowed artists at the very beginning of their careers to freely invent figures in motion and make them appear no less natural than studies from life (cf. pp. 434 and 435). By allowing creative activity to be experienced from the outset as a subjective act of imagination, it imbued the students with a hitherto almost unheard-of self-confidence, in the form of a feeling that in the final analysis it was the soundness of the idea, rather than the manual execution, which established the value of a work of art. But it was not long before the reverse side of the coin also made its appearance. Even by 1520, contrary to what Leonardo had imagined, the art of those trained by the new method was already beginning to alienate itself from its source – i.e. nature. It became artificial, the vehicle not only of lofty ideas, but also of carefully elaborated *maniere* to express them. It finally needed the foundation of a private academy (1582) and the joint methodological efforts of its three young founders, Ludovico, Agostino and Annibale Carracci, to provide a long-term guarantee of that natural vitality which an excessive trust in the power and goodness of pure imagination so quickly destroyed.

Appendices

SFORZA Milan

GONZAGA Mantua

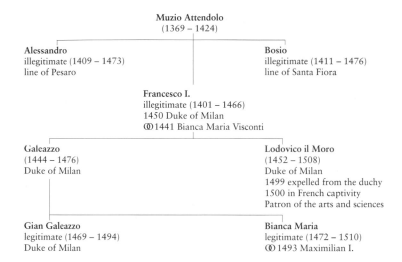

Muzio Attendolo
(1369 – 1424)

Alessandro
illegitimate (1409 – 1473)
line of Pesaro

Bosio
illegitimate (1411 – 1476)
line of Santa Fiora

Francesco I.
illegitimate (1401 – 1466)
1450 Duke of Milan
⚭ 1441 Bianca Maria Visconti

Galeazzo
(1444 – 1476)
Duke of Milan

Lodovico il Moro
(1452 – 1508)
Duke of Milan
1499 expelled from the duchy
1500 in French captivity
Patron of the arts and sciences

Gian Galeazzo
legitimate (1469 – 1494)
Duke of Milan

Bianca Maria
legitimate (1472 – 1510)
⚭ 1493 Maximilian I.

Francesco I.
Signor of Mantua 1382 – 1407
⚭ Agnese Visvonti † 1391;
⚭ Margherita Malatesta † 1399

Gianfrancesco
Signor1407, Marquis 1433 of Mantua † 1444
⚭ Paola Malatesta † 1449

Luigi III., »the Turk«
Marquis of Mantua 1444 – 1478
⚭ Barbara of Brandenburg † 1481

Federico I.
Marquis of Mantua 1478 – 1484

Francesco II.
Marquis of Mantua 1484 – 1519
⚭ Isabella d'Este † 1539

Federico II.
Marquis 1519, Duke 1530 of Mantua
1536 Marquis of Montferrat † 1566

ESTE Ferrara

Borso
(1413 – 1471)
1452 Duke of Modena and Reggio
1471 Duke of Ferrara

Ercole I.
(1431 – 1505)
1471 –1505 Duke of Ferrara, Modena
and Reggio
⚭ Eleonora of Aragon † 1493

Isabella
(1474 – 1539)
⚭ Francesco Gonzaga,
Marquis of Mantua

Beatrice
(1475 –1497)
⚭ Lodovico Sforza il Moro (1491),
Duke of Milan

Alfonso I.
(1476 – 1534)
Duke of Ferrara 1505
Duke of Modena 1505 – 1510 and 1527 – 1534
Duke of Reggio 1505 – 1512 and 1523 – 1534
⚭ Anna Sforza † 1494
⚭ Lucrezia Borgia † 1519

Ercole II.
(1508 – 1558)
Duke of Ferrara, Modena and Reggio
1534 – 1559
⚭ Renata of France † 1575

Popes

155.	Nicholas II., 1058 – 1061	193.	Boniface VIII., 1294 – 1303
156.	Alexander II., 1061 – 1073	194.	Benedict XI., 1303 – 1304
157.	Gregory VII., 1073 – 1085	195.	Clement V., 1305 – 1314
158.	Victor III., 1086 – 1087	196.	John XXII., 1316 – 1334
159.	Urban II., 1088 – 1099	197.	Benedict XII., 1334 – 1342
160.	Paschalis II., 1099 – 1118	198.	Clement VI., 1342 – 1352
161.	Gelasius II., 1118 – 1119	199.	Innocent VI., 1352 – 1362
162.	Calixtus II., 1119 – 1124	200.	Urban V., 1362 – 1370
163.	Honorius II., 1124 – 1130	201.	Gregory XI., 1370 – 1378
164.	Innocent II., 1130 – 1143	202.	Urban VI., 1378 – 1389
165.	Celestine II., 1143 – 1144	203.	Boniface IX., 1389 – 1404
166.	Lucius II., 1144 – 1145	204.	Innocent VII., 1404 – 1406 (Cosma de' Migliorati)
167.	Eugenius III., 1145 – 1153	205.	Gregory XII., 1406 – 1415 (Angelo Correr)
168.	Anastasius IV., 1153 – 1154	206.	Martin V., 1417 – 1431 (Oddo Colonna)
169.	Hadrian IV., 1154 – 1159	207.	Eugenius IV., 1431 – 1447 (Gabriel Condulmer)
170.	Alexander III., 1159 – 1181	208.	Nicholas V., 1447 – 1455 (Tommaso Parentucelli)
171.	Lucius III., 1181 – 1185	209.	Calixtus III., 1455 – 1458 (Alfonso Borgia)
172.	Urban III., 1185 – 1187	210.	Pius II., 1458 – 1464 (Enea Silvio Piccolomini)
173.	Gregory VIII., 1187	211.	Paul II., 1464 – 1471 (Pietro Barbo)
174.	Clement III., 1187 – 1191	212.	Sixtus IV., 1471 – 1484 (Francesco della Rovere)
175.	Celestine III., 1191 – 1198	213.	Innocent VIII., 1484 – 1492 (Giovanni Battista Cibo)
176.	Innocent III., 1198 – 1216	214.	Alexander VI., 1492 – 1503 (Rodrigo Borgia)
177.	Honorius III., 1216 – 1227	215.	Pius III., 1503 (Francesco Todeschini-Piccolomini)
178.	Gregory IX., 1227 – 1241	216.	Julius II., 1503 – 1513 (Giuliano della Rovere)
179.	Celestine IV., 1241	217.	Leo X., 1513 – 1521 (Giovanni de' Medici)
180.	Innocent IV., 1243 – 1254	218.	Hadrian VI., 1522 – 1523 (Adrian von Utrecht)
181.	Alexander IV., 1254 – 1261	219.	Clement VII., 1523 – 1534 (Giulio de' Medici)
182.	Urban IV., 1261 – 1264	220.	Paul III., 1534 – 1549 (Alessandro Farnese)
183.	Clement IV., 1265 – 1268	221.	Julius III., 1550 – 1553 (Giovanni Maria del Monte)
184.	Gregory X., 1271 – 1276	222.	Marcellus II., 1555 (Marcello Cervini)
185.	Innocent V., 1276	223.	Paul IV., 1555 – 1559 (Giovanni Pietro Caraffa)
186.	Hadrian V., 1276	224.	Pius IV., 1559 – 1565
187.	John XXI., 1276 – 1277	225.	Pius V., 1566 – 1572
188.	Nicholas III., 1277 – 1280	226.	Gregory XIII., 1572 – 1585
189.	Martin IV., 1281 – 1285	227.	Sixtus V., 1585 – 1590
190.	Honorius IV., 1285 – 1287	228.	Urban VII. 1590
191.	Nicholas IV., 1288 – 1292	229.	Gregory XIV. 1590 – 1591
192.	Celestine V., 1294	230.	Innocent IX. 1591

Doges of Venice

1400 – 1413	Michele Steno	1478 – 1485	Giovanni Mocenigo
1414 – 1423	Tomaso Mocenigo	1485 – 1486	Marco Barbarigo
1423 – 1457	Francesco Foscari	1486 – 1501	Agostino Barbarigo
1457 – 1462	Pasquale Malipiero	1501 – 1521	Leonardo Loredan
1462 – 1471	Cristoforo Moro	1521 – 1523	Antonio Grimani
1471 – 1473	Nicolò Tron	1523 – 1538	Andrea Gritti
1473 – 1474	Nicolò Marcello	1539 – 1545	Pietro Lando
1474 – 1476	Pietro Mocenigo	1545 – 1553	Francesco Donà
1476 – 1478	Andrea Vendramin		

Glossary

abacus (Lat. "plate"), the uppermost part of a capital.

acanthus (Gk. akantha, "thistle"), a thistle-like Mediterranean plant, whose large, slightly curled leaves were used in the classical era as decorative motifs, for example on the capitals of the Corinthian and Composite orders. It was frequently used in the Renaissance and the Baroque.

acroteria (Gk. "outermost part"), the small plinths, and the statues or carved ornaments they support, at the apex and two ends of a pediment.

aedicule (Lat. "miniature house"), A niche for a statue in Roman temples, a small burial chapel in the Middle Ages. In architecture, the frame of a window consisting of columns supporting a pediment. Since the Renaissance, mainly tombs and altars have been built as aedicules.

alcove (Span. alcoba, "bed chamber"), in Arabic architecture a vaulted niche for a bed, in European architecture a small windowless bedchamber adjacent to the main living quarters.

al fresco (It. "on fresh"), see fresco.

all'antica (It. "after the antique"), a work of art based on a classical model.

alla prima (It. "at first"), method of painting directly onto a surface without the use of underpainting.

allegory (Gk allegorein, "say differently"), a work of art which represents some abstract quality or idea, either by means of a single figure (personification) or by grouping objects and figures together. In addition to the Christian allegories of the Middle Ages, Renaissance allegories make frequent allusions to Greek and Roman legends and literature.

al secco (It. "on dry"), painting which, unlike true fresco, is carried out on plaster which has already dried.

altar (Lat. altaria, "high sacrificial table"), the raised structure consecrated to an act of worship. In classical times, the main altar was erected in front or at the side of the temple. Christian altars, used since the third century for prayers and the Eucharist, occupy a particular position within the church, which has been the apse since the Middle Ages; the *portabile* is a special portable altar, normally expensively decorated. The basic Christian altar consists of the mensa (rectangular slab) and the stipes that bear it. Four types developed: 1. table altar (mainly in Italy), 2. box-shaped altar (hollow-centred entrance to reliquary below), 3. block altar (thick stipes), 4. sarcophagus altar (with a sarcophagus underneath). Artistic decoration was at first restricted to ornamental coverings, the antependium, later altarpieces, then painted wings on either side. The winged altarpiece was developed after the Gothic period (triptych, polyptych), and could be locked (to differentiate between ordinary and holy days); later the reverse side was also painted. In the late 16th century altars without moving panels and bearing sculptural compositions became the norm.

altarpiece, altar painting in the centre of the retable, frequently surrounded by architectural embellishments and stone or wooden figures.

altar utensil, any religious and liturgical container or item needed at the altar during services.

ambulatory, the passageway behind the high altar and around an apse, separated from the choir by open arcades.

anastasis (Gk. "resurrection"), also the Harrowing of Hell, when Christ descended into limbo, the abode of souls who are neither in heaven nor in hell. Christ broke open the gate to hell and brought the chosen souls out into the light. This apocryphal story was often portrayed in Byzantine art.

anatomy (Gk. anatemnein, "dissect"), with reference to classical medical processes, the dissection of dead organisms was especially important in the Renaissance. Scientific knowledge was the purpose of human dissection (the ancients only dissected animals). Anatomical knowledge became a prime part of artistic training. Artists themselves performed such research. Pollaioulo, Michelangelo and Leonardo all conducted anatomical research to help them understand the basic proportions and laws of movement of the human body.

antependium (Lat. "hung in front"), an ornamental covering for the front of an altar, usually of rich fabric or precious metal, also called altar frontal.

Antiquity, the (Lat. antiquus, "old"), the classical age of Greece and Rome began with Greek migrations of the 2nd millennium BC, and ended in the West in 476 AD with the deposition of the Roman emperor Romulus Augustus, it ended in the East in 529 AD when the Platonic Academy was closed by Justinian.

apocrypha (Gk. "hidden"), in Greek times, books that were kept secret and not made available to the public. The term is also used to denote Jewish or Christian additions to the Old and New Testaments excluded from the Canon.

apse (Gk. "arch"), also called exedra. A semi-circular vaulted altar niche in Christian churches, which is added on or into the main building.

arcade (Lat. arcus, "arch"), a series of arches carried on piers or columns.

architrave (Gk. archi-, "top", and Lat. trabs, "beam"), in classical architecture the main beam that usually rests on columns and bears the upper part of the building.

archivolt (It. archivolto, "front arch"), a continuous moulding framing the face of an arch. In Roman and Greek architecture decorated archivolts were often used for triumphal arches and city gates. In Romanesque and Gothic jamb portals, archivolts formed a link with the upper parts of the wall, and were often decorated with sculptures.

"ars liberalis", "ars mechanica" (Lat. "liberal arts" and "mechanical arts"), the "seven liberal arts" (septem artes liberales) were in classical times those branches of knowledge and abilities, which a free man was expected to have mastered. In 400 AD, the writer Marcianus Capella combined them and defined them as the trivium of grammar, arithmetic and geometry, and the quadrivium of astronomy, dialectic, rhetoric and music. It was not until humanist pursuits and sciences such as perspective, proportion, and anatomy were more widespread and established that what we know as the fine arts were raised from the level of "artes mechanicae", from crafts to arts, leading in turn to a rise in the social status of the artist. The "artes mechanicae" thereafter meant those crafts and activities that were considered necessary to life on a practical level, such as building, farming, weaving, hunting, navigation, medicine.

"ars perspectiva", see perspective

atlantes, the term derives from Atlas, the Titan of Greek mythology. In architecture, full or half-length male figures, depicted in the round or in high relief, which are used instead of columns to support an entablature.

atrium (Lat. "entrance hall"), originally the open central court of a Roman house. Later, the colonnaded forecourt of an Early Christian church, on the west side of a basilica.

attic, a storey above the main entablature. It was frequently decorated or bore inscriptions, and was used to conceal the roof line. In classical times, it was used on city gates and triumphal arches; in

Renaissance architecture on churches and secular buildings.

attribute (Lat. attributum, "added"), a symbolic object which is conventionally used to identify a particular saint or deity, such as the stave and winged sandals of Hermes or Neptune's trident. It portrays a characteristic moment from the person's life, or, in the case of martyrs, the nature of their martyrdom.

Augustines, mediaeval order of mendicant monks following the Rule of St. Aurelius Augustinus (354–430), founded 1256, which spread during 14th and 15th centuries. It was influenced by Renaissance Humanism and many members joined the early Reformation movement instigated by their brother Martin Luther; the order also took on an increasing teaching role.

aureole (Lat. aureolus, "beautiful, wonderful"), light shown as encircling the head or body of a sacred personage.

baldachin, originally a textile canopy supported by poles at the four corners, carried over relics and dignitaries. Later, an architectural canopy made of stone or wood, placed over high altars, thrones, the bishop's seat, statues, portals, etc.

balustrade (It. balustra, "banister"), A railing supported by short pillars called balusters.

baptistery (Gk. baptisterion, "wash basin"), from the 4th to 14th centuries, 15th century in Italy, a small building, separate from the main church, in which the rite of baptism was performed. It was often dedicated to St. John the Baptist and mainly circular or octagonal in shape. In the late Middle Ages, the practice of full submersion during baptism was abolished; from then on, a font in the main church was used.

basilica (Gk. basilike stoa, "king's hall"), in Athens it was the government building of the Archon Basileus, in Rome a long hall designed to accommodate markets and legal courts. Christianity adopted the basilica as a community meeting place and church. The basic shape is a rectangular hall church , with a nave flanked by 2–4 narrower, lower side aisles. Light entered through windows in the side aisles and at the top of the nave walls. The nave led to an apse, usually in the east. Later, variations were added, such as a transept, narthex, choir and crypt. The originally plain exterior was embellished with the addition of towers, more elaborate façades and decoration of the portal.

Romanesque interiors were decorated with wall paintings or mosaics; in the Gothic period, which considered architecture to be a symbolic illusion of heaven, sculptures predominated. Italian Renaissance basilicas returned to a clearer, flatter architecture, triggering a new explosion of wall paintings.

bay, a division of a building, either inside or out, which is created by supporting members such as walls, columns and buttresses.

biforium, mediaeval vaulted double window that is divided in half by a column.

blind ornament, an architectural element that is added to a wall as a decorative feature.

boss, a projecting ornament made of stone or wood, often with a rusticated finish. See rustication.

bozzetto (It. "sketch"), first three-dimensional sketch made by a sculptor in preparation for the finished work.

bracket, an architectural member projecting upward and outward from a vertical surface to support something, such as an arch or statue.

bust, sculpted portrait consisting of the head and part of the shoulders. Developed in Greece, and revived in 15th century Italy.

cameo, a gemstone (or sometimes glass, ceramic or shell) which has layers of different colours, carved or moulded so that the design stands out in relief in one colour against the background of the other. The opposite of an intaglio.

campanile (It. campana, "bell"), an Italian belfry, often detached from the main building.

capital, in architecture, the separate member which crowns a column, pilaster or pier. It provides a more efficient support for the entablature than the column alone.

Carmelites (Lat. Ordo Fratrum Beatae Mariae Virginis de Monte Carmelo), a contemplative order of mendicant monks founded in 1247.

cartoon, in its original sense, a full-scale preparatory drawing for a painting, tapestry, or fresco. In fresco painting, the design was transferred to the wall by making small holes along the contour lines and making small marks through them (see sinopia). The cartoon had no intrinsic value.

casino (It. "little house"), a small house or pavilion built in the grounds

of a larger one, later a public saloon for dancing.

cassone (It. "chest"), an Italian marriage chest, used as a seat and often given as a marriage present. A characteristic item of furniture of the Early and High Renaissance, the cassone was often decorated with elaborate wood carvings. Inset panel paintings, or "cassone paintings", were added on the sides, by artists as important as Sandro Botticelli, Paolo Uccello and Andrea del Sarto.

catafalque (Lat. catafalcium, "scaffold"), a temporary timber structure used at a funeral service to support the coffin.

cathedral, a church which contains a "cathedra", the official throne of a bishop.

cenotaph (Gk. kenos, "empty", taphos, "grave"), a commemorative monument erected to an individual or to a group of people whose bodies are lost or lie elsewhere.

central planning, a building whose parts are of equal proportions, with a ground plan that is normally a circle, ellipse, square or rectangle, or Greek Cross type. Ambulatories or small apses are sometimes added. Models for centrally-planned buildings in the Italian Renaissance included the ancient Roman Pantheon, as well as Byzantine (Constantinople, S. Serlio and Bacchus) and Ottoman (Istanbul, Sultan Ahmed Mosque) architecture.

chasing, the process of adding detail and removing imperfections from metalwork by using chisels, files, etc.

chapter house, a large room within, or a building attached to, a monastery or bishopric, which is used for meetings of the governing body (chapter).

chiaroscuro (It. "light-dark"), in painting, the technique of modelling form by almost imperceptible gradations of light and dark. Chiaroscuro is often used to add to the atmosphere of a painting, adding to the drama of the events depicted.

choir (Lat. chorus, "round dance"), term borrowed from Ancient Greek theatre, used for that part of the Christian church reserved for singers and clergy; the area extending from the crossing to the high altar.

choir stalls, the rows of seats set up on either side of the choir for the clergy.

chrysography (Gk. chrysos, "gold", graphein, "write"), writing or painting with gold.

ciborium, a canopy over an altar, a

type of baldachin, supported by columns.

Cinquecento (It. "five hundred"), the period 1500–1600 in Italian art, the High and Late Renaissance. Main artists are Leonardo, Raphael, Michelangelo and Titian.

cladding, a thin layer of one material used externally in building to protect or conceal another, and used to form non-loadbearing exterior walls.

coffering, a system of deep panels or caissons recessed into a vault, ceiling or arch. Coffered ceilings, occasionally made of wood, were frequently used in Renaissance palaces.

colonnade, a row of columns carrying either an entablature or a series of arches.

Colossal (also giant order), any order whose columns or pilasters rise through more than one storey

Composite, architectural order which combines Ionic and Corinthian

console, in classical architecture, an ornamental bracket shaped like a letter S.

contour, the outline that defines a particular form. By using thick contour lines an artist is also able to suggest greater plasticity.

contrapposto (It. "placed opposite"), a way of representing the various parts of the body so that they are obliquely balanced around a central vertical axis. First developed by Classical Greek sculptors as a means of avoiding stiffness, contrapposto was revived in the Renaissance and carried to extremes under the influence of Mannerism.

copper engraving, a method of printing using a copper plate engraved with a pointed instrument such as a burin. The process was invented in south west Germany, c. 1440, is the second-oldest graphic art (after woodcuts).

corbel, a projecting architectural member, of stone, wood, metal, etc., which supports a weight.

Corinthian, architectural order with a capital that represents an acanthus growing in a basket.

cornice, the third and uppermost part of the entablature; a projecting moulding which runs round the top of a building.

Counter-Reformation, action led by the Catholic Church and Catholic rulers between 1555 and 1648 against the Reformation. The leaders of the

Catholic restoration were the Jesuits, who held influential positions in universities and schools, and commissioned many magnificent churches.

crossing, the part of a church where the nave and transept intersect. If the nave and transept are the same length, the result is a central ground plan.

crypt (Gk. cryptos, "hidden"), an underground chamber, usually with a vault, beneath the floor of a church, often housing a tomb or reliquary.

cupola, see dome.

devotional picture, in the art historical sense, is anything from a small to very large picture intended for the devotion, meditation and worship of the individual. It is meant to encourage an inner contemplation of the subject of the picture. The material used is normally wood, the theme usually the suffering of Christ and Mary. This type of picture came into existence, under the influence of mysticism, in 14th century Germany; though motifs and iconographical aspects appear earlier in Italian and Byzantine art of the late Middle Ages. The term is used both for certain statues of the Madonna and crucifixes, and for paintings. The term "devotional picture" is also applied to wood carvings used as covers on religious books.

diptych (Gk. di-ptysso, "folded twice"), in classical times folding writing tablets made of wood or metal. In the Middle Ages, an altarpiece comprising a pair of panels hinged together, without a central part.

dome, or cupola, an evenly curved vault on a circular, elliptical or polygonal base. In cross section it can have any of the configurations of an arch. There is frequently an oculus or a lantern at the highest point to admit light. The earliest known domed structures were Cretan and Mycenaean graves; the most important classical and Byzantine domed buildings were the Pantheon and Hagia Sophia respectively. The main Renaissance domes are those of Florence Cathedral, by Brunelleschi, and St. Peter's in Rome, by Michelangelo.

Dominicans (Lat. Ordo Fratrum Praedictatorum), order of mendicant monks founded by St. Dominic in Toulouse in 1216, to spread and extend the faith by preaching and teaching. The Dominicans were the most influential mediaeval order, and were put in charge of the Inquisition. Important Dominicans included Albertus Magnus, Thomas of Aquinas, and Meister Eckart.

Doric, architectural order, with a fluted

column and a capital with a flat abacus.

dwarf gallery, a low exterior wall passage with an equally low arcade, usually attached to the apse in Romanesque architecture.

Ecclesia (Gk. ekklesia, "gathering", Lat. "church"), gatherings of citizens in the Ancient Greek city states. The term was adopted by Christianity for the community, the room where services took place, and finally the Roman Catholic Church itself, which was represented in art as Ecclesia, a crowned female figure.

entablature, the upper part of one of the orders of architecture, including cornice, frieze and architrave.

exedra, see apse.

façade, the main elevation of a building; sometimes also one of its subsidiary elevations.

faïence, see majolica.

figura serpentinata (Lat. serpens, "snake", serpentinatus, "snaking"), a serpentine figure which was particularly popular in 16th century painting and sculpture, and favoured complex, elongated figures.

fluting, in architecture, closely spaced parallel grooves used to ornament columns, pilasters, etc.

foreshortening, the technique of depicting an object lying at an angle to the picture plane, by means of perspective devices.

Franciscans, order of mendicant monks founded by St. Francis of Assisi in 1223. They sought salvation in asceticism, poverty, safeguarding spiritual welfare and missionary work.

fresco (It. "fresh", affresco intonaco, "fresh plaster"), wall painting, in which mineral or earth pigments are suspended in water and painted onto wet lime or gypsum plaster; the pigments unite with the plaster as they dry.

frieze, the part of the entablature between the architrave and the cornice, sometimes decorated with relief sculpture. Also any relief or painting used decoratively in a long horizontal format.

gallery, an upper storey open on one side to the main interior space. In ecclesiastical architecture, the upper storey over a side aisle (basilica), ambulatory (centrally-planned building) or the west entrance. The gallery was used to separate a particular group from participants in

the service (e.g. women or members of the nobility).

Ghibelline, see Guelph.

Gothic (It. gotico, "barbaric, not classical"), a word now used to describe mediaeval art from the end of the Romanesque period (mid 12th century) to the beginning of the Renaissance. The term was coined by Vasari and used to deride the Renaissance's immediate predecessors as "Goths" or barbarians. The Gothic cathedral was a particularly important architectural development; the separate areas of Romanesque churches were united, and the entire building was very tall. Other features were pointed arches, rib vaults and flying buttresses. Gothic sculpture was mainly used as an architectural ornament, e.g. using statues as columns on cathedral façades. As the architectural detail of Gothic churches left little room for wall paintings, (an exception being Giotto's frescoes at the beginning of the 14th century), Gothic painting was restricted mainly to altarpieces and stained glass.

Greek key pattern, an ornament consisting of lines turning at right angles to one another to form a squared spiral.

grisaille (Fr. gris, "grey"), painting in grey or greyish monochrome, sometimes heightened with gold. It was first used in stained glass windows of churches of the Cistercians, who were afraid that coloured glass would distract monks from their meditations. Painters, from the time of Giotto, have used grisaille as a way of imitating the appearance of sculptures. During the Renaissance, grisaille designs were used by engravers to make it easier to copy paintings.

grotesque (It. grotto, "cave"), a kind of ornament derived by Renaissance architects and artists from Ancient Roman decorations, which they discovered c. 1520 in subterranean ruins, hence the name. The ornament, which was either painted, carved or made of stucco, usually consisted of vines twisting around human figures, birds, animals and monsters.

Guelph and Ghibelline, the names of two rival princely families who were involved in the war between the supporters of Otto IV and Frederick II. In Italy, the Guelphs supported the Pope, and the Ghibellines were on the side of the German emperors.

guilds, associations of artists, craftsmen or tradesmen. These organisations originate in the Middle Ages, and their aims were to regulate the financial, social and political interests of their members. Guilds are

closely connected to the development of towns, and many were still in existence in the 19th century.

hippodrome (Gk. "race-course"), an ancient elliptical course for horse and chariot racing.

Hodegetria, a type of Byzantine Madonna, named after a painting in the monastery of the Hodegon in Constantinople (5th century), which shows the Virgin with the child on her left arm. The style was copied, often in ivory, from the 10th to 12th centuries.

Hortus Conclusus (Lat. "enclosed garden"), a representation of the Virgin and Child in a fenced garden, sometimes accompanied by a group of female saints, angels, and tame animals. The garden is used to symbolism her purity and freedom from sin.

humanism, intellectual movement in Italy, which started in the 14th and lasted into the 17th century. It suggested the ideal of an education that was based on antiquity, and was purely human, not theological, in nature. It included the belief that man himself could improve his own conditions without supernatural help. Petrarch (1304-1374) was considered to be the "Father of humanism"; he re-introduced classical literary forms. Main centres of humanism were Medici Florence, Rome under Pius II, and the courts of Urbino, Ferrara, Mantua and Naples; these were also thriving artistic centres. The most important goals of Renaissance humanism, which encompassed all areas of spiritual life, were the development of individuality and a critical knowledge of the world by means of science, medicine and technology. In philosophy, there was an attempt to return to classical concepts such as those of Plato, which led to the foundation of a Platonic Academy in Florence by Cosimo de' Medici.

icon (Gk. "likeness"), a small, portable painting by a Greek or Russian Orthodox believer on panel, generally of a religious subject, usually Christ, the Virgin Mary or saints. The subject was strictly prescribed by tradition, using an equally strict pattern of representation. Used both as church ornaments and private devotional pictures.

iconography (Gk. "description of a picture"), originally the study and identification of classical portraits. In art history, refers to the systematic investigation of the subject-matter and symbolism of images, as opposed to their style; an important part of this is a research of literary, philosophical and theological sources.

Iconoclasm, the movement to destroy images of Christ, Mary, saints, angels, during the 8th and 9th centuries, which led to Iconoclast art, a type of Byzantine art without figurative religious images. The term was applied analogously to Protestants in the 16th and 17th centuries.

impost, the horizontal moulding of course of stone or brickwork at the top of a pillar or pier.

inlay, a process by which small pieces of materials such as stone and glass are inserted into a large piece of another, softer material, such as plaster and cement, in order to create a colourful pattern.

intaglio, a hollow-cut design, sometimes of a gemstone, the opposite of relief. An intaglio is often used as a matrix from which a relief can be made.

intarsia, a type of marquetry (wooden inlay) used for the decoration of choir-stalls and the panelling of rooms. Materials used included different colours of wood, ivory, tortoise shell, mother of pearl and metal.

intrados, the inner face of an arch.

Ionic, architectural order with slender columns and capitals with symmetrical volutes.

jamb, the side of a window, door, or other wall opening.

Jesuits, Catholic teaching order founded by Ignatius Loyola in 1534 with the express purpose of fighting heresy. It was their intention to spread the faith by missionary work and education, publishing books and scientific studies.

lantern (Lat. lanterna, "lamp"), in architecture, a small turret at the highest point of a dome, fitted with windows or other openings and used to light the space below.

Legenda aurea (Lat. "Golden legend"), a collection of legends about saints, collected from written and oral sources by Jacobus da Voragine (1230–1298/99), Archbishop of Genoa. The *Legenda aurea* was the most important source for artists' pictures of saints.

loggia, a kind of exterior corridor, communicating through an arcade or colonnade with the open air. Can be used on the ground or upper floor, or a sequence of floors. During the Renaissance loggias were usually used for stately functions, or as market places.

lunette (Fr. "little moon"), a semi-circular space, often a window, over doors and windows.

Madonna (It. "my lady"), a picture of Mary, the Mother of God, holding Jesus.

Maestà (It. "majesty"), a representation, popular in 13th and 14th century Italy, of the Madonna and Child enthroned and surrounded by saints and angels.

majolica, low-fired, white or coloured tin-glazed pottery. Majolica, which was invented by the Babylonians, was a technique used to produce pieces ranging from everyday utensils and tiles to magnificent vessels. It was supposedly introduced into Italy around the 12th century from the island of Majorca, and there were, from the 14th century, important majolica workshops in Faenza, Urbino, Orvieto and Florence (della Robbia family).

mandorla (It. "almond"), an almond-shaped glory of light enclosing the whole of some sacred figure, such as the resurrected Christ.

maniera tedesca (It. "German manner"), Giorgio Vasari's term for Gothic, which he considered to be a flawed style of art that had been caused by the migrations of Germanic tribes.

Mannerism (It. maniera, "manner"), term describing European art in the period between the Renaissance and the Baroque, c. 1520–1620. It can, to an extent, be explained as a consequence of the Counter-Reformation, and the destruction of the High Renaissance's anthropocentric view of the world by radical social restructuring and political events. Renaissance ideals were rejected; inventiveness was the main requirement, and logic rather than emotion prevailed. Mannerism was typified by stylistic trickery and a liking for bizarre effects. Typical features of Mannerist art include elongated bodies and anatomically impossible positions, extremely complicated compositions, irrational and theatrical lighting, and a use of colour that was no longer restricted to the object it represented. Main Mannerist artists include Pontormo, Bronzino, Parmigianino and Tintoretto.

meander pattern, see Greek key pattern.

mendicant monks (Lat. mendicare, "beg"), orders which exist solely through hard work or begging for alms. Came into existence in 13th century as a reaction to the growing secularisation of the church (Francis of Assisi). Mendicants saw their task as including the connection of monastic life with spiritual work in the outside world, including spiritual welfare, fighting heresy, teaching in universities and working as missionaries.

mosaic (Arab. muzauwaq, "decoration"), a design made by cementing small pieces of hard, coloured substances (e.g. marble, glass) to a base.

narthex, a single storey porch leading into the main body of an Early Christian or Byzantine church.

nimbus (Lat. "cloud, aureole"), the disc or halo, usually golden, placed behind the head of a saint or other sacred personage to distinguish him or her from ordinary people. It was used in this way in oriental, classical and Indian art, and was adopted by Christian art in the 4th century.

nymphaeum, a shrine to nymphs built in classical times over a spring or the place where a conduit reached the city, and frequently decorated lavishly with architectural structures and statues.

oculus (Lat. "eye"), a small round opening in a wall or dome.

oil painting, painting done with pigments that have been bound with drying oils. It is possible to show very precise gradations of colours and the paint can be applied in a variety of thicknesses, from almost transparent coatings right through to pastos. Oil paintings were at first done on wood, later canvas. It has been shown that oil painting was a technique known in classical times; it was revived, in the 15th century, by the brothers Hubert and Jan van Eyck.

Opera del Duomo, association of all the craftsmen involved in building an Italian cathedral.

orders, a system devised by Vitruvius, the Roman architectural historian, to categorise architecture. See Doric, Ionic, Corinthian, Tuscan (Roman Doric), Composite, Colossal.

ornament (Lat. ornare, "decorate"), a decorative motif that can be painted, inlaid, or sculpted. The decorative motifs used by particular artistic circles, styles or individual painters are called ornamentation. Ornaments do not have any intrinsic narrative properties, and can be divided into geometric and natural (plant) ornamentation. Arabesques (curves, tendrils and flowing lines based on plant forms) and moresques (based on leaves and flowers), and c. 1520 grotesques (above) and scrollwork, were all important forms of Renaissance ornamentation.

palazzo, stately residence or public government building. Many palazzos were built during the Renaissance and Baroque periods, inspired by ancient Roman palaces.

panelling, the decoration of ceilings or walls with wooden panels.

patronage, during the Renaissance, patrons promoted the arts and collected pieces of art, as is clear from the donations they made to public bodies and the free training and many opportunities to find work given to artists. A famous example of a patron-artist relationship was that between Lorenzo de' Medici and Michelangelo.

pedestal, the lowest part of the support for a classical column.

pediment, a gable or gable-like ornament over a portico, door or window. Originally triangular, but sometimes segmental.

peristyle (Gk. peri, "round", stulos, "column"), a courtyard within a building, surrounded by columns; also a continuous colonnade around a building.

perspective (Lat. perspicere, "see through, see clearly"), the method of representing a three-dimensional object on a flat or nearly flat surface. Perspective gives a painting a sense of depth. The most important form of perspective in the Renaissance was linear perspective, in which real or suggested lines converge on a vanishing point on the horizon, often in the middle (centralized perspective) of the composition. It was important not to paint all the perspective effects, however, if it was to be visually effective. The scientific and mathematical basis of perspective was probably discovered by Brunelleschi c. 1420, and was first used by Masaccio c. 1426/27 in his frescoes; L. B. Alberti wrote about it in 1436. An additional important feature in creating a sense of depth is to remember that colours become lighter and appear to lose intensity the further away they are.

piano nobile (It. "noble floor"), the main floor of a large building such as a palazzo, containing the reception rooms.

pier, a large, free-standing pillar, of rectangular, square or composite section, supporting an arch, etc.

Pietà (It. "pity"), abbreviation of "Maria Santissima della Pietà". a representation of the body of Christ lying in the lap of the Virgin Mary.

pilaster, a rectangular pier engaged in a wall and projecting only slightly away from it. It is used as a decorative feature, and also to strengthen the wall, support the entablature and frame portals and windows.

pillar, a free-standing upright, of any regular shape.

pinnacle (Gk. "bowl"), Gothic architectural ornament. Narrow, pointed pyramid crowning a buttress and flanking triangular pediments. The lower part of the usually four or eight-sided pinnacle is often decorated with tracery.

plinth, square base for columns, pillars and statues.

polychromy (Gk. poly, "many"), the art of painting or decorating in several colours.

polyptych, a painting made up of a number of panels fastened together.

portal, an entrance, usually of stately or magnificent construction, to a building. A feature of classical architecture which was developed by the Renaissance, and used on both ecclesiastical and secular buildings.

portico, a roof supported by columns and usually attached to the front of a building.

predella (It. "altar-step"), a painting or carving placed beneath the main scene or series of panels in an altarpiece, creating a king of plinth. Often part of the housing of a reliquary.

presbytery, the raised part of a church reserved for the clergy.

propylæum, the entrance gateway to an Early Christian basilica.

putto (It. "boy"), a small naked boy, with or without wings, often carrying out some playful action.

quatrefoil, a four-lobed decorative motif, especially a four-lobed shape in Gothic tracery.

Quattrocento (It. "four hundred"), the period 1400–1500 in Italian art, the time of the Early Renaissance. Main artists are Filippo Brunelleschi, Donatello, Lorenzo Ghiberti and Masaccio.

reception of antiquity, the deliberate borrowing of ideas, materials and motifs that were considered to be classical and ideal models, together with literary and artistic forms, for one's own purposes. The Renaissance, in particular, returned to classical elements from the areas of philosophy, architecture, painting and literature. The creation of a new image of the world and man rested on classical ideals of man as educated in a range of areas, and was propagated, in Italy in particular, by humanists. The generally accepted formal norms in architecture and painting were derived from ancient texts and archaeological research. Roman works of art or Roman copies of Greek art were rediscovered and collected. Great excitement was caused by discoveries such as the *Laocoön* group and the *Three Graces;* a later influence on Italian Renaissance architecture as well as art theory was Vitruvius' *De Architectura Libri X,* which was discovered in 1415.

relief (Lat. relevare, "raise"), a composition or design made so that all or part projects from a flat surface. The degree of relief is indicated in terms such as *alto rilievo* ("high relief", deeply carved sculpture almost detached from its support), *mezzo rilievo* (figures seen in the half-round) and *bas-relief* (figures projecting less than half their true depth from the background).

reliquary (Lat. reliquiae, "remains"), a container for the sacred relics of a saint.

Renaissance (Fr. "rebirth"), progressive epoch in the arts and intellectual life of southern, western and central Europe, originating in Italy and lasting from the 14th or 15th till the 16th century. The term (*rinascità*) was coined by Vasari in 1550; Vasari meant it to refer to progress beyond mediaeval art, but around 1820 in France it was extended to signify a style. Three periods are distinguished: the Early Renaissance (from c. 1420), the High Renaissance (till c. 1520/30) and the Late Renaissance (or Mannerism, till c. 1600). The culture of the Renaissance was primarily established by visual artists, scholars, philosophers and writers. They were inspired by humanism, which aimed for a new image of humanity, the world and nature and took antiquity as its model. Notably anthropocentric in tenor, the Renaissance evolved the concept of the *uomo universale,* the person of universal learning and all-round intellectual and physical capacity. The Italian city states, which saw themselves in the tradition of the Greek *polis,* were ruled by powerful families (such as the Medicis, the Gonzagas or the Sforzas) who had emerged from the rising affluent merchant classes. Renaissance architecture took its bearings from the theories of Vitruvius and adopted classical features; its major achievements were in palace and church architecture, and centrally-planned buildings were characteristic of the Renaissance. The visual arts emerged from their status as crafts, and with their new independence artists found that their social status had risen too. The arts and sciences were closely tied and influenced each other (in the discovery of mathematical perspective, for example, or in the anatomical knowledge that now went into the portrayal of the human form).

retable, the rear wall of an altar, decorated with paintings and sculptures. From the 14th to the 16th centuries, altarpieces were one of the most important commissions in European art; they saw some of the most decisive developments in painting and sculpture.

reveal, the part of a door or window jamb which lies at an angle to the wall, but is not concealed by the frame.

rilievo stiacciato (It. "flattened relief"), a finely graded low relief developed by Donatello, where the transitions are compressed so as to suggest atmosphere as well as purely three-dimensional effects.

Romanesque (Lat. romanus, "Roman"), term describing the art and architecture of Europe from the end of the 8th until the 12th century (pre-Gothic). It is divided into Early Romanesque (until c. 1080), High Romanesque (until c. 1150) and Late Romanesque (until c. 1240), which ran parallel to the Early Gothic in France. Features of ecclesiastical buildings were the heavy and massive proportions of all architectural elements; the west façade of churches was particularly emphasized as a counterweight to the east side with its transept and apse; the churches had several towers and, c. 1100, the entire building was vaulted.

rood-screen, screen between the choir and the nave, its height making it very difficult to see into the choir.

rosette (Fr. "little rose"), a stylized rose shape, used as an architectural ornament. The rosette is one of the oldest and most wide-spread ornamental motifs.

rotunda, a circular building, or a circular interior space.

rustication, masonry treated to resemble huge square blocks, with a deliberately rough surface finish.

Sacra Conversazione (It. "holy conversation"), A representation of the Virgin and Child surrounded by saints, all of whom seem to be engaged in some kind of dialogue, or at least aware of one another's presence.

sacristy, a store-room attached to a church, used for sacred vessels and for vestments.

sarcophagus, a coffin or tomb-chest usually made of stone, wood or metal.

sinopia, the preparatory drawing used to map out the composition of a fresco, and also the reddish brown chalk used for the purpose.

spandrel, the triangular area of stonework on the outer curve of an arch.

still-life, a painting of inanimate objects such as flowers, fruits, dead animals and household objects. These objects often have a symbolic significance. Still-life was used in paintings from the 14th century, as a result of closer attention to reality, but was not a separate genre of painting until the 16th century, reaching its high point in the Netherlands in the 17th century.

tambour (Fr. "drum"), in architecture, the cylindrical area supporting the dome, usually with windows to light the interior of the dome.

tectonic, to do with building or construction.

tempera (Lat. temperare, "to mix in due proportion"), the form of painting used before oil painting was developed. Traditionally, tempera is made with whole eggs or egg-yolk, though various kinds of glue and gum are also used. As tempera paints dry very quickly, changes of colours can only be shown by adding small lines or dots.

terracotta (It. "baked earth"), fired clay with no glaze which, depending on which clay has been used, can be white, yellow, brown, light or dark red. It is used for architectural ornament and vessels, and it is one of the oldest building materials known to man.

tondo (It. "round picture"), a circular painting or relief sculpture. It derives from classical medallions, and was used in the Renaissance as a compositional device to create an ideal visual harmony. It was particularly popular in Florence, and was often used for picture of the Madonna.

torso (It. "tree-trunk"), a sculptured figure which lacks head or limbs, either by accident or design.

tracery, ornamental stonework, in more or less elaborate patterns, which is used to fill windows or as a relief ornament on solid walls.

transept, the section of a church which lies across the main axis.

Trecento (It. "three hundred"), the period 1200–1300 in Italian art. Main artistic centres were Florence, Siena and Padua; important artists include Andrea Pisano and Giotto di Bondone; writers include Dante Alighieri and Petrarch.

trefoil arch, an arch with tracery in the shape of the three lobes of a clover leaf.

triforium (Lat. "three openings"), an arcade on the side wall of a church or cathedral, facing into the interior of the building.

triglyph (Gk. "thrice carved"), part of the frieze in the Doric order, consisting of three parallel grooves in square blocks of stone; probably derives from the wooden ends of the beams in roofs.

triptych (Gk. "in three parts"), a picture made up of three panels, in particular a mediaeval altarpiece.

triumphal arch, an ornamental gateway in Ancient Rome, erected to celebrate military triumphs. In Christian basilicas it is the choir screen in a church, especially one with a large opening flanked by two smaller ones.

trompe-l'œil (Fr. "deceives the eye"), a type of painting which by means of various illusionist devices persuades the spectator that he is looking at the actual objects depicted. Successful *trompe-l'œil* depends on a thorough grasp of realism and perspective. *Trompe-l'œil* dates back to classical times, and appears in paintings from the 15th century; it is a particular feature of Dutch 17th century still-lives.

Tuscan (Roman Doric), architectural order which is simplified Doric with unfluted columns.

tympanum (Lat. "drum"), the triangular area enclosed by a classical pediment, often decorated with sculptures; in mediaeval architecture, the area over the lintel, enclosed by an arch, which is also often decorated with reliefs or mosaics.

vault, a roof based on the structural principle of the arch, which can, in contrast to domes, be used over longitudinal-plan buildings. Of great structural and aesthetic importance to the development of church architecture. Different types of vaults were favoured at different stages, rib vaults being particularly important to Gothic architecture.

verism (Lat. verus, "true"), the attempt to reproduce reality in art with rigorous and unselective accuracy.
vestibule, a room within the entrance of the building.

volute, a scroll-shaped architecture ornament often found on pediments and capitals. It was first used on Ionic capitals, and reappeared during the Italian High Renaissance; it was an important feature of Baroque architecture.

votive image, a picture or panel donated for a particular reason, such as deliverance from danger or an illness, and frequently portraying the donator.

Bibliography

The bibliography has been arranged in the sequence of essays in this volume. It is both a list of the sources used by the authors and a list of suggested secondary reading matter. As a result, some titles are repeated. It must be emphasized that this is only a limited selection of the available works.

ROLF TOMAN
Introduction
Michael Baxandall, Painting and Experience in Fifteenth-Century Italy, Oxford, 1972.
Gene Brucker, The Civic World of Early Renaissance Florence, New York, 1977.
Jakob Burckhardt, Der Cicerone. Eine Anleitung zum Genuß der Kunstwerke Italiens (1855), Stuttgart, 1986..
Jakob Burckhardt, The Civilization of the Renaissance in Italy, Basle, English trans. 1873, repr. London, 1944.
Peter Burke, The Italian Renaissance. Culture and Society in Italy, Oxford, 1987.
Peter Burke, The Renaissance, Berlin, 1990.
André Chastel, Die Kunst Italiens, Munich, 1987.
André Chastel, Chronik der italienischen Renaissancemalerei 1280–1580, Würzburg, 1984.
Eugenio Garin, Der italienienische Humanismus, Berne, 1947.
Werner Goez, Grundzüge der Geschichte Italiens in Mittelalter und Renaissance, Darmstadt, 1975.
Ernst H. Gombrich, Die Geschichte der Kunst, Stuttgart, 1987, ch. 12–18.
Ernst H. Gombrich, Norm and Form, London, 1966.
Ernst H. Gombrich, Symbolic Images, London, 1972.
Agnes Heller, Renaissance Man, London, 1979.
Johann Huizinga, Das Problem der Renaissance (1920); Renaissance and realism, English trans. in Men and Ideas, New York, 1920.
Michael Jäger, Die Theorie des Schönen in der Renaissance, Cologne, 1990.
Thomas Krämer, Florenz und die Geburt der Individualität, Stuttgart, 1992.
Paul Oskar Kristeller, Humanismus und Renaissance, 2 vols., Munich, 1974–76.
Giovanni Previtali and Federico Zeri (ed.), Italienische Kunst. Eine neue Sicht auf ihre Geschichte, 2 vols., Berlin, 1987.
Erwin Panofsky, Die Renaissancen der europäischen Kunst, Frankfurt, 1979.
Erwin Panofsky, Studien zur Ikonologie. Humanistische Themen in der Kunst der Renaissance, Cologne, 1980.
Herbert A. Stützer, Die italienische Renaissance, Cologne, 1977.
Giorgio Vasari, Lives (ed. G. Milanese, Florence, 1878–81).
Edgar Wind, Pagan Mysteries in the Renaissance, rev. ed. Oxford, 1980.

ALICK MCLEAN
Italian Architecture of the Late Middle Ages

General:
L. B. Alberti, 1404–1472, On painting and On Sculpture, London, Phaidon, 1972.
L. B. Alberti, Opere volgari, 3 vols., ed. Cecil Grayson, Bari, Laterza, 1960–73.
G. Bandmann, Mittelalterliche Architektur als Bedeutungsträger, Berlin, 1979.
W. Braunfels, Mittelalterliche Stadtbaukunst in der Toskana, Berlin, 1979.
C. Burroughs, "A Planned Myth and a Myth of Planning: Nicholas V and Rome", Rome in the Renaissance, The City and the Myth, ed. P. A. Ramsey, Medieval & Renaissance texts & Studies 18, Binghampton: State University of New York at Binghampton, 1982, pp. 197–207.
K. J. Conant, Carolingian and Romanesque Architecture 800–1200, The Penguin History of Art, Harmondsworth, New York, 1987, pp. 372–383.
S. Curçic, "Late-antique palaces: the meaning of urban context," Ars Orientalis 23, 1993, pp. 67–90
E. Guidoni, Arte e urbanistica in Toscana, 1000–1315, Rome, 1989.
P. Jones, "Economia e società nell'Italia medievale: la leganda della borghesia", Storia d'Italia: Dal feudalismo al capitalismo Annali I, ed. R. Romano and C. Vivanti, trans. Carla Susini Jones, Turin, 1978, pp. 187–372.
P. Jones, "La città-stato nell'Italia del tardo Medio Evo", La crisi degli ordinamenti comunali e le origini dello stato del Rinascimento, ed. G. Chittolini, Bologna, 1979, pp. 99–123.
R. Krautheimer, ed., Ausgewählte Aufsätze zur europäischen Kunstgeschichte, trans. Beyer, A. et alia, Cologne, 1988.
A. McLean, Sacred Space and Public Policy: The Establishment, Decline & Revival of Prato's Piazza della Pieve, Ph.D. dissertation, Princeton University, Ann Arbor, 1993.
G. Tabacco, Egemonie Sociali e Strutture del Potere nel Medioevo Italiano, Turin, 1974, pp. 226–427.
M. Tafuri, Ricerca del Rinascimento: principi, citta, architetti, Turin, 1992.
D. Waley, The Italian City-Republics, London, 1983.
C. W. Westfall, In This Most Perfect Paradise: Nicholas V and the Invention of Conscious Urban Planning in Rome, 1447–1455, University Park & London, University of Pennsylvania Press, 1974.
J. White, Art and Architecture in Italy 1250–1400, Harmondsworth, 1987.

The "Proto-Renaissance" and the construction of a Papal Roman Empire:
A. Busignani, R. Bencini, Le chiese di Firenze: il Battistero di San Giovanni, Florence, 1988.
A. Romanini, M. Andaloro, A. Cadei, F. Gandolfo and M. Righetti Tosti Croce, L'Arte Medievale in Italia, Florence, 1988.
M. V. Schwarz, "Mittelalterliches Dekorationsgefüge, Eine Studie über Schauplätze und Methoden von Antikenrezeption", Römisches Jahrbuch der Kunstgeschichte 25, 1989, pp. 118–22.

The Renaissance in Pisa:
P. Sanpaolesi, Il Duomo di Pisa e l'architettura romanica toscana delle origini, Cultura e storia pisana, 4, Pisa, 1975.
M. Seidel, "Dombau, Kreuzzugsidee und Expansionspolitik. Zur Ikonographie der Pisaner Kathedralbauten", Frühmittelalterliche Studien, 11, 1977, pp. 340–369.
C. Smith, The Baptistry of Pisa, Outstanding dissertations in the fine arts, IV, New York and London, 1978.

The effect of orders of beggars on the great trade centres:
G. G. Meersseman, "Origine del tipo di chiesa umbro-toscano degli ordini mendicanti", Il gotico a Pistoia nei suoi rapporti con l'arte gotica Italiana, Pistoia, 1966, pp. 63–77.
J. Raspi Serra, ed., Gli ordini mendicanti e la città, Metologia e storia delle componenti culturali del territorio, Università degli Studi di Salerno, Milan, 1990.
A. Vauchez, ed., Les Ordres mendicants et la ville en Italie centrale (v. 1220–1350) 89, 2, Mélanges d'Archéologie et d'Histoire, Moyen Age – Temps Modernes, l'École Francaise de Rome, Rome, 1977.

Florence Cathedral and the church of Orsanmichele - a return to the monumental:
B. Cassidy, "The Assumption of the Virgin on the tabernacle of Orsanmichele", Journal of the Warburg and Courtauld Institutes, LI, 1988, pp. 174–180.
B. Cassidy, "The Financing of the Tabernacle of Orsanmichele", Source VIII, 1, 1988, pp. 1–6.
G. Fanelli, Firenze, La città nella storia d'Italia, Bari, 1980, 1984.
H. Saalman, Filippo Brunelleschi: The Cupola of Santa Maria del Fiore, London, 1980.
M. Trachtenberg, The Campanile of Florence Cathedral: "Giotto's Tower", New York, 1971.

Siena in the Late Middle Ages:
W. M. Bowsky, A Medieval Italian Commune. Siena under the Nine, 1287–1355, Berkeley, 1981.
E. Guidoni, Il Campo di Siena, Rome, 1971.
A. Perrig, "Formen der politischen Propaganda der Kommune von Siena in der ersten Trecento Hälfte", Bauwerk und Bildwerk im Hochmittelalter: Anschauliche Beiträge zur Kultur- und Sozialgeschichte, Giessen, 1981, 213–31.
P. A. Riedl, M. Seidel, eds., Die Kirchen von Siena 1–, Munich, 1985– .
F. Toker, "Gothic Architecture by Remote Control: An Illustrated Building Contract of 1340", Art Bulletin LXVII 1, 1985, 67–94.

Competition in secular architecture:
D. Abulafia, Frederick II Harmondsworth, 1988, pp. 280–89 (architecture).
K. Bering, Kunst und Staatsmetaphysik

des Hochmittelalters in Italien, Zentren der Bau- und Bildpropaganda in der Zeit Friedrichs II, Essen, 1986.
D. Friedman, Florentine New Towns, Cambridge MA, 1988.
F. Gurrieri, ed., Il Castello dell'Imperatore a Prato, Prato, 1975.
W. Hotz, Pfalzen und Burgen der Stauferzeit, Darmstadt, 1981.
N. Rubinstein, "The Piazza della Signoria in Florence", Festschrift H. Siebenhüner, Würzburg, 1978, pp. 19–30.
M. Trachtenberg, "What Brunelleschi saw: Monument and Site at the Palazzo Vecchio in Florence", JSAH 47, 1988, pp. 14–44.
H. Wenzel, "Antiken-Imitationen des 12. und 13. Jahrhunderts in Italien", Zeitschrift für Kunstwissenschaft 9, 1955, pp. 29–72.

ALEXANDER PERRIG
Painting and Sculpture in the Late Middle Ages

Altichiero (see also: Padua):
H. W. Kruft, Altichiero und Avanzo, Bonn, 1966.
M. Plant, "Portraits and Politics in Late Trecento Padua: Altichiero's Frescoes in the S. Felice Chapel, S. Antonio", Art Bulletin, LXIII, 1981, pp. 406–25.

Assisi, San Francesco (also see: Giotto, Lorenzetti, Martini, Rome, Torriti):
J. Poeschke, Die Kirche San Francesco in Assisi und ihre Wandmalereien, Munich, 1985.
S. Romano, "Pittura ad Assisi 1260–1280. Lo stato degli studi", Arte medievale, III, 1985, pp. 109–40.
I. Hueck, "Die Kapellen der Basilika San Francesco in Assisi: Die Auftraggeber und die Franziskaner", Patronage and Public in the Trecento, ed. V. Moleta, Florence, 1986, pp. 81–104.
W. Schenkluhn, San Francesco in Assisi: Ecclesia specialis. Die Vision Papst Gregors IX. von einer Erneuerung der Kirche, Darmstadt, 1991.
Schwartz, "Patronage and Franciscan Iconography in the Magdalen Chapel at Assisi", Burlington Magazine, CXXXIII, 1991, pp. 32–36.

Reception of Assisi:
M. Meiss, "Fresques italiennes, cavallinesques et autres à Béziers", Gazette des Beaux-Arts, LXXIX, 1937, pp. 275–86.
M. Boskovits, "Gli affreschi della Sala dei notari a Perugia e la pittura in Umbria alla fine del XIII secolo", Bollettino d'Arte, LXVI/9, 1981, pp. 1–42.
D. Blume, Wandmalerei als Ordenspropaganda. Bildprogramme im Chorbereich franziskanischer Konvente Italiens bis zur Mitte des 14. Jahrhunderts. Worms, 1983.
E. Castelnuovo, Un pittore italiano alla corte di Avignone - Matteo Giovannetti e la pittura in Provenza nel secolo XIV, Turin, 1991.

Roger Bacon:
The "Opus majus" of Roger Bacon, ed. J. H. Bridges, London, 1897 (Reprint Frankfurt a.M. 1964).
K. Bergdolt, "Bacon und Giotto. Zum Einfluß der franziskanischen Naturphilosophie auf die Bildende Kunst am Ende des 13. Jahrhunderts", Medizinhistorisches Journal, 1989, pp. 25–41.

Bartolo di Fredi:
P. Harpring, The Sienese Trecento Painter Bartolo di Fredi (c. 1330–1410), Cranbury and London, 1993.
G. Freuler, Bartolo di Fredi Cini (um 1330– um 1410). Ein Beitrag zur sienischen Malerei des 14. Jahrhunderts, Disentis 1994.

Andrea Bonaiuti:
R. Offner and K. Steinweg, A Critical and Historical Corpus of Florentine Painting, sec. IV, vol VI: Andrea Bonaiuti, New York, 1979.
G. A. Schüssler, "Zum Thomasfresko des Andrea Bonaiuti in der Spanischen Kapelle am Kreuzgang von Santa Maria Novella", Mitteilungen des Kunsthistorischen Institutes in Florenz, XXIV, 1980, pp. 251–74.

Confraternities:
G. G. Meersseman, Ordo Fraternitatis. Confraternità e pietà dei laici nel medioevo, Rome, 1977, I–III.
J. Henderson, Piety and Charity in Late Medieval Florence. Religious Confraternities from the Middle of the 13th Century to the Late 15th Century, doctoral thesis. University of London, 1983.
K. Eisenbichler (ed.), Crossing the Boundaries. Christian piety and the arts in Italian medieval and Renaissance confraternities, Kalamazzo, Michigan, 1991.

Buffalmacco (see also: Pisa):
L. Bellosi, Buffalmacco e il Trionfo della Morte, Turin, 1974.

Byzantine art and Byzantium (see also: Coppo di Marcovaldo, Florence, Cult Pictures, Pisano, The Crucifix):
O. Demus, Byzantine Art and the West, New York, 1970.
K. Weitzmann, "Byzantium and the West around the Year 1200", The Year 1200 A Symposium, New York, 1975, pp. 53–93.
V. Lazarev, Studies in Byzantine Painting, London, 1993.

Giovanni Colombini:
C. Gennaro, "Giovanni Colombini e la sua brigata", Bollettino dell'Instituto storico italiano per il medio evo e Archivio Muratoriano, LXXXI, 1969, pp. 237–71.

Coppo di Marcovaldo:
R. W. Corrie, "The Political Meaning of Coppo di Marcovaldo's Madonna and Child in Siena", Gesta, XXIX, 1990, pp. 61–75.

Francesco Datini:
I. Origo, "Im Namen Gottes und des

Geschäfts". Lebensbild eines toskanischen Kaufmanns der Frührenaissance, Munich, 1986.

Dominic, Dominicans, Dominican art (see also: Bonaiuti, Florence, Orcagna, Pisa, Tomaso da Modena):
W. Hinnebusch, History of the Dominican Order, I, New York, 1966.
M. Meiss, Francesco Traini, ed. by H. B. J. Maginnis, Washington, 1983.

Three-nail Crosses:
G. Cames, "Recherches sur les origines du crucifix à trois clous", Cahiers archéologiques, XVI, 1966, pp. 194–200.

Duccio:
J. White, Duccio, Tuscan Art and the Medieval Workshop, London and New York, 1979.
J. Stubblebine, Duccio and his School, Princeton, 1979; La Maestà di Duccio restaurata, Centro Di, 1990.
H. B. J. Maginnis, "Duccio's Rucellai Madonna and the Origins of Florentine Painting", Gazette des Beaux-Arts, CXXIII, 1994, pp. 147–64.

Duecento (see also: Assisi, Byzantine art and Byzantium, Coppo di Marcovaldo, Duccio, Florence, Nicolaus IV, Pisano, Rome):
Federico II e l'arte del Duecento italiana, Rome, 1980, I–II.
L. C. Marquez, La peinture du Duecento en Italie Centrale, Paris, 1987.
A. M. Romanini, M. Andaloro etc., L'Arte Medievale in Italia, Florence, 1988.

Duecento and Trecento (see also: Duecento, Trecento):
La pittura in Italia: Il Duecento e il Trecento, Venice, 1986, I–II.
D. Bomford, J. Dunkerton, D. Gordon, A. Roy, Art in the Making: Italian Painting Before 1400, London, 1989.
C. M. Rosenberg (ed.), Art and Politics in Late Medieval and Early Renaissance Italy: 1250–1500, Notre Dame-London, 1990.
M. A. Lavin, The Place of Narrative. Mural Decoration in Italian Churches, 431–1600, Chicago and London, 1990.
M. Camille, The Gothic Idol. Ideology and Image-Making in Medieval Art, Cambridge, 1991.
J. Gardner, Patrons, Painters and Saints. Studies in Medieval Italian Painting, Aldershot, 1993.

Elias of Cortona:
D. Berg, "Elias von Cortona. Studien zu Leben und Werk des zweiten Generalministers im Franziskanerorden", Wissenschaft und Weisheit. Zeitschrift für augustinisch-franziskanische Theologie und Philosophie der Gegenwart, XLI, 1978, 102–26.

Florence (also see: Bonaiuti, Brotherhoods, Dominikus, Gaddi, Giotto, Giovanni da Milano, Orcagna):
R. Offner, A Critical and Historical Corpus of Florentine Painting, New York,

1930–79, I–XV.
M. Boskovits, Pittura fiorentina alla vigilia del Rinascimento, 1370–1400, Florence, 1975.
D. G. Wilkins, "Early Florentine Frescoes in Santa Maria Novella", Art Quarterly, N.S. I, 1978, pp. 153–59.
U. Baldini and B. Nardini (ed.), Santa Croce. Kirche, Kapellen, Kloster, Museum, Stuttgart, 1985.
G. Andres, J. M. Hunisak. A. R. Turner, The Art of Florence, New York, 1988, I–II.
A. Tartuferi, La pittura a Firenze nel Duecento, Florence, 1990.
M. Schwarz, Die Mosaiken des Baptisteriums in Florenz und die Florentiner Malerei vor Giotto, 1990 (unpublished postdoctoral thesis with a convincing new dating of the cupola mosaic).
M. Königer, "Die profanen Fresken des Palazzo Davanzati in Florenz. Private Repräsentation zur Zeit der internationalen Gotik", Mitteilungen des Kunsthistorischen Institutes in Florenz, XXXIV, 1990, pp. 245–78.
M. Boskovits, The Origins of Florentine Painting (1100–1270), Florence, 1992.
M. Dachs, "Zur ornamentalen Freskendekoration des Florentiner Wohnhauses im späten 14. Jahrhundert", Mitteilungen des Kunsthistorischen Institutes in Florenz, XXXVII, 1993, pp. 71–129.

Francis of Assisi, Franciscans, Franciscan art (see also: Assisi, Reception of Assisi, Bacon, Elias of Cortona, Cult Pictures, Pisa, Rome, The Crucifix):
Tommaso da Celano, Le due Vite e il Trattato dei miracoli di San Francesco d'Assisi, ed. L. Macali, Rome, 1954.
A. Zawart, The History of Franciscan Preaching and of Franciscan Preachers (1209–1927), New York, 1928.

Agnolo Gaddi (see also: Florence):
B. Cole, Agnolo Gaddi, Oxford, 1977.

Taddeo Gaddi (see also : Florence):
A. Ladis, Taddeo Gaddi. Critical Reappraisal and Catalogue Raisonné, Columbia and London, 1982.

Giotto (see also: Assisi, Florence, Padua):
A. Smart, The Assisi Problem and the Art of Giotto, New York, 1983.
L. Bellosi, La Pecora di Giotto, Turin, 1985.
R. Goffen, Spirituality in Conflict. Saint Francis and Giotto's Bardi Chapel, University Park and London, 1988.
G. Basile, Giotto: La Cappella degli Scrovegni, Florence, 1992.
I. Hueck, "Le opere di Giotto per la chiesa di Ognissanti, 'La Madonna d'Ognissanti' di Giotto restaurata (Gli Uffizi. Studi e Ricerche, VIII), Florence, 1992, pp. 37–50.

Giovanni da Milano (see also: Florence):
L. Cavadini, Giovanni da Milano, Valmorea, 1980.

Cult Pictures (see also: Coppo di

Marcovaldo, The Crucifix):
H. van Os, Sienese Altarpieces 1215–1460: Form, Content, Function, Groningen, 1984.
H. Belting, Bild und Kult. Eine Geschichte des Bildes vor dem Zeitalter der Kunst, Munich, 1990.
G. Wolf, Salus Populi Romani. Die Geschichte römischer Kultbilder im Mittelalter, Weinheim, 1990.
K. Krüger, Der frühe Bildkult des Franziskus in Italien. Gestalt- und Funktionswandel des Tafelbildes im 13. und 14. Jahrhundert, Berlin, 1992.
E. Borsook and F. Superbi Gioffredi, Italian Altarpieces 1250–1550. Function and Design, Oxford, 1993.

Ambrogio and Pietro Lorenzetti:
E. Carli, Pietro e Ambrogio Lorenzetti, Milan, 1970.
C. Ferguson O'Meara, "'In the Hearth of the Virginal Womb': The Iconography of the Holocaust in Late Medieval Art", Art Bulletin, LXIII, 1981, pp. 75–87.
C. Volpe, Pietro Lorenzetti, a cura di M. Lucco, Milan, 1989.

Simone Martini:
A. Tartuferi, "Appunti su Simone Martini e 'compagni', Arte Cristiana, LXXIV, 1986, pp. 79–92.
Simone Martini. Atti del convegno Siena, 1985, Florence, 1988.
A. Martindale, Simone Martini, Oxford, 1988.

Maso di Banco (see also: Florence):
D. G. Wilkins, Maso di Banco: A Florentine Artist of the Early Trecento, New York and London, 1985.

Nikolaus IV (see also: Rome, Torriti):
E. Menesto (ed.), Niccolò IV: Un pontificato tra oriente ed occidente, Spoleto, 1991.

Optics ("perspectiva"):
D. C. Lindberg, Auge und Licht im Mittelalter. Die Entwicklung der Optik von Alkindi bis Kepler, Frankfurt am Main, 1987.
K. Bergdolt, Der dritte Kommentar Lorenzo Ghibertis. Naturwissenschaften und Medizin in der Kunsttheorie der Frührenaissance, Weinheim, 1988.

Andrea Orcagna (see also: Florence):
N. Rash-Fabbri and N. Rutenburg, "The Tabernacle of Orsanmichele in Context", Art Bulletin, LXIII, 1981, pp. 385–405.
B. Cassidy, "Orcagna's Tabernacle in Florence: Design and Function", Zeitschrift für Kunstgeschichte, II, 1992, pp. 180–211.

Padua (see also: Altichiero, Giotto, Scrovegni):
L. Gargan, Cultura e arte nel Veneto al tempo del Petrarca, Padua, 1978.
C. Semenzato (ed.), Le pitture del Santo di Padova, Vicenza, 1984.
M. Lisner, "Farbgebung und Farbikonographie in Giotto's Arenafresken. Figurenfarbe und Bildgedanke", Mitteilungen des

Kunsthistorischen Institutes in Florenz, XXIX, 1985, pp. 1–78.
S. Knudsen, An Investigation of the Program of the Arena Chapel: Mariological Considerations, Austin, 1986.

Pisa:
E. Carli, Pittura pisana del Trecento, Milan, 1958, I–II.
M. Bucci e L. Bertolini, Camposanto monumentale di Pisa. Affreschi e sinopie, Pisa, 1960.
M. Mallory, "Thoughts Concerning the Master of the Glorification of St. Thomas", Art Bulletin, LVII, 1975, pp. 9–20.
A. Murray, "Archbishop and Mendicants in Thirteenth Century Pisa", the position and effectiveness of beggars' orders in urban society, ed. K. Elm, Berlin, 1981, pp. 19–75.
J. Polzer, "The 'Triumph of Thomas' Panel in Santa Caterina, Pisa. Meaning and Date", Mitteilungen des Kunsthistorischen Institutes in Florenz, XXXVII, 1993, pp. 29–70.

Giunta Pisano:
A. Tartuferi, Giunta Pisano, 1992.

Nicola und Giovanni Pisano:
M. Seidel, "Studien zur Antikenrezeption Nicola Pisanos", Mitteilungen des Kunsthistorischen Institutes Florenz, XIX, 1975, pp. 307–92.
E. M. Angiola, "Nicola Pisano, Federigo Visconti and the Classical Style in Pisa", Art Bulletin, LIX, 1977, pp. 1–27.
M. L. Testi Cristiani, Nicola Pisano architetto scultore, Pisa, 1987.
A. Middeldorf Kosegarten, "Nicola Pisano, das 'Wolfenbütteler Musterbuch' und Byzanz", Münchner Jahrbuch der bildenden Kunst, XXXIX, 1988, pp. 29–50.
A. F. Moskowitz, Nicola Pisano's Arca di San Domenico and its Legacy. University Park, 1993.

Rome (see also: Torriti):
S. Waetzoldt, Die Kopien des 17. Jahrhunderts nach Mosaiken und Wandmalereien in Rom, Vienna and Munich, 1964.
J. T. Wollesen, "Die Fresken in Sancta Sanctorum. Studien zur römischen Malerei zur Zeit Papst Nikolaus III (1277–1280)", Römisches Jahrbuch für Kunstgeschichte, XIX, 1981, pp. 36–83.
Roma anno 1300, Atti della IV settimana di studi di storia dell'arte medievale dell'Università di Roma "La Sapienza", Rome, 1983.
G. Matthiae, Pittura romana del meioevo secoli XI–XIV, Rome, 1988.
A. M. Romanini (ed.), Roma nel Duecento. L'arte nella città dei papi da Innocenzo III a Bonifacio VIII, 1991.
A. M. Romanini, Eclissi di Roma. Pittura murale a Roma e nel Lazio da Bonifacio VIII a Martino V (1295–1431), 1992.

San Gimignano (see also: Bartolo di Fredi):
G. Cecchini and E. Carli, San Gimignano, Milan, 1962.

G. Freuler, "Lippo Memmi's New Testament Cycle in the Collegiata in San Gimignano", Arte Cristiana, LXXIV, 1986, pp. 93–102.

Scrovegni:
R. H. Rough, "Enrico Scrovegni, the Cavalieri Gaudenti, and the Arena Chapel in Padua", Art Bulletin, LXII, 1980, pp. 24–35.

Siena:
W. Bowsky, U. Feldges, Landschaft als topographisches Porträt. Der Wiederbeginn der europäischen Landschaftsmalerei in Siena, Berne, 1980.
H. van Os, "The Black Death and Sienese Painting: A Problem of Interpretation", Art History, IV, 1981, 237–49.
E. Carli, La pittura senese del Trecento, Milan, 1981; Il Gotico a Siena, Kat. der Ausst., Florence, 1982.

Behaviour of patrons, donations (also see: Scrovegni):
S. K. Cohn, Jr., The Cult of Remembrance and the Black Death, Baltimore and London, 1992.
R. A. Goldthwaite, Wealth and the Demand for Art in Italy 1300–1600, Baltimore and London, 1993.

The Crucifix (also see: Giunta Pisano, Cult Pictures):
L. Bracaloni, "Il prodigioso Crocifisso che parlò a S. Francesco", Studi Francescani, II, 1939, pp. 185–212.
H. Hallensleben, "Zur Frage des byzantinischen Ursprungs der monumentalen Kruzifixe, 'wie die Lateiner sie verehren'", Festschrift für Eduard Trier zum 60. Geburtstag, Berlin, 1981, pp. 7–34.
D. Russo, "Saint Francois, les franciscains et les représentations du Christ sur la croix en Ombrie au XIIIe siècle", Mélanges de l'Ecole francaise de Rome, XCVI, 1984, pp. 647–717.

Tomaso da Modena:
R. Gibbs, Tomaso da Modena. Painting in Emilia and the March of Treviso, 1340–80, Cambridge, 1989.
D. Russo, "Compilation iconographique et légitimation de l'ordre dominicain: les fresques de Tomaso da Modena à San Niccolò de Trevise (1352)", Revue de l'art, 1992, pp. 76–85.

Trecento (see also: Florence, Pisa, Behaviour of patrons):
M. Meiss, Painting in Florence and Siena after the Black Death. The Arts, Religion and Society in the Mid-Fourteenth Century, New York, 1964.
M. Baxandall, Giotto and the Orators. Humanist observers of painting in Italy and the discovery of pictorial composition 1350–1450, Oxford, 1971.
L. Gargan, Cultura e arte nel Veneto al tempo del Petrarca, Padua, 1978.
H. Belting and D. Blume (ed.), Malerei und Stadtkultur in der Dantezeit. Die Argumentation der Bilder, Munich, 1989.
M. S. Frinta, "Observations on the Trecento and Early Quattrocento

Workshop", The Artist's Workshop, ed. P. M. Lukehart, Washington, 1993, pp. 19–34.
G. Cherubini, E Cristiani, L. Gai, A. I. Pini, G. Pinto (ed.), Italia 1350–1450: tra crisi, transformazione, sviluppo, 1993.

Jacopo Torriti: A. Tomei, Jacobus Torriti Pictor:
Una vicenda figurativa del tardo Duecento romano, Rome, 1990.

Venice:
R. Pallucchini, La pittura veneziana del Trecento, Venice and Rome, 1964.
T. Pignatti, 1000 Jahre Kunst in Venedig, Munich, 1989.
B. Bertoli (ed.), La basilica di San Marco (Venezia). Arte e simbologia, 1993.

ALICK MCLEAN
Renaissance Architecture in Florence and Central Italy

The Tempio Malatestiano, Leone Battista Alberti, and the Malatesta family: a bibliography, Monticello, Ill., 1986.
J. Ackerman, Distance Points: Essays in Theory and Renaissance Art and Architecture, Cambridge, Mass., 1991.
J. Ackerman, "The Regions of Italian Renaissance Architecture," The Renaissance from Brunelleschi to Michelangelo: The Representation of Architecture, Milan, 1994, pp. 319–347.
N. Adams, L. Nussdorfer, "The Italian City, 1400–1600, "The Renaissance from Brunelleschi to Michelangelo: The Representation of Architecture, eds. H. Millon & v. M. Lampugnani, Milan, 1994, pp. 205–230.
L. B. Alberti, tr. Rykwert, J. et alia, On the art of building in ten books, Cambridge, Mass., 1988.
L. B. Alberti, Zehn Bücher über die Baukunst. In Deutsch übertragen, eingeleitet und mit Anmerkungen und Zeichnungen versehen von Maz Theurer, Vienna, 1912.
L. B. Alberti, L'architettura (De Re Aedificatoria), ed. and trans. F. Orlandi, P. Portoghesi, Milan, 1966.
L. B. Alberti, ed. C. Grayson, Alberti and the Tempio Malatestiano: an autograph letter from Leon Battista Alberti to Matteo de' Pasti, November 18, 1454, New York, Pierpont Morgan Library, 1957.
G. Brucker, Renaissance Florence, Berkeley, 1983.
H. Burns, "Quattrocento architecture and the antique", Classical Influences on European Culture: AD 500–1500, Proceedings of an International Conference, (King's College, Cambridge, April 1969), Cambridge, 1971, pp. 269–288.
R. Goldthwaite, The Building of Renaissance Florence, Baltimore, 1980.
L. H. Heydenreich & W. Lotz, Architecture in Italy, 1400–1600, Harmondsworth and Baltimore, 1974.
P. Murray, Renaissance Architecture, New York and Milan, 1971.

H. Millon and V. M. Lampugnani, The Renaissance from Brunelleschi to Michelangelo: The Representation of Architecture, Milan, 1994.

The Rediscovery of the Antique in Fifteenth-Century Florence:
Filippo Brunelleschi. La sua opera e il suo tempo, Florence, 1980.
S. B. Bandera & S. Baroni, Il Sacello di San Satiro: storia, ritrovamenti, restauri, Cinisello Balsamo and Milan, 1990.
F. Borsi, S. Borsi, Bramante, Milan, 1989.
F. Borsi et alia, Leon Battista Alberti, Milan, 1973.
C. Elam, "Lorenzo de' Medici and the Urban Development of Renaissance Florence", Mitteilungen des Kunsthistorischen Institutes in Florenz 23, 1979, pp. 153–86.
M. Ferrara, F. Quinterio, Michelozzo di Bartolomeo, Florence, 1984.
F. P. Fiore, M. Tafuri, eds., Francesco di Giorgio, Milan, 1993.
H. Klotz, Filippo Brunelleschi, New York and London, 1990.
A. Manetti, The Life of Brunelleschi by Antonio di Tuccio Manetti, ed. H. Saalman, English trans. by Catherine Enggass, University Park and London, 1970.
P. Morselli, G. Corti, La chiesa di Santa Maria della Carceri in Prato: contributo di Lorenzo de' Medici e Giuliano da Sangallo alla progettaziona, Florence, 1982.
J. F. O'Gorman, The Architecture of the Monastic Library in Italy, 1300–1600, New York, 1972.
H. Saalman, Filippo Brunelleschi: The Cupola of Santa Maria del Fiore, London, 1980.
H. Saalman, Filippo Brunelleschi: The Buildings, London, 1993.
A. E. Werdehausen, Bramante und das Kloster S. Ambrogio in Mailand, Worms, 1990.

Brunelleschi and Perspective:
S. H. Edgerton, Jr., The Renaissance Rediscovery of Linear Perspective, New York and London, 1976.
M. Kemp, The Science of Art: Optical Themes in Western Art from Brunelleschi to Seurat, New Haven and London, 1990.
E. Panofsky, "Die Perspektive also 'symbolische Form", Vorträge der Bibliothek Warburg 1924–1925, Leipzig and Berlin, 1927, pp. 258–330.
K. H. Veltman and K. D. Keele, Linear Perspective and the Visual Dimensions of Science and Art, studies on Leonardo da Vinci I, München, 1986.

The Ideal City:
K. Bering, Baupropaganda und Bildpro- grammatik der Frührenaissance in Flo- renz, Rom, Pienza, Frankfurt am Main and New York, 1984.
W. Braunfels, Abendländliche Stadtbaukunst, Cologne, 1976 [English: Urban design in Western Europe: regime and architecture, 900–1900; trans. by Kenneth J. Northcott, Chicago, 1988].
G. Chittolini, ed., Metamorfosi di un

borgo: Vigevano in età visconteo- sforzesca, Milan, 1992.
D. Friedman, Florentine New Towns, Cambridge, MA., 1988.
C. Mack, Pienza: the creation of a Renaissance city, Ithaca, 1987.
A. Tönnesmann, Pienza: Städtebau und Humanismus, Munich, 1990.

Architectural theory and drawings:
H. Burns, "I disegni di Francesco di Giorgio agli Uffizi di Firenze", Francesco di Giorgio, F. P. Fiore, M. Tafuri, eds., Milan, 1993, pp. 330–357.
M. D'Evelyn, Word and Image in Architectural Treatises of the Italian Renaissance, Ph.D. Dissertation, Princeton University, Ann Arbor, 1994.
A. Avelino or Filarete, Treatise on Architecture, 2 vols., trans. and ed. F. R. Spencer, New Haven and London, 1965.
C. L. Frommel, "Reflections of the Early Architectural Drawings", The Renais- sance from Brunelleschi to Michelangelo: The Representation of Architecture, Milan, 1994, pp. 101–121.
H. Günther, "The Renaissance of Antiquite", Brunelleschi to Michelangelo: The Representation of Architecture, Milan, 1994, pp. 259–305.
M. Horster, "Brunelleschi und Alberti in ihrer Stellung zur Römischen Antike", Mitteilungen des Kunsthistorischen Institutes in Florenz 17, 1, 1973, pp. 29–64.
M. Jarzombek, On Leon Baptista Alberti: HIs Literary and Aesthetic Theories, Cambridge, Mass., 1989.
R. Krautheimer, "Alberti and Vitruvius", Studies in Western Art 2, 1963, pp. 43–52.
H. Mühlmann, L. B. Alberti: Ästhetische Theorie der Renaissance, Bonn, 1992.
M. Mussi, "La trattatistica di Francesco di Giorgio: un problema critico aperto", Francesco di Giorgio, F. P. Fiore, M. Tafuri, eds., Milan, 1993, pp. 358–379.
J. Onians, "Alberti and Filarete", Journal of the Warburg and Courtauld Institutes 34, 1971, 96–114.
A. Palladio, The Four Books of Architecture, New York, 1965.
S. Serlio, The five books of architecture: an unabridged reprint of the English edition of 1611, New York, 1982.
O. M. Ungers, "Ordo, fondo et mensura": the Criteria of Architecture, Brunelleschi to Michelangelo: The Representation of Architecture, Milan, 1994, pp. 307–317.

Church Architecture:
J. Ackerman, "Observations on Renaissance Church Planning in Venice and Florence, 1470–1570", Florence and Venice: Comparisons and Relations, ed. S. Bertelli et alia, 2 vols., Florence, 1980, (2) pp. 287–308.
A. Bruschi, "Religious Architecture in Renaissance Italy from Brunelleschi to Michelangelo", Brunelleschi to Michelangelo: The Representation of Architecture, Milan, 1994, pp. 123–181.
R Wittkower, Architectural Principles in the Age of Humanism, London, 1962.

Palace Architecture:
G. Cherubini, G. Fanelli, Il Palazzo Medici Riccardi di Firenze, Florence, 1990.
C. L. Frommel, Living all' antica: Palaces and Villas from Brunelleschi to Bramante, Brunelleschi to Michelangelo: The Representation of Architecture, Milan, 1994, pp. 183–203.
F. Kent, A. Perosa, B. Preyer, P. Sanpaolesi and R. Salvani, Giovanni Rucellai ed il suo Zibaldone: A Florentine Patrician and his Palace, London, 1981.
M. Naldini, D. Taddei, La piazza, la loggia, il palazzo Rucellai, Florence, 1989.

Villa Architecture:
J. Ackerman, The Villa: Form and Ideology of Country Houses, London and Princeton, 1990.
D. Coffin, The Villa in the Life of Renaissance Rome, Princeton, 1979.

WOLFGANG JUNG
Architecture of the High Renaissance and Mannerism in Rome and Central Italy

James S. Ackerman, The Cortile del Belvedere, in: Studie documenti per la storia del Palazzo Apostolico Vaticano, Vol. III, Rome, 1954.
James S. Ackerman, The Architecture of Michelangelo, London, 1986 (first edition London, 1961).
James S. Ackerman, The Gesù in the Light of Contemporary Church Design, in: Distance Points, Essays in Theory and Renaissance Art and Architecture, Cambridge, Mass., 1991.
Giulio Carlo Argan, Bruno Contardi, Michelangelo Architetto, Milan, 1990.
Horst Bredekamp, Maarten van Heemskercks Bildersturm als Angriff auf Rom, in: Bilder und Bildersturm im Spätmittelalter und in der frühen Neuzeit, Wiesbaden, pp. 203–216.
Arnaldo Bruschi, Bramante, Rome and Bari, 1985 (first edition Rome Bari, 1973).
Jakob Burckhardt, Geschichte der Renaissance in Italien, Stuttgart 1878.
Lidia Cangemi, Fasi e trasformazioni della fabbrica del Casino di Pio IV, in: Materiali per la Storia e il Restauro dell'Architettura, Roma "La Sapienza" – Facoltà di Architettura, Esc. 3, 1990–91.
Tancedi Carunchio, La Villa di Papa Giulio III a Roma, Citta di Castello, 1994.
Baldassar Castiglione, Il Libro del Cortegiano, Introduzione di Amadeo Quondam, Note di Nicola Longo, Milan, 1990.
B. Castiglione, The Ideal and the Real in Renaissance Culture, ed. by R. W. Hanning and David Rosand, New Haven and London, 1983.
David R. Coffin, The villa in the life of Renaissance Rome, Princeton, 1979.
Christoph L. Frommel, Die Farnesina und Peruzzis architektonisches Frühwerk, Berlin, 1961.
Christoph L. Frommel, Der römische palastbau, Tübingen, 1973, vols. 1–3.
Christoph L. Frommel, Stefano Ray,

Manfredo Tafuri, Raffaello Architetto, Milan, 1984.
Eugenio Garin, Rinascite e rivoluzioni. Movimenti culturali dal XIV al XVIII secolo, Rome and Bari, 1990 (first edition Rome and Bari, 1975).
Pirro Ligorio, Artist and Antiquarian, edited by R. W. Gaston, Milan, 1988.
Giulio Romano, Saggi di Ernst H. Gombrich, Manfredo Tafuri, Sylvia Ferino Pagden, Christoph L. Frommel, Konrad Oberhuber, Amedeo Belluzzi e Kurt W. Forster, Howard Burns, Milan, 1989.
Deborah Howard, Bramante's Tempietto. Spanish Royal Patronage, in: Apollo CXXXVI, pp. 211–217.
Richard Krautheimer, Alberti and Vitruvius, in: Studies in Western Art, The Renaissance and Mannerism, Acts of the XXth International Congress of the History of Art, ed. Millard Meiss, Princeton, 1963, pp. 42–52.
Irving Lavin, The Campidoglio and Sixteenth century stage design, in: Essays in Honour of Walter Friedländer, ed. by the Marsyas Board, New York, 1965, pp. 114–118.
Memoria dell'antico nell'arte italiana, Turin, 1984–86, vols. 1–3.
Gabriele Morolli, "Le belle forme degli edifici antichi", Raffaello e il progetto del primo trattato rinascimentale sulle antichità di Roma, Florence, 1984.
Peter Murray, Bramante's Tempietto, University of Newcastle-upon-Tyne, 1972.
Konrad Oberhuber, Raffaello, Milan, 1982.
Pier Nicola Pagliara, La casa romana nella trattatistica vitruviana, in: Controspazio 4, 1972, pp. 22–36.
Erwin Panofsky, Die Renaissancen der europäischen Kunst, Frankfurt am Main, 1984 (first edition: Renaissance and Renascences in Western Art, Stockholm, 1960).
Ludwig von Pastor, Geschichte der Päpste seti dem Ausgang des Mittelalters, Freiburg, 1906.
Raffaello a Roma, Il convegno del 1983, a cura di C. L. Frommel e M. Winner, Rome, 1986.
Rinascimento. Da Brunelleschi a Michelangelo. La Rappresentazione dell'Architettura, a cura di Henry Millon e Vittorio Magnago Lampugnani, Milan, 1994.
Sebastiano Serlio, Sesto Seminario Internazionale di Storia dell'Architettura, Vicenza 31 agosto – 4 settembre 1987, Milan, 1989.
John Shearman, Die Loggia der Psyche in der Villa Farnesina und die Probleme der letzten Phase von Raffaels graphischem Stil, in: Jahrbuch der kunsthistorischen Sammlungen in Wien 60, 1964, pp. 59–120.
John Shearman, The born architect?, in: Studies in the History of Art 17, Raphael before Rome, 1986, pp. 203–210.
Manfredo Tafuri, L'architettura del Mannerismo nel Cinquecento europeo, Rome, 1966.
Manfredo Tafuri, L'architettura dell'umanesimo, Rome and Bari, 1969.

Manfredo Tafuri, Ricerca del Rinascimento. Principi, città, architetti, Turin, 1992.

Christop Thoenes, Bramante e la "bella maniera degli antichi", in: Studi Bramanteschi, Atti del Congresso internazionale, Milano, Urbino and Rome 1970, Rome, 1974, pp. 391–396.

Christof Thoenes, Sprache der Ruinen, zur Antikenrezeption der Renaissance aus der Sicht der Architekturtratate, in: "Roma quanta fuit ipsa ruina docet", Kolloquium Hertziana, April, 1986, p. 29.

Regola delli cinque ordini d'architettura, Di Iacomo Barozzio da Vignola, Rome, 1602.

Rudolf Wittkower, Grundlagen der Architektur im Zeitalter des Humanismus, Munich, 1983 (first edition: Architectural Principles in the Age of Humanism, London, 1949).

Franz Graf Wolff Metternich, Die frühen St.-Peter-Entwürfe 1505–1514, aus dem Nachlaß herausgegeben, bearbeitet und ergänzt von Christof Thoenes, Tübingen, 1987.

Heinrich Wölfflin, Die Klassische Kunst, Basle, 1899.

JEANETTE KOHL
Architecture of the Late Renaissance in Venice and the Veneto

James S. Ackerman, Palladio. Stuttgart, 1980.

Andreas Beyer, Andrea Palladio. Das Teatro Olympico. Frankfurt am Main, 1987.

Caroline Constant, Der Palladio-Führer. Braunschweig, Wiesbaden, 1988.

Herrmann Diruf, Paläste Venedigs vor 1500. Baugeschichtliche Untersuchungen zur venezianischen Palastarchitektur im 15. Jhdt. Munich, 1990.

J. R. Hale, Renaissance Venice, London, 1973.

Deborah Howard, Jacopo Sansovino. Architecture and Patronage in Renaissance Venice, Yale UP, 1975.

Norbert Huse and Wolfgang Wolters, Venedig. Die Kunst der Renaissance, Munich, 1986.

Martin Kubelik, Die Villa im Veneto. Zur typologischen Entwicklung im Quattrocento, 2 vols., Munich, 1977.

Langenskiöld, Michele Sanmicheli. His Life and Works. Uppsala, 1938.

John McAndrew, Venetian Architecture of the Early Renaissance, Cambridge, 1980.

Muraro, Michelangelo, Die Villen des Veneto. Munich, 1986.

Peter Murray, Renaissance. Weltgeschichte der Architektur, Stuttgart, 1989.

Andrea Palladio, I Quattro Libri dell'Architettura. Venice, 1570. English trans., 1738, reprinted New York, 1965.

Lionello Puppi, Andrea Palladio. Das Gesamtwerk. 2 vols., Stuttgart, 1977.

Manfred Wundram and Thomas Pape, Andrea Palladio, Cologne, 1988.

Alvise Zorzi, Paläste in Venedig, Munich, 1989.

UWE GEESE
Italian Renaissance Sculpture

General:
J. Pope-Hennessy, An Introduction to Italian Sculpture, 3 vols.; vol 2: Italian Renaissance Sculpture, London, 1958; vol3: Italian High Renaissance and Baroque Sculpture, London, 1963.

J. Poeschke, Die Skulptur der Renaissance in Italien, 2 vols., "Donatello und seine Zeit", Munich, 1990, and "Michelangelo und seine Zeit", Munich, 1992.

R. J. M. Olson, Italian Renaissance Sculpture, London, 1992.

Martin Warnke, Hofkünstler. Zur Vorgeschichte des modernen Künstlers. Cologne, 1985.

F. Haskell & N. Penny, Taste and the Antique. The Lure of Classical Sculpture 1500–1900, Yale, 1982.

Lorenzo Ghiberti:
R. Krautheimer, Lorenzo Ghiberti, Princeton, N. J., 1956 (last reprint 1982).

A. Perrig, Lorenzo Ghiberti. Die Paradiesetür. Warum ein Künstler den Rahmen sprengt. Kunststück, Frankfurt am Main, 1987.

Nanni di Banco:
M. Wundram, Donatello und Nanni di Banco, Berlin, 1969.

M. Horstner, Nanni di Banco: "Quattro Coronati", in: Mitteilungen des Kunsthistorischen Institutes in Florenz 31, 1987, pp. 59–80.

M. Bergstein, La vita civica di Nanni di Banco, Rivista d'Arte 39, 1987, pp. 55–82.

M. Bergstein, The Date of Nanni di Banco's "Quattro santi Coronati", The Burlington Magazine 130, 1988, pp. 910–913.

Donatello:
Poeschke, Die Skulptur der Renaissance in Italien, vol. 1, "Donatello und seine Zeit", Munich, 1990.

B. A. Bennet and D. G. Wilkins, Donatello, Oxford, 1984.

J. Pope-Hennessy, Donatello, Frankfurt am Main and Berlin, 1986.

Donatello-Studien, Italienische Forschungen 3, 16, Munich, 1989 (chronological bibliography).

Jacopo della Quercia:
C. Freytag, Jacopo della Quercia: Stilkritische Untersuchungen zu seinen Skulpturen unter besonderer Berücksichtigung der Frühwerks, doctoral thesis Munich, 1969.

Jacopo della Quercia, nell'arte del suo tempo, Ausst.Kat., Florence, 1975.

Jacopo della Quercia fra Gotico e Rinascimento, Atti del convegno di studi 1975, Florence, 1977.

C. List-Freytag, Beobachtungen zum Bildprogramm der Fonta Gaia Jacopo della Quercias, in: Münchener Jahrbuch für Bildende Kunst 36, 1985, pp. 57–71.

Luca della Robbia:
M. Lisner, Luca della Robbia. Die Sängerkanzel. Stuttgart, 1960.

C. Del Bravo, L'umanesimo di Luca della Robbia, Paragone 24, 1973, No. 284, 3–34.

J. Pope-Hennessy, Luca della Robbia, Oxford, 1980.

Agostino di Duccio:
M. Kühlental, Studien zum Stil und zur Stilentwicklung Agostino di Duccios, in: Wiener Jahrbuch für Kunstgeschichte 24, 1971, pp. 59–100.

C. Mitchell, Il Tempio Malatestiano, in: Studi malatestiani, publ. by Instituto Storico Italiano per il Medio Evo. Rome, 1978, pp. 71–103.

Bernardo and Antonio Rosselino:
L. Planiscig, Bernardo und Antonio Rosselino. Vienna, 1942.

A. M. Schulz, The Sculpture of Bernardo Rosselino and his Workshop. Princeton, N. J., 1977.

Desiderio da Settignano:
A. Markham, Desiderio da Settignano and the workshop of Bernardo Rossellino, The Art Bulletin 45, 1963, pp. 35–45.

U. Schlegel, Zu Donatello und Desiderio da Settignano. Beobachtungen zur physiognomischen Gestaltung im Quattrocento, in: Jahrbuch der Berliner Museen 9, 1967, pp. 135–155.

Mino da Fiesole:
I. Lavin, On the Sources and Meaning of the Renaissance Portrait Bust, The Art Quarterly 33, 1970, pp. 207–226.

G. C. Sciolla, La sculture di Mino da Fiesole. Turin, 1970.

Benedetto da Maiano:
E. Lein, Benedetto da Maiano. Frankfurt am Main, 1988.

Francesco Laurana:
H.-W. Kruft and M. Malmanger, Francesco Laurana: Beginnings in Naples, The Burlington Magazine 116, 1974, pp. 9–14.

H.-W. Kruft and M. Malmanger, Der Triumphbogen Alfonsos in Neapel. Das Monument und seine politische Bedeutung, Acta ad Archaeologiam et Artium Historiam pertinentia 6, 1975, pp. 213–305.

Guido Mazzoni:
T. Verdon, The Art of Guido Mazzoni, New York and London, 1978.

N. Gramaccini, Guido Mazzonis Beweinungsgruppen, in: Städel Jahrbuch N.F. 9, 1983, pp. 7–40.

Niccolò dell'Arca:
N. Gramaccini, La déploration de Niccolò dell'Arca. Religion et politique aux temps de Giovanni II Bentevoglio, Revue de l'Art 1983, No. 62, pp. 21–34.

U. Hübner, Zwei anonyme Terrakottastatuen unter den Namen des Niccolò dell'Arca, in: Städel Jahrbuch N.F. 12, 1989, pp. 195–208.

Antonio Rizzo:

R. Munman, Venetian Renaissance Tomb Monuments. Doctoral thesis. Harvard University, 1968.

A. M. Schulz, Antonio Rizzo. Sculptor and Architect. Princeton, 1983.

N. Huse/W. Wolters, Venedig. Die Kunst der Renaissance. Munich, 1986.

Andrea del Verrocchio:
Verrochio's Christ and St. Thomas. A Masterpiece of Sculpture from the Renaissance Florence. Exhibition catalogue. Florence and New York, 1993.

Die Christus-Thomas-Gruppe von Andrea del Verrocchio (1436–1488). Öffentliches Kolloquium vom 19.–21. November 1993. Liebieghaus - Museum alter Plastik, Frankfurt am Main (conference journal in preparation).

Small bronzes:
J. Montagu, Bronzen. Stuttgart und Frankfurt am Main, 1963.

H. Beck and P. C. Bol, Natur und Antike in der Renaissance. Exhibition catalogue, Liebieghaus - Museum alter Plastik, Frankfurt am Main, 1985.

D. Blume, Anticos Antike, in: Städel Jahrbuch N.F., 11, 1987, pp. 179–204.

Michelangelo:
So much has been written about Michelangelo that only a few more recent publications are listed here:

D. Summers, Michelangelo and the Language of Art. Princeton, N. J., 1981.

C. Echinger-Maurach, Studien zu Michelangelos Juliusgrabmal, Hildesheim and Zurich and New York, 1991, 2 vols.

F. J. Verspohl, Der Moses des Michelangelo, in: Städel Jahrbuch N.F. 13, 1991, pp. 155–176.

F. J. Verspohl, Michelangelo Buonarroti. Das Wort und das Bild. Mit einem Beitrag von Horst Bredekamp zur ersten Planungsstufe des Juliusgrabes und Zeichnungen von Jörg Friedrich. Kunststück. Frankfurt am Main (appearing shortly).

Tullio Lombardo:
M. Maek-Gerard, Tullio Lombardo. Ein Beitrag zur Problematik der venezianischen Werkstatt bis zu den Auswirkungen des Krieges gegen die Liga von Cambrai. Doctoral thesis Frankfurt am Main, 1974.

M. Maek-Gerard, Die "Milanexi" in Venedig. Ein Beitrag zur Entwicklungsgeschichte der Lombardi-Werkstatt, Wallraf-Richartz Jahrbuch 41, 1980, pp. 105–130.

A. Luchs, Tullio Lombardo's Ca' d'Oro Relief: A Self-Portrait with the Artist's Wife?, The Art Bulletin 71, 1989, pp. 230–236.

Jacopo Sansovino:
B. Boucher, The Sculpture of Jacopo Sansovino, 2 vols. New Haven and London, 1991.

Baccio Bandinelli:
V. L. Bush, Bandinelli's "Hercules and Cacus" and Florentine Traditions, Memoires of the American Academy in Rome 35, 1980, pp. 163–206.

K. Weil-Garris, Bandinelli and Michelangelo: A Problem of Artistic Identity, in: Art the Ape of Nature. Studies in Honor of H. W. Janson. New York, 1981, pp. 223–251.

Benvenuto Cellini:
B. **Cellini**, Leben des Benvenuto Cellini, trans. by Goethe. With an epilogue by Harald Keller. Frankfurt am Main, 1981.
J. **Pope-Hennessy**, Cellini, London, 1985.
A. **Prater**, Cellinis Salzfaß für Franz I. Ein Tischgerät als Herrschaftszeichen. Stuttgart, 1988.

Giambologna (Giovanni da Bologna):
C. **Avery**, A. **Radcliffe**, M. **Leithe-Jasper** (eds.), Giambologna. 1529 bis 1608. Ein Wendepunkt der europäischen Plastik. Exhibition catalogue. Vienna, 1978.

BARBARA DEIMLING
Early Renaissance Art in Florence and Central Italy

The sections on Perugino, Pinturicchio, Signorelli and Piero di Cosimo were compiled by Marlis Fraatz-von Hessert.

International Gothic:
L. **Castelfranchi Vegas**, International Gothic Art in Italy, Leipzig, 1966.
Europäische Kunst um 1400, exhibition catalogue, Vienna, 1962.
Courajods, Léçons professées à l'Ecole du Louvre, 1887–1896, Paris 1901, 3 vols. (Universal Gothic).

Gentile da Fabriano:
A. **de Marchi**, Gentile da Fabriano: Un viaggio nella pittura italiana alla fine del gotico, Milan, 1992.
K. **Christiansen**, Gentile da Fabriano, Ithaca, N. Y. 1982 (considers Gentile da Fabriano to be a Renaissance, not a Late Gothic, painter).

Masaccio:
L. **Berti**, Masaccio, Florence, 1988.

Masaccio and Giotto:
M. **Boskovits**, "'Giotto born again': Beiträge zu den Quellen Masaccio's", in Zeitschrift für Kunstgeschichte, 29, 1966, pp. 51–66.

Masaccio's use of Perspective:
Various essays, in: Marburger Jahrbuch für Kunstwissenschaft, XXI, 1986.

Masaccio's Trinity:
U. **Schlegel**, "Observations on Masaccio's Trinity Fresco in Santa Maria Novella", in Art Bulletin, XLV, 1963, pp. 19–33 (interprets the trinity as a copy of the Golgotha chapel in Jerusalem).
E. **Hertlein**, Masaccios Trinität: Kunst, Geschichte und Politik der Frührenaissance in Florenz, Florence, 1979.
O. **von Simson**, "Über die Bedeutung von Masaccios Trinitätsfresko in Santa Maria Novella", in Jahrbuch der Berliner Museen, VIII, 1966, pp. 119–159 (theological interpretation of the fresco in

connection with the Last Judgement and the last days).

Fra Angelico:
J. **Pope Hennessy**, Fra Angelico, London, 1952.
K. **Bering**, Fra Angelico: Mittelalterlicher Mystiker oder Maler der Renaissance?, Essen, 1984 (overview of the history of the reception of Fra Angelico).

Fra Angelico and San Marco:
W. **Hood**, Fra Angelico at San Marco, New Haven and London, 1993.

The main Altarpiece in San Marco:
J. I. **Miller**, "Medici Patronage and the Iconography of Fra Angelico's San Marco Altarpiece", in Studies in Iconography, XI, 1987, pp. 1–13.
C. **Gardner von Teuffel**, "Lorenzo Monaco, Filippo Lippi und Filippo Brunelleschi: die Erfindung der Renaissancepala", in Zeitschrift für Kunstgeschichte, 45, 1982, pp. 1–30.

Benozzo Gozzoli and the Three-Kings Chapel in the Palazzo Medici:
Benozzo Gozzoli: La Cappella dei Magi, ed. by C. Acidini Luchinat, Milan, 1993 (excellent photographs of the restored frescoes).
R. **Hatfield**, "Cosimo de' Medici and the Chapel of His House", in Cosimo il Vecchio de' Medici, 1389–1464, Essays in Commemoration of the 600th Anniversary of Cosimo de' Medici's Birth, ed. by F. Ames-Lewis, Oxford, 1992, pp. 221–244.

Filippo Lippi:
J. **Ruda**, Fra Filippo Lippi: Life and Work with a Complete Catalogue, London, 1993 (rejects the influence of Flemish art on Filippo Lippi; instead, tries to explain the change in Filippo by means of Tuscan traditions; not altogether convincing; contains a useful bibliography).
R. **Oertel**, Fra Filippo Lippi, Vienna, 1942.

Filippo Lippi's early works:
M. **Boskovits**, "Fra Filippo Lippi, i carmelitani, e il Rinascimento", in Arte Cristiana, LXXIV, 1986, pp. 235–242.

Filippo Lippi and Flanders:
F. **Ames-Lewis**, "Fra Filippo Lippi and Flanders", in Storia dell'Arte, LXIX, 1990, pp. 255–273.
F. **Ames-Lewis**, "Painters in Padua and Netherlandish Art, 1435–1455", in Italienische Frührenaissance und Nordeuropäisches Spätmittelalter, ed. by J. Poeschke, Munich, 1993, pp. 179–202.

The Annunciation of San Lorenzo:
C. **Gardner von Teuffel**, "Lorenzo Monaco, Filippo Lippi und Filippo Brunelleschi: die Erfindung der Renaissancepala", in Zeitschrift für Kunstgeschichte, 45, 1982, pp. 1–30.
F. **Ames-Lewis**, Fra Filippo LIppi's S. Lorenzo Annunciation", in Zeitschrift für Kunstgeschichte, 42, 1979, pp. 155–163.

The Prato frescoes:
M. **Baxandall**, Die Wirklichkeit der Bilder: Malerei und Erfahrung im Italien des 15. Jahrhunderts, Frankfurt, 1984, 169–178 (English edition: Painting and Experience in Fifteenth-Century Italy, Oxford, 1988, pp. 128–135).

Paolo Uccello:
F. and S. **Borsi**, Paolo Uccello, Milan, 1992.
G. **Vasari**, (quotation in) Vite de' più eccelenti pittori, scultori e architetti, vol IV [Florence, 1568], Milan, 1808, pp. 89–90.
J. **von Schlosser**, Künstlerprobleme der Frührenaissance, III, Paolo Uccello, Vienna, 1933, p. 42.

The equestrian portrait of John Hawkwood:
A. **Schmitt**, "Paolo Uccellos Entwurf für das Reiterbild des Hawkwood", in Mitteilungen des Kunsthistorischen Institutes, VIII, 1959, pp. 125–130.
H.-E. **Mittig**, "Uccellos Hawkwood-Fresko: Platz und Wirkung", in Mitteilungen des Kunsthistorischen Institutes, XIV, 1969–70, pp. 235–239 (examines double perspective).
E. **Borsook**, "L'"Hakwood' d'Uccello et la Vie de Fabius Maximus de Plutarque", in Revue de l'Art, no. 55, 1982, pp. 44–51.

The Deluge Fresco in Santa Maria Novella:
H. M. **von Erffa**, Ikonologie der Genesis, vol I, Munich, 1989, pp. 432–511.
V. **Gebhardt**, "Ein Portrait Cosimo de' Medicis von Paolo Uccello: Zur Ikonologie der "Sintflut" von Santa Maria Novella in Florenz", in Pantheon, XLVIII, 1990, pp. 28–35.

The Route of San Romano:
V. **Gebhardt**, Paolo Uccello's 'Schlacht von San Romano': Ein Beitrag zur Kunst der Medici in Florence, doctoral thesis, Frankfurt, 1991.
V. **Gebhardt**, "Some Problems in the Reconstruction of Uccello's 'Rout of San Romano' cycle", in Burlington Magazine, 133, March, 1991, pp. 179–184.

Cosimo de' Medici as ruler and patron:
Cosimo il Vecchio de' Medici, 1389–1464. Essays in Commemoration of the 600th Anniversary of Cosimo de' Medici's Birth, ed. by F. Ames-Lewis, Oxford, 1992.
V. **Gebhardt**, "Beiträge zur Ikonographie und Ikonologie des Palazzo Medici und seiner Ausstattung", in: V. Gebhardt, "Ein Portrait Cosimo de' Medicis von Paolo Uccello: Zur Ikonologie der "Sintflut" von Santa Maria Novella in Florenz" in Pantheon, XLVIII, 1990, pp. 83–138.

Domenico Veneziano:
H. **Wohl**, The Paintings of Domenico Veneziano: A Study in Florentine Art of the Early Renaissance, New York and London, 1980.

"Pittura di luce" in Florence:
Pittura di luce: Giovanni di Francesco e l'arte fiorentina de metà Quattrocento, ed. by L. Bellosi, exhibition catalogue, Milan, 1990, pp. 11–45.
Una scuola per Piero: Luce, colore, prospettiva nella formazione fiorentina di Piero della Francesca, ed. by L. Bellosi, exhibition catalogue, Venice, 1992, pp. 17–34.

Andrea del Castagno:
M. **Horster**, Andrea del Castagno: Complete Edition with a Critical Catalogue, Oxford, 1980.
E. **Borsook**, The Mural Painters of Tuscany: From Cimabue to Andrea del Sarto, London, 1960.
M. **Meiss**, The Great Age of Fresco: Discoveries, Recoveries and Survivals, New York, 1970.
John R. **Spencer**, Andrea del Castagno and his Patrons, Durham and London, 1991.

The Cycle of Famous Men and Women:
R. L. **Mode**, "Re-Creating Adam at Villa Carducci", in Zeitschrift für Kunstgeschichte 47, 1984, pp. 501–514.
E. **Borsook**, "L'"Hakwood' d'Uccello et la Vie de Fabius Maximus de Plutarque", in Revue de l'Art, no. 55, 1982, pp. 44–51, esp. p. 49 (about the erection of statues with inscriptions in niches; also the quotation from Alberti's treatise De Re Aedificatoria).
C. L. **Joost Gaugier**, "Castagno's Humanistic Program at Legnaia and Its Possible Inventor", in Zeitschrift für Kunstgeschichte, 45, 1982, pp. 274–282.

St. Jerome: scholar and penitent:
M. **Meiss**, "Scholarship and Penitence in the Early Renaissance: The Image of St. Jerome", in The Painter's Choice: Problems in the Interpretation of Renaissance Art, New York, 1976, pp. 189–202.

Piero della Francesca:
E. **Battisti**, Piero della Francesca, 2 vols., Milan, 1971 (on the 500th anniversary of his death; English edition with new bibliography, 1992).

Piero's early works and the Baptism of Christ:
L. **Bellosi**, "Sulla formazione fiorentina di Piero della Francesca", in Una scuola per Piero: Luce, colore, prospettiva nella formazione fiorentina di Piero della Francesca, ed. by L. Bellosi, exhibition catalogue, Venice, 1992, pp. 17–54.
M. **Aronberg Lavin**, Piero della Francesca's Baptism of Christ, New Haven and London, 1981.
M. **Tanner**, "Concordia in Piero della Francesca's Baptism of Christ", in Art Quarterly, XXXV, 1972, pp. 1–20 (a political interpretation of the work as a reference to the union of the Western and Byzantine Churches).

The cycle of frescoes in Arezzo and Crusade propaganda:

L. Schneider, "The Iconography of Piero della Francesca's Frescoes Illustrating the Legend of the True Cross in the Church of San Francesco in Arezzo", in Art Quarterly, XXXII, 1969, pp. 22–48.
C. Ginzburg, Erkundungen über Piero: Piero della Francesca: ein Maler der frühen Renaissance, Berlin, 1985 (English edition: The Enigma of Piero, Piero della Francesca: The Baptism, the Arezzo Cycle, the Flagellation, London, 1985).
F. Büttner, "Das Thema der 'Konstantinsschlacht' bei Piero della Francesca", in Mitteilungen des Kunsthistorischen Institutes in Florenz, XXXVI, 1992, pp. 23–49.

The Flagellation:
C. Bertelli, Piero della Francesca: La forza divina della pittura, Milan, 1991, 184.
T. Gouma-Peterson, "Piero della Francesca's Flagellation: An Historical Intepretation", in Storia dell'arte, no. 26, 1967, pp. 217–33, esp. pp. 217–18.
C. Ginzburg, Erkundungen über Piero: Piero della Francesca: ein Maler der frühen Renaissance, Berlin, 1985, pp. 133–141.
C. Ginzburg, The Enigma of Piero, Piero della Francesca: The Baptism, the Arezzo Cycle, the Flagellation, London, 1985, pp. 116–119.

Piero della Francesca and Federico da Montefeltro of Urbino:
G. Vasari, Vite de' più eccelenti pittori, scultori e architetti, vol. V [Florence, 1568], Milan, 1809, 165 (includes the assumption, that Domenico Veneziano introduced oil painting to Italy).
C. J. Hessler, "Piero della Francescas Panorama", in Zeitschrift für Kunstgeschichte, 55, 1992, pp. 161–179.

Verrocchio:
For Leonardo's part in the Baptism of Christ, refer to the list under his name.
G. Passavant, Andrea del Verrocchio als Maler, Düsseldorf, 1959.
K. Oberhuber, "Le problème des premières œuvres de Verrocchio", in Revue de l'Art, XLII, 1978, pp. 63–76.
L. Bellosi, "Andrea del Verrocchio", in Pittura di luce: Giovanni di Francesco e l'arte fiorentina di metà Quattrocento, ed. by L. Bellosi, exhibition catalogue, Milan, 1990, pp. 177–189.

Antonio and Piero Pollaiuolo:
L. D. Ettlinger, Antonio and Piero Pollaiuolo: Complete Edition with a Critical Catalogue, London, 1978.

The Medicis and Hercules:
L. D. Ettlinger, "Hercules Florentinus", in Mitteilungen des Kunsthistorischen Institutes, XVI, 1972, pp. 119–142.
A. Wright, "The Myth of Hercules", in Lorenzo il Magnifico e il suo mondo, Convegno Internazionale di Studi (Firenze, 9–13 giugno 1992), ed. by G. C. Garfagnini, Florence, 1994, pp. 323–339.
W. A. Bulst, "Uso e trasformazione del palazzo mediceo fino ai Riccardi", in Il Palazzo Medici Riccardi di Firenze, ed. by G. Cherubini and G. Fanelli, pp. 98–142,

esp. p. 113.

The body as the prison of the soul:
Quotation in L. D. Ettlinger, Antonio and Piero Pollaiuolo: Complete Edition with a Critical Catalogue, London, 1978, p. 31 (also the thesis of the copperplate engraving as a pattern, pp. 32–35).
P. Emison, "The Word Made Naked in Pollaiuolo's Battle of the Nudes", in Art History, 13/3, 1990, pp. 261–275.
L. S. Richards discusses "Antonio Pollaiuolo: Battle of Naked Men", in The Bulletin of the Cleveland Museum of Art, 55, 1968, pp. 62–70.

Sandro Botticelli:
R. Lightbown, Sandro Botticelli: Leben und Werk, Munich, 1989 (English: Sandro Botticelli: Life and Work, New York, 1989).
R. Lightbown, Sandro Botticelli, Berkeley and Los Angeles, 1978, 2 vols. (with a complete catalogue).
R. Hatfield, Botticelli's Uffizi "Adoration", Princeton, N. J., 1976.

Artistic self-confidence:
M. Meiss, The Great Age of Fresco, New York, 1970, p. 170.
R. Lightbown, Sandro Botticelli, Berkeley and Los Angeles, 1978, vol II, p. 39.
R. Stapleford, "Intellect and Intuition in Botticelli's Saint Augustine", in: Art Bulletin, LXXVI, 1994, pp. 69–80.

The high ideal of love:
J. Shearman, "The Collections of the Younger Branch of the Medici", in: Burlington Magazine, 117, January 1975, pp. 12–27.
W. Smith, "On the Original Location of the Primavera", in: Art Bulletin, LVII, 1975, pp. 31–40.
A. Warburg, Sandro Botticelli's "Geburt der Venus" und "Frühling": Eine Untersuchung über die Vorstellungen von der Antike in der italienischen Frührenaissance, Leipzig, 1893 (reprint in: idem, Gesammelte Schriften, Leipzig und Berlin, 1932, I, pp. 1–58, esp. pp. 32–33).
E. H. Gombrich, "Botticelli's Mythologies: A Study in the Neoplatonic Symbolism of His Circle", in Journal of the Warburg and Courtauld Institutes, VIII, 1945, pp. 7–60.
E. Wind, Pagan Mysteries in the Renaissance, London, 1958, particularly Chapter VII (Primavera), Chapter VIII (Birth of Venus).
H. Bredekamp, Botticelli Primavera, Florenz als Garten der Venus, Frankfurt, 1988.
C. Dempsey, The Portrayal of Love: Botticelli's 'Primavera' and Humanist Culture at the Time of Lorenzo the Magnificent, Princeton, N. J., 1992.
C. Dempsey, Concerning Famous Women, New Brunswick, N. J., 1963, pp. 79–80.

The Medicis in Florence:
J. Hale, Florence and the Medici: The Pattern of Control, London, 1977.
D. Kent, The Rise of the Medici, Oxford, 1978.
G. Brucker, Renaissance Florence,

Berkeley, CA,, 1983.
E. H. Gombrich, "The Early Medici as Patrons of Art", in Italian Renaissance Studies: A Tribute to the Late Cecilia M. Ady, ed. by E. F. Jacob, London, 1960, 279ff.
Cosimo 'il Vecchio de' Medici', 1389–1464: Essays in Commemoration of the 600th Anniversary of Cosimo de' Medici's Birth, ed. by F. Ames-Lewis, Oxford, 1992.
Piero di Cosimo de' Medici: Art and Politics in Fifteenth-Century Florence. Publication of the records of the symposium 5th to 8th June 1991 in Bad Homburg.
Lorenzo il Magnifico e il suo mondo, Convegno Internazionale di Studi (Firenze, 9–13 giugno 1992), ed. by G. C. Garfagnini, Florence, 1994.

Domenico Ghirlandaio:
E. Micheletti, Domenico Ghirlandaio, Antella, 1990.

The frescoes in the Sassetti Chapel:
E. Borsook & J. Offerhaus, Francesco Sassetti and Ghirlandaio at Santa Trinita, Florence: History and Legend in a Renaissance Chapel, Doornspijk, 1981.

The Portinari altarpiece:
B. Strens-Hatfield, "L'arrivo del trittico Portinari a Firenze", in Commentari, XIX, 1968, pp. 315–319.
F. Ames-Lewis, "On Domenico Ghirlandaio's Responsiveness to North European Art", in Gazette des Beaux-Arts, ser. 6, CXIV, 1989, pp. 111–122.

Artists' contracts:
M. Baxandall, Die Wirklichkeit der Bilder. Malerei und Erfahrung im Italien des 15. Jahrhunderts, Frankfurt 1984 pp. 12–25 (English: Painting and Experience in Fifteenth-Century Italy, Oxford, 1988, pp. 3–14, esp. pp. 5–8).

Filippino Lippi:
A. Scharf, Filippino Lippi, Vienna, 1950.
L. Berti & U. Baldini, Filippino Lippi, Florence, 1991 (very good photographs).

The frescoes of the Strozzi Chapel:
E. Borsook, "Documents for Filippo Strozzi's Chapel in Santa Maria Novella and Other Related Papers", in Burlington Magazine, 112, September 1970, pp. 737–747, 800–804.
S. Peters-Schildgen, Die Bedeutung Filippino Lippis für den Manierismus unter besonderer Berücksichtigung der Strozzi-Fresken in Santa Maria Novella zu Florenz, Essen, 1989.

Sienese art of the Quattrocento:
K. Christiansen, L. Kanter and C. B. Strehlke, Painting in Renaissance Siena, 1420–1500, exhibition catalogue, New York, 1988.

Francesco di Giorgio:
R. Toledano, Francesco di Giorgio Martini: Pittore e scultore, Milan, 1987, esp. pp. 82–85.

Francesco di Giorgio e il Rinascimento a Siena, 1450–1500, exhibition catalogue, ed. by L. Bellosi, Siena, 1992.

Giovanni di Paolo:
L. B. Kanter, Italian Paintings in the Museum of Fine Arts Boston, vol. I, 13th – 15th Century, Boston, 1994, pp. 180–182.

Domenico di Bartolo:
C. B. Strehlke, "La 'Madonna dell'Umilità' di Domenico di Bartolo e San Bernardino", in Arte Cristiana, 72, 1984, 381–390.
Una scuola per Piero: Luce, colore, prospettiva nella formazione fiorentina di Piero della Francesca, ed. by L. Bellosi, exhibition catalogue, Venice, 1992, pp. 59–63.

Sassetta:
J. R. Banker, "The Program for the Sassetta Altarpiece in the Church of S. Francesco in Borgo S. Sepolcro", in I Tatti Studies, Essays in the Renaissance, 4, 1991, pp. 11 ff. (with detailed bibliography).
D. Gordon, "The Reconstruction of Sassetta's Altar-Piece for S. Francesco, Borgo San Sepolcro, Postscript", in Burlington Magazine, 135, September 1993, pp. 620–623.

ALEXANDER RAUCH
Painting of the High Renaissance and Mannerism in Rome and Central Italy

Renaissance Painting in Venice and Northern Italy

Livia Alberton and Vinco Da Sesso, Jacopo Bassano, i Da Ponte: una dinastia di pittori, Bassano de Grappa, 1992.
Kurt Badt, Paolo Veronese, Cologne, 1981 (published posthumously).
Fritz Baumgart, Renaissance und die Kunst des Manierismus, Dumont-Dokumente, Cologne, 1963.
Gino Benzoni, etc., Tiziano, exhibition catalogue, Palazzo Ducale Venezia and National Gallery Washington; Venice, 1990.
Bernhard Berenson, Die italienischen Maler der Renaissance, new edition Gütersloh, 1952.
Jan Bialostocki, Spätmittelalter und beginnende Neuzeit, vol 7 Propyläen Kunstgeschichte, Berlin, Frankfurt am Main and Vienna, 1992.
Anna Maria Brizio, Leonardo da Vinci, il Cenacolo, Florence, 1983.
Beverly Louise Brown and Paola Marini, eds., Jacopo Bassano, exhibition catalogue, Bologna, 1992.
Luigi Coletti, La Camera degli Sposi del Mantegna a Mantova, Milan, 1959.
Regid De Campos, Raffaello nelle Stanze, Florence, 1983.
Pier Luigi de Vecchi, Raffaello, La Pittura, Florence, 1981.
Pier Luigi de Vecchi, Michelangelo, Cologne, 1991.
Mario Di Giampaolo, Parmigianino,

Catalogo completo dei dipinti, Florence, 1991.

Luitpold Dussler, Raphael. A Critical Catalogue of His Pictures, Wall Paintings and Tapestries, London and New York, 1971.

Giuseppe Fiocco, Giorgione, Hamburg, Rome and Bergamo, 1941.

Kurt W. Forster, Pontormo, Munich, 1966.

C. Frey, Le Vite di Michelangelo scritte da Giorgio Vasari e da Ascanio Condivi, Berlin, 1887.

Dagobert Frey, Manierismus also europäische Stilerscheinung, Studien zur Kunst des 16. und 17. Jahrhunderts, Stuttgart, 1964.

K Frey, Die Briefe des Michelangiolo Buonarroti, Berlin, 1914.

Rona Goffen, Giovanni Bellini, New Haven and London, 1989.

Ludwig Goldscheider, The Paintings of Michelangelo, London and Hayes, 1948.

Ludwig Goldscheider, Künstlerbriefe, ed. Adolf Rosenberg, Berlin, 1880.

Detlev von Hadeln, Paolo Veronese, Florence, 1978 (published posthumously).

My Heilmann, Florenz und die Medici, Cologne, 1985.

Theodor Hetzer, Venezianische Malerei, vol. 8 of Hetzer's writings, ed. by Gertrude Berthold, Stuttgart, 1985.

Theodor Hetzer, Tizian. Geschichte seiner Farbe, Frankfurt am Main, 1935.

Gustav René Hocke, Die Welt als Labyrinth, Manier und Manie in der europäischen Kunst, von 1520 bis 1650 und in der Gegenwart, Hamburg, 1957 to 1966.

Christian Hornig, Giorgiones Spätwerk, (= Annali della Scuola normale superiore di Pisa, Classe di lettere e filosofia, Serie III, Vol. VI, 3) Pisa, 1976.

Norbert Huse, Studien zu Giovanni Bellini, Reihe Beiträge zur Kunstgeschichte vol. 7, Berlin and New York, 1972.

Norbert Huse and Wolfgang Wolters, Venedig. Die Kunst der Renaissance, Munich, 1986.

Christiane L. Joost-Gaugier, Jacopo Bellini, Selected Drawings, New York, 1980.

Georg Kauffmann, Die Kunst des 16. Jahrhunderts, Berlin 1970. Vol. 8 Propyläen Kunstgeschichte.

Harald Keller, Michelangelo, Bildhauer, Maler, Architekt, Frankfurt am Main, 1976.

Jan Lauts, Carpaccio, Gemälde und Zeichnungen, Cologne, 1962.

Fabrizio Mancinelli and Anna Maria De Strobel, Michelangelo, Le Lunette e la Vela della Capella Sistina, Rome, 1992.

Pietro C. Marini, Leonardo e i Leonardeschi a Brera, Florence, 1987.

Antonio Morassi, Tiziano, Milan, 1964.

Paccagnini, Giovanni and Salmi, Mario, Andrea Mantegna, Milan, 1961.

Paccagnini, Giovanni and Salmi, Mario, Pisanello e il ciclo cavalleresco di Mantova, Electa Editrice, 1972.

Ridolfo Pallucini and Paola Rosi, Tintoretto, Le Opere Sacre e Profane, 2 vols., Milan, 1982.

Erwin Panofsky, "Idea", Ein Beitrag zur Begriffsbestimmung der älteren Kunsttheorie, Leipzig and Berlin, 1924 (English trans. New York, 1968).

Terisio Pignatti, Giorgione, Milan, 1978.

Carlo Pirovano, ed., Raffaello in Vaticano - Raffaello a Firenze, exhibition catalogue, 2 vols., Vatican and Palazzo Pitti, Milan, 1984.

Andreas Prater, Jenseits und diesseits des Vorhangs, Bemerkungen zu Raffaels "Sixtinischer Madonna" als religiöses Kunstwerk, in: Münchner Jahrbuch der bildenden Kunst, 3rd series, vol. XLII, Munich, 1991, pp. 117–136.

Andreas Prater, Mantegnas "Cristo in Scurto", in: Zeitschrift für Kunstgeschichte, vol. 48, 1985 Book 1, pp. 279–299.

W. R. Rearick and Terisio Pignatti, The Art of Paolo Veronese 1528–1588, exhibition catalogue National Gallery of Art, Washington, 1988.

Robin Richmond, Michelangelo und die Sixtinische Kapelle, Freiburg i. Br., Basle and Vienna, 1993.

Giles Robertson, Giovanni Bellini, Oxford, 1968.

Marcel Röthlisberger, Studi du Jacopo Bellini, Venice, 1961.

David Rosand, Titian, New York, 1978.

Marco Rosci, Leonardo, Milan, 1976.

Mario Salmi, ed., Raffaello, L'Opera, Le Fonti, La Fortuna, Novara, 1968.

Emil Schaeffer, ed., Raffaels Sixtinische Madonna als Erlebnis der Nachwelt (anthology), Dresden, 1927 and 1956.

Armando Schiavo, Michelangelo, nel complesso delle sue opere, 2 vols., Rome, 1990.

Norbert Schneider, Porträtmalerei, Cologne, 1992.

Paul Schubring, Die Kunst der Hochrenaissance in Italien, Berlin, 1926.

Le Siècle de Titien. L'âge d'or de la peinture à Venise, exhibition catalogue, Paris, 1993.

Wilhelm E. Suida, Raphael, London, 1948.

Hans Tietze, Tizian, Leben und Werk, Vienna, 1936.

Hans Tietze, Titian, The Paintings and Drawings, London, 1950.

Hans Tietze, Tintoretto, The Paintings and Drawings, London, 1948.

Charles de Tolnay, Michelangelo I–V, Princeton, 1947–1960.

Ernst Ullmann, Leonardo da Vinci, New York, 1975.

Francesco Valcanover, Carpaccio, Florence, 1989.

Giorgio Vasari, Lives of the Artists, trans. by George Bull, Harmondsworth, 1965.

A. Venturi, Storia dell'Arte Italiana I–XI, Milan, 1901–1940.

Herbert von Einen, Michelangelo, Stuttgart, 1959.

Jack Wasserman, Leonardo da Vinci, New York, 1975.

Pietro Zampetti, Carlo Crivelli, Florence, 1987.

Roberto Zapperi, Paul III und seine Enkel. Nepotismus und Staatsportrait, Frankfurt am Main, 1990.

ALEXANDER PERRIG
Drawing and the Artist's Basic Training from the 13th to the 16th Century

Jacopo Bellini:
B. Degenhart and A. Schmitt, Corpus der italienischen Zeichnungen 1300–1450, Teil II, vols., 5–8, Berlin, 1990.
A. Perrig, "Die theoriebedingten Landschaftsformen in der italienischen Malerei des 14. und 15. Jahrhunderts", in: Die Kunst und das Studium der Natur vom 14. zum 16. Jahrhundert, ed. by W. Prinz and A. Beyer, Weinheim, 1987, pp. 41–60.

Benvenuto Cellini:
Opere. Vita. Trattati. Rime. Lettere, a cura di B. Maier, Milan, 1968.
A. Perrig, Michelangelo-Studien IV: Die "Michelangelo"-Zeichnungen Benvenuto Cellinis, Frankfurt and Berne, 1977.

Cennino Cennini:
Das Buch von der Kunst oder Tractat der Malerei des Cennino Cennini da Colle di Valdelsa. Übersetzt von A. Ilg, Vienna, 1888.
Il Libro dell'arte commentato e annotato da F. Brunello, Vicenza, 1971.

Francesco da Barberino:
B. Degenhart and A. Schmitt, Corpus, part I, vol. 1, pp. 31–38.
S. Partsch, Profane Buchmalerei der bürgerlichen Gesellschaft im spätmittelalterlichen Florenz, Worms, 1981, pp. 79–87.

Jean Bourré:
L. Campbell, Renaissance Portraits. European Portrait-Painting in the 14th, 15th and 16th Centuries, New Haven and London, 1990, illus. p. 176.

Lorenzo Ghiberti:
I Commentari, translated into German by J. von Schlosser, Berlin, 1911–12, I–II.
R. Krautheimer and T. Krautheimer-Hess, Lorenzo Ghiberti, Princeton, 1982.
A. Perrig, Lorenzo Ghiberti: Die Paradiesestür, Frankfurt, 1987.

Artistic education:
S. Rossi, Dalle botteghe alle accademie. Realtà sociale e teorie artistiche a Firenze dal XIV al XVI secolo, Milan, 1980.

Amateur drawings (see also: Francesco da Barberino):
W. Kemp, "...einen wahrhaft bildenden Zeichenunterricht überall einzuführen". Zeichnen und Zeichenunterricht der Laien 1500–1870. Ein Handbuch, Frankfurt am Main, 1979 (the quotation on p. 421 appears in the foreword of this instructive book).

Leonardo da Vinci:
H. Ludwig, Leonardo da Vinci: Das Buch von der Malerei, Vienna, 1882.
J. P. Richter, The Literary Works of Leonardo da Vinci, New York, 1970, I–II.
Leonardo da Vinci On Painting. A Lost Book (Libro A), reassembled from the Codex Vaticanus Urbinas 1270 and from the Codex Leicester by C. Pedretti, London, 1965.
K. Clark, The Drawings of Leonardo da Vinci in the Collection of Her Majesty the Queen at Windsor Castle, London, 1968–69, I–III.
C. Pedretti, The Literary Works of Leonardo da Vinci. A Commentary to J. P. Richter's Edition, Oxford, 1977, I–II.
A. Perrig, "Leonardo: Die Anatomie der Erde", Jahrbuch der Hamburger Kunstsammlungen, XXV, 1980, pp. 51–80.
L. H. Heydenreich, B. Dibner, L. Reti, C. Zammattio, A. Marinono, A. M. Brizio, M. V. Brugnoli, A. Chastel, Leonardo, der Erfinder, der Forscher, der Künstler, Stuttgart and Zurich, 1981.

Michelangelo:
C. de Tolnay, Corpus dei disegni di Michelangelo, Novara, 1975–80, I–IV.
A. Perrig, Michelangelo-Studien I, Michelangelo und die Zeichnungswissenschaft – Ein methodologischer Versuch, Frankfurt and Berne, 1976.
A. Perrig, Das Münchener Blatt mit der Kopie nach Masaccios 'Zinsgroschen'-Fresko und die Methoden der Michelangelo-Forschung", Kritische Berichte, X, 1982, pp. 3–35.
A. Perrig, Michelangelo's Drawings - The Science of Attribution, New Haven and London, 1991.
A. Perrig, "Zeichne, Antonio, zeichne", Antiquitäten-Zeitung, XXI, No. 19, 10th September 1993, pp. 569–71.

Studies of models:
C. Ragghianti e G. Dalli Regoli, Firenze 1470–1480, Disegni dal modello. Pollaiolo, Leonardo, Botticelli, Filippino, Pisa, 1975.

Model books:
R. W. Scheller, A Survey of Medieval Model Books, Haarlem, 1963.
J. G. Ruston, Italian Renaissance Figurative Sketchbooks, 1450–1520, doctoral thesis, University of Minnesota, 1976.

Sinopia:
U. Procacci, Sinopie ed affreschi, Milan, 1960.
Fresken aus Florenz, exhibition catalogue for the Haus der Kunst, Munich, 1969.

Drawing (13th to 16th centuries):
B. Degenhart and A. Schmitt, Corpus der italienischen Zeichnungen 1300–1450, parts I–II, Berlin, 1968–80.
M. W. Evans, Medieval Drawings, London, 1969.
F. Ames-Lewis, Drawing in Early Renaissance Italy, New Haven and London, 1981.
W. Strauss and T. Felker, Drawings Defined, New York, 1987.
G. C. Sciolla, ed., Il Disegno. Forme, tecniche, significati, Milan, 1991.
E. Cropper, ed., Florentine Drawing at the Time of Lorenzo the Magnificent. Papers from a Colloquium held at the Villa Spelman, Florence, 1994.

Index